JANE AUSTEN, a lively, headstrong and determined girl, lived a very full and exciting youth. In her thirties, she published four wonderful novels, but did not disclose her name. After she died, in 1817, her family destroyed most of her letters, and they steadfastly refused to discuss her life. One of her nieces wrote, *a memoir of Miss Jane Austen has often been asked for, and strangers..have wondered that the family should have refused to supply the necessary materials.*

Fifty-two years after her death her nephew Rev. James Edward Austen-Leigh, responded to growing public interest, with a *Memoir of Jane Austen*. He said very little about her youth, and he admitted the family had suppressed her early stories, describing them as, *ridiculing the improbable events and exaggerated sentiments which she had met with in sundry silly romances.* He stated that Jane's life was, *singularly barren: few changes and no great crisis ever broke the smooth current of its course;* and declared he had *no definite tale of love to relate.*

Most, if not all of Jane Austen's readers simply didn't believe him.

Virginia Woolf wrote, *I prefer to present her, not in the modest pose which her family determined for her, but rather, as she most frequently presented herself, as rebellious, satirical and wild.*

After more than two hundred years, *Jane & D'Arcy* reveals the story of the enduring love of Jane Austen and D'Arcy Wentworth.

Over time, the Austen's secrecy was reinforced by D'Arcy's silence. A tall, handsome young Irish surgeon, after being tried, and found not guilty of highway robbery at the Old Bailey, he left England for New South Wales, on the other side of the world.

The day before he sailed, Jane's brother, Henry, reflecting his family's sentiments, applauded *the world* for getting *rid of its superfluous inhabitants, all those who have too much cunning or too little money, shipped off with the very first cargo of Convicts to Botany Bay.*

Despite time and distance, D'Arcy was to remain the fixed star in Jane's firmament.

Folly is Not Always Folly is the first volume of *Jane & D'Arcy*, the second, *Such Talent & Such Success,* is to follow. They tell the long lost story of the romance and adventures of Jane Austen and D'Arcy Wentworth.

Jane & D'Arcy

Jane & D'Arcy

Jane Austen & D'Arcy Wentworth

Volume I

Folly is not always folly

Wal Walker

Published by Arcana Trust. April 2017

Copyright ©William Wallace Walker 2017

email: info@janeanddarcy.com

website: www.janeanddarcy.com

The moral rights of the author are asserted. All rights reserved, no part of this book may be reproduced or transmitted in any form, or by any means, electronic or mechanical, including photocopying, recording or by any information storage and retrieval system, without prior permission in writing from the publisher, the Arcana Trust.

The Australian Copyright Act 1968 allows a maximum of one chapter or 10% of this book, whichever is the greater, to be photocopied by an educational institution for its educational purposes, provided that the educational institution (or body that administers it) has given a remuneration notice to the Copyright Agency (Australia), email: info@copyright.com.au.

Every effort has been made to trace the holders of copyright material. If you have any information concerning copyright material in this book, please contact the publisher, Arcana Trust, at the address above.

The American Philosophical Society, Philadelphia, kindly gave permission to reprint extracts from William Shippen's diary, in *William Shippen, Jr,* © Dr B.C. Corner, 1951; Manchester University Press gave permission to quote from *Whig Principles & Party Politics* by E.A.Smith, 1975; and Michael Durey, at Murdoch University, gave permission to quote from his book, *William Wickham, Master Spy*, 2009.

ISBN 978-646-0-90399-6

Cataloguing-in-Publication details are available from the National Library of Australia
www.trove.nla.gov.au

Design by Stephen Smedley, Tonto Design

Index by Alan Walker

Cover: Joseph Lycett, *South view of Parramatta, New South Wales, from the Great Western Road, near the Turnpike House*, 1820.

Wentworth Woodhouse is the two-storey house in the right foreground, seen through the trees. Government House, Parramatta, is in the left foreground, on the rise.
St John's Church is in the centre of the valley.

The painting was purchased by the Mitchell Library in 1979, from descendants of John Thomas Bigge, and is used with the library's permission.

Contents

Preface   7

1. D'Arcy Wentworth   11
2. Jane Austen   23
3. Nabobs, gold mohrs & palanquins   37
4. Jane at home in Steventon   57
5. Names, Names, Names   67
6. Not a bad speculation for a surgeon   79
7. High spirit & strong passions   97
8. Missing Years   119
9. No Turning Back   139
10. Such Probabilities & Proofs   159
11. More Notions than Facts   175
12. To the most remote corner   189
13. Angels & Eagles   207
14. In such a world   237
15. A Colony Abandoned   255
16. The real & consistent Patron   285
17. Antipodean Hell   311
18. The Dwelling Place of Devils   333
19. The Peripatetic Austens   353

Works of Jane Austen   376
Acknowledgements & Apology   378
Abbreviations used in the endnotes   380
Endnotes   381
Index   415

Preface

WHEN MY UNCLE, Bill Wentworth, first told me of the romantic connection between Jane Austen and D'Arcy Wentworth, I took little or no notice. I never asked Bill how he knew the story, or where I might go to verify it. I remember only that it was given as a simple fact. It was of no interest to me, I was busy and had no interest in Jane Austen. I had never read any of her novels.

In the succeeding years I happened to read a newly published book on the Australian Wentworths. I was not really familiar with my family history, and I found D'Arcy, in particular, a heroic figure, even though the writer attempted to tarnish his character, he shone through the book as a fascinating person.

Later, I read David Nokes' biography of Jane Austen, and realised there was a period early in her life where their lives could have crossed. I confirmed this to my uncle, over breakfast at Bittons in March 2002. He directed me to pursue my line of enquiry and to locate correspondence he believed was in Ireland that would verify the story of Jane and D'Arcy.

It seemed, from reading Nokes, there had been a conspiracy to cover over Jane's early life. Little was known of her teenage years, when she wrote the amazing stories of her *Juvenilia*, an early version of *Sense & Sensibility;* and *First Impressions*, which would become *Pride & Prejudice*.

Her *Juvenilia* contains intimate descriptions of London and life in the city, but her biographers tell us Jane had only visited London once, briefly, on her way back to Hampshire from visiting her great Uncle Francis at Sevenoaks.

These vignettes originate from the years prior to her flirtation with Tom Lefroy, for whom she *did not care sixpence,*[1] and prior to the earliest of her remaining letters.

Jane Austen was a reclusive person, virtually unknown to her readers or to other authors of her day. Her publisher, John Murray, he who burnt Byron's biography rather than publish it, made no effort to promote her or introduce her to society.

In 1869, fifty-two years after her death, Reverend James Edward Austen-Leigh, her nephew, responded reluctantly to public demand for more information about her. He was nineteen when Jane Austen died, the youngest person at her funeral. He had years of experience in drafting sermons and had published an intimate glimpse of bygone county life in his *Recollections of the Early Days of the Vine Hunt.* Now seventy-two, he wrote a *Memoir of Jane Austen.*[2]

James Edward told little of her youth, or her youthful writing. The few insights he offered do not capture the élan of those vital, vivacious years. He wrote, *of events her life was singularly barren: few changes and no great crisis ever broke the smooth current of its course.. I have therefore scarcely any material for a detailed life of my aunt.* He claimed there was an almost total dearth of information or anecdotes about her within the Austen family.

He had asked his sisters, Anna, aged seventy-three and Caroline, sixty-one, for their *recollections of Aunt Jane.*[3] It seems he asked for their own recollections, not for other family stories or rumours they may have heard. They knew he did not intend to include confidences, or to touch on family secrets hidden now for over seventy years.

James Edward wrote he had *no definite tale of love to relate*[4] about his aunt. Caroline said she would not contradict his *theory that Aunt Jane never had any attachment that overclouded her happiness.*[5]

When she wrote her own reminiscences, Caroline Austen was careful to allay any concerns that she might reveal hidden family anecdotes or secrets.[6] She opened with a firm statement - *I mean to relate only what I saw and what I <u>thought</u> myself.*[7] She confirmed the Austen family's refusal to discuss Jane's history, *a memoir of Miss Jane Austen has often been asked for, and strangers..have wondered that the family should have refused to supply the necessary materials.*

There was probably a time when my Uncle Bill would have agreed with their stance, considering it could be insensitive, indecent, distasteful or damaging to both families. By 2002, he was of the opinion sufficient time had elapsed, after more than two hundred years, for the story to be made public. While there were now, no doubt, many distant Austen relations, and descendants of D'Arcy, he believed it would be unlikely to result in recriminations or confected outrage from any.

> *All families have secrets. Sometimes they are of the variety that a family keep from outsiders; sometimes they are the sort that a family keeps from itself; sometimes they are the sort whose presence no one consciously admits. But they are almost always there. People have a deep need for secrets. The question is what to do with them and about them, and when to let them go.*[8]
>
> John Lanchester, *Family Romance*

Where did Jane Austen gain the life experience with which she wrote such complex and realistic stories? Her readers have long noticed the powerful emotional songlines that thread across her writings, that still remain largely unexplored and ill defined.

As I read her novels I found it difficult to accept that Jane Austen wrote these stories having never experienced any other life than that of the small remote rural rectory, in a parish of a few square miles, with a population of a few hundred. Many scenes are so emotionally powerful, one senses she is revealing events from her own life.

A few years after Bill's death, battened down for a cyclone in Darwin, I decided to go back to this project, which had been waiting and puzzling me for years, to set down the story of my grandfather's great grandfather, D'Arcy Wentworth, and Jane Austen, and the links between their lives.

I hoped to unravel some of Jane Austen's secrets. She was a very headstrong, determined girl who lived a very full and exciting youth. In the wild, exaggerated, droll and satirical accounts that make up her juvenilia, she wrote about her adolescent life, and she revisited many of these stories in her novels.

> *He knew of no one but himself who was inclined to the work. This is no uncommon motive. A man sees something to be done, knows of no one who will do it but himself, and so is driven to the enterprise.*[9] Arthur Helps, *Life of Columbus*

This is a story held for several generations of my family. It was my uncle's wish that I record it. I hope, in doing so, that I have done it justice, and that you find the re-incarnations of these shadows fresh and interesting.

The story falls into two volumes, the first, *Folly is Not Always Folly*, tells Jane and D'Arcy's early years, until 1806. The second, *Such Talent & Such Success*, begins from that date, and describes their separate achievements and accomplishments.

The relationship of Jane and D'Arcy is sad and lamentable, but it is also exciting and excellent; for in their separation, in time, their lives each blossomed within its narrow confines. It was as if their parting gave each one the opportunity to fulfil their destiny.

Wal Walker
September 2016

Chapter 1

D'Arcy Wentworth

The rapture of delightful expectation

D'ARCY WENTWORTH was born on St Valentine's Day, Sunday 14 February 1762, in Portadown, a market town on the River Bann, in County Armagh, northern Ireland. He was the sixth child of Martha and D'Arcy Wentworth, the youngest of their four sons. He came after William, Samuel, Gerrard, Mary and Dorothy, and behind him followed Martha and Mary Anne.

The Wentworth family had a proud history in Ireland, as determined leaders in the difficult and contentious English administration. In 1632, Thomas Wentworth of *Wentworth Woodhouse,* was appointed Lord Deputy of Ireland by Charles I. His vigorous pursuit of the King's interests in the face of opposition, particularly from a wealthy Anglo-Irish establishment, earned him the nickname, *Blacke Tom Tyrant of Ireland.*[1]

Nine years later, in 1641, Thomas, now the 1st Earl Strafford, was condemned to death by Parliament and executed on Tower Hill. A number of his family left England, to avoid retribution and a similar fate. Michael Wentworth, from South Elmsall in West Yorkshire, sought safe haven in Ireland. He took his family to County Meath, part of the English Pale, loyal to Crown,[2] where his cousin Earl Roscommon had extensive landholdings. He settled at nearby Fyanstown, and his son became steward of the Roscommon estates.

Robert Wentworth, D'Arcy's grandfather, a barrister, was reared at Fyanstown, but by 1730, the family's fortunes were on the wane. Their land was progressively mortgaged and by 1742, was all sold.

Robert sent his son to Portadown to be apprenticed in the linen trade. Six foot three, personable and capable in business, he did well.[3] In 1747 he married his master's daughter, Martha Dixon. He built a family home, *Wentworth House*, on a large parcel of land, a gift from his father, at nearby Derryanvil.[4]

Portadown on the River Bann served flax growers, merchants and weavers in the surrounding country. The river flowed into Lough Neagh, the huge lake to the north,[5] and was navigable by vessels of up to fifty or sixty tons. It was known as a source of fine, large freshwater pearls, sold in the marketplace during the summer assizes.[6]

In March 1742, after a canal opened from Portadown south to Newry[7] dug by two hundred men with picks and shovels, the town became a hub for coal and other materials from the counties around Lough Neagh.[8] Riverboats offloaded their cargoes onto narrow canal barges, towed by horses that walked the narrow towpath to the Sugar Quay at Newry. From there they went along the Newry Canal, to Carlingford Lough, to be loaded onto coastal vessels sailing south to Dublin. Coal from County Tyrone was in high demand, as was stone, slate, and linen.

Barges returned to Portadown with grain, dried fish, timber, tallow, tools and machinery, traded in the market-house or stored in warehouses along the river, that were nudging out the old water mills and linen bleaching yards.

When D'Arcy was born, Portadown was an eighteenth century boom town. Two years later, the pace increased, a new arched stone bridge was built across the Bann, the only carriage crossing for thirty miles, giving easy access to County Down to the east.[9]

D'Arcy's father prospered in the growing local economy, he was now an established linen merchant, he traded in other commodities and managed the inn at Portadown. There, he offered food, drink and lodging for gentlemen traders and travellers, with transport and storage for their goods in his warehouses.

The first great path   Mansfield Park

At school in Portadown, D'Arcy stood out as a talented student. A surgeon-apothecary at nearby Tandragee, Alexander Patton, noticed his ability. D'Arcy had ridden the eight miles several times to call him out, once to tend a man wounded at the Portadown fair, another time carrying an urgent call to a barge due that evening with an injured man. At the fair he had helped hold the patient, as Dr Patton realigned his badly fractured arm.

In 1778, when Dr Patton advertised for an apprentice,[10] D'Arcy applied through his father, and at sixteen was indentured to Dr Patton for seven years.

This indenture sheweth Persuasion

Dr Patton agreed to share his knowledge and skill, and provide D'Arcy with care and moral guidance. D'Arcy promised to be loyal, to labour for his master, obey him, to learn, conduct himself with moral probity, and to keep the secrets of the surgeon apothecary's skills and trade.[11]

> Some years later, an apprentice surgeon-apothecary in Lancashire described some of his responsibilities: *I studied hard; learned the Linnean names and doses of drugs; attended seven surgical operations; worked from nine to nine daily. Sundays included; made mercury ointment in the old style by turning a pestle in a mortar for three days in succession, to amalgamate the quicksilver with the pig's grease; made up what the doctor called his "Cathartic acid bitter mixture", as a sort of fill up for every purgative bottle, and almost every disease that 'flesh is heir to'; made up boluses of a teaspoonful of preserve with half-a-grain of opium, as a sedative; drew a tooth for sixpence; and took four pence if the sufferer had no more.*[12]

D'Arcy lived in Alexander Patton's house at Tandragee, accompanying him at all hours, to call on patients at home and in the fields, patients of all faiths, Catholics, Protestants, Methodists, Quakers. On Sunday they rode to Seagoe, to attend the Church of Ireland, where D'Arcy caught up with his family.[13]

John Wesley who established Methodist congregations in Portadown and Tandragee, noted in his diary – *I do not wonder the Gospel runs so swiftly in these parts. The people in general have the finest natural tempers which I ever knew; they have the softness and courtesy of the Irish, with the seriousness of the Scots, and the openness of the English.*[14]

From Alexander Patton, D'Arcy learnt the art of the surgeon apothecary, and to question, observe and constantly learn from his patients. He saw the attention Dr Patton gave them, his efforts to improve their health and their children's prospects. D'Arcy saw people suffering and dying, he attended accidents and difficult births, he learnt to diagnose and treat patients with detachment and compassion, to act quickly and decisively, to take risks.

The afflicted tenantry and cottagers Persuasion

He came to know families for miles around Tandragee, to understand the rhythm and the rigour of their lives. He saw the effects of harvest failures and the rising price of food, he learnt that health relied on sound diet and hygiene, how overwork or lack of work could blight people's lives, and how drainage, roofing and a supply of fuel could count towards life or death.

D'Arcy watched the troubles between Anglo-Irish landlords and poor Irish farmers growing more fierce and inflamed. He listened to the disquiet of tenant farmers, anxious at ever-increasing taxes and tithes, fearful of being turned off the land, to be left with nowhere to go.

He knew the despair of Catholic linen weavers, their looms smashed beyond repair by Peep O'Day Boys, repaying them for undercutting their Protestant neighbours. He had seen cattle downed, houghed, their leg tendons cut through by Oakboys or the Hearts of Steel, in retaliation for rising rents and food prices.

D'Arcy saw violence growing in the countryside, the damage done in night-time raids by local gangs. He watched the brawls erupt at local fairs and races when Catholic Defenders and Molly Maguires challenged Protestant youths, impatient to declare their grievances with their fists.

He learnt to say little or nothing, to maintain *the famous Northern reticence, the tight gag of place and times.*[15]

All the disturbances, Distresses & Civil Wars in which England for many years was embroiled The History of England

Alexander Patton subscribed to newspapers and journals, and encouraged his apprentice to read them,[16] to follow events unfolding in Ireland and the wider world. D'Arcy read reports of his Whig cousins, Rockingham and Fitzwilliam, in the Westminster Parliament, proud of them, saluting their commitment to Parliament's supremacy above crown and church.

The regimentals of an ensign Pride & Prejudice

England and France went to war in 1778. After four thousand British troops were withdrawn from Ireland to fight the rebel colonies in America, the Mayor of Belfast asked for reinforcements to guard against a French invasion. He was told Ireland should rely on its own defences.

Local volunteer associations began to form, first among Protestants in the north, then across the country, including men of all creeds, united to defend Ireland against the French, American privateers and local unrest. By 1782, the Volunteers numbered over sixty thousand.

Every future hope Northanger Abbey

In February 1782, the Armagh Regiment of Volunteers convened a meeting of volunteer associations at Dungannon in County Tyrone. Delegates from one hundred and forty-three Volunteer corps, in uniform and bearing arms, marched into the Presbyterian church in Dungannon.

They pledged allegiance to the Crown and called for legislative independence for Ireland, for free trade, the opening Irish ports to foreign vessels and elimination of onerous tariffs and duties. They were supported by Guilds and merchants across Ireland, seeking relief from restrictions on trade with the rest of the world, especially America, where Irish linen was in high demand.

A week after the Dungannon meeting, a *Declaration of Independence* was tabled in the Irish House of Commons, but postponed when Parliament rose for the Easter recess. Ten days later, in London, Lord North resigned and the Marquis of Rockingham was appointed to lead the government. He agreed to grant Ireland legislative independence.[17]

On 16 April, the Irish Commons met again, crowded with spectators, and passed the *Declaration* unanimously. Action by the Volunteers had helped to restore independence to the Irish Parliament, and free up restrictions on trade. The Ulster Volunteers had become a voice for independence from English rule.

D'Arcy, now twenty, was inspired by these events. He joined Dr Patton, a Lieutenant in the First Provincial Battalion of the Ulster Volunteers, as an ensign, a junior officer. D'Arcy's commission was signed by George III.[18] He rode each week to Armagh to train; he memorised drills and exercises, and marched in parades and reviews. He enjoyed the evenings, when he and his fellow young ensigns, in their scarlet coats with white facings, sat with the senior officers and listened to them discussing the political issues of the day.

In September 1783, with the Treaty of Paris, Britain ended its war against the American colonies and recognised its independence. The commanding officer of the Ulster Provincial Regiment, Lieutenant Colonel Thomas Dawson, certified D'Arcy served three years in the Regiment, *till it was reduced at the end of the War, all which time he conducted himself as became a good soldier.*[19]

Uncertain where his future lay, D'Arcy looked abroad for opportunities. His eldest brother William was in Holland, a cavalry officer in the Fifth Regiment of Dragoon Guards,[20] his sister Dorothy was making plans for America.

He wanted to seek his fortune in India. He wrote to the Court of Directors of the East India Company, seeking a position as assistant surgeon; he sought a letter of recommendation from Lord Charlemont, Commander in Chief of the Volunteers, and obtained letters of introduction, one to David Killican, based with the Company in Calcutta.[21]

Irish medical apprenticeships were not recognised outside Ireland. Before D'Arcy could be considered for a post in India, he would have to go to London, and be examined before the Company of Surgeons' Court of Examiners.

By May Day 1785,[22] he had completed his apprenticeship, he had the blessing of his father and of Dr Patton to travel to London, to gain formal recognition as an assistant surgeon, and to apply for a post in India.

En route, he wanted to visit his Wentworth relations in Yorkshire. His father wrote to Earl Fitzwilliam at *Wentworth Woodhouse,* to introduce him. Fitzwilliam's reply assured him D'Arcy would be most welcome.

D'Arcy packed his medical chest, his notes and small collection of instruments, and made his farewells. He rode east first, to Downpatrick, to ask St Patrick's blessing, a custom of those leaving Ireland. D'Arcy climbed up to his grave, amidst the hilltop ruins of the old Celtic monastery, torched by Vikings, rebuilt in the twelfth century and destroyed again under orders from Henry VIII.

Then he turned north towards Donaghadee, on the Irish Sea. He waited on the great curved quay for the daily packet to arrive from Portpatrick. The mailbags from the mainland were taken off, replaced with out-going mail, the passengers went aboard, and she was ready to sail. The wind was fair that day, he crossed the narrow strait to Portpatrick in Scotland in less than three hours.

The packet carried several most engaging passengers, with private assignations in Portpatrick. Couples who were underage, or who could not get their parents' consent to marry, could cross to Scotland and marry there, under its more liberal laws. On board were several affectionate and expectant young couples, their happiness and optimism were infectious.

You intend then to go into Yorkshire? Kitty, or the Bower

From Portpatrick, D'Arcy travelled across steep high country to Dumfries. He took a mail coach bound for Manchester, then went on to Sheffield. From there, a rambling local service took him the last twelve miles to Wentworth Woodhouse, the estate of the 4th Earl Fitzwilliam, his distant cousin; and the burial place of Thomas Wentworth, 1st Earl of Strafford.

What D'Arcy saw was breathtaking, *from the entrance to the park*, there were *magnificent woods, spreading waters and elegant temples, breaking upon the eye at every angle.* He looked across *a noble range of hills, dales, lakes and woods, the house magnificently situated in the centre of the whole.* Before him lay *a valley, the water winding through it in a noble stile*, and *on the opposite side was a vast sweep of rising slopes, finely scattered with trees, up to the house, seen distinctly, standing in the point of grandeur from whence it seemed to command all the surrounding country.*

The road wound around a hill, and broke out upon the house, in striking contrast to the first approach, from which it was seen only gradually. D'Arcy learnt it was a deliberate design, that had involved *cutting away a large part of the hill, which projected too much before the front of the house; huge works, that required the removal of upwards of one hundred and forty thousand square yards of earth.*[23]

Earl Fitzwilliam made him welcome, and the two cousins took an immediate liking to each other. Fitzwilliam, thirty-seven, was fourteen years older than D'Arcy, urbane, gracious and serious minded. D'Arcy was twenty-three, tall, boyish, bright of mind, dark haired, with blue eyes and an Irish lilt, described by a contemporary as *one of the handsomest men of his day*.[24] They forged a friendship that would last all their lives.

Fitzwilliam had inherited *Wentworth Woodhouse* just three years earlier, after the death of his uncle, Lord Rockingham. His inheritance had included a great estate in Ireland, *Coolatin,* that took up the greater part of the cultivated land of County Wicklow, and large tracts of the counties of Wexford and Kildare.

Earl Fitzwilliam and his wife Lady Charlotte had been married fifteen years. They had no children, the Countess was frail, at times *so ill as to be despaired of.*[25] The English Wentworths were in decline, its *four great families*[26] became extinct during Fitzwilliam's lifetime.[27] There was an unspoken recognition of their Irish cousins as a senior branch of the family, with a direct male line from the Wentworths of the original *Wentworth Wodehouse.*

About his own home in Ireland   Emma

D'Arcy carried greetings to him from Lord Charlemont, and gave him an account of the achievements of the Ulster Volunteers under his command. He had news from his family in Portadown, and spoke of his work in Dr Patton's practice. Fitzwilliam wanted to hear more from him about Ireland. He found D'Arcy's optimism, his confidence in the spirit and future of the Irish, Catholic and Protestant, encouraging and refreshing.

They talked of the strong ties between the two kingdoms and the great desire of Ireland to be master of its own destiny. D'Arcy was surprised how much Fitzwilliam knew about Irish retaliation against restrictions on trade, how merchants were boycotting British imports, following the example of the American colonies, and the well organised smuggling of goods to Britain's west coast to avoid tariffs.[28]

Fitzwilliam told D'Arcy, that only a few weeks before, Parliament sent His Majesty its resolutions to improve commerce between Britain and Ireland. Its debates on improving trade with Ireland had aroused huge resistance. More than sixty petitions signed by tens of thousands of people all over England, had protested, fearing *an irrecoverable and deadly wound* to local manufactories and trade.[29]

He spoke of the risk of promoting *Jealousy and Dissatisfaction between the two Kingdoms.*[30] Listening, D'Arcy realised something of the determination required to bring about the reforms so passionately desired in Ireland.³¹ He saw with great pride that Fitzwilliam knew and understood Ireland's aspirations, that his interest was not casual, he was committed to reform.

The Great House Emma

D'Arcy marvelled at scale and magnificence of *Wentworth Woodhouse*, its grand front, noble portico, its great halls and library, and the seeming numberless sets of apartments, with their bed chambers and dressing rooms. Thomas Watson-Wentworth, 1st Marquess of Rockingham had built it to replace the original Tudor house of the Earl of Strafford, his great grandfather. Work had commenced in 1724, and it continued over the next twenty-five years.³² After the 1st Marquess died in 1750, the work on the interior proceeded under his son, Lord Rockingham.

D'Arcy explored the grounds, following the *water, winding through the valley in a very beautiful manner. On one slope was a rustic temple, most elegantly backed with a dark spreading wood, and from the wood were winding paths. One led to an aviary, a light Chinese building of a very pleasing design, stocked with canary and other foreign birds, kept alive in the winter by means of hot walls at the back of the building. Another menagerie, in front of a green-house, contained a prodigious number of foreign birds, particularly gold and pencil pheasants, cockatoos, Mollacca doves, etc. etc. The green-house was very spacious, and behind it was a neat agreeable room for drinking tea.*

A man of fortune at once with horses and grooms at his command Mansfield Park

Fitzwilliam took D'Arcy through the stables, planned by Lord Rockingham, still under construction, *a most magnificent pile of stabling; it is to form a large quadrangle inclosing a square of 190 feet, with a very elegant front to the park. There are to be 84 stalls with numerous apartments for the servants attending, and spacious rooms for hay, corn, etc. etc. etc. dispersed in such a manner as to render the whole perfectly convenient.*³³

The expense of those noble animals Mansfield Park

As Fitzwilliam described his programs to improve the breed and the performance of his horses, he realised he had caught his young cousin's attention. Next morning, D'Arcy rose early to watch the horses train, and he went with Fitzwilliam to watch them race at Doncaster, Richmond, New Malton and Wakefield. At the track, he made the acquaintance of another cousin, a full-time racing man, Peregrine Wentworth, who took his thoroughbreds as far afield as Newmarket and Ascot, to race against the Prince of Wales.

He shortly found himself arrived at politics   Northanger Abbey

Earl Fitzwilliam led a busy public life, he was a member of the House of Lords, a leader of the Whig party and actively involved in the work of the Commons.

In July, he went to York for the summer assizes, planning to be back there in August to begin a round of country meetings and inspections. He invited D'Arcy to stay in York until his return, to enjoy something of the city before he had to leave for London, to return to his studies.

Fitzwilliam arranged for him to stay with Robert Sinclair, a barrister and loyal Whig, who rallied support for him, and kept him informed of political currents in York and the Ridings. A few months earlier Sinclair was made the Clerk of Sessions and Clerk of the Register of Tailzies and Inventories of Heirs in Scotland;[34] later he would become Recorder for the West Riding.

Robert Sinclair was very happy to entertain Fitzwilliam's young Irish cousin. He showed him the city and introduced him to the medical fraternity of York. On Thursday evenings they went to the *Good Humour Club* at Sunton's Coffee House in Coney Street, to enjoy supper, a convivial bowl of punch and a little gaming.[35] D'Arcy met a throng of Yorkshire Whigs, older, sedate members of the Rockingham Club and a more ambitious, feistier group at the Yorkshire Club. Though his future lay with medicine rather than politics, he felt great affinity with their liberal ideals and aspirations.

On 27 August, he joined a crowd behind the Minster to watch the launch of a balloon from Kettlewell's Orchard. After rising gently for about forty feet it started falling rapidly. The pilot threw ballast out of the basket, but to no avail. The balloon dashed against the Roman wall at the edge of the orchard. The basket thumped down, entangled between a chimney and the hipped rooftop. The crowd fell back, afraid of fire. Luckily the roof was slate, not thatch. D'Arcy raced forward to help the pilot, who was bruised and in a great fright.[36]

The family were now seen to advantage   Mansfield Park

In August, Fitzwilliam returned to York to enjoy a week of racing. His brother George, brother in law Thomas Dundas, and D'Arcy accompanied him to Doncaster for the St Leger Stakes. Fitzwilliam's three year old *Matron*[37] ran second,[38] and Peregrine Wentworth's *Verjuice*[39] third. Next race, a four mile sweepstakes, Peregrine's colt[40] took third, Fitzwilliam's fourth.[41] In the four mile Corporation Cup, after leading the field, Peregrine's chestnut five year old, *Spectre* ran second. They were days to be remembered!

More vigorous measures, a more complete reformation, a quicker release from debt Persuasion

Cold October weather rolled in as Fitzwilliam's carriage set out for London. As they travelled south, D'Arcy talked of his plans to find a position in India. Fitzwilliam invited him to write with his observations of the country and of the Company. He reminded D'Arcy it was Elizabeth I who granted the Company its charter in 1600, with exclusive rights to trade with India.

Fitzwilliam saw its costly wars in India as contrary to the interests of a trading company. Its Court of Directors had come to Parliament over the past three years seeking financial support, and Parliament had agreed, persuaded if the Company failed it would damage *the whole publick credit of the kingdom*.[42]

The amusements of this vaunted city Lesley Castle

It was early afternoon when Fitzwilliam's coach entered the city from the Great North Road. D'Arcy did not turn from the window. Fitzwilliam sat back to enjoy his young cousin's delight at finding himself at last in the *great world*.[43]

Fitzwilliam was immediately absorbed in parliamentary affairs, but he found time most mornings to walk to a nearby Coffee-house brimming with the rich aroma of coffee, and conversation. That *Coffee-house of good account, not far from Bond-street, called the Mount*,[44] remained their favoured place to meet.

At Fitzwilliam's house in Grosvenor Square,[45] D'Arcy was introduced to a host of his colleagues and friends. He met his loyalist American cousins, John Wentworth, in exile from New Hampshire, and Paul Wentworth, a spymaster in Europe during the American War of Independence. He made friends with a number of the young lawyers and politicians, Whigs and Tories, and members of both Houses who he met there.

I dare say a very clever surgeon The Watsons

D'Arcy found lodgings at No.12 St Martin's-le-Grand, with a window looking over the street and quiet space to read and study. On the first of December 1785, he was one of twenty-two young men examined by the Company of Surgeons' Court of Examiners, on their knowledge of surgical practice, anatomy, diagnosis and surgery. He was one of the ten who qualified as *Mates to Indiamen*, the East India Company requirement for an Assistant Surgeon.[46]

One of the examiners, Percivall Pott, invited D'Arcy to walk the wards during 1786, under his direction. To qualify a Mate to Indiaman, and to obtain a position with the East India Company, he was required to walk the wards for twelve months, in one of the great London charity hospitals.[47] D'Arcy chose St Bartholomew's at Smithfield, under Mr Pott.

> *I preserved my half guinea entire till the day of examination, when I went, with a quaking heart, to Surgeons' Hall, in order to undergo that ceremony... A young fellow came out from the place of examination with a pale countenance, his lip quivering, his looks as wild as if he had seen a ghost... At length the beadle called my name, with a voice that made me tremble as much as if it had been the sound of the last trumpet: however, there was no remedy; I was conducted into a large hall, where I saw about a dozen of grim faces sitting at a long table, one of whom bade me come forward in such an imperious tone, that I was actually for a minute or two bereft of my senses.*
>
> After their interrogation, Random reported –
>
> *The chairman commanded silence, and ordered me to withdraw. In less than a quarter of an hour, I was called in again, received my qualification sealed up, and was ordered to pay five shillings. I laid down my half guinea on the table, and stood some time, until one of them bade me begone; to this I replied, "I will when I have got my change;" on which another threw me five shillings and sixpence...I was afterwards obliged to give three shillings and sixpence to the beadles, and a shilling to an old woman who swept the hall.*[48]
>
> The Adventures of Roderick Random

The power of doing anything with quickness is always much prized by the possessor, and often without any attention to the imperfection of the performance Pride & Prejudice

Pott was a meticulous surgeon, he did much to abolish the use of escharotics or corrosive creams, for treating cancers; and cautery, the application of a red hot iron after amputation, to remove tumours or close off arteries. His patients included Thomas Gainsborough, Samuel Johnson and David Garrick.[49]

Pott performed many successful cranial operations, and developed techniques to make surgery, done without anaesthetic, less unnecessarily painful. He cautioned against working too speedily, it was, he wrote, *productive of the most mischievous consequences.*[50]

Every thing was said that could encourage Mansfield Park

The late 1780's were exciting years to be a student surgeon in London. D'Arcy wrote to Alexander Patton, describing the wards at St Bartholomew's, and the focus on treatment based on evidence and close observation.

His family in Ireland believed he would shortly leave for India, and *soon become a Nabob*. Alexander Patton sent him a thoughtful letter of advice,

I look upon your fortune now in a fair way of being made, if you throw no impediments in its way, Sobriety, Prudence and Industry, with a Great degree of caution and attention to those whom you have to look up to are the great things you must be mindful of. Great People who are to Confer favours look for attention from those they confer them on, their counsel they think ought to be taken and every degree of respect paid to their advice and opinions, however different in may be from our own sentiments.

The short time you have now to remain in London every hour of it ought to be industriously dedicated to improving yourself in your Profession. As you are about bidding a long farewell to Europe, you must endeavour to warn your mind off Pleasure and seriously apply to the Profits of the world. Consider that is the end of leaving it, apply with diligence to whatever vocation you may be appointed to in that quarter of the world where you are going. Never leave till tomorrow what you can do this day. Without industry and application no fortune can be made.

D'Arcy did not need to be reminded of these principles: sobriety, diligence, industry, respectfulness and a sense of family honour were engrained in him.

Dr Patton went further, with prescience and a sympathetic understanding of the young man who had been his charge: *whatever your income is, be sure not to live beyond it, if you save but a little every day at the end of the year it will be something in store... No one more sincerely rejoices at the pleasing prospect that is before you than I do, if you throw no impediment in its way.*[51]

A little time and experience in the world will convince you of the truth of this; Idle, giddy and dissipated company carefully avoid at all times, however agreeable they may appear. It is much easier avoiding such company at first than breaking from them afterwards – there is something so fascinating in the company of some dangerous men that we cannot see it till it is too late. Rather choose the more Orderly and Sober than the Pleasing and the Voluptuous for your Companions.

Alexander Patton's letter was important to D'Arcy, he kept it with him throughout his life. Through travail, and experience of the world, he came to understand the errors of judgement he had been warned against. In time, he did achieve the prudence, diligence and learning Dr Patton commended to him.

Chapter 2

Jane Austen

Perfect Felicity is not the property of Mortals

JANE AUSTEN was born at Steventon, in Hampshire, Sunday 16 December 1775, nearly fourteen years after D'Arcy Wentworth. Her father, Rev George Austen was forty four when she was born, her mother Cassandra, thirty six.

In general they were virtuously inclined & not given to any wicked ways
Edgar & Emma

The seventh of eight children, Jane had five older brothers: James, almost eleven; George, nine; Edward, eight; Henry, four and a half, and Frank, nearly two; and an elder sister Cassandra, almost three. Her younger brother, Charles, was born three and a half years later.

Jane's father came from difficult circumstances, his mother died when he was one year old, and his father before he turned seven. His uncle, lawyer Francis Austen, ensured he had a good education. George did well at Tonbridge School, won a scholarship to St John's College, Oxford, and graduated in Arts and Divinity. In 1755, he was ordained in the Anglican Church.

In April 1764, George, now thirty, married Cassandra Leigh, twenty five. She had grown up in Harpsden, Oxfordshire, where her father, Rev Thomas Leigh, was rector. He retired to Bath, and died there in February 1764. Two months later George and Cassandra married, at St Swithin's Church at Walcot, Bath.

Cassandra was a young woman with good connections, a great granddaughter of the 8th Lord Chandos, James Brydges, and a grand niece of the first Duke of Chandos, whose wife, Cassandra, Duchess of Chandos, was a sister of Thomas Willoughby, the first Lord Middleton.

The couple settled in Hampshire, where George had been rector of Steventon for three years, a living provided to him by his cousin, Thomas Knight, who owned the Steventon and Chawton estates, and lived at Godmersham in Kent.

As his family grew, George took in private students to supplement his modest income. During term time, the Steventon Rectory was a lively boys' school. Day-boys attended from the local neighbourhood and boarders lived in the rectory as part of the family household. George educated his students and his own sons to university entrance level.

While still a babe in arms, Jane was sent from home to a wet-nurse. Her nephew wrote, *her mother followed a custom not unusual in those days, though it seems strange to us, of putting out her babies to be nursed in a cottage in the village. The infant was visited by one or both parents, and frequently brought to them at the parsonage, but the cottage was its home, and must have remained so till it was old enough to run about and talk.*[1]

Jane was almost four when her second eldest brother George, now thirteen, was sent away from home. He joined his uncle Thomas Leigh, under the care and control of Francis Cullum, at Monk Sherborne, eight miles from Steventon.[2] It is thought George had cerebral palsy. In 1770 his father replied to *kind wishes for George's improvement,* without optimism, *God knows only how far it will come to pass. We have this comfort, he cannot be a bad or wicked child.*[3]

Jane would have missed her brother. He did not move far away, but he was never again included in Austen family life.

In 1783, when she was seven, her third eldest brother Edward was sent to live with wealthy childless relatives, the Knights, in Kent, to become their son and heir.[4] Thomas Knight had extensive land holdings around Steventon, he had presented George Austen with the living of Steventon. George served as his representative in the parish, and he allowed him to select one of his sons to become part of the Knight family and carry on its name.

Jane grew up with a sense of insecurity, *Where would she be taken? What would these people who called themselves her mother and father, do with her?*[5]

Placing her at one of the best private schools   Lady Susan

In 1783, aged seven, she and Cassandra, ten, were sent to boarding school in Oxford, with their cousin Jane Cooper, daughter of Mrs Austen's elder sister. The headmistress, Mrs Cawley, was Jane Cooper's aunt, her father's sister, and the widow of a master of Brasenose College, Oxford.

Thirty years later, Jane described the feelings of a child sent away from home:

The little girl performed her long journey in safety...The little visitor...was as unhappy as possible. Afraid of every body, ashamed of herself, and longing for the home she had left, she knew not how to look up, and could scarcely speak to be heard, or without crying.

It required a longer time...to reconcile to...the separation from every body she had been used to. Her feelings were very acute, and too little understood to be properly attended to. Nobody meant to be unkind, but nobody put themselves out of their way to secure her comfort.

The rooms were too large for her to move in with ease; whatever she touched she expected to injure, and she crept about in constant terror of something or other; often retreating towards her own chamber to cry; and the little girl...ended every day's sorrows by sobbing herself to sleep. Mansfield Park

Despite her homesickness and shyness, Jane found the routine and expectations of school were not unfamiliar. She could write and read, her education was already well in train. *I am in the habit of seeing almost every day of my life at home little children first learning their letters and then learning to spell.* [6]

Later that year Mrs Cawley relocated her school to Southampton. She kept the three girls with her, but their stay was brief. There was an outbreak of typhus in the town, most likely carried by returning troops. Jane Cooper sent urgent news home that the three of them had the putrid fever, and their mothers arrived to rescue them. Three weeks later, Mrs Cooper, in Bath, died of the infection. The girls recovered, although Jane was seriously ill for some time.

Where girls might be sent to be out of the way, and scramble themselves into a little education Emma

In August 1785, the three girls were packed off once again to boarding school, this time, enrolled at Abbey House School in Reading. Jane was nine, Cassandra twelve, Jane Cooper fourteen, they were expected *to make good connections there, as the girls are all of the best families.*[7]

Jane was eager to experience the ruined grandeur of Reading Abbey, founded in 1121, by Henry I, fourth son of William the Conqueror. He ensured it was *liberally endowed and filled with an order of monks of singular piety.* William of Malmesbury described the Abbey's *noble pattern of holiness,* and its *example of unwearied and delightful hospitality.* [8]

Reading Abbey sat on a strategic, gravely hill near the confluence of the Kennet and Thames rivers, and raised tithes and taxes from rich agricultural surpluses produced on the fertile river plain. It extended over thirty acres, and grew rich and powerful, dominating the local economy with its scale, royal patronage, and a stream of pilgrims.

Four hundred years later, the Abbot, Huw Cook Faringdon, resisted Henry VIII's reformation. He was willing to acknowledge Henry as head of the Church in England, but tried at the same time to maintain his ties with Rome. In 1539, Henry had him arrested for high treason. He was hung, drawn and quartered in front of the Abbey, and Reading Abbey was destroyed.

Jane later observed that Henry, by *abolishing Religious Houses and leaving them to the ruinous depredations of time has been of infinite use to the landscape of England in general, which probably was the principal motive for his doing it.*[9]

Arriving there, a hundred and fifty years later, she expected that *having been a richly endowed convent at the time of the Reformation,* she would find *a large portion of the ancient building still making a part of the present dwelling.*[10]

The Children of the Abbey
Emma

Jane walked through the entrance to the inner precinct, *the high-arched passage, paved with stone, with peculiar awe.*[11] Inside, she was amazed to find the school was quite modern. *An abbey! – yes, it was delightful to be really in an abbey! – but she doubted, as she looked round the room... The furniture was in all the profusion and elegance of modern taste. The fire-place, where she had expected the ample width and ponderous carving of former times, was contracted, with slabs of plain though handsome marble, and ornaments over it of the prettiest English china. The windows, to which she looked with peculiar dependence, were yet less what her fancy had portrayed... every pane was so large, so clear, so light! To an imagination which had hoped for the smallest divisions, and the heaviest stonework, for painted glass, dirt, and cobwebs, the difference was very distressing.*[12]

They ordered the bells to be rung & distributed ninepence among the ringers
Edgar & Emma

Reading was a large and wealthy city, and Jane responded to its vitality.[13] Barges carrying wheat, hops and produce, bound for London, moved along the canal below the school. From the west the smells and shouts of the Buttery Market carried over the walls; the ten bells of St Laurence rang out great songs for hours on end;[14] and at night, a line of glowing street-lights lit the darkness.

The morning sun rose from behind the walls of the newly opened Reading Gaol, built within the Abbey ruins, close enough for her to hear and sense the inmates. A century later one of the prisoners wrote:

> We banged the tins, and bawled the hymns
> And sweated on the mill
> But in the heart of every man
> Terror was lying still.[15]

The Ballad of Reading Gaol

In the year and a half Jane spent in Reading she matured quickly, moving from childhood into adolescence. She set aside the security of life in a small village, and contemplated the discovery of a bigger, more exciting world. Everything seemed possible and attainable, she could imagine a future without limitations.

The Abbey in a mouldering heap, concealed by aged pines   Ode to Pity

Jane was aware of a huge, half glimpsed medieval drama within the great, broken ruins of the Abbey, *rich in the massy walls and smoke of former days.*[16] Its grand, tragic history could be seen and felt all around.

She had shared in a sober, thorough, boys' education at her father's rectory. She read widely, she had a rich knowledge of history, some Latin, Greek and French. But she found that most of her classmates *knew nothing more... than what a twopenny Dame's School in the village could teach.*[17]

The school principal, Mme La Tournelle, had dubious qualifications. She was *a person of the old school, a stout woman, hardly under seventy, but very active, although she had a cork leg. She had never been seen or known to have changed the fashion of her dress.*[18]

There were lessons in the mornings, and after lunch the girls were left to find their own amusement. *No one so much as said, "Where have you been mademoiselle?"*[19] Cassandra, responsible for her precocious sister, did not discourage her from taking advantage of the indolent atmosphere.

Jane found a hide-away under the pines, in a corner of the Abbey ruins, abutting the school and overlooking the Holy Brook. There she would take her books to read on summer afternoons, often remaining there into the long twilight evenings.

So agreeable a party   Sense & Sensibility

In late summer 1786, the girls had visitors, Cassandra and Jane's brother Edward, and their cousin, Jane Cooper's brother Edward. The two handsome, eighteen year olds *insisted on taking them out to dine in high style at the smartest inn in town.*[20]

The two Edwards had come to Reading to enjoy the annual races on Bulmershe Heath, held between August 29th and 31st. They had been to the Lambourn races, and they carried greetings and gossip for their sisters. They had seen the Fowle brothers at Ashdown House for the Cravens' ball,[21] and Tom in particular had sent them all his greetings. They had met a young Irish surgeon at Lambourn, D'Arcy Wentworth, who was also down for the Bulmershe races. Here he was, entering the *Bear Inn* with his friends!

My Attention was attracted by the appearance of a Young man the most lovely of his Sex, who at that moment entered the Room with another Gentleman and Lady. From the first moment I beheld him, I was certain that on him depended the future Happiness of my Life   Lesley Castle

D'Arcy, his cousin George Fitzwilliam and their friend joined the Austen – Cooper party. They were all soon laughing over the *skullduggery* of the day: *A match for 50 guineas took place between Mr Hilton's dun mare Miss Tiffany, and Mr Frogley's horse. After one circuit of the course Miss Tiffany, the favourite, had the race well in hand when Richard Bullock from nearby Sonning rode onto the course and knocked down the mare, who was subsequently awarded the race. It came to light that Bullock was the real owner of Frogley's horse and had wagered a considerable sum on the outcome of the race.*[22]

Their eyes instantly met   Pride & Prejudice

The town was alive with festivities. Dinner at the *Bear* was a great treat for the girls, released from the tedium of school, out in the company of handsome young men, eating, drinking and enjoying the music and dancing.

When she was introduced, Jane asked D'Arcy if he was connected to the Strafford family. She was delighted when he replied he was, and she immediately considered it quite proper to befriend him as a family connexion.

There was such an air of good humour and Gaiety. Jane, *tho' perhaps not authorised to address him with so much familiarity on so short an acquaintance, could not forbear indulging the natural Unreserve & Vivacity of her own Disposition, in speaking to him, as he spoke to her. She was intimately acquainted too with his Family who were her relations, and she chose to consider herself entitled by the connexion to forget how little a while they had known each other.*[23]

D'Arcy told her he was a surgeon, completing his clinical studies in London, making ready to go out to the East Indies. They spoke of India, not the place of heat and mosquitoes, but of *nabobs, gold mohrs, and palanquins.*[24]

Jane told him of her uncle, Tyso Hancock, Surgeon Extraordinary in the East India Company garrison at Calcutta, and of other medical men in her family. Her father's father, William Austen, a Tonbridge surgeon, who died when her father was just seven, and her great grandfather, Sir George Hampson, a physician at Gloucester.

In her friendships she was enthousiastic   Kitty, or the Bower

D'Arcy *talked with fluency and spirit, there was an archness and pleasantry in his manner which interested, though it was hardly understood by her.*[25]

Jane, whose *imagination was lively, and whose Disposition romantic... was already extremely pleased with him, and of course desirous that he might be so with* her, is as little to be wondered at. *Every moment as it added to the conviction of his liking her, made him still more pleasing, and strengthened in her Mind a wish of knowing him better.*²⁶

Jane was nearly eleven, she could be a tomboy one moment, and the next, converse about the world, books and history with great authority. She was most interested in love, and she took a fancy to D'Arcy.

During the meal the girls gathered little piles of bread crumbs to feed the carp, kept in a channel behind the Bear's stables, closed off from the Kennet.²⁷ Jane insisted they all go down together. Running ahead, she lost her balance and fell, twisting her ankle.

Your ankle wants rest, I see by the position of your foot   Sanditon

D'Arcy lifted her up and carried her back inside, she was *not to think of proceeding till the ankle had been examined.*²⁸ He declared there was no bone broken, but the swelling had started. She must tread carefully for a few days. The whole party walked up the hill, back to school, with D'Arcy carrying her.

When her brother and cousins were later criticised for allowing such familiarity and over-excitement, Jane responded, *our acquaintance with each other renders all such Prudery, ridiculous.*²⁹

She recorded the incident at the *Bear* and her meeting with D'Arcy in her first novel,³⁰ and echoed it in her last.³¹ In two rare scenes of intimate contact, a young girl trips and falls, a young man nearby comes to her rescue, takes her up and carries her to safety.

In *Sense and Sensibility*, Marianne and her sister, caught in a sudden rain storm on the downs, run *with all possible speed down the steep side of the hill.*

Marianne trips, *a false step brought her suddenly to the ground… A gentleman… ran to her assistance. She had raised herself from the ground, but her foot had been twisted in the fall, and she was scarcely able to stand. The gentleman offered his services, and perceiving that her modesty declined what her situation rendered necessary, took her up in his arms without further delay, and carried her down the hill… he bore her directly into the house… and quitted not his hold till he had seated her in a chair in the parlour.*

His manly beauty and more than common gracefulness were instantly the themes of general admiration… Marianne had seen less of his person than the rest, for the confusion which crimsoned over her face, on his lifting her up, had robbed her of the power of regarding him.

He *called at the cottage early the next morning to make his personal inquiries… she saw that to the perfect good-breeding of the gentleman, he united frankness and vivacity.*

She had neither shyness nor reserve in their discussion... Encouraged by this to a further examination of his opinions, she proceeded to question him on the subject of books; her favourite authors were brought forward and dwelt upon with so rapturous a delight, that any young man of five and twenty must have been insensible indeed, not to become an immediate convert to the excellence of such works, however disregarded before.

A fine shady Bower – to tranquillise her mind & quiet her spirits
Kitty, or the Bower

D'Arcy called at the Abbey school next afternoon, to enquire about Jane's progress. He introduced himself to Mme La Tournelle as her cousin, the surgeon who attended her ankle the previous evening. She pointed him to the place Jane was most likely to be found, in a little bower beyond the garden gate, towards the Abbey ruins, overlooking the Holy Brook.

Her imagination was busy, her reflections were pleasant, and the pain of a sprained ankle was disregarded
Sense & Sensibility

Jane was sitting in low golden sunlight filtering through the pines. D'Arcy sat on the ground beside her and asked after her ankle. She tested it and declared that other than *a twinge or two in trying to move her foot*[32] it was recovered.

It is pleasant to be among people who know one's connections and care about them
Letters

Jane was eager to talk with him about the history of the noble connexions they shared, of the Earl of Strafford, his life, his family, and his terrible end.

Perfectly convinced that he *was infinitely superior, both in Natural Abilities, & acquired information,* she took *every opportunity of turning the Conversation on History, and they were very soon engaged in an historical dispute. They were conversing... when he suddenly seized hold of her hand, and exclaiming with great emotion, "Upon my honour you are entirely mistaken," pressed it passionately to his lips & ran out of the arbour.*[33]

Hearing an uneven gait approaching, realising it was Mme La Tournelle, D'Arcy took his leave with an affected romantic gesture. He bowed and kissed her hand, not so much a show of respect as a provocation to approaching authority. Jane smiled with delight, it was a magical moment!

Her spirits were elevated above the influence of Displeasure in any one
Kitty, or the Bower

The headmistress' response was swift and vehement: *She began with great Anger and Asperity, the following harangue: Well; this is beyond anything I could have supposed. Profligate as I knew you to be, I was not prepared for such a sight. This is beyond anything you ever did before; beyond any thing I ever heard of in my Life!... I plainly see that every thing is going to sixes & sevens and all order will be at an end throughout the Kingdom."*

"Not however Ma'am the sooner, I hope from any conduct of mine... for upon my honour I have done nothing this evening that can contribute to the overthrow of the kingdom."

"You are Mistaken Child," replied she; *"the welfare of every Nation depends upon the Virtue of it's individuals, and any one who offends in so gross a manner against decorum & propriety is certainly hastening its ruin."*[34]

The report of the young cousins' dinner at the *Bear* seems to have travelled slowly, taking a month or more to arrive at the rectory at Steventon, no doubt gaining in colour and detail with each retelling. Members of her family deemed it shocking, *a strange thing to allow.*[35]

Mme La Tournelle decided that Jane was *one of the most impudent Girls that ever existed.*[36] She wrote to George Austen *to request that she might be immediately removed. I am afraid she is a perverse girl.*[37]

Reverend Austen took her out of school midway through the Michaelmas term. She was happy to see him, and to hear his news, that her cousin Eliza was coming for Christmas. It was ten years since Eliza had visited Steventon, Jane could not remember her. She looked forward to her arrival, as soon as her father's students finished their lessons and went home for the holidays.

These kind of things are all very well at Christmas   Emma

On 21 December 1786, Eliza Hancock, under her grand new style of the Comtesse de Feuillide, made her long-anticipated entrance, accompanied by her noisy baby, Hastings, and her irrepressible mother, Philadelphia.[38]

Eliza, fourteen years older than Jane, was *delicately fair,* slight and full of life, *her countenance is absolutely sweet and her voice and manner winningly mild.*[39] She captivated Jane with her tales of adventure in faraway places, and her pleasantries, known to rouse the heart of any young man.

Jane heard lively stories of Eliza's conquests, of one of her Tonbridge cousins, young James Walter, who was so overcome by her charms, he *made verses on me in which he compared me to Venus & I know what other divinity, & played off fireworks in the cellar in honour of my charms.*[40]

The vagabond life

Eliza was proud of being *early accustomed to the vagabond life.*[41] She left England for Europe with her mother at age fifteen, arriving in Paris at the end of 1779, after two years travelling through Flanders and Germany.

Two years later, at twenty, she married a handsome French Captain, Jean-Francois Capot de Feuillide, son of a provincial lawyer, with estates in south west France. He was ten years older, with a title, the Comte de Feuillide.

Rev Austen disapproved of Eliza's impulsive marriage to a foreigner, a self-styled aristocrat and a Catholic.[42] She had protested, *the man to whom I have given my hand is everyways amiable both in mind and person. It is too little to say he loves me since he literally adores me; entirely devoted to me... My situation is everyways agreeable.*[43]

Their marriage appeared happy, they acquired a large estate of five thousand acres from Louis XVI. It was largely marshland, but the Comte set about draining and making it productive. Naturally, Eliza and Philadelphia contributed all they could to assist him in his enterprise.

Such a fund of vivacity & good humour
Kitty, or the Bower

Eliza described Paris as *magnificence beyond conception*. At one ball she saw Marie Antoinette, in a *Turkish dress made of silver grounded silk intermixed with blue & entirely trimmed and almost covered with jewels.*[44]

At Versailles, she wore *a corset & Petticoat of pale green lutestring, covered with transparent silver gauze. The petticoat and sleeves puckered and confined with large bunches of roses and an amazing large bouquet of White Lilac. The same flower, together with gauze, Feathers, ribbon & diamonds intermixed with her hair. Her neck was entirely uncovered & she was without gloves.*[45]

Eliza described Longchamps, a monastery in the Bois de Boulogne, where *everybody now goes, not to say their prayers but to show their fine cloaths and fine equipages... the Queen and Royal family are generally there...The number and magnificence of the carriages are incredible. Most people have four to six fine horses, as many lacqueys as possible behind, sometimes in the number of eight, and often running footmen. The élégants or fashionable young men in general either on horseback or in open carriages.*[46]

In London, Eliza enjoyed the fashionable social whirl, she attended receptions at St. James's Palace, and counted the Duke and Duchess of Cumberland amongst her friends.

I have been for some time past the greatest rake imaginable & really wonder how such a meagre creature as I am can support so much fatigue, of which the history of one day will give you some idea, for I only stood from two to four in the Drawing Room & of course loaded with a great hoop of no inconsiderable weight, went to the Duchess of Cumberland's in the Evening, and from thence to Almack's where I staid till five in the morning, all this I did not many days ago, & am yet alive to tell You of it. I believe tho', I should not be able to support London hours, & all the racketing of a London life for a year together.[47]

Christmas gaieties Mansfield Park

Eliza turned twenty-four three days before Christmas. George Austen borrowed a fortepiano for her to play. Philadelphia watched Hastings, while she filled the house with carols, songs and lively dance tunes for them all. Eliza believed, during cold weather, *dancing was the only effectual method of rendering one's existence less uncomfortable.*[48]

Eliza had played from an early age, encouraged by her father, who followed her *Progress in Musick,*[49] and insisted she study with *the best Masters, otherwise she will get a Wrong method of Fingering which can never after be rectified,*[50] and that her harpsichord *be the best, mind not the price*[51]

Mrs Austen saw that Jane was rapt in her husband's niece, every sentence she uttered included Eliza, she asked repeatedly for her to *favour* them all with stories of her *life and adventures.*[52]

Acting this Christmas in Hampshire[53] Eliza de Feuillide

Many of George Austen's students went on to careers in the church or the law. He encouraged them, and his children, to be confident public speakers, to read aloud, to put on and to act in plays together.

Over several memorable Christmas holidays, the Austens and their guests rehearsed and performed popular plays, usually comedies, for amusement. *Nobody is fonder of the exercise of talent in young people or promotes it more, than my father; and for anything of the acting, spouting, reciting kind, I think he always has a decided taste. I am sure he encouraged us in it.*[54]

Theatricals were frustrating, they demanded cooperation, *everybody had a part either too long or too short; – nobody would attend as they ought, nobody would remember on which side they were to come in.*

I shall always look back on our theatricals with exquisite pleasure Mansfield Park

Eventually though, it came together, *there was such an interest, such an animation, such a spirit diffused! Every body felt it. We were all alive. There was employment, hope, solicitude, bustle for every hour of the day. Always some little objection, some little doubt, some little anxiety to be got over. I never was happier.*[55]

This Christmas was memorable and full of laughter, Eliza, Philadelphia and the Coopers took part in two comedies, performed in the rectory barn. Eliza took the leading female roles, Isabella in *The Wonder-A Woman Keeps a Secret,*[56] and Constantia in *The Chances,* with a carried-on part for baby Hastings as the mystery child.[57]

You will rejoice to hear of the return of my amiable Brother from abroad
Amelia Webster

The next Christmas, 1787, Eliza was eager to return. James Austen was home after a year in Europe recuperating from a broken heart and failed engagement. *The air of France had greatly recovered both his Health & Spirits.*[58]

She invited another Austen cousin, Phylly Walter, to join her – *we shall have a most brilliant party & a great deal of amusement, the house full of Company & frequent balls. You cannot possibly resist so many temptations when I tell you your old Friend James is returned from France & is to be of the acting party.*[59]

She told Phylly they would perform two farces.[60] In *Maid of the Oaks* by John Burgoyne she would play Lady Bab Lardoon, *a mole in the sunshine* once out of London.[61] In David Garrick's *Bon Ton,* she would be Miss Tittup, a spirited minx, who declares, *we went out of England, a very awkward, good English family; but half a year in France, and a winter passed in the warmer climate of Italy, have ripened our minds to every ease, dissipation and pleasure.*[62]

Phylly was polite, but had no intention of joining Eliza, telling her brother James, he of the fireworks in the cellar, *the Countess has many amiable qualities… they wish me much of the party and offer to carry me there but I do not think of it.* She mentioned the *dissipated life she was brought up to.*[63]

He thinks it very good fun to be single again
Lesley Castle

James Austen, now twenty-two, was to direct the family theatricals, and he was eager to enjoy Eliza's company. *She is clever and agreeable, has all the knowledge of the world which makes conversation easy, and talks very well.*[64]

Eliza did not star in the salacious romantic comedies she favoured. In the end, in March 1788, well after Christmas, they performed Henry Fielding's burlesque, *The Life & Death of Tom Thumb the Great.*

It was more pleasant than prudent
Mansfield Park

Mrs Austen, acutely conscious of Eliza's flirtations, was *provoked at the artifice.* She considered her extravagant, a wrong influence. The year before, she had seen her effect on Jane, now she saw her with James and Henry: *engaging at the same time and in the same house the affections of two men who were neither of them at liberty to bestow them.*[65]

In *Mansfield Park,* Jane told a story of the Bertram family theatricals, choosing *Lover's Vows* to perform, and vying for parts to allow them a taste of the illicit pleasures of seduction and adultery. Perhaps, disturbed by Miss Tittup's influence, George Austen was prevailed upon to halt the production.

The following Christmas, 1788, Eliza was in Paris when James directed *Bon*

Ton, the final production of the Austen family theatricals.

I have heard that there is a great deal of wine drunk at Oxford   Northanger Abbey

In the new year of 1787, Cassandra left for Abbey House School with Jane Cooper[66] while Jane remained at Steventon, to watch her brothers leaving home, gaining their independence.

Edward was away on his Grand Tour, arranged by the Knight family. Frank returned to the *Royal Academy for Seamen at Portsmouth,*[67] making ready for a naval career. Charles was to join him in just a few years.

James was expected to return to Oxford, where he was in his seventh year. Henry completed his studies at the rectory, preparing for his matriculation. He was to join James at St John's College, and follow his lead, as a scholar working towards a Master of Arts.

Jane was not convinced of their commitment to scholarship, she suspected young men at Oxford passed their days in the style of *Peregrine Pickle*:

> *The heart of our young gentleman dilated at the prospect of the figure he should make with such a handsome annuity, the management of which was left to his own discretion: and he amused his imagination with the most agreeable reveries during his journey to Oxford, which he performed in two days. Here being introduced to the head of the college, to whom he had been recommended, accommodated with genteel apartments, entered as a gentleman commoner in the books, and provided with a judicious tutor, instead of returning to the study of Greek and Latin, in which he thought himself sufficiently instructed; he renewed his acquaintance with some of his old school-fellows, whom he found in the same situation, and was by them initiated in all the fashionable diversions of the place.*
>
> *It was not long before he made himself remarkable for his spirit and humour, which were so acceptable to the bucks of the university, that he was admitted as a member of their corporation, and in a very little time became the most conspicuous personage of the whole fraternity; not that he valued himself upon his ability in smoking the greatest number of pipes, and drinking the largest quantity of ale; these were qualifications of too gross a nature to captivate his refined ambition.*
>
> *He piqued himself on his talent for raillery, his genius and taste, his personal accomplishments, and his success at intrigue; nor were his excursions confined to the small villages in the neighbourhood, which are commonly visited once a week by the students for the sake of carnal recreation. He kept his own horses,*

> *traversed the whole country in parties of pleasure, attended all the races within fifty miles of Oxford, and made frequent jaunts to London, where he used to lie incognito during the best part of the term.*
>
> *The rules of the university were too severe to be observed by a youth of his vivacity; and therefore he became acquainted with the proctor, by times. But all the checks he received were insufficient to moderate his career; he frequented taverns and coffee-houses, committed midnight frolics in the streets, insulted all the sober and pacific class of his fellow-students; the tutors themselves were not sacred from his ridicule; he laughed at the magistrate, and neglected every particular of college discipline.*[68]
>
> The Adventures of Peregrine Pickle

Jane contemplated the freedoms enjoyed by her sister and her brothers. She *had seen the World, had passed two years in one of the first boarding schools, spent a fortnight in Bath and supped one night in Southampton.*[69] Now, it seemed, there was nothing more for her to experience or to enjoy.

Chapter 3

Nabobs, gold mohrs & palanquins

*She left England & I have since heard is at present
the favourite Sultana of the great Mogul*

JANE WAS VERY AFFECTED by the story of her father's childhood, how he and his sisters were orphaned, then separated, their lives taking such different paths. During the Christmas visit of Philadelphia and Eliza, she made *repeated entreaties* to her aunt to recount the story of their *Misfortunes and Adventures*.[1]

Jane's grandmother Rebecca Austen had died in 1732, leaving her husband William with four children, her newborn daughter Leonora; George, Jane's father, aged one; Philadelphia, two; and eleven year old William Hampson Walter, the son of her first marriage.

William Austen, a surgeon in Tonbridge, a market town in Kent, managed alone for four years. In 1736, he married Susanna Kelk, but a year later, at thirty six, he was dead. Susanna, forty-eight, was reluctant to care for his children.[2] George, six, stayed with his aunt, Betty Hooper, in Tonbridge. Leonora, five, and Phila, seven, were sent to London to live with their father's youngest brother, Stephen Austen, *an eminent bookseller in Newgate-street*[3] near St Paul's churchyard.

Jane felt for their fate – *dispersed* and *left in great distress, reduced to a state of absolute dependence on some relations, who though very opulent and very nearly connected with them, had with difficulty been prevailed on to contribute anything towards their Support.*[4]

Portionless girls

Four years later, Francis Austen, one of William's three older brothers, came forward to assist ten year old George. It was decided Philadelphia and Leonora would remain in London in Stephen Austen's care.

Philadelphia showed an early interest in fashion. When she was fifteen, he arranged her apprenticeship to *a celebrated milliner in Bond Street.*[5] Stephen Austen died in December 1750, the year she completed her indenture, and it seems her uncle Francis then took charge of her affairs. A few months later, now twenty-one, she wrote to the East India Company, asking permission to visit Fort St David, a hundred miles south of Madras.[6]

Philadelphia left England in January 1752, on the *Bombay Castle,* an East India Company vessel, *in the adventurous manner often adopted by portionless girls.*[7] After unloading their cargoes of cotton and silk textiles, tea, rock salt and saltpetre, the roomy Indiamen would sail home, carrying lively young "spins," off to India, with marriage in mind. Jane knew the brutal truth about her aunt, *that being without means or prospects she was sent out to India with the object of finding a husband.*[8]

To a Girl of any Delicacy, the voyage in itself, since the object of it is so universally known, is a punishment that needs no other to make it very severe
Kitty, or the Bower

In February 1753, at Fort St David in Cuddalore, Philadelphia, twenty-three, married a forty year old Company surgeon, Tyso Saul Hancock. Her uncle Francis, his agent and attorney, had doubtless arranged the match.

The eldest daughter had been obliged to accept the offer of one of her cousins to equip her for the East Indies and, tho' infinitely against her inclination, had necessitated to embrace the only possibility that was offered to her of a Maintenance; yet it was one so opposite to all her ideas of Propriety, so contrary to her Wishes, so repugnant to her feelings; that she would almost prefer servitude to it; had Choice been allowed her. Her personal Attractions had gained her a husband as soon as she arrived in Bengal, and she had been married nearly a twelvemonth; Splendidly yet unhappily married – United to a Man of double her own age, whose disposition was not amiable and whose Manners were unpleasing, though his Character respectable.

Leonora, eighteen, remained with Stephen's widow Elizabeth, who, two years later, married another bookseller near St Paul's, John Hinton. Leonora stayed on *as a companion,* helping out as she had always done, hurrying along the ginnels threaded between Newgate Street, Paternoster Row and St Paul's, carrying books, orders and messages, and attending to the household chores.

Jane described the arrangement with gentle derision – they *treat her as if she were* their *own daughter. She does not go out into Public with* them *to be sure;*

but…*nothing can be kinder to her than* they are; they *would have taken her to Cheltenham last year if there had been room enough at the Lodgings, and therefore I don't think that she can have anything to complain of.*

Leonora missed Philadelphia, *she was not married, and could yet look forward to a change in her circumstances, but situated for the present without any immediate hope of it, in a family where, tho' all were relations she had no friend, she wrote usually in depressed Spirits, which her separation from her Sister and her Sister's marriage had greatly contributed to make so.*

Phila wrote to her family, her *letters were always unsatisfactory, though she did not openly avow her feelings, yet every line proved her to be Unhappy. She spoke with pleasure of nothing, but of those Amusements which they had shared together and which could return no more, and seemed to have no happiness in view but that of returning to England again.* [9]

The perils of postings

In 1759, the Hancocks sailed a thousand miles north, to Bengal, to Fort William at Calcutta, then upriver to Cossimbuzar. Tyso was appointed Company surgeon there, *at the particular request of Colonel Clive.* He had treated Robert Clive, at Fort St David, and Clive recommended him *as a person of great experience in his profession and particularly attentive to his duty.* [10]

Sir Roger Dowlat [11]

In April 1756, Siraj-ud-daula, just twenty-three, succeeded his grandfather as the Nawab of Bengal. Angered by the expansion of the British military presence at Fort William, he amassed a huge army. In June, with thousands of foot soldiers and horsemen, four hundred battle elephants and eighty cannons, he seized Cossimbuzar, then Calcutta. He imprisoned a large group at the Calcutta garrison, in a tiny cell, where most of them suffocated and died. It became known as the *Black Hole of Calcutta*.

In June 1756, Robert Clive, with just three thousand and two hundred troops, defeated Siraj-ud-daula near Cossimbuzar, in the Battle of Plassey, a victory that established the East India Company's authority in Bengal. In London, one Company director enquired, was Sir Roger Dowlat a baronet?

The Black Hole of Calcutta Letters

Arriving in Cossimbuzar, Phila was reunited with her friend, Mary Elliott. They had travelled to India together on the *Bombay Castle*, seven years before. Phila disembarked at Fort St David, Mary went on to Fort William, and married Captain Buchanan. He died in the Black Hole of Calcutta, leaving her alone with two daughters.

The following year, she married Warren Hastings, he was twenty six and had been in India for eight years.[12] Captured at Cossimbuzar by Siraj-ud-daula, he *suffered ill treatment*[13] at his hands.

Hastings was reared by his grandfather, the rector of Daylesford. His mother died in childbirth, and his father left soon after, for the West Indies. At sixteen, he sat the East India Company entry examination, and arrived in Calcutta on the *London,* in October 1750, appointed to the Fort William Accomptant's Office as a writer.

Hastings had a good ear for languages, he took pains to learn Urdu, Persian and Bangla. He had an even temperament, and could listen sympathetically to Indian grievances. He gained a good standing with local people and the Company. In 1758, he was appointed Resident at the Court of Murshidabad.

When the Hancocks arrived in 1759, Hastings, Mary, their son George and her two daughters were living in Cossimbuzar. In July that year, Mary died in childbirth, her newborn daughter lived just nineteen days.

The duties of friendship Northanger Abbey

Phila helped with his children, and Tyso Hancock became a partner in Hastings' private trading ventures, then permitted, in salt, timber and Bihar opium. Hastings complained constantly that Tyso failed to provide proper accounts or to keep him informed.

Two years after Hancock arrived in Cossimbuzar, the Company's Court of Directors objected to his appointment, ordered the *extravagant* three thousand rupees a year *settled upon him* be *set aside,* that he be paid the usual allowance and no more.[14]

Dispirited by his demotion, Hancock asked for *leave to resign his post as surgeon on account of his Health.*[15] He left Cossimbuzar for Calcutta, where he took up the post of surgeon at Fort William.

Eliza was born there in December 1761, the Hancocks' first and only child, a great treasure after nearly nine years of marriage. She was named Elizabeth, for the Hastings' lost daughter, and he became her godfather.

Hastings also moved to Calcutta that year, promoted with Clive's patronage, to the Council of Fort William. Concerned that three year old George was delicate, he decided to send him home to England.[16] Philadelphia suggested her brother George Austen as foster parent, and it was duly arranged. The child travelled in the care of Francis Sykes,[17] who came to India with Hastings. He was returning home ill; in England, he handed the boy to George Austen.

When Cassandra Leigh and George Austen married in April 1764, six year old George Hastings became their first child. As a young girl, Cassandra knew

Warren Hastings, from visits to her grandparents in Gloucestershire, where the Leigh and Hastings families had known each other for generations.[18]

Impelled in opposite directions   The Watsons

Hastings found his duties on the Fort William Council highly frustrating. He had an ally in the Governor, Henry Vansittart, but they were two against the majority, constantly outvoted by *headstrong, violent and unscrupulous Councillors*,[19] and powerless to deal with abuses of power within the Company.

Conflict on the Council became unmanageable. In 1764, Hastings resigned and Vansittart retired. Both men returned to England on *HMS Medway*, leaving Calcutta shortly after Christmas Day. Dr Hancock's resignation had been accepted and the Hancock family was also on board. It was a journey of nearly seven months to reach England.

A fellow passenger on the *Medway*, wrote, *Mr Vansittart with his usual cheerfulness makes us all very happy & we have all enjoyed good health except Hancock who is generally complaining & often much out of order...he knows too much to hear any Opinion but his own but I think he is Emeticking himself to the next world.*[20]

At the Deane rectory, in Hampshire, George Hastings contracted diphtheria and died. George Austen, devastated, went to meet the *Medway*, to give Warren Hastings the dreadful news. His son's death *left a shadow on his face for years.*[21] George was there to see Phila disembark, to welcome her home, and be introduced to her husband and daughter.

The schemes of amusement at home   Sense & Sensibility

The Hancocks rented a house in Mayfair and a cottage in Surrey. Phila found herself in London, in a comfortable, gracious residence with a husband and daughter, money and servants. She was eager to re-establish relations with her family, to meet her husband's family, and to introduce Eliza.

Phila's mother was one of seven children of George Hampson, a baronet. She had a large extended family, Austens, Walters, Paynes, Freemans, Stanhopes and more. She and Tyso called at a glittering, little shop in Charing Cross, full of sparkling cut-glass, to meet his brother Colbron, and took Eliza to call on his sister Olivia Lightfoot, at Margate in Kent. They exchanged regular visits with Hastings.

After just a few years, the Hancocks found it increasingly difficult to afford their new life. Dr Hancock attributed much of the blame for their predicament to Phila's uncle, Francis Austen, believing he had *neglected his affairs*[22] and failed to give him a true picture of his finances.

Without any alliances but in trade Emma

In 1768, Dr Hancock received permission from the Company to return to India, to reside there for three years to settle his private affairs and recover his effects.[23] He paid his own passage on the *Lioness*, he did not apply for a Company position, he planned to restore his family fortunes through trading.

Hancock knew many Company servants in Bengal who made their fortunes through private trade.[24] His intention was to obtain a licence, or *dustuk*, from the East India Company, to enable him to trade privately under its protection, exempt from paying tolls or customs.

Henry Vansittart was returning to India, and Hancock could rely on his patronage to obtain the *dustuk*, *without which it is impossible to trade here to any advantage*.[25] The Company had appointed Vansittart to examine each department of its Indian administration. He sailed from Portsmouth, with two inspectors Francis Forde and Luke Scrafton, on the *Aurora*, in September 1769. After leaving Cape Town on 27 December, she was never heard of again.

In the East Indies the climate is hot and the mosquitoes are troublesome
Sense & Sensibility

The year Hancock returned to India, the monsoon failed, and a dreadful drought followed, bringing widespread famine to Bengal. *The rains failed; the earth was parched up; the tanks were empty; the rivers shrank within their beds.*[26]

He fell *very ill with severe fever. The great sickliness of Calcutta obliged me to undergo great fatigue… the diseases which have been and continue to be very fatal here are chiefly owing to the putrefaction occasioned by the prodigious number of dead bodies lying in the streets and all places adjacent.*[27]

In March 1769, the Company tightened eligibility for *dustuks*, asserting, *our displeasure at the irregularity committed in the granting of Dustuks to Free merchants and others*. They were to be revoked, and no *Dustuk* granted *to any but the Company's covenanted servants*.[28]

In January 1770, a friend of Hancock recommended him for a post as surgeon at Fort William. It would give him the means to support his family.[29] He reassured Phila, *I hope soon to amend my situation so much that you shall not have Occasion to deny yourself anything which may be agreeable to you.*[30]

The Court of Directors was advised that *in consideration of the long services of Mr Tyso Saul Hancock and his experience in his profession we have been induced to indulge him so far as to appoint him a supernumerary surgeon at the Presidency but not to rise.*[31] The Court approved with bad grace: *in future we shall disapprove of any appointment you may make to persons who have our permission to remain in India only to settle their private affairs.*[32]

After a break of six years, Hancock was unhappy returning to medical duties, he was fifty-eight, he had been a surgeon for over thirty years.[33] He told Phila: *it was intended to be a Sinecure, but it subjects me to attend whenever I am called upon which happens too frequently. You know how much I hate the Practice of Physick yet I am obliged to take it up again: nothing could have induced me to do so but the Hopes of thereby providing for my family.*[34]

When Phila suggested she and Eliza join him, Hancock refused: *You know very well that no girl, tho' but fourteen years old, can arrive in India without attracting the notice of every Coxcomb in the Place... you know how impossible it is for a young girl to avoid being attached to a young handsome man whose address is agreeable to her. Debauchery under the polite name of Gallantry is the Reigning Vice of the Settlement... I am sure that nothing shortens a woman's days so much as her being married when too young...I am certain no Argument can ever induce me to give my consent to the Introduction of my Daughter to so lewd a place as Bengal now is.*[35]

Acquainted with the manners and amusements of London   Sense & Sensibility

Eliza was seven when her father returned to Calcutta in 1768. She would not see him again. Her letters made him happy, he followed all her doings: *pray acquaint me with...the wild duck's eggs...whether you have gotten a little horse and how you ride.*[36]

Phila remained in London with Eliza, assisted by two servants they had brought from India. She wrote regularly to her husband, kept him in touch with Eliza's progress, and muddled through her finances.

Hancock sent detailed instructions for Eliza's education: *I am pleased to hear that she likes Musick; if she attempts the Guitar, I beg she may have the best Masters.*[37] *Pray endeavour to keep Betsy's recollection of me alive, I fear she will only remember me by the name of a Father.*[38]

Phila occasionally sent gifts she hoped he might find useful, but they were not generally appreciated: *If I should receive the third waistcoat, I will, after thanking you most heartily for your intention, return it. I should be the most ridiculous Animal upon Earth could I put any finery upon such a Carcase as mine worn out with age and diseases. The Shoes you sent I have never heard of. The Books I have received: pray do not send more on the subject of Religion; I have neither Time nor Inclination to read them.*[39]

When Phila visited her half-brother William Hampson Walter, and his wife Susanna Weaver in Kent, she would take the opportunity to call on her uncle Francis Austen at Sevenoaks, to go over her finances and gently raise questions around his management of her husband's affairs. The Walters had named their youngest child Philadelphia, in her honour. Phylly Walter and Eliza were the same age, and Phila encouraged their friendship.

Phila went to Steventon, where she helped nurse Cassandra through several confinements. In 1772, Cassandra wrote to Susanna, *I begin to be very heavy and bundling as usual, I believe my sister Hancock will be so good as to come and nurse me again, for which I'm sure I will be much obliged to her.*[40]

As the Steventon rectory filled with the little Austens and George's students, spare rooms were scarce. Eliza wrote, *My Uncle informs us that Midsummer & Christmas are the only Seasons when his Mansion is sufficiently at liberty to admit of receiving his Friends.*[41]

That luckless girl   Evelyn

When Philadelphia returned home to London, her first call was to see her sister Leonora. India and motherhood had changed Phila, Leonora had altered very little. She moved quietly within the narrow confines of her service to the Hintons, seeming almost part of the little tunnel groaning with books and smelling of yellowed pages. Jane noted that she was *dependent even for her Cloathes on the bounty of others, who of course do not pity her, they consider her very fortunate.*[42]

In May 1781, John Hinton, said to be *very rich*,[43] died suddenly. In Tyso Hancock's opinion, *Mr Hinton has behaved very nobly to poor Leonora. He certainly had not the least Obligation to do anything for her.*[44]

Twice widowed, Elizabeth Hinton married a third bookseller in July 1782, Stephen Austen Cumberlege, a protégée of her first husband. By now, Phila was in France with newly married Eliza. Leonora was fifty, she stayed with Elizabeth and her stock of books, perhaps *considered as one of the fixtures of the house.*[45] She died the next year. Jane who was seven, remembered her in a *blue hat*. She asked, *is that not shameful? That she should be so poor? It is indeed, with such wealthy connexions as the Family have.*[46]

In the East Indies   Persuasion

The year after Tyso Hancock returned to India, Warren Hastings, after five years in England, found his savings exhausted, and sought a new appointment in India. The Court of Directors first refused to reemploy him, but with Clive's influence and patronage he was appointed a member of the Madras Council.

Two years later, Clive promoted him, as his successor as Governor of Bengal. Dr Hancock predicted, it will *prove to Him a Crown of Thorns.*[47]

Hastings found Bengal close to bankruptcy. To raise revenue, he accepted a substantial payment from the Nawab of Oudh for the services of a Company brigade to fight against the Afghani Rohillas. His initiative, in deploying Company troops as mercenaries, proved a great thorn indeed. Hastings was seen to have taken sides in an old and brutal conflict, between the Shi'ite, Nawab of Oudh and the Afghani Rohillas, who were Sunni Muslims.

In 1774, after his victory over the Rohillas, Colonel Alexander Champion, commander of the East India Company army, resigned, horrified by the bloody reprisals that followed, the rape, pillage and destruction of Rohilla villages. He was outraged that the Company's army was seen as the enforcer.

Hancock resumed his business ventures with Hastings. *In his later life he attended more to commercial enterprise than to medicine, he was in some respects a protégé of Hastings, who was very liberal to his family.*[48] Some of their projects ended badly, as in the Sunderbunds, where *Tygers of a very large size* attacked the workers; *eight Men* were lost to these *terrible Beasts*.

The ivory, the gold & the pearls, all received their appointment Sense & Sensibility

It was very difficult to send money home from India. To provide for Phila and Eliza, to help support his sister Olivia[49] and brother Colbron[50] and *with great chearfulness,* Phila's sister Leonora,[51] Hancock adopted the risky but not unusual practice of sending home gold and jewels.[52] *I am greatly disappointed in my expectations of remitting you money from this place. Everyone expected that the government would grant Bills at a reasonable rate. But they have determined to grant none payable in less than two years.*[53]

In 1770, he wrote to Phila, *Mr Hastings writes that he will send to England some diamonds on my account. Pray acquaint Mr Austen of this;*[54] *last year Mr Hastings sent 2500 pagodas in diamonds, this produce to be paid to my attorneys;*[55] in 1771, *I now send your four gold Mohurs, quite new from the Mint;*[56] *I have sent you some gold and silver coins;*[57] in 1775 he sent her *four Strings of Pearls in a Philagree Blotter sewed on a Bag.*[58]

There were letters of complaint from both sides – *did I ever accuse you of Extravagance? You perfectly knew the Situation of my Affairs, I have never been deceived in them since our first connection.*

Who at such a distance can foresee Contingencies? Live comfortably and make yourself easy; take care of your own & the Child's health.[59]

In 1772, Hancock wrote proudly to Phila – *a few days ago Mr Hastings made his goddaughter a present, a Respondentia bond for 40,000 rupees to be paid in China.*[60] In 1775 he set up a trust for Eliza with the funds from Hastings, nominating George Austen as trustee. *The interest of this money will produce to you while you shall live nearly £400 per annum & the whole should she marry be a large fortune to Betsy after your death.*[61]

There certainly are not so many men of large fortune in the world Mansfield Park

Hancock remained convinced that Francis Austen was mismanaging his funds.⁶² He complained routinely to Phila of her uncle's failings: *Mr Austen has never acquainted me with the least of his transactions, and therefore I do not know what moneys he has received nor what debts are standing out against me. This embarrasses me very much.*⁶³ In 1773 he worried, *by his Management I may be a fourth time ruined.*⁶⁴

Despite this, he continued to rely on him, telling his wife, *you know how incapable you are of managing such complicated affairs. Oh Phila, had a very few of those hours which were formerly spent in dissipations been employed in acquiring the necessary and most useful knowledge of Accounts, happy it would have been for us both.*⁶⁵

It is hard to judge if Francis Austen failed in his duties, more than likely he found Dr Hancock's finances unusual and complicated to administer. He was a staid, elderly attorney, born in 1698, in the reign of William & Mary. Jane's brother Henry described him as, wearing *a wig like a Bishop and a suit of light grey, ditto coat, vest and hose. He retained a perfect identity of colour, texture and make to his life's end.*⁶⁶

So severa misfortune Pride & Prejudice

The loss of trade which followed the drought and great famine, pushed the East India Company to the brink of insolvency. The Court of Directors attributed the lack of revenue to *the luxurious, expensive and idle manner of life which has too much prevailed for many years... among all ranks, the genuine effects of which have been inattention and negligence in most and dishonesty in many.*⁶⁷

The Company applied to Parliament for assistance, and Lord North set up a Committee to examine its finances. In 1772, Robert Clive, appeared before the Committee, that was eager to censure him. He asked the members to: *consider the situation in which the victory of Plassey had placed me. A great Prince was dependent upon my pleasure; an opulent city lay at my mercy; its richest bankers bid against each other for my smiles; I walked through vaults which were thrown open to me alone, piled on either hand with gold and jewels! At this moment I stand astonished at my own moderation.*⁶⁸

The House of Commons defeated a motion to censure Clive, voting almost unanimously that he *rendered great and meritorious services to his country.*⁶⁹

Happy to be called to such a Council Emma

In 1773, the Fox-North government lent the Company £1.5 million, and placed a new regime of supervision over its operations.⁷⁰ Its administrations in Bengal,

Bombay and Madras were placed under a single authority, the Governor-General of Bengal, based in Calcutta, assisted by a Council of four. Warren Hastings was promoted to the position of Governor-General. He would be reappointed three times and hold the office for thirteen years.

Three councillors were sent from London, joining Richard Barwell, a Company officer in India. Two were former military men, Sir John Clavering had served in the West Indies and Sir George Monson had seen action in India. The third, Sir Philip Francis, was an Irish classical scholar, pamphleteer and onetime chief clerk of the War Office. They were paid ten thousand pounds each a year.

Clavering, Monson and Francis disembarked in Calcutta in October 1774. *They landed in ill-humour,* their arrival was heralded with a mere seventeen gun salute, not twenty-one. Things started badly, and failed to improve, *on the morrow commenced the long quarrel.*[71] The councillors and Hastings had equal voting rights. The three arrivals formed a majority bloc, and persisted in obstructing and frustrating Hastings.

In this period, between 1776 and 1781, Britain was engaged in the American War of Independence, her attention was distracted from affairs in India.

Insufferably hot   Sense & Sensibility

Colonel Monson died in September 1776 after suffering *an outbreak of boils.* General Clavering died a year later, *from the effects of climate.*[72] Hastings found the rashness and interference of Council lessened, but it did not cease, and Philip Francis sought opportunities at every turn to discredit him.

As to an additional servant, the expense would be a trifle   Sense & Sensibility

Francis settled into life in Calcutta, he and three others shared a house, they employed one hundred and ten servants, sixty-two to wait on Philip Francis. *Mr F keeps five horses and according to the cursed fashion of this idle country, has ten fellows to look after them, besides a coachman to keep the whole in order. He has moreover twelve Palanquin Bearers, for no reason that I can learn except him being a Councillor – four Peons, four Hircarahs, two Chubdars (staff-bearers) who carry silver staves, two Jemmadars.*

These are without-doors – Within, a Head Sircar, or Banyan or Agent…A housekeeping-comprador and his mate to go to market, two cooleys bring home what he buys, and Consomar takes charge of it. Cook and two Mates dress it. Baker in the house. Butler and assistant take charge of Liquor, Abdar and his mate cool them. Two Side Board Men wait at Table. House – two Mertrannees (sweeper-women) to clean it, two watchmen to guard it, a Durwan to keep the door.

Tailor, Washerman and Ironing Man for each person. Marshalgees, torchbearers F(rancis) 4, M(acrabie)2, L(ivins) 1, C(ollings)1. Two Mallies or gardeners, Cow and poultry feeder and Pork Man…Let me see, Mr F – 62.[73]

With ease descended by the Ladder Henry & Eliza

In 1778, Francis was caught in the arms of a newly married, sixteen year old beauty, Catherine Grand, after scaling the wall of her compound on a bamboo ladder.[74] George Grand took legal action against him for *criminal conversation* with his wife, and was awarded fifty thousand rupees in compensation. A pasquinade did the rounds of Calcutta:

> A GRAND and a might affair to be sure
> Just to give a light PHILLIP to nature
> How can you, ye prudes, blame a luscious young wench,
> Who so fond is of love and romances,
> Whose customs and manners are tout à fait French,
> For admiring whatever from France – IS![75]

Hastings told the Bengal Council that Francis was *devoid of truth and honour*. Francis responded by challenging the Governor General to a duel. Neither man was experienced with pistols, but Hastings' shot found its mark, fired *through the body*.[76] *The surgeon arrived in about half an hour and Francis had to encounter the danger of being put to death by a well-intentioned, but armed and meddlesome man*.[77] He recovered, resigned, and in 1781, he returned to England, to run a relentless campaign against Hastings.

I am sorry to hear there has been a rise in tea. I do not mean to pay Twining till later in the day Letters

In 1773, Hastings sought to increase Company revenue by strengthening its control over the production and sale of opium. He saw it as the solution to the enormous balance of payments problem that beset Company trade with China. The Company bought increasing quantities of tea in Canton, but Chinese demand for English or Indian goods was not growing at the same rate. *Some product had to be found that China would buy.*[78] *The East India Company began its ruthless marketing of opium.*[79]

Francis opposed the proposal, but Hastings persuaded the Council that opium was too valuable a source of revenue to lose. He argued revenue could be extracted relatively easily from opium users, mainly foreigners, not their concern! Under Hastings, the East India Company over the following decades took monopoly control of India's opium production, and its sale by auction.

I want his directions no more than his drugs Emma

The Emperor of China had banned importation of opium in 1729, but the Hong merchants in Canton, who sold tea to the East India Company, needed payment, and they were induced to accept opium as currency.

In 1766, the Court of Directors warned of the risks of trading opium with China, advising: *introducing it there can be only in a clandestine manner.*[80] By mid-century European factories were established up river from Calcutta, at Patna, to produce and trade opium. Company men traded it privately, as did the French and the Dutch.

Tea was carrying round Emma

In 1782, the Court of Directors wrote, *in regard to a consignment of 2000 chests of ophium, we have been informed that the importation of ophium to China is forbidden by the Chinese Government on very severe penalties. The ophium on seizure is burnt, the vessel on which it is brought to the port confiscated, and the Chinese in whose possession it may be found for sale punished with death. Under any circumstances it is beneath the Company to be engaged in such clandestine trade; we therefore hereby positively prohibit any more ophium being sent to China on the Company's account.*[81]

The Court emphasised that opium was exclusively for the China trade, but did not want the Company to be seen openly indulging in illicit trade. In 1787, it gave the Governor General and Council *latitude to adopt such a Plan as in your Estimation, will best answer that desirable purpose, and at the same time be the most advantageous to the Company in other respects.*[82]

Company relations with China were difficult. European merchants were treated oppressively by officials in Canton and had no means of redress. To establish amicable relations the British Government sent Lord George Macartney to China in 1792, ostensibly to honour Emperor Quianlong's eightieth birthday, but really in an attempt to negotiate, to broaden trade and gain greater access to Chinese markets.

The London press was optimistic: *The Times* declaring: *the Emperor of China will surely be convinced of the vast liberality of the English Monarch when Lord Macartney absolutely lays the Globe at his feet.*[83]

How does Lord Macartney go on? Mansfield Park

Lord Macartney met the Emperor of China, but his efforts proved to be in vain. He was willing to kneel and touch his forehead to the floor to greet him, but only on condition the Emperor's officials kowtowed the same fashion to his portrait of King George III. When they refused to do likewise, so did Macartney.

He left Peking with a letter from the Emperor to George III: *You O King from afar have yearned after the blessings of our civilisation...the Celestial Empire abounds in all things and lacks nothing...Should your vessels touch the shore, your merchants will assuredly never be permitted to land or reside there, but will be subject to instant expulsion. In that event your barbarian merchants will have had a long journey for nothing. Do not say that you were not warned in due time! Tremblingly obey and show no negligence!*[84]

Not content with coming, he actually invited himself to remain here a few days
Lady Susan

In 1774, twenty-one year old Philip Dormer Stanhope, son of Phila's cousin Catherine Hampson,[85] arrived in Calcutta. Tyso Hancock had met him as a teenager in London, and he was not pleased to see him. He wrote complaining dismally to Phila, *It gives me infinite pain to have him recommended to me in the manner he is. Represent to yourself that I have lived many months without entertaining any company or ever going into company, that I have confined my Diet to one Dish a Day and that generally Salt Fish of Curry & Rice, that I eat neither Breakfast or Supper & all this that I may save a little for you. Notwithstanding my circumstances I will treat him with what kindness I can.*[86]

Stanhope, though, found Tyso hospitable, he *enjoyed frequent libations of Mr Hancock's claret* and declared him *a most agreeable companion who though upwards of fifty years of age still retains all the fire and pleasantry of youth.*

Hancock *loaded* him with *favours: He has given me an apartment in his house, has furnished me with a superfluity of all the articles of dress, and even granted me an unlimited order for money on his cash-bearer.*[87]

Hancock told Phila – *He is indebted to me considerably for supplying him with the necessaries as he arrived almost naked*[88]*...he owes me 2000 Rupees.*[89]

A year later, in 1775, Tyso Hancock died, aged sixty-four. He was insolvent, depressed, ravaged by fever, *gout, gravel & many other Disorders,*[90] and likely addicted to the opium he took to suppress the pain of his ills.

An awful legacy for a mother
Persuasion

His death, and her ensuing insolvency, caused Phila great anguish. New problems emerged. Hancock, *patron of the widow and the fatherless*[91] had managed the affairs of a colleague Colonel Forde, lost on the *Aurora*. The Colonel's daughter Louisa requested that funds entrusted to Dr Hancock be repaid. Mrs Davis, wife of another of his associates, returned from America with her two daughters in great distress after her husband's death, to claim monies he had lent to Dr Hancock.[92]

> *They continued the flight to the Continent, which they judged to be more secure than their native land, from the dreadful effects of the vengeance, which they had so much reason to apprehend* Henry & Eliza

Phila considered the attractions of leaving England. The cost of living on the Continent was lower, Eliza could improve her French, and they would be beyond the bounds of English law, free of harassment from Mrs Forde, Mrs Davis and their ilk. She and Eliza left for Europe in 1777.

Do our laws connive at them? Northanger Abbey

Hastings put in place civil justice, and administrative systems dealing with inheritance, caste, marriage, and other religious arrangements or institutions. His understanding and respect for distinct Indian cultures helped establish impartial legal processes that recognised Hindu and Muslim traditions.

He commissioned *professors of Hindoo law* to record their own laws. He translated the document from Sanskrit, and in 1774, sent it to the Lord Chief Justice, Lord Mansfield: *four large volumes of Mahometan law... formed at a time in which the Arabians were in possession of all the real learning which existed in the western parts of this continent.*

He sought Mansfield's advice regarding *the rights of a great nation in the most essential point of civil liberty, the preservation of its own laws.* His objective was *establishing a new form of judicature, and giving laws to a people who were supposed to be governed by no other principle of justice than the arbitrary wills of their temporary rulers.*[93]

Hastings founded a Muslim theological college in Calcutta and was the patron of the Royal Asiatic Society.[94] In his introduction to a translation of the Bhagavad Gita in 1785, he predicted such writings would *survive when the British dominion in India shall have long since ceased to exist.*[95]

A distance of two years from London[96] Hastings

Hastings transformed Calcutta's administration, strengthening its function as a mercantile centre. He placed it under English law, introducing laws of debt, contract and employment, and establishing a Supreme Court with jurisdiction over civil and criminal matters.

His consolidation and reform of the Company's administration met difficulty on all fronts. He dealt with criticism from the Court of Directors in London, strife within the Company in India, rivalry and ill feeling between the Councils of Fort William and Fort St George, religious differences, territory disputes and corruption. He faced ongoing wars with powerful princes, including the Sultan of Mysore, Haider Ali, whose son Tippoo gained support from the French and the Dutch to lead an advance against the English.

The Court of Directors constantly interfered with administrative decisions made in India, and the delay in the exchange of letters often meant that complex arrangements could have been in place for some time before a countermand from London required them to be revoked.

Contrary to the usual course of things — Emma

In March 1784, the Court announced the appointment of twenty-six assistant surgeons from London, and cancelled twenty-four of Hastings' appointments: *We disapprove the appointments made by you…and positively direct that on receipt of this letter you revoke the said appointments. We permit the twenty-four assistant surgeons appointed by you to remain in India to practise in their profession and direct that they be reappointed to vacancies, as they may happen, after the said twenty-six shall have been provided for. We have further resolved that no more surgeons be allowed to proceed till it shall be known whether their services be wanted in India.*[97] It was an edict that would seriously affect D'Arcy Wentworth's future.

Parliament takes on the East India Company

In 1783–84 *evidence of exploitation and rascally behaviour of many of the Company's servants, and political resentment at the power Hastings wielded, brought about an East India crisis in London.*[98] Public upswelling of indignation and anxiety about the behaviour of Company servants in India built up pressure to recall the Governor-General, to give an account of his administration and its abuses.

The nabob, depicted by cartoonists and the press, *faced constant temptation to indulge sensuality and excess, engorging himself amid the vividly imagined corruptions of the Orient,* and he always returned home *very wealthy.*[99]

In 1783, Charles Fox's *India Bill* proposed to make the Company answerable to Parliament. An independent board was to replace the Court of Directors in Leadenhall Street. Earl Fitzwilliam was nominated as First Commissioner.[100]

Edmund Burke spoke in support of the Bill: *I freely admit to the East India Company their claim to exclude their fellow subjects from the commerce of half the globe. I admit their claim to administer an annual territorial revenue of seven millions sterling; to command an army of sixty thousand men; and to dispose (under the control of a sovereign, imperial discretion, and with the due observance of the natural and local law) of the lives and fortunes of thirty millions of their fellow creatures. All this they possess by charter, and by Acts of Parliament (in my opinion) without shadow of controversy…*

> *To whom then would I make the East India Company accountable? Why, to Parliament to be sure; to Parliament, from whom their trust was derived; to Parliament, which alone is capable of comprehending the magnitude of its object, and its abuse; and alone capable of an effectual legislative remedy.*[101]

Fox's *India Bill* failed. The Court of Directors, elected annually by the proprietors or shareholders, was aware of *corruption, licentiousness and total want of public spirit in the Company's service* and *rapacious, oppressive and disobedient conduct* by its servants,[102] the court viewed the *India Bill* as a full frontal attack on its power, it elected a committee to campaign against the *Bill*, and to liaise directly with William Pitt, leader of the Opposition.

With powerful resistance from commercial interests and Company shareholders, George III, advised by William Pitt, instructed the House of Lords to vote the Bill down. The Whig government of Charles Fox and Lord North was defeated, and William Pitt was made Prime Minister.

The following year, Pitt passed the *India Act* of 1784, creating a Government Board to separate the administration of India from the commercial activities of the Company.

There is exquisite pleasure in subduing an insolent spirit   Lady Susan

Philip Francis entered Parliament in 1784. He pursued a crusade against Hastings, accusing him of corruption and maladministration. He convinced Edmund Burke of the validity of his claims. Burke praised him as, *clear, precise, forcible and eloquent in a high degree. No intricate business was ever better unravelled and no iniquity ever placed so effectually to produce its natural horror and disquiet.*[103]

The Whig Opposition took up Francis' campaign, hoping to discredit the Government. Edmund Burke and Richard Sheridan led the charge. As Irishmen they saw India as *subject to the imperial rapacities of the arrogantly Protestant English.*[104] They failed to allow for Francis' malice towards Hastings.

Is India free? and does she wear her plumed
And jewelled turban with a smile of peace,
Or do we grind her still?[105]   William Cowper, 1785

In 1784 Hastings resigned and returned to London to defend himself. He received an audience with George III, and formal thanks from the East India Company for *his firm, unwearied and successful endeavours in procuring the peace.*[106] On 17 February 1786, Burke took the first step to his impeachment in the Commons. In May 1787, Hastings was called before an impeachment committee of the House of Lords to answer twenty detailed charges.

We must not rashly condemn those who living in the world & surrounded by temptation, should be accused of errors which they are known to have the power of committing   Lady Susan

Fitzwilliam was one of nine peers who protested at the process for Hastings' trial, declaring it a *Principle of Justice* that Hastings *should be at Liberty to make his Defence in such form and manner as he shall deem most to his advantage.* The twenty charges against him were of *such Magnitude, Extent and Variety, based on Acts done at Times and Places so distant, relating to Persons so different, and Crimes so distinct from each other in nature and tendency*, that it would be impossible for the Parliament in judging Hastings *to have full, clear and distinct Knowledge of the issues.* The *Mode of Proceeding* proposed, they feared, would *tend to the Degradation of both Houses of Parliament and to diminish the Vigour of Public Justice.*[107]

What is England now? A sink of Indian wealth, filled by nabobs…a gaming, robbing, wrangling, railing nation, without principles, genius, character, or allies; an overgrown shadow of what it was![108]   Horace Walpole

In February 1788, with great popular support, the Commons passed an Act to impeach Warren Hastings. It was a far more deliberate and planned attack than Robert Clive faced fifteen years earlier.

The Hall was crowded. The Prince's box was full, the Peeresses' was likewise well filled. About one hundred and seventy spiritual and temporal Lords assisted. Most of the Foreign Ministers were there, and four hundred members of the House of Commons in their seats.[109]

Edmund Burke spoke for two days, detailing the charges against Hastings: *I impeach Warren Hastings, Esquire of high crimes and misdemeanours. I impeach him in the name of the Commons of Great Britain in Parliament assembled, whose Parliamentary trust he has betrayed. I impeach him in the name of all the Commons of Great Britain, whose national character he has dishonoured. I impeach him in the name of the people of India, whose laws, rights and liberties he has subverted, whose properties he has destroyed, whose country he has laid waste and desolate. I impeach him in the name of human nature itself, which he has cruelly outraged, injured and oppressed, in both sexes, in every age, rank, situation and condition of life.*[110]

Macaulay reported, the *ladies in the galleries, unaccustomed to such displays of eloquence, excited by the solemnity of the occasion and perhaps not unwilling to display their taste and sensibility were in a state of uncontrollable emotion. Handkerchiefs were pulled out, smelling bottles were handed round, hysterical sobs and screams were heard.*[111]

Jurist, Thomas Erskine questioned the integrity of the process: *the person who is the subject of a bill of Empeachment, is treated with hourly calumny and invective before the Grand Jury who are to have the bill before them. The prosecutor, who is also one of the Grand Jury, prints the Bill. It is sold in every shop, and is the conversation of the coffee houses.*

Will any man whose reason is not disordered, say that when Parliament reassembles it can try the object of all this proceeding upon any principle of English justice. Bound by no oaths, limited by no principles of judgement, confined to no rules of evidence, and every man's mind made up on the subject.[112]

Seven years were gone since this little history of sorrowful interest had reached its close   Persuasion

Hastings' impeachment ground on for more than seven years, a political battleground between Whigs and Tories. When Erskine returned to Parliament in 1790, after a six year break, he presented detailed legal grounds against continuing the proceedings, but to no avail.

Warren Hastings was acquitted in April 1795, ruined by the huge expense incurred in defending his reputation. The East India Company eventually provided him with a loan and a pension.

In 1813, he was summoned to the Commons, to give evidence before a committee of the whole, enquiring into the renewal of the East India Company's Charter. Now aged eighty, Hastings stood before the bar of the House for nearly four hours, answering questions from all sides. *When I was ordered to withdraw, and was retiring, all the members, by one simultaneous impulse, rose with their heads uncovered, and stood in silence, till I passed the door of their chamber.*

A few days later, the Duke of Gloucester escorted him into the House of Lords, *where the same honour was paid me, with a more direct intention.* He was provided with a chair, *an almost unprecedented honour,* and the *most marked attention was paid both to his person and his opinions.*[113]

History views Hastings as the man who *restored the affairs of the East India Company, from the highest distress, to the highest prosperity..he ruled with a mild and equitable sway and secured to its inhabitants the enjoyment of their customs, laws and religion, and the blessings of peace.*[114]

Mark Twain said, he *saved to England the Indian Empire, and that was the best service that was ever done to the Indians themselves, those wretched heirs of a hundred centuries of pitiless oppression and abuse.*[115]

The troubles in France[116]   Eliza de Feuillide

After her second Christmas at Steventon in 1787, Eliza remained in England until late summer, before returning home to France. A year later she was in London again, just weeks before the violent outbreak of the French Revolution.

An uncommon sight, we fancied worth going to Philly Walter

In February 1788, she and Phylly Walter went to Westminster Hall to watch Hastings' impeachment proceedings. Phylly reported staying *from 10 to 4 o'clock, completely tired, but I had the satisfaction of hearing all the celebrated orators, viz. Sheridan, Burke & Fox. The first was so low we cd. not hear him, the 2nd so hot and hasty, we cd. not understand, & the 3rd was highly superior to either as we cd. distinguish every word, but not to our satisfaction as he is so much against Mr Hastings whom we all here wish so well.* [117]

Warren Hastings was an important connection for the Austens. The Hancocks relied on his patronage, and Jane's brothers Frank[118] and Charles called on his support when they sought preferment or promotion in the Navy.

The Austen family loyally followed the progress of his impeachment, confident that he would prevail. The lengthy affair entered the family vernacular, years later, Jane wrote to Cassandra, *Like Mrs Hastings, I do not despair.*[119]

She had a friend & the kindness of her cousin Mansfield Park

Jane and Eliza became friends. Eliza had a gift of making others feel alive and happy. Her own life seemed tracked by disaster and adventure, but she had the art of rising above her troubles and living life to the full.

When she was in London, she made Jane welcome. Jane enjoyed her household, her émigré friends, her servants, food, fashion and music, the accents and cadences that echoed through the rooms. More than anything she marvelled at Eliza's art of coquetry and conversation, and she used them in her early stories.

In August 1788, crossing Hounslow Heath, a sudden change in the weather deterred two highwaymen from holding up Eliza's coach: *We returned to town on Sunday and of all the dreadful storms of thunder and lightning and rain I can remember, I think that we experienced on that amicable place called Hounslow Heath was the worst. However, I believe it saved us from being robbed, as afterwards we heard that two highwaymen were at that very moment waiting for their prey, and nothing but the violent storm prevented them robbing us.*[120]

Chapter 4

Jane at home in Steventon

One does not love a place the less for having suffered in it

JANE AUSTEN was her father's daughter, it shines through her writing. She knew he expected great things of her: *My Father will be so good as to fetch home his prodigal Daughter from Town, I hope, unless he wishes me to walk the Hospitals, Enter the Temple, or mount Guard at St James.*[1]

A most affectionate, indulgent father Emma

George Austen respected Jane's intelligence: *He knew her to be clever, to have a quick apprehension as well as good sense, and a fondness for reading, which, properly directed, must be an education in itself.*[2]

Being fond of books and spending the chief of her time in reading Lady Susan

He encouraged his favourite daughter's appetite for books, she explored his library without restriction. In the evening Jane sometimes read her pieces of own writing aloud, with passages often designed for her father's ears.

She teased George Austen with the plot of *Pride & Prejudice*. Her five Bennet daughters were a riposte to his lament that his two girls were an impossible handful. She marked her pleasure in their shared sense of humour and private asides: *His cousin was as absurd as he had hoped, and he listened to him with the keenest enjoyment, maintaining at the same time the most resolute composure of countenance, and, except in an occasional glance at Elizabeth, requiring no partner in his pleasure.*

That lady, I suppose, is your mother   Pride & Prejudice

There was little love lost between Jane and her mother. Jane was *the least dear to her of all her children.*[3] She was very young, learning to form her letters, when she scrawled in the margin of a book, *Mothers angry fathers gone out.*[4]

Mothers certainly have not yet got quite the right way of managing their daughters. I do not know where the error lies. I do not pretend to set people right, but I do see that they are often wrong.[5]

Mrs Austen assisted her husband at his rectory school, and reached out warmly to his students,[6] but the matter-of-fact coldness of her exchanges with Jane survives. Jane *was born to be the torment of her life*. She had *no real love for her daughter and had never done her justice, or treated her affectionately.*[7]

In 1801, they travelled together to Bath, as Jane told Cassandra: *we changed horses at the end of every stage, & paid at almost every turnpike;- we had charming weather, hardly any dust, & were exceedingly agreeable, as we did not speak above once in three miles.*[8]

In 1771, four years before she was born, the Austens moved from the Deane Rectory to Steventon. *Mrs Austen, who was not then in strong health, performed the short journey on a feather-bed, placed upon some soft articles of furniture in the wagon which held their household goods.*[9]

Jane mentions her mother in her letters, most often with details of her ailments and complaints. She presents her as *the sort of woman who gives me the idea of being determined never to be well – and who likes her spasms and her nervousness and the consequence they give her, better than anything else.*[10]

In October 1798: *my mother began to suffer from the exercise and fatigue of travelling so far, & she was a good deal indisposed. She had not a very good night at Staines... At Basingstoke received much comfort from a mess of broth & the sight of Mr Lyford, who recommended her to take 12 drops of Laudanum when she went to bed, as a composer, which she accordingly did.*[11]

Ten years later, she wrote to Cassandra: *For a day or two last week, my Mother was very poorly with a return of* one *of her old complaints – but it did not last long, & seems to have left nothing bad behind it. – She began to talk of a serious Illness, her two last having been preceded by the same symptoms.*[12]

Jane described Catherine's mother in *Northanger Abbey* with a touch of irony, as *a woman of useful plain sense, with a good temper, and, what is more remarkable, with a good constitution.*[13]

Mrs Austen outlived Jane by ten years. In 1817 she was living at Chawton Cottage, she did not make the seventeen mile trip to Winchester to see Jane when she lay ill and dying.

JANE AT HOME IN STEVENTON

No music but Scotch airs
Lesley Castle

After Christmas 1786, Mrs Austen was persuaded to permit a concession to Eliza's influence, Jane was allowed to study the piano. The instrument borrowed for Eliza had been returned to its owners, and her father bought her a fortepiano, *a rare addition in those days to a modest country parsonage.*[14] He arranged for George Chard, the assistant organist at Winchester Cathedral, to give her lessons.[15] Jane practiced with great discipline, and played for pleasure for the rest of her life. *Without music life would be a blank to me.*[16]

A small village, precluded by its size from experiencing any of the evils of civilization
Sanditon

Steventon was a country village, *the house itself stood in a shallow valley, surrounded by sloping meadows, well sprinkled with elm trees, at the end of a small village of cottages, each well provided with a garden, scattered about prettily on either side of the road.*[17]

A yearning which she could not suppose any schoolboy's bosom to feel more keenly
Mansfield Park

For most of the year the Steventon rectory was home to a group of adolescent boys, George Austen's students. Clearly Jane enjoyed their company, and the boys responded. As daughters of their headmaster, the girls might sometimes have had an upper hand, there was doubtless a lively current of teasing and flirtation in the house. Rev Austen may well have decided it would benefit the education of both his daughters and his students to separate them, by sending the girls away to school.

Jane and her sister formed close and lasting friendships with several of the boys. Tom Fowle was at Steventon for five years. In 1783, at eighteen, he went up to Oxford, to join his elder brother Fulwar-Craven and James Austen at St John's College. He and Cassandra became engaged eight years later.

In January 1796, Tom was in the West Indies and Cassandra was staying with his family at Kintbury. Jane wrote reporting on a ball she had attended the night before. John Willing Warren, a friend from the Rectory school was there, *He left his love, &c., to you, and I will deliver it when we meet.*[18]

Five days later, she wrote again, with a message to Mary Lloyd, a cousin of the Fowles, who would becames James Austen's second wife. Mary, she wrote, was welcome to all her admirers, starting with *Mr Heartley & all his estate to her for her sole use and benefit in future, & not only him, but all my other admirers into the bargain wherever she can find them, even the kiss that C. Powlett wanted to give me as I mean to confine myself in future to Mr. Tom Lefroy, for whom I do* not care sixpence. Assure her also as a last and indubitable proof of Warren's indifference to me, that he actually drew that Gentleman's picture for me, & delivered it to me without a sigh.[19]

We seldom parted with merely a Nod & a Smile   Kitty, or the Bower

The path from the rectory to the Steventon church led *as well as to a fine old manor house, of Henry VIII's time, occupied by a family named Digweed, who for more than a century rented it, together with the chief farm in the parish.*[20]

James and Harry Digweed were day-boys at the rectory school. The Digweed and Austen boys rode and hunted together. Jane recorded a riding accident where James Digweed's *animal kicked him down with his forefeet, & kicked a great hole in his head.*[21]

Harry was her favourite, a loyal friend. *Her early impressions were incurable. She prized the frank, the open-hearted, the eager character beyond all others.*[22] He was a keen fox hunter, at a time *there was an abundance of hunting… most country squires and some tenant farmers, kept each his own cry of hounds… and came near to a realisation of that ideal old English gentleman in the song, Who never hawked nor hunted but on his own ground…The Digweed family, who then as now rented the whole parish of Steventon, had a few couples of beagles with which they hunted.*[23]

In 1798, Jane's brother, Edward Knight, gave Harry the right to shoot game on the Steventon estate, a privilege usually reserved for the land owner.[24] After signing the formal privilege document he gave it to Jane to deliver, she referred to it as, *my dear Harry's deputation.*[25]

Her eldest brother, James, enjoyed fox hunting, and joined *The Vyne* Hunt of William Chute, the Member for Hampshire, whose *hounds were renowned for their great strength and good noses.*[26] The Prince of Wales sometimes rode with the Vyne, staying at nearby *Kempshott*, where he kept a pack of stag-hounds.[27] In 1791 James went stag hunting with him and the *Kempshott* pack. The Prince later tried, but failed, to use his stag-hounds for fox hunting.

Jane mentions attending annual balls at *Kempshott House*. In 1799, she obtained an invitation for her brother Charles to attend. She told Cassandra: *Charles is not come yet, but he must come this morning, or he shall never know what I will do to him. The Ball at Kempshott is this Evening, & I have got him an invitation.*

Next day she reported, *I wore my Green shoes last night, & took my white fan with me… I spent a very pleasant evening, cheifly among the Manydown party. There was the same kind of supper as last Year, & the same want of chairs… One of my gayest actions was sitting down two Dances in preference to having Lord Bolton's eldest son for my Partner, who danced too ill to be endured…Charles never came! Naughty Charles. I suppose he could not get superseded in time.*[28]

It was moonlight, and everybody was full of engagements Sense & Sensibility

In the country, nightfall affected household routine, *we are to dine at five,*²⁹ as an *early dinner hour rendered candlesticks unnecessary.*³⁰ A *mild and still* night *was as pleasant as the serenity of nature could make it,*³¹ and full moon was *a perfect time for balls, and a pleasant drive home by moonlight.*³² In Derby, Erasmus Darwin and his Lunar Society met at full moon to share their scientific discoveries.

Ever since there had been balls in the place The Watsons

Balls were an opportunity for *gliding about with quiet, light elegance, and in admirable time,*³³ for *humourous sallies, bonmots and repartees.*³⁴ *Invitations were sent with dispatch, and many a young lady went to bed that night with her head full of happy cares.*³⁵ *A ball was indeed delightful…hopes and smiles, bustle and motion, noise and brilliancy in the drawing-room, and out of the drawing-room, and every where.*³⁶

A ball might also be an occasion for bullying, snobbery and humiliation: 'Have you got a new Gown on?'

'Yes Ma'am. I replied with as much indifference as I could assume.'

'Aye, and a fine one too I think – I dare say it is all very smart – But I must own, for you know I always speak my mind, that I think it was quite a needless piece of expence – Why could you not have worn your old striped one? It is not my way to find fault with people because they are poor, for I always think they are more to be despised and pitied than blamed for it, especially if they cannot help it, but at the same time I must say that in my opinion your old striped Gown would have been quite fine enough for its Wearer – for to tell you the truth (I always speak my mind) I am very much afraid that one half of the people in the room will not know whether you have a Gown on or not…

Hey day, Miss Maria! What cannot you get a partner? Poor Young Lady! I'm afraid your new Gown was put on for nothing!

She was determined to mortify me, and accordingly when we were sitting down between the dances, she came to me with more than her usual insulting importance… and said loud enough to be heard by half the people in the room, 'Pray Miss Maria in what way of business was your Grandfather…was he a Grocer or a Bookbinder.' I saw that she wanted to mortify me, and was resolved if I possibly could to prevent her seeing that her scheme succeeded. 'Neither madam; he was a Wine Merchant.'

'Aye, I knew he was in some such low way.'³⁷

Victuals & Drink! Love & Freindship

Jane took a lively interest in the wines and home brews the Austens made and enjoyed. *Elder wine or Mead; warm ale with a toast and nutmeg;*³⁸ *spruce* beer.³⁹ Most were made with fermented garden produce, that should be ripe and in sufficient quantity: *Yesterday I had the agreeable surprise of finding several strawberries quite ripe...There are more gooseberries & fewer currants than I thought at first.- We must buy currants for our Wine.*⁴⁰ *There is to be no Honey this year, bad news for us, we must husband our present stock of Mead.*⁴¹ *The Orange Wine will want our care soon;*⁴² *I believe I drank too much wine last night... I know not how else to account for the shaking of my hand to day.*⁴³

The yeomen & the labourers, the mansion & the squire Persuasion

Jane knew the local balls were not intended for all the young people. *Who amidst those that perspire away their Evenings in crouded assemblies can have leisure to bestow a thought on such as sweat under the fatigue of their daily Labour.*⁴⁴ She observed the clout of those in control: *Sir George and Lady Harcourt were superintending the Labours of their Haymakers, rewarding the industry of some by smiles of approbation, & punishing the idleness of others, by a cudgel.*⁴⁵

William Cobbett observed young girls working in the Hampshire countryside, near Winchester, where *the turnips are by no means good; but I was in some measure compensated for the bad turnips by the sight of the turnip-hoers, about a dozen females, amongst whom there were several very pretty girls, and they were as merry as larks. There had been a shower that had brought them into a sort of huddle on the road side. When I came up to them, they all fixed their eyes upon me, and, upon my smiling, they bursted out into laughter... These girls were all tall, straight, fair, round-faced, excellent complexion, and uncommonly gay. They were well dressed too.*⁴⁶

I took her to a Haycock & laid her down Henry & Eliza

Late one Sunday he reached East Woodhay, a village six miles from Newbury: *Sunday evening is the time for courting, in the country. It is not convenient to carry this on before faces, and, at farmhouses and cottages, there are no spare apartments; so that the pairs turn out, and pitch up, to carry on their negociations, by the side of stile or a gate. The evening was auspicious; it was pretty dark, the weather mild, and Old Michaelmas (when yearly services end) was fast approaching; and, accordingly, I do not recollect ever having before seen so many negociations going on, within so short a distance. At West Woodhay my horse cast a shoe, and, as the road was abominably flinty, we were compelled to go at a snail's pace: and I should have gone crazy with impatience, had it not been for these ambassadors and ambassadresses of Cupid, to every pair of whom I said something or other.*⁴⁷

To become conversant with the world A Collection of Letters

For all the pleasures of country life, Jane yearned for a wider world: *Alas! (exclaimed I) how am I to avoid those evils I shall never be exposed to? What* probability is there of my ever tasting the Dissipations of London, the Luxuries of Bath, or the stinking Fish of Southampton? I who am doomed to waste my Days of Youth and Beauty in an humble Cottage in the Vale of Uske.[48]

I wonder what we shall do with all our intended visits this summer? Letters
Jane spent periods away from home, visiting friends and family, particularly during term time when her parents had to accommodate their live-in students.

She visited her cousins Edward and Jane Cooper at Sonning near Reading, and later in Bath. Jane stayed in Bath with her mother's brother Richard Leigh-Perrot and his wife. Bath was the setting for *Northanger Abbey*, in which she told a story from 1786, of her brother James' romance and broken engagement.

Cassandra and Jane visited the rectory at Kintbury to stay with the Fowle family. Rev Thomas Fowle and George Austen were colleagues and friends of long standing. The four Fowle sons were educated at Steventon in preparation for university. Charles, the youngest would go on to study law, and William was apprenticed to his uncle, a London surgeon.

Fulwar-Craven and Tom, down from Oxford, drove the two girls to the neighbouring parish, Enborne, to visit another friend of their father, Rev Nowes Lloyd, his wife Martha and their daughters Elizabeth, Martha and Mary.

Jane Fowle and Martha Lloyd, wives of the two rectors, were sisters, cousins of William, Lord Craven, who owned the livings of Kintbury, Enborne and parishes in Berkshire and Shropshire. Their parents were married in the church at Kintbury in 1719, after their father, Charles Craven's three years as Royal Governor of South Carolina, between 1712 and 1715.

Nowes Lloyd became rector of Enborne in 1770. He nursed the eight members of his family through a smallpox epidemic that ravaged the district in 1775. Pock-marked by *the speckled monster*,[49] they recovered, all except his only son Charles, aged seven. His father buried him in St Michael & All Angels, the inscription on his tomb saluting his *pleasing form, with gentlest manners join'd; an infant temper, with a manly mind*.[50]

To Jane, the Church of St Michael & All Angels at Enborne was an austere, contemplative place, very different from the sunlit St Mary the Virgin at Kintbury. Nowes Lloyd stood on the stone floor to address his congregation, standing level with them, eye to eye, shoulder to shoulder.

George Austen came to collect her, *my Father met him with that look of Love, that social Shake, and cordial kiss which marked his gladness at beholding an old and valued freind from whom thro' various circumstances he had been separated nearly twenty years...many events had befallen each during that interval of time*.[51]

In July 1788, Jane accompanied her parents and Cassandra, to escort her brother Henry to St. John's College Oxford, to sit his matriculation and commence his studies there.

She refused to be impressed by Oxford: *I am sure I never wish to go there again – They dragged me through so many dismal chapels, dusty libraries, and greasy halls, that it gave me the vapours for two days afterwards.*[52]

From Oxford, the Austen party went to Sevenoaks in Kent to stay at the *Red House,* with George's uncle, Francis Austen. At a large family gathering next evening, they celebrated his ninetieth birthday and the return of his son John from the West Indies.

Phylly Walter first met Jane there; she described her to her brother James Walter as *whimsical & affected, not at all pretty and very prim.*

The family stayed another day in Sevenoaks, to meet a large gathering of Austen relations. Then they took a coach to London to dine with Philadelphia, Eliza and Hastings, who were staying in a rented house in Orchard Street.

Philadelphia had not attended her uncle's party. Hastings was unwell and having fits, Phylly believed that their *fears were of him being like poor George*, Jane's abandoned brother.[53]

The two families were pleased to see each other again; Eliza thought her uncle *more amiable than ever, what an excellent & pleasing man he is.*[54]

All the racketing of a London life[55] *Eliza de Feuillide*

London, *the great world,*[56] fills Jane's early writing. The twenty nine pieces of her *Juvenilia* range across the kingdom, with London always at the centre. She knew the city intimately, as early as 1787, when she described how Charlotte *threw herself into a deep stream which ran thro' her Aunt's pleasure Grounds in Portland Place.*[57]

Jane observed and explored different areas of London, she knew its layout, and grasped the nuances of class at play within its districts. Much of her first novel, *Sense & Sensibility,* is set within Mayfair and Marylebone, and declares her familiarity with its streets and squares, districts, houses and their residents.

The households and characters in the story are all within walking distance from each other. The two sisters, Marianne and Elinor are staying with Mrs Jennings in Berkeley Street, Willoughby in Bond Street, the John Dashwoods at Harley Street, Colonel Brandon in St James Street, the Middletons in Conduit Street, the Palmers at Hanover Square, and Mrs Ferrars in Park Street.

It was painful to displease her brother but she could not repent her resistance
Northanger Abbey

When James Austen returned to Oxford from Europe, he began a new student magazine, *The Loiterer*, promising, *we shall banish from our Paper, all Party and Politics, and their constant attendants, scurrility and scandal; and that however we at times be dull, insipid, and unentertaining, we shall never be indecent, abusive, or profane.* Over two years, during term-time, he produced sixty weekly issues. Henry assisted him, along with other friends, and edited eight issues. The final issue of *The Loiterer* appeared at the end of the Hilary term, on 20 March 1790.

I wonder what curacy he will get! Sense & Sensibility

James left Oxford at the end of March 1790, to become the full-time curate at St Mary and St Michael, Overton, three miles from Steventon. His patron Henry Ellis St John, a member of a rollicking local family, owned the living.[58]

James aspired to something better than his father's modest livings at Steventon and Deane. In February 1789, he put a mock advertisement in *The Loiterer*: *Wanted--A Curacy in a good sporting country, near a pack of fox-hounds, and in a sociable neighbourhood; it must have a good house and stables, and a few acres of meadow ground would be very agreeable--To prevent trouble, the stipend must not be less than £80.--The Advertiser has no objection to undertaking three, four, or five Churches of a Sunday, but will not engage where there is any weekly duty. Whoever has such a one to dispose of, may suit themselves by sending a line, directed A.B. to be left at the Turf Coffee House, or the gentleman may be spoken with, any tuesday morning at Tattersall's Betting Room.*

Having a curacy where residence was not required Persuasion

The Church of England had nearly ten thousand livings at this time, and more than half of them had no resident clergyman. The owner of the living collected compulsory tithes from its residents, and could make a rich income from the parish. Contrary to the law, many were not *resident and abiding* in the parish, and owned more than one living. They would employ a curate, paying him around £50 a year to attend to the spiritual needs of parishioners.[59]

James was in excellent spirits Northanger Abbey

James, ten years older than Jane, was the favoured Austen son, and heir. The indulgence and forbearance of her parents towards him, roused her on occasions to poke fun at his behaviour and to challenge him.

She did find his magazine *dull, insipid, and unentertaining*. In March 1789, citing its motto, *Speak of us as we are*, she wrote to James and told him so, signing off, *as you behave,* alluding perhaps to his own criticism of her writing.

Women were not admitted to study at university, in his response James asked, *with what subjects do we intend to treat those of our fair friends, whom curiosity, or desire of amusement, may incline to read our work?* He undertook to *carefully select such subjects as may captivate the imagination, without offending the judgment, and interest the feelings, without misleading the heart.* This was clearly not enough to satisfy Jane.

James gave her letter pride of place, under a quotation from Ovid's *Heroides*, the words of Phyllis, daughter of the Thracian king: *non venit ante suum nostra querela diem – you will find my complaint comes not before its time,* suggesting he did not disagree with her sentiments:

To the AUTHOR of the LOITERER

Sir,

I write this to inform you that you are very much out of my good graces, and that, if you do not mend your manners, I shall soon drop your acquaintance. You must know, Sir, I am a great reader...I assure you my heart beat with joy when I first heard of your publication...I am sorry, however, to say it, but really, Sir, I think it the stupidest work of the kind I ever saw... your subjects are so badly chosen, that they never interest one... not one sentimental story about love and honour, and all that.

Why, my dear Sir – what do you think we care about the way in which Oxford men spend their time and money... As for your last paper, indeed, the story was good enough, but there was no love, and no lady in it, at least no young lady... you might have created a little bustle, and made the story more interesting...

Get a new set of correspondents, from among the young of both sexes, but particularly ours; and let us see some nice affecting stories, relating the misfortunes of two lovers...

If you think fit to comply with this my injunction, you may expect to hear from me again, and perhaps I may even give you a little assistance: but, if not, may your work be condemned to the pastry-cook's shop, and may you always continue a bachelor, and be plagued with a maiden sister to keep house for you.

Your's, as you behave,
SOPHIA SENTIMENT.[60]

Jane's own *affecting story*, the misfortunes of Jane and D'Arcy, would unfold relentlessly over the coming months. Though carefully excised from her family history, it would be the wellspring she revisited and explored in all her writing.

Chapter 5

Names, Names, Names

She was really proud of her family & Connexions,
and easily offended if they were treated with Neglect

JANE AUSTEN'S REGARD for her family history was considerable, not merely the *occupation for an idle hour*.[1] She disdained the view that a family was defined solely by its male line, she cherished her mother's connection to Eleanor, daughter of Anne Wentworth, and granddaughter of Thomas Wentworth, 1st Earl of Strafford. At the Bear Inn, and the following afternoon in her little bower in the Abbey ruins, she took great delight in telling D'Arcy her connexion to his family was through her mother's line, the distaff side of her family. Jane and D'Arcy shared all they knew of Strafford, of his noble and tragic history.

The Earl of Strafford The History of England

Jane began her story with Thomas Wentworth, born on Good Friday 1593, heir to *Wentworth Woodhouse*, a great estate in the south of Yorkshire's West Riding, the seat of his ancestors since the Norman Conquest.

Thomas first studied with the Dean of Ripon, Dr Higgins, in his house in Well. She imagined his life there as similar to her father's students at the rectory. At age fourteen he entered the Inner Temple in London, and in 1609, two years later, matriculated at St John's College Cambridge. At eighteen, he married Margaret Clifford, eldest daughter of the Earl of Cumberland. They travelled in Europe where they learnt French, Italian and Spanish.

In 1614, Thomas was elected to the House of Commons as Member for Yorkshire, in the short lived Addled Parliament. That year his father died, and he inherited his baronetcy, and responsibility for the education and careers of his eight younger brothers. Now a member of the House of Lords, Thomas attended successive parliaments called by James I and his son Charles I, during a long and difficult period of struggle between king and parliament.

With the accession of Charles I in 1625, the struggle intensified. The new King believed he ruled by royal prerogative, *that parliaments are altogether in my power for the calling, sitting and continuance of them.*[2]

When he needed funds, especially to wage war, Charles had to call parliament, to seek its agreement to raise taxes. Parliament opposed him raising revenue from sources outside its control, particularly *ship money,* from the coastal and inland counties, and customs duties, or *tonnage and poundage*.

Parliamentary sessions were highly volatile, it was never easy for the King to gain approval for the funds he wanted. Parliament made him wait, as the Commons placed backlogs of its numerous grievances before him. It distrusted him, and after he courted a Spanish Infanta, and later, married a French Catholic, Princess Henrietta Maria, suspected him of papist leanings.

In Parliament, Wentworth *tried to mediate between the king and those who saw the crown's policy as a threat to the privileges of parliament and the ancient liberties of the king's subjects.* He supported a *harmonious union betwixt the king, the nobles and Commons.* He suggested the king *do first the business of the commonwealth,* rather than demand subsidies for foreign wars.[3]

Wentworth warned Parliament *not to enter too deeply into disputes about their privileges and the king's prerogative.* Their liberties, he argued, *would be much safer if they remained 'wrapte up in a sacred and questionable doubtfulnesse' instead of being unravelled by an 'over precise curiosity.*[4]

In 1622, he and his wife fell seriously ill with tertian fever, malaria. Margaret did not recover, she died childless, after eleven years of marriage, and during the following two years, Thomas suffered debilitating bouts of fever.

Three years later, he married Arabella Holles, the beautiful sixteen year old daughter of the Earl of Clare. They had four children, three of whom survived: William, born in 1626, Anne in 1627 and Arabella in 1629.

In 1626, Charles summoned Parliament to raise funds for war against France. It was hostile, delaying, raising grievances and complaints on every aspect of his rule, finally moving to impeach Buckingham, his most trusted advisor. After several months of argument and rejected compromises, Charles dissolved Parliament, he resolved to raise funds by way of loans, and appointed nobles and gentry in every shire, as commissioners to manage their collection.

Seventy six nobles were arrested, for refusing to lend money or for obstructing local collectors. Wentworth was arrested in June 1627, and imprisoned at Marshalsea[5] and Dartford. Released after six months, he was elected in 1628 to a new parliament, and he called on it to vindicate *our ancient, sober, vital liberties*. Wentworth played a key role in drafting the Petition of Right,[6] demanding the King's subjects *should not be compelled to contribute to any tax, tallage, aid or any like charge not set by common consent in Parliament*. Charles gave the Petition his assent though he later claimed it did not bind him.

In December 1628, Wentworth was appointed Lord President of the Council of the North. He proved to be a competent and efficient administrator. He followed his maxim, *to go cheerfully and boldly; if others do not do their parts, I shall be still Thorough and Throughout, one and the same*.

On 10 March 1629, Charles dissolved Parliament and began an eleven year period of personal rule. In November 1629, he appointed Wentworth a Privy Councillor. He and William Laud, Archbishop of Canterbury, were the King's key advisors during this period, and they served him faithfully.

In 1631, Wentworth's wife Arabella died in childbirth, leaving three children, aged five, four and two. Three months later, in January 1632, Charles appointed him Lord Deputy of Ireland. As he prepared to leave England, his greatest concern was his motherless children, *God bless the young whelps*, he wrote, *for the old dog there is less matter*. He decided to leave his two girls in the care of their grandmother, Anne Stanhope Holles, Countess Clare, who had asked several times to have Anne to stay with her. Wentworth wrote to her:

> My lord of Clare having writ unto me, your ladyship desired to have my daughter Anne with you for a time in England… I have at last been able to yield so much from my own comfort, as to send both her and her sister to wait your grave, wise, and tender instructions…

> I was unwilling to part with them, in regard those that must be a stay one to another, when by course of nature I am gone before them. I would not have them grow strangers whilst I am living. Besides, the younger gladly imitates the elder, in disposition so like her blessed mother, that it pleases me very much to see her steps followed and observed by the other…

> Madam, I must confess, it was not without difficulty before I could perswade myself thus to be deprived the looking upon them, to overcome my own affections in order to do their good, acknowledging your ladyship capable of doing them more good in their breeding than I am. Otherways, in truth, I should never have parted with them, as I profess it a grief unto me, not to be as well able as any to serve the memory of that noble lady, in these little harmless infants.

Nan, they tell me, danceth prettily, which I wish (if with convenience it might be) were not lost, – more to give her a comely grace in the carriage of her body, than that I wish they should much delight to practise it when they are women. Arabella is a small practitioner that way also, and they are both very apt to learn that or any thing they are taught.

Nan, I think, speaks French prettily, which yet I might have been better able to judge had her mother lived. The other also speaks, but her maid being of Guernsey, the accent is not good. But your ladyship is in this excellent, as indeed all things else which may befit them, they may, and I hope will, learn better with your ladyship than they can with their poor father, ignorant in what belongs women, and otherways, God knows, distracted…

Their brother is just now sitting at my elbow, in good health, God be praised; and I am in the best sort accommodating this place for him… I do not forget the children of my dearest wife, nor altogether bestow my time fruitlessly for them…I am afraid to turn over the leaf, lest your ladyship might think I could never come to a conclusion; and shall therefore. &c.[7]

In 1632, before he left England, Thomas was married a third time, to Elizabeth Rodes, daughter of Sir Godfrey Rodes of Great Houghton in South Yorkshire. She would bear him a daughter, Margaret.

As he crossed the Irish Sea in 1633, pirates boarded the vessel and carried off his belongings; they were never recovered. He responded energetically, putting down the pirates who had roved Irish coasts and bays since Roman times. By 1637 he could report – *there was not so much as a rumour of Turk, St Sebastian's man, or Dunkirker.*

Wentworth found Ireland bankrupt. He confronted the corruption and cronyism amongst English officials in Dublin: *I find them in this place a company of men the most intent upon their own ends that ever I met with.*

He realised he would have to secure *beaten ways of happiness* for Ireland. He reformed the administration, ridding it of corrupt officials; he strengthened the church, raised an army, promoted manufacture of linen and trade with Spain, and raised customs duties from traders who could now move their goods safely across the Irish Sea. He curtailed monopolies and the tyranny of the wealthy over the poor. His government turned Ireland from a massive drain on the English Treasury to a source of tens of thousands of pounds in revenue.

English diplomat, Sir Thomas Roe, wrote to Elizabeth of Bohemia in 1636: *The Lord Deputy of Ireland doeth great wonders and governs like a king, and hath taught that kingdom to show us an example of envy, by having parliaments and knowing wisely how to use them.* Roe described him as: *severe abroad and in business, and sweet in private conversation; retired in his friendships but very firm; a terrible judge and a strong enemy.*[8]

Wentworth's single minded devotion to the King's interests, and his *thorough and throughout* approach to reforming the finances and administration of the entire island earned him a reputation for systematic, even ruthless methods, and created enemies. *Of all things,* he responded, *I love not to put off my cloaths and go to bed in a storm. If you purpose to overcome evil, you must fall upon the first transgressors like lightning!*[9]

In 1639, on the mainland, Scottish forces gained the upper hand over an untrained and badly disciplined English army. Charles asked Wentworth to return to England as his principal advisor. He left Ireland, *the country prospering, its debts paid, its revenues increased, the army paid and disciplined, the poor relieved, the rich awed and justice done to all alike.*[10]

In January 1640, Charles I created Wentworth, the 1st Earl of Strafford. In April, he summoned Parliament to obtain funds to quash the Scots. The Commons refused to consider supply until he heard and attended to its many grievances. Impatient, Charles dissolved this Short Parliament in less than a month. Scottish forces pushed further south, as far as Newcastle.

In November 1640, Charles, desperate for funds, summoned a new parliament, it would be called the Long Parliament. Angry and frustrated but unwilling to attack him directly, the Parliament turned on Strafford, launching a relentless and virulent attack to undermine his power and influence with the King.

Strafford understood it was part of his role to deflect dissatisfaction and anger from the King. Charles had been clear, *if there be anything to be denied, you may do it and not I.*[11]

Strafford became a scapegoat for the nation's grievances and the army's defeat. It was claimed he had acted treasonably, that he had advised Charles to dissolve the Short Parliament. *Poems libel,* on handbills circulated through London accused him, and Archbishop Laud, of being enemies of the King:

> Landless Will of Lambeth Strand
> And Blacke Tom Tyrant of Ireland
> Like fox and woolfe did lurke
> With many rookes and madgepies
> To picke out good King Charles his eyes
> And then be Pope and Turke[12]

The Long Parliament met on 3 November 1640, Strafford was its first target. He took his seat in the Lords on 11 November, intending to accuse those Members who had invited the Scots into England of treason. Instead the

Commons accused him of high treason and had him arrested. He faced twenty-eight charges, most relating to his rule in Ireland, and was accused of planning to bring in the Irish Army to subdue the English. Charles refused a suggestion that Strafford be allowed to retire from office; he felt he should answer his accusers, and vindicate himself and his policies.

Strafford wrote to his wife from the Tower:

Sweet hart – you have heard before this what hath befallen me in this place, but be confident, that if I fortune to be blamed, yet I will not, by God's help, be ashamed. Your carriage upon this misfortune I should advise to be calm, not seeming to be neglective of my trouble, and yet so as there may appear no dejection in you. Tell Will, Nan, and Arabella, I will write to them by the next. In the mean time I shall pray for them to God, that he may bless them, and for their sakes deliver me out of the furious malice of my enemies, which yet I trust, through the goodnesse of God, shall do me no hurt. God have us all in his blessed keeping.

Your very loving husband,

Strafford.[13]

His trial in the House of Lords began on 22 March 1641, and Strafford defended himself with skill and courage, so ably that the charge of treason could not be proved. At one point in the proceedings, he protested against allegations against him based on private conversations:

If, my lords, words spoken to friends in familiar discourse, spoken in one's chamber, spoken at one's table, spoken ill in one's sick bed, spoken perhaps to gain better reason, to give himself more clear light and judgment, by reasoning; – if these things shall be brought against a man as treason, this, under favour, takes away the comfort of all human society, – by this means we shall be debarred from speaking (the principal joy and comfort of all human society) with wise and good men, to become wiser, and better our lives. If these things be strained to take away life and honour, and all that is desirable, it will be a silent world! A city will become a hermitage, and sheep will be found among the crowd and press of people! And no man shall dare impart his solitary thoughts or opinions to his friend and neighbour![14]

The Long Parliament needed to vent its fury against the King, and Strafford took the full force of its wrath. Having failed in the charge of treason, Parliament did not back down, it sought another means of destroying him.

The Commons resorted to a *Bill of Attainder*, a medieval manoeuvre whereby it was declared by Act of Parliament that a person was attainted, or tainted. The *Bill* declared Strafford a traitor, and condemned him of treason. He was to be executed without further trial, would lose his titles and his children would lose their inheritance.

He argued courageously against the Bill: *My lords, it is hard to be questioned upon a law that cannot be shown. Where hath this fire lain hid so many hundred years, without smoke to discover it, till it thus burst forth to consume me and my children? That punishment should precede promulgation of a law, to be punished by a law subsequent to the fact, is extreme hard! What man can be safe, if this is admitted?*

It is now 240 years since any man was touched for this alleged crime, to this height, before myself. Let us not awaken these sleeping lions to our destructions, by taking up a few musty records, that have lain by the walls so many ages, forgotten or neglected... Do not put, my lords, such difficulties upon ministers of state, that men of wisdom, of honour, and of fortune, may not with cheerfulness and safety be employed for the public. If you weigh and measure them by grains and scruples, the public affairs of the kingdom will lie waste, no man will meddle with them who hath any thing to lose. My lords, I have troubled you longer than I should have done, were it not for the interest of those dear pledges a saint in heaven hath left me. What I forfeit myself is nothing; but that indiscretion should extend to my posterity woundeth me to the very soul. And so my lords, with all tranquillity of mind, I submit myself to your judgement, whether that judgement be of life or death, Te Deum laudamus.[15]

On 13 April 1641, the Commons passed the *Bill of Attainder*, 204 to 59, but it needed to pass the House of Lords and receive the King's consent. On 23 April, the King wrote to Strafford from Whitehall:

> Strafford
>
> The Misfortune that is fallen upon you by the strange Mistaking and Conjuncture of these Times being such that I must lay by the Thought of employing you hereafter in my Affairs; yet I cannot satisfy myself in Honour or Conscience, without assuring you (now in the midst of your Troubles) that, upon the Word of a King, you shall not suffer in Life, Honour, or Fortune: This is but Justice, and therefore a very mean Reward from a Master to so faithful, and able a Servant, as you have showed yourself to be; yet it is as much, as I conceive the present Times will permit, though none shall hinder me from being your constant faithful Friend
>
> Charles R.[16]

The King went to great lengths to keep his promise. He appeared before the Lords on 30 April, saying it was impossible for him to condemn Strafford for treason. He asked for a lesser sentence, he even encouraged a plot to seize the Tower and release him. But the following day, a Sunday, armed crowds gathered shouting for Strafford's blood, and the Lords passed the Bill.

Strafford wrote to the King, releasing him from his promise: *So now to set your majesty's conscience at liberty, I do most humbly beseech your majesty, for prevention of evils which may happen by your refusal to pass this bill, and by this means remove, praised be God, (I cannot say this accursed, but, I confess), this unfortunate thing, forth of the way towards that blessed agreement, which God, I trust, shall ever establish between you and your subjects. Sir, my consent shall more acquit you herein to God, than all the world can do besides. To a willing man there is no injury done.*[17]

Fearful of the mob, Charles signed the Bill, he delivered Wentworth to the axeman. He was granted *three days more of existence*, during which he calmly put his affairs in order. He wrote a petition to the House of Lords asking them to have compassion on his innocent children. He wrote to his wife, *bidding her affectionately to support her courage,* and enclosing a letter of final instruction and advice to his son William, now fourteen:

My dearest Will

These are the last lines that you are to receive from a Father that tenderly loves you. I wish there were a greater Leisure to impart my Mind to you; but our merciful God will supply all things by his Grace, and guide and protect you in all your Ways: to whose infinite Goodness I bequeath you; and therefore not be discouraged, but serve him, and trust in him, and he will preserve and prosper you in all things.

Be sure you give all Respect to my wife, that hath ever had a great Love unto you, and therefore will be well becoming you. Never be awanting in your Love and Care for your Sisters, but let them ever be most dear unto you: For, this will give others Cause to esteem and respect you for it, and is a Duty that you owe them in the Memory of your excellent Mother and myself: Therefore your Care and Affection to them must be the very same that you are to have to yourself; and the like Regard must you have to your youngest Sister; for indeed you owe it to her also, both for her Father and Mother's sake.

Sweet Will, be careful to take the Advice of those Friends, which are by me desired to advise you for your Education… and diligently follow their Counsel…

The King I trust will deal graciously with you, restore you those Honours and that Fortune, which a distempered Time hath deprived you of together with the life of your Father.

Be sure to avoid as much as you can to enquire after those that have been sharp in their Judgements towards me, and I charge you never to suffer Thought of Revenge to enter your Heart; but be careful to be informed, who were my Friends also; and on such you may rely, and bestow much of your Conversation amongst them.

And God Almighty in his Infinite Goodness bless you and your Children's Children; and his same Goodness bless your Sisters in like manner, perfect you in every good work, and give you right understandings in all Things, Amen

Your most loving Father

T.Wentworth

Tower, this 11th of May, 1641.

You must not fail to behave yourself towards My Lady Clare your grandmother with all Duty and Observance; for most tenderly dost she love you, and hath been passing kind unto me. God reward her Charity for it. And both in this and in all the rest, the same that I Counsel you, the same do I direct also to your Sisters and so the same may be observed by you all. And once more do I, from my very soul, beseech our gracious God to bless and govern you in all, to the saving you in the Day of his Visitation, and join us in the Communion of his blessed Saints, where is Fullness of Joy and Bliss for evermore.

Amen Amen[18]

Next morning, Strafford was beheaded on Tower Hill. No less than a hundred thousand people crowded there to witness his execution. As he walked to the scaffold, he doffed his hat frequently to salute people in the crowd, and he received not a word of insult or reproach.

Strafford addressed them from the scaffold, saying he had always believed *parliaments in England to be the happy constitution of the Kingdom and nation, and the best means under God to make the King and his people happy.* Refusing to bind his eyes, he said a prayer, spread forth his hands as a sign to the executioner and faced his death with calm and great courage. His body was later buried at *Wentworth Woodhouse*.[19]

This noble & gallant Earl was beheaded…after having been Lord Lieutenant of Ireland, after having clapped his hand on his sword, and after performing many other services to his Country The History of England

Charles returned Strafford's honours to his son William on 1 December 1641, and Parliament reversed his father's attainder in 1662.

Charles was troubled by his betrayal of Strafford, he felt that in giving way he had passed his sovereign power to the Long Parliament. After sacrificing the ablest and most talented of his advisors, he was never again able to regain the advantage. This single act was the precursor to his demise. Perhaps he thought of Strafford as he walked through the snow to his own execution in 1649.

William, Strafford's only son, died in 1695, childless. His estates passed to his nephew, Thomas Watson, the son of his sister Anne Wentworth, wife of Lord Rockingham, head of the Watson family.

Jane wrote of this period: *Never certainly were there before so many detestable Characters at one time in England as in this period of its history; Never were amiable Men so scarce.* Strafford was one of the few noble and amiable men in the reign of Charles I, *who never forgot the duty of the Subject, or swerved from their attachment to His Majesty.*[20]

The sweets of friendship in an unreserved conversation – they talked much and with much enjoyment
Northanger Abbey

D'Arcy described for Jane, the forest of majestic oaks at Coolattin, in County Wicklow, where he had seen the remains of Strafford's hunting lodge. Over the centuries the park provided timber for Westminster Hall, Westminster Abbey, Christ College Cambridge, and the Stadt House in Amsterdam. The little that remained of the lodge was called 'Black Tom's Cellar' and in the nearby village of Tinahely, was an old inn called Black Tom's Tavern.

D'Arcy told her how during this period of upheaval, his Wentworth forebears, members of Strafford's family, left Yorkshire for Ireland and for America, fearing the hatred that had built up in England against them. In Ireland, his family settled under the patronage of James Dillon, third Earl of Roscommon and his wife Elizabeth, a younger sister of Strafford.

Jane would be pleased to know, their son, Wentworth Dillon, fourth Earl Roscommon, was a fine poet and courtier to both Charles II and James II. Strafford, his godfather, invited him to Yorkshire to study. When the tide turned against Strafford, he went to Caen and later to Italy for further study. After the Restoration he was made Master of the Horse to the Duchess of York.

Alexander Pope praised Wentworth Dillon as the only moral writer of King Charles' reign: *Unhappy Dryden – in all Charles' days, Roscommon only boasts unspotted lays.*[21] Dillon admired Milton, and he was a gambler. He died in 1684 and was buried with great pomp in Westminster Abbey.[22]

I have been connected with his family
Pride & Prejudice

Jane traced the connexions between their two families for D'Arcy. Her mother, was a descendant of Rowland Leigh, eldest son of Sir Thomas Leigh, the Lord Mayor of London from 1558 to 1559. He led the coronation procession of Elizabeth I on 15 January 1559. Rowland's younger brother, Sir Thomas Leigh of Stoneleigh, was succeeded by his grandson Thomas, 1st Baron Leigh, who was succeeded by his grandson, 2nd Baron Leigh.

The Earl of Strafford's eldest daughter Anne married Edward Watson, second Baron Rockingham. Their daughter Eleanor married Thomas, 2nd Baron Leigh of Stoneleigh. In August 1642, his family gave shelter to Charles I at Stoneleigh, after he marched to Coventry, a Parliament stronghold, and found the gates of the city shut against him.

Connected with some of the great men of the day Sense & Sensibility

D'Arcy spoke of Charles Watson-Wentworth, 2nd Marquess of Rockingham, who died in 1782 whilst serving his second term as Prime Minister. He had repealed the *Stamp Act,* that caused such great agitation in America, and he supported independence for the American colonies.

In the early 1760s, his American cousin, John Wentworth, visited London from New Hampshire, as official spokesman for opposition to the *Stamp Act*, he asked Rockingham to convey to Parliament the concerns and disapprobation of the Province of New Hampshire.

John Wentworth was Governor of New Hampshire from 1767 to 1775. He returned to England in 1778, shortly after the legislature passed a Bill of Attainder, condemning him for his military support for the British. He stayed in England during the American Revolution, was received at Court, and enjoyed the hospitality and patronage of Earl Fitzwilliam,[23] D'Arcy had met him at Grosvenor Square.[24]

The effusions of his endless conceit Northanger Abbey

Jane told him the story of General Thomas Wentworth, another Wentworth in her mother's family, who in 1741, sailed fom the Isle of Wight with Admiral Vernon,[25] on an expedition against the Spaniards in South America.

Two years earlier, Vernon was *extolled as another Drake or Raleigh, his praise resounded from all corners of the kingdom* after his celebrated capture of Porto Bello[26] with just six ships.[27] He and Wentworth took Marines and regiments under Lord Cathcart, joined by four battalions raised in the American colonies. Wentworth took command of the land forces after Lord Cathcart succumbed to dysentery, and led the attack on Cartagena de las Indias.[28] After a two year campaign and the loss of nearly 25,000 men from yellow fever, dysentery and inept leadership, he had not succeeded in capturing the port.

Tobias Smollett served as a naval surgeon in the Cartagena campaign, he condemned Admiral Vernon's command of the expedition. In September 1742: *Vernon and Wentworth received orders to return to England with such troops as remained alive: these did not amount to a tenth part of the number which had been sent abroad in that inglorious service. The inferior officers fell ignobly by sickness and despair, without the opportunity of showing their courage; and the commanders lived to feel the scorn and reproach of their country.*[29]

Smollett attributed the failure of the Cartagena campaign to Vernon's weak understanding, prejudice, boundless arrogance, and overboiling passions. He saw Wentworth as lacking in experience, confidence and resolution.[30] *Between pride of one and insolence of another, the enterprise miscarried according to the proverb, "between two stools, the backside falls to the ground."*[31]

The victor was Don Blas de Lezo, a Lieutenant General in the Spanish navy, a Basque, named for his village, between San Sebastian and Irun. He had lost his left leg in the Battle of Gibraltar, his left eye in Toulon, and right arm in the Battle of Barcelona. In the battle for Cartagena he was wounded in his good leg, and he died shortly after the withdrawal of Vernon's fleet.

In Spain, de Lezo remains a great hero, one of the Basques' two great naval figures, along with Juan Sebastian Elcano, who completed the first circumnavigation of the earth after Magellan's death in the Philippines in 1521.

Admiral Vernon was ridiculed by the Spaniards for having had commemorative coins cast to proclaim his victory over Spain. They showed Blas de Lezo on his knees surrendering, a victory that never happened.

On his return to England, General Wentworth was elected to the Commons as Member for Whitchurch, and served from 1743 to his death in 1747. His widow, Elizabeth Wentworth, known in the Leigh family as Aunt Wentworth, lived in Berkshire with her sister Mary Leigh, Jane's mother's great aunt.[32]

Of all people and all names in the world — Persuasion

Jane Austen marked her connexion to the Wentworth and Fitzwilliam families in her stories and novels, including their names and other family references, such as Watson, Woodhouse, Ferrers, Bertram and Musgrave. While the context remained hidden, her readers have long been aware of the deep emotional resonance of these names.

In her lifetime, the name D'Arcy Wentworth would have been immediately identifiable. In *Pride and Prejudice*, she named the hero Fitzwilliam Darcy, his Christian name that of the head of the Wentworth family, Earl Fitzwilliam, using Darcy as his surname.

I dare say you know him by name — Persuasion

It was improper for a young woman, in her day, to address a man by his Christian name, or for a man to address a woman with such familiarity.

In *Sense & Sensibility*, when Elinor overheard Willoughby *addressing her sister by her Christian name alone, she instantly saw an intimacy so decided, a meaning so direct, as marked a perfect agreement between them. From that moment she doubted not of their being engaged.*

Jane had a great desire to hear and to say D'Arcy's name aloud. By making Darcy a surname, she gave her characters the freedom to speak it without reserve. By this means she ensured his name and her great love for him have resounded across the years.

Chapter 6

Not a bad speculation for a Surgeon

*Golden London, and her silver Thames, throng'd with shining spires
And corded ships; her merchants buzzing round like summer bees
and all the golden cities in his land overflowing with honey.*

LONDON IN 1785, a city of nearly a million people, was bursting with commerce, ideas and excess, full of noise and spectacle. *Earth has not anything to show more fair*, said Wordsworth, *dull would he be of soul who could pass by a sight so touching in its majesty.*[1] For a young man from the Irish countryside this was a gigantic and breathtaking adventure.

It was a time of tumultuous change, a new attitude of mind was transforming science, technology and commerce. Riches from the colonies and trade had pumped up the Industrial Revolution, expanding Britain's power and influence. She strengthened her navy to protect her merchant ships along the trade routes, their holds filled with treasure: sugar and rum from the West Indies, cotton, silk and saltpetre from India, furs from North America, tea from China.

Her economy was weathering the turbulence of the industrial revolution, of war, rising food prices, unemployment and urban poverty. After great instability following the loss of America, the middle class, particularly in London, enjoyed unprecedented expansion and was accumulating great wealth.

Living about at his own charge now, at lodgings and taverns   Sense & Sensibility
D'Arcy's rooms on St Martin's-le-Grand, near St Pauls, were an easy walk to St Bartholomew's, the great charity hospital at Smithfield, where he went each day to walk the wards, under the supervision of a senior surgeon.

The hospital, founded by monks in the twelfth century was transferred to the City of London in 1546 by Henry VIII, renamed *House of the Poore in West Smithfield in the Suburbs of the City of London of Henry VIII's Foundation*. In 1666, it survived the Great Fire that burnt for days and devastated the city.

Health, good humour & cheerfulness — Pride & Prejudice

Rebuilt in the 1730's, it comprised four modern three storey buildings around a great open courtyard, housing over four hundred patients, and attended by a hundred or more out-patients each day. D'Arcy found its scale astonishing, it was noisy and crowded, and he could observe and compare the progress of patients at different stages of their complaints and treatment.

He observed a great stream of cases under Mr Pott, and visited other teaching hospitals to observe different treatments and surgical procedures. He went to specialty hospitals, infirmaries, maternities, dispensaries, and to the anatomy theatre at the Company of Surgeons in the Old Bailey building, to watch the statutory dissection of the cadavers of executed criminals.

D'Arcy grasped the many opportunities London offered to progress his medical studies. He saw a great range of diseases, injuries and conditions, and heard the detailed discussion and analysis that took place on the wards. They enlarged and deepened his ideas, and his commitment to his profession.

There is a monstrous, curious stuffed fox there, a badger – any body would think they were alive — The Watsons

He visited the natural history and medical museums and collections, spending many hours in William and John Hunter's museum of comparative anatomy in Leicester Square. Outside was a forty foot long skeleton of a bottle-nose whale, inside a magnificent collection of specimens.

> Carelessly I gazed, roving as through a cabinet
> Or wide museum (thronged with fishes, gems,
> Birds, crocodiles, shells) where little can be seen
> Well understood, or naturally endeared,
> Yet still does every step bring something forth
> That quickens, pleases, stings – and here and there
> A casual rarity is singled out
> And has its brief perusal, then gives way
> To others, all supplanted in their turn.[2]
>
> *William Wordsworth*

A pretty good lecture, upon my word — Mansfield Park

John Hunter held regular public medical levees on Sunday evenings, with up to a hundred people, in the conversazione room at his house. A former student of Pott, he was a man-midwife, a dentist, and surgeon to George III. His medical research and teaching covered gunshot wounds, foetal and child development, venereal disease, the lymphatic system, digestion, dentistry and more. D'Arcy attended a number of his lectures, studied his methods, and used them to help shape his future practice.

The *Medical Register* advertised lecture courses *available in the metropolis, many given by extremely eminent men in physic and materia medica, clinical paediatrics, animation, chemistry, natural history, anatomy, midwifery, surgery, dentistry and natural philosophy.*[3]

It was a time of *unprecedented garrulousness among doctors. Never before in England had members of a single profession devoted such energy to making their views public, a cacophony of competing theories, treatment and triumphs. These activities were due to a genuine interest in the advancement of medical practice and knowledge…and more significant, the desire to attract custom.*[4]

D'Arcy went to the coffee-houses where medical men met and exchanged ideas. He met Drs Thomas Beddoes and Matthew Baillie; and in 1786, heard John Hunter read his paper, *A Treatise on Venereal Disease*, at Young Slaughter's in St Martin's Lane, where Joseph Banks, and Neville Maskelyne, the Astronomer Royal, took coffee.

D'Arcy was committed to following improvements in medical knowledge and practice. He subscribed to specialist magazines and wrote up his own *Medical Notebook*, recording particular challenges he faced, noting observations and opinions he found interesting and helpful, describing symptoms, diagnosis and treatment, and carefully noting his sources.

In quest of this Medicine   Sense & Sensibility

Physicians were the upper crust of the medical world, university trained; they moved and practiced in society and provided charitable services to the poor. They diagnosed imbalances between the bodily humours: blood, bile, phlegm and melancholy, the failure to maintain the precarious state of balance between them. *When the heat of the body turns it acrid and it insinuates itself into the neighbouring parts all about it, it produces sinuses, ulcers, fistulae, caries in bones, opens into some of the cavities, is perhaps absorbed into the mass of the blood, brings on a hectic fever, phthisis pulmonalis, ulcers of the liver.*[5]

They were beginning to examine environmental and psychological factors in disease. Erasmus Darwin analysed the effects of emotional states, irritation, sensation, volition and associated connections, on the condition of the body.[6]

Physicians referred patients to surgeons for remedies such as sweating, vomiting, purging, bloodletting and blistering, and to apothecaries for preparations of simple and compounded medicines. Licensed apothecaries *made up various*

Drugs, compounded into Bolus's, Linctus's, Electuaries, Juleps, Tinctures, Cordial... that the Doctor prescribes.[7]

Unlike physicians and apothecaries, surgeons examined, touched and worked on their patients' bodies. They studied anatomy and surgical skills, and like craftsmen, they had served their apprenticeship to a practicing surgeon.

The Surgeon is employed in the Cure of Wounds, Bruises, Contusions, Ulcers, and Eruptions in the outward Parts, in Trepanning, Cutting, or Scarifying, and Amputations of any of the Limbs or Members, that require these Operations. He applies only topical Medicines, that is, to the outward Parts of the Body affected; such as Plaisters, Cataplasms, Blisters, Cauteries, and the like; but is rarely concerned in any inward Applications; nor is supposed conversant with the Pharmacy of any sort.

Yet a skilful Surgeon generally understands a certain Train of Medicines, that inwardly applied, correct the Humours, prepare the Body, and put it in a proper Habit, fit it to undergo his Operations...To a solid Judgement, quick Apprehension, and a good Memory, he must add a kind of Courage, peculiar to himself. It is vulgarly said, that a Surgeon should have a Lion's Heart, a Hawk's Eye, and a Lady's Hand.[8]

When Roderick Random sought an apprenticeship with surgeon Launcelot Crab, he told him he had studied surgery. Crab laughed, *Oho! You did, Gentlemen here is a complete artist! Studied surgery! What? In books, I suppose...You are to learn'd for me, d—n me. But let's have no more of this stuff. Can you blood and give a clyster, spread a plaster, and prepare a potion?*[9]

Surgeons valued practical skills over academic learning, they worked with their hands, they touched and handled the sick and injured. They dissected corpses to study anatomy and the causes of death, to visualise and understand the progress of disease within the body, to categorise external inflammations, abscesses, ulcers, gangrene, tumours, etc, to understand the patient's symptoms and build up their knowledge to assist future diagnoses.

He studies too much for words of four syllables. Do not you Darcy?

Pride & Prejudice

It was surgeons, committed to observation and the use of evidence, who were transforming medicine. The *vast number of facts collected about organic alterations,* and *the beautiful illustrations with which anatomists illustrated their works,*[10] were leading the advances being made in medical practice.

Their efforts would unify medical practice: *medicine is one and indivisible, it must be learnt as a whole, for no part can be understood if learnt separately. The physician must understand surgery; the surgeon, the medical treatment of disease. Indeed, it is from the evidence afforded by external disease, that we are able to judge of the nature and progress of those which are internal.*[11]

You write uncommonly fast   Pride & Prejudice

Fitzwilliam took an interest in the challenges faced by his young cousin. He wrote D'Arcy letters of introduction to gentlemen in government and trade who might assist him with a post in India.

He was a patron of Samuel Taylor, designer of a *universal system of stenography or short hand-writing* to assist one *to acquire knowledge with unwonted rapidity*.[12] Fitzwilliam recommended the system to D'Arcy, who studied and mastered it, and used it from that time to record his clinical notes.[13]

To walk the Hospitals   Letters

William Shippen, a young surgeon from Philadelphia, was the same age as D'Arcy when he walked the wards in London. His diary gives insights into what the young student doctors saw and learnt there.

> THURSDAY 19 JULY 1759: . Spent in same manner as other Thursdays being taking in Day at hospital Mr. Pawl took off a man's leg very elegantly. Supped with Governor Hamilton, Dr. Smith and Martin.
>
> FRIDAY 20TH JULY 1759: Breakfasted with Martin gave Dr. Smith a letter for Philadelphia. Attended Dr. Smith's lecture at 2. Spent the afternoon and Evening at 3 labours and at 11 o'clock a Fracture of Leg at Guys Hospital.
>
> SATURDAY 21ST JULY 1759: Rose at 7½, went to Hospital at 11 and walked around the Hospital with Dr. Reeve, took down all remarkable cases and prescriptions. After hospital I attended Dr. Smith lecture de Lue Venerea till 3½. Spent the afternoon and Evening at my own apartment. Supp'd about 9 went to bed about 11.
>
> MONDAY 23RD JULY 1759: Rose at 8 being lazy. Breakfasted and went round the Hospital with Surgeon Baker not being Physicians Day, he performed 2 or 3 little operations. Dr. Smiths lecture on Menses and from 2 till 4 drank Tea with Mr. Perkins, and returned home about 9 after reading late York papers.
>
> THURSDAY 26TH.JULY 1759: Rose at 7 breakfasted at 8 and went to Hospital at 9½. Dr Milner took in the Patients being 49, and wrote for them, Dr Reeves wrote for the out Patients and wrote for them made 50. At one o'clock with 3 of the Physicians Pupils went to the Royal College of Physicians and heard Dr Lawrence read a Latin oration or Treatise De Schirro et Garcinomate. Dined with Mr. De Berdt and spent afternoon and Evening at my own apartment; bed about 10½.
>
> MONDAY 30TH JULY 1759: Rose at 7½. Went thro the hospital by myself to examine the patients; at 3 Dr McKensie's Lecture began after which I spent 2 hours in examining a dead Body at Hospital who died suddenly, his os humeri

was broke just below the capsular Ligament of that Joint, his viscera sound and good. Brain supposed to affected. Walked this Evening to Newington, and played Skittles an hour with Perkins who drank Tea with me. Supped and went to bed at 10.30. Lobsters for supper.

SATURDAY 4TH AUGUST 1759: Rose at 7 breakfasted and took coach for the dirty London. Saw Mr. Way surgeon to Guy's hospital amputate a leg above the knee very dexterously 3 ligatures. 3 patients at Enfield all better, one with worms, which B.Jovial cured, one obstructed menses, better much.

WEDNESDAY 8TH AUGUST 1759: To Peckham to ride with good Mrs. Huthwaite, to Shooters Hill which commands the most extensive, and variegated Prospect perhaps in England, the windings of the River Thames in the middle of so fine a Garden, if I may so say, makes the Prospect enchanting.

5 SEPTEMBER 1759: Examined particulars in hospital several smallpox 3 out of 4 die, saw Mr Baker perform 3 operations, a leg, breast and tumour from girls' lower jaw inside, very well operated. Mr Warner extracted a large stone from urethra of a man and pinn'd the incision up as in harelip.

2 NOVEMBER 1759: Went to George's Hospital and saw Hawkins and Bromfield operate, stone and amputation.

7 NOVEMBER 1759: Went to Bartholemews Hospital saw the neatest operation of bubonocele that I ever saw by Mr Pott a very clever neat surgeon.[14]

Your father would depend on your resolution and good conduct, I am sure

Pride & Prejudice

William Shippen's father, a surgeon and a Quaker, knew his son could be at risk, alone in London for twelve months, walking the wards. He contacted fellow Quakers, friends and medical colleagues in London, to help guide and support him, telling his brother, Edward: *Billey goes on board Capt. Dingo's fine ship bound to Liverpool, from thence to London where he will find G. Whitefield and Mr. De Berdt, a Methodist Mercht. Of great reputation as a Trader, who will direct him in regard to a Manly, Genteel frugality in his Expenses and Living – as friendly & as sincerely as well as judiciously as any man in London, and I think from his connections with them and their friends he will be despised by your Rakes and Fops whose acquaintance and commendation would be his disgust and ruin. He is to spend this winter in London with the finest Anatomist for Dissections, Injections, &c in England; at the same time visit the Hospitals daily.*[15]

The India House

Letters

Throughout 1786, D'Arcy awaited confirmation from the East India Company of his posting to India. He was well received when he attended the office in

Leadenhall Street, with his certificates and Fitzwilliam's introduction. He had contacts in India and letters of introduction to present when he arrived.[16] D'Arcy was assured that he had been short listed for the next round of postings of assistant surgeons. He was confident a vacancy would soon arise.

He knew nothing of the Company's current surfeit of assistant surgeons. The long peace in Bengal under Hastings had reduced demand for their services. There was a large reserve in India, with one group recruited from Bengal and another sent by the Court of Directors. Leadenhall Street expected its nominees had been deployed and those engaged by the Council of Bengal would find other positions in India. It was anticipated the demand for assistant surgeons would pick up after a short lull, but all did not go to plan.

A despatch from Bengal to the Court of Directors, in April 1785, transmitted *copies of letters from your Commander in Chief and Surgeon-General and several petitions which accompanied them from the assistant surgeons who were dismissed in consequence of your orders of 16 March 1784. The representations of these gentlemen will point out the hardship of their case. We feel the cruelty of it so forcibly that we must beg leave, in the most earnest manner to recommend it to your favourable attention.*

The despatch was on board the *Hinchinbrooke* when she broke up *on the head of the Long Sand, near Cockerlee Buoy, having put back from stress of weather before the pilot had left her. She proved leaky in her upper works, cargo worth 784,280 rupees was lost.*

A second despatch from Bengal at the end of September reiterated the problem: *The loss of our despatches by the Hinchinbrooke will have retarded your receipt of several memorials from the assistant surgeons who were dismissed in conformity to your orders of 16 March 1784. Duplicates are conveyed in this packet... We feel ourselves exceedingly interested in their behalf from the earnest solicitations that we have received from all ranks of officers of the different detachments they served in and the extreme distress to which your orders have reduced them.*[17]

D'Arcy returned regularly to Leadenhall Street to follow up his application. He was advised politely to be patient, he would be notified in good time. He trusted these undertakings would be honoured. He concentrated on his studies.

A young man so totally independent of every one Pride & Prejudice

On the wards, D'Arcy found engaging colleagues and acquaintances at every turn, cases to follow, theories to speculate and discuss. Outside the hospital, he relished his independence. He explored London, eager to find his place in the modern world. Unlike William Shippen, he had no network at the ready to steer him clear of trouble, or the pitfalls he might encounter.

Acquaintance with Mr Wickham *Pride & Prejudice*

Outside his medical world, D'Arcy enjoyed the company of new friends, some, like William Wickham, he had met in York with Robert Sinclair, others at Grosvenor Square with Fitzwilliam.

Wickham was completing his studies at Lincoln's Inn, ready to be called to the bar the following year, 1786. He and D'Arcy would occasionally breakfast at the *Lock & Key* or the *Kings Head Coffee-house* at West Smithfield, with the booming noise of farmers, barrowmen and young medics from St Barts. Through Wickham, D'Arcy met other young lawyers from the Inns of Court.

Equally worthy of all that friendship could do *Emma*

He made lasting friends with John Villiers, the Member for Old Sarum,[18] and second son of the Earl of Clarendon.[19] A supporter of William Pitt, he had been in Parliament just a year. His youth and inexperience saw him dubbed, *Villiers, comely with the flaxen hair.*[20]

A spy and an intruder *Mansfield Park*

D'Arcy joined friends and companions at country house parties, entertainments and race meetings, enjoying gossip, good company and conversation.

He found a *particular friend* in Paul Wentworth, and *often mentioned* him in letters home.[21] Nearly sixty, Paul Wentworth had lived a life of great adventure. Born on Barbados, educated in New Hampshire, where his family were successive governors, he returned to the West Indies, married at age twenty-six, and moved to Surinam in Dutch Guiana. There he acquired plantations and grew coffee and cocoa for export to Europe.

In 1766, after his wife died, Paul Wentworth left managers to run his estates and moved to London. Governor John Wentworth appointed him Colonial Agent for New Hampshire, a consular role, dealing with ministers, business and the Board of Trade.[22] The American rebellion was gaining momentum.

In 1776, Benjamin Franklin was sent to France, to the Court of Louis XVI, as ambassador for the American Colonies. He wanted French support, moral, financial and firepower, for the War of Independence against England.

I have found a convenient old hollow oak to put our letters in *Amelia Webster*

Rockingham introduced Paul Wentworth to Henry Howard, Earl of Suffolk, Secretary of State in Lord North's government,[23] and Howard sent him to Paris to gather intelligence about Franklin's activities and France's involvement in the American rebellion. Paul Wentworth moved back and forth to France, Portugal, Spain, Holland. He recruited other Americans, loyal to America and to Britain, sifted their intelligence and made his reports to Lord Suffolk. The

Prime Minister, Lord North, called him *the most important and truest informer we have had, everything he told us has been confirmed.*[24]

Wentworth arranged for contacts in Franklin's household to prepare weekly reports, written in invisible ink. On Tuesday afternoons, they were left for him in a boxwood tree on the southern edge of the Tuileries Garden.[25]

De Beaumarchais, the French Foreign Minister said of him, *He is related to the Marquis of Rockingham; is a particular friend of Lord Suffolk; is employed by the minister in difficult matters…This Mr Wentworth speaks French like you and better than I do; he is one of the cleverest men in England.*[26]

By December 1777, when British forces had surrendered at Saratoga, French interest in an alliance with America was gaining momentum. Paul Wentworth was directed to meet Franklin, to discuss the terms under which the American Colonies would accept a peaceful settlement. The mission was a failure, as Franklin was adamant that America wanted its independence. A few weeks later, in January 1778, France signed a Treaty of Alliance with America. Wentworth had already alerted Lord Suffolk to the precise details of the Treaty.

Wentworth also spoke fluent Dutch, and was later deployed in Holland to gather intelligence and dissuade the Dutch from joining with France and America against Britain. Exposed by French agents, he was deported. Holland joined France in the war against England, and supported America with generous loans.

D'Arcy knew Paul Wentworth in his last years in London, when his health and fortune were in decline. They would meet at the *Mount*, at the *New England Coffee-house* in Threadneedle Street, or at his house at Hammersmith, where D'Arcy browsed the library, with its books in many languages, and beautiful coloured maps around the walls.

Paul Wentworth retained his daring, his ability to put himself in jeopardy and take his chances. He speculated in stocks and shares, and finally lost heavily, his own and other's money. Sir John Wentworth, now in Nova Scotia lost a great deal. In 1790 he returned to Surinam, and he died there in 1793.

I shall take the opportunity of calling in Grosvenor-street — Pride & Prejudice

D'Arcy called at Grosvenor Square several times during his first months in London. Lady Charlotte Fitzwilliam, now thirty-nine, was at home, and expecting her first child. *Countess Fitzwilliam, who has been married several years, but hitherto not blessed with children, is now pregnant, and near lying-in; an event which opens the fairest prospects of felicity to that noble family.*[27]

On Thursday 4 May 1786, Fitzwilliam's first and only child, Charles William Wentworth-Fitzwilliam, was born at Grosvenor Square.

Three days later, Fitzwilliam learnt his brother George was dead: *Sunday an express arrived from Bristol with an account of the death of Hon. George Fitzwilliam (who was born after the death of his father in 1757) brother of the present Earl Fitzwilliam and brother of Lady Charlotte Dundas.*[28]

About thirty, not handsome, but in person and address most truly the gentleman…there was a softness in Colonel Fitzwilliam's manners

Pride & Prejudice

George Fitzwilliam was twenty-nine when he died. He had joined the 1st Horse Grenadier Guards at nineteen and risen to the rank of sub-Lieutenant. In 1781, his sister Charlotte's father-in-law, Sir Lawrence Dundas, nominated him for his Yorkshire seat of Richmond. George won the seat and served three years under four prime ministers, one of them, his uncle Lord Rockingham. It was a volatile period, dominated by the American War of Independence and its aftermath, the loss of the American colonies.

"A younger son, you know, must be inured to self-denial and dependence." "In my opinion, the younger son of an Earl can know very little of either. Now seriously, what have you ever known of self-denial and dependence?"

Pride & Prejudice

In Parliament, George Fitzwilliam sided with his brother on most matters. When Fitzwilliam, in the Lords, criticised proposals for peace with America put forward by Rockingham's successor, George voted against them in the Commons. He supported Fox's *East India Bill* that proposed Fitzwilliam as head of a new board in London to direct the East India Company.

In May 1783, he voted against a motion of Charles Grey, for an inquiry into parliamentary reform. His stance reflected his brother's opinion, but it was he, not Fitzwilliam, who lost the confidence of his Whig supporters. He was replaced as the Whig candidate for the seat of Richmond.

In 1783, and again in 1784, Fitzwilliam proposed him for the seat of York, but George was not accepted. Peregrine Wentworth wrote to Fitzwilliam that many in the Rockingham Club in York strongly supported reform of Parliament, and had it *fresh in their minds that Mr Fitzwilliam voted against the reform bill.*[29]

Absolutely refused　　　　　　　　　　　　　　　　　　　　　Lady Susan

The Dean of York wrote, *strong as my wishes are to show my regard to every branch of your family…I could not…ask for a vote for your brother, who it is said voted against all reform.*

Rockingham had commanded the Whig vote in Yorkshire, but after his death in July 1782, loyalties shifted dramatically, as William Pitt and his Tories rode to victory throughout the country. Robert Sinclair wrote from York, *many consider Mr Pitt as the champion of their cause.* [30]

Fitzwilliam moved to *Wentworth Woodhouse* from Northamptonshire after Rockingham's death, but he still had to win the loyalty of Yorkshire voters. Whig candidates suffered numerous defeats there, and he was unable to give George his patronage.

D'Arcy grieved for both brothers, for their sisters, and for the great shadow that had fallen across Fitzwilliam's happiness.

Countess Fitzwilliam, who had always been frail, became *dangerously ill*.[31] London papers reported almost daily on her condition, announcing as last, she was *now likely to recover*,[32] and later *in a favourable way of a speedy recovery*.[33] On 16 May her son was christened at Grosvenor Square.[34]

Little spare money and a great deal of health, activity and independence
Emma

Throughout 1786, D'Arcy worked conscientiously at his studies, making ready to take up a surgical post abroad. The East India Company was recruiting troops for India,[35] but still it had no posts for assistant surgeons. By the Spring of 1786, his fourth month walking the wards, his funds were very low.

To become a qualified surgeon could *be obtained but by great Expence*.[36] *Though it requires no great sum to buy a set of instruments, & yet the youth should have a fortune sufficient to support him like a gentleman.*[37]

Unlike other senior surgeons, Percivall Pott did not charge his students, *he read them gratis*,[38] but despite this saving, like many young Irish surgeons, D'Arcy found the cost of obtaining medical credentials far more than he could afford.

Even when qualified, it took a lot of effort and luck for a doctor to make a living. George Bernard Shaw remembered his Dublin childhood, where: *Doctors are hideously poor. The Irish gentleman doctor of my boyhood…took nothing less than a guinea, though he might pay you four visits for it*.[39]

Many doctors practising in London also found it difficult: *A physician in London assured me that many years had elapsed before his annual income was equal to £800. This was in some measure, to be attributed to the smallness of the fee, never or rarely exceeding half-a-guinea, and his gratis visits, he did not receive more than half that sum on an average* or *more than one guinea for the whole of his attendance during a fit of illness. Consider the time and labour many physicians bestow in attending hospitals, dispensaries, and other charitable institutions; & the many visits they make gratis. Excepting a few of the class, who have really too much employment to do proper justice to their patients, the major part are rarely called in, until it is too late.*[40]

Doctors relied on patronage, social networks and word of mouth. Tobias Smollett detailed the elaborate and fruitless efforts of Dr Fathom, trying to attract patients and establish himself in the profession:

> *Doctor Fathom, resolving to make his first medical appearance in London with some eclat, he not only purchased an old chariot, which was new painted for the purpose, but likewise hired a footman, whom he clothed in laced livery, in order to distinguish himself from the common run of his brethren.*
>
> *This equipage, though much more expensive than his finances could bear, he found absolutely necessary to give him a chance for employment; as every shabby retainer to physic, in this capital, had provided himself with a vehicle, which was used by way of a travelling sign-post, to draw in customers...*
>
> *In his researches, he found that the great world was wholly engrossed by a few practitioners who had arrived at the summit of reputation... and the rest of the business was parcelled out into small enclosures, occupied by different groups of personages... who stood in rings, and tossed the ball from one to another...*
>
> *Fathom... set up his rest in the first floor of an apothecary in the neighbourhood of Charing Cross... His chariot rolled along through all the most frequented streets, during the whole forenoon, and, at the usual hour, he never failed to make his appearance at the medical coffee-house...*
>
> *The other means used to force a trade, such as ordering himself to be called from church, alarming the neighbourhood with knocking at his door in the night, receiving sudden messages in places of resort, and inserting his cures by way of news in the daily papers, had been so injudiciously hackneyed by every desperate sculler in physic, that they had lost their effect upon the public, and therefore were excluded from the plan of our adventurer.*
>
> The Adventures of Ferdinand Count Fathom, 1753.

D'Arcy resolved to remain and complete his studies, whatever the difficulties or risks. He knew other young surgeons in similar straits, and there was little paid work for young medics. By his second winter in London, he had moved to cheaper digs in New Compton Street, and found a reliable source of income.

Most abundantly supplied with coffee Pride & Prejudice

Coffee-houses were the meeting places for men with common interests, where *all manner of opinions are profest and maintain'd... to the last drop of coffee*, due to the sovereign virtue it has to strengthen politic notions.[41] *The Discourses of this kind were the most ingeniose, and smart, that ever I heard, or expect to heare, and bandied with great eagernesse: the Arguments in the Parliament howse were but flatt to it... The roome was every evening full as it could be cramm'd.*[42]

Samuel Butler held that before coffee-houses, *men knew not how to be acquainted, but with their own relations or societies... There people of all qualities and conditions meet, to trade in foreign drinks and newes, ale, smoak, and controversy. They admit no distinction of persons, but gentleman, mechanic, lord, scroundrel mix.*[43]

They met for the sake of eating, drinking & laughing together, playing at cards
Sense & Sensibility

Opportunities for gaming abounded in London, everyone played at cards and fluttered a little. It was something to do together, equals around a table, in the evening, in all weathers. Cards and gaming provided an endless source of conversation, and added colour to everyone's lives.

The wealthy bet on horse races at Tattersalls, in betting rooms at the courses, or wagered in drawing rooms and private clubs. Gaming was the main attraction at clubs like Brook's, that Fitzwilliam and his brother visited with Charles Fox,[44] or White's, a popular haunt that attracted Henry Austen.[45] Large stakes were the rule, and debts were settled as a matter of honour.

Horace Walpole remarked that at Brook's, the new Whig club, *a thousand meadows and cornfields are staked at every throw, and as many villages lost as in the earthquake that overwhelmed Herculaneum and Pompeii*. Charles Fox had run up debts there of £140,000 by the time he was twenty-four.

Henry Fielding conceded, noblemen might gamble, but *in the mean time we may, I think, reasonably desire of these great Personages, that they would keep their favourite Vice to themselves, and not suffer others, whose Birth or Fortune gives them no Title to be above the Terrour of the Laws, or the Censure of their Betters, to share with them in this Privilege.*[46]

For London's burgeoning middle class, Coffee-houses provided facilities for gaming. Many had gaming rooms, with card tables, dice and opportunities to bet on horse races, and future or speculative events of any kind. Patrons could buy tickets in the national lotteries, [47] and to theatres and concerts.

Tories met at the *Cocoa-tree* and Whigs at *St James;* writers gathered at *Wills,* the *Bedford Coffee House* in Covent Garden or *Garraway's* in the City; Lawyers met in *Searle's* at Lincoln's Inn Fields. In time, the Coffee-houses evolved into private clubs, business houses, and even financial institutions like the Stock Exchange, the Baltic Exchange and insurers, Lloyds of London.

For every one played at Cards A Collection of Letters

D'Arcy became one of a number of young surgeons who gambled in order to afford to live in London, to pursue their studies. As apprentices, they had sworn not to play *at cards, Dice or any other unlawful game, during the said Term.*[48] Released from their indentures, they gambled for *profit, not pleasure...with all wariness and discretion.*[49]

They emulated *those prosperous gentlemen who wear clean linen every day, who make their five hundred a year by Whist-playing, and have nothing else to live upon.*[50]

> *I determined, in a fit of despair, to risk all I had at the gaming table, with a view to acquiring a fortune sufficient to render me independent for life; or of plunging myself into such a state of misery, as would effectively crush every ambitious hope that now tortured my imagination.*
>
> *Actuated by this fatal resolution, I engaged in play, and, after some turns of fortune found myself, at the end of three days, worth a thousand pounds; but it was not my intention to stop there, for which cause I kept Strap ignorant of my success, and continued my career until I was reduced to five guineas, which I would have hazarded also, had I not been ashamed to fall from a bet of two hundred pounds to such a petty sum.*[51]
>
> The Adventures of Roderick Random

D'Arcy practiced and mastered skill at cards; he played to win in inns and Coffee-houses around the city. Coffee-house managers happily admitted these lively, well-spoken young men to their tables; they did not cheat, their youth and precision attracted patrons, and they added to the diversions on offer.

This Vice, wrote Chief magistrate and novelist Henry Fielding, *is the more dangerous, as it is deceitful...it flatters its Votaries with the Hopes of increasing their Wealth;...it often betrays the more thoughtless and giddy Part of Mankind into them; promising Riches without Bounds, and those to be acquired by the most sudden as well as easy and indeed pleasant Means.*[52]

Fixed the whole time at the same table in the same room The Watsons

In a piece in *The Loiterer,* James Austen described the discipline they required: *All who have ever been by-standers at a Gaming Table, and observed the extreme attention and anxiety marked in the countenances of those people who are so foolishly called Players... far from being engaged in amusement or play, they are in reality occupied in calculations; compared to which, the problems of Euclid are easy, and the discovery of the Longitude a trifle...*

Gaming strengthens the memory; a perfection which young people can never purchase too dear... a man who can accurately remember all the different calculations of the chances at Hazard, and the order in which every card was played in a game of Whist, might be equally enabled to retain in his head an equal number of Acts of Parliament, Cases, and Precedents; and with very little reading would make an excellent Lawyer. This Science is... adapted to soften men's tempers, and teach them patience and fortitude under the sudden changes in life... there is really a charm in Gaming, so exceedingly bewitching as to make full amends for the loss of Fortune, Reputation, and Health![53]

On entering the drawing-room, she found the whole party at loo Pride & Prejudice

The medical profession did not distance itself from gambling. Horace Walpole reported the popular card game, Loo, was routinely played in homes where John Hunter, the fashionable obstetrician, was attending women in labour: *Loo*[54] *is mounted to its zenith; the parties last till one and two in the morning. We played at Lady Hertford's last week, the last night of her lying-in, till deep into Sunday morning, after she and her lord were retired. It is now adjourned to Mrs. Fitzroy's, whose child the town called Pamela. I proposed, that instead of receiving cards for assemblies, one should send in the morning to Dr. Hunter's, the man-midwife, to know where there is loo that evening.*[55]

Almost always at the Gaming-table. Ah! my poor Fortune where art thou at this time? Lesley Castle

D'Arcy joined several fellow student-surgeons from the *Middlesex Infirmary for the Sick and Lame of Soho,* who played cards at the *Oxford and Cambridge Coffee House* in nearby Newman Street. Women were not admitted to coffee houses, but there were messengers employed to collect their bets, deliver their lottery tickets and present them with their winnings.

"I know little of the game at present," said he, but I shall be glad to improve myself, for in my situation in life – -" Pride & Prejudice

As his skill at cards improved, D'Arcy's winnings paid his mounting expenses. The concentration required suited his temperament, he could give unswerving attention to detail, his memory was well trained, and he could approach a risky situation with a gentle, calm detachment.

He would have been called a *sharper,* they were *typically wellborn men with the benefit of a genteel education.* Curiously, many gentle men preferred the risks of playing with sharpers. Lord Chesterfield explained that when he won from sharpers they immediately settled their debts, while gentlemen offered nothing more than genteel apologies and empty promises to pay.[56]

Henry Fielding, did not agree: *What Temptations can Gamesters of Fashion have, to admit inferior Sharpers into their Society? Common Sense, surely will not suffer a Man to risque a Fortune against one who hath none of his own to stake against it.*

The Dog & Duck

On afternoons when he attended ward rounds at St Thomas' or Guy's Hospital, D'Arcy would sometimes dine with friends at the *Dog & Duck* in St George's Fields, a place of entertainment and some notoriety. In the grounds was a pond where spaniels were sent in to catch ducks. When a duck tried to escape by diving, the dog waited for it to surface, and patrons wagered on the outcome.[57]

The *Dog & Duck* was not far from Lambeth Palace, the residence of the Archbishop of Canterbury. It had once been London's foremost watering spa, its mineral springs recommended by eminent physicians for cure of cancers, rheumatism, stone, gravel, fistulas, ulcers, sore eyes, etc. *They are excellent for cutaneous foulness and scrofulous diseases, have been affirmed to cure, but certainly known to retard the progress of cancer.*

By 1786, the premises were extended to include tea rooms, a bar, a music gallery; a Ladies Bath and a Gentlemen's Bath, each covered by a leaded dome; a pleasure garden, skittle grounds and a bowling green. It become known as a resort for dissolute characters and sharpers.[58]

Being tied up with much gaming at present Mansfield Park

Parliament enacted numerous laws to control gambling, but they were never vigorously enforced. The law had no desire to interfere with people who had ample funds and leisure, and chose to risk their money.

While defaulting on gambling debts was not uncommon, the honour of gamblers prevented informing on defaulters. Informers were detested, and the Court was not interested in cases brought for gaming debts.

In August 1839, *The Sporting Review* stated, *We beg to decline the proposed list of turf defaulters: it is not our design to publish a swindling calendar.* In 1843, Charles Henry Russell, warned off the racecourse, produced a list of more than thirty defaulters, with debts totalling almost half a million pounds.

For many gamblers though, honour was paramount. In 1836 Hon. Berkeley Craven[59] committed suicide after losing thirty thousand pounds at Tattersalls, on the Epsom Derby. His loss was received with surprise and regret.[60]

The consequence of ignorance of the world & want of employment
Sense & Sensibility

Young medics who gambled to live and to pay their way, soon realised, that for many gamblers, honour was secondary when it came to gaming debts.

Coffee-house proprietors were eager to maintain an atmosphere of bonhomie amongst their patrons. All of them, defaulters included, were helped into their coats when they chose to leave, and cordially bid goodnight. No matter if they had failed to honour their debts. Young aggrieved sharpers were dissuaded from following them.

D'Arcy realised that he and his friends were seen as easy targets. Men of substance, upcoming young lawyers, sometimes in small groups, would never pay when they lost at the gaming table. Their own money was never at risk; they knew the young medico-sharpers could never press a case for debt against them, and expected them to absorb their losses.

No invitation came amiss   *Emma*

On a winter evening in late December 1786, D'Arcy dined at the *Dog & Duck* with two colleagues, John Molloy and William Manning. The three young men fell in with a group of worldly, well attired men of business, who appeared well known at the inn, friendly with all comers, comfortable with each other. They were invited to join them next evening at the exclusive Blackheath Golf Club[61] for a game of cards, and they accepted the invitation with pleasure.

John Francis Molloy, a young Irish surgeon, aged twenty, was, like D'Arcy, walking the wards to gain accreditation. William Manning, twenty-three, was the son of a London merchant from St. Kitts in the West Indies, who traded produce from the Caribbean, rum, sugar, molasses, cotton and other goods. Manning had married just a few weeks earlier. His mother had died the previous year, and he was urgently awaiting his inheritance from her estate, including shares in a plantation on the Danish island of Santa Cruz.

A club established among the gentlemen & half-gentlemen of the place   *Emma*

The Blackheath Golf Club was a meeting place for wealthy, middle-ranking merchants, traders and ship-owners. Many were Scots living in Kent, with business interests in the dockyards and warehouses on the south shore of the Thames, servicing the thousands of ships carrying goods to and from London.

Other members were involved in the lucrative slave trade – Thomas King of the slave trading firm, Camden Calvert and King; Francis Baring, plantation owner turned banker; John Julius Angerstein, slave trader and founder of Lloyds Bank; Ambrose Crowley, manufacturer of shackles and collars for the trade. They enjoyed gaming, their wagers were paid in gallons of claret or an equivalent number of guineas.

At Long Reach and Erith Reach, *the Indiamen on their passage up the river, frequently come to an anchor, and lay some time to be lightened of part of their* burthen, *that they may proceed with greater safety up the river.*[62] *This, together with the shipping of goods to and from London*, was an opportunity for local traders in *several kinds of East India goods, procured from on board.*[63]

The rich network of ship owners and traders extended well beyond Kent, linking families, colleagues, the City of London, East and West Indian and African company merchants, marine underwriters and slave traders. Their knowledge of the needs of the Navy Board helped them build vast profits.

Blushed at the idea of paying their Debts Love & Freindship

Their hosts were older, richer and far less intent on their play than D'Arcy and his friends. The stakes were raised, and by the end of the evening they had lost badly. They thanked D'Arcy and his friends profusely for the pleasure of the game, saying they had enjoyed the evening, the company and the pace of play, and they laughed off requests to honour their losses.

D'Arcy was outraged at men of such substance conniving to avoid their gaming debts. The three friends were frustrated and angry. They contrived a plan of direct action to obtain the money owed them.

Reasoning on the game of chance

D'Arcy realised his defaulters would not want it known by the press that they were gamblers who did not pay their debts. He calculated, with a reasonable degree of confidence, there was little likelihood they would prosecute him if he held them up to recover his winnings; that they would not be prepared to appear in court and be themselves exposed.

> *Said Darcy, I have faults enough, but they are not, I hope, of understanding. My temper I dare not vouch for. – It is I believe too little yielding – certainly too little for the convenience of the world. I cannot forget the follies and vices of others so soon as I ought, nor their offences against myself. My feelings are not puffed about with every attempt to move them. My temper would perhaps be called resentful. – My good opinion once lost is lost forever* Pride & Prejudice

Several of his debtors, in the hope of recovering stolen watches or property, reported their suspicion that D'Arcy Wentworth was the masked highwayman who had held them up. Time and again D'Arcy took the calculated risk they would stop short of giving evidence to convict and send him to the gallows.

Debt collection by highway robbery was not new. Thirty-five years earlier Henry Fielding described gambling, as the *School in which most Highwaymen of great Eminence have been bred.*[64]

Chapter 7

High spirit & strong passions

The person who has contracted debts must pay them

FROM SHOOTERS' HILL you could follow the Thames, winding across to Essex, Surrey and part of Sussex, while to the north, lay the whole expanse of London:

> A mighty mass of brick, and smoke, and shipping,
> Dirty and dusky, but as wide as eye
> Could reach, with here and there a sail just skipping
> In sight, then lost amidst the forestry
> Of masts; a wilderness of steeples peeping
> On tip-toe through their sea-coal canopy.[1]
>
> *Lord Byron*

An old Roman road to Dover, through Rochester and Canterbury, tracked down Shooter's Hill and out across Blackheath. *The steepness, narrowness of the ancient road, and the shelter which the contiguous coppices and woods afforded, rendered it almost impossible for a passenger to escape being waylaid by robbers.*[2]

It was here that Henry, Prince of Wales, son of Henry IV, and his dissolute associates, robbed the Sandwich carriers and auditors, carrying money to his father's exchequer.[3]

On account of some debts of honour, which were very pressing Pride & Prejudice

On Wednesday, 10 January 1787, three men, their faces covered by black crape masks, rode out of a wooded section of Blackheath. They halted the coach of James Irwin and Stephen Remnant Esq, and rode off with watches, chains, seals and coins.

Stephen Remnant was the proprietor of the *Jerusalem Coffee House* in Corn Hill, one of the oldest city news-rooms, where shipping-lists, papers and details of arrivals and departures were posted for India, the Far East and ports in between. It was frequented by East India Company men from nearby Leadenhall Street, by merchants and captains involved in commerce with India, China and later, Australia. James Irwin was Surgeon-General of the Artillery at nearby Woolwich Arsenal.

Lay thine ear close to the ground, and list if thou can hear the tread of travellers[4]

Henry IV Part I

The following Saturday, after a long lunch, four men, well fed with beef and claret, emerged from *The Bull*, a public house near the crest of Shooters Hill. William Curtis, accompanied by *three other gentlemen*,[5] Archibald Anderson, Claude Scott, and Mr Jones of Bristol, settled back into the comfortable upholstery of Alderman Curtis' coach. As they moved through the wintry afternoon fog towards Welling, three men on horseback were waiting for them in Oxleas Wood.

He had left gaming debts behind him to a very considerable amount

Pride & Prejudice

It seems William Curtis was the prime target. Known as *Billy Biscuit*, his people were 'sugar bakers' who made their fortune producing ships' biscuits at Wapping. The mile-long Wapping Wall, stretching east from Tower Bridge on the north bank of the Thames, was the centre for victualling and supplying the thousands of merchant vessels that entered the Thames.

Curtis was thirty-five, *a ludicrous figure with his massive paunch, drinker's nose and untutored diction, and a godsend to the cartoonists, who mercilessly caricatured him as the epitome of civic gormandising and corruption, he was ruthless and courageous and nobody's fool.*[6]

He was an Alderman for London's Tower Ward, an active member of the Corporation of the City of London, and remained a prominent Tory in City politics for almost forty years. Lord Mayor of London for a short period, he was elected to the Commons in 1790, and served there until 1826.

Curtis was a patron of a merchant group, Camden, Calvert and King, who dominated the transatlantic slave trade. Their ships carried goods from England to African ports, trading them for the slaves they took across the Atlantic, the *Middle Passage*, to trade in the Americas for raw materials to sell in England, a *terse, efficient triangle*.[7] He was also a ship owner, part-owner of the *Lady Penrhyn*,[8] the ship of the First Fleet that carried the first horses to Australia.

Archibald Anderson, a ships master, had been employed by the East India Company. Claude Scott made his fortune in the corn trade, importing cheap corn when it was scarce and expensive in England. A shareholder in the East India Company, he lived 'splendidly' on an estate near Bromley, in Kent. In 1795 he signed a declaration of loyalty by London merchants to Pitt's government, and in 1797 subscribed £50,000 to a loyalty loan. He and his son entered Parliament in 1802, and he remained a Member until 1812, when he was made a baronet.[9]

James Jones, Bristol's biggest slave trader, owned nine slave-ships, he was one of the hundreds of licensed traders who brought great wealth to Bristol.

> "I remember hearing you once say, Mr Darcy, that you hardly ever forgave, that your resentment once created was unappeasable."
>
> Pride & Prejudice

In danger from the pursuit
Northanger Abbey

Mr Duncan, approaching on horseback through the fog, heard sounds of a robbery, and seeing highwaymen moving off, galloped after them. D'Arcy and Molloy turned quickly, going separate ways, each showing *a fair pair of heels*.[10] Manning headed back across Shooters Hill, Duncan raced after him, and caught up with him at Southend, just beyond Lewisham.

The press reported: **Monday two men were brought before Sir Sampson Wright**, for having stopped Alderman Curtis and another gentleman, on the high road near Shooter's Hill, on Saturday last, about three o'clock in the afternoon, and having taken from them their watches and money to some amount. After a full examination, they were committed to take their trial at the next sessions.

One of the above men was taken just after the robbery was committed, and on searching him a pocket-book was found, which led to the discovery of his accomplice.[11]

WHITEHALL EVENING POST

Manning's pocket-book contained an address in **New Compton Street**, by which means another of the robbers was apprehended, and the magistrates are in hopes of soon finding the third.[12]

DAILY UNIVERSAL REGISTER

D'Arcy was arrested and taken to Bow Street, where he and William Manning were examined by the resident magistrate.

We do not look in great cities for our best morality
Mansfield Park

Henry Fielding, playwright, novelist and barrister, appointed London's Chief Magistrate in 1749, worked from his house in Bow Street, Covent Garden. He kept his office open late, to receive reports as soon as possible after a crime was committed. He employed 'Bow Street runners' or 'thief-takers' to respond quickly, discover and apprehend suspects and bring them in for examination.

If new information came to light after the suspect was committed, Fielding would recall him for "further examination," to answer the additional charge. If there was sufficient evidence, the magistrate would charge and commit the suspect for trial.

His listening so attentively Sense & Sensibility

In 1754, Henry was succeeded by his half-brother, John Fielding, who held the post of Chief Magistrate until his death in 1780. He strengthened policing at Bow Street, using the vigorous London press to publicise crime. He issued descriptions of suspects with dates and times of upcoming examinations. He encouraged witnesses and victims of similar crimes to attend and come forward if they could identify a suspect, to build up evidence for the prosecution case.

John Fielding developed a system for collecting and publicising criminal intelligence. He gathered information from magistrates and constables across Britain on serious crimes and wanted criminals, and published it in *Hue & Cry* and the *Police Gazette*. He was known as the *Blind Beak*, having been blinded at nineteen, in a naval accident. It was said he could recognise three thousand criminals by their voices.[13]

In 1780, he was succeeded by Sir Sampson Wright, Chief Magistrate until 1797. In 1790 Wright made the Bow Street Runners a permanent Foot Patrol, operating across central London during the hours of darkness. In 1805, a Horse Patrol was added, followed in 1821, by a Day Patrol, the forerunner to London's Metropolitan Police, established in 1836.

In slighting too easily the forms of worldly propriety, he displayed a want of caution Sense & Sensibility

Sampson Wright examined D'Arcy Wentworth and William Manning, two young men foolhardy enough to have confronted powerful and wealthy Kent merchants. They were frank with him, each man they targeted *had left gambling debts behind him to a very considerable amount*.[14]

The press reported on Wednesday 17 January 1787: **Yesterday morning, two highwaymen who have committed many robberies on Blackheath and the Kentish roads, during the course of last week, were examined in the publick office in Bow-street. Several gentlemen attended who have recently been robbed, when sufficient proof of their guilt appearing, they were fully committed for trial at the next assizes at Maidstone; they are two handsome young men, and have all the exterior appearance of gentlemen. They said their names were Wentworth and Manning. A third whose name they said was Molloy, escaped his pursuers.**[15]

DAILY UNIVERSAL REGISTER

On trial at Maidstone, March 1787

Highway robbery was a capital offence, and after their examinations at Bow Street, Wentworth and Manning were both committed to take their trial at the next sessions.[16] They were imprisoned to await the Lent Assizes at Maidstone.

It is at this point, that William Manning disappears from the case. There is no record of a decision to release him. His wife Elizabeth most likely sought help from her father and brother, Members of Parliament,[17] to have him freed from Newgate, and help settle his financial problems. Certainly his experience was a salutary one.

To Newgate, gentle youth Love & Freindship

D'Arcy knowing he was to face Court alone, remained at Newgate, confronting the ruin of his hopes and plans, and the prospect of a death sentence. Daniel Defoe described *the horrors of that dismal place: the hellish noise, the roaring, the swearing and clamour, the stench and nastiness, and all the dreadful afflicting things that I saw there, joined to make the place seem an emblem of Hell itself.*[18]

St Valentine's Day, his twenty fourth birthday, was bleak and wintry, *the ground covered with snow, and the atmosphere in that unsettled state between frost and thaw... every morning beginning in rain or snow, and every evening setting in to freeze...for many days a most honourable prisoner.*[19]

I cannot be dictated to by a watch Mansfield Park

The press reported that watches belonging to Alderman Curtis and James Jones were found in D'Arcy's possession. Both men retrieved their watches from Bow Street, but refused to prosecute or become involved in the case. At the time, it was the victim of a crime, not the State, who took the role of prosecutor in court, attending the trial and confronting the accused. The judge examined the prosecutor's evidence, he could question both prosecutor and accused before forming his judgement. Curtis and Jones did not appear in court, and they made sure their names were not recorded in the indictment.

How inexpressibly important Emma

Curtis had no desire to be implicated in a gaming scandal. He was a friend of the Prince Regent, a connexion that assured his advancement. He publicly supported the Prince during his marital troubles with Caroline of Brunswick, and was delighted when the Regent, by then George IV, stayed overnight at his seaside house in Ramsgate in 1821, en route to Hanover.

The assizes, and I am so glad when they are over Persuasion

D'Arcy was taken by coach to Maidstone, marched with other prisoners across the great medieval square to the town hall on High Street, and locked in a chamber, with loose straw on the floor, carved lintels, a fine painted ceiling, and a crowd of men of all shapes and ages.

He faced trial at the Lent Assizes on 27 March 1787, before an elderly judge, Sir Henry Gould, charged with four counts of robbery on the King's highway; with taking goods and money from James Irwin worth £2.17.1, from Stephen Remnant worth £2.11.0, from Claude Scott, worth £15.5.1, and from Archibald Anderson worth 40 pence.

D'Arcy was not permitted to give evidence, he could have called witnesses to give references of his good character, but apparently did not. He did not employ a barrister or legal counsel, this type of defence was then in its infancy. The record of the trial is very scant, but it is clear the prosecutors did not pursue their claims, and he was acquitted.

The abode of noise, disorder & impropriety — Mansfield Park

The press reported: what is remarkable in this affair is, that Wentworth is of good family, and was bred a surgeon, since which he has served as an officer in one of the provincial corps in Ireland. He imputed, in his examination before the Justices, the disgrace and misery of his present situation to a destructive connection that he had formed with Molloy, and other bad characters at the Dog and Duck, in St. George's Fields.[20] — DAILY UNIVERSAL REGISTER

Six months after the trial, action was taken to clean up the *Dog & Duck*: The Magistrates took away the licence. The reason assigned… was that too many people assembled there of very loose characters, and that it consequently became a receptacle of disorderly persons, and a place of assignation destructive of that morality which it was the duty of the law to see preserved.

It is said, and greatly to the honour of his Grace the Archbishop of Canterbury, that his interference operated powerfully in favour of the above event; this, however, we cannot with certainty affirm; but it is not what he has done, it is most unquestionably what he ought to have done.

It is hoped, however, that as the house of call for the frail sisterhood is destroyed, a certain neighbouring den of thieves will be annihilated, as it is a constant receptacle of highway men and housebreakers; and whenever the Bow-street runners want an offender, they are sure to have him there.[21] — DAILY UNIVERSAL REGISTER

John Moore, Archbishop of Canterbury, had good reasons to press for closure of the *Dog & Duck*. His residence, Lambeth Palace, was half a mile away. He was a colleague of Fitzwilliam, both men sat in the House of Lords and were neighbours in Grosvenor Square before Moore became Archbishop.

The Hedgers, owners of the *Dog and Duck*, appealed to the City Corporation, and were granted a new licence on the basis of the Corporation's judicial rights over Southwark.[22] When they sold up in June 1807, the *Dog and Duck* became the new Bethlem Hospital; today it houses the Imperial War Museum.

Whether I did it with a bow or a bluster was of little importance – I am ruined forever in their opinion
Sense & Sensibility

After an absence of almost ten weeks, D'Arcy returned to London. There was now greater urgency for him to secure an appointment, but he found none availing. There were no opportunities in India, and England was moving deeper into recession. Large numbers of troops returning from war in America had led to huge unemployment and an increase in crime. Bruised and chastened, D'Arcy lacked the bravado to seek out a patron to help him secure a posting.

A grove of full-grown Elms sheltered us from the East – A Bed of full-grown Nettles from the West – Before us ran the murmuring brook and behind us ran the turn-pike road
Love & Freindship

Highwaymen, *gentlemen of the road*, were glamorised in popular plays[23] and stories. Jane Austen made a kindly reference to them, in *Northanger Abbey,* where Catherine Morland's journey to Bath, *was performed with suitable quietness and uneventful safety. Neither robbers nor tempests befriended them, nor one lucky overturn to introduce them to the hero.*[24]

Many highwaymen were gentlemen born, they asked for the traveller's purse with grace and courtesy. Horace Walpole,[25] held up and robbed, declared *the whole affair was conducted with the greatest good breeding on both sides.*

By the late 1780's, highway robbery was in its twilight phase. Better policing and restrictions on transporting bullion made the profession less attractive. The expansion of turnpikes, manned and gated toll roads, made it more difficult to make a getaway, and from 1784, the post-boys on mail coaches were replaced with guards on horseback, each armed with a blunderbuss.

The last recorded highway robbery in England was in 1831. In Australia their heyday was just beginning. After gold was discovered in 1851, coaches on roads from the goldfields were routinely targeted by *bushrangers*.[26] The most famous, Ned Kelly, hanged in 1880, aged twenty-five, became a folk hero.

At the will of the present patron
Pride & Prejudice

In mid April, a few weeks after his acquittal, Fitzwilliam was in London briefly, and D'Arcy met him at the *Mount*. He asked how D'Arcy was faring, he knew everything that had occurred over the past winter, and had an uneasy sense he was implicated in D'Arcy's difficulties. He had taken considerable notice of him, had introduced him into London society, not realising D'Arcy was being drawn into habits well beyond his means. D'Arcy had a naive expectation that his confreres at the card table shared his sense of honour and integrity. His efforts at debt collection had failed, *he was too remarkable a figure and too little adept in the profession to escape detection.*²⁷

They spoke of the East India Company, Fitzwilliam observed it appeared to have sufficient young surgeons. D'Arcy was wanting employment, it would be unwise to delay too much longer here in London. He mentioned the fleet commanded by Captain Arthur Phillip, due to leave England shortly for New South Wales, to establish a new colony in the Southern Ocean. Fitzwilliam had followed the scheme over several years; it would be a great adventure to be among the first to go there, and there would certainly be a need for surgeons.

D'Arcy was very glad to have his advice, and eager to learn more. When Fitzwilliam recommended he call on Mr Nepean, at the Home Office, with his compliments, D'Arcy eagerly followed up his suggestion.

Necessary preparations for his removal on board directly — Mansfield Park

The First Fleet was making ready to sail for Botany Bay. On 22 February 1787, two hundred and ten convicts, in thirty guarded wagons, were sent from the Thames hulk at Woolwich, to Portsmouth, and a hundred convicts conveyed from Newgate. Along the route frightened town residents closed their shops and doors, fearful for their lives. The town of Portsmouth filled with the families and friends of the prisoners, coming to say farewell, to see them a last time, before they were transported to the other side of the world.

It was a busy time for the surgeons of the fleet. Many convicts were ill, weak, and suffering malnutrition; the surgeons obtained approval to improve their diet, to assist their chances of surviving the long sea voyage.

On 24 February 1787, all prisoners were taken off the *Alexander;* she was lime-washed to stem the gaol fever, raging on board. On 29 March, she was smoked and washed again to contain the spread of the fever. The *Charlotte* and *Friendship* arrived from Plymouth with prisoners needing attention. Shortly after, women convicts were taken aboard the *Lady Penrhyn,* and the surgeons found themselves delivering babies.

I honour you for your esprit du corps — Mansfield Park

Fitzwilliam's patronage secured D'Arcy a direction from Evan Nepean, under-secretary at the Home Office, to leave without delay for Portsmouth and go aboard the *Charlotte*. There he would find John White, Principal Surgeon, who would advise him of any vacancies on the fleet for assistant surgeons.

He arrived in Portsmouth to find the *Charlotte* had collected her convicts and moved to anchor at the Motherbank Roads, sheltered by the Isle of Wight.

She would remain there until the fleet was ready to sail. He had never seen such a huge ship, more than a hundred foot long, her three masts square rigged.

It was a great object with me, at that time, to be at sea, a very great object. I wanted to be doing something Persuasion

D'Arcy was introduced to the Principal Surgeon John White, and that evening he dined with him and other naval surgeons, William Balmain from the *Alexander*, Dennis Considen from the *Scarborough*, and visitor, John Harris.

He listened to their discussion, the latest rumours of a sailing date, and all that still remained to be done – precautions to prevent disease and maintain the health of the convicts and crew, checking the medical and surgical stores for the voyage. He had found himself among the *gentlemen of the Navy*.[28] He was filled with *admiration and delight* at *their friendliness, their brotherliness, their openness, their uprightness.*[29]

D'Arcy was eager to join the fleet, but when Surgeon White questioned him, he gave him unwelcome news – his credentials from the College of Surgeons were for India, not for the Navy, it was not possible. Even so, he remained on board the *Charlotte* for several days, made welcome to assist the surgeons with preparations for the long journey.

On 2 May, there was a great bustle aboard the merchantman, *Lady Penrhyn*, as Alderman Curtis arrived with Mr Watts to inspect the vessel. Captain William Sever, a co-owner with Curtis, showed them over the ship. The surgeon, Arthur Bowes Smyth was invited to drink tea, and Curtis introduced Mr Watts, the Naval Lieutenant who was to travel on board to China.

Next day Billy Biscuit was returned to Portsmouth in the pinnace.[30] He had given instructions, after she delivered her cargo of convicts to New South Wales, *Lady Penryn* was to sail north east across the Pacific to Nootka Sound on the *North West Coast of America to Trade for Furrs & after that to proceed to China & barter the Furrs & for Teas and other such goods.*[31] She was to carry these goods home to England without delay, and her crew would receive bonus pay for the trip to China.

D'Arcy went ashore, having resolved to obtain the qualifications the Navy required. The First Fleet sailed without him on Sunday 13 May 1787.[32]

Determined to enter on a course of serious study Sense & Sensibility

He stayed in London over the summer and autumn of 1787, found cheaper lodgings at 7 Great Russell Street, and settled down *with some large books before him*.[33] It might require *his studying himself to death,*[34] but he was determined to qualify for appointment to the Navy, as soon as possible.

The focus of his medical study shifted from diagnosis and treatment of disease, to treating injuries in the heat of battle, assessing shattered limbs, amputation, setting bones, repairing flesh torn by swords, guns and cannon shot, treating injuries to head and torso, blood loss, infection and gangrene. He studied the principles of a healthy diet at sea, of supplements to protect against scurvy on long voyages, of maintaining hygiene aboard ship, and many other matters he never encountered in Tandragee, or walking the wards.

To pay for his lodgings and keep food on his modest table, D'Arcy played cards in lesser known coffee houses and inns. He still played a scientific, systematic game, but his focus now was on getting a naval appointment to take him abroad, out of London. He was *bitterly sensible of his imprudence and showed it*.[35] He sought neither diversion nor society, he withdrew, preoccupied and ashamed of all that had unfolded over the past winter.

He had even refused one regular invitation to dinner — Persuasion

On Friday, 6 June 1787, James Dawson, a barrister friend of Dr Patton, invited him to supper at Lambeth Walk. D'Arcy stood him up, for the second time.

Dawson wrote chiding him, saying he asked him, *for my having the Pleasure of your Company. I waited supper till eleven o'clock – this is the second time you have kept me waiting – had you found it out of your Power to call upon me, you should have sent me a line intimating the same, to have prevented me staying at home on purpose in the evening, and waiting Supper each night to a very late hour.* The following week he would have an *opportunity of writing to Ireland by a private hand to Tandragee. I wish to know if you have heard from your father or family, as if you have not I shall write that day to Doctor Patton and mention the circumstances.*[36]

We must not expect a lively young man to be so guarded & circumspect — Pride & Prejudice

D'Arcy's relations with his family in Portadown had broken down. Two years before, they farewelled him, confident he was en route to India, to return a wealthy Nabob, and repay his father with interest, the costs of his education. News of his arrest and trial had shocked and horrified them. They blamed *Fitzwilliam's evil influence*, believing that, *struck* by D'Arcy's *appearance and manners,* he had elevated him into his company and society.[37]

D'Arcy kept in contact only with his elder brother William. He avoided James Dawson, he did not wish to be quoted to Dr Patton or his parents. They were angry, full of recrimination and disbelief at his wanton destruction of his future. He preferred they did not hear of the straightened, hopeless situation in which he now found himself.

I was mightily pleased to find myself qualified for second mate of a third rate
The Adventures of Roderick Random

On Thursday, 5 July 1787, he sat for a second examination at the Company of Surgeons. Percivall Pott was there, on the panel of examiners, he greeted him warmly, offering his encouragement.

D'Arcy qualified as an Assistant Surgeon, Second Mate, Third Rate.[38] The rate determined the class of vessel on which he could serve, according to the number of her cannons: *first and second rates had three continuous decks of guns, fourth and fifth rates had about 50 or 60 guns on two decks.*[39]

To exert whatever interest he might have for getting him on Mansfield Park

Realising there could be objections to his appointment in the Navy, D'Arcy looked for a friend who might exert influence on his behalf within the naval hierarchy, and quash any opposition. He asked John Villiers for a recommendation to Sir Charles Middleton, Comptroller of the Navy. Villiers was not keen, but he did suggest another acquaintance, Henry Russell.

Tho' I would feel no hesitation in answering any enquiries from Sir Charles Middleton, I really do not know how I can trouble him first upon the subject. I would advise you by all means to go to Mr Russel in Lincolns Inn <u>immediately</u> (to whom I have no doubt Mr Taylor will have the goodness to introduce you) & solicit him to write to Sir Charles Middleton upon the subject – I am confident you may rely on every thing that is liberal in that Gentleman if He is satisfied that a mistaken apprehension of his is the occasion of your embarrassment – & a line from him to Sir C.M. is the most satisfactory and most natural way of obviating the objections to your appointment. I have written to Mr Taylor by this Post upon the subject.[40]

Sir Henry Russell Persuasion

The day after he heard from Villiers, Wednesday 11 July, D'Arcy went to the Company of Surgeons at the Old Bailey to collect his new certificate. It seems unlikely he intended to go to Lincoln's Inn to seek Henry Russell's support, but he did run into him, unexpectedly, at the Old Bailey.

Having dawdled about in the vestibule to watch for the end of the conference Pride & Prejudice

As he walked across the Old Bailey foyer, through *all the various noises of the room, the almost ceaseless slam of the door, and ceaseless buzz of persons walking through,*[41] a well dressed man came across the room towards him. He began shouting, that here was the highwayman who robbed him and Alderman Clark nine months earlier. It was Henry Russell, he called for the sheriff, and he sent for Alderman Richard Clark, a colleague of Alderman Curtis.

The Sheriff's servant was sent to guard the door till Mr Alderman Clark was sent for, upon whose arrival he was taken into custody and upon examination appeared to be the celebrated Mr Wentworth.

Russell had second thoughts, and D'Arcy was released. Mr Russell did not think it proper to swear positively to the person of a man after so long a time had elapsed, and Mr Wentworth averring that he intended to quit the kingdom next week, having then a warrant lying ready for him as a Marine Surgeon, at Surgeons' Hall, he was discharged, and very seriously exhorted to depart the kingdom immediately.[42]

DAILY UNIVERSAL REGISTER

Fifteen years later Henry Russell was Chief Justice of Bengal, where he sentenced an East India Company cadet to death for the murder of an Indian. He asserted – *the natives are entitled to have their character, property and lives protected*. The Governor-General, Lord Moira, lauded his *able, upright and dignified administration of justice*.

A trifling, silly young man Emma

The press suggested another reason for D'Arcy being in the court building. Mr Wentworth went to the Old Bailey, to hear the fate of Algar, a native of Diss in Norfolk and son of Algar the noted bruiser, who lately lived at the Oxford Coffee House in Newman Street.[43]

DAILY UNIVERSAL REGISTER

Thomas Algar, aged nineteen, was a waiter at the Oxford and Cambridge Coffee House. His father, a professional pugilist, was known as the *Norfolk and Norwich Champion*.[44]

Algar was at the Old Bailey, charged with highway robbery of a post-chaise carrying Mr and Mrs. Attree, silk mercers, between Kew and Hammersmith. Arrested at the Kensington turnpike, his horse was very warm, and he was carrying a pair of small brass barrelled pistols, a watch, a guinea, silver and a silk purse containing three shillings and sixpence.[45]

Algar had already gained some notoriety after a suicide at the coffee house, A gentleman of fortune who lodged at the Oxford and Cambridge Coffee House, became enamoured with the daughter of a shoe-maker in the neighbourhood who not being inclined to return his passion, he adopted the fatal resolution of infusing some poison in a glass of jelly, which having taken, he remained a few hours in very great agonies, and then expired.[46]

Young Algar foolishly ate some of the jelly, a part of which was left in the glass, which Algar taking, had nearly cost him his life.[47]

DAILY UNIVERSAL REGISTER

At that moment I happened to be passing by the door of the Court Scraps

John Wilkinson, proprietor of the Oxford and Cambridge Coffee House, came to London from Bath to provide a character reference for him: I have known the prisoner six or seven months; he has lived with me as under waiter once, and the second time as upper waiter; I had a very good character with him from Joe's coffee-house in the Temple, and I thought so well of him, I made him upper waiter; he has been intrusted with twenty pounds, fifty pounds, and hundred pounds bank notes to get change, and has always been very punctual and honest.[48]

I know very well that Mr Darcy is not in the least to blame   Pride & Prejudice

Wilkinson saw D'Arcy, detained in the foyer. He spoke to reporters, taking the opportunity to lay blame for Algar's fate squarely on him: This unhappy youth owes his dreadful situation to the above gentleman; of this the master and mistress of the Oxford Coffee-house, Newman-street, are no strangers.

Wentworth used to frequent the Coffee-house before his bad character was known; and the young man being of good temper, and obliging to his master's customers, used to attend upon Wentworth, and carry messages to his ladies, who were pretty numerous. By this means he got a connexion, which unsettled him so much, that he was obliged to leave his place, which Mr and Mrs Wilkinson were much concerned at, as well many of the gentlemen who frequented the Coffee-house, who many times have sent him to their Brokers for considerable sums of money, which he always faithfully brought.

He then formed a connexion with Wentworth, who no doubt gave excellent advice, which in following of will cost him his life, but for the mercy of his Majesty. It is generally believed that was the first night of his going on the highway, his foolish conduct in the business truly bespoke it, and his case is much to be commiserated. Mr Wilkinson's respect for him was such, as to go to the hazard of his life to speak on his behalf, he is but just returned from Bath, and was told it was extremely dangerous to go in the situation he was in.[49]   DAILY UNIVERSAL REGISTER

So say the Papers   Letters

D'Arcy had become a popular villain. The press found yet another incident at the Court to attribute to him. It was claimed, after he was discharged, that a man seated in the gallery, feeling on the ground for his handkerchief which had fallen, discovered a gold watch upon the floor, which he immediately signified publicly to the Court. The strong suspicion was that this was the secretion of Mr Wentworth; and intelligence of these circumstances were immediately despatched to Bow Street, to have him apprehended, when a newspaper was sent back, in which the very watch was advertised, as having been taken from a Gentleman on Hounslow Heath on Saturday night, by a person of similar description.[50]   DAILY UNIVERSAL REGISTER

Oh! do not attack me with your watch!   Mansfield Park

Headlines screamed: Diligent search is making after Wentworth, at present without success.⁵¹ D'Arcy had become the favourite rogue of the London press, a dashing, handsome and irrepressible celebrity. He realised he was once again a wanted man, and saw the dreadful damage being done to his future prospects.

Such an infinity of applications   Emma

D'Arcy called again at India House, only to learn the Company did not require assistant surgeons. Lord Cornwallis, now Governor General of Bengal, was maintaining Hastings' commitment to stable, peaceful government. It would be two years before war broke out again, in Travancore, to boost demand for surgeons and assistants on battlefields across south India.

He went to the Navy Office in Crutched Friars, Aldgate, seeking a position as assistant surgeon on a naval vessel, but his reception there dashed any hopes he had of immediate relief. There could perhaps be something at an unspecified future date, but he was not encouraged to rely on it.

The Lords of the Admiralty have enough of our applications already   Letters

Roderick Random had met a similar reception:

> "Well (says he) you propose to go on board a man of war, as a surgeon's mate." To which I replied with a low bow. "I believe it will be a difficult matter…to procure a warrant, there being already such a swarm of Scotch surgeons at the Navy Office, in expectation of the next vacancy, that the commissioners are afraid of being torn to pieces, and have actually applied for a guard to protect them – However some ships will soon be put into commission, and then we shall see what's to be done.
>
> *The Adventures of Roderick Random*

The profession, either navy or army, has everything in its favour   Mansfield Park

D'Arcy next looked for an appointment as assistant surgeon in the military. He had an understanding of army life, having been a junior officer in the Ulster Volunteers. He asked John Villiers again for support. On 16 November 1787, Villiers replied, *I am just leaving London & shall not return I believe till about the 26th I am sorry that I do not happen to be acquainted in the least with the Gentlemen who have the command of the regiment you mention but I will see if I can do any thing on your behalf when I come to town.*⁵²

Villiers sent his reply to 68 Great Titchfield Street, but D'Arcy, fearful of pursuit by the press had moved abruptly, to Great Russell Street. He had taken up a friend's offer of cheaper lodgings, using the name, Charles Fitzroy. Henceforth he would not use his real name in his dealings in London.

The Postilions had at first received orders only to take the London road

Love & Freindship

At dusk, eleven days later, Tuesday 27 November 1787, a solitary highwayman held up a *poste chaise* at the Powder Mill, near the ten mile stone on Hounslow Heath. Mr John Hurst, a London lawyer, returning to London from Slough with his wife, her friend Mrs Ann Grundy, and his clerk, was robbed of a metal watch, value thirty shillings; a steel chain, value one shilling; a seal, value threepence, and a key, value tuppence. Anne Grundy was robbed of a silk purse, value sixpence, and two guineas. They drove on to London and at Hyde Park Corner their post-boy reported the robbery to the Bow Street Patrol.

Gently brawling down the turnpike road Verse

The press reported, the **noted D'Arcy Wentworth** was apprehended by the Bow Street Patrol at the Notting-Hill Turnpike. **He will be re-examined at the above Office in a few days, when it is apprehended that several other charges will be brought against this unhappy youth.**[53]

DAILY UNIVERSAL REGISTER

After a further examination at Bow Street, D'Arcy faced a second charge of highway robbery, from the previous Friday, when William Lewer Esq., a lawyer, and his Clerk, on their way to Hartley Row in Hampshire in a post-chaise, were held up and robbed on Hounslow Heath. **Mr Lewer of his silver watch, value twenty-five shillings, a steel watch-chain, value a penny, a stone seal set in gold, value one shilling, and a metal watch-key, value a penny.**

My Lord, the sheriff with a most monstrous watch is at the door Henry IV Part I

Mr Lewer provided Bow Street with a detailed description of his missing watch, made for him in 1772 by Thomas Amyot.[54] On the front of its double silver case was an impression of Hercules strangling the Numidian Lion. "my watch is so very remarkable, that perhaps there is not one in the whole Court like it; among the engravings in the brass work, on the edge of the cock of the watch, is my name engraved."

Bow Street circulated London pawn shops with lists of stolen goods: Aldous, a pawnbroker, produced the watch which was pawned to him by a Miss Wilkinson, who lives with Wentworth. Mr Lewer swore to his property with much more agitation of mind than appeared in Wentworth.[55]

On 6 December, the press announced that the **notorious D'Arcy Wentworth, a tall personable man, well known on the road, was removed to Newgate, to take his trial at the old Bailey. Miss Wilkinson is likewise remanded for trial – she is a very pretty young woman.**

DAILY UNIVERSAL REGISTER

Trial at the Old Bailey, 12 December 1787

A week later, he came before the Old Bailey, charged with three counts of highway robbery – of William Lewer and his clerk on 23rd November, John Hurst on 27 November, and Ann Grundy on the same day.

Mary Wilkinson (otherwise known as Looking) was charged with feloniously receiving Mr Lewer's watch, chain and key, knowing them to be stolen.

The dailies were pressing for a resolute and firm judgement in the case: The conduct and apparent fate of D'Arcy Wentworth ought, in an especial manner, to stimulate magistrates to a conscientious discharge of their duty, and particularly that part of it which relates to the suppression of houses where the morals of youth are likely to be contaminated.

This unfortunate young man's ruin was effected by frequenting a certain tea house, where he incautiously formed an acquaintance with certain persons of genteel appearance, who were highwaymen by profession. He has already had several narrow escapes from an ignominious death, but, once initiated in the paths of vice, he found it impossible to stop; and it is highly probable that this last robbery, for which he was apprehended near Kensington Gravel-pits, will terminate his career with shame and repentance.[56]   DAILY UNIVERSAL REGISTER

Standing in the dock, D'Arcy saw the huge crowd of onlookers. He had heard the Great Bell of the Old Bailey, from St Bartholomew's, signalling executions were taking place at Newgate, and he had seen the crowds gathered outside the prison, eager to pay money to watch them.[57]

The Company of Surgeons would claim the corpse to use in anatomy lectures and demonstrations. There was always a crowd in the gallery at the Surgeons' Hall amphitheatre, eager to view it, before the surgeons began their dissections.

Sitting in the dock of the Old Bailey, did D'Arcy contemplate his own cadaver on display, split open, exposed and dissected in elaborate detail, arteries and veins probed, each manoeuvre observed by his medical friends and colleagues?

Dishonesty I must call it   Pride & Prejudice

During the trial he showed *his usual deliberation*, listened as evidence was presented, occasionally asked a question, and observed proceedings with *an earnest stedfast gaze*.[58]

His was the eighth trial of the day,[59] and as it opened he requested the judge, *My Lord, I hope you will have the goodness to order the other witnesses out of the Court*. Sir Richard Perryn, a baron of the exchequer, agreed. It was the first indication D'Arcy anticipated there could be collusion between the witnesses.

A dish of butter that melted at the sweet tale of the sun's   Henry IV Part I

William Lewer took the stand. He declared he could not swear D'Arcy was one of the highwaymen: *"there was a man followed us and called stop, stop; hearing the* voice stop, I turned my head, and though never having been robbed before by high-waymen, I knew it to be so by seeing a large black silk over his face; it is totally impossible to swear to the man, having black over his face."* Lewer could not recollect any thing of his person, *"a man being on horseback is quite different to a man on foot."* Nor could his clerk, Samuel Buckland, identify D'Arcy as the highwayman – *it was impossible, he had crape over his face…I could not distinguish.*

On examining watches Emma

William Aldous was called: *I am a pawnbroker in Berwick Street. I produce a watch I received of the woman prisoner at the bar, on 24th of November, on Saturday in the evening. I never saw her before to my knowledge, she pawned it with me for a guinea, she said she brought it from her brother, and that his name was William Looking, that he lived at No. 24 Greek Street, Soho; she said her name was Mary Looking, that her brother wanted to make up a sum of money to pay a bill; I think, to the best of my recollection that was what she said; on Monday when the list came down, I went to Bow Street; and Jealous and me went to look for the woman in Greek Street, but there was no such person.*

Elizabeth Wilkinson, sworn as a witness, gave her address as Stephen Street, Tottenham Court Road. She stated – *A lady named Wilkinson received a watch in my lodging; she has passed for my sister; she is not my sister.*

She identified the prisoner, Mary Wilkinson, as the lady – *I do not know for what purpose, they came into my lodging; I left the room for half an hour I should suppose; I never saw the gentleman before, he came with the lady; I let them both in; she said, after he was gone, she would pawn the watch.*

D'Arcy asked Elizabeth if he was the person who gave the watch to Mary Wilkinson. *No; it was not you; it was a much shorter man.*

The judge asked whether Elizabeth Wilkinson was examined by the Justice at Bow Street. Samuel Maynard, of the Bow Street Patrol replied, *No; she was waiting at the Brown Bear for them.*

Samuel Maynard was very vague about Mary Wilkinson's involvement: *she said she met a gentleman in the street, and went with him somewhere, to a Coffee-house or some house-bagnio, or what not, and there she had the watch; I am not sure what place she said; I was sent out backwards and forwards.*

Producing the box Emma

Maynard stated, he had *apprehended the prisoner in the Uxbridge Road, at Notting Hill turnpike, I searched him there, when I got him from the horse on the ground; and in his right-hand pocket I found a loaded pistol and this bunch of hair, and this piece of black silk, and a purse; and I found a small key in his waistcoat pocket,* which he said belonged to the chest he had in his lodgings; he would not tell me where he lodged.

Maynard went to D'Arcy's lodgings, opened his *deal box or chest, about a yard and a half long,* and found a seal. He did not recollect if D'Arcy had appeared *to know any thing of the seal, or was ignorant of it.*

He took Elizabeth Wilkinson with him to D'Arcy's room, she *went with me to Wentworth's lodgings to take the things.*

Mary Wilkinson, D'Arcy said, *had a key to the box as well as me. She has freely acknowledged that I did not give her the watch.*

D'Arcy asked leave to ask Maynard, "*whether Mr Maynard knew anything of the box, till I freely told them about it. I really knew nothing of a seal being in my box, if I had I would not have told them.*"

Thomas Little, D'Arcy's landlord was sworn. *I am a carpenter. I live in Titchfield Street, Oxford Market; the prisoner lodged with me four weeks and a few days; he came on the 22nd of October, and staid till the 27th of November; I remember Samuel Maynard coming to my house, the prisoner was not with him; I was with him when he unlocked the box, which was the second or third time he came; I saw him take out several things, I cannot say what they were; I saw him take the seal out, but I cannot describe it.*

Maynard stated twice to the court that D'Arcy, Mary and Elizabeth Wilkinson had been living together *in July or August last, they all lived in Pleasant Row, Islington. They all lived at Islington together about six months ago.*

D'Arcy was at Great Titchfield Street with Mary Wilkinson only five weeks before he was arrested. Realising Maynard was trying to paint a picture of a much longer-term relationship with the two Wilkinsons, he objected: *Did I not live in Great Russell Street at that time?*

Mr. Lewer has not said that I robbed him; I only trust that those paragraphs that have appeared publicly against me, in the papers, may not have any effect on the minds of the Jury; I have been ranked among the most notorious of offenders; and I wish that any person that has published those paragraphs against me, would now come forth like a man.

Mary Wilkinson had taken the sensible precaution of engaging Counsel, who was busy building a case for her acquittal. Mr Newman Knowlys was a member of the Middle Temple, who began practicing in the Old Bailey in 1782. Over twenty years, from 1783 to 1803, he appeared in more than thirteen hundred cases there, and also practiced in other London courts.[60]

Knowlys argued, Mary Wilkinson had cohabited with D'Arcy, and she was therefore entitled to the same protection at law as a wife; that when she pawned

Mr Lewer's watch she had acted *under the immediate coercion of her husband* and could not be found guilty.

From his comments and omissions, Samuel Maynard, the Bow Street Runner, appeared to cooperate with this approach, trying to help Mary Wilkinson.

Everything plain & easy between landlord & tenant — Persuasion

Knowlys questioned landlord Thomas Little at some length about his tenants. It appears to have taken D'Arcy a while to see the drift of these questions.

Did the woman live with him all the time? – Yes, and behaved very well in our house.

In what capacity did she appear? – There was nothing disorderly, they behaved like gentlefolks

By what name did she pass? – I do not know any thing of that, she was always called the lady, and he Mr Fitzroy.

What sort of hours did the prisoner keep? – Very good hours, he was always at home almost, very seldom out; he behaved like a gentleman in my house.

You supposed them to be man and wife? – I had no reason to think to the contrary.

Did they go by the same name? – He went by the name of Fitzroy, and she was called the lady; I understood her to be his spouse of course.

Did they ever pretend to be married? – I can say nothing to that.

Did they ever say they were married, or did they pass for man and wife? – I will not pretend to say, because I know not; it was never mentioned whether they were man and wife or not.

D'Arcy asked Little, *Was it me that took your lodgings or not?* trusting, it seems, that his reply might shine fresh light on his relationship with Miss Wilkinson. But the landlord could not answer – *I know not which; they gave me half a crown, I do not know whether it was given by you or the lady; my wife took it, not me; I was not in the room Mr Wentworth.*

A Lady ready to witness anything for the cause of Justice — Scraps

Mary Wilkinson, of Faversham in Kent, was a niece of coffee house proprietor John Wilkinson. The press reported – **She is a pretty woman, and was genteelly drest; her head dress a near French cap, with a large white beaver hat, and an elegant gold and silver band. This woman and her sister have made great havock amongst the gentleman of the road, and may be titled the Milwoods of the present day.**[61]

Daily Universal Register

Sarah Millwood was a character in *The London Merchant,*[62] by George Lillo, a high class prostitute who seduced and led a young apprentice into crime. He was sent to Newgate and executed. She was described as a *lady of pleasure,* who sought out innocent young men, *who having never injured women apprehend no injury from them.*[63]

Comparing the Wilkinson sisters with the Milwoods told readers a great deal about them, and described D'Arcy's obvious youth and inexperience. He was reported as saying: *if Wilkinson was brought into trouble upon his account, he would destroy himself.*[64] The boyish trill in his voice can be heard, down more than two hundred years.

Mr Knowlys earned his fee, he built his case, presenting precedents and arguments to the jury: *she has no right to question the actions of that person to whom she looks up for assistance, on whom she depends; whose servant she is; who has power to compel to do things at times from fear; it would be hard to call that feloniously receiving from a woman who has not the power to resist.*

Though the Court disagreed, stating *she cannot plead any coercion, she was at full liberty,* the judge, Baron Perryn, recollected the case that Knowlys cited. He had been *on the Rota at the time the indictment was tried,* and agreed with Knowlys argument, *she is entitled to the protection of a wife in my apprehension.*

Knowlys called character witnesses for his client. William Dodd, a farmer from Faversham who had known Mary Wilkinson from infancy, was asked, *Has she been a very good girl? – yes I have no reason to doubt it.*

The jury found both *D'Arcy Wentworth* and *Mary Wilkinson, not guilty.*

The Affair was soon adjusted Scraps

Following their verdict, D'Arcy was indicted for his second charge, the highway robbery of John Hurst. Before any witnesses were examined, he requested that the officers from Bow Street be asked to leave the court.

John Hurst was sworn in, and stated that at five pm on 27 November 1787, he had been in a post-chaise with two ladies, when they were held up by a single highwayman on a very dark chestnut or black horse.

Hurst was quite definite that he could not identify D'Arcy as the highwayman, and that he had stated this at the Bow Street examination. *He appeared to be a tall thin man… the person I saw at Sir Sampson Wright's, which was the present prisoner, appeared to me to be a very different man to the man that robbed me, and I noticed it at the time.* Ann Grundy confirmed his story.

Three men of the Bow Street Patrol were then admitted to give their evidence. Samuel Maynard stated Hurst had reported he was robbed by a *lusty man.*

The opinion of the groom Mansfield Park

John Dunn, a stable-keeper at Three Horse-shoe Yard, Grosvenor-square[65], knew D'Arcy, *I have let him horses before once or twice; in October I let him the* same horse. He hired it by the name of Fitzroy. It was *a light chestnut cropt mare with a white face.*

Dunn collected the horse from Bow Street after D'Arcy's arrest. Maynard confirmed it was the horse that D'Arcy was riding when he was stopped at the turnpike. John Hurst said he was shown the horse: *I saw the mare, it was shewn to me; I was much surprised to see the mare so different in colour.*

A reward on that person who wrote the ablest defence Sense & Sensibility

D'Arcy was not permitted to cross examine witnesses, but in the short interval between the two hearings, he had engaged Newman Knowlys as his counsel. It was clear to him by now, that Knowlys knew what he was doing.

A perjured witness in every public tryal Scraps

Knowlys set about probing Maynard's evidence, questioning him on the inconsistencies between his story and that of Hurst: *I am glad you did not hear Mr Hurst's examination, there is so great a difference.*

Maynard had arrested D'Arcy at Notting Hill Gate, he had told the story of the arrest in the previous case of Mr Lewer, but by now the details had changed: *I went to the gate, he kept his distance, and seeing the prisoner at the bar answer the description, and the horse exactly, I stopped him and searched him, as I attempted to apprehend him, at that time, he turned his mare's head round from me, and put his left hand down in a great hurry to his waistcoat pocket, and flung his arm a great way from him; I said immediately, Sir, you have thrown something…I put him into custody, and searching with a lantern, I found a metal watch at some distance from him.*

Hurst had said it was too dark to see the horseman's face. Knowlys asked Maynard if Hurst had identified D'Arcy at Bow Street, and he replied: *I understood that he swore to him; I mean that he swore to his watch there.*

Knowlys asked Maynard how much he would make if D'Arcy was convicted: *That introduces one question; how much all you get by the conviction of this man? – I cannot tell.*
I knew that would be the answer exactly; how long have you been employed as an officer at Bow Street – Pretty near five years.
And you cannot tell what you would get by the conviction of that man – I cannot tell.

Knowlys asked a second Patrolman, Edward Hughes, the same question. *You are employed at Bow Street? – Yes, I am partner with Maynard.*
He does not know what he shall have for the conviction of this man, perhaps you do not know? – Conviction! Sir it is our duty; we do not think of conviction.

Hughes suggested that Knowlys not ask the third Patrolman, *he is another patrol; he proves nothing more than catching the horse.*

Mr Hurst became impatient, he interrupted the proceedings, contradicting Maynard's report: *My Lord, I beg pardon for interrupting; but I never told the guard that he was a stout, lusty man; I always held this language, that he was a tall, thin man, nor did I ever say he had any thing over his face; but that I judged there might be something, because I could not see his features.*

The jury found *D'Arcy Wentworth not guilty*. He was called to answer a third charge of robbing Ann Grundy, but *there being no other evidence, the prisoner was acquitted.*[66]

The trash with which the press now groans   Northanger Abbey

Transcripts at the Old Bailey criminal trials were taken down in shorthand, printed and sold to the public. Transcripts of D'Arcy's trials are hard to follow but in parts it is clear that insufficient or questionable evidence was produced, and that the pre-trial examinations could not be relied upon.[67]

The press covered the trials, and other independent reporters were often present, who sold their coverage to newspapers. At this time there were nine daily papers in London, eight tri-weekly and nine weekly papers, and their readers had a great appetite for stories about highway robbery.

Reward to behaviour deserving very differently   Lady Susan

Bow Street encouraged press coverage of its pre-trial examinations, and of the work of the Runners. Runners stood to gain a reward if an accused was convicted,[68] and there were instances where they planted evidence, or ensured that more serious charges were laid than warranted by the events, in order to be eligible for a higher reward.

Two years before, Harvey, a constable, was convicted of perjury, sentenced to three years imprisonment in Newgate, and to stand twice in the pillory in the Old Bailey yard,[69] for giving false evidence against two men sentenced to death for highway robbery. He shared a reward of £80 with the prosecutor. **Some years have elapsed since several thief-takers were convicted and pilloried for a similar offence. One of them was killed on the pillory at Smithfield. Conviction-rewards rather create, than amend the evils, which they were intended to prevent.**[70]   Daily Universal Register

Lamenting the blindness of his own pride, and the blunders of his own calculations   Persuasion

Alexander Patton advised D'Arcy to avoid *idle, giddy and dissipated company*. As he surveyed the wreckage of his hopes and his reputation, he rued the day he had sought companionship among *the Pleasing and the Voluptuous*.

Chapter 8

Missing Years

"Very well," was her ladyship's contented answer,
"then speculation, if you please."

IN 1788, Cassandra Austen, at fifteen, was old enough to accompany her elder brothers to the Angel Assembly Rooms to enjoy the monthly Basingstoke ball.¹

The girls were wild for dancing Persuasion

Jane went too. Not yet thirteen, she was full of *bloom and spirits,*² *very attractive, her figure was rather tall and slender, her step light and firm, and her whole appearance expressive of health and animation... She had all the natural grace of sweetness of temper and artlessness in herself.*³

When is your next ball to be? Pride & Prejudice

Mrs Austen was delighted to see her daughters attending the local assemblies. *My girls are out... As their progress in every thing they have learnt has always been the same, I am willing to forget the difference in age, and to introduce them together into Public.* She warned them not to be *swayed by the Follies and Vices of others,* and was assured *they were prepared to find a World of things to amaze and to shock them.*⁴

Jane was not necessarily the youngest at the ball. In *The Watsons*, she tells the story of little Charles Blake, who believed he had a partner for the first two dances. She had promised him, but she dropped him for a smart young officer, Charles *stood the picture of disappointment, with crimsoned cheeks, quivering lips, and eyes bent on the floor...He contrived to utter with an effort of boyish bravery*

"Oh! I do not mind it,"- it was very evident by the unceasing agitation of his features that he minded it as much as ever.

Emma did not think, or reflect;- she felt and acted – 'I shall be very happy to dance with you sir, if you like it," said she, holding out her hand with the most unaffected good humour.

The boy in one moment restored to all his first delight – stepping forwards with an honest and simple "Thank you ma'am," was instantly ready to attend his new acquaintance.

Emma could not be giving greater pleasure than she felt herself – and Charles being provided with his gloves and charged to keep them on, they joined the set which was now rapidly forming, with nearly equal complacency.

To what purpose that freedom would be employed — Sense & Sensibility

D'Arcy was released on 12 December 1787, a bitterly cold morning, after three weeks in Newgate. He savoured his freedom as he walked to Great Titchfield Street to retrieve his medical chest, books and belongings from the lodgings.

Fitzwilliam had instructed his London agent, Thomas Hill, to assist him to make arrangements to leave London. His cousin's determination to take to the road, confront his defaulters and collect his debts, made him very uneasy. D'Arcy was playing a dangerous game, he feared it would end badly.

By mid afternoon, D'Arcy was seated in a coach en route to York. As it moved up the Great North Road, he could make out, through the fog, the rickety gibbets placed along the roadside, where convicted highwaymen were hung.

The present state of a sick horse — Mansfield Park

Staying within Fitzwilliam's orbit, he found work through Peregrine Wentworth with racehorse trainers at Malton and Middleham. He enjoyed the open air, long hours and physical challenges of the training stables. Rapport with horses came easy to him, he treated them using John Hunter's rule, *don't think, be patient, be accurate.* He applied his skills to improving their performance, recalling Hunter's dictum, that *the power of action arose from the particular position of the living parts.* Years later he would write up advice on treating horses in his *Medical Notebook.*

During these months D'Arcy observed close-hand, the fast growing horse-racing industry, its culture and organisation, its regulations, rules and risks. It was knowledge he would put to good use in a future life.

From February to May 1788, Fitzwilliam was occupied in London, his parliamentary work dominated by the proceedings against Warren Hastings. In early March he found a few days to spend at *Wentworth Woodhouse*, and D'Arcy accompanied him when he returned to London.

For two years, after D'Arcy was discharged at the Old Bailey, the press made no mention of him. Details of those years would still exist, *sources of intelligence in former histories and records,* stored in attics or in archives, that will one day shed more light on the *principal facts.*[5] Today, for the important events of those years, the main source remains Jane Austen's own writing.

In consequence of a wish to establish some medical man, which the nature of the advertisement induced him to expect to accomplish Sanditon

From London, D'Arcy took a coach to Alton, he had obtained a post there, as a locum in a family apothecary practice.

Agreed upon between two friends as the only thing to be done Persuasion

He stayed with William Wickham, in a comfortable rented house a few miles away, near Dummer. The two young men had met in York, and had been comrades and friends in London, one studying law, the other medicine.

Miss Bingley is to live with her brother, and keep his house Pride & Prejudice

Wickham was *provided with a good house and the liberty of a manor.* Two of his sisters, Anne and Harriet, taking the opportunity for a change of air, came down from Bingley to stay with him. *They were of a respectable family in the north of England…Though he was now established only as a tenant,* his sister *was by no means unwilling to preside at his table.*[6]

He meant to be at the next assembly with a large party Pride & Prejudice

Handsome and eligible, Wickham was invited to all the local balls, and soon after he arrived, D'Arcy went with him, to a monthly Assembly at Basingstoke.

The ball had commenced when they arrived, the Austen party was already settled. Looking across the room, Jane saw the *great tall fellow*[7] with Wickham, and recognised him immediately, it was D'Arcy Wentworth, the cousin she met while she was at school in Reading.

She was in dancing, singing, exclaiming spirits Emma

He was the same *remarkably fine young man, with a great deal of intelligence, spirit, and brilliancy.*[8] *At the same time* he seemed *haughty, reserved, and fastidious.*[9]

His want of spirits, of openness & of consistency Sense & Sensibility

Jane found D'Arcy very serious, *his manners, though well bred, were not inviting.*[10] She set herself to draw him out. He did not respond when she teased him, though he stood near her with a degree of silent amusement.

She was as bright and delightful as he remembered her. He was not unaffected by her light hearted happiness, but his sense of honour determined him to resist her attentions. He remained separate and reserved, too conscious of her youth, her ignorance of his London world, and all its troubles.

This was but the beginning of other meetings — Persuasion

In *Pride & Prejudice,* Jane recorded the months D'Arcy spent in Hampshire, her ambivalence and her growing attraction towards him.

But who are you looking for? — Northanger Abbey

Jane Austen used the interplay between the two sisters, Jane and Elizabeth Bennet, to describe her own different moods and feelings. Elizabeth is in the foreground, feisty and combative – *from the very beginning…your manners, impressing me with the fullest belief of your arrogance, your conceit, your selfish disdain of the feelings of others.* Jane Bennet is quieter, more reserved, reflecting more stoic, unstated feelings of her namesake – *so pure and uncoquettish were her feelings.*

I do not write for such dull Elves as have not a great deal of Ingenuity themselves — Letters

Jane was writing a true story, disguising it as fiction. She transposed some names and events, invented some characters, and shifted locations. She renamed D'Arcy, *Mr Fitzwilliam Darcy*, akin to Fitzwilliam in status, fortune, great house and estate; with the *pride and insolence* of noble birth. The name she invented for D'Arcy exposed his connection to Earl Fitzwilliam, she reinforced it with a cameo part for Colonel Fitzwilliam, a thinly veiled sketch of Fitzwilliam's younger brother George, who died in 1786.

Jane renamed William Wickham, George Wickham, and as with D'Arcy, his identity is only lightly disguised. Their fictional Christian names are rarely mentioned, they are Darcy and Wickham, and she tells much of their shared history in real-life, and of her changing feelings towards them, during 1788.

A great deal…of real, solemn history…must be invention, and invention is what delights me in other books — Northanger Abbey

Jane created another character, *Charles Bingley,* to share parts of both D'Arcy and Wickham's stories from that spring and summer. She named him Bingley, for a village near William Wickham's home in Yorkshire.

Jane used Bingley to give her story more air, more room to move. She could set Wickham more apart from Darcy, and make him a key axis of the plot.

Darcy and Elizabeth Bennet hold centre stage, with *bravura* parts, sparkling virtuosity, dissonance and skilful dynamics of tone, tempo and cadence. The story of Bingley and Jane forms the *basso continuo,* sustaining a sense of direction and harmony throughout. Bingley is the *sweet tempered, amiable, charming man* who asks Jane Bennet to dance, and *she was the only creature in the room that he asked a second time.* Their immediate compatibility, their quiet pleasure in each other, her stoic unhappiness at losing him, reflect the youthful Jane Austen's feelings for D'Arcy.

Mr Wickham's circumstances *Pride & Prejudice*

William Wickham was born at *Cottingley Hall*, near Bingley, in the West Riding. His forebears on both sides were clergymen, including an early Bishop of Winchester. At twelve he went to Winchester College, later to Harrow, and won a scholarship to Christ Church, the wealthy, prestigious Oxford college and cathedral, noted for its education of the clergy. He spent a year in Geneva studying civil law, and in 1786, received a Master of Arts at Oxford, and was called to the bar at Lincoln's Inn.

His mother, Elizabeth Lamplugh, was from an established Yorkshire family, her grandfather, William Dobson, an apothecary, was mayor of York in 1729. His father Henry Wickham had a long connection with *Wentworth Woodhouse*.

Impudent, extravagant & greatly in debt *Pride & Prejudice*

George III said Henry Wickham was, *the handsomest man in his three regiments of guards*. William Wickham described his father as *tall and well made, a really manly beauty,* Henry, with a *passion for a military life and an aversion to Greek and Latin*, had run away from school at fifteen, enlisted in an infantry regiment, and *marched some time with the corps*. His father caught him, had him discharged, and sent him to school in Leipzig.[11]

Henry decamped once more, this time he enlisted in a Swiss Canton regiment. Two years later, in uniform, standing sentinel at the gates of Alexandria in Egypt, he was recognised by an old school friend. His father relented, and bought him a commission as an ensign in the First Regiment of Foot Guards, where he rose to the rank of Lieutenant Colonel.

After his father's death, Henry sold out of the Guards, and in 1769, he retired to Bingley. He had married Elizabeth Lamplugh there in 1761, and their family was growing. His father-in-law, Rev Lamplugh, gave up *Cottingley Hall* to accommodate them, and Henry settled down to *become an active justice of peace and a resident country gentleman*.[12]

Extravagance or irregularity *Pride & Prejudice*

Jane gave her character, George Wickham, something of Henry Wickham's military history. *It is Mr. Wickham's intention to go into the regulars; and, among his former friends, there are still some who are able and willing to assist him in the army. He has the promise of an ensigncy in General – –'s regiment, now quartered in the North... He left gaming debts behind him, to a very considerable amount.*

Under the greatest obligations to my father's active superintendence
Pride & Prejudice

In Yorkshire, Henry Wickham found a patron in Lord Rockingham, and served him as an Honorary Deputy Lord Lieutenant of the West Riding for almost fifteen years. After his death, Henry remained as a deputy to the two Lord Lieutenants who followed, Charles Howard, 11th Duke of Norfolk, until his removal in March 1798, and Fitzwilliam, from March 1798 to November 1819.

In *Pride & Prejudice*, discussing *Pemberley*, Darcy's family estate, Elizabeth is told – *Wickham passed all his youth there you know*. Wickham tells her, the *estate there is a noble one... I have been connected with his family in a particular manner from my infancy. We were born in the same parish, within the same park, the greatest part of our youth was passed together.*

In the novel, Wickham claims his father *gave up everything to be of use to the late Mr Darcy, and devoted all his time to the care of the Pemberley property*. Darcy tells Elizabeth a different story, that Wickham's father was *unable to give him a gentleman's education,* and his father had supported him as his own, at school and university. Darcy's father *intended to provide for* him in his chosen profession, the church, but after his death, Wickham's plans changed, he now *had some intention of studying the law.*

Wickham has not sixpence of his own
Pride & Prejudice

Henry Wickham, living a new life in Yorkshire society, fell rapidly into debt. He was unable to assist his children to establish themselves. His son described him, *living in very high society in London and vying with county neighbours.*[13]

Lacking dowries, his three daughters never married, William Wickham later supported them. He said of his own prospects, *I can never become a rich man by honest means.*[14] *I went poor into the Publick service.*[15] After Henry's death in 1804, he sold *Cottingley Hall* to discharge some of his debt, and the estate was involved in *an unpleasant Chancellery suit.*[16]

Handsome young men must have something to live on
Pride & Prejudice

It seems D'Arcy Wentworth stayed with William Wickham at *Kempshott*, a country estate three miles from Dummer, leased to Wickham's friend, the Prince of Wales, in 1788.[17]

At the time, Wickham may have been working for an attorney in Alton, to earn an income and gain experience in legal practice. There is a *broad faced stuffy* attorney, *breathing port wine,* in *Pride & Prejudice,* Mr Philips. Perhaps Jane was describing Mr Trimmer, the Knight family lawyer in Alton.

D'Arcy was most likely employed by Mr Curtis[18] a respected apothecary and Quaker, whose family had practiced on Alton's High Street for several generations. William Curtis, sixteen years D'Arcy's senior, had left the practice to publish a highly successful *Botanical Magazine*,[19] that first appeared in 1787.

What were nine miles to a young man? An hour's ride Emma

D'Arcy would have ridden to Alton early in the morning, to begin the day in the dispensary, weighing, measuring, compounding prescriptions. Patients called at the High Street surgery in great numbers on Alton market days. He would have received them and recorded details of their complaints, and in the afternoons, accompanied Mr Curtis on house calls. Like Sam Watson, the young surgeon in *The Watsons*, he was kept busy, *Mr. Curtis won't often spare him, and just now it is a very sickly time in Guilford.*

A delightful evening, a most excellent ball Pride & Prejudice

In *The Watsons*, Sam Watson is in love with Mary Edwards, *has been very much in love with her these two years*, but he is *only a Surgeon, you know*, her *father is decidedly against him, the mother shows him no favour.*

Jane Austen told her niece Anna, *a Country Surgeon would not be introduced to Men of rank*,[20] an assistant surgeon would have had very little standing.

Obliged to go on horseback Pride & Prejudice

In *Pride & Prejudice*, Darcy is Bingley's guest at *Netherfield*. Caroline Bingley invites Jane Bennet to visit, and riding there, she is caught in a storm. Wet and chilled, she develops a fever and remains at *Netherfield* to recover.

Her mother's eyes had *sparkled with pleasure*, when the note arrived from *Netherfield*, inviting Jane to dine. She is determined to flaunt her daughter before a prospective suitor.

"Can I have the carriage?" said Jane.

"No, my dear, you had better go on horseback, because it seems likely to rain; and then you must stay all night."...

"I had much rather go in the coach."

"But, my dear, your father cannot spare the horses, I am sure...

Jane was therefore obliged to go on horseback, and her mother attended her to the door with many cheerful prognostics of a bad day. Her hopes were answered; Jane had not been gone long before it rained hard. Her sisters were uneasy for her, but her mother was delighted. The rain continued the whole evening without intermission; Jane certainly could not come back.

"This was a lucky idea of mine, indeed!" said Mrs. Bennet, more than once.

I am not going to write to my mother Sense & Sensibility

Confined to bed at *Netherfield*, Jane wrote home to her sister, not her mother. "*Well, my dear,*" *said Mr. Bennet, when Elizabeth had read the note aloud, "if your daughter should have a dangerous fit of illness, if she should die, it would be a comfort to know that it was all in pursuit of Mr. Bingley, and under your orders.*"

"*Oh! I am not at all afraid of her dying. People do not die of little trifling colds. She will be taken good care of. As long as she stays there, it is all very well.*"

I shall gradually get intimately acquainted with all the hedges, gates, pools and pollards Emma

Elizabeth walks across the muddy fields to *Netherfield*, to visit her sister. *The distance is nothing when one has a motive; only three miles – I shall be back by dinner.*

The rain continued the whole evening without intermission Pride & Prejudice

She walked alone – *crossing field after field at a quick pace, jumping over stiles and springing over puddles with impatient activity, and finding herself at last within view of the house, with weary ancles, dirty stockings, and a face glowing with the warmth of exercise.*

Never had the exquisite sight, smell, sensation of nature...brilliant after a storm, been more attractive to her.[21] Gilbert White, who lived at Selborne, not far from Steventon, recorded very heavy rain in the area from late June to mid July 1788, and storm damage in the local lanes – *It began with vast drops of rain... the hollow lane towards Alton was so torn and disordered as not to be passable till mended.*[22]

William Cobbett also described the impact of heavy rain on the Alton lanes. *The lanes were very deep; the wet malme just about the colour of rye-meal mixed up with water, and just about as clammy, came in places very nearly up to my horse's belly.*[23]

Very fine ladies...but proud & conceited Pride & Prejudice

Wickham's sisters were much older than Jane, as Bingley's sisters in *Pride & Prejudice* are older and more worldly than the Bennet sisters. In 1788 Anne Wickham was twenty-four, Harriet Wickham a couple of years younger.

You young ladies who cannot often ride in a Carriage never mind what weather you trudge in, or how the wind shews your legs A Collection of Letters

The Bingley sisters look down on Elizabeth: "*She has nothing, in short, to recommend her, but being an excellent walker. I shall never forget her appearance this morning. She really looked almost wild.*"

"*Very nonsensical to come at all! Why must she be scampering about the country, because her sister had a cold? Her hair so untidy, so blowsy!*"

"*Yes, and her petticoat; I hope you saw her petticoat, six inches deep in mud, I am absolutely certain...*"

"*To walk three miles, or four miles, or five miles, or whatever it is, above her ancles in dirt, and alone, quite alone! what could she mean by it? It seems to me to shew an abominable sort of conceited independence, a most country town indifference to decorum.*"

Caroline Bingley *instantly turned towards D'Arcy,* she is interested in him, she tries *to provoke D'Arcy into disliking* Elizabeth.

On the catch for a husband — Lady Susan

Jane described a mother's pressure on her daughter, to ensnare an eligible suitor. When Jane Bennet feels well enough, Elizabeth writes to her mother, *to beg that the carriage might be sent for them in the course of the day.*

It was a grand house, and *Mrs. Bennet, who had calculated on her daughters remaining at Netherfield till the following Tuesday, which would exactly finish Jane's week, could not bring herself to receive them with pleasure before.*

Mrs. Bennet sent them word that they could not possibly have the carriage before Tuesday; and in her postscript it was added that, if Mr. Bingley and his sister pressed them to stay longer, she could spare them very well.

His society became gradually her most exquisite enjoyment — Sense & Sensibility

Jane Austen found herself developing a great interest in D'Arcy Wentworth. *He was not pleasant by any common rule, he talked no nonsense, he paid no compliments, his opinions were unbending, his attentions tranquil and simple. There was a charm in his sincerity, his steadiness, his integrity.*[24]

Artless Affection — Lady Susan

She was certain *her eagerness, her impatience, her longings*[25] must be evident to her family. But though *her father was certainly disposed to take very kind and proper notice of him,*[26] her mother and father, *never once thought of her heart, which, for the parents of a young lady...just returned from her first excursion from home, was odd enough!*[27]

Laugh as much as you chuse — Pride & Prejudice

In 1788, in *Frederic & Elfrida,* Jane lampooned those parents who insist their children must wait until they are older to marry. Mrs Fitzroy has two daughters, the elder, Jezalinda, has *an engaging Exterior,* while Rebecca's *conversation shone resplendent with Wit & Charms. The eldest Miss Fitzroy ran off with the Coachman & the amiable Rebecca was asked in marriage by Captain Roger of Buckinghamshire. Mrs Fitzroy did not approve of the match on account of the tender years of the young couple, Rebecca being but 36 & Captain Roger little more than 63. To remedy this objection, it was agreed that they should wait a little while till they were a good deal older.*

Reading the story aloud to her family after dinner, we can imagine her laughing with them and at her own predicament. She was thirteen, D'Arcy, twenty-six. Would there ever be a right age to marry?

Every charm of person & address that can captivate a woman Pride & Prejudice

In *Pride & Prejudice*, George Wickham is a womaniser. On his arrival in the district he *particularly attended* to Elizabeth, *made her feel that the commonest, most threadbare topic might be rendered interesting*. Jane Austen might well have had a brief flirtation with William Wickham – *At present I am not in love with Mr Wickham, no I certainly am not. But he is beyond all comparison, the most agreeable man I ever saw.*

After Wickham's attention to Elizabeth Bennet wanes, and he moves on to another young heiress, their farewell *was perfectly friendly, on his side even more. His present pursuit could not make him forget that Elizabeth had been the first to excite and to deserve his attention.*

He wanted, she supposed, to cheat her of her tranquillity Mansfield Park

She detected, *in the very gentleness that had first delighted her, an affectation and a sameness to disgust and weary. In his present behaviour to herself, moreover, she had a fresh source of displeasure, for the inclination he soon testified of renewing those attentions which had marked the early part of their acquaintance, could only serve, after what had passed, to provoke her.*

Your character was unfolded Pride & Prejudice

During his twelve month stay in Hampshire, did Jane learnt details of D'Arcy's past, his gaming, or that he had been charged with highway robbery?

There are moments in *Pride & Prejudice*, when the polite banter darkens, an undercurrent of suspense is created, and it seems something unexpected or unpleasant is to be revealed about Mr Darcy.

"Your character...I am trying to make it out".

"And what is your success?"

"I do not get on at all. I hear such different accounts of you as puzzle me exceedingly."

In a fleeting suggestion Darcy is about to be exposed, his cousin Colonel Fitzwilliam asks Elizabeth – *pray let me know what you accuse him of. I should like to know how he behaves among strangers,* and she replies, *You shall hear then – but prepare yourself for something dreadful."*

Jane Bennet is told that Wickham is a gambler, she *heard them with horror.* *"A gamester!" she cried. "This is wholly unexpected, I had not an idea of it."*

Was it William Wickham who told Jane of D'Arcy's recent history? She set down her shock and dismay: *Her feelings were yet more acutely painful and more difficult of definition. Astonishment, apprehension, and even horror, oppressed her. She wished to discredit it entirely, repeatedly exclaiming, "This must be false! This cannot be! This must be the grossest falsehood!"*

He is quite mistaken. There is no Truth in any such report   Persuasion

In the novel, Elizabeth is aware, from her first meeting with Wickham, of something hidden between him and Darcy. She notices that Darcy is *suddenly arrested by the sight of* Wickham. The two men look at each other, *the countenance of both was all astonishment...Both changed colour, one looked white, the other red... What could be the meaning of it? It was impossible to imagine; it was impossible not to long to know.*

She asks Wickham what he knows of Mr Darcy. He assures her, *you could not have met with a person more capable of giving you certain information on that head but myself.* Wickham has *no reserves, no scruples in sinking Mr Darcy's character.*

Darcy responds: *I know not in what manner, under what form of falsehood, he has imposed on you; but his success is not, perhaps, to be wondered at. Ignorant as you previously were of every thing concerning either, detection could not be in your power, and suspicion certainly not in your inclination.*

To question the veracity of a young man of such amiable appearance as Wickham   Pride & Prejudice

Jane's treatment of Wickham in the novel intimates he was disloyal to D'Arcy. She makes him a gambler, indebted to Darcy for several thousand pounds. *Wickham confessed himself obliged to leave the regiment on account of some debts of honour, which were very pressing.* He *left many debts,* which Darcy honoured. To ensure Wickham makes an honest marriage and has a fresh start, Darcy pays the marriage settlement he demands, as well as debts he incurred in his regiment.

Wickham tells Darcy, he *cherished the hope of more effectually making his fortune by marriage, in some other country.* Elizabeth predicts, *Wickham will never marry a woman without some money. He cannot afford it.*

We shall feel the loss of these two most agreeable young men exceedingly   Letters

William Wickham left England in July, and shortly after, on 10 August 1788 he married Eléonore Madeline Bertrand, daughter of a Professor of Mathematics at the University of Geneva.

Jane maintained a very poor opinion of Switzerland – *among the Alps & Pyrenees, perhaps, there were no mixed characters. There such as were not as spotless as an angel might have the dispositions of a fiend.*²⁸

In *Emma*, Frank Churchill, whose deceit caused Jane Fairfax great torment, saw Switzerland as a haven, saying as he looked *over views in Swisserland, "I am sick of England and would leave it to-morrow, if I could."*

The cares & vicissitudes of my past life   _{Scraps}

William and Eléonore Wickham enjoyed nearly fifty years of marriage. He wrote in 1795, *I am a family man, passionately attached to my own home, who never knew what it was to be away from his wife and child before.*²⁹ After her father died in 1814, Eléonore's *fortune was either lost or untouchable in French funds*, frozen during the Napoleonic Wars.³⁰

None of Wickham's private papers remain. His son wrote, h*e was in the habit of preserving the greater part of his official papers, though he destroyed ordinary or family letters.*³¹ Whatever obligations existed or were discharged between him and D'Arcy, the truth behind Jane's innuendo remains hidden.

People did say you intended to quit the place by Michaelmas   _{Pride & Prejudice}

In late September 1788, D'Arcy heard the East India Company would soon recommence recruiting assistant surgeons. He left Hampshire for a brief visit to London, he wanted to be among the first to apply.

Indulging the recollection of past enjoyment & crying over the present reverse   _{Sense & Sensibility}

Jane heard D'Arcy was leaving for London, that he was hopeful there would be an opening in India. She was sure he was looking forward to leaving Hampshire.

I have just received my dispatches and taken my farewell   _{Sense & Sensibility}

She heard he left suddenly, had gone with *no intention of returning.* She suffered a great *oppression of the spirits,*³² and *greater distress...as day after day passed away without bringing any other tidings of him.*³³

Depend upon my thinking of the Chimney-Sweeper   _{Letters}

He met Fitzwilliam at their *snug town coffee-house,* the *Mount.*³⁴ Fitzwilliam asked about Percivall Pott, he understood that his efforts were behind the *Chimney Sweeper's Act,* passed by Parliament a few weeks earlier.³⁵

D'Arcy confirmed that over fifty years at St Barts, Pott recorded an unusually high incidence of cancer of the scrotum among young chimney-sweeps.³⁶ finding it was caused by their frequent exposure to soot, on the bare skin.³⁷

Fitzwilliam wanted to know D'Arcy's plans. He replied, he had called at Leadenhall Street to ask about vacancies for assistant surgeons, and had been to the Naval Office with a similar inquiry, but had received no encouragement from either. He was visiting the Coffee-houses frequented by medics and scientists, and reading every notice posted there, but so far, had found nothing.

Fitzwilliam refused to believe there could be no openings for a young experienced surgeon. He suggested D'Arcy attend one of the *advertising offices*,[38] take the initiative, place his own advertisement, declare his interest in joining a medical practice.

D'Arcy gave the suggestion some thought, agreeing it could perhaps be helpful, but could create further difficulties. The papers might decide to embellish an advertisement with stories of his court appearances, those would surely dissuade any potential employer. Fitzwilliam left him to mull over how best to present himself to advantage.

An advertisement in the medical line, extensive business, undeniable character, respectable references   Sanditon

> **A PARTNERSHIP as SURGEON or APOTHECARY**
>
> A GENTLEMAN of respectable Family Connexion, countenanced by some of the most eminent Physicians in London, who has served a regular Apprenticeship, and attended the principal Hospitals in London, would be glad to receive the Proposals of any Gentleman, well established in the above Professions.
>
> The Gentleman who seeks this Connexion, is of the most unexceptionable Character and Diligence, has never yet been established but is thoroughly grounded on the different Branches of Medical Knowledge; as an Anatomist, Chymist, Botanist, &c, and having Youth and Health on his side, would willingly relieve any Gentle-man of declining health, in the more active Part of the Profession.
>
> A reasonable Equivalent will be given; but it is requested, that only Gentlemen, in a decidedly established Line of Business, will trouble themselves, by directing a Line to C. F. at the Bar of the Mount Coffee-house, Grosvenor-street, stating the average Amount of clear Annual Receipts, and Premium expected.[39]

D'Arcy had called at *The Times* office, and placed an advertisement, under an alias, Charles Fitzroy. The *Mount* was willing to receive any correspondence for him, and to have it delivered to No. 4 Grosvenor Square, close by.

Fitzwilliam agreed, with a laugh, to have any responses received for *Charles Fitzroy*, or even for, *CF care of the Mount*, franked and posted to D'Arcy, in Hampshire.

His advertisement was published on Tuesday, 4 November 1788, and he was pleased to have set things in train to find a new position. D'Arcy stayed another day in London, but he had been away long enough, he took the coach to Alton, where he would be needed by Mr Curtis.

Falling in love with her when she is thirteen — Emma

D'Arcy returned, optimistic he would have a new position in the coming year, when he finished the locum in Alton. Jane had never seen him so happy. In the weeks following his return to Hampshire, their romance blossomed.

The object of open pleasantry — Pride & Prejudice

We can catch the echoes of Jane's happiness with D'Arcy, her *spirits soon rising to playfulness again*,[40] her *lively, sportive manner*,[41] her *power of saying those delightful things which put one in good humour with oneself and all the world*.[42]

She declared, *I assure you I have no notion of treating men with respect. That is the way to spoil them*.[43] *She could perceive that he was rather offended; and therefore checked her laugh*.[44] *She remembered that he had yet to learn to be laughed at, and it was rather too early to begin*.[45] *He has a very satirical eye, and if I do not begin by being impertinent myself, I shall soon grow afraid of him*.[46]

Excessively pleased with my conquest — A Collection of Letters

She enjoyed their exchanges, "*My good qualities are under your protection, and you are to exaggerate them as much as possible; and, in return, it belongs to me to find occasions for teasing and quarrelling with you as often as may be.*"[47]

"I wonder who first discovered the efficacy of poetry in driving away love!"

"I have been used to consider poetry as the food of love," said Darcy.

"Of a fine, stout, healthy love it may. Every thing nourishes what is healthy already. But if it be only a slight, thin sort of inclination, I am convinced that one good sonnet will starve it entirely away."[48]

In a quiet moment together she asked him, "*could there be finer symptoms? Is not general incivility the very essence of love?*[49] "Now be sincere: did you admire me for my impertinence?" He answered *"For the liveliness of your mind, I did."*[50]

We have got a play! Mansfield Park

Christmas at Steventon was always a busy time. George Austen was occupied around the parish and with the Christmas services, and Jane had much to do, helping with preparations for the Austen family gathering.

Plans were afoot for family theatricals, James was directing, and he had decided to revisit *Bon Ton*, the racy farce Eliza wanted to perform at Christmas, 1787, in the starring role of Miss Tittup. It would have been a memorable performance.! Though Eliza was absent this year, they had the playscript, and James suggested they make another attempt.

There is no record of how he cast the two main female roles, Lady Minikin, worldly, pursuing fashion and pleasure, cheating on her cheating husband, an insincere friend to Miss Letitia Tittup, the *minx in a pink cardinal*.[51] It is amusing to imagine that he cast Jane as Miss Tittup, and Cassandra as Lady Minikin, and opened the play himself with a rousing prologue:

> Tis something new!
> Tis losing thousands every night at loo!
> To visit friends you never wish to see;
> Marriage 'twixt those who never can agree;
> Old dowagers, dressed, painted, patched & curled,
> This is Bon Ton, & this we call the world! [52]

In this state of schemes and hopes Emma

In late February, D'Arcy completed his locum with Mr Curtis and left for London. He was losing Jane's society, *her face rendered uncommonly intelligent by the beautiful expression of her dark eyes.*[53]

Thinking of him so much, as she sat drawing or working, forming a thousand amusing schemes for the progress and close of their attachment, fancying interesting dialogues, and inventing elegant letters.[54]

How am I going to introduce him? Is it necessary for me to use any roundabout phrase? – Your Yorkshire friend – your correspondent in Yorkshire; that would be the way I suppose, if I were very bad.[55]

Not one sentimental story about love & honour, & all that Sophia Sentiment

In mid March 1789, Jane's letter to James, editor of *The Loiterer,* signed Sophia Sentiment, has a feistiness and maturity.

She addresses him as, *my dear Sir,* and delivers her critique of his magazine, *the story was good enough, but there was no love, and no lady in it, at least no young lady… you might have created a little bustle, and made the story more interesting.*[56]

Very glad of your company, I am sure, I am much obliged Pride & Prejudice

At the end of March 1789, Jane went to the neighbouring Ashe Rectory, to help out with Madam Lefroy's six children. Anne Lefroy and her husband, the Rev George, were to go to Crondall, for the funeral of her younger sister, Deborah-Jemima Maxwell.

It was a bleak and awful occasion, only the tenants and servants from the Maxwell estate, *Ewshot House,* followed the family to the grave side.[57] *The gentlemen and the neighbourhood offered to attend, but the sorrow of this occasion did not suit with pomp.*[58]

Slumbering on one side of the fire Emma

Deborah-Jemima had been sitting by the fire in the drawing room of her London house, *after dinner, engaged in writing cards of invitation,* wearing *a round calico gown, with an apron of fine muslin, very full and wide.*[59]

A poker fell from the fireplace onto the hem of her gown, and quickly set fire to her clothes. She tried to put out the flames by rolling herself in the carpet, but it was nailed to the floor, she could not lift it.

She ran up the stairs to her bed-chamber, her dress on fire. Servants following her tried to put out the flames with their coats and the bed curtains, but failed. In a few moments the bed, the wainscot and window shutters had all caught fire. The whole household was screaming.

After it was extinguished, Deborah-Jemima lay in bed until early morning, badly burnt, *conscious and uncomplaining.* She died just before dawn, leaving her daughter, eight months old, and her distraught husband.[60]

A week after the funeral, Anne Lefroy decided she must go to London, to do what she could. Henry Maxwell was depressed, unapproachable, withdrawn. Her mother wrote, the baby was in the house, with her nurse, but failing to thrive. The house in Cavendish Square needed urgent repairs and attention. Her mother, very concerned, seemed unable to help or intervene.

Anne Lefroy wrote to Benjamin Langlois, her husband's uncle. He had financed their living at Ashe and often stayed with them. He insisted she use his house in Cork Street, bring the children, and put his servants to good use, for as long as need be. He would come to Ashe and enjoy the company of his nephew, and had no need to return to town before the end of summer.

The attention you have paid to my Convenience & amusement Letters

Anne invited the Austen girls to stay with her in London. It would be an adventure for them, and she knew she could rely on their help with the children. She was fond of Jane, Cassandra she knew less well. It *would be more comfortable for them to be* together... I am sure your mother can spare you very well...Don't fancy that you will be any inconvenience to me, for I shan't put myself at all out of my way for you.

Jane was elated, *your invitation has ensured my gratitude for ever, and it would give me such happiness, yes, almost the greatest happiness I am capable of, to be able to accept it.*

Cassandra less keen, knew how much Jane wanted to go to London, she understood her sister, and...*carried by her eagerness to be with* W. *again, made no farther direct opposition to the plan.*

Mrs Austen was thrilled, "*I am delighted... it is exactly what I could wish... I would have every young woman of your condition in life, acquainted with the manners and amusements of London.*"

Madam Lefroy left Ashe in early April, with her six children and nursemaids. Mrs Austen assured her girls, *you will be under the care of a motherly, good sort of woman, of whose kindness you can have no doubt.* [61] She was sure that under Madam Lefroy's watchful eye they would make good connexions.

We might meet in London were my father disposed to carry me there
Lesley Castle

Jane and Cassandra followed with their father. George Austen had business there next day; he stayed at Cork Street overnight, delighted to be in London. *Sir George is 57 and still remains the Beau, the flighty stripling, the gay Lad, and sprightly Youngster... Our father is fluttering about the streets of London, gay, dissipated, and Thoughtless at the age of 57.*[62]

You must write to me
Mansfield Park

The house was handsome, and handsomely fitted up, and the young ladies were immediately put in possession of a very comfortable apartment. Jane sat down immediately to write to D'Arcy, her letter was *finished in a very few minutes; in length it could be no more than a note; it was then folded up, sealed, and directed with eager rapidity.* Cassandra *thought she could distinguish a large W in the direction.*[63]

Despite *the extraordinary silence of her sister and W. on the subject,*[64] Cassandra had seen *an intimacy so decided, a meaning so direct, as marked a perfect agreement between them.*[65] *When he was present she had no eyes for any one else. Every thing he did, was right. Every thing he said, was clever.*[66]

I wrote him a very kind letter, offering him with great tenderness my hand & heart
Jack & Alice

How happy every body in London must be because you are there. I hope you will be so kind as to write to me again soon, for I never read such sweet Letters as yours. I am my dearest...most truly and faithfully yours for ever and ever.[67]

The common routine of acquaintance, without any danger of betraying sentiments Emma

Anne Lefroy *went thither every morning as soon as she was dressed, and did not return till late in the evening.*[68] She *treated them both with all possible kindness, was solicitous on every occasion for their ease and enjoyment.*[69]

Cassandra and Jane spent part of each day with the children, reading, drawing and singing, settling them into their new routine. Some afternoons they sat with the big girls, Jemima-Lucy, ten, and Julia-Elizabeth, seven, over a sewing basket, showing them how to thread needles, to mend and stitch, discussing fashionable London garments. Jane watched over the youngest, William Thomas, nearly two. Anne, worried about his slow progress, was taking him to be examined by a London physician.

A few weeks spent in London must give her some amusement...benefited by novelty and variety, by the streets, the shops, and the children Emma

Jane and Cassandra explored *the uncertain and unequal Amusements of this vaunted City.*[70] Cassandra *devoured six ices,* met people on the street, took a Hackney Coach to Hampstead, and returned home after having been *absent nearly 7 hours.*[71]

Madam Lefroy *thought it a delightful thing for the girls to be together; and generally congratulated her young friends every night.*[72]

The end of all his anxious circumspection, the happiest, wisest most reasonable end! Pride & Prejudice

D'Arcy called at Cork Street accompanied by his elder brother William, a member of the Green Horse, the 5th Dragoon Guards, visiting from Ireland. Madam Lefroy liked the brothers, *remarkable for their personal appearance,*[73] they were connexions of the Austen girls, and she made them very welcome.

This was the season of happiness Sense & Sensibility

With Madam Lefroy's approval, D'Arcy and William accompanied Jane and Cassandra to enjoy *the amusements so various and pleasing of London.*[74] The brothers talked about home. Jane was eager to know about D'Arcy's life there, she was *quite longing to go to Ireland,* from his account of things.[75]

She had a great taste for the pleasures of London Lesley Castle

D'Arcy took them to Smithfield, they saw great pens and herds of animals for the livestock market, they heard the bells of Old Bailey in the distance, and saw the line to mark where the Great Fire of London halted, more than a hundred and twenty years before.

He showed them the great gate-house of St. Bartholomew's Hospital, built to honour Henry VIII, the magnificent courtyard within the hospital buildings, and the little church of St. Bartholomew the Less. They did not venture into the wards, but they saw patients and their families in the courtyard, and could smell and hear the sick in the wards surrounding the square.

They walked through the great close to the beautiful Norman Priory Church of St Bartholomew the Great, where D'Arcy and other medics attended services. The rector, Owen Perrot Edwardes, Jane discovered was a connexion of her mother's great uncle, Thomas Perrot.

He was a remarkably fine young man, with a great deal of intelligence, spirit & brilliancy   Persuasion

D'Arcy called again at Cork Street, with an Irish naval surgeon, John Harris. Madam Lefroy talked at length with them about the health of her husband's parishioners. How she would *administer medicines to the sick…in a wide surrounding neighbourhood…and had communicated the important benefits of Vaccine Inoculation to upwards of 800 with her own hand.*[76]

They spoke of Lady Mary Wortley Montagu, whose efforts led to the adoption of vaccination against smallpox. Her beloved younger brother, William Pierrepont died of smallpox at the age of twenty. While she survived, badly scarred, her face so disfigured that for some time she wore a mask in public. In Constantinople with her husband, Lady Mary saw the practice of variolation, a form of inoculation to protect against smallpox. She wrote home: *The small pox, so fatal, and so general amongst us, is here entirely harmless.*[77]

D'Arcy described the Sun Monument at Wentworth Castle in South Yorkshire, honouring Lady Mary's role in defeating the ancient scourge of smallpox. Her neighbour and friend, the second Earl of Strafford, had erected an obelisk with a bronze ball on top to catch the sun's rays, and reflect them to her home at Wortley Hall and to her secluded lodge on Wharncliffe Crag.

Of course they had fallen in love over poetry   Persuasion

D'Arcy admired Lady Mary's determination to improve medical knowledge and practice. Jane praised her wit and independent spirit, and quoted from her poetry. For Jane, she was a writer, a cousin of Henry Fielding, who taught herself Greek and Latin, and used her father's library to steal an education.[78]

> A glass revers'd in her right hand she bore
> For now she shunn'd the Face she sought before.
> "How am I chang'd! alas! How am I grown
> A frightful spectre, to myself unknown!"[79]

JANE & D'ARCY

When Corydon went to the fair, he brought a red ribbon for Bess, with which she encircled her hair, and made herself look very fess Frederic & Elfrida

In late August, D'Arcy and Jane went to the Bartholomew Fair at Smithfield. They walked among dense crowds, through smoke from roasting meat and sugar browned to toffee, along rows of sideshows, under tightrope walkers, past musicians, acrobats and entertainers.

Their eager affection in meeting, their exquisite delight at being together Mansfield Park

Madam Lefroy was not unduly concerned by D'Arcy's visits, she liked him, and was happy to see Jane enjoying his company and that of his companions. They *loved with mutual sincerity but were both determined not to transgress the rules of Propriety by owning their attachment, either to the object beloved, or to any one else.*[80] Jane was discreet, *endeavouring to appear indifferent, where I have been most deeply interested.*[81]

I shall take the opportunity of calling in Grosvenor-street Pride & Prejudice

On a warm, golden summer afternoon, D'Arcy took her to Fitzwilliam's house in Grosvenor Square. He introduced her as an aspiring writer and a Wentworth connexion. She found Fitzwilliam very gracious, she told him about her brothers, Frank in the Navy, in the East Indies on board *HMS Perseverance*, James and Henry at Oxford, and their magazine, *The Loiterer*, and Edward, in Rome on the Grand Tour.

There was much talk that afternoon about a garden party Fitzwilliam was planning in honour of the Prince Regent: *Preparations are making with all expedition at Wentworth House, the seat of Earl Fitzwilliam, for the reception of His Royal Highness the Prince of Wales, who is expected to pay a visit there, previous to his honouring the Races with his presence.*[82] Whitehall Evening Post

As they made their farewells, Fitzwilliam said he hoped to see them there, that he would expect them. *These were thrilling words, and wound up* her *feelings to the highest point of exstasy. Her grateful and gratified heart could hardly restrain its expressions within the language of tolerable calmness.*

To receive so flattering an invitation! To have her company so warmly solicited! Everything honourable and soothing, every present enjoyment, and every future hope was contained in it; and her acceptance, with only the saving clause of Papa and Mamma's approbation, was eagerly given. – "I will write home directly," said she, "and if they do not object, as I dare say they will not-."[83]

Chapter 9

No Turning Back

I never spent so happy a summer

JANE WROTE HOME directly. She told her parents D'Arcy Wentworth had invited her to afternoon tea at Earl Fitzwilliam's house in Grosvenor Square. It was magnificent, the greatest square in Mayfair, with fifty-one fine mansions surrounding it. They faced a *central pleasaunce*, a great oval walled park, eight acres of evergreens, flowering trees and shrubs, bordered with elm hedges, an iron gate at each side of the square, opening into a *wildernesse* landscape.[1]

Lord Fitzwilliam spoke to her, and particularly invited her to attend a great party to honour the Prince Regent. It was to take place on the second day of Autumn, at his family seat, *Wentworth Woodhouse – an ancient House & a Park well stocked with Deer.*[2]

Jane received her parents approval by return mail. *Good gracious! Lord bless me! only think! dear me! Mr. Darcy! Who would have thought it! And is it really true? Oh! my sweetest! how rich and how great you will be! What pin-money, what jewels, what carriages you will have!... I am so pleased – so happy. Such a charming man! – so handsome! so tall! – A house in town! Every thing that is charming!...Ten thousand a year! Oh, Lord! What will become of me. I shall go distracted.*[3]

Polite manners were put to some trial on this point Persuasion

Fitzwilliam arranged for the pair to travel in Thomas Erskine's coach. Jane had hoped to have D'Arcy's company to herself for the long drive. He laughed at her disappointment, *I could not have hoped to entertain you with Irish anecdotes during a ten miles' drive.*[4]

Philadelphia was impressed, but she was sure the company at such a grand Whig occasion would be *much against Mr Hastings.*[5] Jane assured her otherwise, Mr Erskine was defending a Piccadilly bookseller charged with seditious libel, for publishing a pamphlet in support of Warren Hastings.[6]

They set off at the sober pace in which the handsome, highly fed four horses of a gentleman usually perform a journey — Northanger Abbey

The long coach journey was full of lively talk and bustle. Jane delighted in Mr Erskine's wit, his *shower of puns, epigrams and anecdotes.*[7] He had joined the Navy at fourteen, as midshipman on the *Tartar,* and spent four years in the Caribbean. His captain was a nephew of Lord Mansfield, who had encouraged him to go to the Bar. Jane told him about Frank, now fifteen, in the East Indies on the *Perseverance.*

There were numerous coaches on the road, carrying guests to the party, and loud greetings from all sides when they stopped to change horses, or for meals. Jane recalled *her admiration of the style in which they travelled, of the fashionable chaise-and-four, postilions handsomely liveried, rising so regularly in their stirrups, and numerous out-riders properly mounted.*[8]

Mr Erskine and his wife, Frances, recalled travelling this same road twenty years before, after he was refused by her father, and they were eloping to Gretna Green. In great spirits, the party travelled to Leicester and Nottingham; through *all the celebrated beauties of Matlock,*[9] *Bakewell,*[10] *Chatsworth, the Peak; from Dove Dale*[11] into South Yorkshire, to Sheffield, thence to Rotherham and *Wentworth Woodhouse.*

She questioned him as to the society of Yorkshire — Emma

Jane, *as they drove along, watched for the first appearance of* Wentworth Woodhouse *with some perturbation.*[12] She began *to feel with some anxiety that all her best manners were on the point of being called into action… She was meditating much upon silver forks, napkins and finger glasses;…but, when they entered the Park, her perceptions and pleasures were of the keenest sort*[13]*…her spirits were in a high flutter.*[14]

The Noise of the Coach & 4 as it drove around the sweep, was…a more interesting sound, that the Music of an Italian Opera — Kitty, or the Bower

They arrived in due time at the place of destination, and as soon as the string of carriages before them would allow, alighted, ascended the stairs, heard their names announced from one landing-place to another in an audible voice, and entered a room splendidly lit up, quite full of company, and insufferably hot.

Without a Blush they entered a large party of superior Rank, whom they had never seen before & took their Seat amongst them with perfect Indifference   Evelyn

When they had paid their tribute of politeness by curtsying to the lady of the house, they were permitted to mingle in the crowd, and take their share of the heat and inconvenience, to which their arrival must necessarily add.[15]

They were shown through a number of rooms, all lofty, and many large ...with shining floors, solid mahogany, rich damask, marble, gilding and carving...of pictures there were abundance.[16] Jane noted: *a room magnificent both in size and furniture – the real drawing-room, used only with company of consequence. – It was very noble – very grand – very charming!*[17] She had heard nothing of... extraordinary talents or miraculous virtue amongst the company, and the mere stateliness of money and rank she thought she could witness without trepidation.[18]

The housekeeper showed Jane and D'Arcy to their rooms, pointing out *all that could relate of the family in former times, its rise and grandeur, regal visits and loyal efforts.*[19] She led them up several staircases, above the grandest guests and their servants, to *a long suite of lofty rooms, exhibiting the remains of magnificent furniture.*[20] She trusted Jane would not find her *Bed too short*, she apologised for *crouding you in such a manner.*[21]

Now they skirt the Park around   Verse

They were quite unconcerned, delighted to have arrived. After changing their clothes, they met and set off *around the park,*[22] *the number of servants continually appearing, did not strike her less than the number of their offices. Wherever they went some pattened girl stopped to curtsey.*[23]

Dinner was exceedingly handsome, and there were all the servants, and all the articles of plate.[24] The huge house was busy and filled with guests, *the entrance of servants with cold meat, cake, and a variety of all the finest fruits in season... the beautiful pyramids of grapes, nectarines, and peaches soon collected them round the table.*[25]

Late that evening she and D'Arcy went to bid Fitzwilliam good night: "*I have many pamphlets to finish,*" said he... "*before I can close my eyes, and perhaps may be poring over the affairs of the nation for hours after you are asleep. Can either of us be more meetly employed? My eyes will be blinding for the good of others, and yours preparing by rest for future mischief.*"[26]

In the morning the whole house came alive, *the breakfast room was gay with company,*[27] *never in her life before had she beheld half such variety on a breakfast-table,*[28] or *number of servants continually appearing.*[29]

We shall have a most delightful party Northanger Abbey

Earl Fitzwilliam gave a magnificent Fete at Wentworth house, in honour of his Royal Highness the Prince of Wales. Nothing could be more superb and sumptuous than the whole of the arrangements. It was in the true style of English hospitality. His gates, on being honoured with the presence of the heir apparent, were thrown open to the love and loyalty of the surrounding country; and not fewer than 20,000 persons partook of his lordship's liberality. The diversions consisting of all the rural sports in use in that part of the country, lasted the whole day, and his lordship's park was the grand stage on which the numerous personages played their parts. The spectators were the prince and his attendants, and the nobility and gentry from every part of the country without distinction. The dinner was an assemblage of every delicacy the world could produce. The ball at night, consisting of more than two hundred ladies, the flower of Yorkshire, with their partners, was the most brilliant ever seen beyond the Humber.[30] THE ANNUAL REGISTER

Jane and D'Arcy, along with hundreds of guests, stayed up the whole evening. There was music, wine, singing and dancing. The lights of the house shone out across the grounds, *every pane was so large, so clear, so light!*[31]

They walked together. He was silent. *She thought he was often looking at her, and trying for a fuller view of her face than it suited her to give.*[32] They followed *the comparatively quiet and retired gravel walk, where the power of conversation would make the present hour a blessing indeed.* [33]

She found her arm drawn within his, and pressed against his heart, and heard him saying, in a tone of great sensibility, speaking low..."My dearest, most beloved... tell me at once. Say "No," if it is to be said."[34]

In the sky, against the light of an almost full moon, they saw a fine light coloured moon-bow.[35] Jane *was now in an exquisite flutter of happiness.*[36]

It might have been a very sad accident Sense & Sensibility

Next day, *in coming to town, from Wentworth-house, the prince encountered an alarming accident. About two miles North of Newark, a cart crossing the road struck the axle of the prince's coach, and overturned it.* [37] THE ANNUAL REGISTER

It was on the verge of the slope, and the carriage fell a considerable way, turned over twice and was shivered to pieces...His Highness was undermost in the first fall, and by the next roll of the carriage was brought uppermost, when he, with his usual activity and presence of mind, disengaged himself, and was the first to disengage and rescue his fellow travellers...The accident happened at ten o'clock at night, and it was a clear moonlight...The Prince and Lord Clermont went forward to Newark, where he slept, and proceeded to London the next morning.[38] WHITEHALL EVENING POST

Upon my word, it is really a pity that it should not take place directly, if we had but a proper licence, for here we are together, and nothing in the world could be so snug and pleasant Mansfield Park

Jane and D'Arcy left *Wentworth Woodhouse* that day, heading north, across the border into Scotland.

I am going to Gretna Green, and if you cannot guess with who, I shall think you a simpleton Pride & Prejudice

They were married at Gretna Green in the second week of September, 1789. *The wedding was very much like other weddings, where the parties have no taste for finery or parade.*[39]

The White Horse Inn, Cannongate, Edinburgh Kitty, or the Bower

They travelled to Edinburgh, and stayed at the *White Hart Inn*. They visited Stirling Castle, where Mary Queen of Scots, *one of the first characters in the world,*[40] was crowned. *A dismal old weather-beaten Castle...it is actually perched upon a Rock.*[41] D'Arcy wrote to his brother William with his news, *We will know where we have gone – we will recollect what we have seen.*[42]

We left on the 28th of last month, and arrived safely in London after a Journey of seven Days Lesley Castle

D'Arcy and Jane travelled back to London with renewed optimism, confident he would have a salaried appointment in Botany Bay, and they would sail there together, to take it up.

I advise you to go out; the air will do you good Mansfield Park

Fitzwilliam had thrown his support behind the scheme, he sent instructions to Thomas Hill, to assist D'Arcy and advance him with whatever he needed for the voyage. Fitzwilliam recommended that D'Arcy call on Evan Nepean, Under Secretary at the Home Office, once more, with his compliments, to formalise his posting to the new Colony.[43]

Mrs Wilson, who was the most amiable creature on earth Henry & Eliza

At the end of October 1789, D'Arcy and Jane moved into lodgings in Clipstone Street, off Great Portland Street, under the name of Wilson. They had been married nearly seven weeks.

Purpose which could not be delayed without risk of Evil Mansfield Park

Thomas Hill called there, under orders from His Lordship, eager to help D'Arcy finalise his arrangements. Fitzwilliam had been definite, he was to board the next ship for New South Wales, equipped with whatever he would need for the long voyage; and the Home Office should be requested to find a medical position for him to fill when he arrived in the Colony. [44]

A surgeon this instant
Persuasion

On the last day of October, a man named Jack Day came to their lodgings for urgent help. He was in great pain, with a bullet lodged in his shoulder. D'Arcy examined the wound, probed it with makeshift instruments, but the bullet was too deep for him to remove. He bandaged the shoulder and summoned another surgeon, who advised he go to hospital without delay. D'Arcy fetched a cab and took him to the Middlesex Hospital

On Saturday night, the 31st ult, a genteel young man called on Mr Connor, a surgeon, and requested his assistance for a person who had received a gunshot wound; the affair, he said, might occasion some uneasiness, and he therefore desired him to take the whole care of it on himself.
<small>Whitehall Evening Post</small>

Assured by the Hospital-Surgeon that the wound is in as favourable state as can be
Letters

Mr C. attended him to Clipstone Street, where the wounded person was; he had the appearance of a servant, and said, that while attending his master's carriage in town, they were stopped by highwaymen, who had fired at and shot him; the ball had struck against one of his coat buttons, and passed from thence across the breast under his arm-pit, where it lodged among blood vessels that rendered it dangerous to attempt extracting it.
<small>Whitehall Evening Post</small>

Testified by the particular direction of the bullet, such a wound could not have been received in a duel – at present he is going on very well, but the Surgeon will not declare him to be in no danger
Letters

The surgeon was convinced that the man had received his wound from a person situated below him, as if he had been on horseback, and fired at from a post-chaise. From this and other circumstances, he concluded him and the gentleman who recommended him to be the highwaymen; the man was with much reluctance, persuaded to go to the Middlesex Hospital, and the master has since been taken into custody and proves to be the celebrated D'Arcy Wentworth. He was examined on Saturday last at Bow Street, and committed for further examination on Thursday next, when it is supposed his wounded friend will be well enough to attend.[45]
<small>Whitehall Evening Post</small>

His circumstances which led to the detection of this offender were as follows: two gentlemen had been stopped by a man on Hounslow Heath, who attempted to rob them; but one of the gentlemen knocked the pistol, which he presented, out of his hand, and immediately fired and wounded the highwayman, who made his escape.

On an information received by Sir Sampson Wright, that a man lay wounded in the Middlesex Hospital, who said he had received the hurt from a highwayman, a suspicion arose that this person might be the highwayman who had been wounded on Hounslow Heath.

They procured the description of those who went in the coach to the hospital with the man, when the officers immediately recognised the person of the famous D'Arcy Wentworth.[46] GAZETTEER & NEW DAILY ADVERTISER

He was waited on and nursed, and she cheered and comforted with unremitting kindness Sanditon

Two of Sir Sampson's officers were sent to the hospital, but had no recollection of the man; and on enquiry found that a woman constantly came once a day to feed him, about three, and remained with him till seven o'clock. WHITEHALL EVENING POST

The Middlesex Hospital was five blocks from Clipstone Street. Did Jane visit Jack Day each afternoon, taking him food and clean clothes and diverting him with company?

On this they agreed to return, and if possible to trace out the lodgings of the wounded man, whom they suspected to have been the person wounded on Hounslowheath. They returned but found the man had contrived to escape out of the window of the ward in which he was lodged. WHITEHALL EVENING POST

Their lodgings were not long a secret Pride & Prejudice

They then met with a surgeon, who said he had been called in to dress the wounds of a man, who said he had received them from a highwayman.

The surgeon informed them that he had been called on to go to No. 23 Clipstone Street, which he did; but found that the man's wounds had been dressed by the person who now appears to be Wentworth, who being originally a surgeon, had probed the wounds, but could not extract the ball. The medical gentleman who had been called in advised the man to go to the Hospital, where Wentworth took him in a Hackney coach, and left him in the name of John Smith.

WHITEHALL EVENING POST

There was time only for the quickest arrangement of mind. She must be collected and calm Emma

On receiving this information, the proper officers repaired to Clipstone Street, but neither Mr Wentworth, who went by the name of Wilson, nor the woman who passed for his wife, by the name of Wilson, were within. They waited a short time, when Mrs Wilson, whose real name appears to be Weaver, came in.

WHITEHALL EVENING POST

No time for recollection!–for planning behaviour, or regulating manners!–There was time only to turn pale Persuasion

They of course secured her; but a great crowd being collected about the door, they thought it necessary to take Mrs Wilson, alias Mrs Taylor, alias Mrs Weaver, away with them, as they knew Wentworth would not come home if he saw any mob about the door.[47] Whitehall Evening Post

Mr Wentworth was the very man Persuasion

He was taken in his lodgings with the woman whom he lived with; he there passed by the name of Wilson – the woman was called Weaver. They were both brought to the Publick Office, and examined before Mr Bond, who took great pains to know from Wentworth who the wounded man was; to which he declared he could give no particular account. The Public Advertiser

She went to the door, but it was locked, she looked at the window, but it was barred with iron Henry & Eliza

The woman denied any knowledge of him, and being questioned who she was, answered that her name was Taylor; that she came from Worcestershire, but did not know any thing of her family at present. In her possession were found two duplicates of watches, which Wentworth acknowledged to be his.[48] The Public Advertiser

He was looking at her with all the Power & Keenness Persuasion

Jane wrote, *she spoke from the instinctive wish of delaying shame…the truth rushed on her; how she could have spoken at all, how she could even have breathed – was afterwards a matter of wonder to herself.*[49]

There was nothing to be done however, but to stifle feelings & be quietly polite Persuasion

Yesterday the notorious D'Arcy Wentworth was brought before Nicholas Bond Esq. The circumstance that led to apprehending this offender, were as follows. A man had been wounded in an attempt to rob two gentlemen on Hounslow- heath. A few days after this robbery, Sir Sampson Wright received information that a man then lay in the Middlesex Hospital, who said he had been wounded by a highwayman.[50] Whitehall Evening Post

At Bow Street, D'Arcy was held on suspicion, to await a witness with evidence for a prosecution. When he was apprehended, he disclaimed all knowledge of the wounded man, but that his name was Jack, and that he had told him he had been wounded with a ball out of a carriage. Notice having been given to a great many persons robbed, that W, was to be brought up for examination.[51] The office was extremely crowded with Gentlemen.[52] The Times

Lamenting the blindness of his own pride, and the blunders of his own calculations   Persuasion

D'Arcy was held in prison throughout November 1789. Nicholas Bond, the Bow-street magistrate, made great efforts to find a witness to prosecute or to supply evidence for a charge of highway robbery. His examinations at Bow Street were well publicised beforehand, to attract people who might identify him.

The press carried the unusual offer of a full pardon to a highwayman prepared to appear against D'Arcy – *What a wonderful advantage have the three companions of Wentworth, the highwayman, now before their eyes, and even the wounded man himself; for agreeable so to the language of the statute. If either of them voluntarily surrenders himself he will be entitled to his pardon for all offences which he may have done before such surrender, and it will be a bar to any appeal brought for any robbery by him committed.*[53]   DIARY OR WOODFALLS REGISTER

Her mind deeply busy in revolving what she had heard, feeling, thinking, recalling & forseeing everything   Persuasion

Jane was released without charge – *It was over, and she had escaped without reproaches and without detection. Her secret was still her own; and while that was the case, she thought she could resign herself to almost everything.*[54]

She returned to Clipstone Street, expecting every day to see D'Arcy again. *She seemed to herself never to have been shocked before. There was no possibility of rest. The evening passed, without a pause of misery, the night was totally sleepless. She passed only from feelings of sickness to shuddering of horror; and from hot fits of fever to cold. The event was so shocking, that there were moments even when her heart revolted from it as impossible.*[55]

Nor among the walkers, the horsemen, or the curricle drivers of the morning   Northanger Abbey

Five times in all, at least once a week, D'Arcy was brought back to Bow-street to submit to further examination. Post-chaise drivers whose passengers had been robbed attended, in order to know if they could identify the prisoner, which however, they could not do; they all declaring that they had not the least recollection of his person.

Several Stable Keepers also attended, of whom it was supposed the prisoner had hired horses on the particular days on which the highway robberies had been committed; but in this also proofs were wanting; all the Stable Keepers but one declaring they did not know his person, and the one that did know the prisoner, said he had not let him a horse to hire these two years.[56]   THE TIMES

The Dutchess, whose friendship with Mrs Wilson would have carried her any lengths Henry & Eliza

D'Arcy was a celebrity of some magnitude, *a great concourse of people attended the hearings, including the Duke and Duchess of Cumberland, brother and sister in law of the King,* friends of Jane's cousin Eliza; *and the Duke of Hamilton, Scotland's premier peer.* [57]

Mr Heywood looked very much astonished Sanditon

John Pemberton Heywood, of Lincoln's Inn, appeared at the second examination, on 12 November. He stated, on a rainy Sunday morning, 5th July, nearly five months before, he with Henry Russell, of Lincoln's Inn, was crossing Finchley Common in a post-chaise when they were held up by two highwaymen.

The 5th of July was very near the day Fitzwilliam departed London for Milton, en route to *Wentworth Woodhouse* to entertain the Prince. On 7 July, the press reported – The Earl of Fitzwilliam and Family are gone to his seat at Milton in Northamptonshire for the Summer season.[58] THE TIMES

Mr Heywood deposed that he left his Chambers in Lincoln's Inn, in a post-chaise accompanied by a gentleman who was going with him on a tour through the north of England; that near the eight mile-stone on Finchley Common, two men on horseback rode up to the chaise, crying out, "Stop, stop." THE BELFAST NEWSLETTER

Many young men, who had chambers in the Temple, made a very good appearance in the first circles, and drove about town in very knowing gigs Sense & Sensibility

Conceiving them to be two honest drunken fellows, who had a mind for a frolic, he let down the front glass of the chaise, and asked what they wanted? Upon which they immediately drew down black crapes over their faces, and one riding to each door, and presenting pistols, answered, "We want your money." While Mr Heywood was producing his money, one of the men said, "Sir, I know you;" and as they rode away with their booty of purses and watches, the wind blew up the crape from one of their faces, and afforded an opportunity to observe him.[59] THE BELFAST NEWSLETTER

Heywood claimed he was robbed of a silk purse, value one shilling; a base metal watch, value 40 shillings; a steel chain, value one shilling; four cornelian seals set in gold, value £8; six guineas; a crown piece; nine shillings; a foreign copper coin, value one farthing; and a red morocco leather tweezer case.

> Prince Hal – Wilt thou rob this leathern-jerkin, crystal-button, not-pated, agate-ring, puke-stocking, caddis-garter, smooth-tongue, Spanish-pouch?
> Henry IV Part I

He turned again to Mr Heywood Sanditon

In evidence, Heywood said, when he told the highwaymen he had no watch, one of them had replied, "*Pho, pho, I know who you are very well, I know you do travel with a watch, give it me.*"

After the men rode off, he had: *immediately observed to his companion, that if D'Arcy Wentworth were in the kingdom, he would say that was he. The greatest part of his face was covered with a crape. Mr. Heywood had seen him once at York. On this evidence Wentworth was committed, and Mr. Heywood was bound over to prosecute.*

John Pemberton Heywood was the only person who attended Bow Street and identified D'Arcy as a highwayman. **Several other Gentlemen who had been robbed attended to look at the person of the prisoner, but they could not identify it.**

At D'Arcy's fifth and last examination: **The postilion who drove Mr Heywood and Mr Russel at the time of the robbery attended, but had not the least recollection of the prisoner's person.**[60] THE TIMES

In a most friendly manner Mr Heywood here interposed, entreating them not to think of proceeding Sanditon

Mr Heywood attended, and addressing Mr Bond, said he would willingly drop all thoughts of prosecuting the prisoner, as he had been informed that if Mr Wentworth was dismissed, his intentions were to immediately quit the kingdom. Mr Bond said that could not now be allowed.[61] WHITEHALL EVENING POST

On a dark November day, a small thick rain almost blotting out the very few objects ever to be discerned from the windows Persuasion

Jane was alone at Clipstone Street, each day she expected D'Arcy to be released, if not today, then surely tomorrow. She wrote him lively, funny letters, wanting him to be cheered. He had told her – *tragedy may be your choice, but it will certainly appear that comedy chuses you.*

He asked her – *visit me in prison with a basket of provisions; you will not refuse to visit me in prison? I think I see you coming in with your basket.*[62] But she was not strong enough to visit Newgate, that *tremendous building*.[63] For her to see him *in so cruel a confinement* would be too overpowering.[64]

The room was now so deserted, occupied by her silent, pensive self Persuasion

Every day Jane was more anxious, more uncertain of what was happening and where it might lead. She waited, entirely alone, too unsettled to call on Eliza, fearful of what Philadelphia might tell her family in Steventon.

Playing a dangerous game, too much indebted to the event for his acquittal

Emma

Until his last examination, on 28 November, D'Arcy was still hopeful he would be released without charge. It was hard that he should be confined so long on a charge of which he was quite innocent; that the ship to which he had been appointed had sailed and got round to Plymouth, and the keeping him in confinement would deprive him of the opportunity of going abroad to provide for himself, and that the consequences must be fatal to him. Mr Bond told him, under the present circumstances Mr Heywood was by the laws of his country bound to proceed against him, and he as a Magistrate was in duty bound to take recognizances.[65]

THE PUBLIC ADVERTISER

A friend of his, a lawyer

Letters

John Pemberton Heywood, six years older than D'Arcy, was a barrister from Wakefield, a member of Lincoln's Inn and a long standing member of Fitzwilliam's Whig network in Yorkshire.[66] D'Arcy had met him in 1785, at Robert Sinclair's house in York.

Two years before, Henry Russell had D'Arcy held at the Old Bailey, accusing him of a highway robbery nine months earlier. He had backed off, saying he could not identify him positively, it was too long ago. Two years on, Russell again declined to prosecute or give evidence against him, he left it to Heywood.

D'Arcy knew them both, and it seems that after a game of cards, which he won, they had refused to pay their losses.

The day after Heywood identified D'Arcy at Bow-street, there was a cryptic notice *To Correspondents* on *The Times'* second page: **Mr Wentworth's back papers shall be sent him with the future, but he must stop the paper sent from the former Hawker whose directions we have not.**[67]

Impossible to understand at this distance, was it suggesting D'Arcy did have a future, that he would not be sentenced to hang?[68]

His trial, held on Wednesday, 9 December 1789, was the first case heard in the Old Bailey December session. Perhaps it was scheduled first, to ensure when released, he would have time to join the fleet at Portsmouth.

Some several of head-piece extraordinary[69]

The Winter's Tale

The Old Bailey was crowded with celebrities: **The Duke and Duchess of Cumberland were present from ten o'clock in the morning till past three in the afternoon.**[70] **The head-dress worn by the Duchess of Cumberland at the Old Bailey, was strongly attractive – the hat was black beaver, exhibiting in front an enormous bow of deep, pink satin ribbons.**[71]

THE TIMES

Within an hour after Mr Harris's arrival, she set off   Sense & Sensibility

On the morning of the trial, John Harris collected Jane from Clipstone Street, and accompanied her to the Old Bailey.

Pray advise him for his own sake, & for every body's sake   Northanger Abbey

Fitzwilliam had asked Thomas Erskine to appear for D'Arcy. He was more than willing, but was scheduled that day to appear before Lord Kenyon, Lord Chief Justice, defending Mr Stockdale, the bookseller of Piccadilly.

Erskine recommended William Garrow, a celebrated barrister, be engaged in his place. The two men most likely discussed the strategy for D'Arcy's defence, it was later said to be *by some ingenious contrivance* of Erskine that D'Arcy was acquitted.[72]

The rusty curb of old father antic, the law   Henry IV Part I

D'Arcy remained silent throughout the hearing. Only Pemberton Heywood was called to give evidence. No witnesses were called. The trial transcript is full of genial exchanges between Garrow and fellow members of Lincoln's Inn, Pemberton Heywood and Judge Baron Perryn, who also presided at D'Arcy's trial in December 1787.

You had some knowledge of the prisoner before?

Yes my lord, he was at York some time, and during one summer assize, I saw him repeatedly at Mr. Sinclair's house, that was four or five years ago; he lived at Mr. Sinclair's house then...and very respectably he behaved; I thought him a very agreeable young gentleman; I know he was introduced by a very respectable gentleman; I believe he is of an excessive good family in Ireland.

Heywood stated that though he did not see his face, he believed Wentworth was one of the two highwaymen. Though physically he had grown and changed, *he has a pretty strong Irish brogue as you will hear.*

The Court did not get the opportunity to hear D'Arcy's brogue. When asked: *would the prisoner say any thing,* Mr Garrow replied: *No my lord, I would not advise him to say anything on this occasion.*[73]

From then on an air of play-acting seemed to envelope the proceedings, as if everybody had considered just how far it was safe to go to achieve a planned result without endangering Mr Wentworth, and without embarrassment to a former judge in the delicate position of a witness on oath.[74]

"Sir," said Mr Heywood with a good humoured smile   Sanditon

At the end of the hearing, the transcript records a telling exchange between Garrow and Heywood:

Garrow: *Soon after the robbery did you meet nobody on the common that you might have communicated this to?*
Heywood: *I had the pleasure to meet you, Sir, on the common soon after.*
Garrow: *And very kindly let me go on to be robbed, I believe?*
Heywood: *I had no idea that you would be robbed.*
Garrow: *I had the good fortune to escape your kind wishes.*
Heywood: *I dare say you had; I do not think you was in any danger of being robbed.*
Court: *Have you any witnesses.*
Mr Garrow. *No.* [75]

There was an air of rehearsed exactitude about everything that happened which might have caused a suspicious nose to scent a peculiar odour about the Court.[76]

The exchange between Garrow and Heywood is open to interpretation. Was Garrow implying that when they met soon after on Finchley Common, Heywood did not tell him that he had been robbed by highwaymen, because it never really happened? Or was Heywood silent because, as he said, Garrow was in no danger of being robbed, perhaps because they both knew that D'Arcy had held up Heywood's coach to collect unpaid gambling debts.

Mr Heywood, it seems, had met Mr Garrow on Finchley Common, in less than half an hour after the robbery was committed, without apprising him of the danger he was in, by communicating to him what had happened; but Mr Heywood excused the omission, by saying, with much pleasantry, that he conceived his learned friend was too well known to the gentlemen of the road, to be in any danger of being robbed by them.[77]   THE BELFAST NEWSLETTER

A report of a most alarming nature   Pride & Prejudice

Another member of Lincoln's Inn was following D'Arcy's travails, Thomas Hill, Earl Fitzwilliam's London lawyer and agent.

My Lord

I forbore to give your Lordship a detail of D'Arcy Wentworth's affair till the conclusion which will be in the course of this week but may now relate it to your Lordship. On receipt of your Lordship's letter I sent to Clipstone Street where he was and told him that your Lordship would assist him with a few Shirts and other necessaries to fit him out and he said he should want some Shirts, some Stockings and a Jacket or two and a bed or Hammock, and that as I had your lordship's Orders I would procure him the things, and he said he would apply to Mr Nepean to know the Ship he was to go on Board and when it would Sail and that he would let me know, and by letter he informed me that he had called but Mr Nepean happened not to be at home, but that he would call of him again –

A few days after that I had a letter from him from New Prison Clerkenwell – he said he had been taken up and was committed there for robbing Mr Heywood of Lincoln's Inn in July last upon Finchley Common: that Mr Heywood said before the Justice he thought it was him but was not certain, but on this evidence he was committed, and it was rather sharping upon Mr Heywood, as his Evidence was not Positive, that this got him bound over to Prosecute – he urged that as his Evidence was not Positive he could not be convicted upon it but as they had got him bound over, it seemed intentionally for the purpose to detain him in Prison.

The Justices or Runners urged that there would be Evidence enough before the Old Bailey Sessions came on, which begins tomorrow, and I have heard of no other Evidence yet: so that in all probability tomorrow or Thursday he will be cleared and I shall see or hear from him –

Mr Heywood I have seen twice on this occasion and its plain he cannot be convicted upon his Evidence, he not being certain of the Person;

When he sent to me from New Prison Clerkenwell he inform'd me he had had no food for 24 hours and beg'd that I would assist him whereupon I sent him a Guinea for he said his Clothes and every thing had been seized by the Justice's people and I had afterwards his thanks for the Guinea, and as he was moved last Thursday to Newgate in order for his trial at the Sessions he sent to me again requesting that I would advance him 24 Shillings to pay his fees on his removal to Newgate, or else he sh'd have no bed to lie upon there –

I sent him the money but represented to him that I was to pursue your Lordship's orders strictly and not vary from it, and that this advancing was going from it that he must expect no more in that way.

On his request I sent twice to the Secretary- States Office to Mr Nepean and a gentleman in the Office there said whenever Wentworth was acquitted, if he call'd at the Office he would give him the name of the Ship bound to Botany bay, and an order for him to go on board and the ship I find is the Neptune and is gone from the River round to Plymouth that it seems as if there would be an expence his going to Plymouth to go on Board the Ship but I will manage this matter as frugally as I can – a small Sum I presume your lordship will not demur at.

I conclude before the close of the Week I shall certainly hear from him, if not to morrow or Thursday.

I am your Lordship's Most obedient & humble Servant

Tho Hill[78]

Excellent news, capital news! Pride & Prejudice

The jury at the Old Bailey found D'Arcy Wentworth not guilty.

After the judgement was announced, it was Heywood, the prosecutor, who requested D'Arcy's release. He told the Court, D'Arcy had *taken a passage in the fleet to Botany Bay; and has obtained an appointment in it, as assistant surgeon, and desires to be discharged immediately.*

The Court agreed: *Let him be discharged.*

The press explained the decision: **Mr Heywood saw the lower part of his face only, and if he had not thought that Wentworth had been abroad, he should have been certain that he was the person. Upon being pressed close, he would not positively swear to the prisoner. There were no other witnesses and the Baron thought it was too much to convict upon such slender circumstances.**[79] THE PUBLIC ADVERTISER

Yesterday, the Sessions began at the Old Bailey when Barrington and D'Arcy Wentworth were each put up to the Bar, and severally acquitted. Nine persons received sentence of death. These trials were neither of them particularly interesting.[80] THE TIMES

Wentworth unshackled and free. She had some feelings she was ashamed to investigate. They were too much like joy, senseless joy! Persuasion

D'Arcy returned to Clipstone Street that evening, exhausted but in good spirits. *She distinguished him on the right hand pavement at such a distance as to have him in view the greater part of the street. There were many other men about him, many groups walking the same way, but there was no mistaking him.*[81]

All their miseries fell away, Jane was cheered by his presence and his energy, they talked excitedly of their future, and the many things to be done before they could leave England.

There is something interesting in the bustle of going away, & the prospect of spending future summers by the Sea or in Wales is very delightful Letters

Over the next few days D'Arcy went several times to Evan Nepean's office. Jane felt able to go to Orchard Street to visit Philadelphia and Eliza, and play with little Hastings.

D'Arcy obtained official permission to travel on the *Neptune* as a paying passenger. The surgeons required for the fleet had all been appointed, and Evan Nepean could not confirm that there would be a medical post available for him in New South Wales.

Earl Fitzwilliam, through Thomas Hill's chambers, advanced D'Arcy money to finance the voyage. Hill's Clerk, Charles Cookney, assisted him to make ready. On 12 December, D'Arcy left for Portsmouth, to go on board the *Neptune*, introduce himself to the captain and secure his cabin for the voyage.

Thomas Hill had urged him to go immediately. The Second Fleet was not due to sail until after Christmas, but this was an urgent duty, by which D'Arcy would demonstrate he was fulfilling his obligation to the Court.

The *Neptune* was anchored in Stokes Bay, off Portsmouth, with two other ships of the Second Fleet, *Surprize* and *Scarborough*. A number of officers of the New South Wales Corps and their families were already on board, along with over five hundred convicts from Newgate, from county prisons and hulks in the Thames and at Plymouth.

D'Arcy *was staying at the Crown*[82] on High Street, next door to the Vicarage. He arranged for Charles Cookney to deliver money to Jane, sufficient for her to make her preparations and to follow him to Portsmouth.

How severely mortified, how cruelly disappointed, in not having it finished while I was in London
Mansfield Park

He would need to go back to London to finalise his affairs, buy instruments and stores for his medical chest, and confirm his appointment in New South Wales. But first, he and Jane would go to Steventon, for George Austen to marry them under English law, and to give them his blessing. They would make their farewells, return to Portsmouth, and board the *Neptune* as husband and wife.

Oh! I am quite delighted with the thoughts of it; I can think of nothing else. I assure you I have done nothing for this last Month but plan what Cloathes I should take with me
Kitty, or the Bower

When Cookney called at Clipstone Street to deliver money to Mrs Wilson, he was unsettled by her youthfulness, and disturbed when she spoke of the clothes she might need on board ship and in the Colony. Not wanting to encourage her, he withheld most of the money he had brought to give her.

It had occurred to her that after so long an absence from home... she... might not be provided with money enough for the expenses of her journey,... it proved to be exactly the case... upon examining her purse.
Northanger Abbey

Jane wrote that Mr Cookney had called, but had not left enough for her coach fare. They were planning to celebrate her birthday in Portsmouth together on the Wednesday, when she would enter her fifteenth year.

On Tuesday, 15 December, D'Arcy wrote to Cookney to remind him of his undertaking to deliver the money to her. He asked if there was mail for him at Grosvenor Square, and said the *Neptune* arrived from Plymouth late on Sunday. On Monday he went on board, he was well received, shown a suitable cabin, and had arranged his passage.

Cookney was a young lawyer, a student of the *strict statutes and most biting laws, the needful bits & curbs to the headstrong.*[83] He knew the background to the charges against D'Arcy, knew those he held up *had pressed a falling man too far*. Perhaps he agreed, it was *virtue* of a sort that had lain him *open to the laws.*[84]

On Thursday, 17 December 1789 he wrote to D'Arcy at the Crown Inn: *tho' I know but little of you, and as such it might be thought why should I care about you, yet believe me, I felt for your situation as much as if you had been related to me, and you have my best wishes for your future welfare.*

What you desire respecting Mrs Wilson I will take care immediately to comply with, my motive was her Interest: indeed I was fearful lest I should pay her the whole that she would set off after you, which would have been a very silly pursuit, but there is no accounting for the actions of a Woman.

Cookney advised no mail had come for him at Grosvenor Square, adding a late postscript: *Since writing the above, thinking you would be better satisfied, I have been to Mrs Wilson's lodgings but she happened not to be at home; however I left word for her to call here, when you may depend upon it I will pay her the remainder of the money.*[85]

By Friday *very little remained to be done*. Jane *had not loitered; she was almost dressed, and her packing almost finished.*[86] She took the coach alone for Portsmouth; *a few hours would take you there; but a journey of seventy miles, to be taken post by you, at your age, alone, unattended!*

The journey in itself had no terrors for her; and she began it without either dreading its length or feeling its solitariness Northanger Abbey

She met with nothing, however, to distress or frighten her. Her youth, civil manners, and liberal pay procured her all the attention that a traveller like herself could require; and stopping only to change horses, she travelled on for about eleven hours without accident or alarm, and between six and seven o'clock in the evening found herself entering Portsmouth.[87]

They drove to the Crown in good time,[88] D'Arcy met her off the coach, and from that moment all was so easy and comfortable, it seemed quite natural to believe this was the new beginning of their life together.

A Prison ship at Portsmouth Letters

They woke to the smell of the sea and the busy noise of the town. After breakfast, they went out to look across at the *Neptune* at Stokes Bay, she looked a strong, sound ship, and there appeared to be many people on board. They walked around the ramparts in the wind, *a fine girl of fifteen, who was of the party on the ramparts, taking her first lesson, I presume, in love.*[89]

Next day, Sunday, they went to the service at the Garrison Church, they could *get there from the Crown in a hop, step, and jump*.⁹⁰ It was almost Christmas, they sang hymns and carols, full of expectation and joy, and afterwards, they went up to stroll along the ramparts once more.

Only walked about snugly together   Letters

The day was uncommonly lovely... mild air, brisk soft wind, and bright sun, occasionally clouded for a minute; and everything looked so beautiful under the influence of such a sky, the effects of the shadows pursuing each other on the ships at Spithead and the island beyond, with the ever-varying hues of the sea, now at high water, dancing in its glee and dashing against the ramparts with so fine a sound...Nay, had she been without his arm, she would soon have known that she needed it, for she wanted strength for a two hours' saunter of this kind, coming...upon...previous inactivity. She *was beginning to feel the effect of being debarred from her usual regular exercise.*⁹¹

In the most private manner imaginable at Portsmouth   Letters

Their few days together in Portsmouth were full of laughter and love. They walked, explored and watched the activity on the harbour. *Spending freely,* they bought bedding and books, ready to take on board ship. D'Arcy *was confident that he should soon be rich; full of life and ardour, he knew that he should soon have a ship, and soon be on a station that would lead to every thing he wanted. He had always been lucky; he knew he should be still. Such confidence* was *powerful in its own warmth, bewitching in the wit which often expressed it.* ⁹²

Late one morning, he *met with some acquaintance at the Crown;*⁹³ John Harris had come to collect him, to go out to the *Neptune*. Harris had sailed from Plymouth on the *Neptune*, and was just now moving onto the *Surprize*.

Jane marked that morning: *The next bustle brought in...the surgeon of the Thrush, a very well-behaved young man, who came to call for his friend, and for whom there was with some contrivance found a chair, and with some hasty washing of the young tea-maker's, a cup and saucer; and after another quarter of an hour of earnest talk between the gentlemen, noise rising upon noise, and bustle upon bustle, men and boys at last all in motion together, the moment came for setting off; everything was ready.*⁹⁴

The weather was most favourable for her, though Christmas-day, she could not go to church   Emma

On Christmas Eve, Jane and D'Arcy left the *Crown* to join the coach to take them to Popham Lane. From there they walked arm in arm across the icy ground to Steventon.

The Austen family was at church; rather than climb up the hill in the dark to join them, they waited quietly at the rectory for their return, each thinking of all that would need to be said and explained.

He is in London tomorrow, some money Negociation Letters

On Boxing Day, D'Arcy left Steventon for London, to obtain letters of introduction to the Governor and the Principal Surgeon in New South Wales, and he trusted, to confirm his employment there.

His return to London did not pass unnoticed. *The Times* reported: **Darcy Wentworth has not fulfilled his engagement with Justice Bond to embark on the Botany Bay fleet, if he escaped from his late prosecution, for he is still about the metropolis.**[95]

To the Neptune Letters

Early in the morning, the last day of the year, D'Arcy Wentworth left London for the last time, for Steventon, and later that evening, went on to Portsmouth.

On 17 January 1790, six weeks after his trial, he sailed alone for New South Wales, broken by Jane's rejection.

Chapter 10

Such Probabilities & Proofs

I cannot speak well enough to be unintelligible

IN THE FIRST MONTHS of 1790, after D'Arcy Wentworth disappeared from her life, Jane Austen came dangerously close to mental breakdown. In her first novel, *Sense & Sensibility*, written in its original form in 1795, she set out with clinical precision the dreadful impact on her of losing him.

Mine is a misery which nothing can do away   Sense & Sensibility

At first she had *shed no tears; but after a short time they would burst out, tears of agony*, in *violent affliction, violent sorrow*. She cried uncontrollably, *a continual flow of tears, agitation and sobs*, and *frequent bursts of grief, tears which streamed from her eyes with passionate violence. Covering her face with her handkerchief, she almost screamed with agony...such grief, shocking as it was, such violent oppression of spirits her voice entirely lost in sobs...she was without any desire of command over herself.*

Dreadfully white...in silent agony, too much oppressed even for tears, her *violence of affliction sunk into a calmer melancholy,* she would experience *a sort of desperate calmness, immediately followed by a return of the same excessive affliction.*

Such grief, shocking as it was to witness it, must have its course   Sense & Sensibility

Almost choked by grief, she neither ate, nor attempted to eat anything, faint and giddy from a long want of proper rest and food, for it was many days since she had any appetite, and many nights since she had really slept. She spent whole hours at

the pianoforte, alternately singing and crying, her voice often totally suspended by her tears. Her *nerves could not bear any sudden noise,* she suffered insomnia, wretchedness...a *most nervous irritability, advised to lie down, for a moment she did so, but no attitude could give her ease, and in restless pain of mind and body, she moved from one posture to another, growing more and more hysterical. She required at once solitude and continual change of place.*

I think it may afford my Readers some amusement to find it out, I shall here take the liberty of presenting it to them The History of England

1789 was the defining year for Jane Austen, the risks she took and choices she made in her fifteenth year, set the groundwork for her life and her life's work. She had been writing little stories and sketches for years, reading them at table in the evening to entertain and tease her family. She kept a record of twenty-nine of these pieces of juvenilia, written between 1786 and mid-1793. All of those written after 1789, contain bright shards of the story of Jane and D'Arcy.

Her writing became the outlet for her grief and frustration, feelings that pervade all her novels, but lie raw and exposed in the juvenilia. She wrote a number of absurdist, picaresque stories, that give her perspective on the events of that tumultuous autumn and winter. She recorded them with comic, improbable plots and absurdist humour, sparkling with knowingness, full of action, romance and misfortune.

Resolving to suppress every particular Pride & Prejudice

Jane Austen's three notebooks of juvenilia were not released until many years after her death. The second volume, *Love & Freindship* was published in 1922, the first volume, eleven years later in 1933, and the third, in 1951, a hundred and thirty four years after her death.

Her nephew, James Edward Austen-Leigh, confirmed that the Austens had suppressed these early stories. *The family have rightly, I think, declined to let these early works be published...some of which must have been composed when she was a young girl, as they amounted to a considerable number by the time she was sixteen. Her earliest stories are of a slight and flimsy texture, and are generally intended to be nonsensical, but the nonsense has much spirit in it....Instead of presenting faithful copies of nature, these tales were generally burlesques, ridiculing the improbable events and exaggerated sentiments which she had met with in sundry silly romances...It would be as unfair to expose this preliminary process to the world.*[1]

Do not imagine me in danger of forgetting Lesley Castle

In the stories Jane wrote, immediately after D'Arcy left England, we read something of the volatility of her moods and of her pressing sense of loss.

In *The Adventures of Mr Harley,* a short piece written early in 1790, Mr Harley, named for the great street of doctors and medical specialists in London, returns home from a voyage, after six months at sea, and fails to recognise his young wife, whom *he had married a few weeks before he left England*. We sense Jane's realisation that she would have to wait much longer than those first, endless six months, before there was a chance of seeing D'Arcy again.

In *Edgar & Emma,* also written that first year, Emma holds her tears until her guests have gone, *when having no check to the overflowings of her greif, she gave free vent to them, & retiring to her own room, continued in tears the remainder of her Life.*

But why all this secrecy? Why any fear of detection? Why must their marriage be private?
Pride & Prejudice

Jane recorded her marriage in *A Collection of Letters,* written at the end of 1791, where *a Young Lady crossed in Love,* confides in a letter to *her freind*: *'I rode once, but it is many years ago' She spoke this in so low and tremulous a Voice, that I was silent. Struck with her manner of speaking I could make no reply. 'I have not ridden, continued she fixing her Eyes on my face, since I was married.' I was never so surprised – 'Married, Ma'am!' I repeated. 'You may well wear that look of astonishment, said she, since what I have said must appear improbable to you – nothing is more true than that I was once married.'*

Why are you called Miss Jane?

I married without the consent or knowledge of my father...It was therefore necessary to keep the secret from him and from every one, till some fortunate opportunity might offer of revealing it.

The Mystery, a short play, dedicated to her father, is a tiny piece of absurdist theatre, mocking the dead hand of collusion in family secrets.[2] Nothing specific is said, the dialogue is full of half stated, unspoken and whispered hints; the characters all understand they are not to speak them aloud.

One asks, *and is he to?* An answer is whispered, nothing is made clear. Are people missing, has someone disappeared? Is the man alluded to, in some unmentionable predicament.

Colonel Elliott enters, *My daughter is not here I see...there lies Sir Edward... Shall I tell him the secret?...No, he'll certainly blab it... But he is asleep and wont hear me...So I'll een venture.* Nothing is resolved. The play ends with the Colonel whispering something into the ear of Sir Edward, still fast asleep.

Her nephew described *The Mystery,* as *the kind of transitory amusement which Jane was continually supplying to the family party.*[3]

I am in love with every handsome man I see Kitty, or the Bower

The *Juvenilia* stories brim over with the excitement of sexual attraction and experience, with Jane's observations, serious and comic, of passion – of men, old and young, in the throes of love and lust.

His transports, his Raptures, his Extacies are beyond my power to describe. A Collection of Letters

His heart was as delicate as sweet and as tender as a Whipt-syllabub, could not resist her attractions. In a very few Days, he was falling in love, shortly after actually fell, and before he had known her a Month, he had married her. Lesley Castle

Yes Madam, I had the happiness of adoring you, an happiness for which I cannot be too grateful. In short madam you are the prettiest Girl I ever saw in my Life. Of that Heart which trembles while it signs itself your most ardent Admirer and devoted humble servant. A Collection of Letters

The lovely Charlotte consents to marry *an aged gentleman with a sallow face & old pink coat* who falls at her feet *declaring his attachment to her & beseeching her pity in the most moving manner.* A short time later, *a young and Handsome Gentleman in a new blue coat, intreated permission to pay to her, his addresses.*[4]... She, with *the natural turn of mind to make every one happy, promised to become his Wife the next morning.* Frederic & Elfrida

Now my Adorable Laura (continued he taking my Hand) when may I hope to receive that reward of all the painful sufferings I have undergone during the course of my attachment to you, to which I have ever aspired. Oh! When will you reward me with Yourself?

'This instant, Dear and Aimable Edward. (replied I.) We were immediately united by my Father, who tho' he had never taken orders had been bred to the Church.' Love & Freindship

In *Scraps* we hear her excitement, as she nears London:
> Where am I? At Hounslow.
> Where go I? To London.
> What to do? To be married. The First Act of Comedy

Love & Freindship

Jane Austen completed *Love & Freindship* in June 1790, in her sixteenth year, six months after D'Arcy Wentworth sailed. Virginia Woolf found the story, *astonishing and unchildish.*[5]

Jane dedicated *Love & Freindship* to Eliza de Feullide, who was staying at

Steventon at the time. Without doubt, she confided in Eliza, the full and detailed history of the folly and misfortunes of Jane and D'Arcy.

She filled *Love & Freindship* with flashbacks of their adventures: the journey to Yorkshire and Scotland, their elopement and marriage at Gretna Green, and his imprisonment in Newgate. She gave the story a subtitle, *deceived in friendship and betrayed in love,* not borne out in the racketing story. Perhaps she was mocking excuses given for her behaviour, within the Austen family.

Jane may well have taken the title, *Love & Freindship,* from lines in *Bon Ton,* spoken by Miss Tittup, the role Eliza coveted. *Pooh, Pooh, Love & Friendship are very fine names to be sure, but they are mere visiting acquaintance; we know their names indeed, talk of 'em sometimes, and let 'em knock at our doors, but we never let 'em in, you know.*

Eliza would have recognised her references to the fearless and affecting romance of Jane and D'Arcy – love at first sight, thefts of money, travelling north by coach, a carriage turning over on the road, visiting generous relatives, and the short duration of their marriage.

Henry Austen had given his advice on love and friendship in the *Loiterer* in August 1789: *let every Girl who seeks for happiness conquer both her feelings and her passions. Let her avoid love and friendship as she wishes to be admired and distinguished. For by these means she will always keep her own secrets and prefer her own interest.*[6]

The story of *Love & Freindship* unravels in letters between Isabel, Laura and Marianne, full of shifts and swift turns between their different perspectives. The characters are hapless victims of fate, their efforts futile, but their suffering and distress, unlike the sentimental novels of the time, are genuine.

Love & Freindship is filled with youthful skits and parody, sending up the postures of sensibility and sentimentality in popular women's novels of the day: *Beware of fainting fits…Beware of swoons Dear Laura…a frenzy fit is not one quarter so pernicious; it is an exercise to the body, and if not too violent, is I daresay conducive to Health in its consequences. Run mad as often as you chuse: but do not faint!*

Laura falls in love with Edward, *the most beauteous and amiable Youth, I had ever beheld… no sooner did I first behold him, than I felt that on him the happiness or Misery of my future Life must depend.* Edward finds himself, not in New South Wales, but South Wales, *tho' I flatter myself with being a tolerable proficient in Geography, I know not how it happened.*

Why should they not go on to Scotland   Pride & Prejudice

Jane included the scene of the Regent's upturned carriage near Rotherham: *an accident truly apropos; it was the lucky overturning of a Gentleman's Phaeton, on the road which ran murmuring behind us... We instantly... ran to the rescue of those who but a few moments before had been in so elevated a situation as a fashionably high Phaeton, but who were now laid low and sprawling in the dust.*

I had not walked many yards before I was overtaken by a Stage-coach in which I instantly took a place, determined to proceed in it to Edinburgh.

Sophia and Laura journey north to Scotland: *"I have a Relation in Scotland"... "Shall I order the Boy to drive there?" said I–but instantly recollecting myself, exclaimed, "Alas I fear it will be too long a Journey for the Horses."... We therefore determined to change Horses at the next Town and to travel Post the remainder of the Journey.* Janetta and M'Kenrie *depart for Gretna-Green, chosen for the celebration of their Nuptials, in preference to any other place.*

To speak more openly than might have been strictly correct   Emma

In a letter to Cassandra in 1814, Jane said of a coach ride from Chawton to London: *It put me in mind of my own Coach between Edinburgh and Sterling.*[7] When he published the letter, her grand-nephew, William Austen-Leigh, realising its association with elopement, corrected and downplayed her reference to Scotland. His footnote protested: *A visit of Jane to Scotland, of which no record is left in family tradition, is so improbable that we must imagine her to be referring to some joke, or possibly some forgotten tale of her own.*[8]

It seems Mr Austen-Leigh had not read Jane's *Lesley Castle*, written in 1792, where her comic impressions of Scotland read like letters home - *I wish.. you could but behold these Scotch giants; I am sure they would frighten you out of your wits.. In the first place they are so horribly tall!...I never can think such tremendous knock-me-down figures in the least degree elegant, and as for their eyes, they are so tall that I could never strain my neck enough to look at them.*

At any rate, she cannot grow many degrees worse without authorizing us to lock her up for the rest of her life   Pride & Prejudice

Thefts of money in *Love & Freindship,* are made light of, described rather, as *gracefully purloined,* or *removed majestically:*

Augustus and Sophia *had been married but a few months when our visit to them commenced during which time they had been amply supported by a considerable sum of Money which Augustus had gracefully purloined from his unworthy father's escritoire, a few days before his union with Sophia.*

By our arrival their Expenses were considerably increased tho' their means for supplying them were then nearly exhausted. But they, Exalted Creatures! Scorned to reflect a moment on their pecuniary Distresses and would have blushed at the idea of paying their Debts.

Sophia happening one day to open a private Drawer in Macdonald's Library with one of her own keys, discovered that it was the Place where he kept his Papers of consequence and amongst them some bank notes of a considerable amount... as Sophia was majestically removing the 5th Bank-note from the Drawer to her own purse, she was suddenly most impertinently interrupted in her employment by the entrance of Macdonald himself, in a most abrupt an precipitate Manner.

In the increasingly chaotic narrative, a gentleman arrives in a *coroneted Coach & 4*, he recognises four of the young people as his missing grandchildren, and gives each of them a £50 note. Sophia and Laura faint, and recover, to find that Gustavus and Philander have disappeared with their banknotes.

Laura encounters them again, and, *whilst the rest of the party were devouring green tea and buttered toast, we feasted ourselves in a more refined and sentimental Manner by a confidential Conversation.* Gustavus and Philander tell her, *when they reached their fifteenth year,* they took the £900 of their mother's shared funds, *kept in a Drawer in one of the Tables which stood in our common sitting Parlour, and ran away.*

Arrest and Newgate

In *Love & Freindship*, Jane recorded D'Arcy's imprisonment in Newgate: *The beautiful Augustus was arrested and we were all undone...To compleat such unparalelled Barbarity we were informed that an Execution in the House would shortly take place...Edward repaired to his imprisoned friend to lament over his misfortunes...Laura and Sophia agreed that, the best thing we could do was to leave the House; of which we every moment expected the Officers of Justice to take possession...*

No Edward appeared... no Edward returned... At length collecting all the Resolution I was Mistress of, I arose and after packing up some necessary apparel for Sophia and myself, I dragged her to a Carriage I had ordered and we instantly set out for London...

"Where am I to drive?" said the Postilion. "To Newgate Gentle Youth (replied I), to see Augustus." "Oh! no, no, (exclaimed Sophia) I cannot go to Newgate; I shall not be able to support the sight of my Augustus in so cruel a confinement–my feelings are sufficiently shocked by the RECITAL, of his Distress...

Ah! my beloved Laura (cried Sophia) for pity's sake forbear recalling to my remembrance the unhappy situation of my imprisoned Husband. Alas, what would I not give to learn the fate of my Augustus! to know if he is still in Newgate, or if he is yet hung.

In *Henry & Eliza*, Jane set down what she would like to do with Newgate prison: *No sooner was she reinstated in her accustomed power... than she raised an* army, with which she entirely demolished... Newgate... and by that act, gained the Blessings of thousands, & the Applause of her own Heart. It was not an impossible prospect, for it had happened, in 1780, during the Gordon riots.

Nothing extravagant in their housekeeping Pride & Prejudice

She described their approach to household budgeting, *Having obtained this prize we were determined to manage it with eoconomy and not to spend it with either folly or Extravagance. To this purpose we therefore divided into nine parcels, one of which we devoted to Victuals, the 2d to Drink, the 3d to Housekeeping, the 4th to Carriages, the 5th to Horses, the 6th to Servants, the 7th to Amusements the 8th to Cloathes and the 9th to Silver Buckles.*

In *Love & Freindship*, Jane recorded the length of time she and D'Arcy spent as man and wife: *Having thus arranged our Expences for two months (for we expected to make the nine Hundred Pounds last as long) we hastened to London and had the good luck to spend it in 7 weeks and a Day, which was 6 Days sooner than we had intended.*

The shackles of parental authority Love & Freindship

Love & Freindship argues vehemently that young people are entitled to follow their hearts desire. Obstinate fathers who press their sons and daughters into arranged marriages are castigated as evil, and morally wrong. Their interference is deemed worse than stealing money, particularly when the money is taken for a life of freedom or romance.

Edward tells his father: *I know the motive of your Journey here- You come with the base Design of reproaching me for having entered into an indissoluble engagement with my Laura without your consent. But Sir, I glory in the Act, it is my greatest boast that I have incurred the displeasure of my Father.*

Laura praises the marriage of Augustus and Sophia, that was *contrary to the inclinations of their Cruel and Mercenary Parents; who had vainly endeavoured with obstinate Perseverance to force them into a Marriage with those whom they had ever abhorred; but with an heroic Fortitude worthy to be related and admired, they had both, constantly refused to submit to such despotic Power. After having so nobly disentangled themselves from the shackles of Parental Authority, by a Clandestine Marriage, they were determined never to forfeit the good opinion they had gained in the World.*

In the society of my Edward and this Amiable Pair, I passed the happiest moments of my Life; Our time was most delightfully spent, in mutual Protestations of Freindship, and in vows of unalterable Love, in which we were secure from being interrupted, by intruding and disagreeable Visitors.

My father was at first highly displeased at so hasty and imprudent a connection; but when he found that they did not mind it, he soon became perfectly reconciled to the match   Love & Freindship

Behind the burlesque and humour of *Love & Freindship*, Jane asserted her feelings, clear and loud. If she read it to her parents, she was telling them of her passion for D'Arcy, her involvement in his world, and her disdain for her father's rejection of him. George Austen would have felt her censure.

Her mother was less kind – *I related to them every other misfortune which had befallen me since we parted… Nay, faultless as my Conduct had certainly been during the whole course of my late Misfortunes and Adventures, she pretended to find fault with my Behaviour in many of the situations in which I had been placed. As I was sensible myself, that I had always behaved in a manner which reflected Honour on my Feelings and Refinement, I paid little attention to what she said… wounding my spotless reputation with unjustifiable Reproaches.*[9]

Wilson brought me word of it   Lady Susan

Jane had been moved to learn her father had gone to London to search for her. In 1791, in *Sir Charles Grandison*, she told how a Mrs Wilson was missing: "Wilson is not come within, Sir."

"Well she must be carried out into the country I think. You go to Paddington, & tell Thomas to go to Hampstead, and see if he can find her, & I will go to Clapham.[10]

In 1793, in *Scraps*, Jane responded to her father's dismay at learning she was questioned by the magistrate at Bow Street. In *A Letter from a Young Lady, Whose Feelings Being Too Strong for Her Judgement Led Her into the Commission of Errors Which Her Heart Disapproved,* she amplifies and exaggerates her misdemeanours, declaring she had committed the unthinkable: *I murdered my father at a very early period of my Life, I have since murdered my Mother. I am now going to murder my Sister. I have changed my religion so often that at present I have not an idea of any left. I have been a perjured witness in every public trial for these last twelve years; and I have forged my own Will. In short there is scarcely a crime I have not committed.*

A little writing will not comprise what I have to tell you   Pride & Prejudice

The last book of the Juvenilia, written in 1792, has just two stories, *Evelyn* and *Kitty, or the Bower*. Here Jane appears more mature, and more confined. The stories are less frenetic and end unhappily. Family authority overshadows young people, ever-present, disapproving parents and guardians watch their every move, determined to assert control over youthful spontaneity and desire.

Generosity overstrained
Sense & Sensibility

In *Evelyn,* Mr Gower, who is looking for a house, is recommended to call on Mr and Mrs Webb in the village of Evelyn. They invite him in, ply him with food: *chocolate, venison pasty, sandwiches, a basket of fruit, ices, a bason of soup, jellies and cakes, an excellent dinner and exquisite wines.*

Mrs Webb gives him her purse, Mr Webb adds another £100. They ask what else he would like, and when he suggests their house and grounds – *it is yours, exclaimed both at once; from this moment it is yours.*

Mrs Webb introduces him to her two daughters, one seventeen the other several years younger: *Our dear friend Mr Gower – He has been so good as to accept of this house, small as it is, & to promise to keep it for ever.* Mr Gower suggests *if they would complete their generosity by giving me their elder daughter with a handsome portion, I should have nothing more to wish for.*

Mr Webb responds: *Take our girl, take our Maria, and on her the difficult task must fall, of endeavouring to make some return to so much Benefiscence. Her fortune is but ten thousand pounds, almost too small a sum to be offered.*

Was Jane satirising her parents' desire to see her married, their eagerness to encourage any suitor they thought respectable, their willingness to hand her to even a complete stranger, with her wishes of no consequence, neglected and ignored. In *Evelyn,* she used burlesque, exaggeration and other attempts at comedy; her *family party* could hear it as yet another piece of her *transitory amusement;* but it falls very flat, the seriousness of Maria's situation is overpowering, her anxiety and her fears, very real.

Mr Gower has a sister, Rose, whose *heart had been engaged by the attentions and charms of a young Man,* of *high rank and expectations.* His father sends him *for a fortnight to the Isle of Wight...with the hope of overcoming his Constancy by Time and Absence in a foreign Country.*

The young Nobleman was not allowed to see his Rosa... He prepared to bid a long adieu to England... They set sail – A storm arose which baffled the arts of the Seamen. The vessel was wrecked on the coast of Calshot and every Soul on board perished.

Such a thought never occurred to Kitty
Kitty, or the Bower

In *Kitty, or The Bower,* Kitty's aunt is *most excessively fond of her, and miserable if she saw her for a moment out of spirits; Yet she lived in such constant apprehension of her marrying imprudently if she were allowed the opportunity of choosing, and was so dissatisfied with her behaviour when she saw her with Young men, for it was, from her natural disposition remarkably open and unreserved...* her aunt *always thought her defective, and frequently complained of a want of Steadiness and perseverance in her occupations.*

Despite confinement and censure, Kitty pursues her amusements and enjoys the company and diversions of handsome young men. Her aunt: *had a most unfortunate opportunity of seeing her Neice whom she had supposed in bed, or amusing herself as the height of gaiety with a book, enter the room most elegantly dressed, with a smile on her Countenance, and a glow of mingled Cheerfulness & Confusion on her Cheeks, attended by a young Man uncommonly handsome, and who without any of her Confusion, appeared to have all of her vivacity.*

Kitty receives *a very severe lecture from her Aunt on the imprudence of her behaviour during the whole evening. There is certainly nothing like Virtue for making us what we ought to be, and as to a Young Man's, being young and handsome & having an agreeable person, it is nothing at all to the purpose for he had much better be respectable.*

Her guardian's *impatience to have them separated conquered every idea of propriety & Goodbreeding…Mrs Percival: immediately began a long harangue on the shocking behaviour of modern young Men, & the wonderful Alteration that had taken place in them, since her time, which she illustrated with many instructive anecdotes of the Decorum & Modesty which had marked the Characters of those whom she had known, when she had been young. This however did not prevent his walking in the Garden with her Neice, without any other companion for nearly an hour in the course of the Evening.*

The young people disregard authority, with *more than their usual haughtiness… Stanley who with a vivacity of temper seldom subdued & a contempt of censure not to be overcome, possessed the opinion of his own Consequence, & a perseverance in his own schemes which were not to be damped by the conduct of others, appeared not to perceive it. The Civilities therefore which they coldly offered he received with a gaiety & ease peculiar to himself.*

Kitty in the meantime remained insensible of having given any one Offence, and therefore unable either to offer an apology, or make a reparation; her whole attention was occupied by the happiness she enjoyed in dancing with the most elegant young Man in the room, and every one else was equally unregarded. The Evening indeed to her passed off delightfully; he was her partner during the greater part of it, and the united attractions that he possessed of Person, Address & vivacity, had easily gained that preference from Kitty, that they seldom fail of obtaining from every one.

You intend then to go into Yorkshire? Kitty asks Camilla.

Edward Stanley leaves for France, on his father's instructions. He and Kitty do not have a chance to say goodbye. *He desired me when we all met at Breakfast* to give... his Love to you, for you was a nice Girl he said, and he only wished it were in his power to be more with you. You were just the girl to suit him, because you were so lively and good-natured, and he wished with all his heart that you might not be married before he came back, for there was nothing he liked better than being here. Oh! you have no idea the fine things he said about you.

But he is gone – Gone perhaps for Years – Obliged to tear himself from what he most loves...In what anguish he must have left the house! Unable to see me, or to bid me adieu.

Yet I should like to have seen him before he went, for perhaps it may be many Years before we meet again.

The plan of an elopement Lady Susan

Jane was the daughter of a clergyman, she knew the law regarding marriage in England. Her father was rector of Steventon when the *Marriage Act* came into force in 1753, it would have been discussed within the family. To be valid, a marriage required parental approval for any party to the marriage aged under twenty-one, and the marriage had to be conducted in a church, by a clergyman, after publication of three banns, or production of a marriage licence.

The *Marriage Act* did not apply in Scotland. Young people whose parents refused consent could marry legally in Scotland. Young couples crossed the border from England to Scotland on a turnpike road that led to Gretna Green, others came from Ireland on the daily packet that crossed the Irish Sea to Portpatrick. Elopement became a popular alternative, it came to be seen as a romantic prospect for a young girl in love.

> In contempt of the Marriage Act, post-chaises and young couples run smoothly on the north road. All this, and more we owe to novels, which have operated like electricity on the great national body.
>
> *The fatal consequences of novels!*
>
> *Heigho! Wentworth! Who would have thought it?-What a foolish thing is a fond fluttering heart!*[11]
> The Annual Register

Elopements and abductions often had covert family support, particularly from the bride's family, as it was usually the groom's family who objected to the match. If elopement was the only course for them to marry, the bride's parents would usually accept it after the event, to protect their daughter's reputation; knowing that after such an escapade her future marriage prospects would be considerably dimmed.

The very important concern of marriage Lady Susan

There are numerous hasty marriages in the *Juvenilia*, some of them quite irregular. Jane carefully recorded their compliance with the *Marriage Act*, whether or no the couple had parental consent, were married within the Church, or had the correct licence.

Some of the couples make a swift decision to marry, without consulting their parents: *Lesley...at Naples, has turned Roman Catholic, obtained one of the Pope's Bulls for annulling his 1st Marriage and has actually married a Neapolitan Lady of great Rank & Fortune.* Lesley Castle

In time, Elfrida observed that she had a rival, a *growing passion in the Bosom of Frederic for the Daughter of the amiable Rebecca.... She flew to Frederic & in a manner truly heroick, spluttered out to him her intention of being married the next Day.* Eventually he is *united to her Forever.* Frederic & Elfrida

A mutual love took place & Cecil having declared his first, prevailed on Eliza to consent to a private union, which was easy to be effected, as the dutchess's chaplain being very much in love with Eliza himself, would be certain to do anything to oblige her.

The Dutchess & Lady Harriet being engaged one evening to an assembly, they took the opportunity of their absence & were united by the enamoured Chaplain.

When the Ladies returned, their amazement was great at finding instead of Eliza the following Note.

'MADAM,
We are married & gone
Henry and Eliza Cecil.' Henry & Eliza

Having so nobly disentangled themselves from the shackles of Parental Authority, by a Clandestine Marriage Love & Freindship

In September 1788, less than a year before she and D'Arcy eloped to Scotland, Jane's cousin Thomas Twisleton went to Gretna Green with Charlotte Wattell. They were both under twenty-one, they had fallen in love during theatricals at Adlestrop, the Leigh family home. Charlotte had played the title role, and Thomas, her lover, in *Julia, Or the Italian Lover*, by Irishman, Robert Jephson.

Both families approved them remarrying under English law, and their elopement was regularised at St Marylebone. Charlotte went on to perform on the London stage. They divorced in 1798 and Thomas took holy orders. He became Archdeacon of Colombo, in Ceylon, where he died in 1815.

Miss Fitzroy ran off with the Coachman Frederic & Elfrida

In 1764, Lord Rockingham's youngest sister, Fitzwilliam's aunt, Lady Henrietta Alicia Wentworth, known as Lady Harriot, eloped with an Irishman, William Sturgeon, one of Rockingham's footmen. She was twenty-seven.[12] They were married shortly after by special licence; they moved to Rouen in France. William Sturgeon became a manufacturer of china but his business was destroyed by the French Revolution. Lady Harriot died in 1789, and Fitzwilliam supported her children.[13]

Twelve days after D'Arcy sailed on the *Neptune*, another of Jane's cousins, Hon Cassandra Twisleton, Thomas' younger sister, not yet sixteen, eloped to Gretna Green with Edward Jervis Ricketts, eldest son of Viscount St Vincent. Her mother, Lady Saye & Sele, said that many of her family *winked approvingly* at their continued attachment, if not the elopement.[14]

Years later, in 1826, Jane's nephew, Edward Knight, her brother Edward's eldest son, then thirty-two, eloped to Gretna Green with Mary-Dorothea Knatchbull, aged nineteen. Mary-Dorothea was the eldest daughter of Sir Edward Knatchbull. Fanny Knight, young Edward Knight's eldest sister, had been Mary-Dorothea's stepmother for six years, she had married Sir Edward when Mary-Dorothea was thirteen.

His library, and all the parish to manage Emma

One day in 1790, Jane opened her father's parish register. One of his duties was to record there, the details of all the couples married at St Nicholas, Steventon. On specimen sheets at the front of the volume, in her tiniest hand, Jane wrote her own marriage banns.

It was a defiant gesture, she was interfering with an official record. It is surprising that it has survived. The register contains the records of the marriages conducted and the banns read at Steventon between 1755 to 1812.[15] If George Austen, or James, his successor, had read Jane's make believe banns, it is unlikely they would have left them there or submitted them as part of the parish record, as James did after 1812. It seems that in the eleven years George Austen was the custodian of the register, and James' eleven years, neither of them glanced at the specimen sheets at the beginning of the volume.

Jane wrote in the parish register that the banns had been issued, and that Jane Austen was married at St. Nicholas, Steventon. She did not record the date, or give the real name of her husband, rather, she gave three different names.

Banns of marriage at Steventon

Jane Austen's Banns announced she was to marry a connection of Fitzwilliam, with Christian names of his friends, and of heroes from English history, names which she later used for lovers and heroes in her novels.

> *The Banns of Marriage between* Henry Frederick Howard Fitzwilliam of London *and* Jane Austen of Steventon.
>
> Edmund Arthur William Mortimer *of* Liverpool *and* Jane Austen *of* Steventon *were married in this Church.*
>
> *This marriage was solemnised between us* Jack Smith *&* Jane Smith late Austen, *in the Presence of* Jack Smith, Jane Smith.[16]

Frederick Howard, 5th Earl of Carlisle, was Fitzwilliam's fellow Whig and a school-friend from his first days at Eton. Charles Howard, 11th Duke of Norfolk was another Whig colleague. Jane would have seen, and perhaps met them at the party at *Wentworth Woodhouse*.

Drawn for the hero of a favourite story   Sense & Sensibility

Charles, Second Lord Howard of Effingham, an earlier Howard, was a relative of the Duke of Norfolk, premier peer of England and first cousin of Ann Boleyn. In 1585, he was made Lord Admiral and commanded the English fleet in the longest naval battle in history, the defeat of the Spanish Armada in 1588.

More important, from Jane's view of history, Howard stood up to Elizabeth I. After the victory over the Armada, to reduce expenditure, she demanded he demobilise the crews and send them home. Howard refused to discharge them unpaid. It was *too pitiful to have men starve after such service,* he wrote, and he was sure Her Majesty would not want it so. He paid out many of the men from his own pocket. He distributed wine, cider, sugar, oil and fish amongst the ships at Plymouth. He wrote to the Queen: God knows I am not rich, but I would rather have never a penny in the world than that they should lack.

There is a nobleness in the name of Edmund   Mansfield Park

Jane wrote a second name for her intended, Edmund Arthur William Mortimer – *there is a nobleness in the name of Edmund. It is a name of heroism and renown; of kings, princes, and knights; and seems to breathe the spirit of chivalry and warm affections.*[17]

Shakespeare depicted Edmund Mortimer, 5th Earl of March, 7th Earl of Ulster, in *Henry IV, Part I,* as a claimant to the throne, a survivor, and a lover who declared, *I understand thy kisses & thou mine.*[18] A chronicle described him as *circumspect in his talk, wise and cautious during the days of his adversity.*[19]

Publishing the Banns of marriage between John Smith & Mary Brown

Sense & Sensibility

Her third entry in the register is the most revealing. Here she named herself and D'Arcy as Jane and Jack Smith, whose marriage was solemnised in their own presence, not by her father, or any other clergyman. D'Arcy sometimes used the name John Smith,[20] perhaps he used it for their Scottish marriage, and Jane gave her name as Mary Brown.

Chapter 11

More Notions than Facts

Their hearts are open to each other... they know exactly what is required and what can be borne

A GREAT PART of the history of Jane and D'Arcy has been lost, some deliberately destroyed, some simply discarded or mislaid during the intervening years. Perhaps letters, or recollections of their *sentimental story about love and honour,* do still exist, awaiting discovery. But until they come to light, the most reliable source will continue to be Jane Austen's own writing.

A profound secret, not to be breathed beyond their own circle   Persuasion

It seems that after Christmas 1789, a family silence gathered around Jane, that became a part of the Austen family culture. Her story and her misfortune were *never admitted by the pride of some, and the delicacy of others, to the smallest knowledge of it afterwards.*[1]

I bring back my heroine to her home in solitude and disgrace   Northanger Abbey

She was accepted, her brothers were not necessarily unkind, but she appears to have been kept at arms length, certainly by James, Edward and Charles, and their wives, and largely disregarded by them, as they moved on with their lives and careers.

It appears as if the mind itself was tainted   Mansfield Park

When her first novels were published, Jane was very anxious about her brothers' reactions to her truth-telling.[2] But over the years, as demand for her work grew, their attitude towards her appeared to soften. Henry and Frank were the exceptions, she always had their loyalty, but the family maintained a united front to protect the secret of her involvement with D'Arcy Wentworth, and to erase the story from their history.

Her word had no weight — Persuasion

That attitude was passed to the next generation. Her nephew James Edward, son of her eldest brother James, read *Sense & Sensibility*, without any idea his aunt was the author. It tells something about a family disposed to ignore, overlook or disdain her. James Edward wrote to her:

> No words can express, my dear Aunt, my surprise
> Or make you conceive how I opened my eyes...
> When I heard for the very first time in my life
> That I have the honour to have a relation
> Whose works were dispersed through the whole of the nation.[3]

What do they do for her happiness, comfort, honour & dignity in the world — Mansfield Park

The silence her family maintained says much about how Jane was perceived and treated. She was in no doubt that *loss of virtue in a female is irretrievable – that one false step involves her in endless ruin.*[4]

Perhaps she found the disregard and censorship around her so suffocating, it strengthened her *interest in what people thought and said about each other and underlying meanings of what was said.*[5] Certainly she developed an uncanny ability to hear and describe nuances and unspoken meanings behind and within conversations.

Her father was a clergyman and he was not in the least addicted to locking up his daughters — Northanger Abbey

After Jane left Cork Street for *Wentworth Woodhouse*, in the weeks between September and Christmas 1789, it is likely she wrote home funny stories of Yorkshire and Scotland, with no mention of her elopement or future plans. *I owed it to my family and friends not to create in them a solicitude about me.*[6]

During her month alone in Clipstone Street, she was withdrawn, she did not write home. She stopped calling on Eliza, she had said nothing to her of D'Arcy's arrest and court appearances, and little of her own situation or state of mind.

The search for a lost daughter

In *Pride & Prejudice,* through the story of Lydia, Jane recorded how her father went to London to search for her, and did not find her. She felt deeply for the panic and anxiety she caused him, and for his own sense of guilt.

In the story, Lydia's aunt and uncle tell Elizabeth and her father what is happening with Lydia and Wickham. It was most likely Philadelphia Hancock, alerted by Eliza, who told George Austen of Jane's distress.

My father is going to London…instantly, to try to discover her. What he means to do, I am sure I know not; but his excessive distress will not allow him to pursue any measure in the best and safest way.

He meant, I believe…to go to Epsom, the place where they last changed horses, see the postilions, and try if any thing could be made out from them…he was in such a hurry to be gone, and his spirits so greatly discomposed, that I had difficulty in finding out even so much as this.

The deepest disgrace Pride & Prejudice

In the novel, Lydia's father returns home, without her, he *made no mention of the business that had taken him away*. When finally asked, *he replied, "Say nothing of that. Who would suffer but myself? It has been my own doing, and I ought to feel it."*

"*You must not be too severe upon yourself*"…

"*You may well warn me against such an evil. Human nature is so prone to fall into it! No… let me once in my life feel how much I have been to blame.*

Oh! my dear mother, you must be wrong in permitting an engagement between a daughter so young, a man so little known, to be carried on in so doubtful, so mysterious a manner! Sense & Sensibility

Jane contrasts the reactions of Lydia's mother and father, when she returns home. *Her mother stepped forwards, embraced her, and welcomed her with rapture.* Her father, *to whom they then turned, was not quite so cordial. His countenance rather gained in austerity; and he scarcely opened his lips.*

In the evening, soon after Mr. Bennet withdrew to the library, she saw Mr. Darcy rise also and follow him, and her agitation on seeing it was extreme. She did not fear her father's opposition Pride & Prejudice

Jane trusted her father would agree to formalise their Scottish marriage. On Christmas Eve 1789, D'Arcy told George Austen they planned to leave for New South Wales, where he was to work as a surgeon. He asked him to arrange a special licence to marry them at Steventon over Christmas. He asked his forgiveness for their precipitate action, and sought Rev Austen's blessing. *She did not fear her father's opposition, but he was going to be made unhappy; and that it should be through her means, that she his favourite child, should be distressing him by her choice, should be filling him with fears and regrets in disposing of her, was a wretched reflection, and she sat in misery till Mr. Darcy appeared again, when, looking at him, she was a little relieved by his smile.*

George Austen told Jane – *I have given him my consent. He is the kind of man, indeed, to whom I should never dare refuse any thing, which he condescended to ask. I now give it to you, if you are resolved on having him. But let me advise you to think better of it. I know your disposition...I know that you could be neither happy nor respectable unless you truly esteemed your husband – unless you looked up to him as a superior. Your lively talents would place you in the greatest danger in an unequal marriage. You could scarcely escape discredit and misery. My child, let me not have the grief if seeing you unable to respect your partner in life.*[7]

Unsoftened by one kind word or look on the part of her sister Persuasion

Cassandra had returned from Kintbury for Christmas, Jane recorded her father's happiness at having them home together, he *though very laconic in his expressions of pleasure, was really glad to see them; he had felt their importance in the family circle. The evening conversation, when they were all assembled, had lost much of its animation, and almost all its sense, by* their *absence.*[8]

Do not trust her with any secets of your own The Watsons

Cassandra was unhappy at the turn of events, that Jane was to marry so soon, to leave with D'Arcy for Botany Bay, an outpost at the end of the earth. Questioned by James, she told what she had seen of their courtship in London. *She could not be surprised at their attachment.*[9] Jane *was everything but prudent,*[10] she had an *unfortunate tendency of setting propriety at nought.*[11]

In the course of the Christmas week Mansfield Park

Jane had come home, it was Christmas, but nothing seemed as it should. In Portsmouth, the garrison church had been full of Christmas warmth, song and cheer. In Steventon, it was a Christmas full of whispers, anxiety and family tension. On Boxing Day, D'Arcy left for London to secure his employment in the Colony, and deal with the unfinished matters relating to their journey.

A most affectionate, indulgent father Emma

After George Austen completed his Christmas duties in the parish, he had time at last to sit down gently and privately with Jane. *Your marriage must have involved you in many certain troubles and disappointments.*[12]

He did not quiz her. Jane knew she could trust him. She told him something of her seven weeks and a day as D'Arcy's wife, and of the nearly forty dreadful days alone without him in London.

Jane told her father they returned from Scotland in October, and had taken lodgings under the name Wilson. She reassured him she had protected his name, that no one ever knew her real name.

An injured man had come to D'Arcy for help. He was in pain and bleeding, his wound was too deep, D'Arcy did not have the instruments he needed. He took him to hospital in a cab. Bow-street Runners came to the lodgings several times, other people had been, looking for D'Arcy.

She was alone; she was frightened, she did not want to say anything or cause more trouble. She gave her name as Weaver, another time as Taylor. The landlord had told them she was Mrs Wilson. She did not give her own name to the officers who came to their lodgings, nor to the magistrate at Bow Street. She had not spoken of Steventon or her family.

George recognised each name as she spoke them. She had not strayed far from her family. His cousin, Francis Motley Austen's wife was Elizabeth Wilson; they had a daughter, Jane, her own age. His half-brother William Hampson Walter's wife was Susannah Weaver; their son Weaver was a curate in Kent who had followed his lead, and took in pupils.

Miss Taylor was a family joke, one Frank told with great relish. On board Naval vessels, sailors were known to survive on *a diet of dry salt beef and maggoty biscuits, washed down with a sour white wine called* mistella*, known to the men as Miss Taylor.*[13]

Jane told him when the Bow Street magistrate, Nicholas Bond, asked her age, she replied truthfully, *I am not one and twenty.*[14] Mr Bond observed she seemed young, he had asked after her family. Jane replied that she came from Leigh, in Worcestershire, and saw nothing of her family at the present time.

Leigh was her mother's family name. Jane was always proud of the Leigh church, dedicated in 1100, to St Eadburga, a learned and wise daughter of a West-Saxon king, who practiced the art of poetry.

By the end of their conversation, Reverend Austen was ashen.

Family attachment & family honour Persuasion

James was down from Oxford, concerned at the news from home. Henry was covering for him, taking responsibility for the next two issues of *The Loiterer*, one was due out on Boxing Day. In the privacy of the rectory library, James Austen told his father what he had read in the newspapers about D'Arcy's arrest and trial, and all he knew of his history.

If you, my dear father, will not take the trouble of checking her exuberant spirits, and of teaching her that her present pursuits are not to be the business of her life, she will soon be beyond the reach of amendment.[15]

James was concerned about the impact on his reputation, his social circle, his future, that presently looked so rosy, and the rest of the family. Surely his father would not listen to Jane! How could she have been allowed to become entangled with such *a character of dangerous impetuosity?*¹⁶ He must not allow her to marry the most notorious highwayman in the kingdom!

I want to be married at home, & my brother will not consent to it. & I know my brother will let as few people be by at the ceremony as possible

Sir Charles Grandison

James was alarmed for his prospects, and for those of Edward and Henry. It was fortunate D'Arcy was to sail without delay to the other side of the world. It might prevent further humiliation and damage to their family's reputation. But Jane should not accompany him. He argued their futures would be irrevocably damaged if his father sanctioned her elopement and agreed to marry them. He had an urgent, sacred duty to protect the family reputation and good name.

A marriage which the whole of your family, far and near, must highly reprobate

Lady Susan

The next morning, as she was going down stairs, she was met by her father, who came out of his library with a letter in his hand.

"I was going to look for you; come into my room."

She followed him thither; and her curiosity to know what he had to tell her was heightened by the supposition of its being in some manner connected with the letter he held...

She followed her father to the fire place, and they both sat down. He then said,

*"I have received a letter this morning that has astonished me exceedingly. As it principally concerns yourself, you ought to know its contents.*¹⁷

It was a long and noisy letter; there were parts she particularly remembered.

The loss of a daughter and a disgrace never to be wiped off

Mansfield Park

I feel myself called upon by our relationship, and my situation in life, to condole with you on the grievous affliction you are now suffering...

The death of your daughter would have been a blessing in comparison...

I am inclined to think that her own disposition must be naturally bad, or she could not be guilty of such an enormity at so early an age...

This false step will be injurious to the fortunes of all the others; for who...will connect themselves with such a family.

*Let me advise you then... to throw off your unworthy child from your affection for ever, and leave her to reap the fruits of her own heinous offence.*¹⁸

I will change the subject & desire it may never again be mentioned; remember it is all forgot
Jack & Alice

George Austen told Jane gently, but very firmly, her clandestine marriage was not legal, she was under-age, he was responsible for her, he believed she had been grievously led astray. *In the very important concern of marriage especially, there is everything at stake; your own happiness, that of your parents, & the credit of your name.*[19]

He had agreed to marry them under a Special Licence, without the need for Banns to be read over three weeks, and he had agreed, reluctantly, to Jane sailing with D'Arcy from Portsmouth to Botany Bay. But events had rapidly altered his view, he had learned of D'Arcy's arrest, his notoriety, his earlier encounters with the law. He blamed himself for her predicament.

Jane could hear her father's great unhappiness and his determination. She could read in his voice, as he moved to withdraw his consent, the outrage and anger of her brother James.

There is nothing more to be said or do
Mansfield Park

Her own misgivings and uncertainties disappeared; the most honourable path for her was to step back, to relinquish everything she had so eagerly anticipated and desired.

She told her father they would not need a Special Licence, she was not asking him to legalise their Scottish marriage. That she did not intend to sail to Botany Bay with D'Arcy. Her respect and love for him prevailed on Jane to set her affair with D'Arcy aside, to deny the exaltation she had experienced, to give ground to his wishes, against her own desires.

Jane asked if she might use his desk, to write immediately to tell D'Arcy that she would not sail on the *Neptune*. She wrote the letter with as much tenderness as she had ever felt towards him, she felt, strangely, that she was sending him a gift, and her blessing.

Our first care has been to keep the matter secret
Sense & Sensibility

The events of the last weeks, her father said, would not be mentioned again, within or without the family. *I shall make no mention of what has passed...say nothing about it yourself.*[20] Such discussion or comment would serve only to destroy of her reputation. It would ruin not only her life, it would reverberate and wreak damage on the future prospects of her entire family, particularly her brothers, who were now entering the world.

When I yielded, I thought it was to Duty
Persuasion

In *Pride & Prejudice,* Jane emphasised her sense of duty towards her father

– You must not let your fancy run away with you. You have sense, and we all expect you to use it. Your father would depend on your resolution and good conduct... You must not disappoint your father.

My father's opinion of me does me the greatest honor; and I should be miserable to forfeit it.

Unaccountable, however, as the circumstances of his release might appear to the whole family   Sense & Sensibility

On 16 January 1790, the day before D'Arcy sailed, Henry Austen published a piece in *The Loiterer,* applauding *the world* for getting *rid of its superfluous inhabitants, both Poets & Pick-pockets Prudes & Prostitutes, in short all those who have too much cunning or too little money...shipped off with the very first cargo of Convicts to Botany Bay.*[21]

There are secrets in all families, you know   Emma

George did not discuss Jane's story with anyone else in the family. James knew something of it, and Cassandra. George asked for their word, and they gave it, they would never mention their sister's perilous youthful folly. But *in spite of his intended silence...it was all known at the parsonage.*[22]

George Austen was an experienced pastor, he understood it was his duty to guide his daughter back to a virtuous life. One of her last letters suggests he made a distinction for her, one lost to our generation, that while the power of original sin had disrupted and threatened to blacken her life, she had the independence to choose a moral path for herself:

She looked so pretty, it was quite a pleasure to see her, so young & so blooming & so innocent, as if she had never had a wicked Thought in her Life – which yet one has some reason to suppose she must have had, if we believe the Doctrine of Original Sin, or if we remember the events of her girlish days.[23]

In her fifteenth year, with *so feeling a heart, so sweet a temper, to be so easily persuaded by those she loved,* [24] Jane Austen agreed to *bury the tumult of her feelings under the restraint of society.*[25]

A blush on Jane's cheek gave it a meaning not otherwise ostensible   Emma

In 1795 and 1796, Jane Austen wrote two full length novels, *Elinor and Marianne,* that she later redrafted as *Sense & Sensibility,* and *First Impressions,* which she revised and renamed *Pride & Prejudice.*

Of all her novels, they resonate with a quality Virginia Woolf described as: *A sense of meaning withheld, a smile at something unseen, an atmosphere of perfect control and courtesy mixed with something satirical, which, were it not directed against things in general rather than against individuals,* *would be almost malicious.*²⁶

The meaning withheld, the thing unseen, was perhaps the story of Jane's own feelings, her suffering and the pride she took in her relationship with D'Arcy Wentworth. She identified herself as a Wentworth. Although their marriage had not been solemnised under English law, she was D'Arcy Wentworth's wife, one of his family. She drew on Wentworth family history and asserted her own place within it through her novels, recording and marking their connexions in subtle and purposeful ways.

The play of the critic   The History of England

Jane Austen's readers have long observed her *preoccupation with truth, and her selection of material only from among observed facts tested by personal experience.*²⁷ Her first independent editor noted her writing was *exceptionally and even surprisingly dependent on family and biographical truth as the basis of imaginary construction.*²⁸

Critics also noted the control exercised by the Austen family over her history: *the major biographies of her for more than one hundred years after her death in 1817 were written by family members, and biographies since then have relied largely on unpublished or obscurely published family manuscripts. Furthermore, the Austen family has been determined from the start to present its most famous member to the world as a figure of exemplary gentility and piety... The public's curiosity was satisfied, and yet the author's dignity was preserved.*²⁹

David Nokes is remembered for his skill to spot terrain missed by other biographers, and to use it to supply a psychological dimension of discomfort which his subjects concealed, while suggesting how their evasions left traces in their literary writings.³⁰ He said of Jane Austen, *there is a restless, reckless undercurrent of frustration in all her early sketches; a violent fantasizing energy, which uses the disguise of fiction to subvert the careful rules and reticences of polite rectory life.*³¹

Virginia Woolf agreed, *I prefer to present her not in the modest pose which her family determined for her, but rather, as she most frequently presented herself, as rebellious, satirical and wild.*³²

Jane Austen wrote about real people, real episodes, events and conflicts, that she disguised as fiction. Over two centuries, sensitive readers and critics have guessed they were dealing with true stories, but they lacked the key to unlock them. Her family kept her secrets closely guarded for generations, somehow preventing critics and historians from probing the key names and events she gave as clues in her novels. D'Arcy, after his few moments of celebrity, disappeared to the other side of the world and never spoke of his past.

A secret which was to be kept at all hazards   Emma

In *Pride and Prejudice,* Jane broke the silence around her relationship with D'Arcy, she named him, revealed his connection to Fitzwilliam, and included characters from his adventures on the King's Highway.

In her first two novels she included sketches of men who had accused D'Arcy with highway robbery – Alderman Curtis from his first arrest, John Hurst from his second, and John Pemberton Heywood from his third. Perhaps Jane was revealing the target of each hold-up, those D'Arcy *could not forget, who had lost his good opinion forever.*

William Curtis

D'Arcy was accused of robbing two coaches on Shooters Hill in January 1787, two men in the first coach, four in the second. Jane included a vignette of William Curtis in *Pride and Prejudice,* renaming him Sir William Lucas. *Sir William Lucas had been formerly in trade... where he had made a tolerable fortune and risen to the honour of knighthood by an address to the King during his mayoralty... his presentation at St. James's had made him courteous.*[33]

Invited to dine at Rosings, Sir William was not overwhelmed. *I am the less surprised...from the knowledge of what the manners of the great really are, which my situation in life has allowed me to acquire. About the Court, such instances of elegant breeding are not uncommon.* At dinner, he *did not say much. He was storing his memory with anecdotes and noble names.*

Mr & Mrs Hurst

D'Arcy was charged with robbing a coach on Hounslow Heath in December 1787. Jane included two of the passengers, Mr & Mrs Hurst, in *Pride & Prejudice* and, perhaps for her family's edification, used them to illustrate D'Arcy's dislike of gambling.

Mr Hurst is a gambler, Mr Darcy prefers not to play: *As for Mr Hurst, he was an indolent man, who lived only to eat, drink, and play at cards. He merely looked the gentleman... a man of more fashion than fortune.*

When tea was over, Mr. Hurst reminded his sister-in-law of the card-table – but in vain. She had obtained private intelligence that Mr. Darcy did not wish for cards; and Mr. Hurst soon found even his open petition rejected. She assured him that no one intended to play, and the silence of the whole party on the subject seemed to justify her. Mr. Hurst had therefore nothing to do but to stretch himself on one of the sophas and go to sleep.

John Pemberton Heywood

Jane watched John Pemberton Heywood give evidence against D'Arcy at the

Old Bailey in December 1789. She included him in a little vignette in *Sense & Sensibility*, discreetly altering his red Morocco leather tweezer case, reported stolen on Finchley Common, to an ornate toothpick case which he selects at Gray's in Sackville Street.

He was giving orders for a toothpick-case for himself, and till its size, shape, and ornaments were determined, all of which, after examining and debating for a quarter of an hour over every toothpick-case in the shop, were finally arranged by his own inventive fancy... a person and face, of strong, natural, sterling insignificance, though adorned in the first style of fashion.

The puppyism of his manner in deciding on all the different horrors of the different toothpick-cases　　　　　　　　　　　　　　　　　　Sense & Sensibility

The ivory, the gold, and the pearls, all received their appointment, and the gentleman having named the last day on which his existence could be continued without the possession of the toothpick-case, drew on his gloves with leisurely care, and... walked off with a happy air of real conceit and affected indifference.

Carrying on a negociation for the exchange of a few old-fashioned jewels
　　　　　　　　　　　　　　　　　　　　　　　　　　　　Sense & Sensibility

In *Sense & Sensibility* Elinor Dashwood goes to Gray's to sell second hand jewellery. *There was not a person at liberty to attend to her*, she is *obliged to wait*. She goes to a counter where there is only one gentleman, it *seems to promise the quickest succession. She is not without hopes of exciting his politeness to a quicker despatch*, but instead she has to watch him toy with an entire range of toothpick cases. *At last the affair was decided* and *she lost no time in bringing her business forward.*

Was Jane revealing another incident from Jane & D'Arcy's story? Was it Jane who waited, anxious and impatient, at Thomas Gray, Jeweller, of 42 Sackville Street, in 1789, to sell jewellery handed over on the King's highway?

You see what a collection I have, I do not offer them as new　　Mansfield Park

Years later, writing *Mansfield Park*, she appears to draw on the same incident. Did she place a *small trinklet box* before Thomas Gray, for him *to chuse from among several gold chains and necklaces*. The prospect causes Fanny Price to *start back at first with a look of horror.*

Endeavouring to appear indifferent where I have been most deeply interested
　　　　　　　　　　　　　　　　　　　　　　　　　　　　Sense & Sensibility

At the heart of both *Sense & Sensibility* and *Pride & Prejudice* are young women careful to never reveal their true feelings, not even to their closest family intimates. Even with her sister, Elinor Dashwood is discreet, *sorry for the warmth she had been betrayed into, in speaking of him.*

In a household where your mother sought to exploit your every chance encounter, to actively commit you to compromising situations, it was important to exercise discretion, to hide your true feelings.

In *Pride and Prejudice*, Darcy dissuades Bingley from his interest in Jane Bennet, for, after observing her closely he believes she does not care for him: *convinced from the evening's scrutiny, that though she received his attentions with pleasure, she did not invite them by any participation of sentiment.*

Gossips! Tiresome wretches! Emma

Discretion is an essential defence against the intrusions of gossip. Lydia in *Pride and Prejudice*, and Marianne in *Sense & Sensibility*, each fall in love with a dashing young man whose surname starts with *W*. Gossip about Lydia's elopement travels fast and wide, and Marianne's attraction to Willoughby is the subject of constant speculation: *By whom can you have heard it mentioned?" "By many – by some of whom you know nothing, by others with whom you are most intimate."*

When Marianne realises her affair with Willoughby is over, she tells her sister: *I cannot stay here long, I cannot stay to endure the questions and remarks of all these people – how am I to bear their pity?*

W's apology

Ann Lefroy invited Jane to visit Ashe Rectory as often as she wished, to spend time with the children, who loved her. On the last day of 1789, Jane walked over to Ashe, to be outdoors, to breathe the cold air, and leave behind the confusion of family questions and criticism.

After reading her letter, D'Arcy made a long, urgent ride from London to see her. Despite its finality and resignation, he still believed they could commence their life together. If she agreed, they would leave for Portsmouth, go out to their little cabin on board the *Neptune*, and make ready to sail to Botany Bay. At Steventon, he found Cassandra alone, and spoke with her.

In *Sense & Sensibility*, Willoughby comes to Cleveland to see Marianne, but she is desperately ill. He makes a passionate apology to her sister Elinor for his failing Marianne, for disrupting her life.

"Why did you call Mr Willoughby?" said Elinor reproachfully, "a note would have answered every purpose. Why was it necessary to call?"

"*It was necessary for my own pride... I could not bear to leave the country... I mean to offer some kind of explanation, some kind of apology, for the past...*

My fortune was never large, and I had always been expensive, always in the habit of associating with people of better income than myself... Her affection for me deserved better treatment... I have injured one, whose affection for me... and who's mind – Oh! How infinitely superior!

"Well sir" said her sister, *who, though pitying him, grew impatient for his departure,* "and is this all?"

A short pause of mutual thoughtfulness succeeded...

"Well let me make haste and be gone. Your sister is certainly better, certainly out of danger?"

"We are assured of it."

"Will you repeat to your sister, when she is recovered, what I have been telling you... Tell her of my misery..., and if you will that at this moment she is dearer to me than ever."

Willoughby's apology is the powerful emotional climax of *Sense & Sensibility*, filled with a sense of finality and loss.

I hoped to obtain your forgiveness, to lessen your ill opinion — Pride & Prejudice

D'Arcy rode from Steventon to the Ashe rectory. He found Jane there, in the drawing room, watching over little William Thomas, sickly and unwell. He *walked into the drawing-room at the cottage, where were only herself and the little invalid.* Jane was silent, depressed, ill with grief. She appeared thinner, taller, pale, withdrawn. *The surprise of finding himself almost alone with her deprived his manners of their usual composure. After calmly and politely saying,* "I hope the little boy is better," *he walked to the window to recollect himself, and feel how he ought to behave.*

Nothing but the strongest conviction of duty could induce me to wound my own feelings — Lady Susan

She was obliged to kneel down by the sofa, and remain there to satisfy her patient; and thus they continued a few minutes, when, to her very great satisfaction, she heard some other person crossing the little vestibule.

Another minute brought another addition. The younger boy, a remarkable stout, forward child, of two years old, having got the door opened for him by some one without, made his determined appearance among them, and went straight to the sofa to see what was going on, and put in his claim to anything good that might be giving away...

He began to fasten himself upon her, as she knelt, in such a way that, busy as she was about Charles, she could not shake him off. She spoke to him, ordered, entreated, and insisted in vain. Once she did contrive to push him away, but the boy had the greater pleasure in getting upon her back again directly.

"Walter," said she, "get down this moment. You are extremely troublesome. I am very angry with you."

In another moment, however, she found herself in the state of being released from him; some one was taking him from her, though he had bent down her head so much, that his little sturdy hands were unfastened from around her neck, and he was resolutely borne away, before she knew that Captain Wentworth had done it.[34]

Her sensations on the discovery made her perfectly speechless. She could not even thank him. She could only hang over little Charles, with most disordered feelings. His kindness in stepping forward to her relief, the manner, the silence in which it had passed, the little particulars of the circumstance, with the conviction soon forced on her by the noise he was studiously making with the child, that he meant to avoid hearing her thanks, and rather sought to testify that her conversation was the last of his wants, produced such a confusion of varying, but very painful agitation, as she could not recover from.[35]

He looked at her with a glow of regard...He took her hand; whether or not she had made the first motion, she could not say – she might, perhaps, have rather offered it – but he took her hand, pressed it, and certainly was on the point of carrying it to his lips – when...he suddenly let it go... the intention, however, was indubitable... It spoke such perfect amity – he left immediately afterwards – gone in a moment.[36] *He had left the country in consequence.*[37]

She was ashamed of herself, quite ashamed of being so nervous, so overcome... but so it was, and it required a long application of solitude and reflection to recover her.[38]

The belief of being prudent, and self-denying... was her chief consolation, under the misery of a parting, a final parting   Persuasion

D'Arcy left Ashe for Portsmouth, where the Second Fleet was gathering, making ready to sail. A quarter of a century later, Jane wrote, *a few months had seen the beginning and the end of her attachment. Her attachments and regrets had, for a long time, clouded every enjoyment of youth; and an early loss of bloom and spirits had been their lasting effect.*[39]

Chapter 12

To the most remote corner

The world is not their's, nor the world's law

DURING Jane Austen's lifetime, England extended its reach into the South Pacific. There it established a new colony, New South Wales, which included the eastern half of the present Australian mainland, the island of Van Diemen's Land or Tasmania, and many newly encountered islands of the South Pacific.[1] England's primary objective was to exclude other European powers, particularly the French.

It was short – merely to announce – but cheerful, exulting   Emma

When he opened Parliament in 1787, George III announced, *A plan has been formed by my direction, for the transporting of a number of convicts in order to remove the inconvenience which arose from the crowded state of the gaols in different parts of the Kingdom.*[2]

A pressing motive behind the decision was the overcrowding of the gaols and hulks – decommissioned ships used as floating prisons, moored on the Thames at Woolwich and Deptford, and in other ports, where the convicts were put to work as labourers.

The loss of the American Colonies had closed off an avenue to transport convicts out of England, and harsh sentencing had rapidly built up prisoner numbers, now in excess of a hundred thousand.

Allowing for the necessary preparations of settlements   Pride & Prejudice

Treasury advanced funds to send seven hundred and fifty convicts, two hundred marines and their families, animals, tools, seeds and two years supply of food to New South Wales. Two Royal Navy ships, six transports and three supply ships were fitted out and assembled at Portsmouth.

> *Let no-one think much of a trifling expense*
> *Who knows what may happen a hundred years hence*
> *The loss of America – what can repay?*
> *New colonies seek for in Botany Bay*[3]   WHITEHALL EVENING POST

In 1786, Captain Arthur Phillip was appointed Captain-General and Governor-in-Chief of the new colony.[4] His commission gave him sovereign naval power to secure the territory claimed by Great Britain, and directed him to establish a penal settlement at Botany Bay.[5]

He was not to transgress the East India Company control of trade between the Cape of Good Hope and Cape Horn.[6] *Every sort of intercourse between the intended settlement at Botany Bay, or any other place which may be hereafter established on the coast of New South Wales and its dependencies, and the settlements of our East India Company, as well as the coast of China, and the islands in that part of the world..should be prevented by every possible means.*[7]

Phillip's broad experience made him uniquely qualified; educated by the Navy, fluent in German, French, Dutch, Portuguese and Spanish, with experience as an able seaman whaling in the Arctic, an officer in the blockade of Havana, and active service in the West Indies during the Seven Years War with France. While assigned as a captain commanding a Portuguese man-of-war, he transported convicts from Lisbon to Brazil and charted the coasts of South America. He had contributed to naval intelligence, had been deployed in France as a spy, and was trusted by both the Admiralty and Home Office.

Phillips first brought the news – well so much the better!   Pride & Prejudice

After prolonged and careful preparation, Phillip sailed from Portsmouth on 13 May 1787, with the eleven ships of the First Fleet. On 20 January 1788, the fleet sailed into Botany Bay. They found themselves in the heat of summer, surrounded by waterless sand dunes and exposed to dangerous winds.

Most favoured by nature & promising to be the most chosen by man   Sanditon

Phillip left the fleet at anchor there on 23 January. He set out by longboat with Captain Hunter and other officers, to explore an inlet to the north that Cook had named Port Jackson. There they found an *eligible Situation for the Colony, & being without exception the finest Harbour in the World.*[8]

After sleeping the night on the beach at Camp Cove, Phillip and his men found a sheltered bay with *the best spring of water and in which..ships can anchor so close to the shore that at a very small expense quays may be made at which the largest ships may unload.* He *honoured* the cove *with the name of Sydney.*⁹

On the same day, Lord Sydney entertained fourteen guests at his home in Grosvenor Square, including Prime Minister William Pitt and the Duke of York.¹⁰

Phillip returned to Botany Bay, and led the fleet north, to the grandeur and safety of Port Jackson. At dawn in Sydney Cove, on 26 January 1788, he raised the British colours.

*The air, the sky, the land, are objects entirely different from all that a Briton has been accustomed to see before..the easy liberal mind will be here filled with astonishment.*¹¹

Six months later, writing a despatch to Lord Sydney from his tent, one shoulder wounded by an Aboriginal spear, he reported thunderstorms, nauseous flies, ants that bit severely, blunted tools, thieving, whoring, drinking and gambling, depravity and wickedness.¹² He predicted - *this country will prove the most valuable acquisition Great Britain ever made.*¹³

Their remoteness & unpunctuality Mansfield Park

Phillip chided the Home Office, *no country offers less assistance to the first settlers than this does; nor do I think any country could be more disadvantageously placed with respect to support from the mother country, on which for a few years we must entirely depend.*¹⁴

The strongest conviction of duty Lady Susan

Phillip's great contribution to the new colony lay in his humane respect and understanding, for the sailors and Marines, for the convicts, whom he believed to be capable and deserving of rehabilitation, and for the Indigenous people whom he was duty-bound to protect.

He was concerned to prevent the abuse of Indigenous women and determined women convicts not be *abused and insulted by the ship's company, which is said to have been the case too often when they were sent to America.* He supposed convicts would marry, and *this should be encouraged.*¹⁵

Phillip insisted no slaves or system of slavery be introduced in the new colony, he had witnessed the inhumanity of slavery in the Americas.¹⁶ In 1775, carrying Portuguese convicts from Rio de Janeiro to Colonia do Sacramento in the Brazils, scurvy depleted his crew. He called on the convicts to assist him, and he acknowledged their contribution by obtaining pardons and grants of land for them in Brazil. His sense of fairness and understanding of his fellow man underpinned his approach in the penal settlement, and it laid the groundwork for the successful future of the Colony.

On half-pay between wars, Phillip farmed land at Lyndhurst in Hampshire, he knew the requirements for successful food production. In 1788, he asked for farmers, carpenters, masons and bricklayers be sent to the Colony, and fewer unskilled convicts, *numbers of those now here are a burthen and incapable of any kind of hard labour.* The Marines were reluctant to supervise the convicts who could work – *unfortunately, we have no proper people to keep those to their labour who are capable of being made useful.*[17]

By rigour and resolution — Emma

The settlement grew up around Sydney Cove, on sandy coastal soil, where all attempts to grow food failed. By October 1788, with supplies running down, Phillip sent Captain Hunter to Cape Town on the *Sirius*, to purchase provisions. She sailed eastwards, via New Zealand, Cape Horn, South Georgia Island, and across the Atlantic, carrying Phillip's despatches to Lord Sydney to be forwarded from the Cape, outlining the Colony's predicament.

In mid-January 1790, Captain Watkin Tench, an officer of the Marines, wrote: *we have now been two years in the country and thirty-two months from England, in which long period no supplies, except what had been procured at the Cape of Good Hope by the Sirius, had reached us. From intelligence of our friends and connexions we had entirely been cut off, no communication whatever having passed with our native country since 13 May 1787, the day of our departure from Portsmouth. Famine besides was approaching with gigantic strides, and gloom and dejection overspread every countenance.*[18]

Such scarecrows as the streets were full of — Persuasion

On 11 April 1790, Phillip reported to Lord Sydney: *the settlement had been at two thirds of the established rations from 1st of November, and it was now reduced to less than half a ration; consequently little labour could be expected from the convicts, and they are only employed for the public in the mornings, leaving the afternoons to attend to their gardens.*[19]

The *Neptune* entered Sydney Cove eleven weeks later, on 28 June 1790, two and a half years after the First Fleet. A ship of despair, she landed apparitions of death and depravity and cast a gloom of horror over the settlement.

A second fleet

The Second Fleet was no voyage of discovery, its objective was to transport convicts cheaply. The Navy Board contracted three of the ships from Camden, Calvert & King, the largest slave trading firm in London, to transport one thousand convicts, and paid £17.7.6 for each convict who embarked, it made no difference whether they were landed in New South Wales or not.

Some of them did decide on going in quest of tea Persuasion

Eyeing further profits, Camden, Calvert & King filled the holds of their three vessels, *Neptune, Scarborough* and *Surprize,* with stores, timber and saleable goods. They followed the lead of their patron William Curtis, and the *Lady Penrhyn,* and made arrangements with the East India Company for their ships to return to England filled with tea from China.

During the few days he spent aboard the *Charlotte,* prior to the departure of the First Fleet, D'Arcy had admired the work of the surgeons on the transports, their efforts to prevent infection and disease, and to improve the diet and health of the convicts. At Tenerife, Phillip provided for their *"present and future wellbeing, giving the marines and convicts one pound of fresh beef per day, with rice, wine and whatever vegetables and fruit were available."* Three weeks into their journey they were *"not so sickly as when they sailed",* and were in *good health & Spirits.* [20]

Neptune, Scarborough and *Surprize,* were "wet" ships, designed to carry slaves from West Africa to the Caribbean in dark prison areas below, awash with seawater and seepage. Transport of slaves across the Middle Passage to the Americas, could take five to twelve weeks, depending on the weather.

Alexander Falconbridge, a surgeon on slave ships to America, wrote in 1788: *The men negroes, on being brought aboard the ship, are immediately fastened together, two by two by handcuffs on their wrists, and by iron riveted on their legs. They are then sent down between the decks... Neither will the height between the decks, unless directly under the grating, permit them the indulgence of an erect posture.*[21]

One should be a brute not to feel for the distress they are in Mansfield Park

The voyage of the Second Fleet took six months. On the *Neptune,* women prisoners and children were allowed on deck, the men were starved and shackled below deck for the entire journey. *The irons used upon these unhappy Wretches were barbarous. The Contractors had been in the Guinea trade, and had put on board, the same Shackles used by them in that Trade; which are made with a short Bolt... not more than three Quarters of a Foot in length, so that they could not extend either Leg from the other, more than an Inch or two at most. Thus fetter'd it was impossible for them to move, but at the risque of both their Legs being broken.*[22]

D'Arcy was horrified at the abysmal situation of the convicts. He was powerless to challenge the inhumanity of Captain Donald Traill, to question the Naval Agent John Shapcote, or the ship's master surgeon, William Gray.

He was a paying passenger on the *Neptune,* with no status as a surgeon, and no certainty of what awaited him in New South Wales. The day before he sailed, Thomas Hill wrote to say Evan Nepean had written to Governor Phillip, to have a position waiting for D'Arcy on his arrival in the Colony. It is unlikely Phillip received the instruction.

So melancholy a reverse   _{Lady Susan}

D'Arcy spent twenty-three weeks on board the *Neptune*. He had been a month in prison and had been bundled out of England. He had been parted from Jane, he felt a great regret for the suffering he caused to her. Every day on board he watched time and distance between them increasing. For D'Arcy the horror of the voyage was a shattering and life changing experience.

He was happy to say he had accepted a commission in their corps   _{Pride & Prejudice}

The Second Fleet carried members of a newly formed New South Wales Corps, the 102nd Regiment, under the command of Captain Nicholas Nepean, sent to relieve the Marines of the First Fleet.

A permanent posting to the remote colony was an unpopular deployment, the Corps had attracted officers on half-pay, with few prospects elsewhere, soldiers paroled from military prisons, troublemakers, all hoping for a better future in the new colony.

One officer, Lieutenant John Macarthur, had successfully challenged Camden, Calvert & King. He was the son of a mercer and linen draper in Plymouth, after serving in the American War of Independence he retired on half-pay to Devon, waiting his chance to return to full pay. A skilful manipulator, he emerged as violent, irascible and an energetic agitator.

Whoever suffered inconvenience, she should suffer none   _{Persuasion}

Macarthur was the only officer accompanied by his family. His wife Elizabeth was pregnant and they had a baby son, Edward, and a maid with them. From the time they boarded the *Neptune* in Plymouth, Macarthur complained about their accommodation, to his superior, Captain Nepean, and to the captain of the *Neptune*, Thomas Gilbert.

Haughty & quarrelsome   _{Kitty, or the Bower}

He told Gilbert *it was impossible to live in his cabbin owing to the stench of the buckets belonging to the convict women of a morning.*[23] Enraged by Gilbert's response, he challenged him to a duel on Plymouth Dock. Both men fired their pistols and both missed.

A message to Mr Harris, & an order for post-horses directly   _{Sense & Sensibility}

John Harris had enlisted in the New South Wales Corps after ten years as a naval surgeon. He witnessed their argument and acted as Macarthur's second in the duel. He gave his view of events: *I sustain'd much scurrility and abuse from Captain Gilbert, which I did not think proper to reply to at that time. As the lieut's were rather illiberal in some conclusions, I thought proper to point out to them the difference between an Army and a Navy mate, with some of my ideas on the subject.*[24]

Captain Nepean sent John Harris to Bath to report the incident to his elder brother, Evan Nepean, Under Secretary for the Navy. From there Harris went to London where he called at Clipstone Street. He accompanied Jane to the Old Bailey, joining a crowd of celebrities at D'Arcy's trial. Later, at Portsmouth, he saw Jane and D'Arcy together at the Crown Inn. He was transferred from the *Neptune*, and sailed to Colony on the *Surprize*.

Hardships which fall to every sailor's share Mansfield Park

Following Evan Nepean's intervention, Camden, Calvert & King removed Captain Gilbert from the *Neptune*, even though he had invaluable experience, as captain of the *Charlotte* in the First Fleet.

He was replaced with Donald Traill, an experienced ships master, hardened by years in the slave trade. The change brought no relief to those on board the *Neptune*. Elizabeth Macarthur found the situation far worse, Traill's *character was of a very much blacker dye.*[25]

Such an office of high responsibility Mansfield Park

Evan Nepean was aware of the conditions on the slave ships, that the convicts were at great risk of sickness, debilitation and death. He instructed naval agent John Shapcote before the fleet sailed, to *examine minutely into the manner of confining the convicts, as it has been represented that they are ironed in such a manner as must ultimately tend to their destruction.*[26]

He drafted a letter from William Grenville, Secretary of State, instructing Phillip to ensure convicts on the Second Fleet disembarked as early as possible, *as from the length of passage from hence and the nature of their food, there is every reason to expect that many of them will be reduced to so debilitated a state that immediate relief will be found expedient.*[27]

Tenacious of his Dignity, & jealous of his rights, forever quarrelling concerning the respect & parade he exacted Kitty, or the Bower

Camden, Calvert & King's three ships sailed on 19 January 1790, travelling separately from other ships of the Second Fleet. At sea, Macarthur's complaints continued, now directed to Captain Traill.

He reported cheating in the allocation of meat to the soldier's mess, he was concerned about the limited water rations, he deplored his accommodation in half the great stern cabin, and wanted lumber and boxes that were blocking the passageways moved. The other half of the great stern cabin had been intended for Captain Nepean, but had been given over to women convicts.

Mrs Macarthur described her ordeal: *No language can express – no imagination can conceive- the misery I experienced. Approaching near the Equator, where the heat of the situation is almost insupportable; assailed with noisome stenches that even in the cold of an English winter hourly effusions of oil of tar in my cabin could not dispel; two sides of it surrounded with wretches whose dreadful imprecations ever rang in my distracted ears; a sickly infant requiring constant medical care; my spirits failing; my health forsaking me.*[28]

Captain Nepean, annoyed by Macarthur's belligerence and increasing tensions with Captain Traill, agreed that as no other suitable accommodation could be found on the *Neptune*, the Macarthur family could be moved to another vessel. On 19 February, mid-ocean, with his wife and son, their maid and baggage, Macarthur was taken off and rowed across to the *Scarborough*.

"The gentlemen and ladies at this table look as if they wondered why we came here – we seem to be forcing ourselves into their party".
"Aye, so we do. That is very disagreeable.
Northanger Abbey

D'Arcy's cabin was located on an upper deck, with those of Captain Traill and his wife, Nepean and Shapcote. He dined with them but otherwise kept to himself. Mrs Macarthur's diary makes no mention of him. She noted *Mrs Trail was on board with her husband, and Mr Shapcote, the agent for the fleet, was also in our ship; but they all lived together, and Capt. Nepean with them, we seldom benefitted from their society.*[29]

Her dislike of Mr Darcy, and her resolution to be civil to him only
Pride & Prejudice

It is inconceivable Elizabeth Macarthur did not meet D'Arcy on the *Neptune*. Airing her grievances to him, she may well have noted an *air of distant civility*,[30] *manners, though well bred...not inviting.*[31] Perhaps she was *offended, probably by the little encouragement which her proposals of intimacy met with, she drew back in her turn and gradually became much more cold and distant... The ill-will which it produced was necessarily increasing.*[32]

D'Arcy certainly took John Macarthur's measure on the *Neptune*, belligerent, *untamed, unabashed, noisy and fearless*.[33] The judgements each made of the other, they would hold for the rest of their lives. At times they would find themselves adversaries, at other times colleagues, and each would have a profound impact on the Colony. They and their sons would influence its political evolution and its path to independence over the next half century.

The Cape of Good Hope Letters

The *Neptune* crossed the equator on 25 March 1790. In sight of the Cape she *met so violent a Tempest, which continued for six and thirty hours*.[34] On 14 April, she anchored at False Bay, twenty miles from Cape Town, to take on fresh water and supplies. The wreckage of the *Guardian*, a transport of the Second Fleet, lay strewn along the beach.

You must build me an elegant Greenhouse & stock it with plants The Three Sisters

The *Guardian* left Spithead in September 1789 and arrived in Cape Town in November. She had a special plant cabin on the quarterdeck, designed by Joseph Banks, with ninety-three pots of fruits, herbs and vegetables for cultivation in the colony, and she carried convicts with agricultural skills.

Banks had sailed with James Cook on the *Endeavour*, and part funded its voyage of exploration and discovery. On his return he lobbied successfully for a British settlement in New South Wales, and over the following decades was a patron and a valuable source of information and influence for officials and settlers going out to the Colony or returning home.

At the Cape, the *Guardian*'s captain, Edward Riou, learnt the *Sirius* had called there for urgent food supplies for the Colony. Seeing an opportunity, he took extra livestock on board: cattle, horses, sheep, goats, rabbits and poultry. He steered the *Guardian* south to catch the Roaring Forties; sighting icebergs, he realised he was dangerously close to the Antarctic.

Setting in to freeze Emma

> The Island of Ice was first seen on the 23rd of Dec. 12 days after the Guardian sailed from the Cape of Good Hope, on her way to New South Wales, the weather was extremely foggy, and the Island was not very distant when first beheld. Lieutenant Riou gave directions to stand towards it, in order to collect lumps of ice to supply the ship with water. This proceeding was judged highly expedient, as the daily demand of water was prodigious, owing to the great quantity of cattle on board: as the ship approached the Island, the boats were hoisted out and manned, and several lumps collected. During this time the ship lay to, and on the supply of water being brought on board she attempted to stand away. Very little apprehension was at this time entertained of her safety, although the monstrous bulk of the Island occasioned an unfavourable current, and, in some measure gave a partial direction to the wind.
>
> On a sudden the base of the Island, which projected under water, considerably beyond the limits of the visible part, struck the bow of the ship; she instantly

swung round, and her head cleared, but her stern coming on the shoal, struck repeatedly, and the sea being very heavy, her rudder broke away, and all her works abast were shivered. The ship in this situation became in a degree embayed, under a terrific bulk of ice; the height was twice that of the mainmast of a ship of the line. The prominent head of ice was every moment expected to break away, and overwhelm the ship. At length after every practicable exertion, she was got off the shoal, and the ice floated past her.

It was soon perceived that she had six feet of water in her hold, and it was increasing very fast: the hands were set to the pumps, and to find out the leaks. They continued labouring incessantly all the 24th, although on the 23rd not one of them had the least rest. The water increased in a moment to ten feet; and the ship being discovered to be strained in all her works, and the sea running high, every endeavour to check the progress of a particular leak proved ineffectual. An immediate project was fixed on to lighten the ship, and the cows, horses, sheep, and all the other live stock, for the colony, were, with their fodder committed to the deep, to perish!

In this hopeless state the ship continued for some days, without a rudder, and wholly unmanageable: but the application to reduce the water in her hold was assumed, whenever the weary crew felt the return the strength and power: and thus was the Guardian kept afloat, till the Dutch packet boat from the Spice Islands and Batavia, providentially steering a high southerly latitude, fell in with her, and affording aid of men and materials, enabled her to make good her way back to the Cape of Good Hope.[35]   PUBLIC ADVERTISER

Assisted by the Dutch vessel, the *Guardian* limped into False Bay, her men came ashore in rags, with long beards, filthy dirty. They set about repairing her, rebuilding sections smashed by the iceberg. Two days before the *Neptune* arrived in False Bay she was torn from her moorings in a violent storm, run aground on the beach and broken up under the fierce surf. Her convicts and their five superintendents were transferred to the *Neptune* and the *Surprize*.

The agonising pain of Doubt and Suspence weighed down his Spirits. Agitated by Greif, Apprehension and Shame he wrote the following letter. You will perhaps unjustly accuse me of Neglect and Forgetfulness   Evelyn

D'Arcy went ashore, the great mountainous landscape looming above him. Native people walked erect to the landing point, carrying fresh fruit, vegetables, on their heads, to replenish the *Neptune* and her sister ships.

The township, controlled by the Dutch East India Company, had a *Propensity to Avarice; their Governors are Merchants, and monopolise the whole Stock of the adjacent Country, and will not supply the Shipping but at an advance of five or six Hundred per cent.*[36]

D'Arcy carried a letter for Jane, and he walked the town, looking for an officer bound for England, one he could trust to carry it. He felt the uncertainty, the impossibility of a few scraps of paper with his markings on them, finding a way back to her. It seemed impossible she would ever hear his voice, from so far away, so removed from her.

He found an officer off the *Guardian*, returning home on the first berth available, who agreed to take the letter, who assured him he would frank and post it, as soon as he landed.

He told me at parting that he should soon write   Emma

It was a long well-written letter, giving the particulars of his journey and of his feelings, expressing all the affection, gratitude and respect which was natural and honourable, and describing every thing exterior and local that could be supposed attractive, with spirit and precision.[37] Jane did not receive it.

They had been all solitary, helpless & forlorn alike; and now the arrival of the others only established them in wretchedness   Mansfield Park

At the Cape, D'Arcy compared notes with John Harris, the treatment and conditions of the convicts uppermost in his mind. D'Arcy believed that scurvy, evident on board the *Neptune*, would become more prevalent, just as it was for slaves on the Middle Passage. It would only be a matter of time after leaving the Cape before the flux, starvation and scurvy set in. Each day on the slave ships, two or three died, and *were dumped overboard to the sharks which hung about the trade ships*.[38]

For the convicts, *inactivity at sea is a sure Bane, as it invites the Scurvy, equal to, if not more than Salt provisions; although the allowance from the Government is ample; Even when attacked by Disease their situations were not alter'd, neither had they any Comforts administer'd.*[39]

Deep in hardened villainy   Sense & Sensibility

After a fortnight at the Cape, on 29th of April, the three vessels set sail. The next two months, as they made their way east, proved the most horrific.

William Hill, Captain of the Marines on the *Surprize*, wrote of *the villainy, oppression and shameful Peculation of the masters of the Transports. The Bark I was on board of, was unfit from her make & size, to be sent to so great a Distance; if it blew but a trifling Gale, she was Lost in the Waters; of which she shipped so much, that from the Cape, the unhappy Wretches, the Convicts, were considerably above their waists in Water... in this situation they were obliged, for the safety of the Ship to be pen'd down.*[40]

Unspeakably welcome Mansfield Park

On 26 June 1790, the *Surprize* anchored in Sydney Cove. Two days later the *Neptune* and *Scarborough* joined her. The Fleet had left Portsmouth in winter, and arrived into another winter in Port Jackson. The sun was shining but it was cold and blustery. The Colony was short of food, the entire settlement, even the Governor, was on reduced rations.

Convicts crowded the shore to welcome the ships. The few clothes they had were thread-bare, they had no shoes, some were near naked. Clothing for women convicts had been left behind in England by the First Fleet. Everyone expected the Second Fleet would bring replenishments, but they saw emerging from the ships the appalling remnants of their human cargo.

Oh, if you had but seen the shocking sight of the poor creatures that came out of the three ships it would make your heart bleed; they were almost dead, very few could stand, and they were obliged to sling them as you would goods, and hoist them out of the ships, they were so feeble; and died ten or twelve a day.[41]

Misery, Ill-health or Vice Evelyn

The Chaplain, Richard Johnson, boarded the *Surprize* and went down amongst the prisoners. He saw numbers lying naked or half-clad, in their own nastiness, without bed or bedding, unable to turn or help themselves. He did not attempt to visit the *Neptune,* still more wretched and intolerable.

As the vessels came up the harbour, bodies of dead convicts had been dumped overboard. Some had died after the harbour had been reached; their bodies were thrown into the sea and cast up naked on the rocks; the landing was truly affecting and shocking; great numbers were not able to walk, nor move hand or foot. Such were slung over the ships side in the same manner as they would sling a cask...; upon being brought into the open air, some fainted; some died upon the deck, and others in the boat before they reached land. When they came on shore, many were not able to walk, to stand, or to stir themselves in the least. Hence some were led by others, some creeped upon their hands and knees, and some were carried on the backs of others.

Ashore the hospital accommodation was insufficient; and a great number of tents, in all ninety or a hundred, were pitched; in each of these there were about four sick people; here they had nothing to lay in a most deplorable situation; at first they had nothing to lay upon but the damp ground, many (having) scarcely a rag to cover them; blankets were issued, one to every four, but the strongest in each case took the blanket... The number of casualties occurring on the Neptune... arose from the conditions in which the convicts were compelled to live. They sat for days up to the middle in water, chained hand and leg and almost starved. For days, bodies washed up on the beaches around Sydney Cove, bloodless hands still fettered.⁴²

Human flesh! You quite shock me Emma

William Hill wrote to William Wilberforce in June 1790: *The slave trade is merciful compared with what I have seen on this fleet, in that it is in the interest of the masters to preserve the health and lives of their captives, they having a joint benefit with the owners; in this, the more they can withhold from the unhappy wretches the more provisions they have to dispose of at a foreign market, and the earlier in the voyage they die the longer they can draw the deceased's allowance to themselves... My feelings never have been so wounded as on this voyage, so much so, that I shall never recover my accustomed vivacity and spirits; and had I been em-powered, it would have been the most grateful task of my life to have prevented so many of my fellow creatures so much misery and death.*⁴³

Living or Dead Persuasion

One hundred and forty-seven men and eleven women died on the *Neptune*. The press in London commented on the death toll: the owners farm the business to the Master of the ship, and therefore the more that die on the passage, the greater his gains...as the matter now stands, the less of his cargo the Captain brings into port, the more profit he makes.⁴⁴ The Times

On the First Fleet, twenty three out of seven hundred and fifty nine convicts died during the eight month journey, a mortality rate of three percent. One thousand and six convicts sailed on the Second Fleet. Two hundred and sixty seven died during the voyage, another one hundred and seventeen within six months of their arrival in Sydney, raising the number of dead to three hundred and eighty four, a mortality rate over thirty eight percent. It became known in the Colony as the *Death Fleet*.

The Slave Carriers

After arriving in Sydney Cove, Donald Traill and his wife set up a stall to sell food from rations denied the convicts, and clothes and possessions taken from the dead. They charged exorbitant prices, and although regarded as pariahs, attracted many customers in need of food and clothing.

Traill was a slave trader, he did not recognise slaves as fellow humans, he saw convicts as no more deserving, and treated them no better. In England public disquiet grew over the fate of convicts in his charge. When the *Neptune* returned to London from China in 1791, several of the crew gave depositions at the Guildhall, before Alderman Richard Clark.

Murder & every thing, of the kind   Northanger Abbey

Thomas Evans, Attorney and a member of the Middle Temple, gathered evidence and lobbied for Captain Traill and his Chief Mate William Ellerington to be prosecuted. He published and circulated handbills with details of the statements made by witnesses. Finally he instituted his own private prosecution against them for murder on the *Neptune* of an un-named convict.

Evans' prosecution was taken over and conducted by the Admiralty Court. The trial lasted three hours. Admiral Nelson travelled to London to defend Traill. During the American War of Independence, Traill served with him on the *Albemarle*, Nelson said of him: *He is the best Master I ever saw since I went to sea.*[45]

Traill and Ellerington were acquitted,[46] and Judge Ashurst and Baron Hotham ordered *Thomas Evans, the Attorney who was the occasion of these trials, be struck off the Roll.*[47]

It has been so many years my province to give advice   Emma

A fortnight later, *Thomas Erskine moved in the Court of the Kings Bench for a rule to show cause why a criminal information should not be filed against Mr Evans, Attorney at Law, in consequence of the acquittal of the Captain and First Mate of the Neptune.* Mr Evans had *published handbills containing the depositions of different witnesses, with an intent to excite the resentment and indignation of the public and prejudice the minds of the jury.*[48]

Donald Traill returned to naval service in 1792, and from 1795 to 1798 was master-attendant in Simon's Town, near Cape Town. He collected fees and taxes, and entered a slave trading partnership. In 1799, he was appointed acting-master of *HMS Temeraire.*[49] He returned to England in 1801 with a fortune of £60,000, bought twenty-eight houses in London, and an estate in Kent, amongst fellow ship owners and merchants.

Kent, the maritime county servicing London, was important to the Navy, and to mercantile and shipping interests. Its long seaboard passed through Deptford, Greenwich, Woolwich and Gravesend, onto the Thanet and around to Deal and Dover. Kent-owned ships carried over seven hundred and seventeen thousand slaves to America; and most of the convicts to Australia.

In a time of heightened anxiety in England at the radicalisation and increasing violence in France, Camden, Calvert & King avoided prosecution.

Everybody's heart is open, you know when they have recently escaped from severe pain   Persuasion

When D'Arcy came on board the *Neptune* he was assigned a servant from the women convicts. Her name was Catherine Crowley.

Being always with her…and his feelings exactly in that favourable state which a recent disappointment gives   Mansfield Park

She soon became his mistress, a relationship which began at a time of his rejection, and of fear, desperation and despair for both of them.

Their arrival in Sydney was a joyless and sobering occasion. They went ashore separately. Catherine was escorted with the other women convicts into overcrowded tents.

D'Arcy, relieved to be on land, saw despair all around him. The arrival of the ships, with sick, hungry convicts, with more military and their families, was creating further pressure on the scarce rations. The colonists were hungry and demoralised, apprehensive of the Aboriginals, thwarted by the barren soil and impossibly hard timber.

Every neighbourhood should have a great lady   Sanditon

Some, like Elizabeth Macarthur, disembarked oblivious to the desperation. She came ashore, escorted off the *Scarborough,* overjoyed to be on land, rid of the horrors of the convict transports.

She had endured extremes of discomfort, the birth of a daughter who died within an hour; constant worry about her sickly son, Edward; her maid ill and miserable much of the voyage; and the sudden collapse and near death of her husband. She was led to a tranquil, rough, wattle and daub hut built for officers who had left for Norfolk Island.

On the *Scarborough,* the Macarthurs shared a cabin with Lieutenant Edward Abbott, from Montreal. The captain, John Marshall did all he could to make their voyage comfortable. The *Scarborough* was one of the First Fleet, and Marshall had spent four months in Sydney Cove. He charmed Elizabeth with cheerful stories about the new settlement.

I have once in my life been fool enough to travel I don't know how many hundred miles…Deuce take me if ever I am so foolish again   Love & Freindship

Mrs Macarthur was determined to see her new surroundings in the most favourable light. *Beyond a certain distance round the Colony,* she observed, *there is nothing but native paths.*[50] She would see beauty in this unfamiliar, strange rural wilderness; in the coves and streams, the gnarled trees and unfamiliar plants, the hopping animals, even the birds that laughed at her. She would never attempt the return voyage.

Those attractive powers for which she is celebrated   Lady Susan

John Macarthur was one of the first officers to bring his wife to the new colony, and she had a unique status. He encouraged her to develop the friendships with other officers, to advance his ambitions in the Regiment. Elizabeth welcomed them to the house, it became their focal point.

Surgeon Worgan enjoyed teaching her to play the Broadwood piano he brought out on the *Sirius*.[51] Lieutenant Dawes introduced her to astronomy and engaged her with his exploration of Aboriginal culture. On her walks, she called on Captain Tench and Mr Dawes.[52] She had a formidable presence, and all the officers, including Captain Nepean, went out of their way to please her.

She wrote home: *This country possesses numerous advantages to persons holding appointments under government;*[53] and she voiced her *very reasonable expectation of reaping the most material advantages.*

Many officers and soldiers found partners among the convict women, for their companionship and their happiness. Others, like John Harris, took a more pessimistic view. To Harris, the Colony was *the most miserable place I ever beheld, whoever gave a flattering account could not be an honest man, or regard the truth.*[54]

To be waiting so long in inaction, and waiting only for evil, had been dreadful Persuasion

On shore, D'Arcy could be useful. John White, the Chief Surgeon, remembered him from the *Charlotte*, and was glad to have his assistance. Convict orderlies erected a hundred tents in front of the hospital to house the newly arrived sick and the dying. They carried them up from the shore and placed them four to a tent, sharing a single blanket against the cold wind.

Glad to be thought of some use, glad to have anything marked out as a duty Persuasion

D'Arcy assisted the surgeons to examine the convicts as they were brought ashore, assessing their condition and their prospects. It was a grave task, many men were in their last hours of life. All of them were emaciated, with symptoms of scurvy, many had dysentery, many were feverish. The grim work went on methodically, calmly, for several days.

The frequent sound of the pestle & mortar Letters

There were limited antiscorbutics available to treat the scurvy. The surgeons deployed convicts to collect a quantity of a strange, bitter fruit and other native plants to give some relief. D'Arcy learnt to identify them, and helped to amalgamate and prepare them into *cordials, restoratives.*[55]

There is a Hospital & capital Surgeons Letters

Aided by a book of instructions, he helped his colleagues to assemble and erect the portable, prefabricated hospital unloaded from the *Surprize*. Its panels had been prepared at St Georges Fields, by architect Jeffry Wyatt. *It was instantly filled, the sick list stood at 488 persons.*[56]

D'Arcy spent his first five weeks in the Colony in *honest toil,*[57] busy in the crowded sick tents and the small hospital above Sydney Cove. He felt positive, stronger, convinced he had begun a new life.

His voyage on the *Neptune* had changed him irrevocably, he was determined to redeem himself. He wanted to return to England, to be accepted by Jane, by his family, and by Fitzwilliam. He wanted their company and their trust again.

Jane may well have advised him *to deplore the pride, the folly, the madness of resentment* that led him into trouble, to *distinguish between the steadiness of Principle and the Obstinacy of self-will.*[58] D'Arcy would find his own path, and he was gaining in confidence to do so.

When you had once made a beginning — Pride & Prejudice

For Governor Phillip, the arrival of boatloads of desperately ill convicts and hungry soldiers in mid-winter served only to increase pressure on his limited food supplies. *Had it not been for the trip of the Sirius to the Cape to bring us six months flour, we should have, long before the arrival of the fleet, been food for the crows. When the transports came into this port, and for three months before, we were reduced to so low a ration of provisions of just pork, flour and rice, every other species of provisions being long expended.*[59]

To avert worsening disaster, Phillip decided to send the stronger and healthier of the new arrivals to the smaller settlement on Norfolk Island, *where the soil is said to be good and the climate a healthy one.*[60]

The tea was well flavoured — Northanger Abbey

By early August, the Camden, Calvert & King ships were ready to leave for Canton. Traill had his orders – *After convicts, stores etc are delivered, you must make the best of your way without loss of time... At New South Wales, or on your passage to China, you are to remove all bulkheads, storerooms, & obstructions of every kind, both in the hold & between the lower and middle deck, & to stow both the hold & lower deck, in the best and most advantageous manner, completely full of teas from one end of the ship to the other.*[61]

Phillip chartered the *Surprize,* smallest of the three, to take nearly two hundred convicts and their superintendents to Norfolk Island.[62] With them he sent a surgeon who had arrived unheralded, D'Arcy Wentworth, the Colony's first fare-paying, free settler.

Every body was shortly in motion for tea — Northanger Abbey

On Sunday, 1st August 1790, the *Surprize* sailed out of Port Jackson. When the *Scarborough* left for Canton, on 8 August, the *Neptune* was ready to leave, but was held back. A number of convicts had sworn before the Judge Advocate that Captain Traill had confiscated their money and possessions, they sought to have them returned.

Mr Collins, with all his solemn composure   _{Pride & Prejudice}

Captain Traill, called before the Judge Advocate, David Collins, asserted he had confiscated only knives, swords and other weapons, and had thrown them overboard. No restitution was made to the convicts. The *Neptune* finally sailed on 24 August. She stopped for two weeks at Macau before going to Canton. In China, almost thirty of her crew deserted the ship.

Going to settle in Norfolk   _{Letters}

David Collins, noted in his diary for Sunday, 1st August 1790 – *Mr Wentworth was now sent to Norfolk Island to act as an assistant to the surgeon there, being reputed to have the necessary requisites for such a situation.*[63]

Governor Phillip had no authority to appoint D'Arcy to a medical position on Norfolk Island, these were appointments made from London. Phillip was aware that D'Arcy had faced trial in London, he was uncertain of his status. Just as he never mentioned a convict by name in his correspondence, he was reluctant to mention D'Arcy. He decided to await instructions. Meanwhile D'Arcy was to act unpaid. It would be seven years before his role as assistant surgeon on Norfolk Island was acknowledged or he received any payment.

A man like him, in his situation! With a heart pierced, almost broken! A man does not recover from such a devotion of the heart to such a woman! He ought not – he does not. _{Persuasion}

Five weeks after going ashore from the *Neptune*, D'Arcy found himself on board the *Surprize*, en route to Norfolk Island, with the sound of waves and wind, of birds overhead, creaking beams, and the canvas sails.

Catherine was on board with the other women. She was pregnant. He would ensure he was there with her to deliver their child. He was looking forward to practicing again as a surgeon, he hoped for a brighter future on Norfolk Island. He would restore his reputation; he would do what was necessary to gain approval to return quickly to England.

> Such wind as scatters young men through the world
> To seek their fortunes farther than at home,
> Where small experience grows.[64]
>   _{*The Taming of the Shrew*}

Chapter 13

Angels & Eagles

I flatter myself for being a tolerable proficient in Geography

LA PEROUSE, the French explorer, brought his ships *Astrolabe* and *Boussole* close in to Norfolk Island on 13 January 1788. It resembled a raised platform surrounded by cliffs and reefs. There were no beaches or natural bays, making it extremely difficult to disembark or unload supplies, impossible in heavy seas. It was far too dangerous to attempt to land. La Perouse declared it a place *fit only for Angels and Eagles*.[1]

Eight weeks later, on 6 March 1788, Lieutenant Philip Gidley King came ashore with a party of convicts. Governor Phillip had been given orders, *as soon as Circumstances will admit of it, to send a small Establishment to Norfolk Island to secure the same to us and prevent it being occupied by the Subjects of any other European Power*. He sent twenty-three people on the *Supply* to settle there.

King, the second lieutenant of the *Sirius,* was superintendent and commander. He landed with a midshipman, two surgeons, two seamen, two marines, nine male and six female convicts. *With great difficulty and danger, the stores sent with Lieutenant King were landed, on account of the rockyness of its shore, and the violence of its surf that almost continually beat upon it.*[2]

King raised the British colours, and took possession of the island. It was *closely wooded*, with water in good supply and soil a *rich black mould*. The group had a four-oared boat, some domestic animals, *provisions of every kind for six months, and tools for cutting down timber, which last employment was the purpose of the mission*.[3]

*When Cook steered Britain's oak into a world unknown, & in his country's
glory sought his own* William Cowper

James Cook had come upon the island in October 1774, on his second voyage to the Pacific, and after sending boats ashore, decided it would be of interest to the Admiralty. It was uninhabited, its forests of tall pine trees[4] could be a source of timber for masts and spars, and its wild flax or hemp plant might be useful for canvas and cordage for naval vessels. He named it *Norfolk Island*, in honour of his patron, the Duchess of Norfolk, wife of Edward Howard, 9th Duke of Norfolk, and their worthy family.

Its abundance of timber…covering a good deal of ground Emma

The Navy was dependent for its supply of hardwood, mast timbers and hemp on the Baltic, particularly Russia. In 1783, Britain imported over twenty-one thousand great masts from the Baltic, nearly eighteen thousand of them from Russia. Her dependence on the region for hemp for ships' ropes was even greater.[5]

From Cook's report, the Admiralty considered Norfolk Island to be a strategic acquisition. Its potential was discussed during high level deliberations on the merit of founding a colony in New South Wales.

Such a great connexion between the Dalrymples & ourselves Persuasion

The East India Company's Alexander Dalrymple was not convinced: *when we consider the situation of Norfolk Island, and the length of the Passage, the inconvenience and expence of affording, an ample and certain supply, to a precarious want, such as that of a Squadron on Service, from a remote place, would in my Judgement, be madness to place such confidence in that supply, as to leave the Squadron dependent on it. Supplies of masts and Cordage may always be provided in India, or from China, in the ordinary course of navigation for a constant, or even an unexpected demand. All the Coasts of Sumatra, Borneo, etc. abound with Masts for either a constant or accidental Supply: for which so small an Island as Norfolk Island is quite incompetent.*[6]

Impelled by the combination of Misfortunes under which I laboured
Love & Freindship

In October 1788, threatened with famine, Phillip despatched Captain Hunter on the *Sirius* to buy food at the Cape, and sent another forty six convicts to Norfolk Island on the *Golden Grove*, trusting its fertile soil would sustain them.

On 10th November the Golden Grove returned from Norfolk Island with a few spars, and some timber for the governor. While she was there, she was obliged to cut her cable and stand at sea, there being (as before observed) no harbour in the whole island where a ship can ride in safety. The master of the ship was swamped in the surf and nearly lost, with his boat and crew.[7]

Phillip sent more convicts to the island on the *Supply* in November 1789, and again in January 1790. He reported to Lord Sydney – *all the people in that island were well…and their crops, so good, that they had grain sufficient for six months bread for every one upon the island, reserving sufficient for their next year's crop…and they had vegetables in the greatest abundance.*[8]

It is a manoeuvring business   Mansfield Park

In March 1790, Phillip was forced to further reduce rations. Captain Hunter took the *Sirius* and *Supply* to Norfolk Island with two companies of marines and more than two hundred convicts. He landed his passengers on 13 March but the weather had turned before he could unload cargo. He moved the ships away, returning on the 19th with fine weather. While they were unloading the wind suddenly changed. Hunter wrote, *Sirius struck upon a reef of coral rocks which lies parallel to the shore, and in a few strokes was bulged*.[9]

Oh! What a loss it will be   Letters

In April 1790, the *Supply* returned to Sydney with news the flagship of the fleet all 512 tons, had foundered on the reef. Her loss was a disaster, the hungry Colony had lost its only secure supply line to the outside world. It was now reliant on one small vessel, *Supply*, a brig of 168 tons, unsuitable for long voyages to the Cape or Calcutta for provisions. John White, the Principal Surgeon wrote, *Should any accident happen to her, Lord have mercy upon us!*[10]

In Sydney, rations were further reduced. Marine Lieut. Watkin Tench wrote, *If a lucky man, who had knocked down a dinner with his gun, or caught a fish by angling from the rocks, invited a neighbour to dine with him, the invitation always ran "bring your own bread." Even at the governor's table, this custom was constantly observed. Every man when he sat down, pulled his bread out of his pocket, and laid it by his plate.*[11]

The *Supply* made ready to sail to Batavia for urgently needed provisions. The Colony had no money at hand to pay for them. Captain Ball was authorised to enter any arrangements deemed necessary by the Governor of Batavia. The supplies were charged to the British Government, and Ball chartered a Dutch vessel, the *Waaksamheyd*, to assist with transporting them to Sydney.

King returned to Sydney from Norfolk Island to travel on the *Supply* to Batavia. There he boarded a vessel to Holland, and from thence he went to London, arriving just before Christmas 1790. He gave a first-hand account of the desperate plight of the forgotten Colony, urging Lord Sydney to send more regular supplies.

A few months earlier, Lord Grenville had written to Lord Cornwallis, Governor of Bengal, to authorise trade between the Colony and India. Supplies could be obtained there *upon more moderate terms*[12] than from England or the Cape.

King arrived in England after the Second Fleet had sailed. He returned on the *Gorgon,* a transport with the Third Fleet. Whitehall had contracted Camden, Calvert and King to transport nearly two thousand convicts on the Third Fleet, double the number they carried on the Second.

A whole camp full of soldiers Pride & Prejudice

During King's absence from Norfolk Island, Major Robert Ross of the Marines was made acting commandant. He administered the narrow society of Marines, soldiers and convicts under martial law. With additional convicts from the *Sirius* and *Supply* and the officers and crew of the *Sirius,* the population rose sharply from a hundred and fifty to *above five hundred souls.*[13] They had to rely on food and supplies from the Commissary. They had salvaged what they could from the wreck but most of the foodstuffs on the *Sirius* were lost.

As she lay aground on the reef, two convicts, James Branagan and William Dring, had volunteered to swim out and release the livestock on board. When this was done, they found the grog store, got drunk and set fire to the ship. The gun deck burnt through and the cannons fell into the hold, trapping the badly needed stores.

There are a prodigious number of birds hereabouts this year, so that perhaps I may kill a few Letters

It was five months before another vessel called at the island, supplies were exhausted, rations inadequate and for a time the settlement faced starvation. *It was a general opinion that we could not have survived so long but for the immensity of birds which we brought in every night from Mount Pitt.*[14]

Providence Petrels[15] came in vast numbers each winter to Mount Pitt, the highest point on the island, nesting in burrows on the mountain flanks. They were curious, they came at the call of men bearing clubs, and yielded meat and eggs for the population, averting starvation. More than 170,000 of them were killed in a season, within eight years their migration all but ceased.

I hate to hear of women on board, or to see them on board Persuasion

D'Arcy left Sydney Cove on the *Surprize* on 1 August 1790. Bound for China, she stopped first off Norfolk Island to deliver the healthier of the Second Fleet convicts, a hundred and fifty seven females and thirty seven males. Catherine Crowley, heavily pregnant, was among the women selected from the *Neptune.*

The night was stormy, the wind had been rising at intervals all afternoon
Northanger Abbey

The *Surprize* had begun landing her prisoners when severe wind and weather closed in. Forced to stand off, she moved around off Cascade Bay on the north of the island, to wait out the storm.

The storm still raged, and various were the noises, more terrific even than the wind
Northanger Abbey

The storm continued to build, a low pressure system developed into near cyclonic conditions, with vivid lightning flashes and violent southerly winds. The ship lurched in every direction at once, bouncing in the turbulent and phosphorescent sea, reflecting each lightening strike, accompanied by driving rain and terrifying claps of thunder.

Catherine had never wanted comfort more
Northanger Abbey

On Friday, 13 August 1790, at the height of the storm, William Charles, D'Arcy Wentworth and Catherine Crowley's first child, was born on the *Surprize*. Catherine was in a state of terror, the baby, premature and tiny, cried lustily. Perhaps the electricity and energy of that wild night entered his spirit, for a dramatic, stormy energy was to define William's life.

A premature baby, under circumstances such as these, faced enormous risks. D'Arcy was determined William would survive, he watched over him day and night, with every skill he possessed. His birth gave D'Arcy new focus and responsibility. It sealed his bond and loyalty to Catherine and gave them the strength and optimism to face the difficulties in their life on this remote island.

William grew into a tall and handsome man, carrying the marks of his precipitate entry into the world – a limp, a cast in one eye, and a lifelong predisposition to respiratory problems.

On August 16th when the wind abated, the *Surprize* returned to Sydney Bay, on the eastern side of the island, to complete unloading. Catherine and her baby were rowed ashore in a longboat, passing close to the wreck of the *Sirius*.

Next day the seas grew heavier, a huge wave overturned a longboat carrying convicts ashore. It was tossed against the rocks and broken up, leaving seven people dead, three convict women, a child, two seamen and a convict[16] who dived into the boiling surf to try to save the victims.

The tragedy affected everyone on the island, it heightened the newcomers' realisation of the precariousness of their existence. Catherine knew the longboat carrying her ashore with William could just as easily have been swamped or thrown over the rocks.

Going in quest of tea   Persuasion

The *Surprize* left Norfolk Island on 29 August 1790 to meet with the *Neptune* and *Scarborough* bound for Canton. In early December they sailed along the China coast to Whampoa, and filled the holds with tea. On 20 March 1791 they joined an East India Company convoy bound for England, via the island of St Helena. The *Neptune* arrived home in the first week of October 1791.

A nightly supply of coarse food   Northanger Abbey

The population of Norfolk Island had risen suddenly to over seven hundred. D'Arcy was housed in the main encampment at Sydney Bay. Catherine and William lived under canvas with the female convicts. Catherine received rations for her son, who was listed as William Crowley.[17]

Irregularity in the fall of the ground & a profusion of old Timber   Evelyn

D'Arcy walked two miles inland each day, from Sydney Bay, up Mount George,[18] across the Longridge to Charlotte Field, a small settlement in an open, relatively treeless area, where the sick and injured convicts were housed.

Another of his duties was to attend floggings, he could intervene if he thought it necessary, and dress any wounds that warranted. He was far more humane than some of his successors. Records show he halted many floggings ordered by Lieutenant Ralph Clark, often a quarter or half way through. He noted, the convict was *unable to bear more*, though Clark might add, *the rest to follow when his back is better*.[19]

There will be work for five summers at least before the place is liveable

                                                                                                                                Mansfield Park

From first light, convict men worked, hacking away at Samson's Sinew,[20] a woody vine as thick as a man's arm, and clearing the tree cover, exposing high, rolling downs for fields and pasture. There was *scarcely a piece of level ground* it was *all hill and dale*.[21] The tall, beautiful Norfolk Island Pines, felled in the hundreds, were found to be too brittle for masts and spars.

The island flax also proved disappointing. Convict women dried the fibres and worked the flax into canvas, it was slow, and results were inferior. Cook had been impressed by the skill of the New Zealand Maori who made nets, clothes and twine from a similar plant.[22] The Maori women wove it with ease, but it defied the skills of the convict women on the island.

Covering a good deal of ground, rambling & irregular   Emma

After the loss of the *Sirius*, Hunter and many of his crew were stranded on the island for nearly a year, awaiting a ship to take them off. Hunter kept his distance from Major Ross, seeking *nothing more than common civility*.[23]

Hunter, fifty-three, twenty-five years D'Arcy's senior, was a Scot from Leith, the port of Edinburgh. He had been at sea since he was a boy. He carried a sketchbook filled with survey sketches of islands, shorelines and reefs, he added watercolours of flowering plants, fish and the Colony's colourful birds. In the evening he might play Scottish reels on his violin.

Hunter liked D'Arcy's intelligence and willingness. He admired his measured approach to both prisoners and officers, to the military and the crew of the *Sirius,* his ability to gain their confidence and respect.

On light summer evenings the two men walked across the cleared slopes of the island. Hunter thought they resembled *the waves of the sea in a gentle wind*.[24] It was more than three years since he had left Europe, they spoke of Edinburgh and London, of upheavals in England and France, of Hastings' impeachment.

D'Arcy's position on Norfolk Island was ambiguous; he was a free man, he had gone freely to the island when requested by the Governor. He was a civilian working within its military establishment, without an appointment and without payment. He was outside the system, and his superiors on the island could offer him no remedy.

Hunter suggested D'Arcy write to the Governor for advice about his status on the Norfolk Island. On 10 February 1791, Hunter left for Sydney on the *Supply,* taking his letter to deliver.

Your resolution & good conduct Pride & Prejudice

Governor Phillip replied to D'Arcy, he was satisfied with his conduct. When he received instructions from the Home Office he would determine his future.

In Sydney, Hunter noticed Phillip's exhaustion and the growing sway of the Corps who arrived on the Second Fleet. In March, he and his crew left for England to face court martial for the sinking of the *Sirius*.[25] They sailed first to Batavia on the *Waaksamheyd,* a frustrating voyage that took six months.

Hunter bought the *Waaksamheyd* and sailed for England with his crew. In a gale near the Cape she lost her anchors and was taken in tow by *HMS Providence,* captained by William Bligh, who was en route to Otaheite, on a second voyage for breadfruit, after the failure of his first, on the *Bounty*.[26]

Linneus, does his Ghost rise up before You? Letters

During his first fifteen months on the island, D'Arcy worked alongside two Irish surgeons from the First Fleet. He was assistant to Dennis Considen, a naval surgeon from the *Scarborough,* the first assistant surgeon to the Colony, under John White. The two respected each other's skills and dedication, they would remain good friends and colleagues.

Thomas Jamison, from County Down, came on the *Sirius* as a surgeon's mate, or apprentice, and was sent to Norfolk Island with King in March 1788. Granted twelve months leave in September 1800, he returned to England, and came back to the Colony in 1802.

D'Arcy's experience in rural Tandragee, assisting with patients of all ages, men, women and children, proved helpful to his naval surgeon colleagues.

If every other leaf were powerless — Persuasion

Dennis Considen, in particular, valued D'Arcy's experience as an apothecary. In Sydney, guided by Aboriginals, Considen identified local plants useful for treating common complaints and diseases. He applied apothecary principles to test and prescribe native plants to his patients, and the Colony's surgeons used them to supplement their limited supply of remedies.

Considen was the first to distil eucalyptus oil and use it as an antiseptic, he noted its anti-inflammatory and decongestant properties. He used red gum[27] and peppermint gum[28] for diarrhoea and stomach problems, native sarsaparilla[29] and currants[30] to treat and protect against scurvy; and the grass tree or "black boy"[31] for respiratory complaints. In 1788 he had sent a variety of specimens to Joseph Banks, with descriptions of his research.

Construction both simple & elegant — Scraps

Convicts under Lieutenant Clark built a small log cabin for D'Arcy at Charlotte Field, renamed Queenborough in 1791. He and Catherine moved there in the first week of April 1791 with William, and in August, they had a daughter Martha. Martha lived only four months; she died during an outbreak of fever brought by convicts from the Third Fleet, who arrived in November, on the *Atlantic* and *Queen*.

In their six and a half years together on Norfolk Island, Catherine and D'Arcy had two more sons, Dorset, born on 23 June 1793, and Matthew, two years later on 13 June 1795. The children took their mother's surname, in accordance with victualling arrangements for convicts, their rations were allocated to her.

Catherine Crowley

Little is known of Catherine Crowley's beginnings, her's is a story still to be told. Her surname is common in Ireland, but it seems likely she was born in England, into a Quaker family. It appears she had some education, and was literate and numerate.

There is no record of her birth in the area where she lived and worked in 1788, not in Newcastle-under-Lyme, Stafford or Stoke-on-Trent. She was possibly related to Ambrose Crowley, who manufactured irons for convicts, his connexions settled around Staffordshire and Worcestershire. A possible forebear, Robert Crowley, born around 1470, who came to England from Wexford in Ireland, had descendants living in Warwickshire.

He was a wine merchant A Collection of Letters

Catherine came to New South Wales sentenced to seven years transportation. She was arrested in Newcastle-under-Lyme, a Staffordshire market town, where she worked as a servant to William Hyatt, Brandy Merchant.[32]

On April 5 1788, at fifteen, she was charged with stealing two pairs of linen sheets from him, and clothing from his house, belonging to Maria Morell.[33] She spent three months in Stafford Gaol before her trial at the Stafford Assizes on July 30, 1788, where she was found guilty.

Catherine listened with a beating heart Northanger Abbey

Her case relied on the testimony of two women, Mary Mulveny and Bridget Podmore, who received the stolen goods. John Worrell had gone to their houses with a search warrant and found William Hyatt's goods in their possession. Both women identified Catherine as the thief, and testified against her. Neither appear to have been questioned for their part as receivers of stolen property.

At the time, Newcastle-under-Lyme was known for its felt-making. We do not know if Mary Mulveny or Bridget Podmore were involved in other instances of receiving stolen clothes or fabrics, or if there was another story behind the charges. Nor do we know who paid Catherine Crowley's gaol fees, or for her transport, later, from Stafford Gaol to Deptford to join the Second Fleet.

Catherine could not relieve the irksomeness of imprisonment by the exchange of a syllable with any of her fellow captives Northanger Abbey

She was held in the overcrowded Stafford Gaol for sixteen months, a *dismal old prison*,[34] filled with misery, damp, rot, suffering and rats. While she was there, the Marquis of Stafford wrote to the Home Secretary, *in the present bad state of the old gaol, there is a constant apprehension of sickness and escapes. The convicts really have not so much room to lye in as the mercenary African merchant used to allow his negroes. The justices therefore desire, if it is possible, that you will dispose of some of these miserable and desperate people.*[35] A number of the prisoners were transported on the Second Fleet, and the gaol was demolished the following year.

Catherine was tired of being continually pressed against by people Northanger Abbey

In October 1789, she was bundled onto the back of a coach with four other women, Hannah Hawkins, Ann Calcut, Mary Cooksey and Frances Handley, and driven a hundred and sixty miles across the autumn landscape, breathing the cold, sweet air, to Deptford. They walked with groups of other prisoners the five miles to Woolwich, on the Thames, and went aboard the *Neptune* on 25 October 1789. They were confined there while she sailed to Plymouth, then Portsmouth, to collect convicts and troops. The *Neptune* remained in the Solent for three months before sailing on 17 January 1790, for New South Wales.

Too wretched to be fearful, the journey in itself had no terrors for her
Northanger Abbey

Hannah Hawkins was sent to Norfolk Island with Catherine,[36] and she likely knew other convicts there from Stafford gaol, as well as from the *Neptune*.[37]

James Colnett, the captain of *HMS Glatton*, transported female convicts from county gaols. He wrote, they *claimed my pity,…having natural expressions of despair, etc, quite of a different appearance to those from Newgate and large jails…many had been private servants, ladies' maids, housekeepers, etc. Many of this class, who I believe, were first offenders…would have escaped unpunished if tried in the metropolis.*[38]

Catherine cheerfully complied
Northanger Abbey

D'Arcy respected Catherine's intelligence, her ability to manage the challenges of their household. She gave him her support, and cared for their young family.

Always wholesome, these the finest beds & finest sorts
Emma

Norfolk Island's role changed during their time there. Enterprises that seemed so promising, tall timbers and flax, both failed. But by the end of their first year, the rich, volcanic soil, up to twelve metres deep in places, was providing bountiful harvests of grain and vegetables. Within four years it was supporting over eleven hundred people. For a short time the island had a larger population and more free settlers than Sydney, and became its major source of foodstuffs.

The early convicts generally behaved well, clearing the ground, sowing corn and potatoes, responding to rewards for industry and good behaviour. In the afternoons they tended their own garden plots and animals, to help feed and benefit themselves. Many found partners and reared children. But as more and more convicts arrived from Sydney Cove, a great number *remained idle and miserable wretches, despite the climate, and their isolation from previous haunts of crime.*[39]

As the fertile land along the Hawkesbury River west of Sydney was settled, Norfolk Island lost its importance as a food producer. It continued to supply salted pork and grain to the main settlement at Port Jackson, but it was run primarily as a penal settlement. Serious offenders were shipped there from Sydney, its isolated location made it virtually escape proof.

A third, it seemed like wilful ill-nature Pride & Prejudice

Lieutenant Governor King and his new bride Anna Josepha left England on 15 March 1791, on the *Gorgon*, one of eleven ships of the Third Fleet. She carried convicts, and passengers, including Captain William Paterson with his wife, Elizabeth, with a detachment of the New South Wales Corps. At the Cape, she took on stores salvaged from the wreck of the *Guardian,* and livestock to replace the animals she had jettisoned.

In April, the *Queen* left Cork with the first load of Irish convicts for the Colony, one hundred and twenty-six men, twenty-one women.

Britannia, another transport in the Third Fleet, a whaler belonging to Samuel Enderby & Sons, collected a cargo of convicts at Plymouth, and a shipment of goods for John Macarthur. Sent by his brother, they including 'slops,' clothing from the Macarthur family business, for resale in the Colony.

Her American captain, Thomas Melville, sailing north from Van Diemen's Land, sighted great numbers of whales. He declared there were more in these waters than he had seen in seven years of whaling on the coast of *the Brazils,* and he intended to pursue them.

The loss of life among convicts on the Third Fleet was around ten percent, with six hundred and seventy six convicts needing medical treatment on their arrival. Phillip reported to Lord Grenville: *Although the convicts landed from these ships are not so sickly as those brought out last year, the greatest part of them are so emaciated; so worn away by long confinement, or want of food, or from both these causes that it will be long before they recover their strength, and which many of them never will recover.*[40] Camden, Calvert & King was awarded no further Government contracts.

They had been hunting together and were in the midst of a good run
Mansfield Park

Leaving Sydney, Melville took the *Britannia* in pursuit of the whales. He was obeying instructions from Samuel Enderby, one of her owners, and a friend of Lieut King. It was the beginning of the Colony's important whaling industry, Melville was followed by members of other American whaling families, Coffin, Folger, Delano, Eber Bunker and others.

King had brought despatches for Governor Phillip, including *His Majesty's Authority for Granting Pardons Absolutely or Conditionally,* and a secret order instructing him to send the officers and crew of the *Sirius,* Marines and thirty colonists, to Nootka Sound on the American west coast, on board the *Gorgon* and *Discovery,* to found a colony there and develop the lucrative trade in furs.[41]

Under the Treaty of Tordesillas of 1494, the west coast of America lay within

Spain's jurisdiction, and the Spanish resisted British attempts to establish a settlement there. A Spanish naval officer, Esteban Jose Martinez seized two British ships at Nootka Sound, the *Princess Royal*, under Thomas Hudson and the *Argonaut,* under James Colnett, and imprisoned and mistreated their crews.

Pitt considered access to the Pacific worth fighting for, he sent a large fleet to threaten the coast of Spain. On 13 October 1790, after much intimidation and negotiation, Spain agreed to allow British traders to settle and trade on the coast between Alaska and California, and to fish in the Pacific; but resisted British demands to permit its merchants to trade directly with Spanish America.[42] Phillip's secret order was never carried out.

She married Philip King The History of England

Two ships of the Third Fleet carried sick and debilitated convicts to Norfolk Island, suffering malnutrition, scurvy, fever and dysentery. The *Atlantic* arrived on 2 November 1791, followed a week later by the *Queen*. Lieutenant-Governor Philip Gidley King was on board the *Atlantic,* returning to his role of Commandant, with his new wife, Anna Josepha.

King wrote to Evan Nepean, to tell him the island now had fifty free settlers, with grants of sixty acres apiece, *eighty acres of wheat and upwards of ninety of maize have a very good appearance… two small towns are built, one nearest the centre of the island called Queenboro*. On his return he was *pestered with complaints, bitter revilings, back-biting*; he noticed *discord and strife on every persons' countenance and in every corner and hole of the island.*[43]

D'Arcy was introduced to King and his wife. She liked and trusted him, and a few weeks later D'Arcy attended the birth of her son, Phillip Parker King, the Commandant's first legitimate child. King had two older sons on the island, Norfolk and Sydney, their mother, Ann Innet was a convict, transported for breaking, entering and stealing with force of arms.

Nobody can be a greater advocate for matrimony than I am Emma

King had brought a chaplain, Rev Richard Johnson, from Sydney, to sanctify the many de facto relationships on Norfolk Island. Over three days, he married more than a hundred couples. Many convicts had wives in England, and bigamy being a transportable offence, not all unions were sanctified. Many of the convict women married in the hope a legal relationship would protect them from the predation of the soldiers.[44]

I am glad you are no enemy to matrimony Northanger Abbey

It was known to his superiors on Norfolk Island that D'Arcy had left a wife in England. The list of landowners on the island for 1796 recorded him as married.[45]

King discreetly overlooked that his union with Catherine Crowley did not have the imprimatur of the Church.

Support & advancement
Mansfield Park

Shortly after King's return, Denis Doidge, the superintendent of convicts at Queenborough, resigned, after sending King two *abusive letters, and some very improper and disrespectful behaviour*. King promptly appointed D'Arcy as his replacement.[46]

From 10 December 1791, he was responsible for overseeing up to a hundred and fifty convict labourers, deployed on building projects, farm work, and in assisting the officers. Most were minor criminals, unskilled products of poverty in England, *convicted of sickness, hunger, wretchedness and want*.[47]

D'Arcy continued to work as assistant surgeon, and after the arrival of the Third Fleet convicts, his workload increased. There were frequent outbreaks of dysentery, the usual illnesses and injuries of convicts and soldiers; he attended floggings, and treated the Commandant, his family, and the settlers.

Dennis Considen had left for Sydney in November 1791, and was given leave to return home in 1792. He was replaced by William Balmain, a Scot, who like Jamison, came out as a surgeon's mate, on the transport, *Alexander*. D'Arcy's apprenticeship in Ireland, his training at St Barts and credentials from the Company of Surgeons, set him apart from his fellow surgeons, but he said little or nothing about his background.

The miseries of waiting
Mansfield Park

It took years for D'Arcy to receive confirmation of his appointment as Assistant Surgeon. It had to come from London, and ships were few, the voyage long and often indirect. Letters from Norfolk Island went via Sydney, and few ships called at either place. It might take up to a year for a letter to reach London. Even a prompt reply could take longer to deliver; and a letter to Norfolk Island could wait in Sydney for four or five months for a ship.

In January 1792, Governor Phillip wrote to King, saying D'Arcy could return to Sydney if he proved deserving, but advised he might do better to stay until a decision was received from the Home Office. In November that year Phillip chided King for listing D'Arcy on his returns as an assistant surgeon. In future, his list of personnel was to record him only as *superintendent*.[48]

Phillip was exhausted and ill. The two years following the arrival of the New South Wales Corps on the Second Fleet had been doubly difficult. When their Commander, Major Francis Grose arrived on the *Pitt,* in February 1792, with a third and final company, Phillip hoped he would improve the discipline and behaviour of the Corps. Instead he had become an advocate for their discontent, increasing pressure on the Governor.

The tendency is gross & illiberal   Sense & Sensibility

As food supplies in the Colony dwindled, Phillip added his private supply of foodstuffs to the public store, and took reduced rations with everyone else. *He wished not to see anything more at his table than the ration which was received in common for the public store, without any distinction of persons; and to this resolution he rigidly adhered, wishing that, if a convict complained, he might see that want was not unfelt even at Government House.*[49]

A few months after he arrived, Grose wrote to Phillip, describing *the situation of the soldiers under my command, who at this time have scarcely shoes to their feet and who have no other comforts than the reduced and unwholesome rations served from the stores.*[50]

He replied: *I cannot acquiesce with you in thinking that the ration served from the public stores is unwholesome; I see it daily at my own table; I am sorry to see that it is neither so good nor in that quantity as I would wish it; and every means in my power has and will be taken to remedy the evil.*[51]

Grose complained to London about Phillip's policy of equal rations for all. *Whenever it happens that a short allowance is issued to the felons, the soldiers' ration is also reduced, and that without the smallest difference or distinction – the Captain of a company, and a convict transported for life, divide and share alike whatever is served.*[52]

In October 1792, he sought the Governor's permission for officers of the Corps to charter the whaler, *Britannia*, to sail to the Cape to purchase provisions, cattle and rum – the name given to all spirits. Grose stated these were intended for the officers, and at their discretion for other members of the Corps. John Macarthur had organised a group of officers to subscribe over £4,000 in £200 shares, to pay for the charter. They could draw on their salaries paid in London by Treasury, a reliable means of payment for the Captain.

A gross violation of duty & respect   Mansfield Park

Phillip did not approve the plan, reminding Grose the *Britannia* would infringe the Royal Charter that gave the East India Company exclusive trading rights to the region.

Macarthur and his fellow officers disregarded him, they arranged with Captain Raven, one of the *Britannia*'s owners, to accept the charter. Phillip had left the Colony when Raven returned to Sydney with enough supplies for a return to full rations; and a quantity of rum and other tradable items for the paymaster, John Macarthur, and company commanders, William Paterson, George Johnston,

Joseph Foveaux and Thomas Rowley. The success of this venture brought the officers wealth, and a taste for further involvement in trade.

On 11 December 1792, Phillip had sailed on the *Atlantic*, weak, ill and in constant pain. He had requested a year's leave in April 1790, in March 1791 and again in November, 1791, but the Home Office did not respond. In October 1792, he wrote that he would await the next ship for a reply, but his return could no longer be delayed.

In 1791, Phillip wrote to Joseph Banks, *I think my old acquaintance Bennillon will accompany me when ever I return to England, and from him when he understands English, much information may be attained, for he is very intelligent.*[53]

He took two Sydney Aboriginals with him, Bennelong and Imeerawanyee, who had befriended and assisted him during the first years of settlement. David Collins described how they *withstood at the moment of their departure, the united distress of their wives and the dismal lamentations of their friends.*[54]

Disgusted with the women Pride & Prejudice

On Norfolk Island, from the beginning, there were problems managing the women convicts. After he returned, King proclaimed eighteen new regulations with specific penalties for women. *Every woman convicted of blasphemous or indecent language, will for the first offence have her hair cut off, for the second offence will be shaved, and for the third offence will be whipped at the cart's tail.* And further – *No cloathing will in future be issued to any convict, male or female, convicted of theft.*[55]

One gets so tumbled in such a crowd Northanger Abbey

Amongst convicts on the Second Fleet, was a young woman of eighteen, Sarah Lyons, sentenced to seven years transportation in May 1788, for the theft of seven yards of silk from a London haberdashery. On the voyage from England on the *Lady Juliana*, she was involved in several escapades. At Tenerife, after drinking a cask of wine, a group of women convicts went ashore, parading through the town, wearing crucifixes and carrying a hastily made cross. They claimed to be devout Catholics, transported for their religious convictions. They won the islanders' sympathy and extracted money and gifts from them.

The women also reaped considerable rewards from ships' crews in St. Jago harbour on Cape Verde Island, and in Rio de Janeiro, where the *Lady Juliana* stayed for several weeks.[56]

A little flogging for men and women too would be the best way to prevent such things Mansfield Park

Sarah was sent to Norfolk Island on the *Surprize* with Catherine Crowley, and employed at Charlotte Field. Lieutenant Ralph Clark, the Marine in charge, considered women convicts *ten thousand times worse than the men*. Sarah received twenty-five lashes for striking and ill-using a fellow convict, Catherine White. Three months later, Clark ordered fifty lashes for her, for abusing D'Arcy, but after sixteen, D'Arcy requested he halt the flogging.

Life improved for Sarah; she met William Tunks, another Marine stationed on the island. Rev Johnson married them in November 1791. William exercised his option to stay in the Colony and transferred to the New South Wales Corps. They moved to Sydney, and today their descendants number over six thousand.

Perrot, wily dame

Sarah Lyons' punishment for stealing haberdashery, highlights the story of Jane Leigh-Perrot, Jane Austen's aunt, who in 1799, was charged with shoplifting a card of lace from a shop in Bath. She was committed to the Ilchester County Gaol, refused bail, and remained there until March 1800, when she was tried at the Taunton Assizes.

Mrs Leigh-Perrot told the Court that as a wealthy, married woman she had no reason to steal: *Placed in a situation the most eligible that any woman could desire, with supplies so ample that I was left rich after every wish was gratified; blessed in the affections of the most generous man as a husband, what could induce me to commit such a crime?...Can you suppose that disposition so totally altered, as to lose all recollection of the situation I held in society – to hazard for this meanness my character and reputation.*[57]

> A pretty, accomplished girl, & two other young ladies, of respectable families, will be transported to Botany Bay in the Hindostan, all for stealing lace at Haberdashers' shops, the first in Bond Street, the other two in the country[58]
>
> BIRMINGHAM GAZETTE

Mrs Leigh-Perrot was acquitted. Had she been found guilty, under the laws of the time, she could have been sentenced to death, or transported, like Sarah Lyons and many others.[59] Jane's aunt may have had kleptomaniac tendencies; for in 1805, she was again charged with stealing; this time, plants from a commercial nursery. She was acquitted a second time.[60]

The friend of the poor and the oppressed! Mansfield Park

D'Arcy understood the thin filament that lay between respectable and criminal society. He saw the misfortune of many convicts, and the injustices they suffered through the cruelty and arrogance of the superintendents and the soldiers. He could identify with them from his own experience, and he advocated for more humane treatment of convicts and settlers on the island.

He forged a reputation as a just, reasonable superintendent of convicts. His *compassion for his convict labourers and his friendly nature encouraged a cooperative spirit at Queenborough. Rather than seeing his qualities as a weakness to be exploited, the convicts responded positively to his manner.*[61]

Joseph Smith, a convict who worked under D'Arcy, said *a better master never lived in the world.*[62] The housekeeper of Pemberley, in *Pride & Prejudice,* echoed this sentiment exactly, describing Mr Darcy's attitude to his tenants and servants, *he is the best landlord, and the best master that ever lived…there is not one of his tenants or servants but will give him a good name… What praise is more valuable than the praise of an intelligent servant?*[63]

Lieut. King recognised that convicts under D'Arcy's supervision worked without discontent or disagreement. Compassion was unfashionable on Norfolk Island, but King valued his counsel.

It would be rather gratifying to him to have enlightened witnesses to the progress of his success — Mansfield Park

In 1792, the London press reported: *Wentworth, the highwayman, acts as assistant to the Surgeon General at Norfolk Island and likewise behaves himself remarkably well.*[64]

THE DAILY ADVERTISER

John Hunter's journal, published in London in 1793 by John Stockdale, stated D'Arcy was superintendent of convicts at Queenborough, that he *behaved with the greatest attention and propriety as assistant surgeon which duty he still continued to discharge.*[65]

Unable longer to bear the confinement — Sense & Sensibility

On 23 April 1793, D'Arcy attended Mrs King at the birth of her second child, a daughter, Anna Maria. Two months later, on 23 June 1793, he assisted Catherine to deliver their second son, Dorset.

Frustrated by continual delays and stonewalling from London, he wrote to Fitzwilliam, asking him to use his influence to have his appointment as assistant surgeon confirmed. Fitzwilliam instructed Charles Cookney to write to the Home Office on his behalf, to request payment for D'Arcy's work on Norfolk Island.

The general goodness of his intentions — Mansfield Park

King provided letters of support to Evan Nepean at the Home Office, in March and May 1792[66] and to Governor Phillip in September.[67] He praised D'Arcy's exemplary behaviour, his propriety, punctuality and his industry; stating that he was of the greatest service, attentive in maintaining law and order, and active in overseeing public works.

In August 1792, King made D'Arcy the constable for the Queenborough district. He attempted to appoint him a magistrate, but D'Arcy would not accept the appointment.[68]

A confinement he could not endure — Emma

D'Arcy made numerous attempts to return to England. To our eyes, he was a free man, he had not been transported, he was not a convict. But regardless, he needed permission from London, and from the Governor, before he could arrange a return passage. He asked Fitzwilliam several times to help him to obtain official approval to return to England.[69]

King wrote to Evan Nepean in March 1793, stating that D'Arcy had served without pay as assistant surgeon for thirty-one months, and as a superintendent of convicts for fifteen, that he wished to leave Norfolk Island, and he would be irreplaceable. He praised his conduct and his contribution, stating that convicts under his supervision had produced 2000 bushels of maize and 500 bushels of wheat. He had received no complaints from D'Arcy or those under him, he called him, a *real treasure...how I shall replace his loss I cannot tell*.[70]

It was a noble gift — Letters

Charles Cookney had some success at the Home Office. Fitzwilliam wrote in June 1793 to say that John King, the under-secretary, had made a commitment that D'Arcy would be the next assistant surgeon appointed to the Colony.

Fitzwilliam wished D'Arcy, *health, happiness and prosperity*, and told him he had sent a box with *an assortment of things that I fancy will be useful*.[71] The box, arrived in Port Jackson on the *William*, but it had been ransacked; its contents, valued in London at £97, were all stolen.[72]

Nothing was omitted on his side of civility compliment or kindness — Mansfield Park

Fitzwilliam's letter offered D'Arcy a wonderful, unexpected opportunity: *I have desired Mr Cookney, clerk to the late Thomas Hill, to act as your attorney, and as you know him, I daresay you will approve the appointment*.[73] His comment *as you know him*, suggests Cookney may have suggested that D'Arcy might find a London agent useful, and even proposed himself for the role.

Thomas Hill, Fitzwilliam's London agent for many years, had, four years before, made Cookney responsible for helping D'Arcy with his eleventh hour arrangements for a passage to the Colony. Cookney had called on Jane at Clipstone Street, and knew her as Mrs Wilson.

A civil, cautious lawyer
Persuasion

Cookney was a member of Staple Inn, an Inn of Chancery that credentialed solicitors, as Inns of Court did barristers. Solicitors of Staple Inn usually worked with barristers of Gray's Inn, but Cookney was articled to Thomas Hill of Lincoln's Inn, and worked in his office at 9 Castle Street, Holborn.

Cookney was a year younger than D'Arcy, he had married two years earlier, at twenty-eight, and in time he and his wife Thomasine had twelve children. He was a long-standing member of the *Royal Society for the Encouragement of Arts, Manufactures and Commerce,* he took a great interest in the Colony and its commerce and he actively assisted D'Arcy to become a successful trader.

Cookney endorsed Adam Smith's view, that *exploring new markets and extending existing ones will ensure a period of tranquillity and a continued course of successive improvement in the general order of the world.*[74] Adam Smith gave an air of high moral endeavor to colonization and commerce. George III had commended him, *I am persuaded that a general increase in commerce throughout the empire, will prove the wisdom of your measures.*[75]

Engaged in trade
Emma

On 2nd November 1793, the whaler, *Britannia,* called at Norfolk Island. Her captain, William Raven was warmly welcomed by Lieutenant King, who learnt the ship was on her way to India, under charter to Major Grose and his officers. and that she made a similar trip for them to the Cape the year before.

King was angry his fellow officers had not offered him a share in the venture: *This indulgence myself and the other officers have been excluded from... It is these, and Similar Neglects, which sours the mind of those who would otherwise be Contented in their Situation.*[76]

He arranged with Captain Raven to purchase supplies for Norfolk Island, and had the settlers compile a list of their requirements, with the maximum weight of five to six pounds per family. King gave D'Arcy and his fellow surgeon Thomas Jamison, permission to order goods through Captain Raven.

King learnt that the *Britannia* occasionally sailed to New Zealand, she had left her second mate and several crew at Dusky Bay, in the remote south island, to hunt seals. He arranged for Captain Raven to take a detour to the north island with him, to return two Maori men, Tuki and Huru, brought to Norfolk Island by force to help establish a flax industry.[77] It was unfortunate that they knew nothing of preparing or working flax, as these were Maori women's skills.

On board the *Britannia,* returning to England, was Captain Nicholas Nepean of the New South Wales Corps, brother of Evan Nepean in the Colonial Office. On the spur of the moment, King made him the Acting Commandant, bypassing Lieutenant Abbott, the commander of the Corps on Norfolk Island.

King took a party of more than twenty with him on the *Britannia*, mostly officers and soldiers of the Corps. At Murimoto Island, off North Cape, the two Maoris left the ship, carried ashore in long canoes by men they knew, who had rowed out to welcome and trade with the ship.

Conversation centred around Sidney Sanditon

Nepean was in charge during King's ten day absence. He and D'Arcy renewed their acquaintance, from the *Neptune*. D'Arcy showed him over the island, and heard about the great changes made by Major Grose, after Phillip's departure.

Nepean had commanded the first of the New South Wales Corps, sent out on the Second Fleet. In May 1791, he transferred them from Sydney to Parramatta, and set up the garrison in the new township. He remained commanding officer until February 1792, when Grose arrived. After serving eighteen months under Grose, realising there was little chance of promotion in the settlement, he had decided to return to active service in Europe.

A most uncommon degree of popularity Emma

Grose, from the first, had displayed a more assertive attitude towards the Governor, and his approach proved very popular with the Corps. Nine months after he arrived, Phillip departed, leaving him in charge. Grose's first action was to quash Phillip's policy of equal rations for all, and to give the officers, soldiers and settlers from the Marines an increase.

Grose granted the soldiers *every indulgence...spirits and other comforts had been procured for them; he had distinguished them from convicts in the ration of provisions;...he had indulged them with women.*[78]

Assiduously pushing their good fortune Persuasion

Phillip refused to approve officers taking up land, whilst they held a commission. Grose rewarded serving officers with land grants, some over a thousand acres, with convict labour to work them.

He appointed John Macarthur as his Inspector of Works, responsible for allocating both land and convicts. As Nepean and fellow officers anticipated, Macarthur made sure he favoured himself.

The hope of an opportunity Mansfield Park

When the *Britannia* arrived at Norfolk under charter to Grose and his officers, it was evident that Phillip's strict regulations on importing liquor had been reversed. Phillip had banned importation without a permit, banned trafficking or trading in liquor, and the sale of liquor to convicts. On one occasion when he instructed all imported spirits be sent to the Commissary store, Macarthur had threatened him with legal action for taking his private property. Nepean confirmed that less than a fortnight after Phillip left on the *Atlantic*, Grose had lifted all of his restrictions.

Early that year, an American vessel, *Hope*, arrived in Port Jackson with a cargo of provisions and 7,500 gallons of rum. Her captain refused to sell any of the provisions until all the rum was sold. With Grose's approval, Macarthur formed a syndicate amongst the Corps officers and purchased everything, rum and provisions. As paymaster, he arranged payment with bills drawn against the officers' accounts in London.

This shipment of rum provided an incentive to induce convicts to work on the officers' farms. Grose permitted them to be paid in rum for work done in their own time, after their scheduled work on government schemes. The convicts willingly participated in the scheme, *rum worked where the lash had failed!*[79]

Coinage was in such short supply in the Colony, that rum had become a currency, traded for food and other necessities.[80] Sydney was rife with drunkenness, gambling and crime.

The *Hope* opened a floodgate, and gave the regiment its name, the *Rum Corps*. It did not take long for shipowners to hear of the opportunities in Port Jackson. Rum started to arrive, particularly on American ships, not answerable to the East India Company. The officers of the Corps controlled the unloading of vessels, and could now purchase as much as they chose, directly from the ships' captains or at cost price through the stores. They traded and on-sold goods and spirits at much higher prices. It was so lucrative they began to charter vessels to bring in rum from the Cape and India.

In the King's service, of course Mansfield Park

Under Grose, the Rum Corps officers soon controlled the price of all imported commodities. Everything was in short supply, they had a monopoly over trading, and they made enormous profits.

So gross & notorious that no one could be ignorant of them at the time, nor can now have forgotten them Lady Susan

Grose handed Rum Corps officers the power to dispense justice in the Colony, replacing the Criminal Court, civil magistrates and justices of the peace. It was said by some he did *more harm to this colony than it would be in the power of any government to do for many years...hostile not only to the British constitution but to ends for which all good government was instituted.*[81]

Rum Corps officers had control of trade and mercantile activities, the port and tariffs, the landing and distribution of goods including rum and spirits, the public stores, the Courts, land distribution, and the distribution of convict labour. The Colony, it's *people and its resources* had become *an inexhaustible source of plunder and profit.*[82]

Nepean left Norfolk Island on the *Britannia* on 21 November 1793, after a stay of less than three weeks. After she was attacked by pirates in the Malacca Straits, he was left at Batavia to recover from a severe bout of fever. He returned to Europe, and by July 1794, he was fighting the French in Corsica, at the siege of Calvi, alongside Sir John Moore and Horatio Nelson. Moore was injured there, and Nelson lost his right eye. Nepean received regular promotion and by 1814 had attained the rank of lieutenant general.

Your portion is unhappily so small Pride & Prejudice

The visit of the *Britannia* increased King's frustration at the neglect of Norfolk Island. Its relatively large population received no share of the supplies landed at Port Jackson. The few ships that did call had already sold their entire cargo in Sydney. There was a lack of necessities such as tea, sugar, clothes and spirits, and a constant air of privation on the island.

There was growing dissatisfaction among settlers on the island. After a bumper crop in 1794, they delivered an oversupply of maize to the government store, but Grose refused to honour undertakings made to pay for the grain. The result was that many settlers left, out of forty-five in March 1793, by March 1795 only twenty-five remained.

D'Arcy took the opportunity to buy two vacant farms, of sixty acres each, originally granted to Marines who had opted to remain on the island. He used one as an enclosed run for goats and pigs, the other he farmed,[83] while continuing to live at Queenborough on his first sixty-acre grant.[84]

The corner of a steepish downy field Mansfield Park

D'Arcy laid out fields for livestock and to raise crops, and planted fruit trees.[85] *As a farmer...he had to tell what every field was to bear next year,...the plan of a drain, the change of a fence, the felling of a tree, and the destination of every acre for wheat, turnips, or spring corn.*[86] He planted sugar cane as a hedge to enclose his fields and to provide feed for his swine.[87] He was soon producing enough maize and pigs to sell a surplus to the Commissary, and to trade with ships calling at the island, in return for tobacco and spirits.

So cruel a confinement Love & Freindship

D'Arcy's accounts to Fitzwilliam of his progress on Norfolk Island assured him that he was living an orderly and industrious life. He had still not been paid for his work as assistant surgeon, and he had realised he was not at liberty to leave Norfolk Island, or the Colony.

King may appear best in the background — Mansfield Park

King faced increasing difficulties managing law and order. Most of his problems stemmed from isolation, from lack of support and poor communication with the settlement in Sydney.

For almost a year, from April 1793 to February 1794, no ship called at the island. Phillip was gone, and King had no means of dealing with the Acting Governor. He found it impossible to refer decisions to Grose, or to seek direction or advice from him, and the stress of his isolation affected his health.

Cares & Alarms — Kitty, or the Bower

King's most corrosive problem was the New South Wales Corps. The soldiers were disgruntled and belligerent, an endless source of unrest and irritation, and his attempts to control them produced more friction.

The Corps required absolute obedience from the convicts, and access to the convict women. They took the same attitude to free settlers on the island, many of them emancipists, former convicts who had served their term. The soldiers expected deference and compliance from them, and their bullying and mistreatment of the settlers became a major source of unrest.

In March 1793, they were relieved by a detachment known as the *Botany Bay Rangers*, under command of Lieutenant Abbott. The soldiers consorted with convicts, and caused friction with the settlers. King reported they had *become very intimate with the convicts, living in their huts, eating, drinking and gambling with them, and perpetually enticing the women to leave the men they were married to.*[88]

There was no avoiding, though, at Christmas — Emma

On, Christmas Day 1793, tensions boiled over. Four soldiers attacked a group of settlers, including William Dring, an emancipist, who retaliated, beating one of the soldiers, who had raped his wife.

Due celebration of that festival requires a more than ordinary share of private balls and large dinners to proclaim its importance — Sense & Sensibility

Christmas Day was observed as a holy day on the island. King noted: *after Divine Service, all the officers did me the pleasure of their company to dinner and…everyone joined the festival with much conviviality and regular behaviour. New Year day was also observed as a Holy day. Those with their Majesties and the Prince of Wales Birthdays and Good Friday are the only standing Holy days throughout the year.*[89]

On Boxing Day, King fined Dring and another sailor-settler twenty shillings each for assault. The soldiers thought this was too lenient, they wanted them given a hundred lashes, and decided to take the law into their own hands.

Four soldiers attempted to set fire to Dring's crops, one thrust the lighted torch into the face of a settler who challenged him. King had them arrested and court martialled. The ringleader was sentenced to a hundred lashes and was required to pay Dring compensation of a gallon of rum.

To King's amazement, Dring and the other settlers begged him to forgive the soldiers. They believed his punishment would only produce further reprisals. King granted their request, and then, during the evening, a group of soldiers attempted to bludgeon Dring to death.

We had always a turn for the stage Love & Freindship

On Friday, 18 January 1794, convicts performed a play at Sydney Bay. *Plays were performed on all publick days.* King *generally went to the play once a month and on the King and Queen's birthdays.*[90] There were disputes over the seating, and after the show, a brawl broke out between soldiers and settlers.

King decided to punish both groups, but after he had a soldier taken into custody, he was confronted by a detachment from the Corps. They argued his reaction was unwarranted, the incident had merely been a few drunken brawls and some intemperate language.[91]

Agitation and alarm exceeded all Mansfield Park

By Sunday 20 January, the mood had intensified, with the soldiers announcing that King was siding with the emancipist settlers. To them, an emancipist was still a convict. They declared they would rise up and put Dring and all the prisoners to death, and took an oath, *not to suffer any of their comrades to be punished for an offence against a convict any more.*[92]

King made a long speech The History of England

Next day, King, determined to prevent a mutiny, convinced the officers of the Corps, Abbott, Beckwith and Piper, to disarm the soldiers. When their weapons were removed, they became even more belligerent, declaring they had been betrayed by their own officers.

To maintain order, King put together an armed militia of settlers and ex-marines, D'Arcy was included in their number. To prevent bloodshed and mutiny, King had the ten leading protagonists arrested.

On Wednesday 23 January, there came a welcome relief to the tension. A ship, the *Frances,* was seen, she was carrying despatches. Bad weather closed in and she stood off the island for ten days. When she left on 2 February 1794, she carried the soldiers under arrest, to be dealt with by Acting Governor Grose.

Grose called a Court of Enquiry on 15 February, to hear evidence.[93] It found *the soldiers were forced into the disorders they committed on the 18th January by the licentious behaviour of the convicts.*

Grose wrote to King that he was *astonished and mortified* at his *ill-judged and unwarrantable proceedings*. He sent him a series of General Orders, asserting military ascendancy over the settlers, convicts and constables and over King's administration. He ordered him to disarm the settlers and to send the weapons to Sydney for distribution to settlers on the Hawkesbury.[94]

Grose forwarded details of the affair to the Home Office. He received a stern reprimand from Portland, Home Secretary, who asserted, *the mutinous detachment that was sent from the island* deserved *much severer treatment* than it had received. Their commanding officer had *improperly permitted* them *to mix and interfere with the other inhabitants, but particularly the convicts, from whom* they should *separate... their conversations and connections.*

King wrote to the Secretary of State – *having incurred Lieut. Govr. Grose's marked disapprobation... compels me, Sir, to request in the most respectful manner, your attention for the reasons I have had for the line of conduct which I found myself obliged to follow*.[95] *What the consequences of seven hundred inhabitants opposing themselves to sixty-five armed soldiers would have been, if not timely prevented, may be easily imagined.*[96]

Portland considered the *General Orders of Lieut.-Govr. Grose... must have been hastily conceived on the pressure of the moment, and without due attention to the principle,* he affirmed that *whenever such disputes do arise, strict and impartial justice must decide between the parties.*[97]

Do not give way to useless alarm, though it is right to be prepared for the worst, there is no occasion to look on it as certain Pride & Prejudice

Isolated, facing a violent and volatile mutiny, King had responded quickly, with courage and impartiality. D'Arcy had supported his actions to prevent mutiny. He commended King's attempts to advance the standing of emancipists on the island, his refusal to accept the oppressive attitude of the military towards them, their assertions that *once convicted they had forfeited their right to any recognition other than that of a convict.*

King asked London to approve a civil court on Norfolk Island, to provide an alternative to the island's flawed system of military justice, controlled by the Corps. He called on D'Arcy and Deputy Surveyor Charles Grimes to assist in hearing civil cases and dispensing justice.

I hope the shoes will fit Letters

D'Arcy's salary as superintendent of convicts was paid in London and he gave Cookney authority to manage his account, and asked him to purchase clothing and other essentials for himself, Catherine and the children.

His family was not alone in needing paper & pens, stockings & shoes, buckles, coats, capes, combs, ribbons, linen, thread, china, soap, brushes and cloth. He asked Cookney to select and send him these things in quantity, and he sold them at reasonable prices and a good profit.[98]

Their alphabets, their box of letters Emma

He asked for writing materials, exercise books and readers to teach William to read and write. When he turned five, D'Arcy enrolled him with a woman of good character, who taught children their lessons. William could *repeat the chronological order of the Kings of England, with the dates of their accession, and most of the principal events of their reign;...the Roman emperors as low as Severus... the metals, Semi-metals, Planets, and distinguished philosophers.*[99]

Shirts, stockings, cravats & waistcoats, hair powder, shoe-string & breeches
Northanger Abbey

Cookney arranged to purchase, pack and forward goods to D'Arcy. He would hurry to catch a particular ship due to sail, sometimes adding extras he thought might be useful. He obtained advances from Fitzwilliam when D'Arcy's funds ran low, and repaid them when his salary was received.

The newest fashions Pride & Prejudice

His letters to D'Arcy, in his fine spidery hand, record the business relationship of two men at opposite ends of the world, based on great trust and friendship. For his fee of two guineas a year, Cookney gave D'Arcy a lifeline back to the world he knew, and kept that line steady throughout his life in the Colony.

Cookney enjoyed his involvement: *I could wish to know if you would have any objection to a little Fashionable Millinery and Mantuas being sent out from time to time, instead of so many gown pieces, etc, as I think it may answer your purpose better and it will not be inconvenient for me to do it for you.*[100]

On 3rd October 1795, the *Asia* arrived at Norfolk Island en route for China. She had come directly from New York, and needed supplies of food and water. She was one of very few ships that had not called first at Sydney. For D'Arcy and other settlers it was a rare opportunity, and they provided her with fresh fruit, vegetables and meat in exchange for tobacco and spirits.

In June 1795, Catherine Crowley gave birth to Matthew, their third son; and in October, D'Arcy attended the birth of Anna King's second daughter, Utricia.

No time for your remaining in London Letters

In February 1794, John Hunter was appointed Governor of New South Wales, succeeding Arthur Phillip. He was to return on the *Reliance*, but she was thrown ashore at Plymouth in wild weather, and it was another year before he sailed.[101] He arrived in the Colony nearly three years after Phillip's departure.

In December 1794, Major Grose, debilitated by his wounds from the American War of Independence, had returned to London, leaving Captain William Paterson, second in command of the Corps, to take his place.

D'Arcy was glad to learn Hunter was the new governor. He was a trusted friend who knew the frustration of awaiting instructions and a ship to take him home.

In July 1795, D'Arcy wrote to David Collins, the Governor's Secretary, applying for leave to return to England. King gave his support, questioning the *propriety of his being detained to perform an office for which he does not receive any Emolument.* He provided a letter confirming D'Arcy held two positions, as *superintendent and having the medical treatment of those under his direction as well as the settlers in his Neighbourhood.*[102]

Beginning a journey Sense & Sensibility

On 7 September 1795, after the long, anxious voyage through French-infested waters, Governor John Hunter arrived on *HMS Reliance,* captained by Henry Waterhouse. He was welcomed into Sydney Cove, he had been Phillip's second-in-command, the captain of *HMS Sirius,* that provided the naval escort for the First Fleet. *How happy is it for the Colony that we have at last a Governor who will make the good of the community at large his particular care, abstracted from all party and dirty pecuniary views.*[103]

Bennelong had come home on the *Reliance.*[104] In London, he had stayed with William Waterhouse, Henry's father, at 125 Mount Street, in Mayfair, close to Grosvenor Square. He had studied English, he had been to the theatre and to observe Warren Hastings' trial at Westminster Hall, where his *appearance excited much curiosity.*[105]

It was snowing when the *Reliance* sailed, the Thames was frozen, and Hunter was concerned for him, *the surviving native man, Benelong, is with me, but I think in a precarious state of health. He has for the last twelve months been flattered with the hope of seeing again his native country – a happiness which he has fondly look'd forward to, but so long a disappointment had much broken his spirit, and the coldness of the weather here has so frequently laid him up... I do all I can to keep him up, but still am doubtful of his living.*[106]

Surgeon George Bass attended Bennelong on the long voyage, and learnt something of his language, Eora. Once home, Bennelong was the chief contact between his people and the settlement, until his death in January 1813.

Impatient to be gone Sense & Sensibility

In October 1795, D'Arcy learnt that two new assistant surgeons had been appointed, and had arrived in Sydney. The undertaking made to Fitzwilliam two years before, that his would be the next appointment, had not been honoured. Confounded by the news, he wrote to Fitzwilliam, *I intend to avail myself of the first opportunity of returning to England.*[107]

In January 1796, he told Fitzwilliam again that he intended to take leave and return to Europe. Without saying so, he wanted Fitzwilliam's approval. D'Arcy assured him he did not intend to stay in London, and would return to New South Wales. *I did not feel myself bound after six years service, to remain any longer in my present situation, I have therefore adopted the only alternative which was left me, that of returning to Europe.*[108]

Those letters are convenient passports, they secure an introduction Persuasion

Over the years, D'Arcy had arranged for friends and colleagues going to London to call at Grosvenor Square with messages and gifts, to fill Fitzwilliam in on events in the Colony. King saw advantages in gaining access to him. *King cherished hopes of impressing a Whig nobleman who might assist in forwarding his claim to the governorship of New South Wales.*[109]

King had seen himself a strong candidate to succeed Phillip as governor, he believed the Governor would have recommended him as a successor. Instead he had been left on a remote island, disregarded and humiliated by Grose, passed over in favour of Hunter.

Suffering from disappointment and drinking heavily, he lost his vitality, he complained of *an almost fixed compression of the Lungs and Breast, with difficulty breathing and a constant pain in the stomach.* D'Arcy prescribed *Portland Cordial,* and recommended a more nourishing diet, with a little *pidgeon-broth.*[110]

There he had learnt to distinguish between the steadiness of principle and the obstinacy of self-will, between the darings of heedlessness and the resolution of a collected mind Persuasion

Governor Hunter gave D'Arcy permission to return to Sydney. D'Arcy farewelled the many people he knew on Norfolk Island – settlers, soldiers, merchants and convicts. He was thanked for his medical skills, his industry, his willingness to make life more endurable, more liveable, in what was a prison camp, ruled by a military garrison.

Graciously pleased to approve
Pride & Prejudice

He left with Catherine and the children, on the *Reliance,* after six years as assistant surgeon, without a break, unpaid, still awaiting recognition from London. Catherine had served her term, D'Arcy felt no obligation to remain.

King sent a letter to Fitzwilliam with the *Reliance,* full of praise for D'Arcy.

I could have wished that his stay here had been longer; as he certainly has acquitted himself very much to my satisfaction, and greatly to the Publick Advantage – not only in the Good Crops he has raised for the Crown, & the uninterrupted Good Order he has preserved in his district for the last Two Years – but also for the Quantity of Grain & Stock that he has raised on Three Farms of Sixty Acres each, which he acquired from Indolent Settlers. These Acquisitions & Mr Wentworth's Industry has turned very much to his pecuniary advantage.

Whatever may have been his former Errors, I have no doubt but that his future Conduct in Life, will be mark'd by the same propriety of behaviour which has procured him the General Esteem of everyone here.[111]

In April 1796, King wrote to D'Arcy in Sydney, that his treatment had proved effective, he was: *quite free of tremor in legs, hand and elbow, and quite recovered every way else.*[112] King sounded cheerful – Hunter had given him leave to return to England, to regain his health.

D'Arcy gave King a letter for Fitzwilliam, recommending him as a friend and a potential future governor.[113] Hunter was nearly sixty, King was thirty-eight, and his aim was to gain the confidence and support of patrons in London, to endorse him as the next governor of the Colony.

Catherine heard, admired, & wondered
Northanger Abbey

The return journey to Sydney was a joyful one. The sounds of the rigging, the activity on board, the slow birds and shoals of fish that followed them for hours were sights to share with William Charles, now five and a half. Catherine sat in a space on the deck, a free woman; Matthew, eight months old, was in her arms, and Dorset, two and a half, sat beside her. They had boarded the *Reliance* as a family, and their children were listed as Wentworths.

She had lived nearly twenty-one years in the world
Emma

1796 was a year that raised unanswerable questions for D'Arcy, about his past and future life. Jane would be twenty-one in December. They had looked forward to the day when she no longer needed her father's approval to be his wife. There were endless complexities, but first he needed approval to leave the Colony and he continued to press for it.

I think you must like Udolpho if you were to read it; it is so very interesting
Northanger Abbey

There was a copy of *The Mysteries of Udolpho,* Ann Radcliffe's novel, in Captain Waterhouse's little library on the *Reliance.* D'Arcy remembered Jane's teasing: *"What think you of books?"said he, smiling. "Books. Oh! No. I am sure we never read the same, or not with the same feelings."*[114]

Chapter 14

In such a world

In such a world, so thorny

JANE'S FIRST YEAR, confined at home, was dreadful, *with regrets so poignant and so fresh,* she was *captious and irritable*[1].

The small pianoforte has been removed...into her dressing room, and she spends great part of the day there; practising it is called, but I seldom hear any noise when I pass that way. What she does with herself there I do not know, there are plenty of books in the room, but it is not every girl who has been running wild the first fifteen years of her life, that can or will read. Poor creature![2]

Poor dear Jane could not bear to see anybody, anybody at all...she was suffering under severe headaches, and a nervous fever Emma

The following Christmas, she was still unwell: *My Freinds are all alarmed for me; they fear my declining health, they lament my want of spirits; they dread the effects of both. In hopes of releiving my melancholy, by directing my thoughts to other objects, they have invited several of their friends to spend the Christmas with us. This is all most kindly meant...; but what can the presence of a dozen indifferent people do to me, but weary and distress me.*[3]

Her present home was unfavourable to a nervous disorder – confined always to one room Emma

Madam Lefroy's interest in her had not waned, there was an open invitation for Jane to walk over to the Ashe Rectory to visit her and the children. *Here we shall in time be at peace, our regular employments, our books and conversation, with exercise, the children and every domestic pleasure.*[4] Jane came to rely on these outings, and Anne Lefroy's encouragement. They both read widely and loved history, and *for private amusement* Anne wrote poetry.[5]

Tis eloquence, that grace of tongue[6]   Verse

Her poems, *easy, elegant and full of...natural graces,*[7] show how she liked to present herself to the world, her temperament, her tone of voice.

At twenty-seven, two years before she married, Anne wrote a *Poetical Epistle to Miss K.B.*, describing the pleasures they shared, trusting *these stupid lines may prove how much my Kitty shares her Anna's love!*

> *Where no beaux flatter, and where shines no belle*
> *Where books and work our harmless hours employ,*
> *And a calm ramble is our highest joy.*

Musing over their *mirthful scenes* and *giddy round*, she is recalled to *truths divine* and *realms of purer light:*

> *Yet still the chosen few my mind approves,*
> *Whom my fond soul with utmost ardour loves,*
> *Cling round my heart:- with them I trace the plains,*
> *Or rise to scenes, where endless pleasure reigns.* [8]

Anne Lefroy set her poem, *On Seeing Some School-Boys in the Green Court at Canterbury with Drums, Fifes, etc*, beside Canterbury Cathedral, where her mother Jemima Brydges lived.

> *Yon tiny elf, on stilts upborne,*
> *A giant stalks the green,*
> *While by those props that raise his form,*
> *His childish folly's seen:*

> *'Tis thus, when rais'd by wealth or birth,*
> *To fill a lofty sphere,*
> *The idle coxcomb's want of worth,*
> *More plainly must appear!*

Her partial favour from my earliest years[9]   Verse

As Jane became, perhaps unwittingly, one of Madam Lefroy's chosen few, she knew *the extraordinary blessing of having one... truly sympathising friend.*[10]

Anne Lefroy took an active interest in her taste in reading: *"Dear creature!...*

when you have finished Udolpho, we will read the Italian together; and I have made out a list of ten or twelve more of the same kind for you."[11]

She encouraged Jane's writing, to vindicate her feelings, give them life, and the strength to stand their ground.

I mean only to vent my spleen against, and shew my Hatred to all those people whose parties or principles do not suit with mine The History of England

In 1791, Jane referred to Anne Lefroy, in *The History of England*, written *to prove the innocence of the Queen of Scotland...this bewitching Princess whose only freind then was the Duke of Norfolk, and whose only ones now are Mr Whitaker, Mrs. Lefroy, Mrs. Knight and myself.*[12]

Suffering as a girl of fourteen, of strong sensibility & not high spirits must suffer at such a time Persuasion

Jane celebrated their friendship, the following year, in *Lesley Castle,* with an exchange of letters between Miss Eloise Lutterell and Mrs Emma Marlowe.

Eloise is in despair over the loss of her lover – *The ill state of Health into which his loss has thrown her makes her so weak, and so unable to support the least exertion, that she has been in Tears all the Morning.*

She writes to her friend Mrs Marlowe: *You must not expect news for we see no one with whom we are in the least acquainted, or in whose proceedings we have the slightest Interest.*

You must expect from me nothing but the melancholy effusions of a broken Heart which is ever reverting to the Happiness it once enjoyed and which ill supports its present wretchedness...

I once thought that to have what is in general called a Friend (I mean one of my own sex to whom I might speak with less reserve than to any other person) independent of my sister would never be the object of my wishes, but how much was I mistaken!

To have some kind and compassionate Friend who might listen to my sorrows without endeavouring to console me was what I had for some time wished for...To find such hopes are realised is a satisfaction indeed, a satisfaction which is now almost the only one I can ever experience.[13]

Mrs Marlowe replies: *How welcome your letter was to me...whether they be grave or merry, if they concern you they must be equally interesting to me...What would my husband and Brother say of us, if they knew all the fine things I have been saying to you in this letter. It is hard that a pretty woman is never to be told she is so by one of her own sex without that person's being suspected to be either her determined Enemy, or her professed Toadeater.*

She had been forced into prudence in her youth, she learned romance as she grew older Persuasion

In her twenty-first year, Jane became friends with Tom Lefroy, a nephew of Madam Lefroy's husband, who was staying at the Ashe Rectory. He had studied law at Trinity College, Dublin, and been admitted to Lincoln's Inn.

A year younger than Jane, with a sweet Irish lilt, he enjoyed flirting with a young woman of experience. Jane gave Cassandra an exuberant account of her *Irish friend, a very gentlemanlike, good-looking, pleasant young man.*

The danger attending any young woman who attempted to draw him in Sense & Sensibility

Jane recorded Madam Lefroy's disapproval of their friendship, *before the arrival of his Aunt in our neighbourhood... his visits to her had been at stated times, and of equal and settled Duration; but on her removal to... within a walk from our house, they became both more frequent and longer... So great was her aversion to her Nephews behaviour that I have often heard her give such hints of it before his face.*[14]

To Cassandra, she mocked the asides and whispers that followed them at local balls and dances – *imagine to yourself everything most profligate and shocking in the way of dancing and sitting down together.*[15]

MADAM - An humble Admirer now addresses you. I saw you lovely Fair one as you passed on Monday last, before our House on your way to Bath. I saw you through a telescope, & was so struck by your Charms that from that time to this I have not tasted human food...

Yours,

Tom Amelia Webster

I am myself a sad example of the miseries in general attendant on a first Love & I am determined for the future to avoid the like Misfortune Jack & Alice

Jane confided in Tom her despair at losing D'Arcy, and she realised he was unwilling to get involved in her problems. *Her heart was too full to contain its afflictions. A confidante was necessary – In Thomas she hoped to experience a faithfull one – for one she must have & Thomas was the only one at Hand. To him she unbosomed herself without restraint & and after owning her passion for young W., requested his advice in what manner she should conduct herself in the melancholy Disappointment under which she laboured.*

She suffered a great deal under such a system of secrecy and concealment Emma

Thomas, who would gladly have been excused from listening to her complaint, begged leave to decline giving any advice concerning it, which much against her

will, she was obliged to comply with. Having dispatched him therefore with many injunctions of secrecy, she descended with a heavy heart into the Parlour.* [16]

The impertinence of these kind of scrutinies   Sense & Sensibility

Anne Lefroy discouraged the friendship – *he is so excessively laughed at about me at Ashe, that he is ashamed of coming to Steventon, and ran away when we called on Mrs Lefroy a few days ago… I can expose myself, however, only once more, because he leaves the country soon after next Friday.* [17]

In *Emma*, Jane described a *most unequal of all connexions…Such an elevation on her side! Such a debasement on his! It was horrible…to think how it must sink him in the general opinion, to foresee the smiles, the sneers, the merriment it would prompt at his expense; the mortification and disdain,… the thousand inconveniences to himself.*

Eight months after Tom's departure from Ashe, Jane was still on friendly terms with Anne Lefroy, she was staying at Cork Street once more as her guest. In a letter to Cassandra, she alluded to the family's view of her visit seven years earlier – *here I am once more in this Scene of Dissipation and Vice, and I begin already to find my Morals corrupted.* [18]

Such another scheme she hoped never to be betrayed into again   Emma

Two years later, her friendship with Anne Lefroy was over: *Mrs Lefroy, with whom, in spite of interruptions from both my father and James, I was enough alone to hear all that was interesting, which you will easily credit when I tell you that of her nephew she said nothing at all, and of her friend very little. She did not once mention the name of the former to me, and I was too proud to make any enquiries; but on my father's afterwards asking where he was, I learnt that he had gone back to London on his way to Ireland, where he is called to the Bar and means to practise.*

The friend of whom Madam Lefroy said very little, was Rev Samuel Blackall, an eligible clergyman she had introduced to Jane. Initially, it appears, he was interested in her, but his ardour cooled as he learnt more about her. Anne Lefroy had said too much.

She showed Jane a letter from him, mentioning her, though not by name: *It would give me particular pleasure to have an opportunity of improving my acquaintance with that family – with a hope of creating to myself a nearer interest. But at present I cannot indulge any expectation of it.*

She had become hardened to such affronts   Persuasion

World weary beyond her twenty-two years, Jane observed: *This is rational enough, there is less love and more sense in it than sometimes appeared before, and I am very well satisfied. It will go on exceedingly well, and decline away in a very reasonable manner. There seems no likelihood of his coming into Hampshire this Christmas, and it is therefore most probable that our indifference will soon be mutual, unless his regard, which appeared to spring from his knowing nothing of me at first, is best supported by never seeing me.*

Mrs Lefroy made no remarks on the letter, nor did she indeed say anything about him as relative to me. Perhaps she thinks she has said too much already.[19]

Such a proof of family weakness, such an assurance of the deepest disgrace
Pride & Prejudice

Jane could guess what was said. Years later in *Emma*, she scrutinised the presumptions behind Anne Lefroy's interference – *with what insufferable vanity had she believed herself in the secret of every body's feelings; with unpardonable arrogance proposed to arrange every body's destiny. She was proved to have been universally mistaken; and she had not quite done nothing – for she had done mischief.*

She wrote, *there was a something of resentment... which increased the desirableness of their being separate... it seemed as if an angel only could have been quite without resentment under such a stroke.* It took four years, after Madam Lefroy's sudden death, for Jane to belatedly acknowledge a debt to her, for *bestowing life, and light, and hope to me.*[20]

If you are still alive, do not think too harshly of me
Evelyn

For years after D'Arcy sailed on the *Neptune*, Jane scanned the newspapers for any mention of him, or of New South Wales. *She had only navy lists and newspapers for her authority.*[21] There were rumours the voyage of the *Neptune*, of the entire Second Fleet, had been disastrous.

Can it be Neptune?
Emma

In October 1791, she read the *Neptune* was home from China,[22] and a *month later that the captain and chief mate were to undergo a severe scrutiny,* that *no less that 179 convicts died on the voyage; and many instances of the most inhuman treatment are being daily brought forward.*[23] By February 1792, questions were being asked in the Commons. Sir Thomas Bunbury, Whig member for Sussex, demanded an account of the convicts on the Second Fleet be tabled, detailing *how many embarked and how many arrived in Botany Bay and their state of health.*[24]

Her mind opened again to an agitation of hope, by an article of news, which then began to be in circulation[25]
Pride & Prejudice

A tiny item in *The Times* in 1792, filled her with relief and joy. D'Arcy was alive and well, *Wentworth, the highwayman,* was working as a surgeon, leading an exemplary life.[26]

I read it aloud by candlelight Letters

In 1794, Jane read Robert Southey's poems, depicting life in Botany Bay. She saw a harsh, anguished world, and D'Arcy at work there, among the convicts.

> Welcome ye savage lands, ye barbarous climes
> Where angry England send her outcast sons...
> Unbroken by the plough, undelv'd by hand
> Of patient rustic; where the lowing herds
> And for the music of the beating flocks
> Alone is heard the kangaroo's sad note
> Deepening in distance. Welcome ye rude climes.[27]

> Yon tree whose purple gum bestows
> A ready medicine for the sick man's woes
> Forms with its shadowy boughs a cool retreat
> To shield us from the noontide's sultry heat.[28]

> Shall the diseased man
> Yield up his members to the surgeon's knife,
> Doubtful of succour, but to ease his frame
> Of fleshly anguish, and the coward wretch,
> Whose ulcered soul can know no human help
> Shrink from the best Physician's certain aid?[29]   Robert Southey

I felt myself to be as solemnly engaged to him, as if the strictest legal covenant had bound us to each other Sense & Sensibility

For a long time, Jane counted the days, waiting to see D'Arcy again. *She felt the want of his society every day, almost every hour.*[30] She felt herself indissolubly bound to him. When she turned twenty-one she would be free to make her own decisions, she would await his return to England, they would be reunited. Until that time, she might enjoy the friendship of the young men in her circle, she had no reason to look for a husband.

Jane was quite longing to go to Ireland Emma

Jane knew of one person who would be in touch with D'Arcy, who could tell her when he might return, his elder brother William, now a barrister in Dublin.

Would it make you happy to write to William? Mansfield Park

She could have made an enquiry or two as to the expedition and the expense of the Irish mails – it was at her tongue's end – but she abstained[31]. D'Arcy had trusted William with their secret, he knew of their marriage, she *had a fond dependence on no human creature's having heard of it from him.*[32] *He had enquired after* her *very particularly.*[33]

Her twenty-first birthday on 16 December 1796, passed without word from D'Arcy. Was he still *condemning her for the past, and considering it with high and unjust resentment.*[34] A few weeks later came the anniversary of their parting – *seven years I suppose are enough to change every pore of one's skin, and every feeling of one's mind.*[35]

Engrossed by writing Persuasion

In 1796, Jane, gaining in confidence, began a full length novel, *Elinor and Marianne*. She finished it, and soon commenced a second, *First Impressions*. In each of them she told the story of Jane and D'Arcy, in the first, the heartbreaking sadness and loss she experienced; in the second, the great delight and happiness they brought each other. There she declared – *I am happier even than Jane, she could only smile, I laugh!*[36]

The strong sisterly partiality Pride & Prejudice

At the centre of both novels are two close-knit sisters, markedly different in temperament. Through Jane and Elizabeth Bennet in *Pride & Prejudice*, and Elinor and Marianne Dashwood in *Sense & Sensibility*, Jane presented her various and, at times, contesting perspectives on feeling, love and lovers.

James Austen realised both sisters in *Sense & Sensibility*, were studies of Jane:

> *On such Subjects no wonder that she shou'd write well*
> *In whom so united those Qualities dwell...*
> *Fair Elinor's Self in that Mind is exprest,*
> *And the Feelings of Marianne live in that Brest*[37]

Action off St Domingo Persuasion

In *Sense & Sensibility*, Jane included a reference to her sister's lover, Tom Fowle, revealing the elder sister, Elinor, is interested in someone whose *name begins with an F*.[38] When Cassandra was nineteen and Tom twenty-seven, they became engaged but could not afford to marry.

The following year, 1793, his mother's cousin, Lord Craven, gave Tom the living of the Church of St John the Baptist, at Allington in Wiltshire. In 1795, Tom accompanied Lord Craven to the West Indies as his military chaplain. He died there, at San Domingo, of yellow fever, in 1797.

Reading aloud the most material passages Northanger Abbey

Jane Austen read her first novels to her parents and Cassandra. In *First Impressions*, later revised as *Pride & Prejudice*, she took the opportunity to tell something of her side of the story, and to illustrate the qualities she loved and admired in D'Arcy.

Jane acknowledged his independent spirit: *he likes to have his own way very well, but so we all do.*[39] She presented him as serious minded and reserved, not one to seek out society: *"I certainly have not the talent which some people possess,"* said Darcy, *"of conversing easily with those I have never seen before. I cannot catch their tone of conversation, or appear interested in their concerns, as I often see done."*

She described *his fine, tall person, handsome features, noble mien;*[40] and the qualities in him she loved most – his wit, his disdain for frivolous society, his enjoyment of intelligent conversation. He was an *intricate character*, to her, the *most amusing.*[41]

She gave his opinion of dancing, *"What a charming amusement for young people this is, Mr. Darcy! There is nothing like dancing after all. – I consider it as one of the first refinements of polished societies."*

"Certainly, Sir; – and it has the advantage also of being in vogue amongst the less polished societies of the world. – Every savage can dance."

There are moments in *Pride & Prejudice* where Darcy's words seem oddly outside the context of the story. *My temper I dare not vouch for. – It is I believe too little yielding – certainly too little for the convenience of the world. I cannot forget the follies and vices of others so soon as I ought, nor their offences against myself. My feelings are not puffed about with every attempt to move them. My temper would perhaps be called resentful. – My good opinion once lost is lost for ever.* Was this confession of his flaws, a means for Jane to give her father an insight into D'Arcy's pursuit of those who cheated him and defaulted on gambling debts.

To secure & expedite a marriage Pride & Prejudice

In *Pride and Prejudice,* Jane deliberately shifted the moral perspective in her story of Lydia and Wickham. *Imprudent as a marriage between Mr. Wickham and our poor Lydia would be, we are now anxious to be assured it has taken place, for there is but too much reason to fear they are not gone to Scotland…that W. never intended to go there or to marry Lydia at all… My poor mother is really ill and keeps her room… and as to my father, I never in my life saw him so affected.*

Was she suggesting that if she and D'Arcy had not eloped to Gretna Green, but simply lived together, George Austen may have insisted on marrying them.

Satisfied that it was so, & feeling it her due Emma

In writing her first two novels, Jane found an outlet for the trauma and grief she carried for seven years, from her fifteenth to her twenty-first year. She did not write to obtain closure, she wanted to rescue her story from damnation and oblivion. Recording her story and her feelings shifted a great burden from her shoulders, and for some years after she lost interest in writing.

She shared the manuscript of *First Impressions* with friends, for them to enjoy. In 1799, Cassandra wrote from Godmersham, asking to read it again. *I do not wonder at your wanting to read First Impressions again,* Jane replied, *so seldom as you have gone through it, & that so long ago.*[42] A few months later she teased Martha Lloyd about her interest in the story, telling Cassandra: *I would not let Martha read First Impressions again on any account, & am very glad that I did not leave it in your power.-She is very cunning, but I see through her design.- she means to publish it from Memory, & one more perusal must enable her to do it.*[43]

Open, candid, artless, guileless[44] — Northanger Abbey

In 1798, Jane began a third novel, *Susan*, set in Bath, in which she turned a satirical eye on her youth and naivety, and on her brother James and his Oxford friends, their drinking exploits, gadding about, womanising and crass stupidity.

Her heroine, Catherine Morland, blatantly manipulated by her brother James and Isabella Thorpe, is used as a cover for their romantic adventures. James' first serious love affair ended badly; *just at present it comes hard to poor James; but that will not last for ever; and I dare say he will be a discreeter man all his life, for the foolishness of his first choice.*

Susan, renamed *Northanger Abbey*, was published in 1817, after Jane's death, thirty years after James' broken engagement.

I flatter myself with the hope of surviving my share in this disappointment — Lady Susan

Jane's life was shuttered in, while her brothers were taking their places in the world. She watched their advance and retreat through all the accepted, time-honoured steps of courtship and commitment.

The expectation of one wedding made everybody eager for another — Pride & Prejudice

In December 1791, Edward, twenty-four, married eighteen year old Elizabeth Bridges. Fanny, the first of their eleven children, was born a year later. Though Austens, they were members of the Knight family, residing in the comforts of Kent. Cassandra would spend weeks and months at a time with them and their growing family, Jane was less welcome.

James married three months after Edward, in March 1792. He met Anne Mathew while he was curate at Overton, and riding to hounds. She was six years older, thirty-three, one of the twin daughters of General Edward Mathew and Lady Jane Bertie, daughter of the Duke of Ancaster.

Their union offered connexions of immense importance to the Austens. Anne's cousin Louisa was married to Samuel Gambier, who became Secretary of the Navy Board in 1795, and First Commissioner the following year. Louisa's sister Jane was the wife of Admiral James Gambier; he became the patron of Frank and Charles Austen, and he assisted their advancement in the Navy.[45]

General Mathew, born in Antigua, was a brigadier-general in the American War of Independence. Under the 1783 Treaty of Versailles, Britain regained control of Grenada from France, and in 1785, he was appointed governor-in-chief of Grenada and the Grenadine Islands.[46]

Grenada's plantation society was diverse, with a large French speaking population and numerous Irish, the remnants of forced labour shipped from Ireland a century before; supplanted by a stream of West African slaves, and growing numbers of Free Coloureds in the islands.

General Mathew served two terms as Governor, from 1785 to 1789. He applied a firm hand to administration of the islands, restoring the island fortifications to defend against the return of the French, and dealing with sectarian tensions between Catholics and Protestants, bloody skirmishes amongst the slaves and threats from runaways.

Their father is a clergyman & their brother is a clergyman, & they are all clergymen together　　　　　　　　　　　　　　　　　　　　　　　Mansfield Park

James and Anne had a daughter, Anna, in April 1793. General Mathew promised £100 a year towards her support, and in 1794, he bought James an army chaplaincy in the 86th Regiment. James employed a curate to perform the duties.

Anne died when her daughter was two. Anna's annuity of £100 stopped immediately, impacting on James' household. General Mathew, meanwhile, was facing unexpected financial difficulties.

Treasury had presented him with a demand for £11,000, the salary for his second term as Governor. His initial appointment was made by George III. On his re-appointment, the King did not ratify his salary, and now insane, could not remember. In 1805, when he died, General Mathew's debt to Treasury, with interest, was calculated as £24,000.

Jane is said to have modelled General Tilney in *Northanger Abbey,* on General Mathew. He demands the *strictest punctuality of family hours,* and dominates and crushes the individuality of his children. Catherine Morland experiences *his unpleasantness, ill-will* and his appalling *breach of hospitality.*

Perhaps Jane used her late sister-in-law as the model for Eleanor Tilney, the General's daughter; and that character's reserve and gentle, stoic qualities reflect something of Anne Mathew.

All the constancy of his wife Emma

Eliza de Feuillide had remained in London since 1789, caring for her son Hastings, and her mother. Philadelphia Hancock died in February 1792, after a long, painful struggle with breast cancer.

Eliza's husband, the Comte de Feuillide, came to London a few weeks later, but *soon received accounts from France which informed him that having already exceeded his Leave of Absence, if he still continued in England he would be considered as one of the Emigrants, & consequently his whole property forfeited to the Nation. Such advices were not to be neglected and he was obliged to depart for Paris.*⁴⁷

He and Eliza spent a fortnight in Bath before his return to France. Eliza is believed to have miscarried after his visit. It was the last time she was to see him, two years later in the escalating violence of the Revolution, he was arrested, tried and guillotined.

*The sound of war has lost its terrors ere it reaches me*⁴⁸ William Cowper

In June, Eliza was caught in a riot near Grosvenor Square – *Tuesday last going thro' Mount Street in my carriage I most unexpectedly found myself in the midst of an immense mob who were contending with a large party of Guards on Horseback... The noise of the populace, the drawn swords & pointed bayonets of the guards, the fragments of bricks and mortar thrown on every side, one of which had nearly killed my Coachman, the firing at one end of the street which was already begun, altogether in short alarmed me so much, that I really have never been well since.*

*The Confusion continued all that day & Night & the following Day, & for these eight & forty Hours, I have seen nothing but large parties of Soldiers parading up & down in this Street...How soon in such a City as this, a Fire, very trifling in its beginning, might be productive of the most serious Consequences.*⁴⁹

Jane followed reports of the riots in the press. In *The Times,* another item caught her attention, the captain and first mate of the *Neptune* had been tried for murder and acquitted.⁵⁰ She *could enjoy no comfort.*⁵¹

Thinking of the French as one cd wish, disappointed in every thing Letters

By September 1792, the Revolution was spiralling into violent bloodshed. In September 1792, France abolished the monarchy, proclaimed a Republic and announced the trial of King Louis XVI. The National Guard was ordered into gaols in Paris and other cities, and murdered over a thousand people, including many political prisoners and Catholic clergy.

In London, Pitt recalled Parliament for approval to call out the militia, to assist with national defence. Henry and James were members, *trained in the use of arms… that in the case of an actual invasion, they would perform such military duties as shall be required.*[52]

The whole party are at war — Lady Susan

The events in France caused enormous tensions amongst the Whigs. Charles Fox welcomed and supported the Revolution, as *liberty rising up against tyranny – how much the greatest event that ever happened in the world! And how much the best!*[53]

Edmund Burke, who supported the American Revolution, condemned the French, who *have shewn themselves the ablest architects of ruin that had hitherto existed in the world…the excesses of an irrational, unprincipled, proscribing, confiscating, plundering, ferocious, bloody and tyrannical democracy.*[54]

Fitzwilliam, a loyal friend to both Fox and Burke, failed to find a bridge between them. After the September Massacres, he wrote to Burke, saying the French cause was *now looked upon with execration, and the fallacy of their system as universally admitted, as the wickedness and cruelty of their proceedings abominated. You will recollect the change of sentiment upon the subject of the American War: on this occasion, the vane has veered not only more suddenly, but more completely too.*[55]

Fitzwilliam gave generously to assist the many Catholic clergy fleeing to England[56] after the massacres. Echoing Henry VIII's dissolution of the monasteries, two hundred and fifty years earlier, France nationalised church property, abolished collection of tithes, and dissolved monasteries, religious orders and congregations, except for those caring for children and the sick.

Eliza, living in Marylebone, found herself surrounded by an ever growing community of displaced French émigrés. Around four thousand refugees had fled to England,[57] they were seen by authorities as a security risk, who might be spying for France. In January 1793, Parliament passed an *Aliens Act*, giving the government control over their landing, registration and passports, their movement and place of residence, with power to arrest and deport them.[58] Through Eliza, Jane met and made friends among the émigrés, and listened to their difficulties.

A neighbourhood of voluntary spies — Northanger Abbey

In 1792, William Wickham was appointed a magistrate, attached to the Whitechapel police office, to investigate and report on possible treasonable activities. In July 1794, he was made Superintendent of Aliens. He set up a system of surveillance to cover the émigré community, alert for spies and revolutionaries. At first it covered only the French, but in the mid-nineties it was extended to exercise control over the hundreds of United Irishmen crossing the Irish Sea to escape the force of the *Insurrection Acts*.

Wickham created Britain's first secret service, gathering intelligence through the Home Office, Foreign Service, the Admiralty and War Office, the Customs service and Post Office, and from informers. He created a *Registry*, with *an alphabetical list of all the persons against whom informations have been made, the nature of the information, when given, and by whom, so that no character of that description may be unknown to Government, whenever his, or her (for we have lady conspirators) name occurs.*[59]

Wickham reported to Lord Grenville, Foreign Secretary, and to Evan Nepean in the Home Office. He took an active interest in groups in London pressing for political reform, including the London Corresponding Society, men from the artisan class, without the vote, who advocated the reform of parliament.

The people who fell martyrs The History of England

Maurice Margarot, who lived in France in the early years of the Revolution, became president of the London Corresponding Society in 1792, advocating electoral reform, shorter parliaments and a broader franchise.

In 1793, he and Joseph Gerrold attended a national convention in Edinburgh, where delegates demanded universal male suffrage, declared their support for the principles of the French Revolution, and called each other *citizen*. Margarot, Gerrold and William Skirving were arrested, charged with sedition, and sentenced to fourteen years transportation. They were sent to New South Wales on the *Surprize*, with Thomas Muir and Thomas Palmer, and arrived in Sydney in October 1794. They were known as the *Scottish Martyrs*.

A system of hypocrisy & deceit, espionage & treachery Emma

In October 1794, Wickham moved to Switzerland, where he endeavoured to disrupt and undermine the revolutionary government in France, and promote restoration of the monarchy. He organised Britain's continental allies into coalitions. Liberally funded by Grenville, he paid them handsomely to pursue military campaigns against the French. His intelligence network reported on French troop movements, shipping and operations. French police records describe his, *Machiavellian cunning and largesse.*[60]

Wickham was the *Scarlet Pimpernel*,[61] who assisted many French aristocrats to escape to England. He arranged with his friend the Prince of Wales[62] for a number of them to stay at *Kempshott*, the country estate the Prince leased near Dummer. *Kempshott was crammed with emigrants, and the hospitable welcome they received from the prince must have been some consolation to them. For their amusement a great stag-hunt was got up.*[63]

Charles-Philippe, Comte d'Artois, brother of Louis XVI, later Charles X, took refuge in England during the Revolution. He thanked Wickham *for the care and zeal with which you have served the common cause, & that of the King, my brother, in particular, while on the important mission which your Government has confided in you.*[64]

Observances which he supposed a regular part of the business   Pride & Prejudice

In 1798, Wickham returned to London as under-secretary in the Home Office. A year later he was back in Switzerland, progressing his operations in France, liaising with troop commanders from Austria and Russia involved in the war against Napoleon. He returned to England in 1801 and was appointed a privy councillor. In August 1802 took up the post of Chief Secretary of Ireland.

In 1803, Robert Emmet, returned to Dublin from exile in Paris to lead a rebellion against the British. Born in Dublin in 1778, at fifteen he attended Trinity College. He joined the College Historical Society, formed by Edmund Burke in 1747, where he debated Jane's *Irish friend,* Tom Lefroy. Influenced by his elder brother Thomas, a friend of Wolfe Tone, he was expelled from Trinity for his involvement with the United Irish.

In July 1803, with inadequate preparation, Emmet issued a declaration in the name of *the Provisional Government,* and with a group of supporters, made an attempt to capture Dublin Castle. His rebellion lasted less than an hour, the authorities knew of his plans well in advance.

It is believed Wickham tricked Emmet into returning home from Paris to lead a revolt, and that Pitt recommended he *be approached for the purpose.*[65] Under Wickham's surveillance, his rebellion was contained and exploited.

Wickham had nearly three thousand men arrested across Ireland, and personally interrogated many of them, *using suggestions of mercy, trickery, polite threats and hints of blackmail to break prisoners' resistance.*[66] The intelligence he obtained enabled him to develop a comprehensive registry of Irish conspirators.

From prison, Robert Emmet wrote to his secret lover, Sarah Curran. Wickham obtained the letter and sent the military to search her home. Her father, a barrister, cast her off as irrevocably tainted.

Emmet's trial lasted thirteen hours, he pleaded guilty to high treason, and gave a powerful oration from the dock. He made only one request, *the charity of silence, let no man write my epitaph,* finishing, *when my country takes her place among the nations of the earth, then, and not till then, let my epitaph be written. I have done.*

Robert Emmet was hung and beheaded on 20 September 1803, aged twenty-five. On the morning of his execution he wrote to Wickham, absolving him of guilt for his death.

Sarah Curran, lived for five years after his death. In November 1805, in Cork, she married a cousin of Fitzwilliam, Captain Robert Henry Sturgeon, a British Army officer who served in Egypt. When she died of tuberculosis in 1808, her father would not permit her to be buried with her elder sister.

Jane Austen commented on Wickham's intelligence activities in a riddle :

Divided, I'm a gentleman
In public, Deeds & Powers
United, I'm a monster, who off
That Gentleman devours.[67]

So respectable a Curate as yourself
The Visit

After Anne Mathew's death in 1795, James Austen was soon eager to marry again. He paid his addresses to his cousin Eliza, who once again found herself engaged in a flirtation with both James and Henry.

James was first to propose, but he faced the trenchant opposition of his mother: *were you not blinded by a sort of fascination, it would be ridiculous in me to repeat the instances of great misconduct on her side, so very generally known. Her neglect of her husband, her encouragement of other men, her extravagance and dissipation were so gross and notorious, that no one could be ignorant of them at the time, nor can now have forgotten them. It is my duty to oppose the match.*[68]

Eliza returned to London, unwell, with a lump in her breast. Remembering her mother's suffering, she sought treatment, and was prescribed poultices of bread and milk. She found this treatment *excessively inconvenient as it confines me entirely to the house and prevents the admittance of any Visitors, a few insipid females excepted.*[69]

The poultices proved ineffectual, and in December 1796, her physician, Sir Walter Farquhar, operated without anaesthetic, to remove the growth, and he treated a remaining lump with caustic. Eliza's letters made no complaint. Fifteen years later, after a similar operation, Fanny Burney described *a terror that surpasses all description, and the most torturing pain.*[70] Eliza lived seventeen years after her surgery, Fanny, twenty eight.

I have had the smallpox, and must therefore submit to my unhappy fate
Lesley Castle

In January 1797, James married Mary Lloyd, one of the three daughters of Rev Nowes Lloyd and Martha Craven. Jane was close to Martha Lloyd, but she and

Mary were never friends. She may have had her in mind in her portrayal of Mary Musgrove in *Persuasion*, who complains she is not given *the precedence that was her due.*⁷¹

I cannot remember the time when I did not love Eliza Sense & Sensibility

On the last day of December 1797, Eliza married Henry Austen, ten years her junior, now an officer in the Oxford Militia, in London on leave. There was no time for banns to be read, they were married by a special licence. Their marriage was a happy one, and they welcomed Jane to enjoy the society and culture of their London life.

Henry is different, he loves to be doing Mansfield Park

Jane dedicated *Lesley Castle* to Henry in 1792, with a mock promissory note: *Messrs Demand & Co.- please to pay Jane Austen Spinster the sum of one hundred guineas on account of your Humble Servant. £105. H. T. Austen*

It was an accurate prediction of the important role Henry would later play in her life. He was the brother who encouraged her writing, found her publishers, undertook negotiations for her, who made sure agreements were in place for her to be paid, and for a time, at least, ensured she remained anonymous.

Henry said of Jane, that *neither fame nor profit mixed with her early motives.*⁷² She had certainly considered them; at sixteen, in her dedication to *Kitty, or the Bower* she suggested her novels might obtain *a place in every library in the Kingdom, and run through threescore Editions.*

The feelings of her father Emma

Throughout the 1790s, George Austen watched over his favourite daughter. He had hoped Jane would pick up her old life anew, but he saw her sense of herself and her destiny were irrevocably changed. She was more independent minded. She enjoyed the company of young men, she flirted, but with detachment, with a laugh. Without declaring it, she considered herself married, and silently awaited her husband's return.

People that marry can never part Northanger Abbey

Her father knew from the first that Jane's expectations were fruitless, he saw only disappointment awaiting her. He believed she had escaped *the most irremediable of evils, a connection for life with an unprincipled man.*⁷³ But he suffered periods of considerable regret that he had contributed to her unhappiness. He encouraged her writing as unobtrusively as he could.

It is in no ones power to make me happy A Collection of Letters

George Austen recognised Jane's talent, he asked her to keep a record of the many pieces she wrote to amuse the family. He gave her three notebooks into which she copied her juvenilia. On the front of the second volume she noted, *Ex dono mei Patris,* a gift from my father, and he wrote inside the front cover, *Effusions of Fancy by a very Young Lady consisting of Tales in a Style entirely new.* On her nineteenth birthday, he bought her *a small mahogany writing desk with one long drawer and glass inkstand compleat.*

With Caution & Care I Commend to Your Charitable Criticism
A Collection of Letters

George Austen found *Elinor & Marianne* bleak and heartbreaking. Perhaps Jane began *First Impressions,* in part, to alleviate the pain it caused him. He was delighted with it, and was prepared to finance its publication. In November 1797, he wrote to Cadell & Davies, publishers, and asked their terms to publish it *at the author's risk.* Cadell declined his proposal *by return of post.*[74]

Her father's encouragement of her writing, his efforts to have her published, were proof to Jane of his pride in her creative resilience, his relief that she was not crushed by events, and his confidence that the solace she sought through her writing could blossom into something marvellous.

My sister, poor girl! She still laments his death with undiminished constancy
Lady Susan

Tom Fowle's death in 1797 bound the Austen sisters closer, they threw their lot in with each other, facing the limited horizons of their lives together. Jane's relationship with Cassandra was a source of protection and strength for her, though at the same time, she *really lived remote in great reserve.*

After her first two novels, Jane *Austen never again gives us a picture of two intimately united sisters... Nowhere does she give any picture of united family happiness... at Longbourn, or Mansfield, Northanger or Kellynch. This, to any one who understands Jane Austen's preoccupation with truth, and her selection of material only from among observed facts tested by personal experience, speaks volumes, in its characteristically quiet way, for her position towards her own family.*[75]

I will not say...I have not had some happy moments; but I can say, that I have never known the blessing of one tranquil hour
Emma

The outcome of her affair with D'Arcy, was Jane's confinement within the narrow Austen family ambit for the remainder of her life. *It was to be her last independent adventure in the outside world. Thereafter, for the rest of her life, she never strayed outside the enclosure of her family circle.*[76]

Chapter 15

A Colony Abandoned

We none of us expect to be in smooth water all our days

ON SATURDAY 5 MARCH 1796, D'Arcy Wentworth and Catherine Crowley stood on deck with their sons, as the *Reliance* came through the heads into Port Jackson. When the sailors pointed out the *Sow & Pigs* reef, William called out excitedly, he could see them foraging amid the waves.

Looking over the foreground of unfinished buildings, waving linen & tops of houses to the sea, dancing & sparkling in sunshine & freshness   Sanditon

The town had grown and stretched in six years, huts and boatsheds nestled in bays and inlets, and new buildings crowded round the Cove. On the ridge above, a tower was going up for a town clock, and there was talk on board about a new play-house![1]

Six months earlier, on his return, Governor Hunter ordered a muster, which reckoned the population at 3,211. He proclaimed the town of Sydney, marked it into four divisions, *King, Nepean, Maskelyne*[2] and *Banks,* ordered the houses numbered, and the water supply protected.[3]

Reliance anchored in Sydney Cove, dwarfed by a merchantman, *Marquis Cornwallis,* standing nearby. She had arrived three weeks earlier with more than two hundred Irish convicts and exiles, guarded by the New South Wales Corps. She was to stay in port three months, while a Court of Inquiry investigated the shooting of seven convicts on board, and heard details of floggings, mutiny and death during the voyage.

A Capital season'd Hunter Mansfield Park

D'Arcy called on Governor Hunter shortly after he landed. He was immensely grateful for his permission to leave Norfolk Island. He wanted his approval to leave the Colony, and sail with his family to England.

John Hunter gave him a warm welcome, glad to see him here in Sydney. He told D'Arcy he could do little more, the Home Office had failed to respond to previous requests on his behalf. At this time, he could see no possible benefit in pressing the matter of his returning to England.

Throughout Hunter's period as governor, D'Arcy remained in the shadows. Hunter heeded Phillip's example, never mentioning him in despatches, believing rightly or wrongly that London would not condone his formal recognition.

Before she went out of harbour Mansfield Park

A letter waiting for D'Arcy from Charles Cookney told him he had goods on the *Marquis Cornwallis*. He went on board to claim them, to meet Michael Hogan, the owner and captain, an educated Irishman from County Clare.

Hogan spoke about the convicts he had transported. Of the two hundred and thirty three taken on board the *Marquis Cornwallis* from Cork, seventy were Defenders, Catholics agitating for social and political reform.

He invited D'Arcy to join him for St Patrick's Day, and on the afternoon of March 17, *fair weather and pleasant,* D'Arcy stood on the deck, overlooking the town, celebrating Ireland and her history. Hogan gave *the ships company double allowance of Grogg & afterwards permitted them to go on shore.*[4]

A Man of Business Letters

With the goods he received from Cookney, D'Arcy could commence trading in Sydney immediately. He had saved nearly £800, his profits from farming and trade on Norfolk Island,[5] and he had a reliable London agent. *He was confident… he had always been lucky; he knew he should be still.*[6]

Very impolitic too – for it is provoking me to retaliate Pride & Prejudice

He knew it would be difficult to set up as a trader, he had to tread warily. He would be in competition with Rum Corps officers, with their wealth and power, their sense of superiority and arrogance,

A few weeks before, the Corps had dealt with John Boston, a free settler who arrived with his wife and three children on the *Surprize*, in October 1794. An experienced brewer and distiller,[7] he began brewing and selling beer made from Indian corn, using Cape gooseberries instead of hops for a bitter flavour.

A young private, William Faithfull, had shot Mr Boston's fine sow. When Boston shouted *"murder,"* the Quartermaster ordered Faithfull to thrash him.

Boston took a civil action for assault and Faithfull was fined forty shillings. He appealed, but Hunter upheld the decision, calling it a very lenient punishment. The officers were outraged at a member of the Corps being disciplined by a magistrate, angered by the Governor's dismissal of his appeal, and his censure.

Thomas Fyshe Palmer, one of the Scottish Martyrs, wrote, *the Bostons, firmly, but in guarded language, insisted on the rights of British subjects to carry on any trade, not prohibited, in one of his Majesty's harbours. This irritated the whole governing despotic power of the settlement against them. They were refused a grant, (and) servants.*[8]

Bustle & shopping
Pride & Prejudice

Cookney had sent clothing, cloth, linen and household goods for the Sydney market, and D'Arcy set up as a merchant. He could rely on trade for a living in Sydney, he could not earn *a single shilling* as a surgeon. He wrote to Fitzwilliam, reiterating his plans to return, after six years of *disagreeable circumstances*, reassuring him he would not stay in London.[9]

A year later, D'Arcy sent a Treasury Bill for £502.10.0, to repay Fitzwilliam for the funds he advanced for Cookney to purchase the goods. Cookney sent his congratulations, *there is reason to think that the things sent out to Mr Wentworth found a good market.*[10]

Goods from Cookney soon formed only part of D'Arcy's trading stock. With his colleague William Balmain, in direct conflict with the Rum Corps, he began buying shares in the cargoes brought in by speculative captains.

Thomas Fyshe Palmer wrote: *the destructive and oppressive monopoly of the military officers forbad everyone to purchase of the ships that came into the harbour. The military officers alone bought, and resold to all the colony at 1,000 per cent profit and often more.*[11]

To the Rum Corps officers, D'Arcy was an interloper, attempting to breach their unofficial monopoly. They did nothing directly to stop him trading, but they went to great efforts to denigrate him and undermine his reputation, with repercussions that continued long after his death. He told Fitzwilliam of their *Whim & Caprice*, doing *everything in their power to render my Residence in this Colony disagreeable to me.*[12]

Exorbitant charges & frauds
Mansfield Park

In May 1796, the *Britannia* returned again from India with cargo for the Corps. *Great and tumultuous was the joy and ludicrously extravagant was the exhibition of it on the arrival and landing... Captain Raven was met and attended by the principal officers of the colony, the military band playing and a chaise belonging* to Colonel Paterson, the military commandant, was brought by the soldiers to the landing place in which his ponderous body was placed and dragged by a circuitous route to the barracks amidst the noisy huzzas of the soldiers of the town in an uproar and the music at one time even struck up the military air, He comes, he comes, the Hero comes.[13]

One of the *Britannia*'s crew described the Rum Corps officers: *Land added to their own possessions, purchased with enormous priced articles of the Soldiers under their command. Publick duty neglected, the Officer standing forth in different characters – A Publican – Money Lender – Farmer – Chandler – and an Officer of the New South Wales Rum Corps, which must strike a man of common feelings, with horror and detestation.*[14]

Mrs Macarthur saw things differently – *The officers of the colony with a few others possessed of money or credit in England, unite together and purchase the cargoes of such vessels as repair to this country from various quarters. Two or more are chosen from the number to bargain for the cargo offered for sale which is then divided amongst them in proportion to the amount of their subscriptions. This arrangement prevents monopoly and the imposition that would otherwise be practiced by the masters of the ships.*[15]

Aye, I knew he was in some such low way — A Collection of Letters

Whilst it was not unacceptable for military officers to be in wholesale trade, it was seen as improper to set themselves up in retail. The Rum Corps used their convict servants and common-law wives to on-sell their rum and other imports.

Exertions which had never cost half so much before — Emma

Their trading enterprise, begun with the *Britannia,* rapidly became the engine for the development of the Colony's internal economy. The officers followed precedents set in other places, particularly India, where civil and military officers made substantial profits from trade.

In India army officers operated in a vibrant market with many players, they were never able to acquire monopoly control. Trade by the military in New South Wales had a very distinctive aspect, with virtually no competition, the Rum Corps achieved an immediate monopoly.

The Wealth of Nations

Under the Rum Corps, private enterprise grew and flourished. Despite its unpalatable impacts, the officers' enterprise attracted ships and goods, reduced the Colony's impossible dependence on Britain, and overcame the restrictions on trade imposed by the East India Company. Theirs was the first effective endeavour to transform the penal colony into a trading nation.

John Macarthur wrote home – *the changes we have undergone since the departure of Governor Phillip are so great and extraordinary that to recite them all might create some suspicion of their truth. From a state of disponding poverty and threatened famine that this Settlement should be raised to its present aspect in so short a time is scarcely credible.*[16]

It was a ringing endorsement of Adam Smith's theory that self-interest added to the public good: *It is not from the benevolence of the butcher, the brewer, or the baker, that we expect our dinner, but from their regard to their own interest. We address ourselves, not to their humanity, but to their self-love, and never talk to them of our own necessities, but of their advantages.*[17]

Bad things for the country, sure to raise the price of provisions & make the poor good for nothing Sanditon

As the Rum Corps tightened their control over imports, they drove up prices. The emancipated convicts, no longer on government rations, were unable to pay for goods. When they bought food and necessities they were price-gouged by the officers. If they provided labour to the officers and wealthy settlers, they were exploited for negligible reward.

Many went into debt and bankruptcy, abandoned their land grants or sold them cheaply to the officers. Many crowded back to Sydney Town to live, or to await an opportunity to join a ship going home.

A sailor confronts the military

John Hunter returned to find the culture of New South Wales completely altered, no longer a place of benevolent ideals, under an enlightened Governor. The military oligarchy, in control for three years, had extended its political and financial power throughout the Colony. The populace, subject to the whims of the Rum Corps, was riven with divisions and hostilities.

Within a few days of his arrival, he travelled to Parramatta and called on the Macarthurs at *Elizabeth Farm*. As Inspector of Public Works, John Macarthur allocated convicts to public works, and to the many officers who received land grants from Major Grose. He was known as the *Governor of Parramatta*.

Hunter knew Grose relied on Macarthur, that he was the most influential of the officers, the one with business acumen. Hunter needed to work with him to gain support and cooperation from the Rum Corps, and hoped to gain his allegiance.

And rather better pasturage for their cows Sense and Sensibility

He accepted Macarthur's hospitality, he was shown the farming districts, where Macarthur pointed out the many achievements of officers and wealthy settlers.

What he saw confirmed that *private enterprise had been a very great success...the farms of the different officers and...settlers afforded great abundance, which did not succeed in the hands of the emancipated convicts...he was compelled to acknowledge that cattle of all kinds throve much better in the hands of individuals than in those of the government.*[18]

Particularly attached to these young men Pride & Prejudice

At home with his accomplished wife, Macarthur reigned over the social life of Sydney. Elizabeth Macarthur was gracious and welcoming, *Elizabeth Farm* was a meeting place for Rum Corps officers, where they enjoyed musical evenings and reminders of the life they left behind in England.

On a visit to Parramatta, John Price, surgeon of the *Minerva*, called on Mrs Macarthur, *I found her sitting alone with two stout athletic natives who were perfectly naked, & conversing with them with the greatest composure.*[19]

James, Macarthur's fourth son, recalled their relations with the Aboriginals, *as far back as I can recollect the Aboriginal natives came about our house at Parramatta generally a few families only, but occasionally in large parties.*

I will distinguish two, Tjedboro[20] *and Harry, at that time both fine young men. The former was the son of Pemelway, notorious in the earliest years of the Colony for his wild, untameable spirit and his hostility to Europeans; he was shot I believe in a skirmish before I was born. Tjedboro was a mere boy at this time. My father, as I have heard him say, took him in hand to reclaim him.*

He was accordingly brought in and treated with kindness, and for a time he was quite happy and docile. After a lapse of a few weeks, my father being out walking with the boy, and wishing to go in one direction while the boy wished to go in another, and finding persuasion to no avail, he used the tone of command. The young savage immediately took to the woods, and was not seen by our family for many months. He then resumed his old habits, coming and going as he liked but always kindly treated and without attempts to restrain him. He always called my father "Master" but I do not think he would ever employ himself about any useful occupation.

He used to say he should "Like to be a White Man," that is civilised, that he might be a gentleman; but the idea of being controlled he could not endure.[21]

Conscious superiority rather than any solicitude to oblige Mansfield Park

Initially, Hunter relied on twenty-eight year old Macarthur, but he never gained his full cooperation. His intimate knowledge of the Colony and his influence over his fellow officers ensured he held a position of dominance. Macarthur had been, and was still, the virtual administrator of the Colony. As paymaster and inspector of public works, he received extensive land grants, his salary was doubled, and he had unrestricted access to convict labour. His pursuit of wealth and his complicity in the commercial activities of the Corps created unresolvable conflict with Hunter.

In his role as assistant to Lieutenant-Governor Grose, and now to Governor Hunter, Macarthur gained credibility with the administration in London. Despite his best efforts, Hunter, in his sixties, realised he was no match for Macarthur and the Rum Corps. His authority was continually undermined, and his power as Governor under challenge.

Hunter wrote to the Under Secretary of State, *there is not a person in this colony whose opinions I hold in greater contempt than I do this busybody's, because I have ever observed that under the most specious and plausible of them has always been cover'd a self interested motive.*[22]

Law being the worst wilderness Mansfield Park

One of Hunter's first actions was to remove the legal processes from military control. He appointed a new judge advocate, new magistrates and justices of the peace, depriving many officers of power they had enjoyed, and in many cases used for their own advancement. They still served on the Governor's Court and juries, but Hunter had signalled the restoration of civil government.[23]

He reported that his reinstatement of civil magistrates was not welcomed by some, who *began to show a disposition to annoy the civil power by every indirect means they cou'd contrive.*[24]

Hunter found his greatest problem in the Colony was that *in matters of law the Governor could only consult his law books, he had no person to advise with; that was a great inconvenience.*[25]

Lo! The cattle sweetly feeding scamper, startled at the sound Verse

In December 1795, Hunter sent good news to London, cattle that escaped from Sydney town in 1788 had been found, living wild, in very verdant pasture. In a valley he named *Cowpastures*, some fifty miles to the south west, the Governor had counted sixty-one beasts of the Cape of Good Hope breed.[26]

Hunter did not include Corps officers in his search party, and he declared the area out of bounds to them and to settlers. Macarthur, though, was soon pressing to appropriate the *Cowpastures* land and the cattle grazing there.

There might not be a remedy found for some of these evils Mansfield Park

A few weeks after D'Arcy arrived in Sydney, Samuel Leeds, a surgeon recently sent out, proved *incapable of doing his Duty for being in an almost constant State of Drunkenness for several months.* Hunter accepted his resignation, he offered

D'Arcy his position, appointing him without authority from London. William Balmain, his colleague from Norfolk Island, was Principal Surgeon.

D'Arcy told Fitzwilliam, Hunter *has without any solicitation on my part, been pleased to confer this vacant appointment upon me. I trust therefore the hour is come, when no possible objections can be made to this appointment.*[27]

The first start of its possibility   Emma

D'Arcy began work at the long, rectangular hospital in Sydney Cove, he had helped to assemble six years before. It was badly in need of repair, and Hunter allocated two acres at Dawes Point to re-erect it on stone foundations, with a new hospital store, a dispensary and accommodation for the surgeons.

The hospital building was given a new lease of life, but its limitations were soon obvious. The convict population had rapidly expanded, while the number of surgeons remained static. The hospital relied on untrained, unpaid convicts, working as nurses, attendants, assistants and hospital orderlies, as gardeners, janitors and storemen. The store of surgical instruments was depleted, it had not been replaced, and pilfering was rife, especially of food and drugs.

I wish to have my name put down as a subscriber   Letters

Through Cookney, D'Arcy ordered new instruments and medical journals. His August 1797 account includes medical books from Lee & Hurst, seven volumes of *Bells Surgery*, £2.16.00, *Bells on venereal disease*, 14/- and *Wallis on Diseases* 8/-. He asked Cookney to subscribe to periodicals for him, *Medical and Chirurgical Review*, *Edinburgh Medical and Surgical Journal*, and the *Medical and Physical Review*.

I must confess myself surprised by your application   Pride & Prejudice

In May 1796, Hunter decided to create three new positions to command the outlying settlements. D'Arcy saw the opportunity to use his experience on Norfolk Island, to work with Hunter and to involve himself in the development of the Colony. He decided to apply, and with new confidence, wrote to Fitzwilliam, asking him to support his application. Hunter's proposal came to nothing, but D'Arcy's interest in serving in the administration of the Colony had been roused.

A hasty departure   Pride & Prejudice

He kept Fitzwilliam informed, in May 1796, although *little or no news worth mentioning to your Lordship prevails here at present,* he sent him the news of the Scottish Martyrs. *Mr Muir has made his escape in an American ship a few weeks ago and Messrs Gerrard and Skirving are both dead from dysentery. I have reason to suppose that Mr Fyshe Palmer will follow Mr Muir's example very soon.* [28]

Muir, a friend of Tom Paine, had been arrested in Portpatrick in 1793, en route to America. He escaped from the Colony in 1796, rowing out of the harbour to the *Otter*, an American vessel bound for Nootka Sound.[29] Fearing recapture at Nootka, he found his way onto a Spanish vessel. She encountered a British squadron, and during the skirmish, Muir was shot in the face and lost an eye. News of his plight reached Paris, the French Directory sent a delegation to his hospital in Cadiz, and he was taken back to Paris in February 1798. He died less than a year later, of his wounds.

In the Colony, Hunter provided the Scottish Martyrs with a *mild and paternal administration*.[30] Muir wrote, *of our treatment here I cannot speak too highly, gratitude will forever bind us to the officers, civil and military*.[31]

Fyshe Palmer built small boats, and became a trader in partnership with John Boston. Hunter noted – *he is said to be a turbulent restless kind of man; it may be so, but I have seen nothing of that disposition in him since my arrival*. When his sentence expired, Palmer bought a decrepit Spanish prize, *El Plumier*, and sailed to Guam, where she was condemned. He died there in 1802.

Even you, used as you are to great sums, would hardly believe! Emma

In May 1796, D'Arcy asked Fitzwilliam to help him obtain payment for his work on Norfolk Island – *My long service in a double capacity, that of Assistant Surgeon, and Superintendent of Convicts, for which I find from Mr Cookney I have been only paid £40 per Annum, ought I presume to be a sufficient Recommendation, not but I still hope his Majesty's Ministers will think me deserving of some extra Emolument for acting in a double situation. I think it my Due & I am sure every Officer in this Country is of the same opinion. I hope your Lordship will suppose I ought to have some extra allowance, if so, I am not without Hope that your Lordship will interest yourself on my behalf*.[32]

He wrote again in August 1797, *I hope that the Duke of Portland will do me that justice to which I think I am entitled for my long and faithful service... If this should not be the case how mortifying must my situation be... I hope to be able to accumulate a handsome fortune in a few years, to live in peace and quietness for the remainder of my days.* [33]

A situation such as you deserve, & your friends would require for you, is no everyday occurrence Emma

That Home Office told Fitzwilliam, that as D'Arcy was not appointed from London, he could not be paid the usual rate. Fitzwilliam's advocacy won him £40 a year as Assistant Surgeon and £75 a year as superintendent of convicts. Cookney urged him to accept it – *considering the many changes in affairs and* the ill treatment which Lord Fitzwilliam had experienced from Lord Portland on his vice-royalty to Ireland, we succeeded so well, and I don't think it would be advantageous in any way at present to show ourselves dissatisfied with this consideration.[34] In 1798, D'Arcy was paid arrears of £160 for his six years work on Norfolk Island.[35]

The apprehension of disgrace in the corps   Pride & Prejudice

Hunter's relationship with Macarthur disintegrated within six months of his arrival. The final straw was an incident involving soldiers from Macarthur's company.

In February 1796, an emancipist, John Baughan, argued with a soldier, and noticed him leave his sentry post, his gun unattended. Baughan handed the gun to his sergeant, and the soldier was disciplined. He went to Baughan's cottage, with several others from Macarthur's company, to teach him a lesson.

The soldiers brutalised Baughan, held him down with an axe above his head, threatening to chop it off, they cut away the corner posts of his house, destroying it, and wrecked his furniture and outhouses.

Baughan identified the men responsible, and a warrant was issued for their arrest. Macarthur offered him compensation, undertook to make good his loss, and prevailed on him to withdraw the charges against his men. Baughan, fearing further reprisals, agreed, and the Governor ordered the warrant withdrawn.[36] Macarthur apologised to the Governor on the Corps' behalf, promising, *future conduct to wipe away the odium.*[37]

William Balmain, newly appointed as a magistrate, told Baughan he had compounded the felony by withdrawing his charges, and insisted he continue, or he would have him prosecuted. Balmain's action displeased the Rum Corps officers, who accused him of *malevolent interference.* Insults were traded, Balmain challenged Macarthur to a duel, which he did not accept.

Balmain's frustration with Macarthur was not new. He interfered in the running of the hospitals; Balmain's *assistants were not permitted to manage the concerns of their own departments in the public hospitals, thro' his improper interference... known to be of malicious prejudice.* [38]

Hunter wrote to Captain Paterson, insisting *the military must not, they shall not, dictate laws and rules for the government of this settlement...Their violence upon this late occasion shall be laid before the King... I shall consider every step they may go farther in aggravation as rebellion.*[39]

The severity and danger of this attack   Sense & Sensibility

The attack on Baughan ended any possibility of a working relationship between Hunter and Macarthur. It also damaged Hunter's credibility with the Home

Secretary, Lord Portland, who criticised him for being too lenient: *the conduct of the military…is of so flagrant a nature, and so directly tending to endanger the safety of your government, that I cannot well imagine anything like a justifiable excuse for not bringing the four soldiers who were deposed against to a Court-martial and punishing them with the utmost severity.*[40] Hunter received Portland's censure twenty-seven months after the incident.

The airs & interference of such a person Persuasion

In February 1796, Hunter accepted Macarthur's resignation as Inspector of Public Works *without reluctance*. He told Portland, Macarthur possessed *a restless, speculating, troublesome, dissatisfied, ambitious and litigious disposition.*[41] *Scarcely anything short of the full power of the Governor would be considered by this person as insufficient for conducting the dutys of his office…I saw it absolutely necessary to forbid any interference in the departments of the other officers…I was not dispos'd to allow any power to any officer in this colony which cou'd be exercis'd to the annoyance of other responsible persons, or to the disturbance of that peace and harmony on which I consider'd the happiness of the people at large and the progressive improvement of the colony depended so much.*[42]

Hunter looked elsewhere for advice, intelligence and support, to help counter the power and schemes of Macarthur and the Rum Corps. He turned increasingly to men he could trust, William Balmain, John Palmer, the Commissary, and D'Arcy Wentworth.

Every part of it brought pain & humiliation Emma

Macarthur found his influence and power significantly reduced. He retaliated with a relentless campaign against Hunter, becoming his most active and vocal opponent. He wrote to Portland, charging Hunter with extravagance, with *putting men on the land who could not cultivate it, men who should be in the service of a vigilant master…He concluded with an attack on the moral condition of the Colony, in which he asserted that vice of every description was openly encouraged while positions of trust were held by men whose characters were disgraceful to the British nation.*[43]

Out of spirits, which appeared perfectly natural Emma

The Corps' hostility increased, as the Governor moved to control the rum trade. When Hunter left for London on the *Waaksamheyd* in 1791, there was no rum in the Colony.[44] Four and a half years later he found it awash with spirits.

This turbulent and refractory colony[45] John Hunter

Lord Portland gave his instructions, *it is certainly in your power, as well as it is your duty, to prohibit, by the most positive orders, all officers of the government, civil or military, from selling any spirituous liquors to the convicts and settlers.*[46]

Hunter issued Government Orders to curb the rum trade, but had no power to enforce them. He could not rely on the military, the officers controlled the import of spirits and would simply ignore the order. Unable to control the import of spirits, he was forced to accept the reality and acquiesce.

In August 1796, he told Portland he was helpless to enforce prohibitions against the landing of spirits, he could not rely on the co-operation of the military and lacked the manpower necessary to police its prohibition. *I have taken every step in my power to prevent the smuggling of spirits from ships to the shore, but ineffectually, notwithstanding having a guard on board… We have taken every means, but it is so much sought that they will smuggle it; they will go to Botany Bay, or Broken Bay, or any of those places, and purchase it if they are able. To prevent the importation of spirits entirely, my Lord, is next to an impossibility, unless I had more assistance to depend on.* [47]

Hunter's efforts at reform, to restore civil administration and to curb the rum trade, met with absolute retaliation. He wrote to Portland, the *characters who have been considered as disgraceful to every other regiment in His Majesty's service, have been thought fit and proper recruits for the New South Wales Corps… and often superior in every species of infamy to the most expert in wickedness amongst the convicts.*[48]

Spirits sinking — Mansfield Park

Campbell & Clarke of Calcutta had a distillery at Howrah, on the Hooghly, capable of producing a hundred and twenty thousand gallons of spirits per annum. They bought an old expendable Indian Country ship, *Begum Shaw*, renaming her *Sydney Cove* to signal their new venture.

On 10 November 1796, the tired, three-masted vessel left Calcutta, with Guy Hamilton, an old Glaswegian, at the helm. One of the first non-official vessels from Calcutta, sent to trade with the Colony, she had a speculative cargo: horses, textiles, foodstuffs, luxury goods, and seven thousand gallons of Bengal Rum. Hamilton steered her far south, to the Roaring Forties, turned east, cleared Van Diemen's Land, and headed north to Sydney.

Once in the open sea, *Sydney Cove* started taking in water. Her pumps were manned the whole journey. By 9 February 1797, water was up to the lower deck hatches, she was in danger of sinking. Hamilton beached her north east of Van Diemen's Land, on an island in the Furneaux Group he named *Preservation Island*. All hands made it to shore, and they secured the rum on a small island nearby.

A longboat with seventeen men was sent north to take the news to Sydney. Landing on the south coast of the mainland, they set off, walking northwards along the coastline to Sydney. It was a four hundred mile journey, and only three men survived. Eleven weeks later, on 16 May 1797, Mr Clarke, the Supercargo and two Lascars were found at *Watta-moo-lee* just south of Sydney. They had trekked through the southern rain forest, east of the Great Dividing Range, proving the length of the east coast was penetrable, fertile and habitable.

Captain Hamilton and the rest of his crew were rescued from the island. The disaster became part of colonial folklore, with many attempts made to find and salvage the rum. Fortune-hunters came from America and escaped convicts tried to locate the wreck, some died in the attempt.

The rum had been taken off with Hamilton on the *Francis*.[49] He persuaded Hunter to purchase 3500 gallons on the government's account, and the balance was sold to the settlers at enormous prices.

Campbell knows his business Emma

In Calcutta, Campbell and Clarke were not discouraged. Robert Campbell was despatched to Sydney to develop their trading interests. He arrived in June 1798 on the aptly named, *Hunter,* with more rum, and bought land from Captain Waterhouse and the unfortunate John Baughan, to build his sandstone warehouses. They still stand today in Sydney Cove.

It is a new circumstance...I acknowledge, & dreadfully derogatory
Northanger Abbey

The Colony had no newspapers, no vehicles for public debate. The use of *pipes,* anonymous letters or verses, filled with political and derogatory comment, and left in public places, was commonplace.

On 15 September 1795, *an anonymous writing of an inflammatory and seditious tendency was found affixed to one of the posts of the Boat house, such a writing being a direct breach of His Majesty's peace, and evidently tending to subvert the good order of this Government.*

Hunter issued a Government & General Order: *His Excellency is hereby pleased to make known his determination to punish with the utmost severity of the Law any person or persons who shall be convicted of having advised, written, or published the said paper or any paper of a like tendency which may be written or published hereafter in this Settlement.* [50]

In 1797, he told the Home Office, a *pipe* was dropped on a Sydney street, *in which the author is endeavouring to lay my name into that vortex of dirty traffic which I have been labouring to put a stop to.*[51]

Macarthur wrote to the Duke of Portland, to the Commander in Chief of the Army, and to colleagues in London, accusing Hunter of trafficking in rum.

The pipe claimed, *the traffic is not confined to officers, but is carried on in the Government House.*

Stop your confounded pipe, or I shall be after you Mansfield Park

In June 1799, a *pipe* was circulated within the Corps and its wider Sydney circle, denouncing D'Arcy Wentworth as a man of serious ill-repute, who should be ostracised by any member of the Corps who valued his position.

This *pipe* was in the form of a letter from Major Grose, now in England, to Joseph Foveaux, Commander of the Rum Corps.[52] It stated some officers of the Corps had been so indiscreet as to admit Wentworth to their company, and warned, if Duke of York learnt that an officer had disgraced himself by such an association, he would turn him out of the service.

The *pipe* came from within the Rum Corps, circulated for its amusement to discredit D'Arcy. He had been on Norfolk Island at the time Grose was in the Colony, they had never met. The *pipe* also misspelt Foveaux's name. Its circulation confirms that D'Arcy had friends among the officers, that others in the barracks were irritated by his trading activities and support of Hunter.

These gentlemen must have some very interesting point to discuss... how to make money, how to turn a good income into a better Mansfield Park

On 15 January 1800, a small snow *Thynne*, arrived in Port Jackson, chartered from Bengal by Rum Corps officers. She carried nine thousand gallons of spirits, tea, sugar and other goods. Hunter knew nothing in advance of her arrival. John Macarthur, William Balmain, and Williamson, the Acting Commissary signed the request to land the cargo on behalf of the officers. It stated the rum would be divided amongst officers in the settlement and on Norfolk Island, for the benefit of their respective farms; that divided into smaller quantities it would facilitate the payment of labour, and not cause inconvenience.

A great deal of very painful import Persuasion

On the same day, another group of small traders, free settlers and former convicts, including Simeon Lord, John Boston, Rowland Hassall – a bitter critic of the rum trade, Francis Oakes – a former missionary, now constable at Parramatta; and others, requested Hunter's permission to land thirteen hundred gallons of rum from the *Minerva,* to assist their farms in hiring labour.

Hunter allowed both shipments to land, knowing he was powerless to prevent the officers landing spirits from the *Thynne*. He noted: *if the officers receive permission to land what they want, and the others refus'd, then we will be accused of encouraging monopoly in the hands of the officers, and refuse those comforts which are wanted by others.*[53]

Hunter knew if he refused the settlers permission, their portion would be sold to the Rum Corps. He was aware of the huge profits made by the Corps. They would buy rum for eight or nine shillings a gallon and sell it to the settlers for £1 to £4 a gallon.[54] He also understood that rum was necessary for payment of labour and as currency.

He attempted to contain the Corps' monopoly by allowing competition. He allowed traders like Robert Campbell to import rum, and did not oppose settlers or civilian officers like D'Arcy and Balmain competing in the trade. Emancipists began to get a foothold in trading, using the profits from retailing spirits, farming, boatbuilding, sealing, whaling and sandalwood.

Such importation of novelties — Emma

For early entrepreneurs, like Andrew Thompson, James Underwood, Simeon Lord and Henry Kable, some of their trading was export oriented. D'Arcy operated on a smaller scale, importing much sought after consumer items. Hunter encouraged his endeavours, Cookney forwarded his goods in convict transports, addressed to: *D'Arcy Wentworth at Hunter's Store.*

The trouble and expense of it — Mansfield Park

From the outset, Hunter faced criticism from the Home Office on the cost of running the Colony. He arrived to find the Government stores depleted, and a food crisis looming. It was necessary to purchase supplies to prevent starvation, and he was held responsible for the expense.

The cost of living and perennial shortages created other pressing problems. Food was expensive, and luxuries like tea, sugar or soap, in short supply. There were shortages of food, clothing, coinage and necessaries of every kind. This had long been known in London, but the government that appointed Hunter ignored his concerns, neglected the Colony and in time, abandoned him.

The state of the harvest — Mansfield Park

Early on, Portland sent plainly unworkable instructions, which Hunter, wisely disregarded. Portland questioned the practice of assigning convicts to officers, men already fed and clothed by the Crown. Hunter recognised the Rum Corps officers, with large holdings and convict labourers, paid for their extra efforts with rum, were effective food producers, who had improved the production of wheat and maize.

Only having the probable credit of it, which went sorely against the grain — Pride & Prejudice

The Rum Corps officers controlled receipt of grain into the Government Store. It was opened from time to time to purchase certain quantities of grain. Once they were received, it closed. The quantity required was frequently lodged by a few individuals, leaving small farmers forced to sell their grain at half price. Farm labourers paid in grain, had to negotiate with Rum Corps traders, who might accept it from them as payment for highly priced imported goods, at a discount of fifty to sixty percent of its value.

Many soldiers in the Corps were ex-convicts, who were paid in rum and grain. *The practice was to pay soldiers only in goods, for every ten shillings worth the soldiers paid twenty, and if they objected to this mode of payment they were most probably sent to the guard house, tried in a Court Martial, for mutiny, and sentenced to imprisonment.*

The soldier would take his monthly pay in property he did not want, and then would endeavour to dispose of what he had received, to some person who had money, generally selling it for less than half the price he was charged by his Captain. This system of monopoly and extortion compelled the soldier to serve his Majesty for half his nominal pay.[55]

The system led to increased crime: *The soldiers as guardians of the public stores have been the principals in stealing there from; their not being able to receive any other pay from their officers than spirits and other commodities at very exorbitant rates.*[56]

Hunter failed to remove the Rum Corps influence over the Government Store. In 1800, he received complaints from nearly two hundred Hawkesbury settlers, that the Corps controlled the receipt of wheat and pork for their own advantage, leaving other settlers without access to deliver their produce. They complained of insufficient labour to till their land, *that the officers and other favourites have men allowed to them out of number.*[57]

Hunter was directed to reduce the price paid for local grain. He anticipated the inevitable results – poverty and bankruptcy amongst the smaller settlers, leaving the officers to buy their land for a pittance, with farm labourers, most of them emancipists, left destitute, increasing their desire to return home.[58]

He ignored the instruction, knowing lower prices would save the government money, but if a crop was not profitable, settlers would not bother to plant it, increasing the risk of a return to starvation. He was proved right, his successor reduced the price, production fell, and the Government *was obliged to send out flour to the amount of £70,000 sterling.*[59]

Pleasure Grounds in Portland Place *Frederic & Elfrida*

In January 1797, Hunter travelled from Botany Bay, up the Georges River for twenty-five miles, then across country, via the Nepean and Hawkesbury Rivers, to Parramatta. He opened the route to a new settlement at the junction of the Hawkesbury and Colo rivers, which he named *Portland Place.*[60]

A ship not fit to be employed Persuasion

Hunter wrote to Evan Nepean about the parlous state of the *Reliance* and *Supply*, neither was considered safe or seaworthy. He requested Nepean *to lay before their Lordships the enclos'd report of a survey... of the feeble and leaky state of the Reliance. She return'd from the Cape to this port, as the Supply had done, with her pumps going.*[61] The *Supply* was condemned, moored as a hulk in Sydney Harbour and used for storage.

On 1st July 1798, came welcome news, when a sixteen ton sloop, *Norfolk*, arrived in Sydney. With the heavy repairs required by the *Reliance*, there was less frequent contact with Norfolk Island. Captain Townson, who acted as Commandant after King's departure for England in 1796, had built the sloop on Norfolk Island on his own initiative.[62]

I am sure I told her to bring some coals half an hour ago Mansfield Park

In 1796, Hunter was pleased to inform London that fishermen sheltering in the mouth of a river north of Sydney, had found deposits of coal. George Bass also discovered coal to the south of Port Hacking.[63]

Portland wrote to the Secretary of State for Home Affairs: *As the exportation of coals from hence to the Cape of Good Hope is attended with a very heavy expence to the public, I cannot but think that a great saving may be made by sending them to the Cape from New South Wales in the Government vessels on that station, which are under your command. You will therefore despatch the Buffalo and the Porpoise, loaded with coals, to the Cape as soon as possible after the receipt of this letter, directing them to return with as large a supply of live stock for the use of the settlement, as they can conveniently stow.*[64]

Portland expected the first coal to arrive at the Cape by Christmas 1799. Hunter was glad to meet his deadline with a modest cargo.

Finding a play that would suit every body proved to be no trifle Mansfield Park

In 1797, news of a playhouse in Sydney caught the interest of the London press: *Lord Kenyon, though not a play-going man himself, has furnished a company to Botany Bay. The players there, by the last accounts, have performed: The Honest Thieves, The Conjurors, Neck or Nothing, The Devil to Pay, All's Well that ends Well, The Robbers, The Lyar, The Jovial Beggars, and The Female Swindler. George Barrington is Acting Manager and Darcy Wentworth Grand Proprietor. The Village Lawyer is in rehearsal, but until the Adelphi Hero arrives, it cannot be performed.*[65] THE TIMES

Barrington, a renowned Irish con-man and pickpocket, found guilty in 1790 of stealing a gold watch at the Enfield racecourse, was transported for seven years. He redeemed himself with *irreproachable conduct* at Toongabbie, and received a conditional pardon. In 1796, Hunter made him chief constable at Parramatta. He died on 27 December 1804, and is still remembered for immortal lines from his prologue to *The Revenge,* performed at the Playhouse:

> *True patriots we, for be it understood*
> *We left our country for our country's good.*

D'Arcy received letters of introduction from a number of his friends. John Villiers,[66] now Member for Dartmouth, James Dawson,[67] Charles Cookney, and his brother William, all asked for his assistance to settle the new arrivals to the Colony they commended, including convicts, constituents and family members.

One should be a brute not to feel for the distress they are in   Mansfield Park

Hunter took his duty of care towards the convicts very seriously. He wrote numerous times requesting clothing and blankets for them. In 1798 – *Suffer me here, my dear Sir, to beseech you to recollect that... no clothing worth mentioning has been received here for more than two years.*[68] In 1799 – *I am constrained to recur to my many official letters on the subject of slop cloathing and blankets... People... put on board ship in England with the cloaths only in which they stood, consequently arriv'd here naked, where cloathing is not to be found... Let me conjure you to use every means in your power to have us supplied in some way or other without loss of time.*[69]

Hunter later told a parliamentary inquiry, *I had so many of them working in a gang, of four or five hundred, naked as they were born, they have gone into the fields to work... I was concerned for them.*[70]

He was also concerned at the exclusion of emancipists from society – *it is much regretted that a man... because once having offended the laws of this country, shou'd be ever afterwards consider'd as unworthy of its favour.*[71]

Irish, I dare say   Persuasion

The 1786 *Insurrection Act* gave magistrates and military officers in Ireland the discretion to arrest and punish anyone suspected of treason or of committing treasonable acts. Thousands had their property confiscated, were flogged, impressed into the navy, transported or executed, without trial.

Boatloads of dissident Irish convicts arrived in the Colony, many without any documentation of their crimes or sentences. A number of them, as a result, served terms longer than those given by the courts.[72]

In 1794, Hunter wrote several times to Portland, that it was *extremely unjust to be obliged to compel the men to longer servitude than the law has directed...They have more than once threatened opposition to all authority if they are not liberated when their time of servitude is expired, a circumstance we continue to be left in ignorance of.*[73]

Rivetts the Chains of those unhappy Beings whose Passion it is impossible not to pity
Lesley Castle

D'Arcy had seen young Catholic Defenders embroiled in sectarian violence around Armagh. By the mid 1790's their influence had grown across Ireland, their aspirations sharpened by the revolutions in America and France.

In April 1796, a month after Ireland was declared in a state of insurrection, Hunter wrote to the Home Office, concerned at the number of desperate Irish convicts who arrived on the *Marquis Cornwallis*. By November he was concerned at *those turbulent and worthless characters called Irish Defenders* who *threatened resistance to all orders*.[74]

There was an air of unreality in London about the seriousness of the situation in Ireland. Opening Parliament in November 1798, George III laid the blame for the uprising that year squarely on the French:*In Ireland the Rebellion which they had instigated has been curbed and repressed; the troops which they landed for its support have been compelled to surrender... Those whom they misled or seduced must be awaken to their Duty; and a just sense of miseries and horrors, which these traitorous designs have produced, must impress on the minds of My faithful subjects the necessity of continuing to repel with firmness every attack on the Laws and established Government of their country.*[75]

Obliged to volunteer
Sense & Sensibility

In September 1799, spooked by the fear of an uprising, Hunter used volunteer associations to prevent seditious assemblies and civil unrest. In August 1800, D'Arcy, with his Irish brogue, was appointed Lieutenant of the Loyal Parramatta Association Corps. As a public official he could not refuse to serve. He understood the predicament of his countrymen, and endeavoured to advocate for them, a cause that was increasingly difficult and unpopular.

Many were members of the United Irishmen, formed in Belfast in 1791, uniting Catholics and Protestants in a campaign for an independent, republican Ireland. They included articulate, well educated and well born men, transported to remove their influence.

They have found themselves entirely deceived, & been obliged to put up with exactly the reverse
Mansfield Park

On 11 January 1800, the *Minerva* landed nearly two hundred Irish convicts, many had been sent into exile without sentence, and promised their freedom in the Colony. They were kept under guard, treated as criminals, put into work gangs or assigned as servants or labourers.

A number tried to return home to continue the struggle. On 9 February, four men stowed away on the *Minerva*, the following day another ten were uncovered, hidden in the hold. All were sent ashore under guard.

The *Minerva's* surgeon recorded: *Major Foveaux having received information of a conspiracy being formed by a number of convicts to board us in the night & make us get under weigh, he got the regiment under arms, & surrounded the house in which they were assembled, & took about forty desperate fellows, most of them of those which we brought out. It has been likewise discovered, that a plan was formed last night of seizing the Magazine, & of putting every person to death that should oppose them, in consequence of this the guards are doubled & those are to be severely punished.*[76]

Hunter was told of Irish convicts holding seditious meetings, and in September 1800, he held an inquiry into their activities. It was unable to uncover an organised body, but reported the felons it interviewed *proved evasive, equivocal and Jesuitical, and not prepared to inform on each other.*[77]

Samuel Marsden ordered one of their number to be flogged until he reveal where the pikes of the conspirators were concealed... They flogged him (Galvin) on the back till it was raw; they flogged him on the bottom; they flogged him again on the back. When he still refused to inform, even Marsden admitted that Galvin would die rather than reveal anything. But Marsden as a magistrate had stooped to the temptation that the truth could be flogged out of a man... To restore order and recall these deluded Irish to their senses, some were sentenced to one thousand lashes, some to five hundred, some to two hundred, and some to transportation to Norfolk Island where the baneful influence of their example could not be experienced.[78]

We must stem the tide Pride & Prejudice

By October 1800, the Colony had received a thousand, two hundred and seven Irish convicts. Hunter asked that fewer be sent, as they were a threat to *that order so highly essential to our well being,*[79] a desperate set of villains.

He is a clever man, a reading man Persuasion

D'Arcy's work in the public hospital brought him close to the convicts and to the poorest and most damaged people in the settlement. As a doctor he was reserved, his patients knew they could confide in him, that he respected their dignity and privacy.

In 1801, George Howe, the Government Printer, an emancipist, thanked him, *for the great Care & Attention you were pleased to shew towards me during my painful & dangerous malady. My Cure is at length perfected & that to your exalted skill & increasing Attention. I tender my most grateful Acknowledgement and sincere thanks. I shall ever esteem you Sir as the Preserver of my Life in restoring me to the use of my Limbs.*[80]

Most fortunately having it within our power to introduce you to a very superior society   Pride & Prejudice

John Price described Sydney in early 1800, as a *tattling town*, full of *tales, by scandal dress'd... Their society is very small and even then divided into party quarrels, which are fomented by an incendiary sett.*[81]

D'Arcy did not seek out society. He was a loyal and discreet friend to the governor, he kept his distance from gossip and small talk, and his home life was completely private. His reserve did nothing to endear him to Sydney's exclusives. He and his children were largely ostracised by the emerging elite.

Seeing Wentworth under his own roof, & welcoming him to all that was strongest and best in his cellars   Persuasion

Hunter was unmarried. His nephew, Captain William Kent, accompanied him to the Colony, in command of the Supply, and William's wife, Eliza, did *the honours of Government House,* as his hostess.

Hunter lived mainly at Government House in Parramatta. He built *an elegant new home there, equal if not superior to the Government House at Sidney. There is an excellent garden before the house in which are the finest grapes, melons, peaches, cauliflowers, etc.*[82]

When D'Arcy arrived there for Christmas dinner in 1798, he was welcomed by Hunter and the Kents. Hunter ensured it was an enjoyable occasion.

We were very pleasant – Jeu de violin etc   Letters

A few weeks later, D'Arcy enjoyed their hospitality, along with the young Irish surgeon from the *Minerva*, John Price, who noted, *a large and agreeable company, composed of the principal officers of the Colony, civil and military, and the officers of the Reliance, enlivened, graced and adorned with the presence of the most amiable ladies of the Colony... We spent the afternoon with the greatest pleasure and harmony being entertained with some beautiful songs by the ladies, after which the Governor having played on the violin, we had some minuets and country dances.*[83]

Delighted to connect anything with history already known   Mansfield Park

There is a record of a wager made by D'Arcy on 29 November 1798: *I deposited fifty guineas in the hands of Mr James Williamson, Acting Commissary, being the amount of a wager with Captain Maum of the Marquis Cornwallis, that the French* were not been in possession of the Electorate of Hanover, on the fifteenth day of November 1798. Captain Maum deposits the like sum of fifty guineas in Mr Williamson's hands on the same account, both which sums are to be given up to either Mr Wentworth or Captain Maum, when the aforesaid wager, is determined as Won.[84]

The *Marquis Cornwallis* had brought news of the resurgence of Napoleon's troops in Europe. The two men bet on whether an event had taken place two weeks earlier. It tells us something of D'Arcy's interest in the wider world, he had been out of Europe for nearly nine years. There would have been few people in the Colony curious enough or confident in their grasp of the intricacies of the war, to have bet fifty guineas.

Marquis Cornwallis was in port for five weeks, she sailed on 3 December 1798 for Bengal, with several runaway convicts on board. D'Arcy won the bet, the French Republican Army had not taken George III's Electorate of Hanover, though the news to confirm his win would take several more months to arrive.

That village of wonderful Elasticity, which stretches itself out for the reception of everybody
Letters

On 11 May 1799, D'Arcy was appointed the assistant-surgeon at Parramatta, in charge of the hospital there, replacing James Mileham, who was later court martialled for refusing *to attend the settlers, free people, and others.*[85]

He took up duty at Parramatta hospital, *two long sheds, built in the form of a tent, and thatched... capable of holding two hundred patients.*[86] It was *large and clean and has a large vegetable garden attached to it.*[87]

William was nine when the family moved. He later described *the town of Parramatta, situated at the head of Port Jackson Harbour, at the distance of about eighteen miles by water and fifteen by land, from Sydney. This town is built along a small fresh water stream which falls into the river. It consists principally of one street about a mile in length. It is surrounded on the south side by a chain of moderately high hills; and, as you approach it by the Sydney road, it breaks suddenly on the view when you have reached the summit of them, and produces a very pleasing effect. The adjacent country has been a good deal cleared, and the gay mimosas, which have sprung up in the openings form a very agreeable contrast to the dismal gloom of the forest that surrounds and o'er tops them.*[88]

It might not be a bad speculation for a surgeon to get a house at the top of the hill
Sanditon

In 16 May 1799, Hunter granted D'Arcy a fourteen year lease over six acres and twenty roods, on a knoll at Parramatta, overlooking the river. The grant extended to Clay Cliff Creek, and adjoined the Military Barracks.[89]

He planted a dozen young Norfolk Island pines along the ridge line, and built a comfortable, two storey house, which he named *Wentworth Woodhouse*.⁹⁰ John Price described it as, *charmingly situated and, as Milton says, "Bosomed high in tufted trees."*⁹¹

An age since they had met Pride & Prejudice

Parramatta Hospital served a large area of the outlying settlements. *The Assistant Surgeon at Parramatta was frequently sent for, twenty miles or further, and was sometimes obliged to walk that distance at night.*⁹²

Among D'Arcy's colleagues in the district was another Irish surgeon, a convict who had practiced in the Hawkesbury for the past five years. He relied on Parramatta hospital for medical supplies, and referred serious cases to them, if they could be carried safely. His name was John Francis Molloy.

To remember the day, the hour, the party, the occasion – to feel the same consciousness, the same regrets Emma

It was more than a dozen years since they rode to Blackheath with William Manning. After Molloy got away, he left London, and found employment in Bath. In October 1790, he returned with his wife and two small children. He took a room at the Black Bear Inn in Piccadilly and left his family there. He hired a horse and rode out to Blackheath.

On Tuesday evening a single highwayman, well mounted, followed the Dover Diligence for about a mile on Blackheath and then came up with a stopt it. He made a tolerably good collection from the passengers, amounting to upwards of £30 and then rode off towards Charlton.

He was apprehended on Tuesday night at a public house in Brewer Street. Near him was a great coat, which there is every reason to believe is his. Wrapt in this coat were found a brace of pistols. He was on Wednesday brought before Sir Sampson Wright and underwent an examination, which was but short, as the persons robbed did not attend.

*He was committed and will undergo a further examination. He is suspected of having committed three highway robberies on the day he was taken. This Molloy was the associate of the notorious D'Arcy Wentworth; is an Irishman, and, like his friend, was bred a surgeon.*⁹³ PUBLIC ADVERTISER

Molloy remained in prison five months before appearing at the Kent Assizes. *This day the trial of John Francis Molloy, commonly called Dr. Molloy, came on for highway robbery, when the prisoner was capitally convicted.*⁹⁴ THE TIMES

Evan Nepean received an appeal for clemency from County Longford, from a man of standing, the Very Reverend Dean Thomas Lewis O'Beirne. He asked that Molloy be pardoned, *or at worst to have his sentence changed to transportation. He is very decently connected in this country and served his time to a very eminent surgeon...who assures me that he never knew him act either dishonourably or dishonestly.*[95]

Molloy's death sentence was commuted to seven years transportation. He arrived in Sydney on the *Pitt,* in February 1792. He worked for three years in Sydney Cove hospital under John White, and in July 1795, with three years still to serve, he was sent by William Paterson, the Acting Governor, to the growing settlement on the Hawkesbury River, forty miles north-west of Sydney.

Not a medical man within reach — Letters

Molloy was granted thirty acres on the western bank,[96] that he named *Charlotte Farm*. He joined more than four hundred ex-convict settlers, supported by convict labour, who had taken up land thirty miles along the banks on both sides of the river. The land was fertile and productive, but inundated by frequent and destructive floods.

It was a frontier settlement. In March 1795, the *Britannia* arrived in Sydney with 25,000 gallons of rum for the officers. Richard Atkins, the Judge-Advocate, declared, *the new settlement on the Hawkesbury is one continual scene of drunkenness... It would be impossible to describe the scenes of villany and infamy that passes at the Hawkesbury... a bottle of liquor for a bushell of corn and no questions asked is the common price... since then drunkenness and robberys to a very alarming degree have taken place.* [97]

In 1795, the principal surgeon, William Balmain, requested more medical staff. Perhaps to bolster his claim, he stated the Hawkesbury was served by a *convict who has not much professional skill*.[98]

In July 1796, Molloy was called to a farm on the opposite bank, where a dying man, John Lane, lay, shot by his master John Fenlow. Molloy gave evidence at the Fenlow's trial. He was found guilty, executed and his body given to the Colony surgeons for dissection, while a large group of settlers looked on.[99]

How very little trouble it can give you to understand the motive of other people's actions — Northanger Abbey

In the reports of his examinations at Bow Street, Molloy appears impatient, and bad tempered. The same traits show in the scant records of his medical practice in the Hawkesbury. He seemed unable to negotiate sound working relationships with his patients, neighbours or employees.

He took nearly a dozen civil actions to recover money owed him for medical services and farming activities, and several counter actions. In 1798, he sued his neighbour, the Sydney trader, Thomas Reibey, for *the sum of ten pounds and upwards for medical and surgical attendance.*[100] At the background of this litigation may have been a determination to be paid in cash, during a period of a great shortage of coinage, most severe in remote areas of the Colony.

Private actions open to the world   Pride & Prejudice

On 11 February 1800, Molloy took out a writ against the Commander of the Rum Corps, Joseph Foveaux, to have him arrested and brought to court. The matter was settled quickly, the next day, the Provost Marshall declared that it had been accommodated, and it lapsed. The detail behind his action has been lost, but it demonstrates his fearlessness, and perhaps, foolhardiness, taking on a powerful man with a hard reputation.[101]

Conscious of the Charming Character which in every Country, and every Clime in Christendom is Cried   A Collection of Letters

On 14 October 1799, Molloy gave evidence at the trial of five settlers charged with murdering two Aboriginals, one of several pay-back killings that followed the murder of two settlers who lived with an Aboriginal girl.

Molloy stated *that in the course of his practice for four years and a half Twenty-Six White People had been killed by the Natives and thirteen Wounded on the Banks of the Hawkesbury and that several of them were wounded in defending their property against the depredations of the Natives.*

White settlement along the Hawkesbury River had blocked the traditional owners, Dharug people, from access to the river and their food sources. When they helped themselves to crops and livestock, *reprisals by the Whites led to guerrilla warfare over a large part of the Cumberland Plain.*[102]

In June 1795, Acting Governor Paterson *sent two subalterns and sixty privates of the New South Wales Corps to the river, as well as to drive the natives to a distance, as for the protection of the settlers...It gives me concern to have been forced to destroy any of these people, particularly as I have no doubt of their being cruelly treated by some of the first settlers who went out there, however, had I not taken this step, every prospect of advantage which the colony may expect to derive from a settlement formed on the banks of so fine a river as the Hawkesbury would be at an end.*[103]

The Court comprised the Judge Advocate, three Royal Navy officers and three officers of the New South Wales Corps. It found Constable Powell and settlers Freebody, Metcalfe, Timms and Butler guilty, but reserved judgement: *under all its peculiar circumstances... until the sense of His Majesty's Ministers at home is known on the subject.* [104]

To you he will talk of farming Emma

Molloy and others along the Hawkesbury River endured a series of disastrous floods that ruined their crops and reduced the availability of grain, flour and fresh fruit and vegetables in the Colony. In March 1800: *The weather had, for upwards of twenty days, been very wet, which was unfortunate, as the maize was now ripe; the wind blew a heavy gale, accompanied with so much rain, that the river Hawkesbury, and all the creeks, rose beyond their banks, laying the flat country under water.*

Many of the people were taken from the ridges of their houses by a few boats they had amongst them just in time to save their lives, for most of the dwellings were cover'd, and the whole country here appear'd like an immense ocean.[105]

On 14 January 1800, with fourteen other Hawkesbury settlers, Molloy signed a submission, *Expenses of Farming at the Hawkesbury,* to Governor Hunter. It detailed the costs of cultivating an acre of wheat, and the average price of necessary articles of life bought from Sydney, adding, *the above charges are to be considered at the Sydney price to the settlers, who vend it again at the Hawkesbury from 50 to 100 per cent advance.*[106]

John Francis Molloy died two years later, on 18 July, 1802, a few weeks before his thirty-fifth birthday. He was buried in St John's churchyard at Parramatta.

Such news as the country afforded Pride & Prejudice

Governor Hunter sent regular despatches to Lord Portland and under-secretaries at the Home Office. The replies, when they came, were slow and often unhelpful. In 1797, he sent eighteen despatches, and in time received ten replies, seven of them arrived on the same vessel in September 1798. He sent twenty five despatches in 1798, and received sixteen acknowledgements, twelve of these arrived together in November 1799. He did not receive a single reply to the forty despatches he sent in 1800, though twelve were received in 1801, by his successor.[107]

No character however upright, can escape the malevolence of slander Lady Susan

On 15 April 1800, Hunter received a letter of recall, it was a wounding experience. The Duke of Portland wrote, *To express my disapprobation of the manner in which the government of the settlement has been administered by you in so many respects – I am commanded to signify to you the king's pleasure to return to this kingdom by the first safe conveyance which offers itself.*[108]

To be neglected before one's time must be very vexatious Mansfield Park

Portland's letter arrived on the *Speedy,* along with Hunter's successor, Philip Gidley King. King had returned to England in May 1796, and spent four years lobbying the Home Office, the Admiralty and potential patrons, for promotion.

In May 1798, he finally received a *dormant commission*, giving him authority to act as governor *in the case of the death or during the absence of Captain John Hunter*. The press reported that he obtained it, *through the interest of Sir Joseph Banks, whose collection he has much enriched.*[109]

King had spent time in Kent, with ship owners and merchants involved in commerce and trade in the Pacific. He collaborated with the Enderby family, whose *Southern Fishery* had sent whaling ships to the southern Atlantic from 1773. The East India Charter prevented them trading in the Pacific. In 1794, Samuel Enderby lent King money for his trading ventures,[110] and offered to carry his cargo in the *Speedy*, the transport that finally took him back to the Colony in 1800.

In August 1800, on King's advice, Enderby wrote to Earl Liverpool: *The Americans, hearing that New South Wales is considered within the chartered waters of the East India Company, and that no British merchant can send goods to that colony without the risque of seizure, have at times sent small vessels there... and have benefitted themselves so much thereby, that there is no doubt, if the restrictions are still continued against British merchants sending goods there, that they will monopolise all the advantages of the trade to New South Wales, and this country will have all the expense of supporting it.*[111]

The following month, King wrote to Lord Portland, criticising the statutory restrictions on trade, and suggesting the whalers could be used to carry convicts to the Colony of their outward voyage – *much advantage will arise to the colony, not only from the frequent intercourse it will produce between it and England, but also the advantage of bringing convicts and stores out on lower terms than have hitherto been paid.*[112]

While Hunter treated him with every consideration, King displayed *little dignity, overpowering conceit, and a jealous, suspicious and hasty, and ungovernable temper.*[113] He began proclaiming *Government & General Orders* before Hunter's departure, and claimed he was acting under royal instructions.

Not one of those who neglect the reigning power to bow to the rising sun
Persuasion

In Hunter's final five months in the Colony, D'Arcy provided friendship, assistance and undivided loyalty. His support rankled King. John Grant, an emancipist, commented, *Governor King hates Hunter's friends.*[114]

For he is in the Opposition, you know
Sense & Sensibility

In March 1799, D'Arcy received a dampening response to his request to Fitzwilliam to approve his return to England. Cookney replied, saying at this time, his Lordship was unable to assist D'Arcy. *My Lord Fitzwilliam seems much satisfied with your conduct and I would not advise your being too hasty in your return to England. Whatever is in His Lordship's power to do for you, I am sure he will. Circumstances don't give him that influence at present as you imagine and I know in the present situation of affairs he would not like to solicit any favour from Government.*[115]

A very good house, in… a lofty, dignified situation   Persuasion

Before Hunter left the Colony, he granted D'Arcy a hundred and forty acres at Parramatta, adjacent to Government House,[116] making him the Governor's neighbour. D'Arcy later ceded a portion of this land to the Governor's domain, and their shared boundary became the line of ponds on the south eastern side of Government House, that drained into the Parramatta River.[117]

A watch is always too fast or too slow   Mansfield Park

D'Arcy asked Hunter to call on his watch-maker in Cornhill, to enquire about problems he was having with his watch. It was losing time, it had been for some years, though he used it, accurate or not. A watch was indispensable to a doctor, to take a patient's pulse or time the progress of a woman's labour. D'Arcy described its problems, and he asked Hunter to enquire from the watchmaker if there was some adjustment he could make to remedy it.

John Brocklehurst, the watchmaker, was very obliging, and wrote to D'Arcy: *It really is a very fine piece of workmanship and we were uncommonly attentive to its accurate performance… should the pendulum spring require a little taking in or letting out, Governor Hunter assures me it can be done by those you have got with great safety, and in that case the watch will not require taking to pieces and the person will do it in ¼ of an hour in your presence.*[118]

This amiable woman, an untimely, unmerited Death   The History of England

On 6 January 1800, D'Arcy's new found security was shattered by Catherine's sudden death. She was twenty-seven. She was out walking with the children near the Government Wharf at Parramatta when she was bitten by a red-back spider.[119] Her funeral was conducted by Reverend Samuel Marsden, and she was laid to rest in St John's churchyard at Parramatta.

We men are sad fellows   Emma

Catherine's death was devastating for D'Arcy and their three sons. Their relationship had been happy and fulfilling, he had found stability with her after the turbulent and reckless years in London. William was now almost ten, Dorset, nearly seven, and Matthew, nearly five, the *little lads wept with heavy hearts. The boys deeply loved their mother.*[120]

William wrote later, *my playful childhood's thoughtless years flew swift away, despite of childhood's tears.*[121] He and D'Arcy were always close. There is a description of them after Catherine's death, William, nine years old, red-headed, hopping alongside his tall handsome father down the streets of Sydney and Parramatta, accompanying D'Arcy as he went about his medical and business commitments.

Write to me by return of post, judge of my anxiety, & do not trifle with it. Tell me the real truth Mansfield Park

In the first months after Catherine's death, D'Arcy continued with his workload at the hospital, he mourned quietly, retreating into himself, gathering his boys around him. In September, nine months after her death, John Hunter was making ready to depart. Spring had arrived, the air full of birdsong, trees heavy with blossom, when he began a letter to Jane, *you will perhaps unjustly accuse me of Neglect and Forgetfulness.*[122]

His anxiety about her health – his concern that she should have no happier prospects Emma

D'Arcy asked how things were with her. He told her he intended to return to England, he wanted to see her again, *he had meant to forget her, and believed it to be done. He had imagined himself to be indifferent, when he had only been angry; and he had been unjust to her merits, because he had been a sufferer from them. Her character was now fixed on his mind as perfection itself.*[123] He addressed the letter, care of the Wheat Sheaf in Popham Lane, and he entrusted it to John Hunter; he hoped he might call on her.

His diligence in his duty, & the strict propriety of his general conduct

Hunter's last official action as Governor was to sign a certificate of D'Arcy's service to the Colony. He wrote, *he has conducted himself, not only in his Official Situation but upon all other occasions with the most exact propriety. I have therefore pleasure in giving him this Testimony of my perfect approbation of his diligence in his duty, & the strict propriety of his general conduct.*[124]

John Hunter left the Colony on 28 September 1800, on *HMS Buffalo*, captained by his nephew, William Kent. He had in his care a little girl of three and a half, William Balmain's daughter Jane. George Johnston, who had been his aide-de-camp for four years, went with him.

A person to employ on the errand The Watsons

Hunter arrived at Spithead on 24 May 1801, and he immediately requested an inquiry into the charges made against his administration. He wrote to the Duke of Portland, *I ask only for common justice... I desire to stand or fall on my own actions. They have been such in that wicked profligate & abandoned colony that were they known to your Grace, & to the whole world, I need not be ashamed of them. I am of opinion had they been more clearly understood, I should have been found to have merited commendation, instead of the treatment I have experienced.*[125] Portland made no reply.

Hunter wrote to Lord Pelham, now the Secretary of State: *it was scarcely possible that an officer holding such situation as I have held could have experienced anything so extraordinary in the common course of public service, or of public justice.*[126] When no action was taken, Hunter was obliged to retire on half pay, as a captain, *without even the shadow of proof to his dishonour.*

Captain Hunter had a great deal to do, and his reputation to retrieve, after the *vile and contemptible endeavours which have been used to traduce my character.*[127] But he did not forget his undertaking. D'Arcy had entrusted him with a letter, asked him to tell his young wife something of his life in the Colony, to reassure her of his diligence in his duty, the strict propriety of his general conduct, and of his great desire to return to her.

Chapter 16

The real & consistent Patron

The different sorts of friendship in the world

IN 1756, when William Wentworth-Fitzwilliam was eight, his father died, and he was made the 4th Earl Fitzwilliam. His family seat, *Milton House*, was in Northamptonshire, with estates in several other counties. His estates were placed under the guardianship of Sir Matthew Lamb, grandfather of Lord Melbourne, until he reached his majority.

That same year, Fitzwilliam was sent to Eton, where he made lifelong friends, including Charles Fox, and Frederick Howard, later Lord Carlisle. At sixteen, he went on the Grand Tour. In France, when he found himself short of funds, his mother cautioned him against extravagance. He replied to her, *I shall not forget (as you seem to imagine) how small my income is, you may assure yourself, I will not throw my money away unnecessarily, but shall not deny myself what is necessary.* In April 1767, he arrived in Italy, and told her, *I like this place beyond expression.*[1] There he met up with Fox and Carlisle. In Naples they stayed with Sir William Hamilton, the British envoy, a noted antiquarian and vulcanologist, and his wife, Lady Catherine.

Fitzwilliam returned home in January 1769, with fourteen Italian paintings, including eight beautiful late Canalettos. In the following year, he married Lady Charlotte Ponsonby, youngest daughter of William, 2nd Earl of Bessborough,[2] and Lady Caroline Cavendish, daughter of the Duke of Devonshire. The Ponsonbys were an Irish political family with estates in Cork and Kilkenny.

The Great House   Persuasion

In January 1790, Fitzwilliam, now twenty-one, joined Lord Rockingham, his uncle, leader of the Whigs, in the House of Lords. He watched as the King entered the chamber in his crown and regal garments, and opened Parliament with the King's Speech. Fitzwilliam was immediately involved with burning issues of power and principle at home, and across the globe.

George III first acquainted his Lords with a *great Calamity – Distemper among the Horned Cattle;* he assured them of his *fixed Purpose to preserve the General tranquillity,* before he turned to the most pressing issue of the day – *the serious Attention of My Parliament to the State of My Government in America.*

I have endeavoured on My Part, by every means to bring back My Subjects there to their Duty, and to a due sense of lawful Authority. It gives Me much Concern to inform you that the Success of My Endeavours had not answered my Expectations; and that in some of My Colonies, many Persons have embarked in Measures highly unwarrantable, and calculated to destroy the Commercial Connection between them and the Mother Country.[3]

Between session & session, the first prepossession may rouse up the nation   Verse

Five years earlier, at the King's insistence, Parliament passed the Stamp Act – *applying certain Stamp Duties, and other Duties in the British Colonies and Plantations in America, towards further defraying the Expenses of defending, protecting, and securing the same.*[4]

The *Act* was intended to reduce Britain's soaring debt, a result of the Seven Years War with France, the ongoing war with the American Indians, and protection for the colonists. It required Americans to pay stamp duty on newspapers, magazines, legal and other documents and paper. In the House of Lords, Rockingham and others voted against it.[5]

John Wentworth, Governor of New Hampshire, gave Rockingham, his cousin, his opinion of those who voted for the *Act.* They were *alarmed at the prosperity and security of the provinces, that they are blessed with a spirit of liberty, and having no French or Indian savages to massacre them, believe that it is necessary to load them with taxes to prevent their revolt; thus humanely proposing that two million loyal subjects should be made poor, miserable, useless and burdensome to their mother country, lest they should be wicked enough (under more favourable circumstances) to grow rich, happy useful and a support to her.*[6]

American colonies had their own legislatures, Britain normally imposed taxes only on their external trade and commerce. The *Stamp Act* taxed internal transactions. The colonists cried foul, *No taxation without representation!*

The *Act* taxed newsprint, and there was swift reaction from pamphleteers and the publishers of the colonial newspapers, stirring up resistance and opposition. Its unpopularity was fanned by an ever-growing popular press; in 1763 there were twenty-one colonial newspapers, by 1775 there were forty-two, and their campaign quickly turned into denunciation of British rule.

Large scale American resistance led to petitions, violent street protests, and boycotts of imported goods that were highly damaging to British mercantile and manufacturing interests. In several colonies, traders ceased making payments for English goods until the *Stamp Act* was repealed, and they soon owed as much as £4.5 million.

In October 1765, delegates from nine of the thirteen colonies met at the Stamp Act Congress in New York, and drafted a formal petition to Parliament. Lord Rockingham and his secretary, Edmund Burke, organised a lobby group of powerful merchants to urge Parliament to repeal the Act, and deal with the threat of rebellion across the Atlantic.

The villainous Bill may be forced to lie still, against wicked men's will   Verse

Benjamin Franklin, who spent some years in England as the Colonial Agent for Pennsylvania, arranged meetings with members of Parliament. He hoped to improve dialogue, and to avert tensions from developing into war between Britain and her colonies.

In July 1765, Rockingham became Prime Minister, replacing George Grenville, architect of the *Stamp Act*. He invited Franklin to a confidential examination before the House of Commons on 13 February 1766. Edmund Burke likened the meeting to *an examination of a master, by a parcel of schoolboys*.

Franklin told the House, the temper of America towards Great Britain, once *the best in the world*, was now *greatly lessened*. Asked the cause, he replied, *To a concurrence of causes: the restraints lately laid on their trade, by which the bringing of foreign gold and silver into the Colonies was prevented; the prohibition of making paper money amongst themselves, and then demanding a new and heavy tax by stamps; taking away, at the same time, trials by juries, and refusing to receive and hear their humble petitions.*

The Stamp Act says we shall have no commerce, make no exchange of property with each other, neither purchase nor grant, nor recover debts; we shall neither marry nor make our wills, unless we pay such and such sums; and thus it is intended to extort our money from us or ruin us by the consequence of refusing to pay it.[7]

Franklin asked the Commons to repeal the *Act*. Lord Chatham, Pitt the Elder, supported its repeal, saying England *could not take money out of their pockets without consent*, but the King, unable to comprehend the seriousness of the situation, refused to compromise.

A month later, on 18 March 1766, Rockingham secured its repeal with a vote of 275 to 167. George III acquiesced: *I told Lord Rockingham I had on Friday given him permission to say I prefer'd repealing to enforcing the Stamp Act... consistent with the honour of this country.*[8]

Burke described Rockingham's achievement, *every thing, upon every side, was full of traps and mines... It was in the midst of this complicated warfare against publick opposition and private treachery, that the firmness of that noble person was put to the proof. He never stirred from his ground; no, not an inch. He remained fixed and determined, in principle, in measure, and in conduct. He practised no managements. He secured no retreat. He sought no apology.*[9]

America celebrated its relief, though it was short lived. Parliament passed the *Declaratory Act*, asserting it *had, hath and of right ought to have, full power and authority to make laws and statutes of sufficient force and validity to bind the colonies and people of America...in all cases whatsoever.*

Rockingham remained Prime Minister for just a year, one of a rapid succession of Prime Ministers, as the American struggle for independence wreaked ongoing instability in Britain's entire body politic.

The expense of such an undertaking — Mansfield Park

In June 1767, the government of Pitt the Elder enacted the *Townshend Revenue Acts*, seeking once again to recover the costs of protecting the American colonies. The King, responding to anger in Britain at the impertinence of the colonials, spurred Parliament on, to take these measures.

In April 1770, four months after Fitzwilliam entered parliament, violent reaction from America resulted in the repeal of *Townshend Acts* on all items except tea. The Boston Tea Party followed, and American resistance built up to the American War of Independence. Britain, convinced she would win the war, was reluctant to negotiate or resolve the conflict. In 1775, Lord North's government commenced military action against the colonists.

Edmund Burke called for peace with *our English brethren in the Colonies*, accusing George III, of German-descent, of employing *the hireling sword of German boors and vassals* to destroy their English liberties.[10]

Rockingham wrote to him, concerned at the growing power of the King, *It is much too probable that the power and influence of the Crown will increase rapidly... I fear indeed the future struggles of the people in defence of their constitutional rights will grow weaker and weaker. If we do not exert now, we may accelerate the abject state to which the Constitution may be reduced.*[11]

Her mind is unconfined, like any vast savannah Verse

In January 1775, Pitt the Elder, a former Whig Prime Minister, pressed for resolution of the conflict. He moved, *That an humble address be presented to his Majesty, humbly to desire and beseech his Majesty that, in order to open the way towards a happy settlement of the dangerous troubles in America, by beginning to allay ferments and soften animosities there; and, above all, for preventing in the meantime any sudden and fatal catastrophe at Boston...: it may graciously please his Majesty that immediate orders be despatched...for removing his Majesty's forces from the town.*

But as I have not the honour of access to his Majesty, I will endeavour to transmit to him, through the constitutional channel of this House, my ideas of America, to rescue him from the misadventure of his present Minister.

He stressed *the importance of the Colonies to this country, and the magnitude of danger hanging over this country from the present plan of misadministration practised against them.*

My lords, if the ministers thus persevere in misadvising the King, I will not say that they can alienate the affections of his subjects from his crown; but I will affirm that they will make the crown not worth his wearing. I will not say that the King is betrayed; but I will pronounce that the kingdom is undone.[12]

His resolution was defeated in the House of Lords, by sixty-eight to eighteen.

In March 1775, Burke, in a *Speech for the Conciliation with the Colonies*, asserted, the Americans, descended mainly from Englishmen, would not back down in the face of force. America, he predicted, *which at this day serves little more than to amuse you with stories of savage men, and uncouth manners; yet shall, before you taste of death, shew itself equal to the whole of that commerce which now attracts the envy of the world.*[13]

Frances Wentworth, wife of the Governor of New Hampshire, wrote to Lady Rockingham: *The Kings troops have too mean an opinion of the Americans. They think them Fools and Cowards, but indeed My lady, they are neither. Undisciplin'd and to be conquer'd they no doubt are, but they are far from the despicable set thought for. Their numbers make them formidable and they take all possible pains to improve themselves in military skill.*[14]

Sauntering politicians Persuasion

Rather than appointing a viceroy to go directly to America to conciliate and resolve the inflammatory situation, in November 1775, Parliament appointed Lord George Germain, Secretary of State for America. He was permitted to remain in London, brushing aside suggestions he could not direct effective tactics to resolve a distant dispute. The war, directed from London, faced delays of three to four months to correspond with the front.

Four days after the Declaration of Independence of 4 July 1776, Fitzwilliam asked Rockingham to send a *Remonstrance* to the King, so Americans *could see that there is still in the country a body of men of the first rank and importance, who would still wish to govern them according to the old policy.*[15]

John Moore, an acquaintance of the Austens, wrote from Vienna of surprise in Europe, at *our disputes with the colonies* and of the English *taking no trouble to conciliate.*[16]

Horrors in London Northanger Abbey

The impact of the war was felt across Britain. In June 1780, *a year pregnant with mischiefs, rapine, and riots,*[17] Fitzwilliam helped defend Rockingham's house in Grosvenor Square during the Gordon Riots. They were sparked by fears the *Papist Act* of 1778, by improving the status of the Roman Catholics, might return Britain to Catholic domination, with a loss of freedom of speech, religion and freedom of assembly, typical of most Catholic countries in Europe.

Lord Gordon, president of the London Protestant Association led a peaceful march to Parliament House calling for repeal of the Act. It descended into large scale rioting by mobs protesting against the war, and other social and economic issues. *An union of folly, enthusiasm, and knavery had excited alarms in the minds of some weak people.*[18]

One mob *entirely demolished*[19] Newgate Prison, after releasing the prisoners. Others burned looted houses, *on the evening of the second day's riot the avowed design was to destroy by fire the houses of the Lord Chancellor and the Lord Chief Justice. It burst upon Lord Mansfield without him being prepared in the slightest manner to resist. He escaped with his life only. The fatal consequence was the irreparable loss of all his books and manuscripts, ever to be deplored.*[20]

A mob of three thousand men assembling in St. George's Fields, the Bank attacked, the Tower threatened, the streets of London flowing with blood, a detachment of the Twelfth Light Dragoons, (the hopes of the nation,) called up from Northampton to quell the insurgents Northanger Abbey

Twelve years earlier, in May 1768, a crowd of fifteen thousand gathered at St George's Fields, shouting *No King, No liberty*! *Damn the King, Damn the Parliament, Damn the Justices!* Authorities feared the mob would break into King's Bench Prison, to free John Wilkes, a radical member of the Commons. The army was sent in to disperse them, the troops fired on the crowd killing seven people, and riots in London followed.

John Wilkes had criticised George III for his praise of the Treaty of Paris, at the opening of Parliament in 1763. The Treaty, signed after Britain's defeat of France in the Seven Years War, guaranteed the protection of Roman Catholics in territories ceded to Britain, including Canada and parts of Louisiana.

He was entitled to give his views under parliamentary privilege, but the Commons determined that privilege did not extend to Wilkes publishing seditious libel in his journal, *The North Briton*. *Wilkes & Liberty* became the catchcry for freedom of speech. On his return to England, after some years abroad, he was imprisoned and held for two years without trial. Wilkes believed in defending the institutions of civilised society. In 1780, during the Gordon riots, he took up arms to protect the Bank of England against a mob.

The mischief to be soon at peace Persuasion

On October 19 1781, after five years of bloody and destructive war, General Cornwallis faced a combined French and American force led by General Washington. His supply lines were cut after the French navy successfully defended the mouth of Chesapeake Bay against the British. Cornwallis' defeat was assured, and he surrendered at Yorktown.

A fair judge in this case Emma

After leading Britain for much of the war, in March 1782, Lord North resigned as Prime Minister. Lord Germain's career came to an end, and George III called on Lord Rockingham once again to form government.

Rockingham pressed for an end to the war, and for recognition of America's independence. He garnered the support necessary for a vote for independence for the American colonies, but he died without achieving it. He did succeed in enacting a *Relief of the Poor Act* to ameliorate the problem of sharply rising unemployment, but tragically he held office for only nineteen weeks. He died during an influenza epidemic in July 1782, aged fifty-two.

On the Death of a late Noble Marquis

> Alas Britannia; mourn & weep
> Thy Wentworth is no more
> For him who ne'er was wont to sleep
> When Guardian of thy shore.
>
> Pale Death has rob'd thee of his worth
> In this, thy time of need
> A man who stands in danger forth
> Must be a friend indeed.

> Happy, Oh Albion, was thy race
> When guided by his hand
> Retrieving was he in great haste
> This almost ruin'd land.
>
> The loss then truely, must be great
> Depriv'd of such a man.
> Can we sufficiently regret
> The Noble Rockingham.[21]

PUBLIC ADVERTISER

Rockingham died childless, his estate passed to the son of his eldest sister, Anne Wentworth, widow of the 3rd Earl Fitzwilliam. Fitzwilliam's inheritance included *Wentworth Woodhouse,* with fourteen thousand acres of agricultural land, quarries, mines and woodlands, passed down from the Earl of Strafford, and vast estates in Ireland. Aged thirty-four, he became successor to the history and fortunes of the Wentworths, Watsons and Woodhouses.

A valuable legacy indeed! Sense & Sensibility

Fitzwilliam succeeded Rockingham as leader of the Whigs in the House of Lords. As part of his inheritance, he took on responsibility for promoting and championing Whig values, with ideals of constitutional government and the rights of Parliament against the Crown and executive.

Whigs saw themselves as the protectors of the Englishman's liberties, guardians of the post-1689 constitution and the Bill of Rights.

> Five positions which Whigs maintain
> Are the positions of Civil Rule and Liberty;
> That Men are equal – born and free –
> That Kings derive their lawful sway
> All from the People's yea and nay –
> That Compact is the only ground,
> On which a Prince his rights can found.[22]

Fitzwilliam was committed to Whig principles: the acceptance of an ordered society, with respect for differences in birth, rank and status, not rigid or overly authoritarian, but not a society of equals. It was indissolubly bound together by reciprocal rights and responsibilities, common interests and duties, freedom of the individual within a structured legal system, and a civil jurisdiction that protected constitutional liberties against the Crown and executive.

There were important differences between the Whigs and the Tories: *If the two principles of the Whig party are a general religious toleration and jealous* *vigilance upon the gradual increase of influence of the Crown; the two principles of the Tories are the maintenance of the ecclesiastical as well as the civil constitution of the kingdom, and the assiduous support of such a degree of power in the King, as maybe an adequate counterpoise to the aristocratic union of the great Whig families.*²³

D'Arcy met Fitzwilliam three years after Rockingham's death. He was now in opposition, and would become the dynamic force who transformed the Whigs from a party of the landed aristocracy to a popular party supported by the growing middle class and poor in the cities.

The division of the party Mansfield Park

Most Governments during the reign of George III were coalitions of individual conservatives from both parties, brought together under the leadership of a strong Prime Minister. Whigs embraced a broad spectrum of ideas and philosophies, and the Whig party Fitzwilliam inherited was very fragmented. It was not unusual for it to divide three or more ways on issues, led by its more charismatic and strident members, including radical reformers like Charles Fox, moderates like Edmund Burke and conservatives.

Rockingham was followed as Prime Minister by Earl Shelburne, who attracted criticism for the terms of peace he endorsed to end the war with America. It was deemed excessively generous to grant the former colonies control of the lands beyond the Appalachians. Shelburne was brought down in April 1783, replaced by a coalition of Lord North and Charles Fox, with Lord Portland, leader of the House of Lords, as figurehead.

The Fox North government signed the Treaty of Paris on 3 September 1783. It lost power three months later, after its *India Bill* was defeated, having aroused opposition from the King. Young Tory, William Pitt came to the fore, cutting a swathe through Whig Party supporters. He was Prime Minister from 1783 to 1801, and from 1804 to his death in January 1806.

Much of the drive for political reform in England came from the north, from the industrial heartland of Yorkshire, stronghold of Rockingham and Fitzwilliam. The Yorkshire Association, led by Rev Christopher Wyvill, campaigned for shorter parliaments, more equal representation, and reduction in misappropriation of taxes. Fitzwilliam advised Wyvill, *adhere strictly to one object, to reduce the influence of the Crown, as the true source of every evil.*²⁴

Fitzwilliam accepted change was inevitable, but it must be lawful, within the constitution, not a radical discarding of the established system of government through revolution, as had happened in France. He understood the ever present potential for civil uprisings and how they weakened support for reform.

I am by no means convinced that we ought not all be Evangelicals, & am at least persuaded that they who are so from Reason & Feeling must be the happiest and safest Letters

In 1787, William Wilberforce approached Fitzwilliam to join his *Proclamation Society*. He wanted to recruit *persons of consequence* to prosecute the offences set out in the King's *Proclamation for the Discouragement of Vice*,[25] including *excessive drinking, blasphemy, profane swearing and cursing, lewdness, profanation of the Lord's day, and other dissolute, immoral, or disorderly practices.*[26] Wilberforce wanted bishops to instruct their clergy to cooperate with civil authorities *to repress the general spirit of licentiousness.*[27]

Fitzwilliam suspected some of those promoting the Society did so to keep the poor in their place. He advised Wilberforce to *consider twice* before introducing penal statutes to enforce purity of manners. *I agree there was a great deal of debauchery, much looseness of behaviour, and very little religion, but I could not agree with him, that it ever would be otherwise.*

Fitzwilliam viewed such laws as a reduction of liberty, *a disgrace to our Statute book for their absurdity and folly...and a still greater disgrace on account of the partial, time-serving and hypocritical motives which have given rise to them. Having seen London in flames only seven years ago, we do not wish to put the potent and zealous arm of enthusiasm under the guidance of hypocrisy so soon again.*[28]

Wilberforce entered Parliament as an independent in 1780, aged twenty-one. His support for Pitt in 1783, ended the Whig government of Lord Shelburne. He was an orator, an energetic and effective motivator, and a loyal friend to Pitt, and leader of the *Saints,* an evangelical group in the Commons. In 1783, Wilberforce met Rev James Ramsay, author of a pamphlet on the inhumanity of the slave trade, and his direction was set.[29]

Ramsay had been a surgeon on slave ships, and a medical supervisor on plantations on St. Kitts. Now a vicar at Teston in Kent, he attracted an evangelical group who advocated abolition of the slave trade. Its members included Frank Austen's patron, Rear Admiral Sir Charles Middleton. In 1786, they asked Wilberforce to bring a bill to Parliament to abolish the trade.

Like many other great moralists & preachers, eloquent on a point in which his own conduct would ill bear examination Persuasion

Fitzwilliam knew Wilberforce for many years before he espoused the anti-slavery cause. He neither joined the abolitionists nor supported Wilberforce's campaigns, *not on any anti-humanitarian principle but partly on account of the strong economic arguments about interference with the rights of property and the possible disruption of the West Indian economy, and partly on new grounds that the abolitionists were working hand-in-hand with popular radicalism.*[30]

Fitzwilliam was committed to the people of Yorkshire. Those employed in mining and manufacturing relied on trade through the port of Liverpool for their exports, and much of this export was shipped by the slave traders.[31] Wilberforce, the popularly elected member for Yorkshire from 1784 to 1812, turned his back on the struggles of Yorkshiremen in emerging industrial cities. He opposed the repeal of suspension of *habeas corpus*, and legislation to improve factory conditions. In 1812, unwell, after a long addiction to opium, he shifted to a quieter seat, Bramber in Sussex, until his retirement in 1825.

They descended the hill, crossed the bridge and drove to the door Pride & Prejudice

Thomas Paine, a father of the American Revolution, was born in Norfolk in 1737. On Benjamin Franklin's recommendation, he left for America in 1774. Made editor of the *Pennsylvania Magazine,* in January 1776 he published a pamphlet, *Common Sense*, supporting American independence and a republic. It sold half a million copies in America during the Revolution and influenced public opinion. Washington used passages from Tom Paine's *American Crisis* to inspire his troops.

In 1788, Paine returned to England to promote his invention, an arched cast iron bridge. After it failed to generate interest in Philadelphia or Paris, he sent the design to Sir Joseph Banks, and applied for a British patent. Banks and the Royal Society later inspected a prototype constructed in London.

Edmund Burke recommended the project to Fitzwilliam, and Paine was commissioned to design a ninety foot iron arch to span the River Don, three miles from Rotherham. He stayed nearby for three months to oversee its casting at the Walker family foundry. Fitzwilliam came to the foundry with Burke to inspect progress and invited Paine to stay at *Wentworth Woodhouse.*

By December 1789, with the first half of the arch completed, Paine returned to London. In 1790, he went to Paris, eager to witness the French Revolution.

Many pamphlets to finish Northanger Abbey

In 1790, Edmund Burke wrote *Reflections on the Revolution in France,* a pamphlet highly critical of the French Revolution. It went through ten printings in England and ten in France. In 1791, Tom Paine responded with *Rights of Man,* which sold over a million copies. It spurred movements for social and political reform in England and Ireland.

Rights of Man gained a great following in Yorkshire's industrial cities. Joseph Gales, publisher of the *Sheffield Register,* encouraged by Paine, printed a cheap edition. Gales was an office bearer in the Sheffield branch of the London Corresponding Society, and published *Sheffield Patriot,* promoting radical political reform and religious freedom.

On 29 July 1791, shortly after Paine left Sheffield, there were riots at nearby Stannington and Hallam over the enclosure of common land. Fitzwilliam hastened to Sheffield, and was glad to inform Burke that the disturbances were neither political, nor caused by *practical Painism*.[32]

In 1792, Paine published a second volume of *Rights of Man,* sold at a more modest price, to increase its circulation. His effigy was burnt at Leeds by merchants and industrialists, and Fitzwilliam's representative intervened in Barnsley, to prevent a similar reaction. In 1792, Paine, now in France, was charged with seditious libel. He was defended by Sir Thomas Erskine, in absentia; the jury found him guilty without even retiring to discuss the case.

Though this king had some faults The History of England

George III was torn by the pressures of governing. As early as the introduction of the *Stamp Act*, he showed signs of a mental break-down. The whole disastrous affair, resulting in the loss of the American colonies, took a profound toll on his mind. George III considered he was responsible, he blamed himself, without acknowledging the poor advice received from his ministers. It was said that he wished to abdicate, but feared his son, the Prince of Wales, was inadequate to take up the duties of king.

At first it was believed his malady was physical, perhaps a result of eating too many pears, but by the summer of 1788, his behaviour was unpredictable and confused, and by the autumn he was an embarrassment, he could not perform his duties.

A frenzy fit is not one quarter so pernicious Love & Freindship

Fanny Burney, Queen Charlotte's Keeper of the Robes, wrote in October 1788, *the King was prevailed upon not to go to chapel this morning. I met him in the passage from the Queen's room; he stopped me, and conversed... with that extreme quickness of speech and manner that belongs to fever... He is all agitation, all emotion, yet all benevolence and goodness, even to a degree that makes it touching to hear him speak. Nobody speaks of his illness, nor what they think of it.*

His Ministers heard reports that at Windsor the King tried to shake hands with a tree, that he babbled incoherently, believing at times he was King of Prussia, at others that London was under water. It was said he attacked one of his pages and the Prince of Wales.

Pitt delayed the appointment of the Prince of Wales as Regent, knowing he favoured the Whigs. He allowed months to pass while Parliament debated the legal intricacies of a regency. Fitzwilliam argued his proposed restrictions on the Prince of Wales were unconstitutional,[33] but by February 1789, when the *Regency Bill* was passed by the Commons, the King had recovered.

It was only in 1810, after several more bouts of madness, and following a period of intense grief at the loss of his youngest daughter, Princess Amelia, that George III was declared insane. Parliament transferred his powers to the Prince of Wales, who officially became Prince Regent.

The two brothers stepped forward, feeling the necessity of doing something
Mansfield Park

In late 1789, in an attempt to rally loyalty and personal support, the Prince of Wales toured Northern England, accompanied by his brother the Duke of York. On 31 August, they went to the races at York on horseback. Later, Fitzwilliam took them into the City of York in his carriage. Entering the Micklegate Bar the horses were released, and the coach was drawn by the loyal citizens of York.

Fitzwilliam received the royal party at *Wentworth Woodhouse,* one of the great Whig country houses of the period. Lord David Cecil said: *There is something easy-going and unofficial about them…Even the great rooms themselves, with their roomy writing tables, their arm-chairs, their tables piled with albums and commonplace books, seem less designed for state occasions than for private life: for leisure and lounging, for intimate talk and desultory reading. And the portraits that glow down from the walls exhibit a similar character…these houses convey an effect of splendid naturalness. In this they are typical of the society which was their creator.*[34]

The enumeration of the windows in front of the house and the relation of what the glazing had originally cost
Pride & Prejudice

Wentworth Woodhouse is a grand Palladian villa, twice as wide as Buckingham Palace, covering one hectare. The East Front, 607 feet long, is the longest country house façade in Europe. It has 365 rooms, five miles of passageways and over a thousand windows.

Many more rooms than could be supposed to be of any other use than to contribute to the window tax, and find employment for housemaids
Mansfield Park

The *'window tax'* was introduced in Britain in 1696, in the reign of William III, to tax the prosperous, in lieu of income tax. At the time income tax was considered an unacceptable government intrusion into personal affairs, to require someone to disclose their income was seen to threaten their liberty.

Most houses were taxed two shillings a year, with the tax increased according to the number of windows (for ten to nineteen windows there was additional tax of four shillings).

In 1785, Fitzwilliam argued against an increase in the tax, calling it a grievous imposition upon the community at large, imposed to cover a reduction in the tax on tea, and meet the extra cost of discouraging tea smuggling; levied solely to benefit the East India Company. *It may fairly be said to be transferred from the pocket of the individual to the Treasury in Leadenhall Street.*[35]

In the picture-gallery were many good paintings, many family portraits
Pride & Prejudice

Wentworth Woodhouse's magnificent art collection, included *a noble collection of portraits... Among them the most celebrated is that of Lord Strafford and his secretary, by Van Dyck.*[36] *The Picture Gallery...was a long red and white room stretching fifty yards, bisected by impressive stone columns. There was a portrait of Shakespeare that had once belonged to Dryden, a cupid by Guido, a Raphael and a painting of Mary Magdalene by Titian.*[37]

Sound, thick, black profound
Verse

Wentworth Woodhouse sat above of a rich coal seam. Coal had been mined there, in shallow pits, since the sixteenth century, used as domestic fuel, by blacksmiths, to fire pottery and for glassmaking. Much of the income of Fitzwilliam and his successors came from coal. Increasing demand and the growth of steam power led to deeper, underground mines. As Yorkshire coalfields became a major source of fuel for the Industrial Revolution, pit-heads marked the landscape along with church steeples.

Regal visits & loyal efforts
Mansfield Park

On 2 September 1789, the royal party entered the gates of *Wentworth Woodhouse* into a huge garden party, welcomed by forty thousand people in the grounds and hundreds of Fitzwilliam's invited guests in the house. *In the true style of ancient English hospitality, his gates were thrown open to the loyalty and love of the surrounding country...The diversions, consisting of all the rural sports in use in that part of the kingdom, lasted the whole day; and the prince, with the nobility and gentry, who were the noble earl's guests, participated in the merriment. The company in the house were about 200 and they comprehended all the beauty and fashion of the neighbourhood, without distinction of party. The dinner was in the highest stile of magnificence, and the Fete concluded with a Ball.*[38]

Earl Fitzwilliam presented gifts to his patrons, the Prince of Wales, the Duke of Norfolk, and leaders of the Whig Party received mementos of the occasion.

The World used Fitzwilliam's party and the politesse of patronage to satirise the Prince of Wales and leading Whigs:

> *Subsequent to the Gala, the noble Lord, with every possible accomplishment of useful splendour, has presented some elegant little memorial, to his more particular friends, and fellow-labourers in the politics of party!*
>
> *In a present, says Swift, it is not the value of the thing – but it should be that which you cannot buy. These presents from Wentworth House, are thus enhanced with rarity either of Nature or Art, with select appropriation, and here and there, it is said, with some apposite innuendo, most elegantly conveyed. All the presents would make too long a list – but these, I hear are some of them.*
>
> *To the Prince, a most invaluable Mabuse, the master of Rubens. It is Harry V, not only dismissing his bad companions, but in the full recovery of his noble nature, receiving the Chief Justice and his father's other venerable friends.*
>
> *To the Duke of Norfolk – the Duke de Bouillon, mentioned by Cardinal de Retz.*
>
> *To Mr. Burke, a blood horse, Rubens never did anything finer, with uncommon powers about the head; but now blind and broken winded, seemingly not worth a guinea, blundering downhill without his breeching. Rubens made his animals think and feel. This animal makes all think and feel around him; and it is as true as the rest of the anecdote, that when the Prince, who is easily impressed, first saw it; he sighed and shook his head – and wrote with a pencil on the frame, "Semper Acerbum."*[39]
>
> *To Mr. Fox, what is singular – a very large piece of cut glass, the first ever made, dated 1163. As the prismatic power is valuable, and it is curious, though not useful to divide and subdivide our rays, Mr Fox is rich indeed. Though the Duke of Cumberland said with some naiveté, he could not see anything in it!* [40]

The Prince, since his return from Yorkshire, has checked his tendency to corpulence very much, and looks the better for it Public Advertiser

The London press calculated the cost and benefit of Fitzwilliam's extravaganza

The expences that Lord Fitzwilliam has been at in entertaining the Royal Brothers at Wentworth Castle, are computed at six thousand pounds. Two hundred persons sat down to dinner each day within the walls of the house; besides the vast concourse of people regaled in the park.

The whole party are at war Lady Susan

On 1 February 1793, France declared war on Britain. The Whigs joined with Pitt when he declared war on France's Revolutionary Government. With Fitzwilliam's support, Lord Portland and four other Whigs joined Pitt's Ministry.

Fitzwilliam refused a place, saying, *I can be ten times more service to the common cause out than in... Let me act in my sphere, to work without doors.*[41] He was made Lord President of the Council in July 1794, and in November was appointed Lord Lieutenant of Ireland, nominated by Portland, who had been Lord Lieutenant in 1782. Portland was now the Secretary of State, responsible for Ireland and for New South Wales.

Lord Lieutenant of Ireland The History of England

As war with France intensified, there were grave fears the French would land in Ireland to join forces with Irish dissidents, against the British. The ideals of the Revolution – liberty and democracy, found fertile ground in Ireland. In April 1794, United Irishmen resolved, if the French invaded, they would collaborate with them, and the French Republic undertook to supply arms to the Irish in an invasion. For England, the involvement of the radical French Republic in its Irish affairs was a worrying development.

Fitzwilliam realised the urgent need to avert an alliance between the Irish and revolutionary France. He worked directly to Portland, he accepted the post believing he had his and Pitt's concurrence to relieve the burdens on the Catholic majority in Ireland. *He hoped that by extending the privileges of the Roman Catholics, and by introducing an impartial system of government, he might restore the alienated affections of the people to their sovereign.*[42]

He wanted to implement Whig principles of civil and religious liberty in Ireland. He relied on support from Portland and Pitt to achieve them, knowing reform would arouse resistance from the Protestant Ascendancy, the great landowners who had controlled political power in Ireland for centuries.

Fitzwilliam followed the footsteps of two of his forebears, Thomas Wentworth, Earl of Strafford, appointed Lord Lieutenant of Ireland by Charles I, and Sir William Fitzwilliam, who held the post three times under Elizabeth I, between 1560 and 1594. In August 1588, over twenty ships of the Spanish Armada, fleeing home after their defeat, were driven ashore in a storm. Sir William had the survivors rounded up along five hundred kilometres of the west coast, from Antrim to Kerry, and executed.

My advice, I certainly do feel tempted to give Emma

Lord Portland's former chaplain and private secretary, Rev Thomas Lewis O'Beirne, offered his services to Fitzwilliam. He urged him to act quickly and decisively, to replace members of the Protestant Faction holding key positions of authority.

O'Beirne was a staunch Irish Whig, born a Catholic, intended for the priesthood, he was educated with his brother at Saint-Omer in Flanders. He left his studies at the Irish College in Paris, and became a clergyman in the Church of Ireland. Described as a man of *rapacious ambition,* with an appetite for patronage that was *predatory and insatiable,* he assured Portland his role as private secretary would not debar him from being made a bishop, and requested a seat on the Irish bench.⁴³

Rev O'Beirne officiated at the private marriage between the Prince of Wales and Mrs Maria Fitzherbert in December 1785. In March 1791, he sought clemency from Evan Nepean, for a young Irish surgeon, John Francis Molloy, convicted of highway robbery.⁴⁴

Such an agreement as may be beneficial to himself and not offensive to his patron
Pride & Prejudice

Among correspondence Fitzwilliam received anticipating his new appointment, was a letter from John Pemberton Heywood. Five years earlier he had prosecuted D'Arcy, now he asked Fitzwilliam for an appointment in Ireland. *I presume now upon the kindness your Lordship has long been so good as to shew me – though perhaps late to render my humble services if I can be useful in any Capacity either now or at any future period during your residence in that Country – where from natural connection I have always looked forward with pleasure to a settlement – I cannot expect or indeed desire any Arrangement was broken in upon on my account – but confiding on the long attachment of my family to the House of Wentworth I trust to your goodness for pardon for this Intrusion and if your Lordship should have an opportunity of doing any thing for me I hope I shall shew that I am not ungrateful.*⁴⁵

Meeting in Dublin
Emma

On 4 January 1795, expectant crowds welcomed Fitzwilliam and his family to Dublin, word had reached Ireland he was bringing justice and liberty.

He began immediately to reform the bureaucracy, he *proceeded to dismiss the "King's friends" and to supply in their places a more virtuous set of politicians.*⁴⁶ He retired several key officials representing the interests of the Protestant Ascendancy, including the First Commissioner of Revenue, John Beresford, leader of the Protestant faction; the Undersecretary; and Solicitor General. Others were induced to agree to resign. He promoted sympathetic Whig reformers, among them, his cousins, William and George Ponsonby.

There was immediate backlash. Pitt was anxious to support those who had served his government in Ireland, and to thwart what was seen as an attempt by the Whigs to impose their regime there. One under-secretary who lost his position wrote to Evan Nepean, in Portland's office, accusing Fitzwilliam of trying to wrest control of Ireland out of the hands of the Crown, and vest it in the Whig aristocracy.[47]

Fitzwilliam arranged for Henry Grattan to lay an *Emancipation Bill* before the Irish House of Commons on 12 February 1795. It allowed propertied Catholics to stand for Parliament and hold senior positions in the civil service. During the previous century, the Catholic majority was progressively stripped of rights, with Catholic property owners disenfranchised in 1728.

Fitzwilliam believed these reforms would strengthen the spirit and loyalty of Catholics, and improve the relationship between England and Ireland. His strategy failed, *as the Whig revolution in Ireland got underway consternation spread through the Protestant faction and their friends in London.*[48]

To become law, the *Emancipation Bill* needed the approval of both houses of the Irish Parliament, and the King. Pitt, realised George III would not support any move towards Catholic emancipation, believing he would be violating his Coronation Oath, to protect the Church of England. He instructed Fitzwilliam to postpone its introduction. On 20 February 1795, after less than seven weeks in Dublin, Fitzwilliam was recalled.

Defended it through every criticism Emma

Indignation and sorrow spread across the whole country, among Catholics and Protestants alike. An undergraduate of Trinity College, Dublin, the *great centre of Protestant learning*, reported the reaction of the Irish House of Commons: *Lord Fitzwilliam had been sent over as a popular Viceroy, and on his sudden recall a strong feeling of disappointment prevailed. On a night when the subject was brought before the House, our gallery was full, and I remember well the inexpressible excitement that seemed to actuate us all.*

At length it broke out. Grattan rose to deprecate the measure as one calculated to cause the greatest disturbance in Ireland, by what was considered the perfidy of the Government, first exciting the high hopes of the people promise measures of liberal policy, and then dashing them by the sudden removal of the man who had been sent over expressly to accomplish them. At the conclusion of Grattan's inflammatory speech, the enthusiasm of the gallery was no longer capable of restraint. We rose as one man, shouting and cheering.

The Trinity students were banned from the parliamentary gallery: *a sergeant at arms with a posse of messengers entered among us. We were pushed out in a heap, without the slightest ceremony, and were never again suffered to enter.*[49]

After having been Lord Lieutenant of Ireland   The History of England
Fitzwilliam left Ireland on 25 March, 1795; *the day of his departure from Dublin was hailed as one of national misfortune, and the inhabitants took every means of manifesting their gratitude, their sorrow, and their disappointment. The shops were all closed. The people dragged the carriage to the point of embarkation. The name of every friend of Fitzwilliam was received with loud approving cheers, and of every opponent with groans and execrations.*[50]

Four days earlier, in the House of Lords, Lord Moira criticised his recall, *at a time when all Ireland was in favour of the measures he pursued, when that country gave the fairest prospect of tranquillity – the surest pledge of assistance and support to Britain, in the arduous circumstances in which she was placed. To the impolicy of that measure, the distracted state of Ireland was now to be imputed. He declared the British Cabinet had interfered successfully for what he deemed an impolitic and mischievous purpose.*[51]

On 24 March 1795, Charles Fox rose and spoke in the Commons: *I was told, touch not upon Ireland, that is a subject too delicate for discussion in this House... Earl Fitzwilliam was sent over as Lord Lieutenant to Ireland. He states it is intended to give emancipation to the Roman Catholics of Ireland. The Irish Parliament are told that abuses are to be reformed. They see the dismissal of several persons known to be connected with the old abuses. They consider all this as the omen of approaching liberty; & that all the people of Ireland are without distinction about to enjoy those rights & and privileges to which they are in justice entitled, & which they ought always to have enjoyed.*

All this passes day after day without the least opposition on the part of the Cabinet of Great Britain. All of a sudden things unfortunately took a different turn. Whether it is owing to the Duke of Portland I know not.

The Ministers here then quarrel with this popular Lord Lieutenant... That the whole blame in this business is to be imputed to His Majesty's Ministers is a matter about which no living man can dispute. They gave up Earl Fitzwilliam rather than Ireland should receive from this country the benefits to which she is in common justice entitled.

Roman Catholics make up five-sixths of the population of Ireland. I no longer dread any danger from disputes between Roman Catholics and Protestants. They have but one common interest – to preserve the country against a corrupt and oppressive administration. I dread that the Irish nation in consequence of the support of abuses & corruption, may become less connected with, & less attached to, the English nation. I dread the alienation of the Irish people from the English government. Is not Ireland in danger? No man will deny it![52]

We met by appointment, he to defend, I to punish his conduct. We returned unwounded
Sense & Sensibility

Following Fitzwilliam's dismissal, the Irish Protestant leader, John Beresford challenged him to a duel, claiming he was unjustly defamed by Fitzwilliam in conversations with Lord Carlisle, and demanding satisfaction.

Fitzwilliam chose Lord Moira as his second, but as he was too closely watched, Lord George Cavendish took his place. The pair arranged to meet at Marylebone Fields, but finding a large crowd gathered there, moved to a field near Paddington. A magistrate then appeared and arrested Fitzwilliam, who gave up his pistol. He apologised to Beresford, who declared himself satisfied, and the two combatants shook hands. After Fitzwilliam's recall Beresford was reinstated as first Commissioner of Revenue.

Narrow souls & prejudicial judgements
The History of England

Just as George III and Parliament misunderstood the American colonists, they misread the Irish situation. The King did not grasp the urgent need for recognition and reconciliation in Ireland. If he had supported the introduction of the *Emancipation Bill* in 1795 and a reduction in the power of the Protestant Ascendancy, Fitzwilliam's strategy as Lord Lieutenant may have prevented two centuries of violence, and avoided the partition of Ireland.

> Fitzwilliam went to Ireland, but he was deemed unfit to stay
> He scarcely could explain himself, ere he was dragged away
> Too frank, too firm, too honest, for Court maxims he appears
> And earned more praise in three short months,
> than some in three long years.[53]
>
> LONDON CHRONICLE

Mr Pitt or the Lord Chancellor
Kitty, or the Bower

Fitzwilliam remained an independent Whig voice in the House of Lords, always conscious of impending tragedy in Ireland. He was resentful of the treatment he received as Lord Lieutenant, and reluctant to ever again give his support to Pitt or Portland.

The Duke of Norfolk
The History of England

On 24 January 1798, Fitzwilliam attended a banquet at the *Crown and Anchor Tavern* in London, to celebrate Charles Fox's birthday. In the company of several Lords and a great many others, the Duke of Norfolk raised his glass to *the rights of the people; Constitutional Redress of the Wrongs of the People; A speedy and effectual Reform in the Representation of the People in Parliament; The genuine Principles of the British Constitution; The people of Ireland, may they be speedily* *restored to the blessings of Law and Liberty; and the Majesty of the People.*⁵⁴

The Duke of Norfolk's sentiments were not well received by the King. He was dismissed from his position as Lord Lieutenant of the West Riding of Yorkshire, for proposing seditious toasts.

Charles Howard, Duke of Norfolk, was no stranger to political controversy. He was one of the last Peers to renounce his Catholicism, he voted against going to war with the American colonies, and he supported Fitzwilliam's efforts to progress Catholic emancipation in Ireland. On 2 March 1798, Fitzwilliam was appointed to replace him as Lord Lieutenant of the West Riding.

My mind is always trembling for the fate of Ireland ⁵⁵   Fitzwilliam, November 1796

The British repudiation of Fitzwilliam let the revolutionary movement run wild in Ireland. Within three years of his departure, rebellion had broken out, and the Irish rebels crushed by systematic military atrocities.

Fitzwilliam was succeeded by Lord Camden, an opponent of Catholic rights, allied to the Protestant Ascendancy. His turbulent period in office culminated in the Battle of Vinegar Hill, twelve days after he was replaced by Lord Cornwallis, late of Yorktown and India, now Lord Lieutenant and Commander-in-Chief.

Cornwallis described, *the ferocity of our soldiers, who delight in murder, who butchered without discrimination, the numberless murders that are hourly committed by our people without any process or examination whatever.*⁵⁶

After the rebellion broke out, Fitzwilliam supported Opposition attacks on the Government in Parliament, voting for resolutions criticising its Irish policies, and censuring the Irish administration.

When Fitzwilliam's West Yorkshire militia volunteered to go and assist in Ireland, he declared, *I cannot lend myself as a firebrand or bayonet of Lord Cornwallis, against the miserable and helpless, nor as the instrument to chastise those who resist, even by force, such oppression.*⁵⁷

Being on the watch, heard distinctly & was sadly alarmed   Emma

Fitzwilliam dated the origin of the rebellion from his own recall. The United Irishmen had made *but little way amongst the Catholics until the recall of Lord Fitzwilliam*,⁵⁸ which created the opportunity for *certain leading conspirators to persuade the Catholics to join the disaffected Presbyterians.*⁵⁹ *The Irish*, he said, *have become most inveterate rebels. Ireland will never be tranquillised till the people give credit to a fundamental change of system.*⁶⁰

He wrote to Edmund Burke in November 1796, *Ireland every day, every hour, confirms the ticklish state of that poor country. The north in rebellion against the constitution; the mass of the people disaffected to the government and panting for the arrival of a foreign enemy, that they may throw off the yoke of their task-masters. The army, one half, at least, is as disaffected as the mass of the people, and owing to the same causes. The Protestant Ascendancy..they may overthrow a host of patriots, but they will never overthrow an army of insurgents. (Pitt) is determined not to make friends with the Irish.*[61]

Two weeks later, Fitzwilliam wrote again, *Ireland is in a state of most odious oppression and abject slavery for the great body of the people – there are there two laws and two constitutions, one for the rich, and one for the poor.*[62]

Lord Cornwallis believed union with England was possible, but he agreed with Fitzwilliam it would require Catholic emancipation. George III could not be convinced. Cornwallis resigned over the impasse, It was a sad, grievous and costly failure, not to recognise the aspirations of the Irish Catholics.

I shall feel myself under an obligation to anyone who is the means of sending my brother home   Lady Susan

Robert Sinclair, in York, was affected by events in Ireland. After the rebellion, in June 1798, his brother William was arrested and sentenced to *peremptory transportation for life to Botany Bay.*

Rev William Sinclair had gone to Ireland in 1775, after graduating from the University of Glasgow. In 1786, he was preaching in County Down; by 1791 he had joined with Wolfe Tone, advocating for Protestants, Catholics, and Dissenters, all Irishmen, to unite and break their connection with England.

Wolfe Tone, a Protestant, born in 1763, studied law at Trinity College, and was a member of the Middle Temple. He called himself a Northern Whig, to distinguish his views from Irish Whigs like Henry Grattan, who wanted to achieve parliamentary reform and Catholic emancipation while remaining loyal to England and the Crown. In Belfast, in October 1791, with William Sinclair and ten others, he had launched the Society of United Irishmen, bringing a new dimension to the political aspirations of the Irish, the desire for an independent republic.

In August 1798, Robert Sinclair replied to *a kind and friendly letter* from Fitzwilliam, telling him William's sentence had been *mitigated to voluntary removal to America*, and thanking him: *were it possible for me to be impressed with stronger feelings of respect and gratitude for the many civilities and acts of kindness I have met with from your Lordship, this last instance would certainly have such effect.*[63]

Very extraordinary talents   Emma

Fitzwilliam opposed Pitt's *Act of Union*, uniting Ireland and Great Britain. It came into force in 1 January 1801, and shortly afterwards, Pitt put up his own proposal for Catholic emancipation in Ireland. George III remained intransigent, he refused to support him, and Pitt resigned on 16 February.

Pitt was replaced as Prime Minister by Henry Addington, Viscount Sidmouth, who held office until 10 May 1804. Pitt returned, but died in office on 23 January 1806. A fortnight later George III appointed William Grenville, Pitt's first cousin, to replace him. With the country in the midst of war with Napoleon, Grenville wanted a strong, united government. His new Whig coalition was mocked with the name, the *Ministry of All Talents.*

Fitzwilliam, now fifty-eight, did not want a position in the new ministry, *with respect to office, it was the wish of my heart and my determination to have none.*[64] Fox implored him to join the Cabinet, he was not interested in a Ministry, but did accept the post of Lord President of the Council.

Charles Fox, Foreign Minister in the new government, tried but failed to conclude a peace agreement, to end the long wars with France. He did succeed in having the *Foreign Slave Trade Bill* passed, and on 10 June 1806, his resolution to abolish the slave trade was passed by both Houses. Fox declared it his proudest achievement in forty years in Parliament. He died in September 1806, and the King assented to the *Slave Trade Act* six months after his death.

The Act had been put to Parliament in 1804 under Pitt, who failed to get the numbers to pass it. The *Ministry of All Talents* had a greater commitment to liberal ideals, and a willingness to take on the contentious issue driven by Wilberforce, but it would be another twenty-six years before slavery was finally abolished.

After Fox's death, Prime Minister, Lord Grenville called an election, hoping to increase the *Ministry of All Talents* numbers in the Commons. But by March 1807, the Government was in crisis, locked in major disagreement with George III, over his mulish rejection[65] of Catholic emancipation. Grenville declined to give the King the pledge he required,[66] to never again propose concessions to the Catholics, and he resigned on 31 March 1807.

On 12 March, Portland had written to the King, and proposed a new ministry that would resist claims from the Catholics. On 31 March 1807, he was made Prime Minister, the *Ministry of All Talents* was finished, the Tories returned to power and Parliament was dissolved on 27 April 1807. Portland had betrayed his colleagues once again. The Whig coalition lasted one year and forty five days, a brief interlude in Government in its long, half century in Opposition.

An only son, & the representative of an ancient family Lady Susan

In the election of 1807, Fitzwilliam encouraged his twenty-one year old son, Lord Milton, to stand for the seat of Yorkshire, that elected two members to the Commons. Wilberforce held one, and was certain to retain it. Lord Milton would have to stand against the Tories and defeat Henry Lascelles, Lord Harewood's son.⁶⁷ It was a battle between two great Yorkshire families.

Mrs Lascelles announcing the speedy return of herself and her husband to England Kitty, or the Bower

The election campaign was dominated by the economic concerns of local merchants and clothiers. Henry Lascelles proved inept at handling their grievances, and was defeated by Lord Milton.⁶⁸ The Lascelles fortune relied on profits from their West Indian plantations, the election cost them over £93,600, Fitzwilliam spent around £100,000.

This is an illnatured sentiment to send all over the Baltic Letters

Fitzwilliam returned to Opposition, but he retained his involvement in matters of power and principle. In the summer of 1807, he criticised the Government for its bombardment of Copenhagen, and the theft of seventeen ships of the Danish fleet, captured in the surprise raid and taken back to Britain. He saw the expedition as the action of buccaneers, violent and unjust, which alienated a potential ally. Britain must now contend with French power, *not only without an ally, but without the good wishes, without the favourable disposition of any part of Europe or America.*⁶⁹

In the Peninsular War, between 1807 and 1814, he praised Spanish resistance to Napoleon as *a glorious crusade for liberty,* declaring, *the Spaniards are a fine people, by their own energy they will emancipate themselves.*⁷⁰

An American War Letters

Fitzwilliam censured the British hostilities against America between 1812 and 1815, he deplored the Government's policy of *drubbing the Americans into submission,* and its apparent desire to achieve *nothing short of the subjugation of America.*⁷¹

While staying with her brother Henry in London in September 1814, Jane Austen commented, *with regard to an American War, they consider it as certain, & as what is to ruin us. The Americans cannot be conquered, & we shall only be teaching them the skill in War which they may want. We are to make them good Sailors & Soldiers, & gain nothing ourselves- If we are to be ruined, it cannot be helped.*⁷² The American War ended a few months later, on Christmas Eve.

Noble kindred and extensive patronage Pride and Prejudice

Though not a Yorkshireman by birth, Fitzwilliam dedicated himself to the County of Yorkshire, he gave financial support to hospitals, local schools, to the York Races and the upkeep of prisoners in the city gaol. During periods of scarcity or when corn prices were high, he funded emergency food supplies and soup kitchens. He financed building projects, including the Ouse Bridge, and the Pocklington canal, and supported Friendly Societies and savings banks, to encourage self-reliance.

He was a humane and generous landholder and employer, he kept his tenanted properties well maintained, reduced rents and cancelled arrears in difficult times, provided cheap food, and gave the elderly free coal and blankets. His contributions were a part of his responsibilities as Lord and patron, and his successors continued those traditions into the twentieth century.

In October 1819, after the Peterloo massacre, Fitzwilliam, as Lord Lieutenant of the West Riding, put resolutions to a county meeting endorsing the right to public assembly, condemning unlawful interference with that right, and demanding an enquiry into events at Peterloo. Two weeks later he was dismissed as Lord Lieutenant.

The claims of our friends or the opinion of the world   Lady Susan

Fitzwilliam did not condone D'Arcy's foolhardy pursuit of his defaulters, but he remained his loyal friend and patron. He enjoyed D'Arcy's intelligence and his vitality, he found him *full of life and ardour*,[73] and he helped him to escape from London for a new life in New South Wales.

From his earliest days in the Colony, D'Arcy relied on Fitzwilliam, for encouragement, practical help and support. Arranging Charles Cookney to act as his London agent, was a turning point in D'Arcy's life and fortunes. Isolated on a remote island, he was assured of Fitzwilliam's friendship and support.

For D'Arcy, as for others in the Colony, there was no avenue of redress or appeal against unjust, arbitrary decisions of the governor or the Colonial office. Without Fitzwilliam's effort and advocacy, time and again, D'Arcy might have been stranded on Norfolk Island, never recognised or employed as a surgeon, or paid for his work. D'Arcy prevailed because he had an influential friend and patron in England, who actively assisted him, who enjoyed and respected him.

Fitzwilliam saw D'Arcy as a cousin and a friend, their friendship is visible in the warmth of their correspondence. Through him, D'Arcy met many enlightened Whigs, and was attracted to their liberalism, philosophy and politics. His advice to Governor Hunter, and to later governors, reflected those ideals and principles. He instilled Whig principles in his son William, who championed political reform in the Colony.

It is clear from their correspondence that D'Arcy wanted Fitzwilliam to approve his return to England. He asked for it numerous times over the years. Fitzwilliam never refused directly, but he tried to dissuade him, and D'Arcy understood that his patron had reservations about him returning.

JANE & D'ARCY

He proceeded a little farther, reading to himself & and then with a smile observed, "Humph! a fine complimentary opening"   Emma

In January 1813, *Pride & Prejudice* was published, its hero Fitzwilliam Darcy, with *splendid property, noble kindred and extensive patronage.* His seat, *Pemberley,* closely fitted the description of *Wentworth Woodhouse,* and the story included *Colonel Fitzwilliam, the younger son of his uncle, Lord –.*

It is unlikely Fitzwilliam heard of the book immediately. A few weeks earlier, between 5 October and 10 November 1812, he was preoccupied with a general election, campaigning, mobilising candidates, counting the results. It was, he said, *the most unfortunate general election in my recollection, because not one occurs to me in which so much talent and character, on the side of the opposition, has been lost.*[74] Parliament was opened by the Prince Regent on 28 January 1813, and Fitzwilliam spent some time in London.

Fitzwilliam was patron and confidante to numerous aunts and female cousins. He had five sisters, four of them unmarried. His married sister, Charlotte, Lady Dundas, had seven daughters and seven sons. Fitzwilliam would had have heard quite early from within the family that it was a love story involving D'Arcy. A second edition of *Pride & Prejudice* was published in October 1813, as its reputation grew, numerous sources would have mentioned the anonymous novel set so literally within his family and estate.

Fitzwilliam met Jane on several occasions, and he remembered the young aspiring writer. He was aware she and D'Arcy went on to Scotland after his great party at *Wentworth Woodhouse.* A quarter of a century later, reading her novel, he would have known it was her, writing about her love for D'Arcy, still on the other side of the globe. Fitzwilliam would have smiled at such delightful *mischief.*[75]

Having performed all these noble actions   The History of England

In 1823, a year after the death of his wife Lady Charlotte, Fitzwilliam, now seventy-two, married her cousin, the Hon. Louisa Ponsonby, widow of William Brabazon, 1st Lord Ponsonby. She died sixteen months later, aged seventy-four.[76] Fitzwilliam lived another ten years, he died six years after D'Arcy, on 8 February 1833, in his eighty fifth year, at *Milton House* in Peterborough. He left one son, Charles, Lord Milton, now 5th Earl Fitzwilliam, four grandsons and six granddaughters.

Chapter 17

Antipodean Hell

Brooding over Evils which cannot be remedied,
& conduct impossible to understand

AFTER CATHERINE'S DEATH, D'Arcy left Parramatta. He bought a house in Sydney, in High Street, close to the port. Goods shipped from London could be easily transported, stored and traded there. John Harris owned the house next door. King gave D'Arcy approval to buy six feet of land from him, to build a new detached kitchen, removing the stove and copper from the house, to reduce risk of fire.[1] He kept a horse and chaise, and five horses between Sydney and Parramatta, to move quickly between the hospitals.

As to my dear little boys   Emma

In 1801, D'Arcy had two convicts assigned to him, one, Catherine Melling,[2] lived in and cared for his three sons. A year later, she left to be married, and was replaced by Maria Ainsley, an emancipist and a widow, who brought her own young son to live with them.[3] D'Arcy adopted new Christian names for his two younger sons, Dorset became D'Arcy, and Matthew became John.

No happiness in veiw but that of returning to England again   Kitty, or the Bower

He continued to work as a surgeon, and increased his investment in trade, he aimed to make sufficient profit to finance his return to England with his sons. He had asked Fitzwilliam several times, to help him obtain approval to return. In October 1800 he asked again – *I informed your Lordship of my determination to leave this country as soon as possible...but how soon that Time may be, is not in my Power at this moment to tell.*[4]

Nothing but a thorough change of sentiment could account for it   Sense & Sensibility

King's return as governor had brought D'Arcy unexpected trouble. He was shocked to find King had turned his back on him; his change of attitude defied explanation. On Norfolk Island they had worked with trust and cooperation. Now King singled him out, and seemed determined to destroy him.

There is a strong appearance of duplicity in all this   Pride & Prejudice

King's change of heart occurred during his years in England, where he became a silent partner of ship-owner Samuel Enderby.[5] He assisted Enderby & Champion to gain exemption from East India Company regulations, allowing them to carry cargo to Sydney on the outwards voyage of their whalers.[6]

King favoured them, he *guaranteed an artificially lucrative market*[7] for goods received from the whalers into the Government Store, and he discouraged and curtailed the activities of other traders in the Colony. He wanted to have all imported goods sold through the Government Store, and to control their prices.

King returned to Sydney on an Enderby whaler, *Speedy,* carrying a hundred and twenty nine convicts, and goods for the Government Store. He continued to profit from his association with the Enderbys, without disclosing it.

In 1798, Cookney told D'Arcy: *King informed me that it was not in his power to get leave for the trunk containing your things to be shipp'd on board the Porpoise.. Not being satisfied with this I wrote to my Lord Fitzwilliam requesting him to write to the Comptroller of the Navy Board which his Lordship did and leave was granted immediately to have them shipp'd on board the Porpoise.*[8]

An order indefinite as to time, to depend upon contingencies & conveniences   Emma

King was in an awkward position when he returned, unlike Phillip and Hunter, he was neither *captain-general* nor *governor-in-chief*. His dormant commission merely instructed him to *discharge the duties of Governor*. He understood the limits of his appointment, he signed his despatches, *Acting Governor*,[9] but he did not disclose his limited authority to Hunter or anyone else.

The practised politician, who is to read every body's character, and make every body's talents conduce to the display of his own superiority   Emma

The uncertainty of King's position made him particularly anxious to please his superiors in London, to demonstrate he could make and enforce tough decisions. He grew impatient when Hunter stayed on for twenty weeks as Governor, and relations between them broke down. Hunter wrote to him that he *conspicuously manifested an indelicate impatience,* with conduct *injurious to my character in the administration of public justice.*[10] He referred to King's *mean, dark and contemptible attempts to asperse my character.*[11]

Hunter agreed to King appointing Major Foveaux as commandant of Norfolk Island. From King's experience, the isolation of the settlement and the potential for volatility between convicts and soldiers living in a close proximity made it one of extraordinarily high risk. He gave Foveaux a lengthy, detailed set of orders,[12] and directed him to be draconian in his management of the convicts.

As to Spirits & Appetite   Letters

King presented himself as the Governor sent to stop the import of rum, to end the entrenched authority of the Rum Corps, limit government expenditure and bring economic prosperity to the Colony. On Monday 8 September 1800, three weeks before he was due to take up his appointment, he issued orders to curb the importation of spirits.

Aware of the contempt in which he was held by the military, King chose not to read it himself. He directed Lieut Governor William Paterson, Commander of the Corps, to read his proclamation to a meeting of all civil and military officers. Under King's administration, importers would need the Governor's permission to import rum and other tradable items; a vessel arriving in Port Jackson could not land spirits without his prior consent and a written permit; and any officer disobeying these rules would be sent home. King made Paterson responsible for enforcing the orders within the Rum Corps.[13]

Two days later he wrote to Portland to inform him of the firm stand he was taking against the Rum Corps and their importation of spirits.[14]

Unfavourable circumstances had suddenly arisen at a moment when he was beginning to turn all his thoughts towards England   Mansfield Park

D'Arcy was greatly concerned at King's new trade regulations. To finance his return to England, he had speculated all the capital he could raise on imported goods. He had invested in substantial stocks, ten chests of tea, three thousand gallons of spirits, and other goods. Under King's new rules, he was forbidden to sell them. His colleague William Balmain was in a similar predicament, with a store of 1359 gallons of spirits and seven chests of tea.[15] Both of them were civil officers, answerable to the governor.

On Sunday, 14 September, six days after King's proclamation, doubtless after discussion with Hunter, D'Arcy and Balmain each wrote to King, opening with, *it becomes my duty to state to you,* and declaring a quantity of goods, including spirits and tea, that *I became possessed of previous to your arrival and before His Majesty's pleasure on this head were made known to me, a single article of which I shall not attempt to dispense of without your permission and approbation, although* my loss will be more than my circumstances can possibly sustain, if every means of getting rid of them is utterly denied me.

I therefore take the liberty of offering them to you, on account of Government, at such an advance as may compensate for laying out my money and cover any other incidental risque or loss; or if you are pleased to direct that I should adopt any other measure which may operate in my favour, without clashing with your orders, I will thankfully embrace it.[16]

A most lively interest in the state of his finances, & live in hopes of his soon being ruined Letters

King replied on Tuesday, 16 September, *Gentlemen – in answer to yours of 14th instant in which you so cordially and fairly state your circumstances and property.* He asked for details of the goods they had, and for the *rate at which you would resign them to the Government.* [17] D'Arcy and Balmain replied the same afternoon, with an inventory of their stocks, stating they were prepared to sell their rum to the Government Store for twenty shillings per gallon, their tea at the same price per pound.

The opportunity was too fair, & his feelings too impatient Mansfield Park

Though Hunter was still governor, King was in the ascendant. Wentworth and Balmain, two civil officers, had come forward, declaring they had a quantity of rum intended for sale. He would not agree to them selling their stores to the Government Store, instead he issued them with new orders, preventing them from marketing the goods freely.

Contractions & restrictions every where Persuasion

King's approval was required before any sale could take place, nothing could be sold, *without my permission and approbation of the purchaser.* He set the price, no more than twenty shillings for a gallon of rum or a pound of tea.

King required monthly returns of what had been sold and what remained, and *an assurance in writing that they will not enter into any future speculations or purchases contrary to the tenor of His Majesty's Instructions – otherwise it will become my duty to take a proper notice of it.*

On Thursday, 18 September, he wrote to Paterson, informing him of the strict conditions he had set for Balmain and Wentworth to dispose of their stores, advising him, *the military may take advantage of the same concessions.*[18]

King took the opportunity to impress his superiors in London that he, unlike Hunter, was prepared to take control of the rum trade. To demonstrate his resolution and vigour, he sent Portland copies of his correspondence with Paterson, Balmain, and D'Arcy.

He wanted to be seen as a strong and effective governor, who made rules and enforced them. He expected his forceful action against the two surgeons to act as a warning to the Rum Corps officers, and to individual traders like Simeon Lord, and Robert Campbell, who was importing rum directly from India.

It was easy for him to single out two civil officers, who risked losing their positions if they did not comply. He did not confront the entrenched power of the Rum Corps officers. He was aware of their rampant abuses and entrenched privilege, but he did not pursue them. The Rum Corps did not answer to him, he issued orders to them through their commander, with no expectation they would comply. He had fallen out with the Corps over the mutiny on Norfolk Island, he wished to appear conciliatory. As Governor he might need to call on them. Not one of the officers declared their trading stocks.

Three months later King permitted the *Royal Admiral* to land seven thousand gallons of rum. He sent five thousand gallons to the Government Store, to be released later as the Governor granted, and allowed the officers, soldiers and settlers the balance. He permitted the Corps to sell the rum at a profit of thirty to forty percent, *a direct encouragement for traffic by the military*.[19] He did not attempt to suppress their trade in rum, but he pursued D'Arcy with a vengeance.

Greater severity & restraint Mansfield Park

On 28 September 1800, Hunter sailed on *HMS Buffalo*. King took control of the Colony, and as D'Arcy and Balmain attempted to dispose of their stocks of tea and spirits, both men faced his vigorous opposition.

Two weeks after Hunter left, D'Arcy wrote to Fitzwilliam and Cookney, outlining his predicament, asking for their advocacy with the Home Office to allow him to return. He gave the letters to Captain Waterhouse on the *Reliance*.

In his first three months as governor, King issued *an extraordinary series of General* Orders, often very lengthy, frequently appealing to *imaginary royal instructions*.[20] Power had gone to his head. He set a maximum price for all imported goods to remedy the *exorbitant demands of creditors* on the free settlers. He established a *public warehouse*, to sell goods to the public at a fixed fifty percent above the cost, to cover transport and overheads.[21]

For my own peace of mind, I should leave this place as soon as I can

D'Arcy told Fitzwilliam the new regulations spelt his ruin. He outlined the onerous constraints King had put on his terms of sale, the financial difficulties caused by his actions; he feared King would dismiss him. *Some restrictions which Governor King has put upon me on the sale of these Articles of Merchandise which*

I am now in possession of & in which I am sorry to say, my whole property is embanked…so that I shall be the loser of at least two Thousand Pounds by these Restrictions – I was in expectation of returning to England with a fortune of six or seven or eight Thousand Pounds, but I now fear I shall not be able to realize more than five Thousand and even in accompanying this, I shall not be surprised if I am compelled to relinquish my situation.[22]

He asked Waterhouse to call on Fitzwilliam – *if he had the opportunity of seeing you to explain my reason…how necessary it was for my own peace of mind, that I should leave this place as soon as I can.*[23]

Of all things in the world, inconstancy is my aversion   Northanger Abbey
Your Lordship, I dare say will think it strange I should say that Governor King has conducted himself towards me since his late arrival in this country, in a manner I little expected from his former profession of Friendship, but so it is…but be assured my Lord, I will not be put in his Power to do so from any Impropriety in my conduct.[24]

Cookney responded – *I can't say but that you surprise me not a little when you inform me that Gov. King and you are not upon Terms of Friendship. He spoke so highly of you when in England that I thought his return a fortunate circumstance for you.*[25]

Darcy, at whom it was all aimed   Pride & Prejudice
Fitzwilliam called on Under-Secretary Sullivan at the Colonial Office. Sullivan wrote to the Governor, advising him to settle matters with D'Arcy and Balmain by purchasing their rum and tea at a moderate mark-up.[26] King was angered by the advice, seeing it as an attempt by D'Arcy to use his London connexions with *art, cunning & fraud*,[27] to circumvent and thwart his authority.

In July 1801, with King's approval, Balmain left on the *Albion*[28] to take leave in England. He gave D'Arcy his power of attorney; and he was replaced as principal surgeon by Thomas Jamison.

All were attracted at first by the plants or the pheasants   Mansfield Park
Balmain took a collection of native birds with him, gifts from D'Arcy to Fitzwilliam, and letters to post. He arrived in England on 25 March 1802, and shortly after, waited on Fitzwilliam. He was received, he told D'Arcy, *like a Prince*. They spoke at length about the Colony: *I can assure you that Lord Fitzwilliam is your warm friend, himself has told me so and such you will find him.*[29]

Fitzwilliam wrote to D'Arcy, Lady Charlotte was delighted with the three parrots, and he thought so highly of the fine pheasant, he had it stuffed and mounted.[30]

And spurning a friendship which could no longer be serviceable, hastened to contradict all that he had said before   Northanger Abbey

Balmain wrote to D'Arcy of King's *cankered heart. I am sorry King, tho' a stranger to gratitude, could not have prevailed upon himself to show a little modesty of conduct... Tyrants while they are dependent will apparently overflow with the full tide of thankfulness, but when placed in Power throw off the Mask and cannot brook the restraint which a retrospect of former obligations necessarily imposes on them, and thus it often turns out that he who served them in adversity is now an object hateful to their sight and the earliest victim of their rankling hearts, and such is that man.*[31]

No one can be really esteemed accomplished, who does not greatly surpass what is usually met with   Pride & Prejudice

King had a need to control, telling Portland, *nor can the affairs of the colony be transacted in any other manner than by the Government's immediate direction and control in every and the most minute public transaction*. He said of the Government Store, *nor is there a nail issued but by my written order.*[32]

King reduced dependence on the Government. He cut back the number of those eligible for government rations, and limited the number of convict servants assigned to an officer, to two. In 1800, when he took office, 72% of the population was victualled by the Crown, by 1806 the figure was 32%.

King encouraged improvements in agriculture, increasing the number of convicts on public farms from 30 to 324. By 1803, he had quadrupled the public acreage. He continued to grant land to convicts who had served their time, and he ensured seed and tools were made available to them.

To be reprobated and forbidden   Mansfield Park

To further reduce government spending, he stopped issuing Treasury bills. This reduced the money supply, and created hardship in the cash strapped settlement, preventing many from buying necessities as well as luxuries. Along with the shortage of rum to pay the wages of labourers, it slowed the development of the Colony. Governor King gradually lost the confidence of every sector, civil and military officers, settlers and convicts.

Upon the whole I commend my own conduct in this affair extremely   Lady Susan

In mid-1801, King prevented two American vessels, *Follensbe* and *Missouri*, from unloading twenty thousand gallons of rum and eighteen thousand gallons of wine, and he turned back sixteen thousand gallons of rum from India. He reported to Portland, *I have forbidden a great quantity of spirits being landed.*[33]

But although he sent large quantities of spirits away, King permitted an enormous quantity to be landed. Between September 1800 and October 1802, he refused entry to 37,691 gallons, and gave entry to 69,880 gallons. His decisions on the landing of spirits were capricious, and showed *some feeling against vessels from America and India.* [34]

Bass & human nature *Pride & Prejudice*

The constraints King imposed on the market had disastrous consequences for another young surgeon, George Bass, from *HMS Reliance*. Encouraged by Hunter, who found him *a young man of much ability*,[35] he had made an attempt to cross the Blue Mountains; explored and mapped the coast south of Port Jackson with two friends from the *Reliance*, Matthew Flinders and William Martin; and with Flinders, explored the waters around Van Diemen's Land.

After four years in the Colony, Bass took twelve months leave from the Navy to try his hand at trading. He returned to London with Charles Bishop, raised £10,000 from a syndicate of family and friends, he bought a small brig, *Venus*, and loaded her with goods to sell in New South Wales. In England, he courted and married Elizabeth Waterhouse, sister of Henry, his captain on the *Reliance*. They had spent ten weeks together when he sailed from Portsmouth on 9 January 1801.

Bass arrived in Sydney in August 1801, where he learnt Hunter had been recalled, and that King was restricting trade and controlling prices. He found no buyers for his goods. He wrote home, *glutted market, empty purses, treasure house dry. Hands full of goods, all sellers, no buyers. Distraction!*[36]

In October 1801, King had the Government Store purchase the entire cargo of Enderby's whaler *Britannia*. Bass told Henry Waterhouse, the market was: *glutted on two accounts, from the quantity of goods far exceeding the consumption, and glutted also because the new system of Government is built upon a plan of the most rigid economy. It issues very little or no bills. We can sell very little of our cargo here and what we do sell is to but very little advantage.*

Bass offered his cargo, or any part of it, to King, at half price, for the Government Store, but *he declines it for wont, he says of sufficient authority.*[37] In February 1803, anxious about his debts, Bass left Bishop in Sydney, with part of their cargo, and sailed for South America, well-knowing the danger. Under the agreement between Spain and Britain, following the Nootka Sound crisis, British ships were forbidden to trade with the Spanish settlements in America.

In 1804, Captain William Campbell arrived in Sydney on the *Harrington*, from the coast of Peru, with news Bass and his crew had been captured by Spaniards and sent inland to the work in the mines. George Bass was never seen again.[38]

The trade of coming out
Mansfield Park

Exports of whale oil and sealskins grew under King, the only viable export from the struggling colony. In 1805, a massive shipment of twenty thousand seal skins and three hundred tons of whale oil, taken to London by Robert Campbell on the *Lady Barlow*, was seized by Customs for breaching the East India Company monopoly, at the behest of the Enderby brothers. Sir Joseph Banks helped to resolve the matter, and Campbell was given permission to land a second cargo from the Colony.

On one side or the other, it was a continual repetition of, Oh; no, that will never do. Any thing but that, my dear
Mansfield Park

It was widely known in the Colony that *the military hate King abominably*.[39] It was the officers' champion, John Macarthur, who put forward their demands and grievances.

A long dispute followed this declaration
Pride & Prejudice

Macarthur and King fell out over a personal dispute. When Lieut Marshall slapped his face, Macarthur had challenged him to a duel. The duel failed to take place, and Macarthur had Marshall charged with assault. He was found guilty, fined £50, and given twelve months imprisonment.

Governor King ordered the Judge-advocate to reconvene the court and reconsider the judgement, but the five military members of the court refused. After angry correspondence with them, King signed a remission of Marshall's sentence.[40] The officers then boycotted him.

When King invited Rum Corps officers and their wives to dine, but excluded the Macarthurs, some of the officers took exception and refused his invitation. Macarthur attempted to get Paterson to withdraw his acceptance, but failed.

As Commander, Paterson was under an obligation to support the Governor. He and his wife and the Kings had travelled from England together on the *Gorgon* in 1791, and they had been friends ever since.

With Major Foveaux on Norfolk Island and Captain Johnston en route to England on the *Buffalo* with Hunter, Captain Macarthur was Paterson's second in command. Their families were friends, the Macarthurs often stayed with the Patersons when they came to Sydney from Parramatta.

Macarthur saw Paterson's friendship with King as *treacherous betrayal*. He showed fellow officers a letter his wife Elizabeth had received from Mrs Paterson, and made it the butt of jokes around the mess.[41] Their wives fell out[42] and tensions increased between the two men.

A little too much of the rattle perhaps Lady Susan

On 14 September 1801, Paterson challenged Macarthur to a duel, in defence of his wife's honour. The two men faced each other. Macarthur's shot hit Paterson in the right shoulder, seriously injuring him. Three surgeons attended, they agreed the ball had penetrated too deeply to be removed.

For some days Paterson remained critically injured, and indeed he never fully recovered. The duel between the two men, close colleagues in a very small, remote settlement, was a dreadful affair.

King had Macarthur, and his second, Captain John Piper, arrested, and held until Paterson's condition was known. He ordered Macarthur sent to England for court-martial. He wrote to Evan Nepean, *the conduct of Capt'n John Macarthur brought on a duel between him and the Lt. Col'l, which had nearly deprived H.M. service and this colony of a valuable officer.*[43] A few weeks later, Macarthur sailed on the *Hunter*, taking his eight year old daughter Elizabeth, and son John, six, with him, to join their elder brother Edward at school in England. He carried numerous deputations from his supporters, criticising King's administration.

The *Hunter* was dismasted in a cyclone near Amboyna, a mountainous island in the Malukus.[44] Macarthur and his children went ashore there, to await an East Indiaman, *Princess Charlotte,* to take them to Bengal.

The delay was fortuitous, Macarthur made the acquaintance of the Resident, Sir Robert Farquhar. He had successfully attacked a Dutch settlement on Ternate, an important spice island, and was facing severe censure from the East India Company, for exceeding his authority.

Macarthur had no flair for apologies, he advised Farquhar to stand firm, *they are not fully aware of the position, or the circumstances.* His encouragement did not help the Resident, who was demoted and recalled.

He gave Macarthur an introduction to his father, Sir Walter Farquhar, physician to the Prince of Wales and Comtesse Eliza de Feuillide. Sir Walter *embraced him with open arms,* and gave him assistance and support in London.[45]

If the evidence of sight might be trusted Northanger Abbey

King took extra precautions with the documents detailing the charges against Macarthur. Rumours were circulating in Sydney that they would be stolen. He sent them to Portland in triplicate.

His aide-de-camp, Lieutenant Mackellar, had been Paterson's second in the duel. His evidence was crucial, King sent him to London on an American schooner, *Caroline*, with his despatch, the depositions and evidence against Macarthur, and Macarthur's sword. The *Caroline* was lost at sea with all hands.

King sent a second copy of the papers with Lieutenant Grant on the *Anna Josepha*. The despatch box arrived in London, but had been interfered with, the despatch and the documents for the court-martial had vanished.

A third copy of the documents and the despatch went on the *Hunter* with Macarthur, under cover of a letter to the Marquis of Wellesley, in Calcutta, asking him to forward them to Portland. Macarthur arrived in London in December 1802, thirteen months later.

By January 1803, when the Commander in Chief considered Macarthur's arrest and conduct, the charges from Governor King had still not arrived. Macarthur was severely censured and released from arrest, after the Army's judge-advocate decided he could not be court martialled in England. He informed King in January 1804, that *for the sake of harmony,* he would *pass over any seeming irregularity.*[46] On 24 February 1803, Lord Hobart acknowledged receipt of the despatches from the *Hunter*.

William Balmain wrote to D'Arcy, *Macarthur has been relieved from his arrest in consequence of no specific charge being urged against him by the Governor, but in every other respect he has got the worst of his contention whatever he may write to the contrary, vast indeed is the difference he finds between this place and New South Wales, we are all very small fishes here.*[47]

Despite Balmain's reservations, Macarthur made influential friends in London. He did everything in his power to damage King's reputation, and to rid the Colony of him.

He had a very fine flock — Emma

During his exile, Macarthur promoted Australian wool, with its suitability for uniforms and blankets for the troops fighting against Napoleon. In 1800, when Foveaux was transferred to Norfolk Island, he bought thirteen hundred cross-bred sheep from him. Macarthur now owned the largest flock in the Colony, and estimated it should double in size every two and a half years.

In July 1803, his *Statement of the Improvement and Progress of a Breed of Fine Woolled Sheep in New South Wales,* was delivered to Lord Hobart, Secretary of State for War and the Colonies, and found a receptive audience.[48]

In 1800, Joseph Banks advertised a *Project for Extending the Breed of Fine-wooled Spanish sheep now in the Possession of His Majesty, into all Parts of Great Britain, where the growth of fine clothing Wool is Found to be Profitable.*[49] He invited interested parties to purchase fine-wool sheep at a livestock sale at Kew.

The sheep were offspring of five rams and thirty-five ewes from the flock of the Marchioness del Camp di Alange, who had been persuaded in 1792, to present them to His Majesty, in exchange for eight fine English coach horses.

He had been bid more for his wool than anyone in the country   Emma

In 1803, Macarthur asked Governor King, from London, to send samples of his fleece to Joseph Banks, with his recommendation.[50] Banks obtained expert opinion that rated the finest of the fleeces *nearly as good as the King's Spanish wool at Oatlands*. It boosted Macarthur's pride, his credibility and status in London, and heralded the beginning of the Australian wool industry.[51]

In 1804, Macarthur was permitted to purchase some of His Majesty's Spanish sheep. He met Sir Joseph Banks when he bought eight of them to improve the quality of his flock at Parramatta. It is unlikely Banks knew that Macarthur had shot Colonel Paterson, one of his protégés; nor would he have guessed he would be the nemesis of another, Governor William Bligh.

In Banks' view, the sheep were being sold to improve wool produced in Britain, he was confident an export embargo would prevent Macarthur sending any of them to the Colony. However, Lord Camden, Secretary of State, arranged a Treasury warrant to permit their export. Camden indicated to Macarthur that he should be given a grant of ten thousand acres; five thousand immediately, with the promise of a further five thousand once his sheep breeding venture succeeded.

Tensions arose between Macarthur and Banks over the legality of a Treasury warrant overriding the embargo regulation. Macarthur called Banks a *venal and debauched old rascal*.[52] It was said that some years later, *Bligh received instructions from Banks to hold up any grant in excess of 5,000 acres*[53] to him. Regardless, on 21 July 1805, King wrote to Banks, *Macarthur intends writing to you and speaks highly of your politeness to him at the sale of the Spanish sheep in England*.[54]

Considering a removal from that Corps as highly advisable   Pride & Prejudice

In August 1802, His Royal Highness, Commander in Chief of the British Army wrote to the Secretary of State – *positively commanding that the officers be not permitted on any account whatever to engage in the cultivation of farms, or in any occupations that are to detach them from their military duties.*[55]

Macarthur, the biggest landowner in the Colony, obtained Lord Camden's permission in 1805, to resign from the army and to return to New South Wales, to develop a wool industry.

On 7 July 1805, he sailed home triumphant, on the *Argo,* its figurehead a golden fleece. He had nine Spanish merino rams and a ewe from the Royal flock at Kew, and the possibility of a grant of ten thousand acres. Walter Davidson, nephew of Sir Walter Farquhar, accompanied him, to take up an adjoining land grant at Cowpastures.

The England they departed was preoccupied with the war against Napoleon, Nelson was crossing the Atlantic at full sail to the West Indies, in pursuit of the Franco-Spanish fleet. In three months he would meet them in his final encounter at Trafalgar.

The necessity of an enlargement of plan & expense — Mansfield Park

Balmain was grateful for D'Arcy's attention to his affairs in Sydney. In 1803, he warned him he would need substantial funds to return to England. *I cannot but lament the trouble I give you and am fearful that pressed as you must be with your own concerns you will be greatly inconvenienced by attending to mine and therefore I must request that you will on no account suffer your care of me to clash with your own interest. I am anxious that you should consolidate some of your own money and remit it without loss of time to Mr Cookney for the purpose of placing it to your advantage, for be assured my Dear Sir such is the state of things in this Country that you cannot think of returning to it without something substantial to depend upon.*[56]

It was a medicinal project — Mansfield Park

Dennis Considen wrote to D'Arcy in February 1804. He had seen Hunter in London, and he sent news: *we are daily threatened with invasion for which the most extraordinary preparations are made.* He had been *advised not to leave the country*, but had written to Governor King asking for *a grant of some acres of land for my service in New South Wales, richly merited, but I find he had refused my request.*

After leaving the Colony, Considen worked in the Army Medical Service as a hospital mate. Put on half pay in 1800, he enrolled at Edinburgh University to pursue his long held ambition to study medicine. He wrote to Major Johnston, requesting he send him *a native skeleton which Dr Munro begged I would provide.*[57] Alexander Monro was his professor of anatomy.

He asked D'Arcy to send him natural history specimens from the Colony, *some of the shells which the natives fasten to their throwing sticks, called Cadangs, with some of the long Whelks called Hercules's Club, of those there is great abundance every where in the Harbour.*

He asked for native birds, and fur, for a muff for his daughter Constance. Considen usually referred to her as his niece, and to Constantine, his son, as his nephew; their mother, Ann Cowley, had been a convict.[58]

Sending instantly for Mr Harris — Sense & Sensibility

On Norfolk Island, King had seen D'Arcy as someone who could be useful to him. In Sydney, he patronised others better placed to progress his ambitions. He considered John Harris had *the most respectable character as a gentleman, joined to an unwearied activity and intelligence.* Harris, as surgeon to the Corps, could provide intelligence from within its ranks. King promoted him to important public offices and provided him with valuable grants of land.

John Harris, an Irish Protestant, born in Moymucklemurry, Londonderry, had studied for a period at Edinburgh University, joined the Navy as a surgeon, and spent ten years on naval vessels in the East Indies. In December 1791, the year after he arrived on the Second Fleet, he was appointed surgeon to the Corps at Parramatta, and he was based there for the next ten years. In April 1793, he was granted 100 acres, and by 1800 he was one of the leading officer farmers, with 315 acres and 413 head of stock.

King made him a magistrate, Deputy Judge Advocate in the regimental courts martial, head of the police establishment, and a committee member of the Orphan Fund. In July 1801, Harris replaced Balmain as Naval Officer for Port Jackson, responsible for collecting customs, excise and port fees, and entitled to a percentage of all monies collected.

Harris's willingness to assist King brought him into conflict with comrades in the Corps. He assured King that he was – *Conscious of my Rectitude, Integrity and Impartiality, in this Arduous and Unpopular task assigned me by your Excellency, I shall (as I have always done) receive the Orders of my Superiors with readiness, whether it is to Vindicate my Honor and Character, or on any other point of Service and Duty.*[59]

King asserted, *Mr Harris has long been the object of secret resentment for his assiduity in assisting me to carry the King's Instructions respecting Spirituous Liquor into effect.*[60]

Now looked very grave on Mr Harris's report Sense & Sensibility

In 1802, Harris was charged with *ungentlemanlike conduct* for reporting private conversations from the barracks to King. In 1803, he was charged with *scandalous and infamous behaviour*[61] for disclosing how two fellow officers had voted at a court martial. He pointed to an error in the charge, that stated the offence occurred on the 19th *ultimo*, rather than the 19th *instant*. He was acquitted, but removed from his civil appointments until 1804, when King reinstated him.

King considered Harris *a most indefatigable and useful assistant to the Governor, from his general knowledge of every person in the colony.*[62] He stated that he undertook his duties *to the evident public benefit and conspicuous general good of His Majesty's services without neglecting an hour's duty as surgeon of the corps. Nor is there an officer in the Colony on whose Honor & Integrity I place so great a confidence in as I do on Mr Harris's to delegate him to Vindicate my Insulted Honor & Reputation by those under my Command.*[63]

In 1804, Harris obtained a grant of land on Sydney harbour that he named *Ultimo*, celebrating the judicial error. He built a grand house there and imported a herd of deer from India, to roam and adorn his estate.⁶⁴

So earnestly grateful, so full of respect   Sense & Sensibility

A *pipe* from 1803, shows the extent to which King's standing had deteriorated:

> From the Orphan Collection, I take what I dare
> Of Whaler's Investments I own I've a share
> Tythes, Taxes and Quit-rents unto me belong
> And Duties on Spirits, I claim as my own.

Having lost the support of the military and many civil officers, King sought to create new allegiances. He looked to a group in the Colony indebted to him for their liberty, the convicts he had emancipated. King took a more liberal stance in issuing pardons, and the convicts he pardoned began to take part in all spheres of colonial life, other than the commissioned ranks.⁶⁵

Major George Johnston, Commanding Officer of the Corps, disagreed with his approach. King replied, *this Colony was formed for the express purpose of receiving Prisoners; that the King and the Legislature's Humanity, in giving the Governor power to Emancipate, did not consign the offender to the Laws of his Country to Oblivion & disgrace for ever. I will aver & support that the Objects of the Mercy become as Free and Susceptible of every right as Free Born Britons as any Soul in this Territory, whether their Emancipation is Absolute or Conditional.*⁶⁶

Sir Joseph Banks wrote to King in 1804 to express his disapproval – *there is only one part of your conduct as Governor which I do not think right – that is your frequent reprieves.*⁶⁷

I have a great mind to go back into Norfolk directly, and put everything at once on such a footing as cannot be afterwards swerved from   Mansfield Park

D'Arcy concentrated on his medical duties, he continued to dispose of his and Balmain's store of goods, while he awaited approval from London for leave to return to England. In July 1802, he saw an opportunity to remove himself from beneath King's yoke, and applied for a vacancy that had arisen for a surgeon on Norfolk Island. King agreed, and published an order that D'Arcy was to *hold himself in readiness to embark for Norfolk Island in about three weeks.*⁶⁸

He resolved to defer his Norfolk journey, resolved that writing should answer the purpose of it, or that its purpose was unimportant, and staid

Mansfield Park

When King refused his request to take his unsold stores with him, or to leave them in Sydney with an agent, to sell on his behalf, D'Arcy decided to remain in Sydney and continue to trade his way out of his difficulties.[69]

A real, honest, old fashioned boarding school — Emma

In October 1802, D'Arcy sent his two eldest sons to school in England, he would follow them as soon as he was able. William, now twelve, and D'Arcy, nine, sailed via China and Calcutta, on the *Atlas*, in the care of her captain, Richard Brooks. As a boy, Brooks had sailed on his father's ship, *Henry & Honoria*, and he had William and young D'Arcy climbing masts, repairing ropes and sails, and poring over the charts, mastering the arts of navigation.

The family circle became greatly contracted…they could not but be missed — Mansfield Park

D'Arcy missed them, he *felt this break-up of the family exceedingly.*[70] Charles Cookney wrote that they had arrived safely, they were starting school, though not studying French. In October 1803, he enrolled them with his three sons at Rev Richard Midgley's boarding school at Bletchley. Cookney became their guardian, and kept D'Arcy informed about their progress.

The two boys visited Lord Fitzwilliam at Grosvenor Square, he gave them each a guinea.[71] William Balmain wrote – *it will give me great pleasure to show them every attention in my power.*[72]

Instances of blunders & failures — Mansfield Park

King was resentful of anyone who might challenge his status or authority. He was displeased by their presence, their ideas, recommendations or requests. Captain James Colnett, a very senior Naval colleague, arrived in Port Jackson on *HMS Glatton* in 1803, with 270 male and 130 female convicts, and 30 settlers. He was critical of King's administration, his ship was not met by a pilot, and at the entrance to the harbour, the channels around the Sow and Pigs shoal were not marked. King was very sensitive to his criticism, and was not prepared to make him welcome. At the same time, he demanded favours from Colnett, who was required to give him a personal supply of 180 gallons of rum.

Among the female prisoners who came on the *Glatton*, was nineteen year-old Mary Sergeant, convicted at Stafford Assizes of the theft of nine Five Guinea notes. Her friends and family campaigned against her conviction and secured a letter from Mr Capper, an official at the Home Office, under Lord Pelham. It recommended the remission of part or all her sentence if she behaved well once she arrived at the Colony. Colnett gave King the letter, as he had undertaken to do, but King was not prepared to grant a remission, or to allow her to return to England on the *Glatton*.

The *Glatton* brought a gift for D'Arcy, a quarter cask of Madeira from Balmain. King had it seized and confiscated, along with the small boat used to bring it ashore. When questions were raised about the legality of his actions, he referred it to the Judge Advocate, who ruled the seizure was not legal, as the Governor had signed a permit to receive the wine. King called a specially convened bench of magistrates to reconsider the matter. They likewise found no illegality, and *recommended to His Excellency to direct the wine and the boat to be given up.*

His Excellency, notwithstanding, confirmed the seizure, and the wine was distributed to the wharfinger and amongst the other parties concerned in the seizure; and the boat, the property of Mr Mileham, was confiscated for the use of the Government.

D'Arcy wrote to Lord Hobart seeking redress for his property and that of Mr Mileham, which had been *oppressively wrested from him, illegally withheld, and unjustly disposed of.*[73]

Hobart was not only confronted with D'Arcy's grievances, Captain Colnett called on him with a litany of complaints about King's management of the Colony, his sycophantic appointments, the poor management of the port, the inadequacy of the wharf, the lack of a police presence; how King had delayed the ship's departure and failed to provide signatures for supplies taken from the *Glatton*. It was Captain Colnett's visit that would seal the Governor's recall.[74]

Interest had to be taken in the matter Sense & Sensibility

In March 1803, Balmain sent a packet of Bigarou cherry stones, suggesting D'Arcy *put half in your ground, the other half cause to be planted at my brush farm at the Hawkesbury.*[75] Eight months later, aged forty, he was dead.

Dennis Considen was Balmain's executor, D'Arcy administered his estate in the Colony. He had managed Balmain's affairs for over two years, and he found the most onerous task, despite his experience in such matters, was collecting monies owed to Balmain, much of it from defaulters. At the same time, D'Arcy collected debts that he himself was owed, in preparation for his intended return to England.

A good chance of escaping his lawsuit Letters

George Crossley was their most notorious defaulter. He was a solicitor, transported for perjury, *for having sworn that he witnessed the signature to a will while life was in the body of the signatory, the life being that of a fly which he had placed in the mouth of the dead man, while he (Crossley) guided the lifeless hand that traced the signature.*[76]

Crossley arrived on the *Hillsborough,* in 1799, with his wife. He had paid her fare to accompany him. At the Cape, he purchased goods to sell in the Colony and issued three Bills of Exchange to pay for them. One was drawn on a man named Schell, a pauper in an English workhouse.

Crossley received a conditional pardon from King, who was led to believe, wrongly, that a pardon was necessary to allow him to be sued.[77]

Crossley refused to honour his debt to Balmain of £1,886, but the Court found in D'Arcy's favour as executor. Threatened with having his goods seized, Crossley appealed to the Governor. Despite owing far more than he could pay, he avoided debtor's prison. King permitted him to continue trading on the unlikely condition he pay off his debts.

Crossley failed to meet these conditions, and King, tired of his pleas and appeals, ordered the seizure of his goods. D'Arcy went to Crossley's home with the Provost Marshall, and removed them. Crossley sued them for trespass, they were acquitted, and Crossley's subsequent appeal to the Privy Council lapsed for lack of funds.

D'Arcy succeeded in having him repay the money he owed, though Crossley made a joke of it, *he was compelled to accept payment in pennies of a debt amounting to £400 – due by Crossley, the notorious attorney.*[78] The London press reported, *Crossley the Attorney, has a law-suit at Botany Bay with another celebrated person, D'Arcy Wentworth.*[79] The Times

Crossley's affairs were tied to the property of a Parramatta innkeeper, Richard Robinson, whose wife Ann Inetts was a former mistress of Governor King, the mother of his two sons, Norfolk and Sydney. Despite her claim that he used threats and intimidation, D'Arcy was able to recover Balmain's debts.

I cannot approve of it Northanger Abbey

In 1802, D'Arcy asked Fitzwilliam once again, to apply on his behalf for leave to return. Fitzwilliam did not oblige, he advised D'Arcy not to leave his property, to stay and continue to work in the Colony.

Another world must be unfurled Verse

Fitzwilliam gave him a promising view of his future: *The circumstances of the Colony must afford to the contemplative mind, constant subjects of admiration and speculation, a New World rising into consideration, for you are young enough to live to see it reach a point of considerable importance…I hope…you will leave the name of Wentworth, one of the most considerable and most respectable in this New World.*[80]

D'Arcy acknowledged his confidence and approbation, but did not respond to Fitzwilliam's advice he remain in the Colony: *Nothing in this life could give me greater pleasure than that Part of Your Lordship's letter wherein you are pleased to express your satisfaction at the Line of Conduct I have pursued in this Country & I think I may venture to hope that my future Behaviour through Life will merit Your Lordship's approbation.*[81]

The prospect of being miserably crowded — Emma

In late 1802, Parramatta hospital was overcrowded with cases of dysentery. D'Arcy wrote to Thomas Jamison, principal surgeon, about the problems there: *I must request that you will represent to His Excellency how necessary it is, that the Hospital should have a compleat and speedy repair. It is really impossible for me to describe to you the wretched State of the Patients as to Bedding, which there is almost a total lack of nor have I had a single grain of either Oatmeal, Barley or Sago for some time past. I beg you will order me the Necessaries and Medicines mentioned in the enclosed list, being very much in want of them.*[82]

Obliged to give up the attempt and to consider it as fruitless — Kitty, or the Bower

In May 1803, D'Arcy, frustrated, anxious to see his children again, and renew his relationship with Jane, turned to Fitzwilliam once more. He asked him to use his influence with Lord Hobart for approval for him to retire from his position as surgeon. *It is with real concern I am obliged to say that the conduct which Governor King still pursues towards me is of the most distressing Nature for there is hardly any thing within his Power but what he has done to render my situation uncomfortable to me, he has even done the most unjustifiable cuts to injure me in my private Fortune.*[83]

Cookney had written to D'Arcy three months earlier, their letters had crossed at sea. He told him Fitzwilliam was not prepared to help: *Lord Fitzwilliam and myself are both sorry that nothing more could be done for you but His Lordship said that he did not want to stir farther in the business. And at present he thought it would not be advisable to obtain leave of absence for you as he cannot see how you could well leave your property.*[84]

Cookney knew D'Arcy's great desire to return to England, and his frustration with the impasse he had reached with King. His advice was not to act contrary to his interests, to remain in Sydney to recover the money he had outlaid. *Lord Fitzwilliam could not advise you to leave the country till you had disposed of all your property as His Lordship justly observed that if you did, you would be sure to be a great sufferer by it.*[85]

Nothing less than a very smart indeed — Pride & Prejudice

Despite everything, D'Arcy maintained a cordial demeanour with King and his wife. In 1804, he sent Mrs King a gift of two bonnets, one for herself, one for her daughter Elizabeth. Her letter of thanks blamed the alteration in the governor's behaviour on Balmain. *I have always experienced your kind attention to me, and mine – and not withstanding the Duplicity of your friend Mr Balmain yet you have not better Wellwishers for your prosperity than King & myself, had you ever chosen to show me the letter you had received from Mr Balmain, I would have Convinced you of his Double Heart.*[86]

Escalate, backlash and crack down, polarisation and long-standing hate[87]

Seamus Heaney

After disorder and revolt in Ireland in 1798, came an influx of Irish convicts. *In May that year there was open rebellion in the counties of Wicklow, Carlow, Dublin, Wexford, Antrim, Meath, and Kildare. On the 25th May a detachment of the Antrim militia encountered three or four thousand of the insurgents, and defeated them, killing three hundred. On the 26th, another considerable body of insurgents supposed to amount to 4000, cut off 100 men of the Cork militia. At Monsteraven, the insurgents lost 400 men; and 50 at Carlow.*

On 20 June, Marquis Cornwallis arrived in Dublin, as Lord Lieutenant and Commander in Chief of the armies of Ireland. On the succeeding day a squadron gained possession of Wexford, drove the insurgents out of it, and took prisoners two of their generals, Hay and Roche.

An attack was made on Hacketstown by several thousands of the insurgents; which was so completely repelled by troops, that thirty cart loads of their killed and wounded were said to have been carried off by them in their retreat; and thirty of their dead were found in the streets and ditches.

A small French squadron landed about 800 men at Killala, where they were joined by great numbers of the insurgents. They remained in the country till the 8th of September, when they surrendered. During the residence of the French in Ireland, vast numbers of the insurgents are reported to have fallen.[88]

Six thousand Irish, many of them well educated and well born, were sentenced to death after the rebellion. Those given reprieves were sent to the hulks in Cork and Wexford to be transported. They brought simmering political grievances with them, and they transformed the social fabric of the Colony.

In September 1800, King reported *a horrible plot* amongst Irish rebel convicts at Parramatta, and the action he had taken to suppress it. He ordered sixteen men flogged, the five deemed ringleaders to be given a thousand lashes each.

In April 1802, he issued a proclamation against sedition, limiting assemblies to a maximum of twelve people, without his permission; with punishment by death if two or more people met for more than half an hour after having been required to disperse by a magistrate.[89]

In December 1803, *upwards of twenty prisoners absconded from Castle Hill. They were chiefly Irish. They did not proceed far before they rushed into a house of a French emigrant settler. After stripping the house of almost every necessary article, they proceeded to some others, taking away the firearms and such things that engaged their attention.*

Large parties were sent in quest of them, and by informing the natives, the latter soon traced them out, and they were apprehended by the former... It seems they had been too free with the Frenchman's wine, as they were divided into three or four parties and apprehended in different places.[90]

Sent after them 300 armed men with orders not to return without their bodies, dead or alive
Henry & Eliza

On Sunday evening, 4 March 1804, a hut was set alight on the Government Farm at Castle Hill, signalling the start of a rebellion. Nearly five hundred convicts were housed at Castle Hill, D'Arcy went there regularly to attend the sick and injured, and as an observer at floggings.

A month earlier, news of Robert Emmet's rebellion in Dublin reached Sydney. Many of the United Irishmen wanted to return home to join him.

The leader of the rebellion, Philip Cunningham, from County Kerry, was the overseer of Government stonemasons at Castle Hill. He was a veteran of the 1798 uprising, a former publican and stonemason in Tipperary. Charged with sedition in 1799, for helping to organise the United Irish network in the south of Ireland, he was transported for life. He arrived in the Colony on the *Anne* in 1800, one of a group of rebels who mutinied en route. In 1802, he was given 100 lashes in for attempting to escape on board a departing French ship.

The rebel plan was for convicts from Parramatta, Seven Hills, Baulkham Hills, Prospect, Toongabbie, Hawkesbury and Nepean to meet and *to proceed to Sydney...and then embark on board the ships... They were assured of their force being augmented to 1100 men.*[91]

That evening, Mrs Macarthur and two of her children were dining with Rev. Marsden and his family at Parramatta. They heard the drums beating at the Barracks nearby, a mob of convicts was outside the gates of the Government House Park. They could see the fire at Castle Hill as they hurried to the river. Marsden, his wife, Mrs Macarthur, two other women, and children, took a boat and fled downriver to Sydney in the darkness. Mrs Macarthur wrote: *You can have no idea what a dreadful night it was and what we suffered in our minds.*[92]

King declared martial law. The Irish were subdued by force, twelve killed, six wounded, twenty-six taken prisoner.[93] Major Johnston reported, *Philip Cunningham, one of the rebel chiefs, was brought in here alive and I immediately*

– *with the opinion of the officers – ordered to be hung up.*[94] Eight ringleaders were tried and hanged, a large number given 200 to 500 lashes.

> Old Days! The wild geese are flighting,
> Head to the storm as they faced it before!
> For where there are Irish there's bound to be fighting,
> And when there's no fighting, its Ireland no more!
> Ireland no more![95]
>
> Rudyard Kipling

The rebels declared themselves United Irishmen,[96] their loyalty to Ireland and resistance to England transcending religious differences. King held the Irish Catholic priests responsible, even though four of the nine men hanged were Protestants. He announced a new penal settlement for Irish convicts on the Coal River,[97] and sent over thirty men there, to cut cedar and mine coal.

Irish! Eh, I remember The Watsons

D'Arcy had an Irish brogue, he worked among the convicts, he was known to be approachable to his fellow Irish. He understood and identified with the distress of the Irish political prisoners. There is no record of his response to the rebellion at Castle Hill, but on the list of officers of the Loyal Parramatta Association, dated 5 March 1804, the day after the uprising, his name had been removed. The entry under Lieutenant, the rank he held, is blank.[98] It was no coincidence that early the next year King removed him from Sydney and sent him back to Norfolk Island.

Chapter 18

The Dwelling Place of Devils, the Doubly Damned

Lost, every consolation in the possibility of acquitting him

D'ARCY UNDERSTOOD his appointment to Norfolk Island was a form of exile. He did not resist, he leased his house, appointed the merchant Simeon Lord as his Sydney agent,[1] and instructed him to dispose of the remainder of his stores, as best he might.

The resolution he has taken of travelling, as it will perhaps contribute to obliterate from his remembrance those disagreeable Events which have so lately afflicted him

Love & Freindship

On 10 May 1804, he boarded the *Betsy* and sailed the thousand miles to Norfolk Island, arriving ten days later. He took his youngest son, John, now nine, and Maria Ainslie and her son with him. Maria was employed as his housekeeper, she cared for John, he had come to regard her as a mother. She had also become D'Arcy's mistress.[2] It was four years since Catherine's death, he was forty-two.

There was a fellow Irishman on board the *Betsy*, General Joseph Holt, a Protestant from County Wicklow and a United Irishman. He was a leader in the 1798 uprising, he surrendered and was sent into exile without trial. Holt and his wife Hester arrived in New South Wales on the *Minerva* in January 1800. A fellow passenger, William Cox, had employed him to manage his property *Brush Farm*, five miles north-west of Parramatta.

In Sydney, Holt found many old comrades, he assisted them where he could, with employment or in difficulties with the authorities. He was detained twice, on suspicion of conspiring with dissident convicts at Castle Hill and Toongabbie. King had ordered him sent to Norfolk Island to prevent any further involvement with them.

A sort of half circle around the fire — Emma

Betsy rounded the island on the cold autumn afternoon of 20 May. Boats were rowed out to bring them ashore. Settler families were gathered on the narrow beach. There was a bonfire for warmth, to dry those who walked the last few yards ashore through the surf. D'Arcy saw many familiar faces in the firelight, and people came forward to greet him and welcome him back.

Over the next days he saw how the island had altered in eight years. The population had more than doubled, to nearly eleven hundred people.[3] In 1790, it was heavily timbered with towering Norfolk Island Pines. There was an urgency to clear the land, to help feed the hungry settlement in Sydney Cove. Huge trees were logged and a solid mass of vines and undergrowth cleared to produce food for the Colony's survival. Now that urgency had passed, and many of the early settlers had left to work the rich alluvial farmland along the Hawkesbury, west of Sydney. Settlers on Norfolk Island now produced food for local consumption, and pigs to send to Sydney as pork.

> *We have killed a porker, there will be the leg to be salted and the loin to be dressed. They must not over-salt the leg. It is eaten with a boiled turnip, and a little carrot, or parsnip.* — Emma

On his return many surprises were awaiting him — Mansfield Park

In his first years on the island, D'Arcy supervised convicts and he worked as a constable. By 1804, these jobs were filled by ex-convicts, presiding over larger, more resentful gangs of convict labourers. Foveaux had built a gaol at Sydney Bay. D'Arcy knew the chief gaoler, Robert Buckey, as a convict. He was sent to the island in 1789, and King gave him a conditional pardon in 1795.

In the early years the problems were *grubs, rats, hurricanes and occasionally troublesome convicts.*[4] Now, the sounds and scent of sadism, cruelty and fear hung over the island; it was a more violent and repressive place: *a barbarous island, the dwelling place of devils in the human shape, the refuse of Botany Bay, the doubly damned.*[5]

At your house in Norfolk, I mean when you are settled there — Mansfield Park

D'Arcy returned to his house and farm at Queenborough, and resumed his medical duties among the convicts. Buckey said of him, *Doctor Wentworth* although holding such a high position as Chief Surgeon was a most generous kind hearted and considerate man he would at all times pay attention to the poorest of prisoners.[6]

In Norfolk, business called him   Mansfield Park

He arranged for Charles Cookney to send him medical journals, books to read, and goods to sell. He resumed trading on a modest scale.

Two umbrellas for us, from Farmer Mitchell's   Emma

James Mitchell, the Norfolk Island shopkeeper, acted as agent for his imported goods, and both men sold goods sent from Sydney by Simeon Lord. Mitchell had been on his way to Tahiti as a missionary, when he abandoned his calling in Port Jackson, to become a store-keeper on Norfolk Island.

Buckey wrote: *Mr Mitchell a store keeper and trader would exchange his stores for rum, his flour was bad and his pork was soft. I believe he came out here as a missioner but gave up that profession as there was more money in trading. He had a beautiful young woman name Lirya McCann who was as cunning as himself who could drink more rum than most of the Hardened Soilders and took every opportunity to make herself disagreeable to the other Females who would dare venture within her store; her greatest Pride would be her clothes in Silks and a bonnet with feathers on them. Mr Mitchell usually wore a dark Coat white trousers and Vest of a Bright red Color with a large black hat brought out from England to order for him.*[7]

Necessary preparations of settlements   Pride & Prejudice

In January 1802, a French expedition led by Nicholas Baudin, in *Le Geographe* and *Le Naturaliste*, mapped the coast of Van Diemen's Land. Though France and Britain were at peace at this time, King became suspicious of their intentions. Aware of Britain's tenuous claim to the island, and advised the Secretary of State, Lord Hobart, that quick action was required to secure it in His Majesty's name.

In September 1803, King sent a small group on the *Lady Nelson* and the *Albion* to establish a settlement at Risdon Cove on the Derwent, under a twenty-three year old, Lt. John Bowen. His inexperience and failure to understand the intentions of local Indigenous groups resulted in hostilities and bloodshed.

Hobart responded to King's concerns; on Sir Joseph Banks' advice he appointed David Collins to locate a settlement at Port Phillip, to secure the Bass Strait. Collins, who had served under Governor Phillip, was in London, on half pay, pressing for recognition of his service.

In October 1803, Collins entered Port Phillip Bay, in present day Victoria, with *HMS Calcutta* and *Ocean,* carrying nearly three hundred convicts, fifty Marines and fifteen staff. He found the sandy soil unsuitable, and after three months King ordered him to abandon that site and move to the Derwent. Collins established a new settlement at Sullivan's Cove, that would become Hobart Town. The group at Risdon Cove moved there, across the Derwent.

In October 1804, instructed from London, King sent Lt. Col. William Paterson from Sydney, with a detachment of soldiers and seventy-five convicts, to position a settlement in the north of Van Diemen's Land, at Port Dalrymple.

A great connexion between Dalrymple & ourselves   Persuasion

Shortly after he arrived, D'Arcy learnt Norfolk Island was to be evacuated, that King had instructions from Lord Hobart to commence relocating the soldiers, settlers and convicts to Port Dalrymple. Hobart considered Norfolk Island was too expensive, that it was a great distance from Port Jackson and lacked a harbour and a safe sea anchorage.[8] D'Arcy realised King had known these plans before he left Sydney. He had been tricked.

As a civil officer, D'Arcy could not leave Norfolk Island without King's permission and he could not refuse an order to move to Van Diemen's Land. He wrote to King asking to return to *Headquarters*, that he not be sent to the new settlement at Port Dalrymple.[9]

Commandant, Joseph Foveaux' announcement of an evacuation plan caused great uncertainty and consternation amongst the emancipists and settlers. Many had arrived as convicts, they had stayed after serving their sentences, built houses, and cultivated their land. They took a petition to Foveaux saying they had families to support, they were too old to begin farming again, and there was no inducement or compensation offered to persuade them to leave.

The outward wretchedness of the place, and recall the still greater   Emma

The sealers and whalers who called at Norfolk Island were questioned from all sides about Van Diemen's Land. They spoke of cold and hunger, and most unsettling to the islanders, of a large Aboriginal population and the growing conflict with the new settlers.

This belief produced another dread   Emma

D'Arcy had thought himself familiar with the world of a convict settlement, but on Norfolk Island he saw the failings of humankind in high relief. Joseph Foveaux had been the Commandant for four years. He had found the island undeveloped and rundown, *the settlement swarmed with bastard children, some two hundred of them, rather more than a fifth of the island population, all illiterate and wild, with the schoolteacher in gaol for debt.*[10] He had rebuilt public works, increased convict workloads and penalties, and built the island's first gaol, at Sydney Bay, all with *stern resolution.*[11]

More difficult, re-offending convicts were sent to Norfolk Island, with an increasing number of *ringleaders* of *seditious and mutinous Irish* dissidents.[12] In 1801, Foveaux brutally crushed a disturbance, executed two prisoners and had a group of others flogged for twenty days. He was finding the command of a remote island increasingly difficult, and his health suffered.

Cold civility and hard-hearted indifference — Persuasion

It was said Foveaux made Norfolk Island into the worst hell hole in the English speaking world, Mitchell claimed, *during his governorship convicts, both male and female were held as slaves. Poor female convicts were treated shamefully. Governor King being mainly responsible. Many were sold as slaves.*

Mr Kimberley was chief gaoler or constable, a very unfeeling and somewhat hasty man. Ignorant and untrustworthy. Many stories are told of his cruelty. One to be remembered by all there was his love for watching women in their agony while receiving punishment on the Triangle. A too common occurrence. What a pleasure to be sure! To watch poor unfortunate wretches being flogged. And afterwards made to walk around the square naked.

It is usual to remit a part of the sentence on condition that they would expose their nakedness it being considered a part of the punishment. And poor wretches were only too glad to save their flesh and pain.[13]

The Irish officer who is talked of for one of them — Persuasion

In early August 1804, surgeon James Mileham wrote from Sydney, with the unlikely hope D'Arcy would be appointed Principal Surgeon.[14] A few days later, D'Arcy was called to attend Joseph Holt, he had collapsed and was very cold. He was on hard rations and hard labour in a gang of convicted felons.

I was fourteen weeks and two days in torture from my landing on Norfolk Island…he put me to hard labour, to try if it would break my heart, and only for Doctor Wentworth, would my life have been the sacrifice.[15]

Buckey called him, *a fiery and plain spoken man. He gave me more trouble than the worst class of criminals. I believe he was an Irish rebel. He was the only man among the gang who would answer the Major, or murderer, as many called him.*[16]

Holt wrote, *the dirtiest work was appointed for me…two hours before daylight every man should get up and tie his bed and carry it out to leave it in the yard until night, let it rain or shine…hard labour, want of sufficient food…I was kept at the heaviest work…at last between fasting and hard work, I fell down…Mr Wentworth* came he felt my pulse, shook his head, and in a very sad tone of voice, said, "Poor fellow! – you are suffering." He then ordered some medicine for me and went to the Commandant – that tyrant Foveaux.[17]

Mr Darcy called, and was shut up with him for several hours   Pride & Prejudice

D'Arcy *talked no nonsense, he paid no compliments, his opinions were unbending, his attentions tranquil and simple.*[18] Holt was almost fifty, a political prisoner, not a criminal. D'Arcy asked Foveaux to restore him to full rations and give him more compassionate treatment.

Holt said that D'Arcy *believed Foveaux was acting beyond his power and that if I died from the effects of labour and from want of proper food, he should feel it to be his duty to make a notation accordingly. Foveaux replied, in a grim manner, "Then we'll exempt him," Mr Wentworth desired me to go to my unhappy lodging, and not to do any more work until he directed it.*[19]

I accept your offer, extraordinary as it may seem, I accept it, & refer myself to you as a friend   Emma

Foveaux responded to D'Arcy's *sincerity, his steadiness, his integrity,*[20] he trusted his word. He was on Norfolk Island only four months under Foveaux, but in that time they became friends. His influence on Foveaux, on his attitude to punishment and towards the Irish convicts, endured.

Foveaux had little respect for convicts, but he came to see his own behaviour in a different light, that brutal treatment made little sense, that treating felons as individuals could be more effective. He backed away from the Governor's insistence that he impose severe corporal punishment, and in so doing, realised he was in conflict with his instructions from King.

D'Arcy spoke frankly with Foveaux about King, of his double standard towards the convicts, how he looked to them for political support, and had recognised and rewarded many with conditional emancipation.

Foveaux also listened to his convict lover, Ann Sherwin. Holt wrote, *many a man's prayers have I heard offered up for her, for she was always ready to intercede for the oppressed, and many thousand of lashes has her interference saved, especially to unfortunate Irishmen, to whom she was always partial.*[21]

An attack of the asthma   The Watsons

In August 1804, D'Arcy watched the first group of forty-one people taken off the island for Van Diemen's Land. They were being sent to the settlement on the Derwent established the year before, to forestall French ambitions.[22]

The following month Foveaux left for England, on the whaler *Albion*, on extended sick leave, suffering severe asthma. Exactly a year earlier, after a very bad attack, he had gone to Sydney to recuperate. His asthma may have been a result of stress, but could have been triggered by the late spring flowering of the Norfolk Island Pines, propelling huge quantities of pollen into the air.

James Mitchell remembered only the worst facets of his period as commandant, *the departure of Major Foveaux was one great rejoicing for all concerned, we had been under a tyrant long enough... His nature was one of those hard and unfeeling kind. One to remember and better forget.*[23]

On board the *Albion,* Foveaux watched whales being hunted, and their blubber rendered into oil on a brick fireplace in the bow of the ship. His health recovered, and nearly a year later, on 3 March 1805, he arrived at Gravesend.

D'Arcy had given him a packet of letters to frank and post, and asked Foveaux to visit to his sons in Bletchley and deliver their letters in person. He called to see them and he took an interest in them. In the summer holidays William and young D'Arcy visited him, and told their father, *he received us very kindly.*[24]

In discussions with colonial officials in London, Foveaux affirmed D'Arcy was to be trusted and respected. He added his support to Hobart's view that the penal settlement on Norfolk Island should be abandoned, that it would never be economic or effective. He also proposed that settlers relocated from Norfolk Island to Van Diemen's Land be granted equivalent landholdings.

He never speaks much unless among his intimate acquaintances. With them is he remarkably agreeable Pride & Prejudice

Captain John Piper replaced Foveaux as Acting Commandant. He was the son of a Scottish doctor, thirty-one, good looking, a larger than life character. He joined the New South Wales Corps in 1791, aged eighteen, as an ensign, and arrived in Sydney on the *Pitt* in 1792. He and D'Arcy had been friends for over ten years, they first met in 1793, when Piper was deployed on Norfolk Island for two years. They renewed their friendship when he lived at the Parramatta garrison. Piper returned to the island in February 1804, when D'Arcy arrived they resumed their friendship, enjoying each other's company.

D'Arcy congratulated Piper on his appointment. Joseph Holt called him *a humane and worthy gentleman of honour.*[25] Under Piper's more relaxed style, conditions on Norfolk Island improved.

Buckey noted, *the appointment of Captain Piper was looked upon with much hope for improvement, nor were they mistaken. The commencement of his governorship began a new era for the welfare of the prisoners... They consisted of no flogging for women, extra two pounds of flour, two pounds of salted pork and one measure of ground corn...The women were to receive an extra allowance of clothing with extra blankets and other minor necessities.*[26]

A languor, a want of spirits, a want of Union Emma

The following month, Piper allowed an American ship, *Union,* to land and sell rum on the island, something Foveaux had never permitted. Piper had sailed on the *Union* from Sydney earlier that year, he knew Captain Pendleton. He allowed him to take eleven men on the *Union,* to obtain sandalwood from the Friendly Islands. Pendleton, his supercargo and six men were killed at Tongataboo when they went ashore for sandalwood.

King was highly displeased by these events, he wrote to Hobart, *I learned that a quantity of spirits I had refused permission to be sold was taken to Norfolk Island, landed and sold, and as I cannot but suppose the transaction was with the knowledge and consent of the officer in command... I cannot but consider that officer reprehensible.*[27]

Thrown into no little alarm Sense & Sensibility

On 7 November 1804, watchmen on Mt George[28] saw nine large ships approaching the island from the south-west. They were thought to be French. In the ongoing war against France and her allies, Britain directed her naval power against their colonies, and there was fear of retaliation.

When Captain Piper and Mr Wentworth had examined these ships through the spy-glass, they expressed themselves much alarmed as at that time the French flag was victorious in many parts of the world.[29] Piper *conjectured they were the enemy*[30] and he prepared for invasion. The gaolers imprisoned the Irish convicts, fearing they would go over to the French.

The gate was locked Mansfield Park

Holt wrote, *I was put in gaol and sixty five more along with me...they were weak enough to think that if all the Irishmen were not confined, we would turn upon them and kill them, which they knew they deserved. They got the soldiers to surround the gaol and place scaffolds all around it and if the fleet had proved to be French men-of-war, they would have set fire to the gaol and have burned us all alive. In this manner things remained all night, the guilty consciences of these wretches rendering them more afraid than the innocent men whom they planned to burn alive.*[31]

At 7 o'clock next morning, *the Fleet were standing into Cascade Bay. They fired a gun to leeward and hoisted the English colours. We returned a Gun and made a signal for a Boat (there not being any at Cascade). They stood off and on for five hours before they attempted to hoist one out which induced us to believe that their hoisting the English colours was used only as a decoy, particularly as we were not able to form an Idea what they were.*[32]

Soldiers, settlers and free men assembled at Cascade, they lugged one of the island's small cannons down to the shore. *One old man had ordered the whole island to be searched, and all the broken bottles to be brought to him; and he swore that he would charge the two six-pounders with these fragments of glass, which would cut the French to pieces if they attempted to land...About ten o'clock one of the ships sent her boat ashore, and when it was found that the fleet was not that of an enemy we were all liberated.*[33]

This unlucky illness made every ailment severe Sense & Sensibility

The ships were part of a British China fleet under convoy of *L'Atheniene*. She sent a pinnace ashore, carrying Lieutenant Little, who told Piper they had left England in June, and come through Bass Strait, en route to the Philippines. They had lost contact with one of their ships, the *Taunton Castle*, six weeks before. Her officers and some of the seamen were in a *sickly state* with scurvy, and *much in want of refreshment*.[34] They called at Norfolk Island to learn if she had been sighted. The nine ships took on fresh water and provisions, and sailed later that afternoon.

Three days later, the *Taunton Castle* dropped anchor in Cascade Bay. Her master, Thomas Pierce, came ashore for provisions and reported the serious outbreak of scurvy on board. She remained at anchor for two days. Livestock were provided by the settlers, and D'Arcy supplied a large quantity of lemons.

When Holt was released, he went to see Piper. *Off I set to seek the Captain and ask him if he had any hand in planning such a death for men who had not committed any fault whatsoever.* Piper *declared his innocence of this wicked conspiracy*, he called the gaolers and *immediately broke and displaced those with knowledge... I said it would have been the most barbarous act that ever was committed. If these Irishmen had been guilty of a fault or a crime in their own country, they had suffered for it...it was no excuse for murdering them.*[35]

Piper accepted Holt was a political prisoner, not a felon, and he gave him the freedom of the island. Holt spent his last months there fishing, *I took eels by spearing. Having held a lighted torch for some time over the water, the eels soon began to rise to the surface, and to play about. With this torch in my left hand, and a short hand-spear in my right, I have taken as many as three hundred eels in a night.*[36]

> *The conversation soon turned upon fishing, and she heard Mr. Darcy invite him, with the greatest civility, to fish there as often as he chose while he continued in the neighbourhood, offering at the same time to supply him with fishing tackle, and pointing out those parts of the stream where there was usually most sport.*
> Pride & Prejudice

All my anxieties & Labours towards you during your Education

A Collection of Letters

At the end of February 1805, a whaler *Alexander* anchored off the island. She left England more than three years earlier to hunt seals and whales in the Southern Ocean, and was now bound for home, with 22 tons of whale oil, 14,000 seal pelts and kangaroo skins.

D'Arcy knew her master, Robert Rhodes, and the mate, Jörgen Jörgensen, from two years before, when they spent six months in Sydney, refitting the ship. He made a snap decision to send John on the *Alexander,* to join his brothers at school. Norfolk Island was no place for him. An order could come at any time for them to embark for Port Dalrymple, there was no future for him there.

He entrusted John to the care of Rhodes, confident he and Jörgensen, the lively twenty-five year old mate, would look after him, and keep him occupied. Rhodes had made the voyage before, in 1799, as master of the *Hillsborough*.

Before the *Alexander* had raised anchor, word got out that Irish exiles had stowed away on board. Piper had the ship searched, they were found and taken off, and her longboat impounded. D'Arcy supplied Rhodes with a replacement of his own, and the *Alexander* left at full-sail, heading for New Zealand, then Tahiti, Cape Horn, St Helena and home.

Such an adventure as this

Emma

She took fifteen months to reach Gravesend. Captain Rhodes was not one to hurry, on the return voyage of the *Hillsborough,* he had spent eight months at Desolation Island, in the sub-antarctic Indian Ocean. There he chased black right whales, took more than four hundred soundings of the seabed around the island, and prepared a set of detailed and beautiful charts of the coastline.

John Wentworth spent the voyage as a captain's boy, a junior midshipman, learning the arts and science of seamanship from Jörgensen, a spirited Dane, who had been apprenticed on a British collier and served in the British navy.

Just three years later, Jörgensen took over the government of Iceland, after the arrest of the Danish governor, Count Trampe. He declared it an independent republic, and assumed the title of *his Excellency the Protector of Iceland, Commander in Chief by Sea and Land,* promising the Icelanders, *undisturbed tranquillity and a felicity hitherto unknown.*[37]

Jörgensen spent two years spying for England in Europe during the Napoleonic Wars. In April 1826, he was transported for life to Van Diemen's Land, where he explored the north and northwest of the island. He married an Irish convict, Norah Corbett in 1831. Among his many ventures, he wrote, published and acted as scribe for the illiterate. He died in Hobart in 1844.

In June 1806, John Wentworth, just ten, disembarked, very ill with scurvy, full of tales of seafaring and shipboard life. Cookney had been waiting anxiously for news, afraid the *Alexander* was captured by the French. He took John home, and he and Thomasine nursed him back to health. Only some months later, was John well enough to join his brothers at school.

The *Alexander* had carried the mail to Norfolk Island from Sydney. There was a letter to D'Arcy from Dennis Considen, now in the final year of medicine at Edinburgh. He asked for *some seed, logs of Beefwood, alias Live Oak, and some of the gums of the country, particularly yellow and green.*[38] In his thesis, on tetanus, *De Tetano,* Considen had written up his work in the Colony on eucalyptus oil.

He graduated as doctor of medicine in 1804, and went to London, but found himself *at a loss where to practice,* and returned to County Clare. From there went to the Cape, where he continued his analysis of native plants. In 1806, he asked D'Arcy to send him eucalyptus specimens there.[39]

To banish myself from the very houses & friends I should turn to for consolation Sense & Sensibility

In December 1804, King complained to Lord Hobart of *the great backwardness of the settlers in giving their names to remove from Norfolk Island and the dislike they had expressed at being removed before their crops were ripe.*[40]

The *Investigator* took all military personnel, except for thirty privates, off the island, on 1 March 1805, along with a great proportion of the convicts, and eight settler families, to be resettled at Port Dalrymple. But by the end of the year, when the *Buffalo* and *Sydney* came to Norfolk Island, not one of the remaining settlers would agree to leave.[41]

It is shameful to have you exiled Lady Susan

In May 1805, Cookney wrote – *I flatter myself I shall see you soon.*[42] D'Arcy was anxious to return to England, to Jane and to his sons, but all his requests for leave of absence remained unanswered. Norfolk Island was being closed down, a third of the population had already been taken off. He knew King wanted to send him to Van Diemen's Land, he could not contemplate starting life in another, more remote settlement.

Despairing, he took the only action he could, he wrote to friends in England, and asked for their help to rescue him from further banishment. Fitzwilliam, Villiers, Cookney, John Hunter, Dennis Considen, Henry Waterhouse were among those who responded, who lobbied the Colonial Office for him to be given leave of absence, to be paid the salary and remuneration due to him and be allowed to return to Sydney, rather than sent to Van Diemen's Land.[43]

He was not only pardoned, they were delighted with him   Persuasion

D'Arcy's assistant surgeon on Norfolk, was William Redfern, twelve years his junior. Examined by the Company of Surgeons, at twenty two, he qualified as a *third mate, any rate,* and joined the Navy in January 1797. He was appointed to *HMS Standard*. Three months later, his eldest brother Robert was sent from Belfast to Dublin's Newgate Gaol, charged with high treason.

On 16 April 1797, mutiny broke out at Spithead, mainly over pay and conditions. On 12 May, the Nore mutiny followed, it was highly political, the mutineers declared themselves to be a "floating republic." United Irishmen, among the many Irish sailors in the Navy, were involved, they demanded peace with republican France and the abdication of George III.

On 15 May, the Spithead mutiny ended, with promises of improved pay and rations and a royal pardon for the mutineers. On 29 May, *HMS Standard* was at the Yarmouth Roads, flying the red flag of mutiny. By 31 May, she had moved to the Nore, a sandbank at the mouth of the Thames, planning to blockade commerce on the river. On 12 June, up river, she raised the blue flag of peace. Two days later, Redfern was discharged at Gravesend, and taken to Maidstone Gaol, his wages forfeited for mutiny and rebellion. Between August 17 and 25 fifty-nine men from *HMS Standard* were tried, with an original charge of treason changed to mutiny.

Redfern was accused of hiding two ship's pistols and ammunition in the dispensary, and having a seditious letter and political pamphlets in his possession. He was sentenced to death. Given a reprieve, he served four years in prison, and was then transported with thirteen other mutineers on the *Canada,* landing in Sydney in December 1801.

In May 1802, Redfern was sent to Norfolk Island as assistant surgeon. Buckey described him as *one of those blunt and outspoken of men. He at all times listened attentively to prisoners...he was well liked for his many kindnesses and liberal ways.*[44] Later that year, Foveaux gave him conditional emancipation on the island, and the following June, King granted him an absolute pardon.

Redfern found a patron in Foveaux and another in D'Arcy. In 1804, he became D'Arcy's assistant; they were friends and colleagues. Joseph Holt thought them *both excellent men, they both came from the North of Ireland.*[45]

In June 1807, Holt returned to Sydney and was given a free pardon. He left the Colony in 1812 on the *Isabella,* she was wrecked off the Falklands, he did not reach Dublin till April 1814. He always regretted leaving New South Wales.

Gazing on it in motionless wonder   Northanger Abbey

In the second week of May 1805, D'Arcy, standing on a slope above the cliffs, witnessed *a considerable influx of the sea...the tide first ebbed to a great distance; when suddenly, an unusual swell was seen coming in, which occasioned considerable alarm in the colony, to whom such a circumstance was entirely novel; it rose to a great height, and retired to its channel.*

A second time it revisited the shore, and flowed to a more considerable height than before; a second time it retreated; and once again returned, with a fury surpassing its former efforts; paralysing the spectators with terror, who were unable to imagine where the extraordinary swellings might pause. For the last time, however, the ocean left the shores, without having caused any material damage; and, in its regress, it opened the secrets of the deep, and displayed to mortal ken rocks which had remained until now undiscovered.[46] On his return to Kingston, he found a great panic, the tsunami had swept one house away and damaged many others.[47]

The quiet, the retirement of such a life, would have answered all my ideas of happiness. But it was not to be — Pride & Prejudice

1805 was a year when D'Arcy might have felt a degree of contentment,[48] he had a friend and ally in Captain Piper, a competent assistant in William Redfern, he was at ease among the remaining settlers, soldiers, convicts and ex-convicts with whom he worked. He had sold the backlog of stock that had so bedevilled him, his farm was profitable, he traded his produce with whalers and other vessels that called at the island.[49] Cookney wrote, *it gave me much pleasure to hear of your having disposed of your property, and the flattering account you give of your affairs.*[50]

Dr Davies was coming to town — Sense & Sensibility

In 1805, James Davies, an emancipist surgeon, returned to Norfolk Island, to work at Sydney Bay, walking distance from Queenborough. He had been sent there in June 1795 as an assistant surgeon, recommended by the governor's secretary as *well qualified for the situation.*[51] After serving his term, he had worked at Sydney Cove hospital with D'Arcy, from 1802 to 1804.

Davies, a naval surgeon, also known as Davis or Christopher Theakston, had been charged with a highway robbery in 1790. The Bow Street patrolman who arrested him stated he had asked, *what had become of Molloy, and said he knew Wentworth well.* Molloy had been captured two days earlier. He was re-examined with Davies, *under the idea that they were companions.*

At the examination – *a woman, in whose house the prisoner slept on the Sunday night last, after the robbery was committed, swore...that he slept there that night with a woman; that he had been in the habit of sleeping there with women for some time, and passed by the name of Davies.* THE TIMES

> *Miss Steele only wanted to be teased about Dr Davies to be perfectly happy*
>
> *Dr. Davies was coming to town, and so we thought we'd join him in a post-chaise; and he behaved very genteelly, and paid ten or twelve shillings more than we did."*
>
> *"Oh, oh!" cried Mrs. Jennings; "very pretty, indeed! and the Doctor is a single man, I warrant you."*
>
> *"There now," said Miss Steele, affectedly simpering, "everybody laughs at me so about the Doctor, and I cannot think why. My cousins say they are sure I have made a conquest; but for my part I declare I never think about him from one hour's end to another. 'Lord! here comes your beau, Nancy,' my cousin said t'other day, when she saw him crossing the street to the house. My beau, indeed! said I–I cannot think who you mean. The Doctor is no beau of mine."*
>
> *"Aye, aye, that is very pretty talking–but it won't do–the Doctor is the man, I see."*
>
> *"No, indeed!" replied her cousin, with affected earnestness, "and I beg you will contradict it, if you ever hear it talked of."*
>
> Sense & Sensibility

Confronted in a second examination, Molloy and Davies denied knowing each other. Davies said *he came up to London for the purpose of being examined, and receiving his diploma to act as a surgeon. He said he had then thirty guineas in his pocket, had never been a gambler, though he sometimes kept the company of women, and gave them a bottle of wine.* [52]   THE TIMES

James Davies was tried at the Surrey Assizes, found guilty and sentenced to seven years transportation. He and Molloy travelled on the *Pitt* with four hundred other felons. D'Arcy was on Norfolk Island when they arrived in Port Jackson on Valentine's Day 1792.

D'Arcy returns to Sydney

In February 1806, D'Arcy learnt the lobbying of his London friends had borne fruit. He was recalled to Sydney, he would not be sent to Van Diemen's Land.[53] He was relieved, though apprehensive about returning there under King. He wanted only to return to England, but his application for leave remained unanswered.

D'Arcy had served fifteen years, longer than any other surgeon practicing in the Colony. Those surgeons who came on the First and Second Fleets had all returned home, a few came back, after a comfortable period of leave.

He wrote to Cookney, asking again if Fitzwilliam had obtained approval for him to return. If yes, he wanted to leave without delay. He was disturbed by the prospect of returning to Sydney: *believe me I am most heartily tired of living under the present Government.* [54] Norfolk Island, ironically, had become his sanctuary, a place of sanity.

In October 1805, Cookney wrote – *Governor King is removed & I sincerely hope Mr Bligh his successor will behave to you satisfactory to your wishes.*[55]

When are calculations ever right? Letters

D'Arcy made ready to leave, he had his pigs slaughtered and salted, and a large cargo of pork shipped to Sydney. He collected a quantity of seed around the tallest, most stately pines, to propagate and plant in Sydney.

He asked Cookney to send him a still and a worm – a spiral pipe for distilling oils from native plants, and a copy of the *Encyclopaedia Britannica*.[56]

> "You are always buying books."
>
> "I cannot comprehend the neglect of a family library in such days as these."
>
> Pride & Prejudice

William Redfern was moving into his house, with its *borders of strawberries, roses, bulbs, sweet briars, grapevines, fig trees, orange trees, oak trees and a quantity of tobacco plants.*[57]

After his return from Norfolk Mansfield Park

D'Arcy left Norfolk Island for the last time, on the *Argo,* on 30 March 1806, and landed in Sydney on 7 April. He was worried about his children, desperately anxious for news of John, nothing had been heard of him for over a year. He had waited on every ship to learn if he was in the land of the living.[58]

He had agreed to William moving to Dr Crombie's school at Greenwich, where he would learn French. He was now fourteen, tall, 5 ft 8ins, and Cookney was asking for directions about his future. Mrs Cookney doubted he could be a surgeon with the cast in his eye. William was familiar with navigation, interested in the navy, though Cookney felt his size might better suit the army.

On 15 April 1807, D'Arcy was put in charge of Parramatta Hospital, he moved back to *Wentworth Woodhouse,*[59] *the best private house in the colony.*[60]

It was a melancholy change Emma

That month, everything went badly wrong, the *Governor King*, carrying his pork to Sydney, was wrecked at the Coal River Settlement in the Hunter River. In June, he was injured in a *severe accident which befell me, having confined me to my house for nineteen weeks past.*[61]

In August, *a quantity of linen apparel* was stolen from *the garden ground* of his house. *Mrs M. Ainsley deposed, that she had laid the articles enumerated in the indictment to bleach, and in the evening discovered that they had been stolen.* John Stephen appeared before the Parramatta Court. *The whole of the property was found in his possession.* [62]

He is sometimes impertinent & troublesome Lady Susan

William Redfern wrote to D'Arcy, asking for his help. It was not the last time he would call on D'Arcy when he found himself in trouble, he had come to rely on his support. *You will be astonished to learn that Captain Piper has ordered me to hold myself in readiness to embark on the first vessel that may arrive here for the purpose of removing the inhabitants to the Derwent.*

His boyish manners make him appear the worse Lady Susan

James Elder, a missionary from Otaheiti, had come to Norfolk Island in search of a wife. When he was recommended to Mary Edge, a girl at the Orphan School, Redfern intervened: *I, unluckily for me, thought it a pity that a man should be saddled with a whore, and candidly told him… What I said to him was merely with a view of committing an act which he might have cause to repent as long as he lived.*

When Elder told him he *had strong suspicions of an intercourse between Captain Piper and her – from the knowledge he had of his character…I incautiously admitted that there might be some truth in his suspicions.*

When Elder declined to accept Miss Edge, Piper sent for Redfern. Elder, he told D'Arcy, *not withstanding his solemn promises, gave up my name.*

Piper *taxed me with circulating reports injurious to his character.* Piper said the *Government had no longer any occasion for my Services – he took away the Servant and took me and my family off the Store, and said to hold myself in readiness to board the first vessel to the Derwent.*

Piper told Redfern, that when he left the island, his house would become government property. *I said the House had never been settled for, and I considered myself as only holding it in trust for you – consequently if any enquiries be made of you, you will take this hint.*

He asked D'Arcy for advice about his pigs: *I shall be glad to know what price you would be willing to give for salted pork.*[63]

A missionary into foreign parts
Mansfield Park

James Mitchell knew Elder, and he gave him a letter of introduction to D'Arcy. They had sailed together from England on the *Royal Admiral,* two of five missionaries sent to Tahiti by Joseph Banks. Elder called on D'Arcy in Sydney. He found a suitable wife, Mary Smith, the daughter of a free settler. they were married at Parramatta in July 1808, and he returned to Tahiti with her.[64]

The inconvenience & expense of so sudden a removal
Sense & Sensibility

Between 1804 and 1810, Captain Piper oversaw the relocation of numbers of convicts and settlers to the Tamar and Derwent Rivers in Van Diemen's Land, but closure of the settlement proved difficult.

In March 1805, convicts were taken off on the *Harrington*, but their numbers were soon replaced. The island had an excellent harvest that year, and Piper wrote to King suggesting the settlement be retained. Piper was unable to relocate everyone in the settlement. There were not enough ships available to move the more than seven hundred people and their possessions, and many free settlers wished to stay on Norfolk Island.

In March 1806, King reminded Earl Camden that Norfolk Island had provided food for the populace in Sydney, its fertile soils could support 6000 people, and it had the potential to serve as a base for whaling in the Pacific.

Regardless of King's views, the two governors who followed him were told to complete the task, given in 1804. Bligh, King's successor, was eager to comply, ready to use force if necessary to remove the settlers from the island. He could not afford to hire ships, and in 1808 he sent *HMS Porpoise* and *Lady Nelson*, vessels used for essential duties, to carry 115 people to Hobart.

In December 1808, Foveaux chartered the *City of Edinburgh* from Port Jackson and sent twenty eight families, two hundred and fifty souls, to Hobart. Bligh, on board the Porpoise moored in the Derwent, reported to London: *she left them in a state of wretchedness, almost naked...I have to observe it is an increase of evils which would never have attended my administration.*[65]

Macquarie, Bligh's successor, found the expense of sending supplies to the island, large, *extremely hazardous and inconvenient.* Foveaux briefed him on the long delays in evacuating the island, and he had the removal completed by February 1814. The last people were taken off on the brig *Kangaroo,* and save for a few dogs, goats and pigs, the island was abandoned, buildings burnt and flattened, the work of a generation of convict labour destroyed.

Dalrymple must be waited for
Persuasion

Surgeon James Davies was evacuated to Port Dalrymple in December 1807. By

1818, he was practising in Hobart, and in 1822, he transferred to a new penal settlement on Sarah Island, in Macquarie Harbour, in the remote south-west. It was a place of secondary punishment for escapees and intractable, one of harshest penal settlements, a place of degradation, depravity and woe.

Convicts worked in chains, in gangs, cutting and hauling Huon Pines from the heavily forested areas around Macquarie Harbour, and manned a ship-building operation on Sarah Island. They built a tall stone wall along the windward side, to shelter the shipyards from the Roaring Forties that blasted up the harbour.

Very little food was produced there, malnutrition, dysentery, and scurvy often raged among the convicts, in the overcrowded conditions. The Sarah Island penal settlement was closed in late 1833, the remaining convicts were relocated to Port Arthur, but no record remains of what happened to James Davies.

Dipping their own Souls in Scarlet Sin — Letters

In November 1806, D'Arcy heard Piper was to be replaced by Captain Kemp, and wrote to tell him. He ended his letter, gently mocking him for his interest in young girls on the island; he already had a child with fourteen year old, Mary Ann Shears. *Make good use of your time amongst the young girls. Don't forget my old friend, Mary G.*[66] Mary G, once a love interest of dashing Captain Piper, was known on the Island as wild, desirable, and uncontrollable.

Buckey told the story of the gaoler *Ted Kimberley, a bright and intelligent Irishman. I can well remember the time he fell in love with Mary Ginders, a married Convict woman. He ran along the road in front of the gaol, Ginders following with an axe in his hand. He told her that if she did not come and live with him he would report her to the Major and have her placed into the Cells.*

That woman gave us more trouble than any one on the Island. She was the leader of the dances in the barrack Room and was well liked among the soldiers. The amusements consisted mainly of dancing in the Barrack Room on Thursday evenings when all the women would join in the dances of the mermaids. Each one being naked with numbers painted on their backs so as to be recognised by their admirers who would clap their hands upon seeing their favourite perform some grotesque action. I well remember the fight between Mary Ginders and Bridget Chandler in respect to their position as favourites among the Soilders which ended in Bridget receiving a broken arm.[67]

As D'Arcy was writing to Piper, Mary G was making her escape on the *Sydney,* bound for Van Diemen's Land. Holt recorded *she was concealed in a sack of cabbages and was stowed away snug enough.*[68] Her husband William followed her a few years later. Piper wrote to a friend in Sydney, *the girls on the island are too much for me, I need some help.*[69]

Redfern wrote to D'Arcy in September 1807, *Let me entreat you to favour me with all the information you have been able to obtain relating to the coming out of Colonel Foveaux. His arrival here is expected with the utmost impatience, being destined, in the public opinion, to bring the Ultimate Fist of Government respecting the fate of this island.* It was a letter filled with complaints, and Redfern anticipated D'Arcy was to leave for Europe. [70]

Friendship & Cordiality Scraps

D'Arcy and John Piper remained friends for life, they shared a great love of horses and racing. Piper imported a fine stallion, *Wellington,* and built a race track on his land at Rose Bay. D'Arcy successfully extricated him from a series of financial embarrassments and acted as his banker for many years.

Long antipodean voyages in small ships had aged and weakened him[71]

After nearly six years, King's period as Governor was coming to a close. Captain William Bligh, *Breadfruit Bligh,* of the *Bounty,* was on his way to Sydney, to succeed him as governor.

Alcohol had taken its toll on King, along with the stress of unrelenting conflict with the military and civil officers. Though only forty six; the responsibility of governing New South Wales and the distant settlements of Norfolk Island and Van Diemen's Land, had broken him physically and, for a time, mentally.

Trunks & Bird cages. Quite amusing! Letters

King left for England on 10 February 1807, on the *Buffalo.* D'Arcy was pleased to see him go, he described his regime as *a Government conducted on the Principles of Tyranny, oppression and injustice.*[72]

King's wife Anna promised D'Arcy she would visit his sons, and he gave her two guineas for each of them. He also arranged for four black swans and several parrots to be carried on board, for delivery to Fitzwilliam.[73]

After boarding the *Buffalo,* King collapsed, and it was some time before he was well enough to sail. He arrived home in November 1807, after a very stormy, difficult voyage around Cape Horn. He died less than a year later, in September 1808, aged only fifty. His two illegitimate sons, Norfolk and Sydney became lieutenants in the Navy. His legitimate son, Phillip Parker King became a navigator and surveyed the Patagonian and Australian coasts. A daughter, Anna Maria, married Hannibal Macarthur, John Macarthur's nephew, in 1812.

JANE & D'ARCY

I look upon the event as so far decided that I resign myself to it in despair

Lady Susan

D'Arcy contemplated the unpromising prospect of his own return to England. He was forty-four, Jane was thirty. His promise to her that he would return was still unfulfilled. He remained trapped, unable to leave the Colony.

> *The autumn... the declining year, with declining happiness, and the images of youth and hope, and spring, all gone together.*   Persuasion

Chapter 19

The Peripatetic Austens

More at large & likewise, more at small

WHERE WERE the celebrations to farewell the glorious eighteenth century, or the great civic events to welcome in the nineteenth? There seem to have been no public festivities, and probably few private resolutions.

In Steventon, the new century heralded a significant alteration in Jane Austen's circumstances, an end to the familiar and stable rhythm of her family life. In December 1800, she turned twenty-five. Her father, who had *for more than forty years been zealously discharging all the duties of his office, was now growing too infirm for many of them.*[1] George Austen decided to retire to Bath with his wife and daughters. Jane fainted with shock when she heard the news.

No second attachment, the only thoroughly natural, happy and sufficient cure, at her time of life, had been possible...in the small limits of the society around them   Persuasion

One of his motives for a move to town, was George Austen's desire to widen his daughters' society, to see them married. Jane heard her mother's complaints: *You will know that it was merely to oblige the Girls & you, that I left the most commodious House situated in the most delightful Country & surrounded by the most agreeable Neighbourhood, to live 2 years cramped up in Lodgings three pair of Stairs high, in a smokey & unwholesome town, which has given me a continual fever & almost thrown me into a Consumption.*[2]

His eldest son had duties to call him earlier home Mansfield Park

George Austen decided to pass the Steventon rectory and its living to his son James, by-passing his curate, James Digweed, their Steventon neighbour. Cassandra was at *Godmersham*, helping with Edward's children, Jane teased her about him. *James Digweed left Hampshire today, I think he must be in love with you, from his anxiety to have you go to the Faversham Balls, & likewise from his supposing, that the two Elms fell from their grief at your absence.- Was not it a gallant idea?*³

Having a curacy in the neighbourhood Persuasion

George offered James Digweed, Deane, his second, much smaller parish. Jane saw the offer as a *necessary compliment... tho' without considering it as either a desirable or an eligible situation for him.* She wondered if he had taken Cassandra's feelings into account, and asked her, *Were you indeed to be considered as one of the fixtures to the house!*⁴ A week later she reported, *James Digweed has refused Deane curacy I suppose he has told you himself – tho' probably the subject has never been mentioned between you.*⁵

Two months later, it seems the flirtation was over. Jane asked, *Why did not JD make his proposals to you? I suppose he went to see the Cathedral. That he might know how he should like to be married in it.*⁶

Regret & resentment Northanger Abbey

In 1801, the Austens and their daughters prepared to move to Bath, while James Austen and his wife, Mary, prepared for their move to Steventon. Jane was conscious, *my father's old Ministers are already deserting him to pay their court to his Son.*

She noted James' moves to take her father's place: *the brown Mare, which as well as the black was to devolve on James at our removal, had not the patience to wait for that & has settled herself even now at Deane.*

James had one of his own horses put down, *the death...tho' undesired was not wholly unexpected, being purposely effected, has made the immediate possession of the Mare very convenient; & everything else I suppose will be seized by degrees in the same manner.* ⁷

Undo all the work of the morning, and pack her trunk afresh Pride & Prejudice

Jane was busy with moving, and felt badgered by her family, *you are very kind in planning presents for me to make, & my mother has shewn me exactly the same attention – but as I do not chuse to have Generosity dictated to me, I shall not resolve on giving my Cabinet to Anna till the first thought of it has been my own.*

Dear me! What can you possibly have to do? Persuasion

A great many things, I assure you. More than I can recollect in a moment; but I can tell you some. I have been making a duplicate of the catalogue of my father's books and pictures... I have had all my little concerns to arrange – books and music to divide, and all my trunks to repack, from not having understood in time what was intended as to the waggons. And one thing I have had to do, of a more trying nature; going to almost every house in the parish, as a sort of take-leave. I was told that they wished it. But all these things took up a great deal of time.[8]

There are plenty of books Lady Susan

She was concerned about her books, and her father's – *my father has got above 500 volumes to dispose of; I want James to take them at a venture at half a guinea a volume,*[9] but James did not oblige.

A clearance sale was held at Steventon after they left. She wrote to Cassandra; *I fancy you know many more particulars of our Sale than we do... Eight for my Pianoforte, is about what I really expected to get; I am anxious to know the amount of my books, especially as they are said to have sold well...Mary is more minute in her account of their own Gains than in ours.*[10] *The whole World is in a conspiracy to enrich one part of our family at the expence of another.*[11]

Her irritation with James did not subside; a few years later, she reflected after a visit from him, *I am sorry & angry that his Visits should not give one more pleasure; the company of so good & clever a Man ought to be gratifying in itself; but his Chat seems all forced, his Opinions on many points too much copied from his Wife's, & his time here is spent I think in walking about the House & banging the Doors, or ringing the Bell for a glass of Water.*[12]

A little sea-bathing would set me up forever Pride & Prejudice

George Austen's retirement and the closure of his rectory school meant they were free to travel, to have holidays! Jane started planning for them well in advance, telling Cassandra*; Sidmouth is now talked of as our Summer abode, get all the information therefore about it that you can.*[13] She was looking forward to a holiday by the sea, and to visiting friends at *Manydown.*

She reported her encounters, romantic and otherwise, to Cassandra, *Your unfortunate sister was betrayed last Thursday into a situation of utmost cruelty. I arrived at Ashe Park before the Party from Deane, and was shut up in the drawing room with Mr Holder alone for ten minutes... nothing could prevail on me to move two steps from the door, on the lock of which I kept one hand constantly fixed... On Friday I wound up my four days of dissipation by meeting William Digweed at Deane.*[14]

Henry & Eliza Juvenilia

Henry Austen was serving in Ireland, part of the reinforcements sent to support Lord Cornwallis, after the rebellion in 1798. Eliza had remained in Surrey with Hastings, who was now entering his teens.

Eliza seemed to enjoy her life as an officer's wife, *her Brother Officers and Brother Officers Wives* whose *visitations succeeded invitations to Parties which are as thick in this Country as Hops in yours, and besides these parties there is at least one Ball every Week.*

As war with France worsened, she feared a French invasion, *I do believe that they will make an attempt on this Country, and the Government appears to be convinced of it.* There were fears they would cross the Channel on *Rafts to be worked with Wheels which have the effect of oars... bordered with cannon, and support a Tower filled with Soldiers.* [15]

In 1801, after Henry Austen resigned his commission, he and Eliza, and Hastings moved to Upper Berkeley Street. Henry was entering the world of London finance, with partners, Henry Maunde and James Tilson, he opened a bank in St James.

Eliza had the skills and desire for a more elegant style of life, their marriage agreement had stipulated *possession of a comfortable income*. She would have hoped Jane's observation, that *when a man has once got his name in a banking house, he rolls in money*, would apply to Henry.[16]

In February 1801, when Cassandra spent three weeks in London with them, Jane asked her to observe *everything worthy of notice, from the Opera House to Henry's office in Cleveland Court; and I shall expect you to lay in a stock of intelligence that may procure me amusement for twelvemonths to come.*[17]

If you had been a week later at Lisbon, last Spring, you would have been asked to give a passage Persuasion

That month, Charles Austen came home on shore leave from the *Endymion*. He had spent three pleasant days in Lisbon, and had lots of tales to tell.

The King's sixth son, Prince Augustus Frederick, sailed back to Portsmouth on the *Endymion* with them, *they were well satisfied with their Royal passenger whom they found fat, jolly and affable, who talks of Ly. Augusta as his wife & seems much attached to her.*[18]

While travelling in Italy, the Prince had met Lady Augusta Murray. In April 1793, they married in secret in Rome, and again secretly in London, in December, at St Georges in Hanover Square. They did not have the King's approval, as the *Royal Marriage Act* required, and their marriage was not recognised. They had two children.[19]

Many a noble fortune has been made during the war Persuasion

The escalating war against Napoleon had an impact on the Austen household. Jane saw how it affected the lives and fortunes of her naval brothers, Frank and Charles. Edward and his family, at *Godmersham* in Kent, less than twenty miles from the Channel, exposed to the increased mobilisation and efforts to secure the coast.

Frank Austen, commanding the *Peterel*, wrote in July 1800, to say he was *with the rest of the Egyptian Squadron off the Isle of Cyprus, whither they went From Jaffa for Provisions etc & whence they would sail in a day or two for Alexandria, to wait the result of the English proposal for the Evacuation of Egypt.*[20] In October he wrote from Cyprus, that he had been to Alexandria, and would return there in three or four days. In November he captured a Turkish ship, driven into port in Cyprus by bad weather, and was forced to burn her.

In February 1801, Jane heard from Charles that both he and Frank were on their way home. Frank had captured forty vessels in the Mediterranean, and shared in prize money. He left the *Peterel* in Rhodes, and he carried important despatches from General Abercromby.

Dispatches from Sir Ralph Abercrombie Letters

Sir Ralph Abercromby, with five thousand troops, sailed to the Mediterranean in April 1800 to confront Napoleon, drive the French army out of Egypt, and complete Nelson's naval victory at Aboukir Bay.

He had been the Commander-in-Chief of the Army in Ireland between 1797 and 1798. Finding the country close to revolt, he had *laboured to maintain the discipline of the army, to suppress the rising rebellion, and to protect the people from military oppression.*[21]

Abercromby, who had studied law at Leipzig, refused to allow the army to be called out to incidents between landlords and poor tenants, or between local gangs of young Protestants and Catholics. He sought to have these matters dealt with by civil authorities and the courts, but Lord Camden, now Lord Lieutenant, the Protestant Ascendancy and the Irish government, all preferred to call on military muscle rather than re-establish civil power.

Abercromby failed to gain their support and resigned his commission in Ireland in 1798. His departure was lamented and it was swiftly followed by the bloody rebellion. Its *true origin*, he said, was *the oppression of centuries.*[22]

Orders for taking Troops to Egypt Letters

On 8 March 1801, British troops, packed tightly in small landing boats, were rowed ashore at Aboukir. Despite strenuous opposition and heavy casualties,

Abercromby and his brave Highlanders cleared the French army from the beach and the surrounding dunes. Abercromby was wounded after the landing, in a skirmish near Alexandria. A ball embedded in his back could not be removed, and he died seven days later.

She was quite impatient to know how the Bath world went on Northanger Abbey

In May 1801, Cassandra, Jane and their mother left Steventon, bound for Bath. They stayed with Mrs Austen's brother, James Leigh-Perrot, and his wife, when they arrived. Jane was delighted to have her own room, she could anticipate a new life, *Bath is a charming place... there are so many good shops... one can step out of doors and get a thing in five minutes.*[23] But despite its comforts, *Bath was depressingly like Basingstoke, full of dull people attending each others dull parties.*[24]

Every morning now brought its regular duties; – shops were to be visited; some new part of the town to be looked at; and the Pump-room to be attended, where they paraded up and down for an hour, looking at every body and speaking to no one Northanger Abbey

The Austen sisters knew very few people in Bath; it was a tourist town, with new people constantly arriving to take the waters. They had lost the standing they had in Steventon, as daughters of the rector, and found there were limited prospects of forming lasting friendships or connexions. Jane wrote: *It is uphill work to be talking to those whom one knows so little.*[25]

There was no one there to introduce them into society; they could not rely on the Leigh-Perrots, who appeared to have few friends.

She longed to dance, but she had not an acquaintance in the room... Catherine began to feel something of disappointment – "How uncomfortable it is," whispered Catherine, "not to have a single acquaintance here!"...

"Yes, my dear," replied Mrs. Allen, with perfect serenity, "it is very uncomfortable indeed. I wish we had a large acquaintance here."

"I wish we had any; – it would be somebody to go to."

"Very true, my dear; and if we knew anybody we would join them directly..."

Dear Mrs. Allen, are you sure there is nobody you know in all this multitude of people? I think you must know somebody."

"I don't, upon my word – I wish I did. I wish I had a large acquaintance here with all my heart, and then I should get you a partner. I should be so glad to have you dance." Northanger Abbey

To retire for the rest of his life The History of England

A few weeks later, George Austen joined them, and leased a house at 4 Sydney Place, overlooking Sydney Gardens.

As yet you have seen nothing of Bath Persuasion

Smollet's Squire Mathew Bramble, described the society of Bath, *Every upstart of fortune, harnessed in the trappings of the mode, presents himself at Bath, as in the very focus of observation. Clerks and factors from the East Indies, loaded with the spoils of plundered provinces; planters, Negro-drivers, and hucksters, from our American plantations, enriched they know not how; agents, commissaries, and contractors, who have fattened, in two successive wars on the blood of the nation; usurers, brokers and jobbers of every kind; men of low birth, and no breeding, have found themselves suddenly translated into a state of affluence, unknown to former ages; and no wonder their brains should be intoxicated with pride, vanity and presumption.* The Expedition of Humphry Clinker, 1771

Unmeaning luxuries if Bath Love & Freindship

Jane had read the accounts of the town as full of diversions, scandal and levity. Daniel Defoe saw it as, *taken up in Raffling, Gameing, Visiting, and in a Word, all sorts of Gallantry and Levity... The whole Time indeed is a Round of the utmost Diversion. At the Cross-Bath: the Ladies and the Gentlemen pretend to keep some distance, and each to their proper Side, but frequently mingle... and the Place being but narrow, they converse freely, and talk, rally, made Vows, and sometimes Love; and having thus amus'd themselves an Hour, or Two, they call their Chairs and return to their Lodgings.* A Tour through the Whole Island of Great Britain, 1742

In my Bath life I have seen instances of it! Emma

Jane was disappointed at not finding Bath rife with scandal. The only evidence she saw, was her own cousin, Mary-Cassandra Twisleton, now the mistress of Charles Taylor, Member for Wells; and a drunken Mr Badcock, being pursued by his equally inebriated wife around the Upper Rooms.

She had never met Cassandra Twisleton, but knew it was her, immediately: *I am proud to say that I have a very good eye for an Adultress... I fixed upon the right one from the first.— A resemblance to Mrs Leigh was my guide... she was highly rouged, & looked rather quietly and contentedly silly than anything else.*[26]

She disliked Bath, and did not think it agreed with her, and Bath was to be her home Persuasion

Jane missed the countryside, the open air, the landscape, the changing seasons – *It was sad to lose all the pleasures of Spring.* She had not known before what *pleasures she had to lose in passing March and April in town. She had not known before, how much the beginnings and progress of vegetation had delighted her... To be losing such pleasures was no trifle; to be losing them because she was in the midst of closeness and noise, to have confinement, bad air, bad smells, substituted for liberty, freshness, fragrance and verdure, was infinitely worse.*[27]

Now she hoped for some beneficial change — Persuasion

Her life had entered a protracted period of change and upheaval. On the surface, it appeared leisurely, with sightseeing, holidays by the sea, balls and entertainments. But for more than eight years, she was constantly on the move, travelling from one abode to the next, in a seemingly continuous round.

Do you know, I get so immoderately sick of Bath — Northanger Abbey

One consequence of the Austens' life of leisure was the great lack of privacy: *The sort of necessity which the family-habits seemed to produce, of every thing being to be communicated, and every thing being to be done together, however undesired and inconvenient.*[28]

In another person's house one cannot command one's own time or activities — Letters

In Steventon, Jane had recorded her most important stories, after she moved to Bath, her creative life lost momentum. Her peripatetic years were a long period of distraction, sapping her confidence and energy. She lacked the peace of mind, the sense of security and focus she needed to work at her writing. She was disinclined to unpack her private papers, her manuscripts remained in her writing box.

In Devonshire pursuing fresh schemes, always gay, always happy — Sense & Sensibility

While they waited for renovations to be completed at Sydney Place, the family left on a long awaited holiday to the Devon Coast. Jane had found the summer in Bath close and oppressive: *sunshine appeared to her a totally different thing in a town and in the country. Here, its power was only a glare, a stifling, sickly glare, serving to bring forward stains and dirt that might otherwise have slept. There was neither health nor gaiety in sun-shine in a town. She sat in a blaze of oppressive heat, in a cloud of moving dust.*[29]

Jane was so admired — Pride & Prejudice

During their summer holiday in Devon, she and Cassandra enjoyed sea bathing. It is said Jane had a fleeting encounter with a handsome man, but his name is unknown. Her niece Caroline told the story, *they parted – but he made it plain that he would seek them out again – and shortly afterwards he died.*

At the end of September 1801, the Austens returned to Hampshire to stay at the Steventon Rectory with James and Mary. Jane spent a pleasant day with Madam Lefroy at Ashe, and the Lefroys came to Steventon for dinner.

On 5 October, their renovations complete, they returned to Bath. Jane, *dreading the possible heats of September in all the white glare of Bath, and grieving to forego all the influence so sweet and so sad of autumnal months in the country.*[30]

Sufficiently composed to give necessary orders for the funeral   Evelyn

On 9th October, Eliza's son Hastings died, he was fifteen. The fits that had begun in his infancy, had continued and worsened. Dr Baillie, the specialist, was unable to save him. Eliza buried him at Hampstead, beside her mother.

I am Captain Hunter   The Watsons

On 13 October 1801, Jane had an unexpected visitor, a white haired naval officer, past middle-age, with bright blue eyes, who introduced himself as Captain Hunter. He had gone first to the Wheatsheaf at North Waltham, he told her, only to learn that she and her parents were in Bath, at 4 Sydney Place.

Jane apologised for their absence, they were in London for the funeral of their grandson, her brother Henry's stepson, Hastings.

The terrors that occurred of what this visit might lead to were overpowering   Mansfield Park

Captain Hunter told Jane he was in Bath on business, and was happy to have found her at home. She asked if he had travelled far. Indeed, he said, Sydney Place was quite a distance from Sydney-town in New South Wales.

He had been asked to deliver a letter to her, he took it from his coat and held it out. Jane saw her name on the envelope, in D'Arcy's strong, energetic hand.

She took it gently, and as he spoke, she *began not to understand a word* he said.[31] *It was the only thing approaching a letter she had ever received from him; she might never receive another…to her the handwriting itself, independent of anything it might convey, is a blessedness. Never were such characters cut by any other human being.*[32]

Captain Hunter told her he was recently the Governor of New South Wales, that D'Arcy was in Sydney, a surgeon at the free hospital. He wished to return to England to see her again, he hoped she was well, he sent her his best wishes. He stayed only a short time, it was a formal, polite, gentle visit. He left her *deep in the happiness of such misery, or the misery of such happiness.*[33]

Jane, Jane, my dear Jane, where are you?   Emma

Jane carried the letter close to her before she opened it to read, she was light-headed, she had forgotten how it felt to be so happy, so open-hearted.

Above all, above respect and esteem, there was a motive within her of good will which could not be overlooked. It was gratitude. – Gratitude, not merely for having once loved her, but for loving her still well enough to forgive all the petulance and acrimony of her manner in rejecting him, and all the unjust accusations accompanying her rejection.[34]   Pride & Prejudice

She opened his letter in this state of confusion, *nor could she, for many hours, learn to think of it less than incessantly. I shall know how to understand it. I shall then give over every expectation, every wish of his constancy.*[35]

Such a letter was not to be soon recovered from. An interval of meditation, serious and grateful, was the best corrective of every thing dangerous in such high-wrought felicity; and she went to her room, and grew steadfast and fearless in the thankfulness of her enjoyment.[36]

She felt such a great desire to see him again. She had thought constantly about what she would say to him, and about herself, how he might find her changed. *Eleven years could not pass away even in health without making some change.*[37] She thought of D'Arcy, a world away, with three sons. He would be a different person.

He waited in the most anxious expectation for an answer to his Letter, which arrived as soon as the great distance would admit of   Evelyn

Jane replied, she told him that although more than ten years had passed, her father continued to maintain his silence and resolve, neither he nor her brothers would accept their reunion. But she promised when he returned, nothing would separate them again, and that promise lightened her heart.

She danced twice with Captain Hunter   The Watsons

In *The Watsons,* Jane made Tuesday, 13 October, the date of the first winter assembly at the White Hart Inn. Captain Hunter arrives *with an air of empressément,* and asks *young* Mary Edwards to dance.

Sam Watson, a young surgeon, *very much in love* with Mary, is not at the ball, his employer *Mr Curtis won't often spare him.* Mary, dominated by her parents, cannot reveal her true feelings. Approached by Captain Hunter, she looks *rather distressed, but by no means displeased,* there is a blush on her cheek.

After the ball, Mary is quizzed by her parents, *'So you ended with Captain Hunter Mary, did you?' said her father. 'And who did you begin with?' 'Captain Hunter' was repeated, in a very humble tone.*

At the White Hart Inn in Edinburgh, Jane had felt perfect happiness. The scene where Mary dances with Captain Hunter, described the feelings his visit had re-awakened in her.

We have long maintained a private Correspondence Amelia Webster

Jane and D'Arcy's correspondence, across the world's oceans, began that day. There they exchanged again those feelings of attachment.

Here, said he, ended the worst of my state; for now I could at least put myself in the way of happiness, I could exert myself, I could do something. But to be waiting so long in inaction, and waiting only for evil, had been dreadful.[38] None of their letters survive, and in Jane's collected letters there is a gap of three years from this time.

The post-office is a wonderful establishment! All that it does so well! Emma

Jane had long been responsible for collecting her family's mail from the *Wheatsheaf*, a coaching inn on Popham Lane, at North Waltham. It was a pleasant walk, a little over a mile, through woods and fields. Her parents did not object to her receiving private correspondence, and she knew the post office would hold her mail. When she *received a letter, as, at that time, happened pretty often, they always looked the other way…the torments of absence were softened by a clandestine correspondence.*[39]

It is throwing time away to be mistress of French, Italian & German Lady Susan

On 25 March 1802, the Peace of Amiens was signed, ending the war with France that began in 1793. France kept Venice, the Rhineland, and her northern conquests, but ceded Rome and Naples. Britain kept Ceylon, won from the Dutch, and Trinidad from Spain.

Charles Austen was paid off from the *Endymion*, and joined his family at Sydney Place. In April, James and Mary came to Bath to stay, bringing Anna, James' nine year old daughter.

That summer, the Austens returned to Devon with Charles, and went on to visit Wales. They returned to Hampshire in August, and from there they went to Portsmouth to see Frank, who was being paid off *HMS Neptune*.

Jane and Cassandra visited the Fowles at Kintbury and the Lefroys at Ashe; they called at Steventon, then went to Kent to stay with Edward and his growing family. They remained with him at *Godmersham* until late October, when Charles took them back to Steventon.

A secret which was to be kept at all hazards Emma

At Steventon, Jane called at the *Wheatsheaf*, and found there was a letter waiting. Within the family, her correspondence with D'Arcy must be kept a secret, but she was *absolutely indifferent to the observation of all the world.*[40]

The letter, when she was calm enough to read it, brought little comfort Sense & Sensibility

She wanted to read that D'Arcy was on his way to her, but his letter gave only reasons why his return must be delayed. *There seemed every probability of him being permanently fixed there.*[41]

All the terrors of expectation   Northanger Abbey

He thanked her warmly for her reply, he was happy to know Captain Hunter had called and given his letter into her hands. He assured her he was working with only one goal in mind, to leave the Colony and return to England. He was making arrangements to send his eldest sons ahead of him, to attend school in England the following year.

He needed to remain a while longer, to realise his investments, to sell the quantity of tea and spirits he had imported. His was awaiting a response from London to his request for leave, he had asked Fitzwilliam to assist him. After that, he would need the Governor's approval. She should not expect him immediately. He wanted to hear from her again, and he asked her particularly about her writing.

It was not the reply Jane had hoped for or expected. How was she *to check her agitation, to wait, at least, with the appearance of composure?*[42] When would she see him again?

The proposal was his own   Northanger Abbey

A month later, on 28 November 1802, she and Cassandra went to stay with friends, Catherine and Alethea Bigg, at *Manydown*. According to James' wife, Mary, the visit took an unexpected turn. Her daughter Caroline, born in 1805, told the story years later, for her brother James Edward to include in his *Memoir*. The Bigg sisters' younger brother, Harris Bigg-Wither, she told him, had proposed to Jane one evening, and she had accepted, but next morning withdrew the acceptance, packed up and left *Manydown*.[43]

Mama will never forgive me, & I shall be worse off than ever   Lady Susan

Austen family values were writ large as Caroline retold her mother's story: *All worldly advantages would have been to her – and she was of an age to know this quite well. My aunts had very small fortunes; and on their father's death, they and their mother would be, they were aware, but poorly off. I believe most young women so circumstanced would have gone on trusting to love after marriage.*

& the natural turn of mind to make every one happy, promised to become his Wife the next morning   Frederic & Elfrida

Harris Bigg-Wither, six years younger than Jane, was heir to *Manydown*. She was two weeks away from her twenty-seventh birthday, an age when, she would declare, *a woman can never hope to feel or inspire affection again.*[44]

Clearly that night, his interest in her was aroused. The general view was that a young woman of limited means should have capitalised on that interest. She could have enjoyed a secure and comfortable life in familiar surroundings.

Nobody ever feels or acts, suffers or enjoys, as one expects!   Letters

I have very little to say for my own conduct. I was tempted by his attentions, and allowed myself to appear pleased…my vanity was flattered, and I allowed his attentions…I thought them a habit, a trick, nothing that called for seriousness on my side. He has imposed on me, but he has not injured me. I have never been attached to him.[45]

Whatever did take place that evening did not dampen the friendship between the Austen and Bigg sisters, Jane and Cassandra continued to visit *Manydown*. Perhaps the only lasting damage from the incident was criticism Jane received from her family, like that echoed in *Mansfield Park*:

> "Am I to understand… that you mean to refuse Mr C…?"
>
> "Yes, Sir."
>
> "Refuse him?"
>
> "Yes, Sir"
>
> "Refuse Mr C…! Upon what plea? For what reason?"
>
> "I – I cannot like him, Sir, well enough to marry him."
>
> "This is very strange!" said Sir Thomas, in a voice of calm displeasure. "There is something in this that my comprehension does not reach. Here is a young man wishing to pay his addresses to you, with everything to recommend him; not merely situation in life, fortune and character, but with more than common agreeableness, with address and conversation pleasing to every body. And he is not an acquaintance of to-day, you have now known him some time. His sister, moreover, is your intimate friend."

There never were two people more dissimilar. We have not one taste in common. We should be miserable.   Mansfield Park

From Caroline's story, something definitive occurred overnight. Next morning Jane and Cassandra left *Manydown* suddenly. Alethea and Catherine Bigg assisted, they drove them to Steventon. From there, Jane insisted James take them to Bath, and he did so.

Perhaps, that evening Jane allowed things to go too far. Did she have *too great a relish for her Claret,* and finding herself, *somewhat heated by wine (no very uncommon case) determined to seek a relief for her disordered Head & Love-sick Heart.*[46]

It was not only that her feelings were still adverse to any man save one…She

had seen too much of the world to expect sudden or disinterested attachment anywhere.[47]

Jane knew a refusal of marriage at this juncture in her life would disturb her father and invite censure from her mother. Other members of the family would see her as wilful, as failing to accept that her financial survival relied on marriage. She was expected to forget that she had once married, that she was married; and this was an inconvenient truth.

In *Sense & Sensibility*, Jane caught a brother's patronising, urging tone; his entitlement to discuss her affairs with whomever he wished, to judge her, to interpose his wishes on her. '*Of one thing, my dear sister,' kindly taking her hand and speaking in an awful whisper, I may assure you: and I will do it, because I know it must gratify you. I have good reason to think – indeed I have it from the best authority, or I should not repeat it, for otherwise it would be very wrong to say anything about it – but I have it from the very best authority…That, in short, whatever objections there might be against a certain – a certain connection – you understand me – it would have been far preferable…It would have been beyond comparison…the least evil of the two…But, however, all that is quite out of the question – never to be thought of or mentioned; as to any attachment, you know – it never could be – all that is gone by. But I thought I would just tell you this, because I knew how much it would please you.*

A secret which was to be kept at all hazards   Emma

After her stay at *Manydown*, Jane returned to the discipline and consolation of writing. She took out *Susan*, finished three years before, set aside a little space and commenced revising her manuscript.

Henry, aware that she was once again the focus of family censure, was concerned for her. When Jane mentioned she was re-writing *Susan,* he asked if she would entrust him the manuscript. In 1803, on her behalf, he sold the copyright of *Susan* to Richard Crosby & Co for £10.

Invigorated by the sale of *Susan*, Jane began work on *The Watsons*. There she commented on her own predicament – *I could do very well single for my own part.– A little company, and a pleasant ball now and then, would be enough for me, if one could be young forever, but my father cannot provide for us, and it is very bad to grow old and be poor and be laughed at.*

He commands the Sea Fencibles here   Letters

In 1801, Napoleon acquired Louisiana from Spain, he onsold it to the United States, and used the proceeds to finance a new military campaign. In February 1803 he invaded Switzerland. The poorly negotiated Amiens treaty had lasted fourteen months, and in May 1803, war with France resumed. Hostilities would continue another twelve years, until the Congress of Vienna in 1815.

Henry and Eliza were in France when the war broke out again, hopeful that Eliza might claim something from the Comte de Feuillide's estate. After war with Britain was declared, they had to leave quickly to avoid detention.

Prime Minister Henry Addington, later Lord Sidmouth, established the *Sea Fencibles,* to protect the British coastline from French invasion. It was made up of volunteers – a Home Guard of fishermen, pilots, old sailors, old soldiers even smugglers. They were armed, maintained shore batteries and installations and were at the ready to man small boats.

Frank Austen was ordered to Ramsgate, in Kent, to command a group of *Sea Fencibles.* He was not very excited by this posting, but he met Mary Gibson there, who became his wife on 26 July 1806.

Five years after returning home from New South Wales, Captain Arthur Phillip was appointed Post Captain of the *Sea Fencibles*. Anne Lefroy's brother, Sir Egerton Brydges, commanded a troop of Fencible Cavalry, and served with them in different parts of England.[48]

The Admiralty was concerned at men volunteering for the *Sea Fencibles,* to protect themselves from impressment into the Navy, where they were needed. Volunteers were still subject to the *Mutiny Act* and *Articles of War,* they could be prosecuted for mutiny or desertion. Their lingering fear was that they might be impressed into service in the Navy.

Lord Keith, a Scottish Admiral, Commander-in-chief in the Mediterranean, observed: Sea Fencibles of Dover, Deal and Folkestone, *regard themselves in a manner completely independent from the service, having a kind of prescriptive right to defraud the revenue and pillage individuals.*

Cornwallis did not agree, he wrote in December 1803, *no man, whether civil or military, will persuade me that 300,000 men, trained as the volunteers at present, do not add very materially to the confidence, and to the actual security of this country*[49].

Charles Austen was sent to Bermuda, in charge of the sloop, *HMS Indian,* well away from the war in Europe. He was to spend six and a half years patrolling the eastern seaboard of America.

A tour to the seaside Emma

The Austens spent part of the summer on the Dorset coast. Jane explored the beaches and the sea with new eyes. D'Arcy had written about the delightful climate of New South Wales, with, *the finest, purest sea breeze on the coast— acknowledged to be so—excellent bathing—fine hard sand—deep water ten yards from the shore—no mud—no weeds—no slimy rocks.*[50]

His letters have been exactly what they ought to be – cheerful & amusing
Letters

From his very first letter, D'Arcy told her about life in the Colony, describing the country and its marvels. In their correspondence they spoke of his return to England, their hopes of being together once more, of never again being parted.

When it was clear that at best, he might be granted twelve months leave, he suggested Jane return to Sydney with him. After long English winters, he felt *a warm climate may be prescribed for her,*[51] and *sea-bathing recommended.*[52]

Wild for Lyme Persuasion

In September, the Austens went to *Godmersham* in Kent, to stay with Edward. Jane and Cassandra visited Frank at Ramsgate, then went to Ashe to stay with Anne Lefroy. The family returned to Bath on 24 October 1803, and in November they left for Lyme Regis.

In Lyme, *after securing accommodations, and ordering a dinner at one of the inns, the next thing to be done was unquestionably to walk directly down to the sea. They were come too late in the year for any amusement or variety which Lyme, as a public place, might offer. The rooms were shut up, the lodgers almost all gone, scarcely any family but of the residents left.*[53]

Beauties of Nature, her curiosity to behold Love & Freindship

The scenes in its neighbourhood, Charmouth, with its high grounds and extensive sweeps of country, and still more, its sweet, retired bay, backed by dark cliffs, where fragments of low rock among the sands, make it the happiest spot for watching the flow of the tide, for sitting in unwearied contemplation.[54]

A very reasonable weariness Mansfield Park

In October 1804, Rev Austen gave up his lease on Sydney Place. Now seventy-three, he was unwell. He had three months more to live. Jane returned to Bath, to their new home at 3 Green Park Buildings East. She described in *The Watsons*, her comfort in his company: *Her father, if ill, required little more than gentleness and silence; and being a man of sense and education, was, if able to converse, a welcome companion. In his chamber, she was at peace from the dreadful mortification of an unequal society, and family discord…she still suffered from them in the contemplation of their existence; in memory and in prospect, but for the moment she ceased to be tortured by their effects. – She was at leisure, she could read and think…the dissipation of unpleasant ideas which only reading could produce, made her thankfully turn to a book.*[55]

Frank Austen's tour of duty with the *Sea Fencibles* ended, he became engaged to Mary Gibson of Ramsgate, and he took command of *HMS Leopard*, patrolling the sea approaches to Boulogne.

In London, Henry moved his office to the *Albany* in Piccadilly, he and Eliza moved from Upper Berkeley Street into a small terrace house in Michael's Place, overlooking the fields and gardens of Brompton.

A great deal to agitate & grieve her — Emma

On 16 December 1804, Jane's twenty-nine birthday, Madam Lefroy died. She was killed in a fall from a runaway horse. The shock of her death was overtaken by George Austen's rapidly failing health, and his death a few weeks later. On 21 January 1805. Jane wrote to her brothers to give them the melancholy news.

James hurried to Bath from Steventon. Henry, at *Godmersham*, came quickly, but Edward was delayed. The funeral on 26 January 1805, was at the Walcot church, where George Austen had married Cassandra Leigh forty years earlier.

A valuable legacy indeed! — Sense & Sensibility

In his retirement, Rev Austen had enjoyed a small annuity from the church that provided for the family in Bath. It ceased on his death, leaving his widow and two unmarried daughters dependent on the generosity of his sons.

James urged his mother to return to Steventon to live with him and his family in the rectory, but she was adamant that she would not intrude on his family life, nor surrender her independence.

On 25 March 1805, when the lease on 3 Green Park Building expired, the three women moved to cheaper lodgings at 25 Gay Street. Cassandra was called to help Martha Lloyd care for her sick mother. Mrs Lloyd died on 16 April, and after her funeral it was agreed that Martha would live with the Austens in Bath. Jane liked Martha, she looked forward to enjoying her companionship.

A great secret & known only to half the neighbourhood — Letters

In early 1805, Jane's aunt, Mrs Leigh-Perrot was accused of a second charge of theft, this time it was a plant from a greenhouse in Bath. The charge was not pursued, but gossip went around the district; that when the plant was found in her pocket, *she burst into tears and entreated that it might not be put in the papers.* The mayor and magistrate of Bath, Dr Harington, was credited with a squib about the incident:

Sub judice lis est

To love of plants who has the greater claim,
Darwin the bard or Perrot's wily dame?
Decide the cause, Judge Botany, we pray,
Let him the laurel take and her the Bay.[56]

It was said that *since Mrs Perrot's stealing the plants everybody has dropped her acquaintance and she is universally shunned.*[57]

Despite the scandal and embarrassment, the Austen family remained loyal to their wealthy uncle and his tiresome wife, who had *neither beauty, genius, accomplishment, nor manner.*[58] Jane wrote to Cassandra, *Uncle & Aunt drank tea with us last evening, I thought it was of the first consequence to avoid anything that might seem a slight to them. I shall be glad when it is over.*[59]

The care of an aunt   The Watsons

In June, the Austen women went to *Godmersham*, visiting Steventon en route. James wife, Mary was expecting her second child, and her stepdaughter, James' eldest daughter, Anna, accompanied them to Kent. She was twelve, the same age as Edward's daughter, Fanny. During their stay Jane and Cassandra entertained the children, and with happy memories of Austen theatricals in the barn at Steventon, they arranged play acting in the evenings.

At the end of July, Mrs Austen took Anna home to Steventon, to meet her new sister, Caroline Mary Craven. Jane and Cassandra remained in Kent until mid September, staying with Edward at *Godmersham*. Jane moved about, she stayed with Edward's mother-in-law, Lady Fanny Bridges at *Goodnestone Park*, and with her sister, Sophia Deede, at *Sandling Park*.

She did not like the proposal   The Watsons

During August, 1805, it seems Elizabeth's brother, Edward Bridges, became interested in Jane. *He had been, strange to tell, too late for the cricket match, too late at least to play himself, and, not being asked to dine with the players, came home. It is impossible to do justice to the hospitality of his attentions towards me; he made a point of ordering toasted cheese for supper entirely on my account. We had a very agreeable evening.*[60]

Perhaps her brother Edward's later coldness towards Jane, was an indication he and Bridges family were not happy about the flirtation.

In September 1805, Edward Knight escorted Jane and Cassandra to Worthing on the Sussex coast, to join their mother and Martha Lloyd. The four women stayed in lodgings there, until the end of the year, using *the actual space to the best possible account, to supply the deficiencies of lodging-house furniture, and defend the windows and doors against the winter storms to be expected.*[61]

You are only going from one set of friends to another   Mansfield Park

In the first years of her father's retirement, Jane had enjoyed their holidays on the coast and visits to places of interest, but it had palled. She disliked Bath, and the continual round of family and friends had lost its charm.

After his death, the Austen women kept moving, with a cheerless, slightly desperate air. Jane described the anxiety of women constantly on the move. *She has been my intimate friend for years. But I have not the least inclination to go near her...I wish I had settled not to go to her till after Easter, a much better time for the visit – but now I cannot put her off. And when I have done with her, I must go to her sister because she was rather my most particular friend of the two; but I have not cared much for her these three years.*[62]

Sea Battles

In October 1805, the Navy was running a blockade off Cadiz. Frank Austen's ship, the *Canopus,* was sent to Gibraltar for supplies, water and stores. As a result he missed the battle of Trafalgar. Nelson expected the *Canopus* would return in time for the battle with the French fleet. He told Admiral Louis, *The enemy will come out, and we shall fight them; but there will be time for you to get back first. I look to the Canopus as my right hand.*[63]

Villeneuve, commander of the French fleet, received intelligence from Paris that he was to be replaced. He learnt six British ships had sailed, and decided to break through the blockade. On 21 October 1805, he led his five squadrons out of Cadiz to be overwhelmed by the British fleet.

Lord Nelson lost his life in the battle of Trafalgar. Frank Austen lamented his death, as his commander, and as his patron, whose respect and influence might have assisted his career. Frank was concerned at having missed the engagement at Trafalgar, it meant he would return to England, *thrown out of any share of credit or emolument which would result from an action.*[64]

Sent off to the West Indies Persuasion

In February 1806, Frank was part of a successful action at St Domingo,[65] in the West Indies, where the British fleet captured or destroyed five French ships, interrupting France's stranglehold on the production of sugar and coffee.

Frank's fortune and prospects improved when the *Canopus* captured four French ships. He was rewarded with a gold medal, the thanks of both Houses of Parliament, and a £100 vase from the Patriotic Society of Lloyds.[66]

The Austens returned to Bath from Worthing, and gave up the house in Gay Street. They stayed at Steventon most of January 1806. Jane and Cassandra then went to *Manydown* to stay with the Bigg sisters until late February.

Happy feelings of escape Letters

The Whigs returned to power, in February 1806, after the death of Pitt, with a coalition dubbed the *Ministry of All Talents*. Earl Fitzwilliam and Thomas Erskine were now two of the four Great Officers of State, Fitzwilliam, the Lord President of the Council, Lord Erskine, the Lord Chancellor.

Jane privately rejoiced, Fitzwilliam had the power to ensure D'Arcy could return to England, she trusted him to do so without delay. She wrote eagerly to D'Arcy, confident they would see each other before the end of the year.

The object of the Admiral's fraternal kindness   Persuasion

In March 1806, the Austen women moved into new lodgings in Trim Street, in the busy centre of Bath. Four years earlier, Jane was determined to *do everything in her power to avoid Trim Street.*[67]

On an early Spring morning, Jane, *walking up Milsom Street, had the good fortune to meet*[68] Captain Hunter again. He was in Bath to visit Arthur Phillip, the Colony's first governor, and his commander from the First Fleet, who had retired and was living in the nearby village of Bathampton.

Captain Hunter had rejoined the Navy in 1803, and he was now the paymaster at Portsmouth. After great persistence, his service as governor had been recognised. Eighteen months after his return, Portland, who initially refused to acknowledge him, had written to Lord Hobart, supporting his application for a pension: *Captain Hunter's statement of his services is perfectly correct – in the execution of that service he experienced great difficulties, and suffer'd very great distress. I have always considered him intitled to be remunerated at the publick expense.*[69]

Since their first meeting, Jane had eagerly followed his progress. From the *Naval Chronicle,* she knew he had received a pension for his very valuable services to New South Wales,[70] that he was an accomplished painter,[71] and he had designed an 'unsinkable lifeboat.'[72]

He is rear Admiral of the White   Persuasion

Jane had *the navy lists and newspapers for her authority.*[73] Two years later, in April 1808, she read of his promotion to Rear Admiral of the White.

Hunter had reached the rank of Vice Admiral of the Red by 1815, when Jane began *Persuasion*. Jane used him, *with all his usual frankness and good humour,* as the model for Admiral Croft. In the novel, she described meeting him again, *standing by himself at a printshop window, with his hands behind him, in earnest contemplation of some print, and she not only might have passed him unseen, but was obliged to touch as well as address him before she could catch his notice.*

Ha! is it you? Thank you, thank you. This is treating me like a friend. Here I am, you see, staring at a picture. I can never get by this shop without stopping. But what a thing here is, by way of a boat. What queer fellows your fine painters must be to think that any body would venture their lives in such a shapeless old cockleshell as that…as if they were not to be upset the next moment, which they certainly must be.[74]

I would not venture over a horsepond in it Persuasion

In *Persuasion*, Admiral Croft and Captain Wentworth converse about the poor quality and the risk of some naval ships. Wentworth is satirical, cynical, *The admiralty entertain themselves now and then, with sending a few hundred men to sea, in a ship not fit to be employed. But they have a great many to provide for; and among the thousands that may just as well go to the bottom as not, it is impossible for them to distinguish the very set who may be the least missed.* It was a statement which echoed Hunter's own experience, but Jane graciously had Admiral Croft respond, *Phoo! Phoo! What stuff these young fellows talk.*

Jane Austen's brothers Frank and Charles reached the rank of Admiral, long after her death, Frank in 1830, Charles in 1846. Among her family, it would have been quite a coup for her to count an admiral as her friend.

We shall drive directly to Clifton Northanger Abbey

The Austen women remained at Trim Street until they left Bath in July 1806. They went via Clifton and Bristol, then to Adlestrop in Gloucestershire, for a gathering of the Leighs, Mrs Austen's family.

Their family connexions, which had often surprised her Sense & Sensibility

They stayed at Adlestrop House, Mrs Austen's family home, for ten days at the end of July, and met her cousin Rev Thomas Leigh at the Adlestrop Rectory. The Hon. Mary Leigh had died earlier that month at Stoneleigh Abbey, part of the Leigh family estate. Confusion had arisen over the title to the estate. Various Leigh relatives had come to the Abbey to put forward claims to the late Lord Leigh's estate. Rev Thomas took them there, so Mrs Austen could join the list of claimants. Jane found herself in the house of Thomas Leigh and his wife, Eleanor Watson Wentworth, the Earl of Strafford's grand-daughter.

The Austens went on to Staffordshire, where they stayed with Edward Cooper, now the Rector of Hamstall Ridware. In late September, they returned to Steventon, and from there, they went to Southampton, to join Frank and his fiancée, Mary, and to look for a new home.

A clandestine correspondence Northanger Abbey

Amid the constant rambling of her peripatetic years, Jane's correspondence with D'Arcy became her centre of gravity. She awaited his return to England. She moved about with her family, detached from day to day affairs. She lived only to see him again, and for their private correspondence.

"I went only to the post-office,' said she, 'and reached home before the rain was much. It is my daily errand. I always fetch the letters when I am here. It saves trouble, and is something to get me out..."

"The post-office has a great charm at one period of our lives. When you have lived to my age, you will begin to think letters are never worth going through the rain for."

There was a little blush, and then this answer, "I must not hope to be ever situated as you are, in the midst of every dearest connexion, and therefore I cannot expect that simply growing older should make me indifferent about letters."

"Indifferent!...Letters...are generally a positive curse."

"You are speaking of letters of business; mine are letters of friendship."

"I have often thought them the worst of the two," replied he coolly.

"I can easily believe that letters are very little to you, much less than to me... You have every body dearest to you always at hand, I, probably, never shall again; and therefore till I have outlived all my affections, a post-office, I think, must always have power to draw me out, and in worse weather than today..."

"Time will generally lessen the interest of every attachment not within the daily circle...As an old friend, you will allow me to hope...that ten years hence you may have as many concentrated objects as I have."

It was kindly said, and very far from giving offence. A pleasant 'thank you' seemed meant to laugh it off, but a blush, a quivering lip, a tear in the eye, shewed that it was felt beyond a laugh...

"My dear Jane, what is this I hear? Going to the post-office in the rain!

This must not be, I assure you. You sad girl, how could you do such a thing?... The man who fetches our letters every morning shall inquire for yours too and bring them to you..."

"You are extremely kind," said Jane; "but I cannot give up my early walk...I must walk somewhere, and the post-office is an object..."

"My dear Jane, say no more about it...consider the point as settled."

"Excuse me," said Jane earnestly, "I cannot by any means consent to such an arrangement..."

Jane's solicitude about fetching her own letters had not escaped Emma. She had heard and seen it all; and felt some curiosity to know whether the wet walk of this morning had produced any...She thought there was an air of greater happiness than usual – a glow both of complexion and spirits.

> *She could have made an inquiry or two, as to the expedition and the expense of the Irish mails; it was on her tongues end, but she abstained.* Emma

Nearly five years had passed since Captain Hunter brought her D'Arcy's first letter. Mail travelled very slowly, few ships came directly to England, and often made long stops along the way. When D'Arcy went back to Norfolk Island, her letters could wait months in Sydney for a ship to carry them there.

In his last letter, he told Jane he had asked Fitzwilliam to help him get leave to return to England. Otherwise it seemed likely he would have to go to Van Diemen's Land. Jane trusted Fitzwilliam to help him, but she had heard nothing. She truly hoped there would be no more letters, that instead, there would be a rap at the door, and D'Arcy would be standing there before her. Each letter, much longed for, brought happiness and greater heartache.

Works of Jane Austen

Juvenilia, Volume the First
Frederic & Elfrida
Jack & Alice
Edgar & Emma
Henry & Eliza
Mr Harley
Sir William Mountague
Mr Clifford
The Beautifull Cassandra
Amelia Webster
The Visit
The Mystery
The Three Sisters
Detached Pieces
    A Fragment
    A Beautiful Description of the Different Effects of Sensibility on Different Minds
    The Generous Curate
Ode to Pity

Juvenilia, Volume the Second
Love & Freindship
Lesley Castle

The History of England from the Reign of Henry the 4th to the Death of Charles the 1st
A Collection of Letters
    From a Mother to Her Friend
    From a Young Lady in Distress'd Circumstances to Her Freind
    From a Young Lady Rather Impertinent to Her Freind
    From a Young Lady Very Much in Love to Her Freind
Scraps
    The Female Philosopher
    The First Act of Comedy
    A Letter from a Young Lady
    A Tour through Wales
    A Tale

Juvenilia, Volume the Third
Evelyn
Kitty, or the Bower

Novels
Sense & Sensibility
Pride & Prejudice
Northanger Abbey
Mansfield Park
Emma
Persuasion
Lady Susan

Minor & unfinished works
The Watsons
Sanditon
Sir Charles Grandison, or The Happy Man
Plan of a Novel, according to hints from various quarters
Opinions of Mansfield Park
Opinions of Emma
Three Evening Prayers
Miscellaneous Verse
Charades

Letters
Letters to her sister, Cassandra, and others

Acknowledgements & Apology

STARTING OUT on this project was a daunting task. I felt I lacked the knowledge and ability to do the story justice. I was prepared to write an outline, a few quick notes to give to someone else who had the experience to turn it into a reality. Alas, I never found the willing scribe, and the few I approached could see risks in tackling such a complex and speculative history. I continued to do the research and to give a great deal of thought to how best to tell Jane and D'Arcy's story.

At the Darwin library, I found some assistance from John Richards, a bemused librarian, and his partner, Diane. While they did not exactly give me encouragement and hope, they directed me to useful source material and arranged loans of helpful books from other libraries.

Again, apprehension, anxiety and fear of failure led me to write a few thousand words which I submitted to the London Review of Books, as I felt that someone in England might be interested to take over the story. Needless to say, it was returned, rejected.

At this point, I decided to visit the places where Jane Austen had lived and worked, in Hampshire, Kent and London, and to follow D'Arcy's movements from Ireland to Yorkshire and London. My wife Victoria and I received some valuable help from libraries, archives and record offices, particularly in Sheffield, Stafford and London. At last, it seemed the project was becoming a reality.

ACKNOWLEDGEMENTS & AN APOLOGY

I felt, if Tyso Saul Hancock could send me a cask of Constantia from the old Cape vineyards, I could sit back with a glass, like Elinor Dashwood in *Sense & Sensibility*. Perhaps Warren Hastings could supply some rich Madeira, to help light my passageway down two hundred years.

After reading all of Jane Austen's writing, from her earliest juvenilia to her last verses, we realised the story of Jane & D'Arcy was the key to understanding the recurring themes and connections in her stories, her sensitivities and her pride. It was a key that her readers and scholars had sought for centuries, and strangely, had missed.

Victoria has edited and given the story a consistent voice. I thank her first. Then the readers along the way who gave me helpful comments and encouragement, Ruth Brebner in Darwin, the McNamara family in Melbourne, Alexandra Shiga and Alan Walker in Sydney, and Giles and Ursula de la Mare in London.

My hope is that all readers will find enjoyment and satisfaction in *Folly is Not Always Folly*, the first of two volumes recording the lives of Jane Austen and D'Arcy Wentworth.

I apologise to Jane Austen for my wilful intimacy, in calling her by her Christian name throughout the story. For our generation such use is quite proper, but speaking of her character, Jane Fairfax, in *Emma*, she made it clear she loathed the familiarity of being addressed as Jane.

Jane indeed! – You will observe that I have not yet indulged myself in calling her by that name, even to you. Think, then, what I must have endured in hearing it bandied..with all the vulgarity of needless repetition, and all the insolence of imaginary superiority.

Wal Walker

Abbreviations used in the endnotes

ADB	Australian Dictionary of Biography
AONSW	New South Wales State Archives
BT	Bonwick Transcripts
CO	Colonial Office document
HMC	Historical Manuscripts Commission, UK
HRA	Historical Records of Australia
HRNSW	Historical Records of New South Wales
JASNA	Jane Austen Society of North America
JRAHS	Journal of the Royal Australian Historical Society
ML	Mitchell Library, Sydney
NLA	National Library of Australia, Canberra
THRA	Tasmanian Historical Research Association
WWM	Wentworth Woodhouse Muniments, Sheffield

Endnotes

Preface

1. Jane Austen to Cassandra Austen, Thursday, January 14, 1796.
2. J.E. Austen-Leigh, *Memoir of Jane Austen*, Richard Bentley & Son, London, 1871, cited hereafter as *Memoir of JA*.
3. Anna Lefroy to James Edward Austen Leigh, December 1864.
4. *Memoir of JA*, Chapters I and II.
5. Caroline Mary Craven Austen, *My Aunt Jane Austen*. Jane Austen Society, 1952, page 1–2.
6. Caroline had been a part of James Edward's household for more than twenty years, since the death of their mother, Mary Lloyd.
7. Caroline Austen, *op cit*.
8. John Lanchester, *Family Romance*, Prologue. Faber & Faber. London. 2007.
9. Arthur Helps, *Life of Columbus*, George Bell & Sons, London, 1868, page 32.

Chapter 1
D'Arcy Wentworth
The rapture of delightful expectation
Sense & Sensibility

1. From *Lambeth Will: Lambeth Strand*, 1640, included in *Early Stuart Libels*, a web based edition of early seventeenth century poems libel from manuscript sources.
2. The English Pale comprised four eastern counties: Dublin, Kildare, Louth and Meath.
3. D'Arcy Wentworth Sinnamon, *Ellis Papers*, ML. D'Arcy's father was one of 119 linen merchants, exporters and dealers in County Armagh, *Belfast Newsletter*, 7 July 1758.
4. The house on the Killicomaine Road, inherited by D'Arcy's elder sister Martha Sinnamon, remained in the family until the 1960s when it was demolished and sub-divided. It now forms part of *Craigavon*.
5. Lough Neagh, the largest lake in Great Britain, is bordered by five counties: Armagh, Tyrone, Londonderry, Antrim and Down.
6. Sir R. Reading wrote to the Royal Society in 1688: *One pearl was bought for fifty shillings which weighed 36 carats and was worth fully £40*. Doyle,T, *Tours of Ulster*, Hodges & Smith, Dublin. 1854.
7. Newry Canal, the first major canal in Britain, nearly 20 miles long, was built between 1731 and 1741, linking the Tyrone coalfields to the Irish Sea. Two hundred men with picks and shovels dug and bricked the canal, built a network of fourteen locks, towpaths, bridges, laybys, stables and bothys.
8. *Belfast Newsletter*, 7 July 1758, 29 April 1759, 22 November 1763
9. *Belfast Newsletter*, 1 February 1765.

10 *Belfast Newsletter,* 23–27 October 1778.
11 *The Surgeons of Dublin, since the time of Queen Elizabeth, have been incorporated with the company of Barbers. Repeated applications have been made to Parliament, to procure an act of incorporation for the Surgeons; but notwithstanding the example of the most polished nations in Europe, every attempt to dissolve this absurd and disgraceful union has hitherto been unsuccessful... As there is no distinct corporation of Surgeons, so there is no regular mode of surgical education...The only esteemed regular method in Dublin, of educating a young man to Surgery, is, by indenting him for five years to a Surgeon. After serving his time, he is considered as a Surgeon, and may commence practitioner. The Medical Register for the Year 1783,* London, page 165.
12 J. Taylor, *Autobiography of a Lancashire Lawyer,* Bolton. 1883, page 22.
13 *Belfast Newsletter,* 16–20 March 1795.
14 *The Works of Rev, John Wesley,* Volume III, London, 1829, diary entry April 1767.
15 Seamus Heaney, *Whatever you say, say nothing,* from *North,* Faber & Faber, 1975.
16 *Belfast Newsletter,* 17 January 1800.
17 The Irish Declaration of Independence did not address discrimination against Irish Catholics and their entrenched disadvantage.
18 *Belfast Newsletter,* 3–7 January 1783.
19 Thomas Dawson, *Testimonial,* 27 January 1786. Wentworth Papers, ML.
20 William Wentworth (D'Arcy's nephew) to his cousin William Bucknall, 17 June 1821, ML.
21 J. Archocky to David Killican, 22 December 1785. Wentworth Papers. ML.
22 *Belfast Newsletter,* 11–15 March 1785.
23 Arthur Young, *A Six Months Tour through the North of England,* Volume I, London 1771, page 245–270.
24 J. Hill to D'Arcy Wentworth, 19 February 1822, quoting Rev Blacker of Carrick. *Blacker Manuscripts,* Armagh County Museum.
25 *Daily Universal Register,* 30 June 1785.
26 *The Gentleman's Magazine,* November 1809, Volume 79, Part 2, page 1024.
27 The Wentworths of North Emsal became extinct on the death of Sir Butler-Cavendish Wentworth, on 3 December 1741; the Wentworths of Woolley and Hickleton, on the death of Godfrey Wentworth, on 18 January 1789; the Wentworths of West Bretton, on the death of Sir Thomas Blacket Wentworth in 1792. Wentworths descended from the Earl of Strafford, became extinct on the death of the 5th Earl Frederick Thomas Wentworth, grandson of Peter Wentworth of Henbury, brother of the 1st earl, on 7 August 1799.
28 Alice Effie Murray, *History of the Commercial and Financial Relations between England and Ireland from the Period of the Restoration,* King & Son, London, 1907, Chapter 12.
29 *Journal of the House of Lords,* Volume 37, 13 July 1785. British History Online.
30 *Ibid,* 18 July 1785.
31 The Irish Parliament did not agree to Pitt the Younger's resolutions for improving commercial intercourse. There was no compromise to satisfy objections by British traders and those of the Irish.
32 Architect, Ralph Tunnicliffe based his design on Colen Campbell's plans for Lord Tylney's *Wanstead House* in Essex. Colen Campbell, a Scottish architect, progressed the Georgian Palladian style of architecture highly desired by the Whig landowners. He aligned his work with Roman architect Vitruvius Pollo, who believed a building should be solid, useful & beautiful, *firmitas, utilitas* & *venustas.* Jane Austen used the name Tilney in *Northanger Abbey.*
33 From Arthur Young, *op cit.*
34 *The Daily Universal Register,* 28 February 1785. A tailzie was a deed that enabled a landowner to set conditions on the disposal of his property after his death. From 1688 the Register of Tailzies was used to determine the validity of the title. To ensure continuation of the family name in the district, the tailzie might restrict the line of inheritance to males, as in *Pride & Prejudice,* or to a female member of the family whose husband would take his wife's surname, effectively becoming a member of her family. Jane Austen's brother Edward and his heirs took the name Knight. Mrs Austen's brother James Leigh added Perrot to his surname to inherit the estate of his mother's uncle, Thomas Perrot. Only after 1848 could land be removed from entailment.
35 Isaac Newton was a Secretary of the Good Humour Club. Laurence Sterne, author of *The Life & Opinions of Tristram Shandy Gentleman,* was a patron.
36 *Daily Universal Register,* 1 September 1785. Three months before, a hot air balloon had crashed in Tullamore starting a fire that

spread across thatched rooves and burnt as many as 130 houses.
37 By *Florizel* out of *Maiden*, from James Weatherby, *Racing Calendar*, London 1785.
38 The first Great St Leger stakes, run on 24 September 1776, was won by Lord Rockingham's brown bay filly by *Sampson*.
39 By *Highflyer* out of *Mopsqueezer*. Weatherby, *op cit*, page 121.
40 *Ibid*, by *Alfred* out of *Rosebud*.
41 *Ibid*, by *Tantrum* out of *Pilgrim's Filter*.
42 *State of the East India Company's Affairs with a View to the Intended Bill*, Pamphlet, 1768.
43 Jane Austen, *Persuasion*, Volume I, Chapter I.
44 William Mason, *The Dean & the Squire, a Political Eclogue*, J. Debrett, London, 1782.
45 Grosvenor Square is part of the Mayfair property of the Duke of Westminster. Earl Fitzwilliam inherited the lease on 4 Grosvenor Square from his uncle, the Marquess of Rockingham, whose father had purchased it in 1742. The family remained in the house for 190 years, surrendering the lease in 1931, when the Italian Ambassador, who resides there today, was granted a 200 year lease.
46 Royal College of Surgeons. *Company of Surgeons Examination Book, 1745-1800*, page 11. Mate was a Royal Navy rank, and included a Boatswain's Mate and a Carpenter's Mate.
47 London, Westminster, Middlesex, St George's, St Bartholomew's, Guy's and St Thomas's hospitals.
48 Tobias Smollett, *The Adventures of Roderick Random*, London, 1748, Chapter XVII.
49 *The Annual Register* in 1788 reported Gainsborough's death: August 2nd. *At his house in Pall Mall about 2 o'clock in the morning, Mr. Gainsborough, the painter, one of the greatest geniuses that ever adorned any age or any nation, died. His death was occasioned by a wen on the neck, which grew internally and so large as to obstruct the passages. The effects of it became violent, a few months since, from a cold caught one morning in Westminster Hall at the trial of Mr. Hastings.*
50 Percivall Pott, from his Preface to *Observations on the Fistula Lachrymalis*, 1775, page 176. Quoted by Jessie Dobson in her profile of him for the Hunterian Museum, Royal College of Surgeons.
51 Alexander Patton to D'Arcy Wentworth, 30 November 1785, Wentworth Papers, ML.

Chapter 2
Jane Austen
Perfect Felicity is not the property of Mortals
A Collection of Letters

1 *Memoir of JA*, Chapter III.
2 Francis Cullum was paid to care for Thomas Leigh and George Austen. Thomas died aged 74 in 1821. Francis cared for George Austen until his own death in 1834. His son took over as carer for four years until George's death aged 72, in 1838.
3 Rev George Austen to Susannah Walter, 8 November, 1772. *Austen Papers*, page 28.
4 *Until the mid-late 18th century, an heir was effectively the trustee of a family estate, a protection against it being divided; an important consideration for a family's social status. The laws of probate in England were governed by primogeniture – the right of the first born male to inherit an entire estate, and entailment. That right transferred to a male descendent where there was no first born son. If there was no heir creditors were more exposed, making it far more difficult to obtain credit, hence the attraction of entailing an estate on another male descendant. Only when there were no males left would an estate be broken up equally amongst surviving females. This was a catastrophe – each parcel would then pass to each woman's eldest male heir, in accordance with the prevailing laws, basically meaning each woman got nothing, and the estate would be broken up and unable to produce a sizeable income. Everyone lost.* Ruth Brebner. SFNT. August 2012.
5 David Nokes, *Jane Austen, A Life*, London, Fourth Estate, 1997, page 77.
6 Jane Austen, *Northanger Abbey*, Volume I, Chapter XIV.
7 Jane Austen, *Lady Susan*.
8 J. A. Giles, *William of Malmesbury's Chronicle of the Kings of England*, London, 1847, page 491.
9 Jane Austen, *The History of England*, Juvenilia, Volume the Second.
10 Jane Austen, *Northanger Abbey*, Volume I, Chapter II. The destruction was complete by the time Jane came to Abbey House School. The Abbey had been pillaged extensively for building materials; the lead, glass and facing stone had been removed to re-use elsewhere;

but the ruins that remained were enormous, even today the huge flint cores of the walls are a stark reminder of the power of the medieval church. One can understand Henry's desire to consolidate his own position in England following the War of the Roses; without being beholden to the Church of Rome. It was more than just an argument over a divorce.
11 *Ibid*, Volume II, Chapter VIII.
12 *Ibid*, Volume II, Chapter V.
13 Ranked by the sum of tax raised, Reading was the tenth biggest city in England.
14 The Reading Youths were enthusiastic bellringers. The *Reading Mercury* reported on 4 May 1756, that to honour of the Duke of Cumberland's birthday, on 26 April, they rang *Ten Thousand and eighty Quadruple changes, otherwise Grandsire Cators, which was performed in Six Hours and Thirty Minutes, being the first Time of their attempting the Peal*.
15 Oscar Wilde, *The Ballad of Reading Gaol*, 1898.
16 Jane Austen, *Northanger Abbey*, Volume II, Chapter VIII.
17 Jane Austen, *Detached Pieces*, Juvenilia, Volume the First.
18 R.A. Austen-Leigh, *Austen Papers 1704–1856*, Spottiswoode Ballantyne, Colchester, 1942, page 37. cited hereafter as *Austen Papers*.
19 W. & R.A. Austen-Leigh, *Jane Austen Her Life and Letters, a Family Record*. London, Smith Elder & Co, 1913, Chapter II. Cited hereafter as *A Family Record*.
20 David Nokes, *op cit*, page 85.
21 Lord Craven established racing at Lambourn on the Berkshire Downs in 1777, his Craven Stakes are still run at Newmarket. Today Peter Townsend, leader of *The Who*, lives at Ashdown House.
22 See Nigel Sutcliffe, *Reading: A Horse-Racing Town*. Two Rivers Press, Reading. 2010, page 16.
23 Jane Austen, *Kitty, or the Bower*, Juvenilia, Volume the Third.
24 Jane Austen, *Sense & Sensibility*, Volume I, Chapter X.
25 Jane Austen, *Northanger Abbey*, Volume I, Chapter III.
26 Jane Austen, *Kitty, or the Bower*, Juvenilia, Volume the Third.
27 Rev. Gilbert White, *The Natural History of Selborne*. Volume I, London, 1822, pages 175–176.
28 Jane Austen, *Sanditon*, Chapter I.
29 Jane Austen, *Kitty, or the Bower*, Juvenilia, Volume the Third.
30 Jane Austen, *Sense & Sensibility*, Volume I, Chapter IX.
31 Jane Austen, *Persuasion*, Volume I, Chapter XII.
32 Jane Austen, *Sanditon*, Chapter I.
33 Jane Austen, *Kitty, or the Bower*, Juvenilia, Volume the Third.
34 *Ibid*.
35 Anna Austen Lefroy, quoted in *A Family Record*, page 49.
36 Jane Austen, *Kitty, or the Bower*, Juvenilia, Volume the Third.
37 Jane Austen, *Lady Susan*.
38 David Nokes, *op cit*, page 87.
39 Jane Austen, *Lady Susan*.
40 Eliza de Feuillide to Phylly Walton, 27 March, 1782. *Austen Papers*, page 101.
41 Eliza de Feuillide to Phylly Walton, 7 May, 1784. *Austen Papers*, page 111.
42 *A Family Record*, Chapter III.
43 Eliza de Feuillide to Phylly Walter, 27 March 1782, *Austen Papers*, page 100.
44 Eliza de Feuillide to Phylly Walton, 27 March, 1782. *Austen Papers*, page 101.
45 Eliza Hancock to Phylly Walter, 16 May 1780, *Austen Papers*, page 90.
46 Eliza de Feuillide to Phylly Walter, 1 May 1783, *ibid*, page 107.
47 Eliza de Feuillide to Phylly Walton, 9 April, 1797, *ibid*, page 123.
48 Eliza de Feuillide to Phylly Walter, 7 May 1784, *Austen Papers*, page 112.
49 T. S. Hancock to Eliza Hancock, 20 December 1770, *ibid*, page 53.
50 T. S. Hancock to Philadelphia Hancock, 23 September 1772, *ibid*, page 66.
51 T. S. Hancock to Philadelphia Hancock, 31 January 1772, *ibid*, page 60.
52 Jane Austen, *Jack & Alice*, Juvenilia, Volume the First.
53 Eliza de Feuillide to Phylly Walter, 16 November 1787, *Austen Papers*, page 126.
54 Jane Austen, *Mansfield Park*, Volume I, Chapter XIII.
55 *Ibid*, Volume I, Chapter XVIII.
56 *The Wonder-A Woman Keeps a Secret*, 1714 by Susannah Centlivre (1667–1723).
57 *The Chances*, 1647 by John Fletcher, adapted by David Garrick in 1773.
58 Jane Austen, *Lesley Castle*, Juvenilia, Volume the Second.

59 Eliza de Feuillide to Phylly Walter, 16 November 1787, *Austen Papers,* page 126.
60 *A Family Record,* Chapter IV.
61 John Burgoyne, *Maid of the Oaks,* 1774.
62 David Garrick, *Bon Ton,* op cit.
63 Phylly Walter to James Walter, 19 September 1787, *Austen Papers,* page 126.
64 Jane Austen, *Lady Susan.*
65 Ibid.
66 George Austen paid Mme La Tournelle at Abbey House School, £35.19.00 on 20 August 1785, £36. 2. 6 on 23 January 1786, and £16.10.0 on 2 January 1787. See Deirdre Le Faye, *A Chronology of Jane Austen and Family,* Cambridge University Press, 2006.
67 Jane Austen, *The Generous Curate,* Juvenilia, Volume the First.
68 Tobias Smollett, *The Adventures of Peregrine Pickle*. Volume I, Chapter XXI, London, 1751.
69 Jane Austen, *Love & Freindship*, Juvenilia, Volume the Second.

Chapter 3
Nabobs, gold mohrs & palanquins
Sense & Sensibility

She left England & I have since heard is at present the favourite Sultana of the great Mogul
Frederic & Elfrida

1 Jane Austen, *Love & Freindship.* Juvenilia, Volume the Second.
2 Susanna died thirty one years later, in 1768. She was buried with William, his first wife Rebecca and their first child, a daughter Hampson, born two years before Philadelphia, who died aged two.
3 *Daily Advertiser,* 31 December 1750, quoted by Ian Maxted, *Exeter Working Papers in Book History,* online.
4 Jane Austen, *Kitty, or the Bower,* Juvenilia, Volume the Third.
5 Jane Austen, *The beautiful Cassandra,* Juvenilia, Volume the First.
6 *A Family Record,* Chapter III.
7 William Austen-Leigh and Montagu George Knight, *Chawton Manor & Its Owners,* London, Smith Elder & Co, 1911, Chapter VII.
8 *Austen Papers,* page 34.
9 Jane Austen, *Kitty, or the Bower,* Juvenilia, Volume the Third.
10 President & Council of Fort William in Bengal to Hon'ble Court of Directors for the Affairs of the Hon'ble United Company of Merchants of England Trading to the East Indies, 29 December 1759. *Fort William - India House Correspondence,* Volume II, Public Series, ed. B.A Saletore, National Archives of India, Delhi, 1957, page 451.
11 *Five Letters from a Free Merchant in Bengal to Warren Hastings Esq.* London, 1777.
12 Fort William to Court, 4 February 1750. *Fort William – India House Correspondence,* Volume I, ed., K. K. Datta, National Archives of India, Delhi, 1958, page 477.
13 Fort William to Court, 30 January 1757, *Fort William -India House Correspondence,* Volume II, *op cit,* page 185.
14 Court to Fort William, 13 March 1761. *Fort William -India House Correspondence,* Volume III, Public Series, ed. R.R.Sethi, National Archives of India, Delhi, 1968, page 88.
15 Fort William to Court, 12 November 1761, *ibid*, page 375.
16 *Austen Papers,* page 36.
17 G. B. Malleson, *Life of Warren Hastings,* London 1894, page 81.
18 The Hastings' family estate at Daylesford had been sold, but his grandfather and guardian still served there as rector. The Leighs lived in the neighbouring village of Adlestrop.
19 L.J. Trotter, *Warren Hastings,* Oxford Clarendon Press, 1892, page 27.
20 Anselm Beaumont, *Letterbooks,* Letter 117, Cape of Good Hope 1765, online.
21 *A Family Record,* Chapter III.
22 *Austen Papers,* page 37.
23 Hon'ble Court of Directors for the Affairs of the Hon'ble United Company of Merchants of England Trading to the East Indies to President & Council of Fort William in Bengal, 16 March & 11 November 1768, *Fort William -India House Correspondence,* Volume V, Public Series, ed. S.N. Sen, National Archives of India, Delhi, 1949, pages 89 & 151.
24 Lord Robert Clive to the House of Commons, 30 March 1772.
25 Tyso to Philadelphia Hancock, 23 November 1769, *Austen Papers,* page 40.
26 R. Walsh, E. Littell, J. Smith, eds, *Life of Lord Clive,* Volume 38, *Museum of Foreign Literature, Science and Art*. Philadelphia, 1839, page 377.
27 Tyso to Philadelphia Hancock, 7 September

1770. *Austen Papers,* page 50.
28. Court to Fort William, 17 March 1769, *Fort William -India House Correspondence,* Volume V, *op cit,* page 196.
29. Tyso to Philadelphia Hancock, 28 November 1769. *Austen Papers,* page 40.
30. Tyso to Philadelphia Hancock, 17 January 1770, *ibid,* page 42.
31. Fort William to Court, 25 January 1770. *Fort William -India House Correspondence,* Volume VI, ed. K.D.Bhargava, National Archives of India, Delhi, 1960, page 182.
32. Court to Fort William, 10 April 1771, *ibid,* page 106.
33. Tyso Hancock was accredited as a surgeon in 1738 by the Worshipful Company of Barber-Surgeons in London. He went out to India in 1743.
34. Tyso to Philadelphia Hancock, 23 November 1769. *Austen Papers,* page 40.
35. Tyso to Philadelphia Hancock, 23 September 1772. *ibid,* page 65.
36. Tyso to Eliza Hancock, 4 April 1772, *ibid,* page 61.
37. Tyso to Philadelphia Hancock, 31 January 1772, *ibid,* page 60.
38. Tyso to Philadelphia Hancock, 29 March 1772, *ibid,* page 60.
39. Tyso to Philadelphia Hancock, 22 June 1773, *ibid,* page 70.
40. Mrs George Austen to Mrs William Hampson Walter. 8 November 1772, *ibid,* page 28.
41. Eliza de Feuillide to Phylly Walter, 23 May 1786, *ibid,* page 118.
42. Jane Austen, *Kitty, or the Bower.* Juvenilia, Volume the Third.
43. Ian Maxted, *op cit.*
44. Tyso to Philadelphia Hancock, 17 January 1770. *Austen Papers,* page 43.
45. Jane to Cassandra Austen, 8 January, 1801.
46. Jane Austen, *Kitty, or the Bower.* Juvenilia, Volume the Third.
47. Tyso to Philadelphia Hancock, 6 December 1771. *Austen Papers,* page 58.
48. Brigade Surgeon Henry Elmsley Busteed, *Echoes of Old Calcutta,* London, 1908, page 138.
49. Tyso to Philadelphia Hancock, 23 November 1769, *Austen Papers,* page 39.
50. J. Woodman to Warren Hastings, 26 December 1781, *ibid,* page 98.
51. Tyso to Philadelphia Hancock, 17 January 1770, *ibid,* page 43.
52. In 1786, the Company acknowledged the risks of the trade in precious stones used to remit money home. *The Calcutta Gazette* of 19 October 1786 reported: *The Honourable Court of Directors having permitted Mr Leon Prager to proceed to Benares and reside there for the purpose of trading in Pearls, Diamonds and other precious Stones, in order to afford to individuals means of remitting their property to Europe, and to secure to the Company their accustomed duties.*
53. Tyso to Philadelphia Hancock, 23 November 1769, *Austen Papers,* page 39.
54. Tyso to Philadelphia Hancock, 15 March 1770, *ibid,* page 48.
55. Tyso to Philadelphia Hancock, 7 September 1770, *ibid,* page 51.
56. Tyso to Eliza Hancock, 8 April 1771, *ibid,* page 55.
57. Tyso to Philadelphia Hancock, 21 November 1771, *ibid,* page 57.
58. Tyso to Philadelphia Hancock, 22 May 1775, *ibid,* page 81.
59. Tyso to Philadelphia Hancock, 28 August 1771, *ibid,* page 56.
60. Tyso to Philadelphia Hancock, 11 December 1772, *ibid,* page 68.
61. Tyso to Philadelphia Hancock, 25 March 1775, *ibid,* page 79.
62. Tyso to Philadelphia Hancock, *ibid,* pages 37, 66 and 74..
63. Tyso to Philadelphia Hancock, 23 September 1772, *ibid,* page 66.
64. Tyso to Philadelphia Hancock, 7 November 1773, *ibid,* page 74.
65. Tyso to Philadelphia Hancock, 3 September 1773, *ibid,* page 73.
66. Henry Austen to James Edward Austen-Leigh, *ibid,* page 17.
67. *Fort William -India House Correspondence,* Volume II, *op cit,* page xlii.
68. *Brick Lane Circle* website, *Robert Clive.*
69. *Journals of the House of Commons,* 21 May 1773, Volume 34, page 330.
70. Under the terms of the *Regulating Act,* 1773.
71. Thomas Babington Macaulay, "Warren Hastings" *Edinburgh Review,* LXXIV, Oct 1841, page 160.
72. Busteed, *op cit.*
73. Alexander Macrabie, Sheriff of Calcutta, 1775. Quoted in S.Chaudhuri, *Calcutta the Living City,* Oxford University Press, 1990, Volume 1, page 46.
74. Mme Grand later settled in Paris and became the wife of Talleyrand, first Prime Minister of France. He called her *stupid as a rose.*

Comparing her to his former mistress Mme de Staël, he said, *one must have loved a genius to appreciate the happiness of loving a fool.*
75 Quoted by D.Kincaid, *British Social Life in India,* Routledge & Kegan Paul, London, 1938, page 113.
76 Macaulay, *op cit.*
77 Busteed, *op cit,* page 116.
78 Eric Rolls, *Sojourners.* University of Queensland Press. 1992, page 385.
79 *Ibid,* page 19.
80 Court to Fort William, 26 March 1766, *Fort William -India House Correspondence,* Public Series, Volume IV, ed. C.S. Srinivaschari, National Archives of India, Delhi, 1962, page 151.
81 Court to Fort William, 12 July 1782, *Fort William -India House Correspondence,* Volume IX, *op cit,* page 61.
82 Court to Fort William, 27 March 1787, *Fort William -India House Correspondence,* Public Series, Volume X, ed. R.Sinh, National Archives of India, Delhi, 1972, page 20.
83 *The Times,* 3 August 1792.
84 E. Backhouse & J. Bland, *Annals & Memoirs of the Court of Peking,* Boston, 1914, p. 331.
85 G.W. Collen, *The Baronetage of England, Revised, Corrected & Continued,* London, 1840, page 257.
86 Tyso to Philadelphia Hancock, 26 August 1774, *Austen Papers,* page 76.
87 Philip Dormer Stanhope, *Genuine Memoirs of Asiaticus,* London, 1784, Letter VII, October 1774.
88 Tyso to Philadelphia Hancock, 20 February 1775, *Austen Papers,* page 78.
89 Tyso to Philadelphia Hancock, 20 May 1775, *ibid,* page 79.
90 Tyso to Philadelphia Hancock, 7 November 1773, *ibid,* page 74.
91 Philip Dormer Stanhope, *ibid,* Letter XIX, May 1778, Madras.
92 Philadelphia Austen to Warren Hastings, 3 March 1780, *Austen Papers,* page 86.
93 Warren Hastings to Lord Mansfield, 21 March 1774.
94 Today, the Aliah University in Kolkata, West Bengal.
95 *The Bhagvat-Geeta or Dialogues of Kreeshna & Arjoon,* translated by Charles Wilkins Senior Merchant in the service of the Honourable the East India Company, on their Bengal Establishment, London, 1785.
96 Warren Hastings, evidence to the House of Commons, 1787.
97 Court to Fort William, 16 March 1784, *Fort William -India House Correspondence,* Volume IX, *op cit,* page 151.
98 *Fort William -India House Correspondence,* Foreign & Secret, Volume XV, eds. C.H. Phillips & B.B. Misra, National Archives of India, Delhi, 1963, Introduction, page i-ii.
99 Brian Young, "A Cheat, a Sharper and a Swindler," *London Review of Books,* 24 May 2001
100 *A Bill for Vesting the Affairs of the East India Company in the hands of certain Commissioners, for the benefit of the Proprietors and the Public.* 24 Geo. III, Journals of the Commons, page 743.
101 Edmund Burke, 1 December 1783, *Writings & Speeches,* Volume II, London 1787.
102 *Fort William -India House Correspondence,* Public Series, Volume V, *op cit,* page i.
103 Edmund Burke to Elizabeth Francis, 20 April 1787, *Correspondence of the Rt Hon. Edmund Burke, between the year 1744 and the period of his decease 1797,* edited by Charles William, Earl Fitzwilliam and Lieut. General Sir Richard Bourke, KCB, London,1844, Volume III, page 56.
104 Brian Young, *op cit.*
105 William Cowper, *The Task,* 1785.
106 *Fort William -India House Correspondence,* Public Series, Volume IX, *op cit,* page iv.
107 *House of Lords Journal,* Volume Thirty Eight, proceedings 21 February 1788.
108 The Hon. Horace Walpole to Sir Horace Mann, Letter CCVIII, July 13, 1773.
109 *Daily Universal Register,* 18 February, 1788.
110 Edmund Burke, *Works of the Rt Hon Edmund Burke,* Volume 10, Boston, Little Brown, 1865–67.
111 Macaulay, *op cit,* page 183.
112 Thomas Erskine to Bishop Shipley, quoted in Busteed, *op cit,* page 344.
113 Quoted by Patrick Turnbull, *Warren Hastings,* New English Library, London, 1975, page 222.
114 From the inscription on the memorial monument to Warren Hastings in Westminster Abbey.
115 Mark Twain, *Following the Equator,* 1897, Chapter 52
116 Eliza de Feuillide to Phylly Walter, 22 August 1788, *Austen Papers,* page 133.
117 Phylly Walter to James Walter, 21 April 1788, *ibid,* page 129.
118 George Austen to Warren Hastings,

8 November 1794. *Austen Papers*, page 226.
119 Jane to Cassandra Austen, 30 November 1800.
120 Eliza de Feuillide to Phylly Walter, 22 August 1788, *Austen Papers*, page 133.

Chapter 4
Jane at home in Steventon
One does not love a place the less for having suffered in it
Persuasion

1 Jane to Cassandra Austen, 18 September 1796.
2 Jane Austen, *Mansfield Park*, Volume I, Chapter II.
3 Jane Austen, *Pride & Prejudice*, Volume I, Chapter XVIII.
4 Reproduced in C. Tomalin, *Jane Austen a Life*, Vintage Books, 1999, page 40.
5 Jane Austen, *Mansfield Park*, Volume I, Chapter V.
6 Mrs Austen wrote a cheerful letter in verse to Gilbert East, who was late returning to school, encouraging him to return with: *we study all day, except when we play.*
7 Jane Austen, *Lady Susan.*
8 Jane to Cassandra Austen, 5 May 1801.
9 *Memoir of JA*, Chapter I.
10 Jane to Frank Austen, 25 September 1813.
11 Jane to Cassandra Austen, 27–28 October 1798.
12 Jane to Cassandra Austen, 17–18 January 1809.
13 Jane Austen, *Northanger Abbey*, Volume I, Chapter I.
14 Constance Hill, *Jane Austen, Her Homes & Her Friends*, 1923, Chapter VIII.
15 George Chard (1765–1849) was appointed assistant organist in 1787. He composed many anthems and glees. His French harpsichord is in the Victoria & Albert Museum.
16 Jane Austen, *Emma*, Volume II, Chapter XIV. The music she enjoyed playing included a collection of Scots songs, and pieces by Handel – a minuet and a song.
17 *Memoir of JA*, Chapter II.
18 Jane to Cassandra Austen, 9 January, 1796.
19 Jane to Cassandra Austen, 14 January 1796
20 *A Family Record*, page 16.
21 Jane to Cassandra Austen, 18 December 1798.
22 Jane Austen, *Persuasion*, Volume II, Chapter V.
23 J. E. Austen-Leigh, *Recollections of the Early Days of the Vine Hunt*, London 1865, page 8.
24 *Shooting was one of the major pursuits of both the aristocracy and the gentry, who protected their monopoly rights over beast and bird by savage game laws...No tenant, however extensive his farm, might shoot so much as a rabbit on it... night poaching carried with it the penalty of transportation, and in years to come many a prosperous Australian could trace his ancestry to some sturdy but unlucky poacher.* D. Marshall, *Industrial England 1776–1851*, Routledge & Kegan Paul, London, 1973, p. 64.
25 Jane to Cassandra Austen, 24 & 27 October, 1798.
26 Aesop, *Sporting Reminiscences of Hampshire from 1745 to 1862*, London, Chapman & Hill, page 33.
27 J.E. Austen-Leigh, *op cit*, page 22.
28 Jane to Cassandra Austen, 8 & 9 January 1799.
29 Jane Austen, *Mansfield Park*. Volume I, Chapter IX.
30 *Memoir of JA.*
31 Jane Austen, *Mansfield Park*, Volume I, Chapter X.
32 Jane Austen, *Mansfield Park*, Volume I, Chapter VI.
33 *Ibid*, Volume II, Chapter VII.
34 Jane Austen, 'The Female Philosopher,' in *Scraps*, Juvenilia, Volume the Second.
35 Jane Austen, *Mansfield Park*, Volume II, Chapter VIII.
36 *Ibid*, Volume II, Chapter XI.
37 Jane Austen, *A Collection of Letters*. Juvenilia, Volume the Second.
38 Jane Austen, *The Visit*, Juvenilia, Volume the First.
39 Jane Austen, *Emma*, Volume III, Chapter IV.
40 Jane to Cassandra Austen, 6 June 1811.
41 Jane to Cassandra Austen, 8 September 1816.
42 Jane to Cassandra Austen, 1 July 1808.
43 Jane to Cassandra Austen, 20 November 1800.
44 Jane Austen, *A Fragment Written to inculcate the Practise of Virtue*, Juvenilia, Volume the First.
45 Jane Austen, *Henry & Eliza*, Juvenilia, Volume the First.
46 William Cobbett, *Rural Rides*, Hampshire, 6 August 1823, London, 1830, page 176.
47 *Ibid*, Hampshire, 6 August 1823, page 424.
48 Jane Austen, *Love & Freindship*, Juvenilia, Volume the Second.
49 *The Gentleman's Magazine*, Volume C, 1807, page 327.

50 *The European Magazine*. Volume XLVI, July 1804. Quoted *from the tablet on the South wall above his tomb in the Church of St Michael at Enborne*. It no longer appears to be there.
51 Jane Austen, 'The Female Philosopher,' in *Scraps*, Juvenilia, Volume the Second.
52 Sophia Sentiment to the Editor, *The Loiterer*, No 9, Saturday, March 28, 1789.
53 Phylly Walter to James Walter, 23 July 1788, *Austen Papers*.
54 Eliza de Feuillide to Phylly Walter, 22 August 1788, *Austen Papers*.
55 Eliza de Feuillide to Phylly Walton, 9 April, 1797, *Austen Papers*, page 123.
56 Jane Austen, *Persuasion*, Volume I, Chapter I.
57 Jane Austen, *Frederic & Elfrida*, Juvenilia, Volume the First. Charlotte's Aunt's house would have been on the eastern side of Portland Place, adjacent to the Tybourne, one of London's three vanished streams. It rose in the hills of Hampstead Heath, flowed through Regents Park, crossing Baker and Oxford Streets on its way south. It divided to define the Isle of Thorney, graced with Westminster Abbey, and entered the Thames below Vauxhall Bridge.
58 Henry Fielding was said to have modelled Squire Western in *Tom Jones*, on Henry Ellis St John's grandfather, Sir Paulet St John.
59 Lord Walsingham, in addition to a pension of £700 a year, was Archdeacon of Surrey, Prebendary of Winchester, Rector of Calbourne, Rector of Fawley, perpetual Curate of Exbury, and Rector of Merton. William Cobbett, *Legacy to Parsons*, London, 1819, noted 332 parsons shared the revenues of 1496 parishes, and 500 others, those of 1524 parishes.
60 *The Loiterer*, No 9, Saturday, March 28, 1789.

Chapter 5
Names, Names, Names
She was really proud of her family & Connexions, & easily offended if they were treated with Neglect
Kitty, or the Bower

1 Jane Austen, *Persuasion*, Volume I, Chapter I.
2 *Oxford Dictionary of National Biography*. "Charles I," Volume 11, OUP, 2004, page 96.
3 *Ibid*, 'Wentworth, Thomas first Earl of Strafford,' Volume 58, page 142.
4 *Ibid*.
5 Marshalsea in Southwark was a brutal prison where men served sentences for debt, sedition, and crimes at sea. It became a notorious London debtor's prison.
6 The *Petition of Right*, as important as the Magna Carta, remains in force in Great Britain and many countries of the Commonwealth, including Australia, and was a precursor to the third, fifth, sixth and seventh amendments to the Constitution of the United States.
7 J. Forster, *Eminent British Statesman*, Cabinet Cyclopaedia, Volume II, London, 1836, page 362–6.
8 *Encyclopedia Britannica*, 11th Edition, 1911.
9 J. Forster, *op cit*, page 372–373.
10 *Ibid*.
11 William Knowler, ed., *The Earl of Strafforde's Letters and Dispatches*, London, 1739.
12 The first of thirteen stanzas of a *poem libel* attacking Strafford and Laud, published in full on the website: *http://www.earlystuartlibels.net*.
13 J. Forster, *op cit*, page 380–381.
14 *Ibid*, page 391.
15 *Ibid*, page 394–5.
16 *Earl of Strafford's Letters and Despatches*.
17 J. Forster, *op cit*, page 401.
18 *Ibid*, page 406–407.
19 *Ibid*, page 409–410.
20 Jane Austen, *The History of England*, Juvenilia, Volume the Second.
21 *The Works of Samuel Johnson*, Volume the Ninth, London 1806, page 218.
22 *The New Annual Register or General Repository of History, Politics and Literature for the Year 1797*, London 1800, page xxi.
23 *The Times*, 24 March 1792.
24 In 1792, Sir John Wentworth was appointed Surveyor General of the King's Woods in Nova Scotia. He assisted the Royal Navy, locating and protecting land suitable for fine timber, particularly the American white pine, ideal for masts, booms and rigging for ships of the fleet.
25 Jane Austen used the name Vernon in *Lady Susan*. George Washington named his house in Virginia, *Mount Vernon*, after his half-brother Laurence served with Admiral Vernon in the capture of Portobello, a glorious prelude to the disaster of Cartagena.
26 In present day Panama.
27 Tobias Smollett, *A Complete History of England from the Descent of Julius Caesar, to*

the *Treaty of Aix la Chapelle, 1748, Containing the Transactions of One Thousand Eight Hundred and Three Years,* Volume the Eighth, London, 1758.
28 In present day Colombia.
29 Tobias Smollett, *A Complete History, op cit.*
30 *Ibid.*
31 Tobias Smollett, *Roderick Random*, Volume 1, Part 2, Chapter XXXIII, London, 1748.
32 *Austen Papers, op cit,* page 290.

Chapter 6
Not a bad speculation for a Surgeon
Sanditon

Golden London, and her silver Thames, throng'd with shining spires
And corded ships; her merchants buzzing round like summer bees and all the golden cities in his land overflowing with honey
William Blake, King Edward the Third,

1 William Wordsworth, from *Upon Westminster Bridge,* 1802.
2 William Wordsworth, from *The Prelude.*
3 Quoted by Joan Lane, "The Role of Apprenticeship," in W.F.Bynum & R. Porter, *William Hunter & the Medical World of the Eighteenth Century*, Cambridge, 1985, page 89.
4 O.M. Brack, *Tobias Smollett, Scotland's First Novelist.* Associated Univ Presses. New Jersey. 2007. For example see, "State of the Controversy between Mr Gataker and Mr Guy, Concerning the Cure of Cancers", *The Gentleman's Magazine,* Volume 34, 1764, page 526.
5 Wellcome Institute for the History of Medicine, MS.934.
6 Erasmus Darwin, *Zoonomia,* 1794–96.
7 R. Campbell, *The London Tradesman,* 1747, page 40.
8 *Ibid,* page 47–48.
9 Tobias Smollett, *The Adventures of Roderick Random*, Chapter VII, London, 1748.
10 P. Rayer, *Sommaire d'une historie abrégée de l'anatomie pathologique,* Paris 1818. Quoted by Othmar Keel in "The politics of health and the institutionalisation of clinical practices in Europe in the second half of the eighteenth century," in Bynum & Porter *op cit,* page 211.
11 J. Abernathy, *Hunterian Oration* 1819, quoted *ibid,* page 229.
12 Samuel Taylor, *A Universal of Stenography or Short Hand-writing,* London, 1786.
13 There are examples of D'Arcy's use of Taylor's shorthand in his *Medical Notebook,* ML.
14 B.C.Corner, *William Shippen, Jr.* American Philosophical Society, Philadelphia, 1951. During the American Revolution, Shippen was made Director of Hospitals for the US Continental Army.
15 William Shippen to his brother Edward, 1 September 1758, in B.C. Corner, *op cit*, page 7.
16 J. Archockey to David Killican, 22 December 1785, Wentworth Papers, ML.
17 *Fort William – India House Correspondence,* Public Series, Volume IX, ed. K. D. Bhagava, National Archives of India, Delhi, 1959, page 556–564.
18 Old Sarum, the most notorious of the "rotten boroughs", a constituency that returned two members of parliament from a barren hill with no residents, was abolished by the *Reform Act* in 1832.
19 John Villiers (1757–1838) took the title third Earl of Clarendon on the death of his brother in 1824.
20 *Criticisms on the Rolliad,* Part 2, an anonymous political satire on the government of Pitt the Younger, Villiers' patron, published in the *Morning Herald* during 1784 to 1785.
21 William Wentworth to William Bucknell, 12 June 1824, Ellis Papers, ML.
22 In London, Edmund Burke was the Colonial Agent for New York, and Benjamin Franklin served as Colonial Agent for Pennsylvania, New Jersey, Georgia and Massachusetts.
23 Henry Howard, Earl of Suffolk, Secretary of State for the Northern Department, 1771 to 1779.
24 *History of Parliament Online.*
25 Paul Wentworth's informants included Edward Bancroft, Franklin's secretary, and Silas Deane. Bancroft made the invisible ink, a compound of cobalt chloride, glycerine and water that became visible when heated. It was superseded by a "sympathetic stain" using one chemical as ink and a second to develop it.
26 Pierre de Beaumarchais to the Comte de Vergennes, 17 December 1777. Quoted by S.F.Bemis, "British Secret Service & the

French-American Alliance," *The American Historical Review*, Volume 29, No.3, April 1924. Pierre de Beaumarchais was a spy and a playwright. His *Le Mariage de Figaro* was the basis for Mozart's opera, and *Le Barbier de Séville* for Rossini.
27 *Daily Universal Register*, 4 April 1786.
28 *Daily Universal Register*, 9 May 1786.
29 *History of Parliament Online*.
30 Ernest Anthony Smith, *Whig principles and Party Politics*, Manchester University Press, 1975, p.73.
31 *General Evening Post*, 18 May 1786.
32 *Ibid*, 20 May 1786.
33 *Morning Herald*, May 23 1796.
34 *General Evening Post*, 17 June 1786.
35 The East India Company received a license *to enlist 2,500 recruits for five years, to deposit and keep them in the Isle of Wight until they can be sent to India*, Journals of the House of Commons, Vol. 43.
36 R. Campbell, *op cit*, page 57.
37 Joseph Collyer, *The Parent's and Guardian's Directory and the Youth's Guide London*. 1761. quoted by Joan Lane, *op cit*, page 94.
38 Surgeons to John Hunter, 27 May, 1793, G.C. Peachey, *A Memoir of William Hunter*, Brendon, Plymouth, 1924, page 288.
39 G. B. Shaw, *The Doctor's Dilemma: Preface on Doctors*. 1909. Shaw was born in 1856.
40 J. M. Adair, *Medical Cautions for the Consideration of Invalids*. Bath. 1786, page 166–168.
41 Samuel Butler, *Characters & Passages from Notebooks*, ed. A.R.Waller, Cambridge UP, 1908.
42 John Aubrey, *Brief Lives, Chiefly of Contemporaries*, ed. A.Clark, Oxford UP, 1898.
43 Samuel Butler, *op cit*.
44 E.A. Smith, *op cit*, page 22.
45 Jane to Cassandra Austen, 23 June, 1814.
46 Henry Fielding, *An Enquiry into the Causes of the Late Increase in Robbers*, London, 1751, Part III.
47 Government lotteries began in England in 1567, used to fund public works, such as repair of harbours. In the 1730s lotteries raised sufficient money to pay for the Westminster Bridge. In the 1750s British Museum lotteries raised £35 million for the Seven Years War, and £70 million for the war with the American colonies.
48 From an Indenture of Apprenticeship signed in 1771 by William Almon, quoted in A.E.Marble, *Surgeons, Smallpox and the Poor*, McGill Queens Press, Canada, 1993.
49 A. Steinmetz, *The Gaming Table Its Votaries and Victims*, London, 1870, page 23.
50 A. Steinmetz, *op cit*.
51 Tobias Smollett, *The Adventures of Roderick Random*, London, 1748, Chapter LX.
52 Henry Fielding, *op cit*.
53 *The Loiterer*, No.56, Saturday, February 20, 1790.
54 Loo or Looterloo was a popular card game of the time. Considered a great pastime by the idle rich it later gained a bad reputation as a vicious tavern game. In one version the pool of funds supplied by the players could reach astronomic proportions in a short space of time, often resulting in spectacular ruins, giving the game a bad reputation. The name Pam was given to the Jack of Clubs, the trump card. Pope's *Rape of the Lock* included the couplet (iii,62)
Even mighty Pam, that Kings and Queens o'erthrew
And mow'd down armies in the fights of Lu.
55 Horace Walpole to George Montagu, Esq., 2 June, 1759, *Letters of Horace Walpole*, Volume III, 1753–1759, Samuel Bentley, London, 1840.
56 David G. Schwartz, *Roll the Bones, The History of Gambling*, Gotham Books, NY. 2006, page 161.
57 See, Ivor Brown, "The Inn", in *The Legacy of England*, Pilgrims' Library, London, 1941, page 196.
58 I. Darlington, Ed. *Survey of London*, Volume 25-Chapter 6: St. George's Fields, from *British History Online*.
59 Berkeley was the youngest of seven children of the 6th Baron Craven and Lady Elizabeth Berkeley who separated in 1783, after thirteen tempestuous years. Lady Elizabeth took Berkeley to Europe, where she remarried and became the Margravine of Brandenburg-Ansbach-Bayreuth. On her return to England she was initially spurned by her son, Lord Craven.
60 *The Gentleman's Magazine*, June 1836, Obituary, page 673, and *Sydney Monitor*, 7 January 1836.
61 Later the Royal Blackheath Golf Club, the oldest Golf Club in England, its records date back to 1784. In 1792 it had a 5–7 hole course, with 45 members.
62 Erith, Deal and Dover Islands, named by George Bass and Mathew Flinders in 1798,

form the Kent group of islands in Bass Strait, North of Tasmania.
63 *British History Online.*
64 Henry Fielding, *op cit*, page 36–7.

Chapter 7
High spirit & strong passions
Mansfield Park

The person who has contracted debts must pay them
Persuasion

1 Lord Byron, *Don Juan*, Canto X.
2 David Hughson, *Circuit of London*, Volume V, Holborn Hill, 1808, page 135.
3 Thomas Philipot, *Villare Cantianum*, Kent 1776, page 136. In *Henry IV Part I*, Shakespeare set this incident further east along the Kent Road, at Gads Hill.
4 William Shakespeare, *Henry IV, Part I*, Act II, Scene II.
5 *Daily Universal Register*, Thursday 18 January, 1787. On 1 January 1788 it was renamed *The Times*.
6 *History of Parliament Online*. 1820–1832, *Curtis achieved his apotheosis as an unconscious buffoon by appearing at the levee at Holyrood House on 19 August 1822 in full but ill fitting and wholly unsuitable Highland uniform including a dangerously short kilt.*
7 C. Johnson, P. Smith, *Africans in America*. Harcourt Brace. New York. 1998. page 70. In 1807, slave trading was made illegal for British subjects. In 1822, Curtis's ship, the *Emma*, was condemned as a prize at Sierra Leone, for being engaged in the slave trade.
8 Alderman Curtis was part owner of the *Lady Penrhyn* with Alderman George Macaulay
9 From *History of Parliament Online*. 1790–1820.
10 William Shakespeare, *Henry IV, Part I*, Act II, Scene IV.
11 *Whitehall Evening Post*, 16 January 1787.
12 *Daily Universal Register*, Wednesday 17 January 1787.
13 *The late blind Justice Fielding walked for the first time into my room when he once visited me, and after speaking a few words said, this room is about 22 feet long, 18 wide and 12 high; all which he guessed by the ear with great accuracy.* Erasmus Darwin, *Zoonomia*, 1796. Volume II, page 487.
14 Jane Austen, *Pride & Prejudice*, Volume III, Chapter VI.
15 *Daily Universal Register*, Wednesday 17 January 1787.
16 *The Whitehall Evening Post,* January 16–18 1787.
17 William Manning's wife Elizabeth, was the daughter of Nottingham banker Abel Smith, an MP from 1774 to 1788; her brother Robert had been an MP since 1779 and two other brothers Samuel and George would later enter the House of Commons.
18 Daniel Defoe, *Moll Flanders*, Chapter XX, 1722.
19 Jane Austen. *Emma*, Volume I, Chapter XVI.
20 *Daily Universal Register,* 18 January 1787.
21 *Daily Universal Register,* 14 September, 1787.
22 Ivor Brown, *op cit*.
23 *The Beggars Opera* by John Gay was performed nearly every year between 1728 and 1886. Sir John Fielding wrote to theatre managers *"concerning its impropriety"* that it was *"never represented on stage without creating an additional number of real thieves."*
24 Jane Austen, *Northanger Abbey*, Volume I, Chapter II.
25 Horace Walpole, son of Robert Walpole, the first British Prime Minister, who served from 1721 to 1742. He resigned after the debacle of the Battle of Cartagena.
26 A Cobb & Co coach *on the way to Forbes was bailed up by bushrangers. Among the passengers were the famous lawyer, the Rt.Hon. William Bede Dalley, PC., and Judge Windeyer; Dalley as ever immaculately dressed in frock-coat, gloves and shiny top hat. All were searched and robbed, Dalley having two hundred pounds in his wallet, besides his valuable gold watch and fob. "Who's them blokes in top hats?" asked the head of the gang to the coachdriver. "Well," came the answer, "the little fellow is lawyer Dalley going up to defend your pal at the trial, and the big bloke is Windeyer, the judge who is going to hang him." Thereupon Dalley's watch and money were returned to him with profuse apologies, while they took the unfortunate judge and heaved him into the nearest waterhole.*
G. Nesta Griffiths, *Point Piper, Past and Present*. Ure Smith Sydney 1970, page 79–80.
27 Rev Blacker of Carrick, *op cit.*
28 Jane Austen, *Persuasion*, Volume I, Chapter III.
29 Jane Austen, *Persuasion*, Volume I, Chapter XI.

30. Arthur Bowes Smyth, surgeon of the *Lady Penrhyn, Journal 1787–1789.*
31. G. Fidlon, & R.J. Ryan, *The Journal of Arthur Bowes Smyth, Surgeon Lady Penrhyn,* Sydney, Australian Documents Library, 1979. Page 86. *Lady Penrhyn* did not sail to Nootka Sound, after problems en route she turned back to Tahiti, went to Canton, loaded a cargo of tea and sailed home.
32. John Harris, Evidence to the Bigge Inquiry, 16 August 1820, B.T. Box 1, page 272, ML.
33. Jane Austen, *Persuasion,* Volume I, Chapter X.
34. *Ibid,* Volume I, Chapter X.
35. Rev Blacker of Carrick, *op cit.*
36. J. Dawson to D'Arcy Wentworth, 11 June 1787, Wentworth Papers, ML.
37. Rev Blacker of Carrick, *op cit.*
38. Royal College of Surgeons, *Company of Surgeons Examination Book, 1745–1800,* page 22.
39. *Naval and Military surgeons,* by the Royal College of Surgeons.
40. John Villiers to D'Arcy Wentworth, 10 July 1787, Wentworth Papers, ML.
41. Jane Austen, *Persuasion,* Volume II, Chapter VIII.
42. *Daily Universal Register,* 13 July 1787.
43. *Daily Universal Register,* 20 June 1787.
44. On 14 September 1773, *The Morning Chronicle* published a tribute to Algar, the noted bruiser, following his death:
    Let Ber-street's sons bestow one solemn tear,
    And awful weep around the mighty bier
    Algar is dead! their champion and their pride,
    Whose Herculean strength mankind defy'd;
    Let them their loss, their dreadful loss deplore,
    Their hero's fall'n, and fall'n to rise no more;
    And to his memory erect a stone,
    To tell the living what the dead has done;
    What numbers own'd his prowess on the stage
    Felt his strong arm, and trembl'd at his rage;
    What mighty feats have eternis'd his name,
    And placed him foremost in the lists of fame.
45. *Daily Universal Register,* 20 June 1787.
46. *The Gentleman's Magazine,* Volume 61, page 270.
47. *Daily Universal Register,* 18 July 1787.
48. Tim Hitchcock, Robert Shoemaker, Clive Emsley, Sharon Howard and Jamie McLaughlin, *et al., The Old Bailey Proceedings Online, 1674–1913.* 11 July 1787, hence forth *Old Bailey Proceedings.*
49. *Daily Universal Register,* 18 July 1787.
50. *Daily Universal Register,* 13 July 1787.
51. *Ibid.*
52. John Villiers to D'Arcy Wentworth, 16 November 1787, Wentworth Papers, ML.
53. *Daily Universal Register,* 30 November 1787.
54. Thomas Amyot was a Huguenot, a descendant of Jacques Amyot, Bishop of Auxerre, and tutor to French Kings Charles IX and Henry III. He came to England on the revocation of the Edict of Nantes in 1685. The Edict had guaranteed rights for the Huguenots, who were Calvinists. Thomas Amyot settled in Norwich, where his brother was a clockmaker. His son Peter Amyot was also a clockmaker, His grandson Thomas was private secretary to William Windham, Prime Minister,
55. *Daily Universal Register,* 3 December 1787.
56. *Daily Universal Register,* 1 December 1787.
57. In 1783 public executions were moved from Tyburn Hill to gallows built at the Old Bailey. Ninety six people were executed there between February and December 1785. *British History Online.*
58. Jane Austen, *Pride & Prejudice,* Volume II, Chapter IX.
59. *Old Bailey Proceedings,* 11 July 1787.
60. *Oxford Dictionary of National Biography, op cit,* Volume 31, page 995.
61. *Daily Universal Register,* 3 December 1787.
62. *The London Merchant,* a play by George Lillo, was first performed in 1736.
63. *Ibid,* Act 1, Scene 3
64. *Daily Universal Register,* 3 December 1787.
65. On his visits to Fitzwilliam at Grosvenor Square, D'Arcy occasionally hired a horse from John Dunn's stables nearby.
66. *Old Bailey Proceedings,* 12 December 1787.
67. The Court transcript was taken in shorthand by E. Hodgson, Professor of Shorthand. His numerous transcripts were offered for sale, price three shillings and sixpence.
68. Treasury expended large sums each year in rewards for successful prosecution. It was a strategy to tackle increasing crime, rewards gave an incentive to witnesses to come forward in Court to assist in the prosecution of offenders.
69. *Offenders frequently stood in the pillory in the Old Bailey, and there, no doubt, were often, as was customary, stoned by the mob, and pelted with rotten eggs, and other equally offensive missiles. The pillory generally consisted of a wooden frame, erected on a scaffolding, with holes and folding boards for the admission of the head and hands of him whom it was*

desired to render thus publicly infamous. Thornbury, W., *Old & New London*, Volume II, 1878, *British History Online*.
70 *Daily Universal Register*, 12 October 1785.

Chapter 8
Missing Years
"Very well," was her ladyship's contented answer, "then speculation, if you please."
Mansfield Park

1 J.E. Austen-Leigh, *Recollections, op cit.*
2 Jane Austen, *Persuasion*, Volume I, Chapter IV.
3 *Memoir of JA.*
4 Jane Austen, *A Collection of Letters*, Letter the First, Juvenilia, Volume the Second.
5 Jane Austen, *Northanger Abbey*, Volume I, Chapter XIV.
6 *Ibid*, Volume I, Chapter XIV.
7 Jane Austen, *Pride & Prejudice*, Volume I, Chapter X.
8 Jane Austen, *Persuasion*, Volume I, Chapter IV.
9 Jane Austen, *Pride & Prejudice*, Volume I, Chapter IV.
10 *Ibid*, Volume I, Chapter IV.
11 *The Correspondence of the Right Honourable William Wickham from the year 1794*, ed. William Wickham, London, Richard Bentley, 1870, F/N page 1–2.
12 *Ibid*, page 3.
13 Wickham Papers, Hampshire Record Office, quoted by Michael Durey, *William Wickham, Master Spy*, London, Pickering & Chatto, 2009, page 7.
14 William Wickham to the Duke of Portland, 12 October 1800, *ibid*, page 189.
15 *Ibid.*
16 William Wickham to Lord Redesdale, 21 March 1804, *ibid*.
17 Prince Regent to William Wickham, 30 March 1807, WWM.
18 Jane Austen, *The Watsons*.
19 William Curtis produced thirteen volumes of the *Botanical Magazine*, still published today as *Curtis' Botanical Magazine*.
20 Jane to Cassandra Austen, 18 August 1814.
21 Jane Austen, *Emma*, Volume III, Chapter XIII.
22 Gilbert White to Thomas Pennant Esq, 5 June 1784, Letter LXVI, *The Natural History of Selborne*, Whittaker & Co, London 1836.
23 William Cobbett, *Rural Rides*, near Selborne on 7 August 1823, page 189.
24 Jane Austen, *Mansfield Park*, Volume I, Chapter VII.
25 *Ibid*, Volume III, Chapter IX.
26 Jane Austen, *Pride & Prejudice*, Volume II, Chapter IX.
27 Jane Austen, *Northanger Abbey*, Volume I, Chapter XVII.
28 *Ibid*, Volume II, Chapter X.
29 William Wickham to Lord Grenville, 13 January 1795, quoted by Michael Durey, *op cit*, page 17.
30 *Ibid*, page 189.
31 William Wickham, Introduction to *Correspondence, op cit*, page IX.
32 Jane Austen, *Sense & Sensibility*, Volume I, Chapter XV.
33 Jane Austen, *Pride & Prejudice*, Volume I, Chapter XXIII.
34 William Mason, *The Dean & the Squire, a Political Eclogue*, J. Debrett, London, 1782, page iii. Mount Street was named for a local landmark named Oliver's Mount, a raised earthwork, the remnant of one of the fortifications erected during the Civil War.
35 The *Chimney Sweeper's Act* 1788, prohibited the apprenticeship of boys under eight; required the master sweep to obtain their parent's permission, to provide his apprentices with proper clothes and accommodation, and ensure they attended church on Sunday.
36 *Daily Universal Register*, 10 July 1787.
37 Percivall Pott was the first to identify the risk of contracting cancer in a specific occupation, from exposure to a carcinogen.
38 Jane Austen, *Emma*, Volume II, Chapter XVII.
39 *The Times*, November 4, 1788.
40 Jane Austen, *Pride & Prejudice*, Volume III, Chapter XVIII.
41 *Ibid*, Volume III, Chapter XIX.
42 Jane Austen, *Lady Susan*.
43 Jane Austen, *Northanger Abbey*, Volume I, Chapter VI.
44 Jane Austen, *Pride & Prejudice*, Volume I, Chapter X.
45 *Ibid*, Volume III, Chapter XVI.
46 *Ibid*, Volume I, Chapter VI.
47 *Ibid* Volume III, Chapter XVIII.
48 *Ibid*, Volume I, Chapter IX.
49 *Ibid*, Volume II, Chapter II.
50 *Ibid*, Volume III, Chapter XVIII.
51 David Garrick, *Bon Ton*, 1775. A cardinal was a three-quarter cloak with a hood.

52 George Colman, *Prologue to Bon Ton,* 1775.
53 Jane Austen, *Pride & Prejudice,* Volume I, Chapter VI.
54 Jane Austen, *Emma,* Volume II, Chapter XIII.
55 *Ibid,* Volume II, Chapter XVI.
56 *The Loiterer,* No 9, Saturday, March 28, 1789.
57 Henry Maxwell bought *Itchel Manor* in 1773, from the estate of Nicholas Linwood, a director of the East India Company, and renamed it *Ewshot House.* He died in 1818, and left it to Madam Lefroy's eldest son, Rev John Henry George Lefroy.
58 *The Gentleman's Magazine,* Volume 59, Part 1, 1789, page 374.
59 *Ibid.*
60 Letter from Abbott of the Inner Temple to the *Whitehall Evening Post,* March 31, 1789 – April 2, 1789; and *Public Advertiser,* April 2, 1789.
61 Jane Austen, *Sense & Sensibility,* Volume II, Chapter III.
62 Jane Austen, *Lesley Castle,* Letter the First, Juvenilia, Volume the Second.
63 Jane Austen. *Sense & Sensibility,* Volume II, Chapter IV.
64 *Ibid,* Volume I, Chapter XIV.
65 *Ibid*, Volume I, Chapter XII.
66 *Ibid,* Volume I, Chapter XI.
67 Jane Austen, *A Collection of Letters,* Juvenilia, Volume the Second.
68 Jane Austen, *Sense & Sensibility,* Volume II, Chapter XIV.
69 *Ibid,* Volume II, Chapter IV.
70 Jane Austen, *Lesley Castle,* Juvenilia, Volume the Second.
71 Jane Austen, *The Beautifull Cassandra.* Juvenilia, Volume the First.
72 Jane Austen, *Sense & Sensibility,* Volume II, Chapter XIV.
73 Rev Blacker of Carrick, *op cit.*
74 Jane Austen, *Lesley Castle,* Letter the Tenth, Juvenilia, Volume the Second.
75 Jane Austen, *Emma,* Volume II, Chapter I.
76 *The Gentleman's Magazine,* December 1804, Obituary, with Anecdotes, page 1178.
77 Lady Mary Wortley Montagu to Sarah Chiswell, 1 April 1717. Lord Wharncliffe, ed., *The Letters & Works of Lady Mary M.W. Montagu,* Richard Bentley, London. 1837.
78 *In her twentieth year she translated the Enchiridian of Epictetus; a manual for living. The Gentleman's Magazine,* 1822, page 470.
79 Lord Wharncliffe, *op cit,* Volume III.
80 Jane Austen, *Frederic & Elfrida,* Juvenilia, Volume the First.
81 Jane Austen, *Sense & Sensibility,* Volume III, Chapter I.
82 *Whitehall Evening Post,* July 14–16 1789, Country News.
83 Jane Austen, *Northanger Abbey,* Volume II, Chapter II.

Chapter 9
No Turning Back
I never spent so happy a summer
Mansfield Park

1 See *British History Online,* Chapter Eight.
2 Jane Austen, *Sir William Mountague,* Juvenilia, Volume the First.
3 Jane Austen, *Pride & Prejudice,* Volume III, Chapter XVII.
4 Jane Austen, *Mansfield Park,* Volume I, Chapter X.
5 Eliza de Feuillide to Phylly Walter, 21 April 1788, *A Family Record,* page 41.
6 John Stockdale, bookseller with a *fashionable lounging place* opposite Burlington House, Piccadilly, was charged with libel for publishing *Review of the Charges against Warren Hastings,* by Rev John Logan in June 1788. Defended by Erskine he was acquitted on 9 December 1789. The case was instrumental in the passing of the *Libel Act* in 1792.
7 From Charles Fox' description of Erskine, footnote to a letter from the Hon Thomas Erskine, 8 February 1793, *Correspondence of the Rt Hon. Edmund Burke,* op cit, Volume III, page 127.
8 Jane Austen, *Northanger Abbey,* Volume II, Chapter V.
9 Jane Austen, *Pride & Prejudice,* Volume II, Chapter XIX.
10 *Ibid,* Volume III, Chapter I.
11 *Ibid,* Volume II, Chapter XIX.
12 *Ibid,* Volume III, Chapter I.
13 Jane Austen, *Mansfield Park*, Volume III, Chapter XV.
14 Jane Austen, *Pride & Prejudice,* Volume III, Chapter I.
15 Jane Austen, *Sense & Sensibility,* Volume II, Chapter VI.
16 Jane Austen, *Mansfield Park,* Volume I, Chapter IX.
17 Jane Austen, *Northanger Abbey,* Volume II, Chapter VIII.
18 Jane Austen, *Pride & Prejudice,* Volume II, Chapter VI.

19. Jane Austen, *Mansfield Park*, Volume I, Chapter IX.
20. Jane Austen, *Northanger Abbey*, Volume I, Chapter XI.
21. Jane Austen. *The Visit,* Juvenilia, Volume the First.
22. Jane Austen, *Pride & Prejudice*, Volume III, Chapter XVIII.
23. Jane Austen, *Northanger Abbey*, Volume II, Chapter VIII.
24. Jane Austen, *Pride & Prejudice*, Volume II, Chapter VI.
25. *Ibid*, Volume III, Chapter III.
26. Jane Austen, *Northanger Abbey*, Volume II, Chapter VIII.
27. *Ibid*, Volume II, Chapter IX.
28. *Ibid*, Volume II, Chapter V.
29. *Ibid*, Volume II, Chapter VIII.
30. *The Annual Register*, Volume XXXI, 1789, editor Edmund Burke, London, page 221.
31. Jane Austen, *Northanger Abbey*, Volume II, Chapter V.
32. Jane Austen, *Emma*, Volume III, Chapter XIII.
33. Jane Austen, *Persuasion*, Volume II, Chapter XI.
34. Jane Austen, *Emma*, Volume III, Chapter XIII.
35. *The Annual Register*, Volume XXXI, *op cit*, *Iris lunaris, or Moon Rainbow*, The moon sometime exhibits the phenomenon of an iris or rainbow by the refraction of her rays in drops of rain in the night time. *Very early this morning, some hours before day, a very fine rainbow appeared, more brilliant than that of August 17, 1788.*
36. Jane Austen, *Emma*, Volume III, Chapter XIV.
37. *The Annual Register*, op cit.
38. *Whitehall Evening Post*, July 14–16, 1789.
39. Jane Austen, *Emma*, Volume III, Chapter XIX.
40. Jane Austen, *The History of England*, Juvenilia, Volume the Second.
41. Jane Austen, *Lesley Castle*, Juvenilia, Volume the Second.
42. Jane Austen, *Pride & Prejudice*, Volume II, Chapter IV.
43. Thomas Hill to Earl Fitzwilliam, 8 December 1789. WWM.
44. *Ibid*.
45. *Whitehall Evening Post*, November 10, 1789.
46. *Gazetter & New Daily Advertiser*, 13 November 1789.
47. *Whitehall Evening Post*, November 12, 1789.
48. *Public Advertiser*, Monday, November 16, 1789
49. Jane Austen, *Mansfield Park*, Volume III, Chapter XV.
50. *Whitehall Evening Post*, November 12, 1789.
51. *The Times*, 13 November 1789.
52. *The Times*, 20 November 1789.
53. *Diary or Woodfall's Register*, 15 November 1789.
54. Jane Austen, *Mansfield Park*, Volume III, Chapter V
55. *Ibid*, Volume III, Chapter XV.
56. *The Times*, 17 November 1789.
57. See John Ritchie, *The Wentworths*, Miegunyah Press, Melbourne, 1997, p. 20.
58. *The Times,* 7 July 1789.
59. *Belfast Newsletter*, 18–22 January, 1790.
60. *The Times*, 1 December 1789.
61. *Whitehall Evening Post*, November 14–17, 1789.
62. Jane Austen, *Mansfield Park*, Volume I, Chapter XIV.
63. Jane Austen, *Lesley Castle*. Juvenilia, Volume the Second,
64. Jane Austen, *Love & Freindship*, Juvenilia, Volume the Second.
65. *Public Advertiser*, 1 December 1789.
66. See John Pemberton Heywood to Earl Fitzwilliam, 28 February 1784. WWM.
67. *The Times*, 13 November 1789.
68. *The Times* often published a column on page two: *To Correspondents*, addressed to reporters paid for copy, and to those who freely contributed items of interest. The column gave readers a taste of the variety of stories coming across the editor's desk, what he might select or reject; it might give a hint of an upcoming story, or a snippet of gossip.
69. William Shakespeare, *The Winter's Tale*, Act I, Scene II.
70. *The Times*, 11 December 1789.
71. *The Times*, 12 December 1789.
72. William Charles to D'Arcy Wentworth, 13 April 1817. Wentworth Papers, ML.
73. *Proceedings of the Old Bailey*, 9 December 1789.
74. M.H. Ellis, *Ellis Papers*, ML.
75. *Proceedings of the Old Bailey*, 9 December 1789.
76. M.H. Ellis, *Ellis Papers*, ML.
77. *Belfast Newsletter*, 18–22 January, 1790.
78. Thomas Hill to Earl Fitzwilliam, 8 December 1789. WWM.
79. *Public Advertiser*, 11 December, 1789.
80. *The Times*, 10 December 1789, and *Public

Advertiser, 30 December, 1789, noted both Wentworth and Barrington were surgeons: *It is rather singular that the two chief leaders of the depredatory gang should have both been bred surgeons: which was the case with Messrs Barrington and Wentworth.*

81 Jane Austen, *Persuasion,* Volume II, Chapter VII.
82 Jane Austen, *Mansfield Park,* Volume III, Chapter X.
83 William Shakespeare, *Measure for Measure,* Act I, Scene III.
84 William Shakespeare, *King Henry the Eighth,* Act III, Scene II.
85 Charles Cookney to D'Arcy Wentworth, 17 December 1789. Wentworth Papers. ML.
86 Jane Austen, *Northanger Abbey,* Volume II, Chapter XIII.
87 *Ibid.*
88 Jane Austen, *Emma,* Volume III, Chapter II. Brian Southam notes in *Jane Austen and the Navy,* London, Hambledon, 2000, that Lord Nelson stayed at the *George* in Portsmouth, that the *Crown* was patronised by middle ranking naval officers and known as the Navy House. A friend of the Austens, Mrs Powys, had *an elegant dinner* there in 1792, but found it *as dirty an Inn as I was ever at.*
89 Jane Austen, *Mansfield Park,* Volume III, Chapter XII.
90 Jane Austen, *Emma,* Volume II, Chapter V.
91 Jane Austen, *Mansfield Park,* Volume III, Chapter XI.
92 Jane Austen, *Persuasion,* Volume I, Chapter IV.
93 Jane Austen, *Mansfield Park,* Volume III, Chapter X.
94 *Ibid,* Volume III, Chapter VII.
95 *The Times,* 30 December 1789.

Chapter 10
Such Probabilities & Proofs
Sense & Sensibility
I cannot speak well enough to be unintelligible
Northanger Abbey

1 *Memoir of JA,* Preface and Chapter 3.
2 Jane Austen, *The Mystery,* Juvenilia, Volume the First. The play has curious echoes in the opening scene of Caryl Churchill's, *Love and Information,* 2012.
3 *Memoir of JA,* Chapter 3.
4 Jane Austen, *Frederic & Elfrida,* Juvenilia, Volume the First.
5 Virginia Woolf, *The Common Reader,* Chapter 12, London, 1925.
6 Henry Austen, "Thoughts on Education," *The Loiterer,* No. 27, 1 August 1789, Oxford.
7 Jane to Cassandra Austen, Tuesday, 23 August 1814.
8 Footnote to Jane Austen's letter of 23 August, 1814, *A Family Record, op cit.*
9 Jane Austen, *Love & Freindship,* Juvenilia, Volume the Second.
10 Jane Austen, *Sir Charles Grandison,* Act I, Scene I.
11 "A Miscellaneous Essay," in *Annual Register for the Year 1772,* pages 185, 188 & 186.
12 Horace Walpole to the Earl of Hertford, 1 November 1764. *Letters of Horace Walpole, op cit.*
13 See E.A. Smith, *op cit,* page 26.
14 A.P.W. Malcomson, *The Pursuit of the Heiress,* Ulster Historical Foundation, 2006, page 155.
15 Hampshire County Council, *Hantsweb Heritage 100.*
16 Marriage Register of St .Nicholas Church, Steventon, 1755 to 1812, Hampshire Record Office.
17 Jane Austen, *Mansfield Park,* Volume II, Chapter IV.
18 William Shakespeare, *Henry IV, Part I.*
19 The fourteenth century Wigmore Chronicle, from Wigmore Abbey in Herefordshire.
20 *Whitehall Evening Post,* November 12, 1789.

Chapter 11
More Notions than Facts
Letters
Their hearts are open to each other... they know exactly what is required and what can be borne
Northanger Abbey

1 Jane Austen, *Persuasion,* Volume I, Chapter IV.
2 Jane to Cassandra Austen, 29 January, 1813.
3 *Memoir of Jane Austen.*
4 Jane Austen, *Pride & Prejudice,* Volume I, Chapter I.
5 Queenie D. Leavis, "A Critical Theory of Jane Austen's Writings," In Collected Essays, Cambridge UP, 1983.
6 Jane Austen, *Sense & Sensibility,* Volume III, Chapter I.
7 Jane Austen, *Pride & Prejudice,* Volume III, Chapter XVII.
8 *Ibid,* Volume I, Chapter XII.
9 Jane Austen, *Sense & Sensibility,* Volume I, Chapter XI.

10 *Ibid*, Volume I, Chapter I.
11 *Ibid*, Volume I, Chapter XI.
12 *Ibid*, Volume III, Chapter XI.
13 David Nokes, *op cit*, page 149.
14 Jane Austen, *Pride & Prejudice*, Volume II, Chapter VI.
15 *Ibid*, Volume II, Chapter XVIII.
16 Jane Austen, *Persuasion*, Volume II, Chapter XII.
17 Jane Austen, *Pride & Prejudice*, Volume III, Chapter XV.
18 *Ibid*, Volume III, Chapter VI.
19 Jane Austen, *Lady Susan*.
20 Jane Austen, *Mansfield Park*, Volume III, Chapter I.
21 Henry Austen, "The Science of Physiognomy Not to Be Depended On," *The Loiterer*, No.51, 16 January 1790, Oxford.
22 Jane Austen, *Mansfield Park*, Volume III, Chapter II.
23 Jane Austen to Fanny Knight, 20 February 1817.
24 Jane Austen, *Northanger Abbey*, Volume I, Chapter XIII.
25 Jane Austen, *Mansfield Park*, Volume II, Chapter II.
26 Virginia Woolf, "Personalities" in *Collected Essays*. Hogarth Press. London. 1966.
27 Reginald Farrer, "Jane Austen", *Quarterly Review*, 228, July 1917.
28 Robert W. Chapman, *TLS*, 10 December 1931.
29 Bruce Stovel, *Further Reading*, Chapter 13, *The Cambridge Companion to Jane Austen*, eds E. Copeland & J. McMaster, CUP, 1997.
30 Clare Brant, "Obituary: David Nokes." *The Guardian*, 7 December 2009.
31 David Nokes, *op cit*, page 115–116.
32 Virginia Woolf, *The Athenaeum*, December 1923.
33 Jane Austen, *Pride & Prejudice*, Volume I, Chapter V.
34 The troublesome boy D'Arcy unfastened from Jane's neck, four year old Edward Lefroy, became a British Commissary Judge in Surinam, where he laboured to suppress the slave trade. Little William Thomas Lefroy never got well, he died at Ashe two months before his fourth birthday, three months after the birth of his brother Benjamin, Anne's seventh and last child. Jane lived to see Benjamin marry her beloved niece, Anna, James Austen's eldest daughter.
35 Jane Austen, *Persuasion*, Volume I, Chapter IX.
36 Jane Austen, *Emma*, Volume III, Chapter IX.
37 Jane Austen, *Persuasion*, Volume I, Chapter IV.
38 Jane Austen, *Persuasion*, Volume I, Chapter IX.
39 *Ibid*.

Chapter 12
To the most remote corner
The Watsons
The world is not their's, nor the world's law
Emma

1 The Colony's easterly sea boundary was not clearly defined, later governors differed on where it lay. King regarded Tahiti as within his jurisdiction. Macquarie considered he held sway over the north island of New Zealand, and appointed a Justice of the Peace for the Bay of Islands.
2 *British Parliamentary History*, XXVI, page 211.
3 *Whitehall Evening Post*, 21 November 1786.
4 The boundaries recognised the 1494 *Treaty of Tordesillas*, under which Pope Alexander VI divided the New World between the great maritime powers of the day, Portugal and Spain. The line of the *Treaty* divided the new continent in two. The eastern border of the State of Western Australia lies along longtitude 129° East, which would have placed that State under the control of Portugal, with the seven States and Territories to the east, under the control of Spain. Portuguese influence had long been supplanted by the Dutch. Unwilling to unsettle Dutch interests, England continued to use the name, *New Holland,* for the continental mainland, and Van Diemen's Land for Tasmania, but the Dutch had no interest in the penal settlement. The eastern side had received little attention from Spain, and Britain had no hesitation in claiming it from her Spanish rival, naming it New South Wales.
5 G.R. *Instructions for our trusted & well beloved Arthur Phillip Esq, our Captain-General & Governor-in Chief in and over our Territory of New South Wales. HRA*, Series I, Volume I, page 11.
6 The East India Company monopoly covered an area between longitude 57°E and 180°.
7 G.R. *Instructions etc*, op cit, *HRA*, Series I, Volume I, page 15.

8. Governor Arthur Phillip to Marquis of Lansdowne, 3 July 1788. Manuscript, ML.
9. Governor Phillip to Lord Sydney, 15 May 1788, *HRNSW*, Volume I, Part II, page 122.
10. *The Times*, Court Circular, 23 January 1788.
11. Thomas Watling, convict, artist, 1794.
12. See C.M.H. Clark, *A History of Australia*, Volume I, Melbourne University Press, 1962, page 117.
13. Governor Phillip to Lord Sydney, 9 July 1788. *HRNSW*, Volume I, Part I, page 51.
14. *Ibid.*
15. Governor Phillip to Lord Sydney, 28 February 1787, 'Phillip's views on the conduct of the Expedition & the treatment of convicts', *HRNSW*, Volume I, Part II, page 51–2.
16. *Ibid*, page 53.
17. Governor Phillip to Under Secretary Nepean, 9 July 1788. *HRA*, Series, 1 Vol. l, page 55–56
18. Watkin Tench, *A Complete Account of the Settlement of Port Jackson*, London, 1793.
19. Governor Phillip to Lord Sydney, 11 April 1790. *HRA*, Series 1, Volume I, page 167.
20. Governor Phillip to Lord Sydney, 5 June 1787. *HRNSW*, Volume I, Part II, page 106.
21. Alexander Falconbridge, *An Account of the Slave Trade on the Coast of Africa*. London, 1788.
22. Captain William Hill to Jonathan Waltham, 26 July 1790. *HRNSW*, Volume I, Part II, page 367–8. William Hill, commander of a NSW Corps detachment on board *Surprize*, sent an account of the voyage to William Wilberforce.
23. Surgeon Harris's Account of the Quarrel between Captain Gilbert and Lieutenant Macarthur, *HRNSW*, Volume II, page 427.
24. *Ibid.*
25. Elizabeth Macarthur, *Journal*, *HRNSW*, Volume II, page 489.
26. Evan Nepean to John Shapcote, December 1789, PRO HO 42/15/402.
27. William Grenville, Secretary of State, to Governor Phillip, 24 December 1789.
28. Elizabeth Macarthur, *op cit*, page 491.
29. *Ibid*, page 488.
30. Jane Austen, *Pride & Prejudice*, Volume III, Chapter XI.
31. Jane Austen, *Pride & Prejudice*, Volume I, Chapter IV.
32. Jane Austen, *Emma*, Volume II, Chapter XV.
33. Jane Austen, *Pride & Prejudice*, Volume III, Chapter IX.
34. William Hill, *op cit*.
35. *Public Advertiser,* 30 April 1790.
36. William Hill, *op cit*.
37. Jane Austen, *Emma*, Volume II, Chapter XIII.
38. Oliver Ransford, *The Slave Trade*. Readers Union, Newton Abbot, Devon. 1972, page 84.
39. William Hill, *op cit*.
40. *Ibid.*
41. *Ibid.*
42. A.C.V. Melbourne, *William Charles Wentworth*, Discovery Press, Penrith, 1934, page 5 & 6, from the Records of the Colonial Office in the Public Records Office, London.
43. William Hill, *op cit*.
44. *The Times*, 18 November 1791.
45. Quoted in Roger Knight, *The Pursuit of Victory, The Life and Achievement of Horatio Nelson*, Penguin, 2005, pages 77 and 129.
46. *The Times*, 9 June 1792.
47. *Ibid.*
48. *The Times*, 24 June 1792.
49. *HMS Temeraire*, made famous by J.M.W. Turner's painting.
50. Elizabeth Macarthur, *Journal*, op cit.
51. Elizabeth Macarthur, *Letter to a Friend*, 7 March 1791, *HRNSW*, Volume II, page 499.
52. *Ibid*, page 498.
53. Elizabeth Macarthur to Bridget Kingdon, 1 September 1775. *HRNSW*, Volume II, page 509.
54. Quoted by M.H. Ellis, *John Macarthur*. Angus & Robertson, Sydney, 1955, pages 30 & 41.
55. Jane Austen, *Persuasion*, Volume I, Chapter XII.
56. Jane to Cassandra Austen, 17 January 1809.
57. Jane Austen, *Persuasion*, Volume II, Chapter XI.
58. *Ibid*, Volume II, Chapter XI.
59. "A letter from Sydney", *Morning Chronicle*, 8 September 1791.
60. A letter dated 24 March 1791, published in *The Bee*, Edinburgh, 15 May 1792.
61. Messrs Camden, Calvert & King to Captain Donald Traill, Portsmouth 19 December 1789. Reprinted in *The Diary, or Woodfall's Register* on 3, 4 and 6 August 1792.
62. Governor Phillip sent two superintendents and a deputy commissary in charge of thirty-seven male and one hundred and fifty-seven female convicts to Norfolk Island on the *Surprize*.

63. Captain David Collins, *Diary*, 1 August 1790. ML.
64. William Shakespeare, *The Taming of the Shrew*, Act I, Scene II.

Chapter 13
Angels & Eagles
I flatter myself for being a tolerable proficient in Geography
Love & Freindship

1. *Public Advertiser*, 31 December 1790. *The Gentleman's Magazine*, January 1791, page 532, reported, *In the Admiralty Islands – it is thought the two vessels under M. La Peyrouse, viz the Boussole and Astrolabe, perished with all their people, or fell into the hand of savages, particularly as the Sirius English frigate, navigating here in 1790, had seen savages dressed in the uniforms of French marines, and other persons who wore European stuffs*.
2. Surgeon John White, *Journal of a Voyage to New South Wales*, 1790, pages 34 and 36.
3. *Ibid*.
4. *Araucaria heterophylla*.
5. See Roger Knight, *Britain against Napoleon, The Organization of Victory, 1793–1815*. Allen Lane, London. 2013, page 17.
6. Alexander Dalrymple, *A Serious Admonition to the Publick on the intended Thief-colony at Botany Bay*. London. 1786.
7. Surgeon John White, *op cit*, 1790, page 57.
8. Governor Phillip to Lord Sydney, February 13, 1790, *The Gentleman's Magazine*, Volume LXI. 1791, page 272–273.
9. Captain John Hunter, *An Historical Journal of the Transactions at Port Jackson and Norfolk Island, With the Discoveries That Have Been Made in New South Wales and the Southern Ocean Since the Publication of Phillip's Voyage*. John Stockdale, London, 1793, Chapter XXIV.
10. *Ibid*.
11. Lieutenant Watkin Tench, *op cit*.
12. Lord Grenville to Lord Cornwallis, 6 September 1790. *HRA*, Series I, Volume I, page 752.
13. Lieutenant Ralph Clark, *Journal*. ML.
14. Governor Phillip to Lord Grenville, 1 March 1791. *HRA*, Series 1, Volume 1, page 245–6.
15. *Pterodroma solandri*.
16. The convict's name was Jonathon Roberts.
17. Despite the great bond that flourished between father and son, there have long been questions about William's parentage, given his birth on 13 August 1790, was less than nine months after D'Arcy first boarded the *Neptune*.
18. Now Flagstaff Hill.
19. Lieutenant Ralph Clark, *Journal*, ML, page 216.
20. Samson's Sinew, *Callerya australis*, Fabaceae.
21. Aaron Price, *Diary of Norfolk Island 1825–1854*, ML.
22. The New Zealand flax (Phormium tenax) known as Harakeke is not related to the European flax (Linum usitatissum). It looks more like an aloe, with long rank leaves of up to three meters long.
23. Lieut. Ralph Clark to Captain Campbell, 10 February 1791. ML.
24. John Hunter, *An Historical Journal*, op cit, page 196.
25. John Hunter left Sydney on 10 December on the Dutch snow, *Waaksamheyd* that arrived in Sydney on 19 September 1790 with relief supplies from the Cape. His voyage home took thirteen months; he disembarked in Portsmouth in April 1792.
26. F.M. Bladen, 'Notes an the Life of John Hunter,' *JRAHS*, Part 3, 1901, page 23.
27. *Eucalyptus resinifera*
28. *Eucalyptus piperita*
29. *Smilax glyciphylla*. A similar sasparilla plant, *Smilax aspera* had been used in the Dutch East Indies in the 17th century by Jacobus Bontius and Robert Durie. Like other herbal remedies used in Batavia it may have been documented in Chinese herbal medicines, but it appears to have been used by the Portuguese apothecary Garcia da Orta. It is recorded in his book, Notae in Garciam ab Orta published in 1631, or in his Colloquies of 1605; earlier than the Dutch in the east indies. Cook, Harold J., *Matters of Exchange; Commerce, Medicine, and Science in the Dutch Golden Age*, Yale University Press, 2007, page 198
30. *Leptomeria acida*. Sour currant- a parasitic plant from the eucalypt forests; high in Vitamin C and used by the aborigines.
31. *Xanthorrhoea spp*.
32. It has been claimed that Catherine Crowley lived on the Fitzwilliam estates in Staffordshire. Her name does not appear in records held at the Stafford Archives; Crowley was not a local name, there is no record of her birth or baptism there.
33. A large amount of linen and clothing is listed in the charge against Catherine Crowley: two pairs of linen sheets, a linen cap, two muslin caps, a laced bodice, a gauze

bodice, three pieces sattyn and two pairs muslin ruffles, goods of William Hyatt. Plus one crape gown, one cloth cloak, one linen bed gown and one linen jacket and petticoat, goods of Maria Morrell, spinster, in the dwelling of William Hyatt.
34. Jane Austen, *Mansfield Park,* Volume I, Chapter VI.
35. Marquess of Stafford to Rt Hon W.W. Grenville, 27 September 1789, *HRNSW,* Volume II, p.426.
36. Anne Needham, *The Women of the 1790 Neptune.* Self Published, Dural, 1992.
37. At the Stafford Assizes on 30 July 1788, among those sentenced to transportation were Joseph and Thomas Genders, Edward Fisher, Thomas Baker, Howell, James Hadon, Saul Aston, James Dodd.
38. Captain James Colnett, *A Voyage to New Holland & Round the World,* ed. G.A.Mawer, Rosenberg, Sydney, 2016, quoted, page 27.
39. C.M.H. Clark, *A History of Australia,* Volume I, *op cit,* page 115.
40. Governor Phillip to Lord Grenville, 5 November 1791. *HRA,* Series I, Volume I, page 274.
41. Nootka Sound had become an important trade link for the British, Captain George Vancouver went there on the *Discovery,* after conducting surveys on the New South Wales coast and in the Pacific. He spent three years surveying the North West Coast of America. During that time New South Wales remained his only link with Britain. The storeship *Daedalus* was sent from Sydney on two occasions with supplies. By December 1794 Vancouver had completed his surveys, and he returned to England.
42. Captain James Colnett, *op cit,* page 15.
43. Lieut. Governor King to Evan Nepean, 23 November 1791, *Historical Records of New Zealand,* Wellington, 1908, page 139.
44. *Present State of His Majesty's Settlement on Norfolk Island.* 18 October 1796, ML.
45. *Ibid.*
46. Lieut. Governor King to Governor Phillip, 29 December 1791, *HRNSW,* Volume I, Part II, page 575.
47. Tobias Smollett, *The Expedition of Humphry Clinker,* 1771.
48. Governor Phillip to Lieut. Governor King, 30 November 1792. ML.
49. Captain David Collins, *op cit.*
50. Major Grose to Governor Phillip, 4 October 1792. *HRA* Series I, Volume I, page 381.
51. Governor Phillip to Major Grose, 4 October 1792. *HRA,* Series I, Volume I, page 381–382.
52. Major Grose to Under Secretary Lewis, 22 October 1792, *HRA,* Volume I, page 236.
53. Governor Phillip to Sir Joseph Banks, 3 December 1791, *Papers of Sir Joseph Banks,* ML.
54. David Collins, *HRNSW,* Volume II, page 230.
55. Lieut. Governor King, *Journal of Transactions on Norfolk Island,* ML.
56. John Nicol, *Life and Adventures 1776–1801,* ed. Flannery, Text Publishing, Melbourne. 1997.
57. *A Family Record,* page 97.
58. *Birmingham Gazette,* 2 August 1802.
59. *Austen Papers,* page 179
60. Mrs Leigh-Perrot, nee Jane Cholmeley, was well connected. In January 1801, Jane reported her niece, Mrs Welby "has been singing Duetts with the Prince of Wales."
61. Kathleen Dermody, *D'Arcy Wentworth 1762–1827, A Second Chance.* PhD thesis, Australian National University, April 1990, page 72.
62. Samuel Sidney, *The Three Colonies of Australia,* London 1852, Page 58. Joseph Smith told his story to Caroline Chisholm in 1845. He was transported in 1790, aged fourteen, aboard the *Neptune,* for seven years, for stealing clothing. He recorded in the days and weeks after the arrival of the Second Fleet, hearing the fighting and howling of dingoes eating the bodies of dead convicts in the open pit where they had been thrown. *There was plenty of hardship then, I have often taken grass, and pounded it, and made soup from a native dog.* On Norfolk Island he was in charge of Lieutenant Governor King's garden, and later worked for D'Arcy Wentworth.
63. Jane Austen, *Pride & Prejudice,* Volume III, Chapter I.
64. *The Daily Advertiser,* 20 January, 1792
65. John Hunter, *An Historical Journal, op cit,* Chapter XXIV, page 579.
66. Lieut. Governor King to Evan Nepean, 9 March and 8 May 1792. ML.
67. Lieut. Governor King to Governor Phillip, 21 September 1792. ML.
68. Lieut. Governor King, *Journal,* page 81–85, ML.
69. Earl Fitzwilliam to D'Arcy Wentworth,

24 June 1793, WWM; D'Arcy Wentworth to David Collins, July 1794; D'Arcy Wentworth to Earl Fitzwilliam, 23 January 1796. ML
70. Lieut. Governor King to Evan Nepean, 4 March 1793. ML.
71. Earl Fitzwilliam to D'Arcy Wentworth, 24 June 1793. Wentworth Papers, ML.
72. David Collins to D'Arcy Wentworth, 18 October 1793, Wentworth Papers, ML.
73. Earl Fitzwilliam to D'Arcy Wentworth, 24 June 1793. WWM.
74. Adam Smith, *An Inquiry into the Nature & Causes of the Wealth of Nations,* Glasgow, 1776.
75. George III, the King's Speech, 5 December 1782.
76. Lieut. Governor King, *Journal,* ML.
77. The two Maoris were taken to Sydney on the *Daedalus*, the supply vessel for Captain Vancouver's Nootka expedition, and landed on Norfolk Island in April 1793 from the *Shah Hormuzear*.
78. Captain David Collins, *op cit*.
79. Governor Hunter to the Duke of Portland, 10 August 1796, *ibid,* page 593.
80. Sugar and tea were also commonly used in place of coinage. At the theatre, a seat in the gallery cost one shilling and the box office accepted flour, meat or rum as payment.
81. Richard Atkins, *Journal of a Voyage to Botany Bay and South America, 1791–1810,* NLA.
82. J.N. Rawling, *The Story of the Australian People*, Modern Press, Sydney, 1938, part 3, page 202.
83. Lieut. Governor King to Earl Fitzwilliam, 19 February 1796. WWM.
84. Lot 88, the original title of the sixty acres granted to D'Arcy Wentworth in 1791.
85. Lieut. Colonel Ross to Governor Phillip, 11 February 1791, *HRA,* Series I, Volume I, page 234–5.
86. Jane Austen, *Emma,* Volume I, Chapter XII.
87. Lieut. Governor King, *Journal 1791 – 1796.* NLA, manuscript, page 11.
88. Lieut. Governor King to Rt Hon Henry Dundas, 10 March 1794, *HRNSW,* Volume II, page 14–15.
89. Lieut. Governor King, *Journal of Transactions on Norfolk Island,* ML.
90. *Ibid*.
91. Lieut. Governor King to Rt Hon Henry Dundas, 10 November 1794, *HRNSW,* Vol. II, page 135–173.
92. Lieut. Governor King to Rt Hon Henry Dundas, 10 March 1794, *HRNSW*, Volume II, page 154.
93. The Court comprised Captain William Paterson, Captain Joseph Foveaux, Captain George Johnston, Lieutenant John Macarthur, Lieutenant John Townson, Lieutenant John Prentice, Lieutenant Thomas Rowley, Ensign McKellar, Ensign Lucas, and Quarter-master Laycock. *HRNSW*, Volume II, page 127.
94. Lieut. Governor Grose to Lieut. Governor King, 25 February 1794, *HRNSW*, Vol. II, page 125–129.
95. Lieut. Governor King to Rt Hon Henry Dundas, 10 March 1794. *HRNSW,* Volume II, page 135–70
96. Lieut Governor King to Lieut Governor Grose, 30 January 1794, *HRNSW,* Volume II, page 105.
97. Duke of Portland to Governor Hunter, *HRA,* Series I, Volume I, page 496.
98. *Account Book,* Wentworth Papers, ML.
99. Jane Austen, *Mansfield Park,* Volume I, Chapter II.
100. Charles Cookney to D'Arcy Wentworth, 1 August 1798, Wentworth Papers, ML.
101. Governor Hunter to Under Secretary King, 25 January 1795. *HRNSW,* Volume II, page 280–281.
102. Lieut. Governor King to David Collins, 12 July 1795. *HRNSW,* Volume III, page 44.
103. Richard Atkins, *Journal of a voyage to Botany Bay and South America, 1791–1810,* NLA.
104. Imeerawanyee died in May 1794, he was buried at Eltham in Kent.
105. *The World,* 17 April 1794.
106. Governor Hunter to Under Secretary King, 25 January, 1795, *HRNSW*. Volume II, p. 281.
107. D'Arcy Wentworth to Earl Fitzwilliam, 1 May 1796, D'Arcy quotes from an earlier letter, WWM.
108. D'Arcy Wentworth to Earl Fitzwilliam, 23 January 1796. WWM.
109. John Ritchie, *Wentworths, op cit,* page 66.
110. Lieut. Governor King, *Journal of Transactions*, December 1795, ML.
111. Lieut. Governor King to Earl Fitzwilliam, 19 February 1796.
112. Lieut. Governor King to D'Arcy Wentworth, 10 April 1796, Wentworth Papers, ML.
113. D'Arcy Wentworth to Earl Fitzwilliam, 10 September 1796. WWM.
114. Jane Austen, *Pride & Prejudice,* Volume I, Chapter XVIII.

Chapter 14
In such a world
In such a world, so thorny
William Cowper, The Task

1. Jane Austen, *Emma,* Volume III, Chapter XII.
2. Jane Austen, *Lady Susan.*
3. Jane Austen, *A Collection of Letters,* Juvenilia, Volume the Second.
4. Jane Austen, *Lady Susan.*
5. *The Gentleman's Magazine,* December 1804, page 1178.
6. Jane Austen, *To the Memory of Mrs Lefroy.*
7. *The Gentleman's Magazine,* December 1804, page 1178. In 1800, her younger brother, Sir Egerton Brydges, had three of her poems, written twenty-five years earlier, published in The Poetical Register *and Repository of Fugitive Poetry for 1801,* with several literary labours of Rev Osmund Beauvoir, his headmaster at the King's School, a collection of obscure Antient Poetry, and a sonnet of his own.
8. Anne Brydges, *The Poetical Register,* London, 1801, pages 32, 36, 112–3.
9. Jane Austen, *To the Memory of Mrs Lefroy.*
10. Jane Austen, *Persuasion.* Volume I, Chapter IV.
11. Jane Austen, *Northanger Abbey*, Volume I, Chapter VI.
12. Jane Austen, *The History of England,* Juvenilia, Volume the Second.
13. Jane Austen, *Lesley Castle,* Juvenilia, Volume the Second.
14. *Ibid.*
15. Jane to Cassandra Austen, 9 January 1796.
16. Jane Austen, *Edgar & Emma,* Juvenilia, Volume the First.
17. Jane to Cassandra Austen, 9 January 1796.
18. Jane to Cassandra Austen, 23 August 1796.
19. Jane to Cassandra Austen, 17 November 1798.
20. Jane Austen, *To the Memory of Mrs Lefroy.*
21. Jane Austen, *Persuasion,* Volume I, Chapter IV.
22. *The Times,* 6 October 1791.
23. *The Times,* 9 November 1791.
24. *The Times,* 16 February 1792.
25. Jane Austen, *Pride & Prejudice,* Volume III, Chapter XI.
26. *The Times,* 21 June, 1792.
27. Robert Southey, *Botany Bay Eclogue: Elinor,* 1794.
28. Robert Southey, *Botany Bay Eclogue: William,* 1794.
29. Robert Southey, *Botany Bay Eclogue: Frederic,* 1794.
30. Jane Austen, *Mansfield Park,* Volume II, Chapter XI.
31. Jane Austen, *Emma,* Volume II, Chapter XVI.
32. Jane Austen, *Persuasion,* Volume I, Chapter IV.
33. *Ibid,* Volume II, Chapter XI.
34. *Ibid,* Volume I, Chapter X.
35. Jane to Cassandra Austen, 8 April 1805.
36. Jane Austen, *Pride & Prejudice,* Volume III, Chapter XVII.
37. James Austen, *To Miss Jane Austen the reputed author of Sense & Sensibility, a Novel lately published,* lines 1–2 & 5–6, in *The Poetry of Jane Austen & the Austen Family,* ed. David Selwyn, University of Iowa Press, 1997, page 50.
38. Jane Austen, *Sense and Sensibility,* Volume I, Chapter XII.
39. Jane Austen, *Pride & Prejudice,* Volume II, Chapter X.
40. *Ibid,* Volume I, Chapter III.
41. *Ibid,* Volume I, Chapter IX.
42. Jane to Cassandra Austen, 9 January, 1799.
43. Jane to Cassandra Austen, 11 June, 1799.
44. Jane Austen, *Northanger Abbey,* Volume II, Chapter X.
45. Jane to Cassandra Austen, 18 December & 24 December, 1798.
46. Ten years earlier Sir Joseph Banks encouraged the Governor in Chief of Grenada to plant botanical gardens in the West Indies, and grow spices: nutmeg, mace, cinnamon, ginger and cloves. Banks provided advice, seeds and seedlings from Kew. It was a strategy to increase British trade and reduce the influence of the Dutch, who controlled the spice islands, Ternate and Tidore, in the Moluccas.
47. Eliza de Feuillide to Philly Walter, 7 June 1792, *Austen Papers,* Chapter III.
48. William Cowper, *The Task.*
49. Eliza de Feuillide to Philly Walter, 7 June 1792. *Austen Papers.*
50. *The Times,* 9 June 1792.
51. Jane Austen. *Evelyn,* Juvenilia, Volume the Third.
52. *Hampshire Chronicle.* 7 April 1792 & 23 May 1798
53. Charles Fox to Richard Fitzpatrick, 30 July 1789.
54. Edmund Burke to the House of Commons, 9 February 1790. In November 1790 Burke had published *Reflections on the Revolution in*

France, a best seller on both sides of the Channel.
55   Earl Fitzwilliam to Edmund Burke, 27 September 1792, WWM.
56   E.A. Smith, *op cit*, page 148.
57   *The Annual Register*, 1792, page 39.
58   *The Annual Register*, 1793, Appendix to the Chronicle, page 110–113.
59   Lord Redesdale to Prime Minister Henry Addington, Lord Sidmouth, 11 August 1803, quoted in Michael Durey, *op cit*, page 109.
60   Quoted by Harvey Mitchell, *The Underground War Against Revolutionary France*, Clarendon Press, Oxford, 1965, page 243.
61   Wickham was the model for Baroness Orczy's *The Scarlet Pimpernel*, London, 1905.
62   Prince Regent to William Wickham, 30 March 1807, WWM.
63   Aesop, *Sporting Reminiscences in Hampshire, 1745 to 1862*, Chapman & Hall, London, 1864, p 29.
64   Charles-Philippe, Comte d'Artois to William Wickham, 15 April 1798.
65   Patrick Geoghegan, *Robert Emmet, A Life*, McGill, 2002, quoted page 39.
66   Michael Durey, *op cit*, page 179.
67   The solution is *Agent*.
68   Jane Austen, *Lady Susan*.
69   Eliza de Feuillide to Philly Walter, 13 December 1796. *Austen Papers*.
70   Fanny D'Arblay to Esther Burney, 22 March 1812.
71   Jane Austen, *Persuasion*, Volume I, Chapter VI.
72   Henry Austen, *Biographical notice to Northanger Abbey and Persuasion*.
73   Jane Austen, *Sense & Sensibility*, Volume II, Chapter VII.
74   *Memoir of JA*, Chapter 8.
75   Reginald Farrer, "Jane Austen," *Quarterly Review*, 228, July 1917.
76   David Nokes, *op cit*, page 86. Nokes dated her confinement from the end of 1786, when she was brought home from school in Reading. It began three years later, in the last days of 1789.

Chapter 15
A Colony Abandoned
We none of us expect to be in smooth water all our days
Persuasion

1   In 16 January 1796, a play house opened in Sydney. A number of the well behaved convicts were given permission to perform.
2   Nevil Maskelyne, Astronomer Royal from 1765 to 1811, presided over projects to assist navigation, the calculation of a standard latitude and longitude, and the adoption of the Greenwich meridian, that became the basis for the global calculation of longitude.
3   *Government & General Order*, 9 November 1796. McGuanne, J.P. "The Humours and Pastimes of Early Sydney." JRAHS, Volume I. 1901, page 36.
4   Captain Michael Hogan, *Logbook of the ship Marquis Cornwallis*, Manuscript, ML.
5   D'Arcy Wentworth to Earl Fitzwilliam, 1 May 1796 & 10 September 1796. WWM
6   Jane Austen, *Persuasion*, Volume I, Chapter IV.
7   John Boston to Evan Nepean, 5 December 1793. ML.
8   Rev Thomas Fyshe Palmer to Mr Lindsey, 15 September 1795. Quoted in, John Cobley, *Sydney Cove 1795–1800, the Second Governor*, Volume V, Angus & Robertson, UK, 1986.
9   D'Arcy Wentworth to Earl Fitzwilliam, 23 January 1796, WWM.
10 Charles Cookney to Earl Fitzwilliam, 10 July 1798, WWM.
11 David Blair, *The History of Australasia from the first dawn of discovery in the Southern Ocean to the Establishment of self-government*, 1879.
12 D'Arcy Wentworth to Earl Fitzwilliam, 11 October 1800, WWM.
13 Daniel Paine, *Journal 1794–1797*, ed. R.J.B. Knight and Alan Frost, Library of Australian History, Sydney, 1983, page 23. Paine was a master boat builder who came to the Colony in 1795, with Governor Hunter, on the *Reliance*.
14 Quoted in Robert Murray, *The Britannia Journal*, Port Jackson, New South Wales 1792–1794. *JRAHS*. June 1974, Volume 60, Part II, page 80.
15 Elizabeth Macarthur, 1 September 1795, *HRNSW*, Volume II, page 512.
16 John Macarthur to his brother James, *Macarthur Papers*, ML.
17 Adam Smith, *op cit*.
18 M.H. Ellis, *Macarthur, op cit*, page 75.
19 John Washington Price, *Minerva Journal*, 29 January 1800, ed. P.J. Fulton, Meigunyah Press, Melbourne, 2000, page 150.
20 Tedbury was the son of Pemulwuy, the great Aboriginal warrior.

21 James Macarthur, *A few Memoranda respecting the Aboriginal Natives,* Macarthur Papers, ML.
22 Governor Hunter to Under Secretary King, 1 June 1797, *HRA,* Series I, Volume II, page 203.
23 Frederick Watson, Introduction, *HRA,* Series I, Volume II, page xi.
24 Governor Hunter to Under Secretary King, 1 June 1797, *HRA,* Series I, Volume II, page 203.
25 Vice-Admiral John Hunter, evidence, 19 Feb.1812, *Report of Select Committee on Transportation,* 10 July 1812.
26 Governor Hunter to Duke of Portland, 21 December 1795, *HRNSW,* Volume II, page 344.
27 D'Arcy Wentworth to Earl Fitzwilliam, 1 May 1796, WWM.
28 *Ibid.*
29 In 1797, Lord Portland, Home Secretary and Henry Dundas, Secretary of State for War, considered using Sydney as a base for a squadron deployed to the West coast of America to harass Spanish shipping, but decided to leave this to privateers. Several were captured and taken to Sydney by South Sea whalers. In April 1799, *Nuestra Señora de Bethlehem* was taken and renamed *Hunter*. In July 1799 three whalers took the 250 ton, *El Plumier*; in November 1799 the *Betsey* captured *Euphemia*, she was renamed *Anna Josepha*; in 1801 *Ruby* captured *La Fortuna*. That year Bishop and Bass were given authority – a letter of marque – for the *Nautilus* to take prizes.
30 T. Muir, T. Fyshe Palmer & W. Skirving to Governor Hunter, 25 October 1795. *HRA* Series I, Volume II, page 545.
31 Thomas Muir to a friend in London, 13 December 1794.
32 D'Arcy Wentworth to Earl Fitzwilliam, 1 May 1796, WWM.
33 D'Arcy Wentworth to Earl Fitzwilliam, 19August 1797, WWM.
34 Charles Cookney to D'Arcy Wentworth, 30 August 1797, Wentworth Papers, ML.
35 Charles Cookney to D'Arcy Wentworth, 1798, Wentworth Papers, ML.
36 J.N. Rawling, *The Story of the Australian People* Part 3, Modern Publishers, Sydney 1938, page 203.
37 Duke of Portland to Governor Hunter, 10 August 1796, *HRA* Series I, Volume II, page 579

38 Surgeon Balmain to Governor Hunter 18 June 1798, *HRA,* Series I, Volume II, pages 163 and 173.
39 Governor Hunter to Captain Paterson, 7 February 1796, *HRA,* Series I, Volume I, page 577.
40 Duke of Portland to Governor Hunter, 18 May 1798, *HRA,* Series I, Volume II, page 148.
41 Governor Hunter to Duke of Portland, 25 July 1798.
42 Governor Hunter to Duke of Portland, 14 September 1796. *HRA,* Series I, Volume I, page 661–662.
43 C.M.H. Clark, *A History of Australia,* Volume I, *op cit,* page 146.
44 Governor Phillip to Lord Grenville, 4 March 1791, *There are neither pease nor butter in the colony, nor any spirits. HRA,* Series I, Volume I, page 249.
45 Governor Hunter to Under Secretary King, 1 June 1797, *HRNSW,* Volume III, page 213.
46 Lord Portland to Governor Hunter, 18 September 1798, *HRNSW,* Volume III, page 490.
47 Governor Hunter to Duke of Portland, 20 August 1796, *HRNSW,* Volume III, page 574. *Ibid.*
48 Governor Hunter to Duke of Portland, 10 August 1796, *HRA,* Series I, Volume I, page 574.
49 In 1977, the wreck of the *Sydney Cove* was located near Preservation Island and bottles of beer were found intact inside the hull. More than twenty strains of yeast were identified, and beer was brewed from these historic cultures, and tested for anti-scorbutic properties. See *Afloat,* October 2016.
50 *Government and General Order,* 20 September 1795.
51 Governor Hunter to Under-Secretary King, 1 June 1797, *HRNSW.* Volume III, page 213.
52 The author of the pipe did not appear to know that D'Arcy Wentworth was on Norfolk Island the entire period Major Grose was in the Colony, and that they had never met.
53 Governor Hunter to Duke of Portland, 15 January 1800. *HRA,* Series I, Volume II, page 439.
54 Governor Hunter to Duke of Portland, 1 February 1800, *Settlers' Appeal to Secretary of State, HRA,* Series I, Volume II, page 442.

55 Joseph Holt, *Memoirs of Joseph Holt, General in the Irish Rebellion in 1798*, Volume II, page 294.
56 Daniel Paine, *Journal, 1794–1797*, eds. R.J.B. Knight, & A. Frost, Sydney, 1983, page 35.
57 *Settlers' Appeal to Secretary of State*, op cit, pages 445–6.
58 Frederick Watson, Introduction, *HRA*, Series I, Volume II, pages xi–xiii.
59 Vice-Admiral John Hunter, *evidence*, 19 Feb.1812, *op cit*.
60 Portland Place, below the junction of the Hawkesbury with the Colo River, now Lower Portland.
61 Governor Hunter to Secretary Nepean, 19 November 1797, *HRA*, Series I, Volume II, page 112.
62 Governor Hunter to the Duke of Portland, 1 July 1798, *HRA*, Series 1, Volume II, page 158.
63 *HRA*, Series 1, Volume II, Note 51, page 713.
64 Duke of Portland to Rt Hon Henry Dundas, 19 December 1798.
65 *The Times*, 17 August 1797. Lord Kenyon, Lord Chief Justice, 2 June 1788 to 11 April 1802.
66 John Villiers to D'Arcy Wentworth, 13 December 1798, ML.
67 James Dawson to D'Arcy Wentworth, 16 February, 1800, ML.
68 Governor Hunter to Under-Secretary King, 1 October 1798, *HRA*, Series I, Volume II, page 237.
69 Governor Hunter to Under-Secretary King, 28 July 1799, *HRA*, Series I, Volume II, page 378.
70 Vice-Admiral John Hunter, *evidence*, 19 Feb.1812, *op cit*.
71 Governor Hunter to Under Secretary King, 19 November 1797, *HRNSW*, Volume III, page 74. His comment referred to George Barrington, then a constable at Parramatta.
72 Governor Hunter to Duke of Portland, 1 May 1799, *HRA*, Series I, Volume II, page 366.
73 Governor Hunter to Duke of Portland, 25 June 1794, 1 November 1798, *HRA*, Series I, Volume II, pages 31 and 236.
74 Governor Hunter to Duke of Portland, 12 November 1796, *HRA*, Series I, Volume I, page 674.
75 George III, *the King's Speech*, House of Lords, 20 November 1798.
76 John Washington Price, *op cit*, page 165.
77 Governor Hunter to Duke of Portland, 21 February 1799, *HRA* Series I, Volume II, page 278.
78 *Proceedings of Inquiry, The Irish Conspiracy*, *HRA*, Series I, Volume II, page 575–583, and 639–51.
79 Governor Hunter to Duke of Portland, 10 January 1798, *HRA*, Series I, Volume II, page 118.
80 George Howe to D'Arcy Wentworth, 16 November, 1801, Wentworth Papers. ML.
81 John Washington Price, *op cit*.
82 *Ibid*.
83 *Ibid*, page 165.
84 *Manuscript*, ML.
85 Thomas Jamison, Principal Surgeon to Earl Camden, 20 July 1805. *HRNSW*, Volume V, page 667.
86 Watkin Tench, *A Complete Account of the Settlement of Port Jackson*, op cit, Chapter XVI.
87 John Washington Price, *op cit*.
88 W.C.Wentworth, *A Statistical, Historical and Political Description of the Colony of New South Wales and its Dependent Settlements in Van Diemen's Land*, 2nd edition, London, 1820, page 15.
89 The site was fourteen miles from Sydney, on the south east of the main road, south of the present Parramatta Town Hall, extending beyond Fitzwilliam Street. In 1810 D'Arcy received a grant of twelve acres that included the lease area.
90 *Wentworth Woodhouse* at Parramatta stood on the top of the knoll behind Firehorse Lane, above the present-day railway station, near Darcy Street and Fitzwilliam Place.
91 John Washington Price, *op cit*. He quoted from John Milton' *L'Allegro*, "*Towers & battlements it sees, Bosom'd high in tufted trees.*"
92 J. Frederick Watson, *The History of Sydney Hospital from 1811 to 1911*, Sydney, 1911, page 6.
93 *Public Advertiser*, Friday 8 October 1790.
94 *The Times*, 19 March 1791.
95 Rev Dean O'Beirne to W Baron Hotham, 31 March 1791, British National Archives.
96 Near Wilberforce.
97 Richard Atkins, *Journal 1791–1810*, Manuscript. ML.
98 Acting Principal-Surgeon Balmain to Governor Hunter, *HRA*, Series 1, Volume 1, page 539.

99. R. Darvall, "The First Bad Debt" in *Australia's Quest for Colonial Health*, eds. J. Pearn, and C. O'Carrigan, Royal Children's Hospital, Brisbane. 1983, page 476.
100. *Ibid*.
101. *Ibid* for details of Molloy's litigation.
102. P. Turbet, *The Aborigines of the Sydney District before 1788*. Kangaroo Press, Kenthurst, 1989.
103. William Paterson to Rt. Hon. Henry Dundas, 15 June 1795. *HRA*, Series I, Volume I, page 499–500.
104. Governor Hunter to Duke of Portland, 2 January, 1800, *HRA*, Series I, Volume II, page 422. The Court comprising the Judge Advocate, three Royal Navy officers and three officers of the NSW Corps found Constable Powell and settlers Freebody, Metcalfe, Timms and Butler guilty.
105. Governor Hunter to Duke of Portland, 1 May 1799, *HRA*, Series I, Volume II, page 354.
106. Governor Hunter to Duke of Portland, 7 January 1800. *Expenses of Farming at the Hawkesbury*. *HRA*, Series I, Volume II, page 234–436.
107. *Synopsis of Despatches*, *HRA*, Series I, Volume II page 757 to 760.
108. Duke of Portland to Governor Hunter, 5 November 1799. *HRA*, Series I, Volume II, page 392.
109. *Dublin Evening Post*, 27 January 1798.
110. See Jonathon and John King, *Philip Gidley King-A Biography of the Third Governor of New South Wales*. Methuen Australia, 1981.
111. Charles, Samuel & George Enderby, Alexander & Benjamin Champion to Earl Liverpool, 1 August 1800, *HRA*, Series I, Volume III, page 2.
112. A/Governor King to Duke of Portland, 28 September 1800, *HRA*, Series I, Volume II, page 613.
113. Frederick Watson, Introduction, *HRA* Series I, Volume III, page xii–xiii.
114. John Grant to his mother and sister, 13 July 1804, John Grant Papers, NLA.
115. Charles Cookney to D'Arcy Wentworth, 4 March 1799, Wentworth Papers. ML.
116. *Account of Lands Granted 6 February 1800*, *HRA*, Series I, Volume II, page 462.
117. *Evidence of James Meehan*, Bigge Report transcripts. BT Box 2262-3.
118. John Brocklehurst & Co, Cornhill to D'Arcy Wentworth, 30 March 1802.
119. See Colinridge Rivett, *Australia's Blacktown From 1788*, Pioneer Media Productions, Sydney, 1986, page 81.
120. *Ibid*. Comment attributed to Francis Oakes, later Chief Constable at Parramatta.
121. W.C.Wentworth, *Australasia*, lines 5–6.
122. Jane Austen, *Evelyn*, Juvenilia, Volume the Second.
123. Jane Austen, *Persuasion*, Volume II, Chapter XI.
124. Governor Hunter, *Letter of Recommendation for D. Wentworth*, 20 September 1800, WWM.
125. John Hunter to Duke of Portland, 10 June 1801, *HRNSW*, Volume IV, page 396.
126. John Hunter to Lord Pelham, 14 August 1801.
127. Governor Hunter to Under Secretary King, 25 September 1800, *HRA* Series I, Volume II, page 554.

Chapter 16
The real & consistent Patron
Mansfield Park

The different sorts of friendship in the world
Mansfield Park

1. Quoted by E.A. Smith, *op cit*, page 9.
2. Lady Charlotte was a granddaughter of the 3rd Duke of Devonshire. Her niece, Lady Caroline Lamb, the daughter of her brother Frederick Ponsonby and his wife, Lady Henrietta Spencer, was a novelist. She was a confidante of Lord Byron. Her husband, later Lord Melbourne, was Prime Minister and a mentor to the young Queen Victoria.
3. *Journal of the House of Lords*, 9 January 1770, Volume 32, page 393–399.
4. The *Stamp Act* was passed in March 1765.
5. The Lords who voted in dissent were Rockingham, Fitzwilliam, Manchester, Portland, Richmond, Scarborough, Devonshire, King, Craven, Abington, DeFerrars, Effingham, Abergavenny, Ponsonby.
6. Governor John Wentworth to Lord Rockingham, 1 September 1765. WWM.
7. Ed. W.J. Bryan, *The World's Famous Orations*, Volume VIII, New York, Funk & Wagnalls, 1906.
8. Quoted in, Stanley Ayling, *George the Third*, Alfred A. Knopf, New York, 1972. pages 301–2.
9. Edmund Burke, 'Mr Burke's Speech on American Taxation,' *The works of the Right Hon Edmund Burke*, Volume I, Dublin,

1792, page 167.
10. Paul Langford, 'Burke, Edmund (1729/30–1797)', *Oxford Dictionary of National Biography*, 2004.
11. Lord Rockingham to Edmund Burke, 14 February 1771.
12. Lord Chatham, *Speech on the Government Policy in America*. House of Lords, 20 January, 1775. From W. Clarke, ed. *Political Orations, from Wentworth to Macauley*. London 1889.
13. Edmund Burke, House of Commons, 22 March 1775.
14. Frances Wentworth to Lady Mary Rockingham, 13 June 1775.
15. E.A. Smith, *op cit*, page 18.
16. John Moore, *A View of Society and Manners in France, Switzerland and Germany*, 1780, p. 290–91.
17. *The New Annual Register or General Repository of History, Politics and Literature for the Year 1797*, London, 1798, page 47.
18. *Ibid*.
19. Jane Austen, *Henry and Eliza*,
20. *New Annual Register*, op cit.
21. *Public Advertiser*, 9 July 1782.
22. William Mason, *The Dean & the Squire, a Political Eclogue*, J.Debrett, London, 1782, page i.
23. *Public Characters of the Year 1828*, London, 1828, p.360.
24. Earl Fitzwilliam to Rev Christopher Wyvill, 9 March 1780, Wyvill Papers, iv, page 127.
25. William Wilberforce to William Hey, 29 May 1787.
26. George III, *Proclamation for the Discouragement of Vice*, 1 June 1787.
27. *Morning Chronicle*, 25 July 1787.
28. Earl Fitzwilliam to Rev H Zouch, 2, 11, 22 September 1787.
29. James Ramsay, *Essay on the Treatment and Conversion of African Slaves in the British Sugar Colonies*, 1784.
30. E.A. Smith, *op cit*, page 134.
31. Abolition of the slave trade in 1807 had a profound economic impact on the port of Liverpool, and on its ship owners and marine tradesmen.
32. Edmund Burke to Earl Fitzwilliam, 4 August, 1791.
33. On 29 January 1789, the Commons passed five resolutions to limit the power of the Prince Regent to act in the King's name. It was not to extend to creating peers of the realm; not to grant office, salary or pension, except as law required, for life or good behaviour; not to extend to granting any part of His Majesty's real or personal estate, except renewal of leases; and the Queen was to be responsible for the King's physicians. Fifty one members of the House of Lords protested against them.
34. David Cecil, *The Young Melbourne*, Constable, London, 1939.
35. Earl Fitzwilliam to Rev Henry Zouch, 21 January 1785, WWM. The window tax was increased during both the American War of Independence and the Napoleonic Wars. In 1851 it was replaced by a tax on inhabited houses.
36. *The Gentleman's Magazine*. December 1804, page 1126.
37. Catherine Bailey, *Black Diamonds*, Penguin, London, 2008, page 52.
38. *Whitehall Evening Post*, July 14–16, 1789.
39. *Semper acerbum* – 'always bitter.'
40. *The World*, 30 September 1789.
41. Earl Fitzwilliam to Lord Portland, 12 and 15 June, 1794. WWM.
42. Footnote to a letter from Fitzwilliam to Rev Mr Addison, 7 August 1793, the *Correspondence of the Rt Hon. Edmund Burke*, eds, Earl Fitzwilliam and Sir Richard Bourke, op cit, Volume III, page 131.
43. E.A. Smith, *op cit*, page 188.
44. Rev Dean O'Beirne to W Baron Hotham, 31 March 1791, British National Archives.
45. John Pemberton Heywood to Earl Fitzwilliam, 7 October 1794, WWM.
46. *Correspondence of the Rt Hon. Edmund Burke*, op cit, Volume III, page 131.
47. Edward Cook to Evan Nepean, 27 January 1795. Cook was an Under Secretary who had been retired.
48. *Correspondence of the Rt Hon. Edmund Burke*, op cit, Volume III, page 192.
49. W. Macneile Dixon, *College Histories Dublin Trinity College*, London, 1902.
50. *Correspondence of the Rt Hon. Edmund Burke*, op cit, Volume III, page 131.
51. *The New Annual Register or General Repository of History, Politics and Literature for the Year 1797*, London, 1798, page 191.
52. *The Speeches of the Right Hon Charles James Fox in the House of Commons*, 24 March, 1795, page 38–43. London, Aylott & Co, 1853.
53. Quidam, "A scrap of truth," *London Chronicle*, 3 March 1795.
54. *The Scots Magazine*, Volume LX, January, 1798, page 143.

55 Earl Fitzwilliam to William Ponsonby, November 1796, quoted by E.A. Smith, *op cit*, page 230.
56 W.E.H. Lecky, *A History of England in the Eighteenth Century*, London, 1913. Volume VIII, page 179–183.
57 Earl Fitzwilliam to French Laurence, 25 June 1798.
58 *Memorial of the State Prisoners in Ireland*, 29 July 1798, quoted E.A. Smith, *op cit*, page 251.
59 Earl Fitzwilliam to French Laurence, 25 June 1798.
60 Earl Fitzwilliam to French Laurence, 14 October 1798, quoted by E.A. Smith, *ibid*.
61 Earl Fitzwilliam to Edmund Burke, 10 November 1796, *Correspondence of the Rt Hon. Edmund Burke*, op cit, Volume IV, page 355.
62 Earl Fitzwilliam to Edmund Burke, 27 November 1796.
63 Robert Sinclair to Earl Fitzwilliam, 14 August 1798. WWM.
64 *The Scots Magazine*, Volume LX, January, 1798, page 143.
65 Marquis of Buckingham to Lord Grenville, 11 February, 1807, HMC, *Dropmore*, ix, page 34–36.
66 Lord Grenville to Lord Bathurst, 18 March 1807, HMC, *Bathurst*, page 56.
67 S.M. Lee, *Parliament, Parties and Elections (1760–1815)* in *A Companion to Eighteenth Century Britain* edited by H.T. Dickinson, John Wiley, Oxford, 2006, page 71.
68 In *Mansfield Park*, the Lascelles were at Wimpole Street, an area where wealthy West Indian plantation owners lived.
69 Earl Fitzwilliam to Lord Grenville, 6 December 1807.
70 Earl Fitzwilliam to Charles Grey, Viscount Howick, 22 July 1808.
71 Earl Fitzwilliam to Charles Grey, Viscount Howick, 22 October 1814, 14 April 1813.
72 Jane Austen to Martha Lloyd, 2 September 1814.
73 Jane Austen, *Persuasion*, Volume I, Chapter IV.
74 Earl Fitzwilliam to Charles Grey, Viscount Howick, quoted by E.A. Smith, *op cit*, page 327.
75 Jane Austen, *Northanger Abbey*, Volume II, Chapter VIII.
76 Louisa was the widow of Charlotte's cousin, William, 1st Lord Ponsonby, and daughter of Richard Molesworth, 3rd Viscount Molesworth.

Chapter 17
Antipodean Hell
Brooding over Evils which cannot be remedied, & conduct impossible to understand
Letters

1 Governor King, *Authorisation*, M.H. Ellis Papers, ML. John Meehan's map of Sydney, 31 October 1807, shows Harris' house on the east side of High Street (now George) immediately North of what is now Bond Street.
2 Catherine Melling arrived as a convict on *Marquis Cornwallis* in 1786, from Dublin, Ireland.
3 In 1795, aged twenty-one, Maria and her sister-in-law Elizabeth, both widows, were sentenced to seven years transportation for stealing a brass pot and pan. They arrived in Sydney on 30 April 1796 on the *Indispensable*.
4 D'Arcy Wentworth to Earl Fitzwilliam, 11 October 1800. WWM.
5 Enderby owned three ships that had brought supplies to Sydney, a storeship, *William*, and two whalers, *Speedy* and *Britannia*. The two whalers each carried stores and a small number of convicts outbound from England, *Speedy* carried 53 female convicts, *Britannia*, 96 female convicts. See Charles Bateson, *The Convict Ships 1787–1868*, Brown Sons and Ferguson, Glasgow, 1969 pp.147 & 157
6 Messrs Enderby & Champion to Earl Liverpool, 1 August 1800, *HRA* Series I, Volume III, page 3, & A/Governor King to Duke of Portland, 8 July 1801, page 110–111.
7 See D.R. Hainsworth, *The Sydney Traders, Simeon Lord and His Contemporaries 1788–1821*. Melbourne, Cassell, 1981, page 49.
8 Charles Cookney to D'Arcy Wentworth, 1 August 1798. Wentworth Papers, ML.
9 King's full commission was sent to him on 5 May 1802, more than two years after he left England.
10 Governor Hunter to Lieutenant Governor King, 8 July 1800. *HRA*, Series I, Volume II, p.658.
11 Governor Hunter to Lieutenant Governor King, 11 July 1800. *HRA*, Series I, Volume II, p.662.
12 Instructions to Major Foveaux, *HRA*, Series I, Volume II, page 512–523.

13 Lieut. Governor King to Paterson, 8 September 1800. *HRA*, Series I, Volume II, p. 542–3.
14 Lieut. Governor King to the Duke of Portland, 10 September 1800.
15 William Balmain to Lieut. Governor King, 16 September 1800, *HRNSW*, Volume IV, page 142.
16 William Balmain to Lieut. Governor King, 14 September 1800.
17 Lieut Governor King to William Balmain and D'Arcy Wentworth, 16 September 1800. *HRNSW*, Volume IV, page 141.
18 Lieut. Governor King to Major Paterson, 18 September 1800, *HRNSW*, Volume IV.
19 Frederick Watson, Introduction, *HRA*, Series I, Volume III, page xviii.
20 *Ibid*, page xviii & xxi.
21 Lieut. Governor King to Duke of Portland, 18 September 1800, *HRA*, Series I, Volume II, page 542.
22 D'Arcy Wentworth to Earl Fitzwilliam, 11 October 1800. WWM.
23 D'Arcy Wentworth to Earl Fitzwilliam, 12 May 1803. WWM.
24 D'Arcy Wentworth to Earl Fitzwilliam, 11 October 1800. WWM.
25 Charles Cookney to D'Arcy Wentworth, 2 June 1801, Wentworth Papers, ML.
26 Charles Cookney to Secretary Sullivan, 10 December 1802; Charles Cookney to D'Arcy Wentworth, 8 February 1803, Wentworth Papers, ML.
27 Governor King to Secretary King, 8 November 1801, *HRNSW*, Volume IV, page 613.
28 Government & General Order 27 July 1801: *William Balmain Esq, Principal Surgeon, having the Governor's consent to avail himself of the Secretary of State's leave of absence. HRNSW*, Volume IV, page 444.
29 William Balmain to D'Arcy Wentworth, 25 March 1803, Wentworth Papers, ML.
30 Kathleen Dermody, *op cit*, page 122.
31 William Balmain to D'Arcy Wentworth, 25 March 1803, Wentworth Papers, ML.
32 A/Governor King to Duke of Portland, *HRA*, Series 1, Volume III.
33 A/Governor King to Duke of Portland, 8 July 1801, *HRA*, Series 1, Volume III, page 117.
34 Frederick Watson, *op cit*, page xvi.
35 Governor Hunter to Evan Nepean, 3 September 1798, *HRA*, Series I, Volume II, page 132.
36 George Bass to Thomas Jamison, 15 May 1802, quoted by Michael Roe, New Light on *George Bass, Entrepreneur and Intellectual*, JRAHS, Volume 72, Part 5, 1987.
37 George Bass to Henry Waterhouse, 4 October 1801, *ibid*.
38 *HRNSW*, Volume III, Note, page 312.
39 John Grant to his mother and sister, 13 July 1804, John Grant Papers, NLA.
40 Frederick Watson, Introduction, *HRA*, Series I, Volume III, page xix.
41 J. & J. King, *Philip Gidley King*, Methuen, Sydney, 1981, page 88.
42 Lieut Col. Paterson to Acting Governor King, 25 September 1801, *HRA*, Series 1 Vol. II, page 317.
43 Governor King to Secretary Evan Nepean, 31 October 1801, *HRA* Series I, Vol. III, page 273.
44 Today Ambon, in Indonesia.
45 M.H. Ellis, *John Macarthur*, *op cit*, page 212.
46 A.G.L. Shaw, 'Philip Gidley King (1758–1808),' *ADB 1788–1850*, Part 2, page 55.
47 William Balmain to D'Arcy Wentworth, 25 March 1803, *Wentworth Papers*, ML.
48 Printed statement delivered by Captain Macarthur at the Right Honourable Lord Hobart's office, London, 26 July 1803.
49 *The New Annual Register or General Repository of History, Politics and Literature for the Year 1800*, London, 1801, page 175.
50 En route to London in 1796, King had called at Cape Town, where the widow of the late Colonel Gordon was selling his flock of merino sheep. King's family had been in the cloth trade and he realised the sheep could supply the foundation for a wool industry in the colony. He and Paterson purchased three each and he prevailed on Captain Waterhouse of the Reliance and Captain Kent of the Supply to purchase the remaining twenty six, and to take them all to Sydney.
51 Introduction, *HRNSW*, Volume V, page xxii.
52 Quoted by Alan Atkinson 'British Whigs and the Rum Rebellion,' *JRAHS*, September 1980, page 79.
53 H.V. Evatt, *Rum Rebellion*, Angus & Robertson, Sydney, 1938, page 10.
54 *HRNSW*, Volume V, page 674.
55 Major-General Brownrigg to Under Secretary King, 4 August 1801, *HRA*, Series 1, Vol II, p.445.
56 *HRNSW*, Volume III, Note, page 312.

57 Dr Munro was most likely Alexander Munro (tertius) who held the Chair of Anatomy at Edinburgh University, as had his father and grandfather, and whose students included Charles Darwin.
58 Dennis Considen to D'Arcy Wentworth, 20 and 27 February, ML.
59 *HRA*, Series I, Volume IV, page 178.
60 Governor King to Lord Hobart, 9 November 1802. *HRNSW*, Volume IV, page 973.
61 Major Johnston to Governor King, 23 February 1803, *King Papers*, ML.
62 Governor King to Lord Hobart, 1 March 1804. *HRA*, Series I, Volume IV, page 541.
63 Governor King to Major Johnston, 23 February 1803, *King Papers*, ML.
64 That area of Sydney is still called Ultimo today.
65 *HRA*, Series 1, Volume IV, Introduction, pages xi–xii
66 Governor King to Major Johnston, 18 February 1803, *HRA* Series I, Volume IV, page 216.
67 Sir Joseph Banks to Governor King, 29 August 1804, *Banks Papers*, ML.
68 *Government and General Order*, 6 July 1802. *HRNSW*, Volume IV, page 798.
69 D'Arcy Wentworth to Earl Fitzwilliam, 12 May 1803, WWM.
70 Jane Austen, *Persuasion*, Volume I, Chapter V.
71 W.C & D.Wentworth, Jnr to D'Arcy Wentworth, 24 July 1804, ML.
72 William Balmain to D'Arcy Wentworth, 25 March 1803, Wentworth Papers, ML.
73 D'Arcy Wentworth to Lord Hobart, 14 May 1803. *HRNSW*, Volume V, page 143.
74 Captain James Colnett, *op cit*.
75 William Balmain to D'Arcy Wentworth, 25 March 1803, Wentworth Papers, ML.
76 J.P. McGuanne, *Humours & Pastimes, op cit*.
77 http://www.austlii.edu.au/au/cases/nsw/NSWSupC/1802/2.html, Note, Page 12.
78 J.P. McGuanne, *op cit*.
79 *The Times*, Friday, 19 July 1805.
80 Earl Fitzwilliam to D'Arcy Wentworth, 30 July 1802. WWM.
81 D'Arcy Wentworth to Earl Fitzwilliam, 12 May 1803. WWM.
82 D'Arcy Wentworth to Thomas Jamison. 1 January 1803. Wentworth Papers, ML.
83 D'Arcy Wentworth to Earl Fitzwilliam, 12 May 1803. Wentworth Papers, ML.
84 Charles Cookney to D'Arcy Wentworth, February 1803. Wentworth Papers, ML.
85 Charles Cookney to D'Arcy Wentworth, June 1803. Wentworth Papers, ML.
86 Mrs Anna King to D'Arcy Wentworth, 18 July 1804. Wentworth Papers, ML.
87 Seamus Heaney, from *Whatever you say, say nothing*, from *North*, Faber & Faber, 1975.
88 *The Scots Magazine,* Edinburgh, Volume LX, January 1798, page iii–iv.
89 *Proclamation* 2 April 1802, *HRA*, Series I, Volume III, page 618.
90 *HRNSW*, Volume V, page 300.
91 'Castle Hill Rebellion,' *Sydney Gazette*, 11 March 1804.
92 Elizabeth Macarthur to John Piper, 14 April 1804, *Piper Papers*, ML.
93 Major Johnston to Lieut. Colonel Paterson, 9 March 1804, *HRA*, Series I, Volume IV, page 570.
94 Major Johnston to Governor King, 6 March 1804, *ibid*, page 568.
95 Kipling, R. *The Irish Guards*, in ed. Laski, M. *Kipling's English History*. BBC. 1974.
96 Surgeon Arndell to Rev Marsden, 4 March 1804, *ibid*, page 567.
97 Today Newcastle, New South Wales.
98 *Return of the Parramatta Associated Company*, 5 March 1804, *HRA*, Series I, Volume IV, p. 578.

Chapter 18
The Dwelling Place of Devils, the Doubly Damned
Joseph Holt

Lost, every consolation in the possibility of acquitting him
Sense & Sensibility

1 *By persevering industry, I know many who were convicts, to be now worth from 10 to 15000£. There is a young man here of the name of Lord, he was a convict & is only 22 years of age, who beside having large farms, keeps a shop socked with soft goods & Haberdashery of every description; he keeps the only bake house in Sidney and auction Rooms, and has now a ship coming from Bengal on his own account*. John Washington Price, *op cit*, page 162.
2 Their union was far from unique in New South Wales. No more than 360 couples were married. Among the civil and military officers and landholders alone, 203 kept concubines; there were 900 legitimate and 908 illegitimate children in the colony.

3. A muster on 10 & 12 July 1804, counted 101 soldiers and 11 civil officers; 211 male and 40 female convicts; 16 settlers; 224 free men, 146 free women and 311 children. *HRNSW*, Volume V, page 431.
4. A.G.L. Shaw, 'Philip Gidley King (1758–1808),' *ADB 1788–1850*, Part 2, page 55.
5. Joseph Holt, *op cit*, page 219.
6. Robert Buckey, *Recollections of 13 Years Residence in Norfolk Island and Van Diemen's Land*. Sydney, Transcript, June 15, 1823. ML.
7. *Ibid*.
8. Lord Hobart to Governor King, 24 June 1803, *HRA*, Series I, Volume IV, page 304.
9. D'Arcy Wentworth to Earl Fitzwilliam, August 14, 1804, WWM.
10. Robert Hughes, *The Fatal Shore*, Collins Harvill, London, 1987, page 114.
11. Jane Austen, *Persuasion*, Volume II, Chapter IX.
12. Governor King to Lord Portland, 10 March 1801, *HRA*, Series I, Volume III, page 8.
13. James Mitchell, *Norfolk Island 1804 to 1809*. ML.
14. James Mileham to D'Arcy Wentworth, 14 August 1804, ML.
15. Joseph Holt, *op cit*, pages 230 & 270.
16. Robert Buckey, *op cit*. Holt wrote of Buckey, *gaoler superintendant, tale-bearer, persecutor, planner of all evil. His father and two brothers were concerned in many robberies and this wretch went and prosecuted the father and two brothers and all three died*. Holt, *op cit*, page 383.
17. Joseph Holt, *op cit*, page 228–229.
18. Jane Austen, *Mansfield Park*, Volume I, Chapter VII.
19. Joseph Holt, *op cit*. page 228–229.
20. Jane Austen, *Mansfield Park*, Volume I, Chapter VII.
21. Joseph Holt, *op cit*, page 224.
22. The first group from Norfolk Island were settled at Sullivans Cove, the site of present day Hobart.
23. James Mitchell, *op cit*.
24. D'Arcy Jnr to D'Arcy Wentworth, 4 July 1805, Wentworth Papers, ML.
25. Joseph Holt, *op cit*, page 238.
26. Robert Buckey, *op cit*.
27. Governor King to Lord Hobart, 20 December 1804, *HRA*, Series I, Volume V, page 167.
28. Today, *Flagstaff Hill*.
29. Joseph Holt, *op cit*. page 232–5.
30. Commandant Piper to Governor King, 30 April 1805, *HRA*, Series I, Volume V.
31. Joseph Holt, *op cit*. page 232–5.
32. Commandant Piper to Governor King, 30 April 1805, *HRA*, Series I, Volume V.
33. Joseph Holt, *op cit*. page 232–5. He commented on the plan to cut the French down with broken glass: *how ridiculous the defence they could have made would have proved*.
34. Commandant Piper to Governor King, 30 April 1805, *HRA*, Series I, Volume V.
35. Joseph Holt, *op cit*. page 232–5.
36. *Ibid*, page 258.
37. See W.H.Auden & Louis MacNeice, *Letters from Iceland*, London, Faber & Faber, 1967, page 76.
38. Dennis Considen to D'Arcy Wentworth, 27 September 1804, ML.
39. *Eucalyptus consideniana* was named in honour of Dennis Considen.
40. Governor King to Lord Hobart, 20 December 1804, *HRA*, Series I, Volume V, page 645.
41. Governor King to Lord Camden, 15 March 1806, *HRA*, Series I, Volume V, page 646.
42. Charles Cookney to D'Arcy Wentworth, May 1805, Wentworth Papers, ML.
43. *Statement of facts on behalf of D'Arcy Wentworth*, to Earl Camden, undated; and D'Arcy Wentworth to Earl Fitzwilliam, November 1806, WWM.
44. Robert Buckey, *op cit*.
45. Joseph Holt, *op cit*, page 229.
46. David Dickinson Mann, *The Present Picture of New South Wales*, London. 1811, page 15–16.
47. Australian Government Bureau of Meteorology, *Records of Tsunamis affecting Australia*.
48. Charles Cookney to D'Arcy Wentworth, 31 December 1805. Wentworth Papers, ML.
49. D'Arcy made £1277 in 1804 for meat and grain sold to the Commissariat store; and in 1805 £1493.
50. Charles Cookney to D'Arcy Wentworth, 3 December 1805. Wentworth Papers, ML.
51. Captain David Collins to Lieut. Governor King, June 1795. ML.
52. *The Times*, 16 October 1790.
53. Thomas Jamison to D'Arcy Wentworth. 8 February 1806, Wentworth Papers, ML.
54. D'Arcy Wentworth to Charles Cookney, 12 May 1806, Wentworth Papers, ML.

55 Charles Cookney to D'Arcy Wentworth, 8 October 1805, Wentworth Papers, ML.
56 D'Arcy Wentworth to Charles Cookney, 12 March 1806, Wentworth Papers, ML. The *Encyclopaedia Britannica* was first published in 1771. Cookney sent D'Arcy the third edition, that was issued in 300 weekly sections between 1788 and 1797, and sold over 10,000 copies.
57 Aaron Price, *Diary of Norfolk Island 1825–1854*, ML.
58 D'Arcy Wentworth to Charles Cookney, 12 May 1806, Wentworth Papers, ML.
59 *Wentworth Woodhouse* at Parramatta stood in what is now Fitzwilliam Street, near the Railway Station. King acknowledged D'Arcy's improvements to the property, and extended his lease. In 1810 it was converted to a grant.
60 D'Arcy Wentworth to Earl Fitzwilliam, 12 May 1803, WWM.
61 D'Arcy Wentworth to Earl Fitzwilliam, 4 November 1806, WWM.
62 *Sydney Gazette*, Sunday, 31 August, 1806.
63 William Redfern to D'Arcy Wentworth, undated, in papers presented by Dorothy Wentworth, ML.
64 It was said Mary Smith suffered a prolonged nervous collapse after the suicide of the captain of the *Perseverance,* who had professed his love for her.
65 Governor Bligh to Viscount Castlereagh, 10 June 1809, *HRA,* Series I, Volume VII, page 114.
66 D'Arcy Wentworth to Captain Piper, 29 November 1806, *HRNSW,* Volume 6, page 204.
67 Robert Buckey, *op cit.*
68 Joseph Holt, *op cit,* page 240.
69 Quoted by Marjorie Barnard Eldershaw, *The Life & Times of John Piper,* Sydney, 1973, page 76.
70 William Redfern to D'Arcy Wentworth, 16 September 1807, ML.
71 M.H. Ellis, *Macarthur, op cit,* page 164.
72 D'Arcy Wentworth to Charles Cookney, undated, Wentworth Papers, ML.
73 D'Arcy Wentworth to Lord Fitzwilliam, 4 November 1806, WWM.

Chapter 19
The Peripatetic Austens
More at large & likewise, more at small
Letters

1 Jane Austen, *Persuasion*, Volume I, Chapter IX.
2 Jane Austen, *Edgar & Emma,* Juvenilia, Volume the First.
3 Jane to Cassandra Austen, 20 November 1800.
4 Jane to Cassandra Austen, 8 January, 1801.
5 Jane to Cassandra Austen, 14 January, 1801.
6 Jane to Cassandra Austen, 21 January 1801.
7 Jane to Cassandra Austen, 8 January, 1801.
8 *Ibid.*
9 Jane to Cassandra Austen, 14 January, 1801.
10 Jane to Cassandra Austen, 12 May, 1801.
11 Jane to Cassandra Austen, 21 May, 1801.
12 Jane to Cassandra Austen, 8 February, 1807.
13 Jane to Cassandra Austen, 14 January, 1801.
14 Jane to Cassandra Austen, 25 January 1801
15 Eliza de Feuillide to Phylly Walton, 16 February 1798. *Austen Papers, op cit,* page 160–170.
16 Jane Austen, *Lady Susan*, Chapter V.
17 Jane to Cassandra Austen, 25 January, 1801.
18 Jane to Cassandra Austen, 11 February, 1801. Prince Augustus, the Prince Regent's younger brother, had an impressive military career as Duke of York. Of his several illegitimate children, two came to live in Australia: John Molloy, born in 1780, emigrated to Western Australia in 1830, and founded the settlement of Augusta, he was a pioneer and magistrate. He had three daughters. John Gibbes, born in 1787, arrived in Sydney in 1834. He served as collector of customs, and was later a member of the Legislative Council. He had two sons, one named Augustus, and three daughters.
19 Prince Augustus remarried, he is remembered as Queen Victoria's favourite uncle.
20 Jane to Cassandra Austen, 1 November 1800.
21 *Encyclopaedia Brittanica*, ninth edition, Volume I.
22 W.E.H. Lecky, *A History of England in the Eighteenth Century*, London, 1913. Volume VII, p.170.
23 Jane Austen, *Northanger Abbey*, Volume I, Chapter III.
24 David Nokes, *op cit,* page 236.
25 Jane Austen to Fanny Knight, 30 November, 1814.

26 Jane to Cassandra Austen, 12 May 1801.
27 Jane Austen, *Mansfield Park,* Volume III, Chapter XIV.
28 Jane Austen, *Persuasion*, Volume I, Chapter X.
29 Jane Austen, *Mansfield Park,* Volume III, Chapter XV.
30 Jane Austen, *Persuasion*, Volume I, Chapter V.
31 *Ibid*, Volume II, Chapter XI.
32 Jane Austen, *Mansfield Park*, Volume II, Chapter X.
33 Jane Austen, *Persuasion*, Volume II, Chapter XI.
34 Jane Austen, *Pride & Prejudice*, Volume III, Chapter II.
35 Jane Austen, *Mansfield Park*, Volume III, Chapter XV.
36 Jane Austen, *Persuasion*, Volume II, Chapter XI.
37 Jane to Cassandra Austen, 30 August 1805.
38 Jane Austen, *Persuasion*, Volume II, Chapter XI.
39 Jane Austen, *Northanger Abbey*, Volume II, Chapter XVI.
40 Jane Austen, *Sense & Sensibility,* Volume II, Chapter IX.
41 Jane Austen, *Emma*, Volume II, Chapter II.
42 Jane Austen, *Sense & Sensibility*, Volume II, Chapter VI.
43 What occurred that evening is unclear. Sixty-eight years later, in 1870, Jane's niece Caroline Austen, then sixty-five, wrote to her niece Amy Austen-Leigh of *some peculiar comings and goings coinciding exactly with what my Mother more than once told me of that affair.* Her mother, Mary Lloyd was not known for her friendship with Jane or her generosity towards her.
44 Jane Austen, *Sense & Sensibility,* Volume I, Chapter VIII.
45 Jane Austen, *Emma*, Volume III, Chapter XIII.
46 Jane Austen, *Jack & Alice*, Juvenilia, Volume the First.
47 Jane Austen, *Persuasion*, Volume II, Chapter V.
48 *Public Characters of the Year 1828*, London 1828, page 346.
49 *Ibid,* page 270.
50 Jane Austen, *Sanditon,* Chapter I.
51 Jane Austen, *Emma*, Volume III, Chapter VI.
52 Jane to Cassandra Austen, 24 August 1805.
53 Jane Austen, *Persuasion*, Volume I, Chapter XI.
54 *Ibid.*
55 Jane Austen, *The Watsons.*
56 Quoted by Sarah Markham, *A Testimony of Her Times*, Michael Russell Publishing, 1991, a diary entry of Penelope Benwell, November 1804. She refers to Erasmus Darwin, Charles Darwin's grandfather, who wrote his treatises on the natural sciences in verse.
57 *Ibid.*
58 Jane Austen, *Northanger Abbey*, Volume I, Chapter II.
59 Jane to Cassandra Austen, 21 April 1805.
60 Jane to Cassandra Austen, 27 August 1805.
61 Jane Austen, *Persuasion*, Volume I, Chapter II.
62 Jane Austen, *Mansfield Park,* Volume III, Chapter V.
63 Quoted by Brian Southam, *Jane Austen and the Navy, op cit,* page 97.
64 *Ibid,* page 98.
65 Now Haiti.
66 Brian Southam, *Jane Austen and the Navy, op cit,* pages 53&126–7.
67 Jane to Cassandra Austen, 3 January 1801.
68 Jane Austen, *Persuasion*, Volume II, Chapter VII.
69 Duke of Portland to Lord Hobart, 3 October 1802, *HRNSW*, page 847–848.
70 *Naval Chronicle*, Volume IX, January to July 1803, page 80.
71 *Naval Chronicle,* Volume XIII, January to June 1805, page 1–44.
72 *Naval Chronicle,* Volume XXV, January to July 1811, page 144.
73 Jane Austen, *Persuasion*, Volume I, Chapter IV.
74 Jane Austen, *Persuasion*, Volume II, Chapter VI.

Index

A
Abbott, Edward (Lieutenant), 203, 226, 229–30
Abercromby, General Sir Ralph, 357–8
Aboriginal people
  New South Wales, 191, 203–4, 214, 221, 234, 260, 279, 323
  Van Diemen's Land, 335–6
Ainsley (or Ainslie), Maria (emancipist), 311, 333, 348
Aldous, William (pawnbroker), 111, 113
Alton (Hampshire), 121, 125–8, 132
American colonies. *see also* New Hampshire; United States
  British trade, 17
  Franklin as Ambassador, 86
  loss of, 14–15, 77, 79, 88, 189–90, 286–91, 296, 304, 308
  loyalists, 217
  transportation to, 306
American War of Independence (1776-81), 20, 77, 86–8, 103, 194, 202, 233, 247, 249, 273, 286–91, 293, 295, 305
Amyot, Thomas, 111
Anderson, Archibald, 98–9, 102
Anglican Church
  Austen family, 23–4, 65, 137
  Catholic emancipation, 302
  history, 26
  Jane's references to, 171–2
Anglo-Irish establishment, 11, 14

apothecaries, 12–13, 81–2, 90, 121, 123, 125, 131, 214, 343
Argo (ship), 322
Armagh (County), 11, 15, 273. *see also* Portadown, County Armagh
Ashe (Hampshire), 134–5, 186–8, 237–41, 355, 361, 363, 368
Atkins, Richard (Judge-Advocate), 227, 233, 278–9, 319, 327, 403n81, 403n103
Austen, Anna (Jane-Anna-Elizabeth) (1793-1872) Jane's niece, daughter of James & Anne, 125, 247, 354, 363, 370, 399n34
Austen, Anne, née Mathew (1758/9-1795) 1st wife of Jane's brother James, 246–8, 252
Austen, Caroline Mary Craven (b. 1805) Jane's niece, 8, 360, 364–5, 370
Austen, Cassandra, née Leigh (1739-1827) Jane's mother
  ancestors & relatives, 23–4, 67, 76
  family life, 23–4, 40, 44, 58, 64, 119, 135, 139, 168, 252, 353, 363, 369
  Jane's relationship with, 23, 33–4, 58–9, 127, 167, 186
  life after George's retirement, 358, 366, 370, 373
Austen, Cassandra (1773-1845) Jane's sister
  early life, 23–5, 27–8, 35–6, 56, 58, 63–4, 119, 133–6, 178, 182, 186
  engagement to Tom Fowle (1791-97), 59, 63, 244, 254
  later life, 60, 164, 240, 246, 353–6, 358, 360,

415

363–5, 368–73
Austen, Charles (1779-1852) Jane's brother, later Admiral, 23, 35, 56, 60, 175, 247, 356–7, 363, 367
Austen, Edward (1767-1852) Jane's brother. *see* Knight, Edward
Austen, Elizabeth ('Eliza' or 'Betsy') (1761-1813) Jane's cousin
  childhood & early life (as Eliza Hancock), 31–2, 40–1, 43–5, 51
  as Comtesse de Feuillide (1781-94), 31–4, 37, 55–6, 59, 64, 133, 148–9, 154, 162–3, 176–7, 248–9
  as widow (1794–97), 140, 386n5
  as wife of Jane's brother Henry (from 1797), 252–3, 320, 356, 361, 367, 369
Austen, Elizabeth (widow of Stephen). *see* Cumberledge, Elizabeth
Austen, Francis (b. 1698, fl. 1788) lawyer, of Sevenoaks; Jane's great-uncle, 7, 23, 37–8, 41, 43, 45–6, 64
Austen, Frank, later Admiral Sir Francis (1774-1865) Jane's brother, 23, 35, 56, 138, 140, 175, 179, 247, 294, 357, 363, 367–8, 371, 373
Austen, Rev George (1731-1805) Jane's father
  family life, 31, 33–5, 40–1, 64, 127, 135, 139, 166–8, 179–82, 241, 362–3, 366
  forebears & relatives, 23–4, 28, 32–4, 37–8, 45
  Jane's relationship with, 57–9, 161, 176–9, 235, 245, 253–4
  as rector of Steventon, 23–4, 63, 65, 133, 155, 170, 172, 174, 353–4
  rectory school, 27, 44, 58, 63, 67
  retirement & death, 353–5, 358–9, 362–3, 366, 368–70
Austen, George (1765-1838) Jane's brother, 23–4, 64
Austen, Rev Henry Thomas (1771-1850) Jane's brother, 23, 34, 46, 64–5, 91, 138, 163, 175–80, 182, 249, 252–3, 308, 356, 361, 366–7, 369
Austen, Rev James (1765-1819) Jane's brother
  early life at Steventon & Oxford (1765-92), 23, 34, 36, 59–60, 63, 65–6, 92–3, 133, 138, 179
  Jane's relationship with, 175–6, 178–82, 241, 244
  marriage to Anne Mathew (1792-95), 172, 176, 178, 246–7, 249
  marriage to Mary Lloyd (1797-1819), 252, 354–5, 361, 363–5, 369–70
Austen, Jane (1775-1817)
  (1775-1786) birth & early years, **23–31,** 33, 35–6
  (1783) at Mrs Cawley's school, Oxford &
  Southampton, 24
  (1785-1786) at Abbey House School, Reading, 25
  (1787-1789) D'Arcy's missing years, **119–38**
  (1789) northern trip, 139–43, 163–4, 310, 362
  (1790s, after D'Arcy's departure) at home in Steventon, **237–49,** 252–4
  (1800s) at home in Steventon & travelling in England, **353–75**
  alias Smith, 174
  alias Taylor, 146, 179
  alias Weaver, 145–6, 179
  alias Wilson, 143, 145–6, 155–6, 167, 178–9
  banns (make-believe), 172–4
  connections with D'Arcy Wentworth (*see* Wentworth, D'Arcy)
  family history interests, **67–78,** 183
  friendship with cousin Eliza, 56, 59
  at home in Steventon, **57–66,** 119–30, 132–4
  Indian connections, 37–8, 56
  London visits & interests (*see* London)
  publishers, 8, 253–4, 366
  relations with Phylly Walter, 64
Austen, Jane (1775-1817): writings, 121, 175, 182–3, 239, 244, 246, 253–4, 360, 366
  The Adventures of Mr Harley, 161
  A Collection of Letters, 161
  Elinor and Marianne, 182, 244, 254 (*see also Sense & Sensibility*)
  Emma, 130, 242, 374–5
  Evelyn, 167–8
  First Impressions, 7, 182, 244, 246, 254 (*see also Pride & Prejudice*)
  Henry & Eliza, 165–6
  The History of England, 239
  Juvenilia, 7, 64, 160, 162, 167, 171, 254
  Kitty, or the Bower, 167–70, 253
  Lesley Castle, 164, 239, 253
  The Loiterer (contributions by 'Sophia Sentiment'), 64, 133
  Love & Freindship, 160, 162–7
  Mansfield Park, 34, 185, 365
  The Mystery, 161
  Northanger Abbey, 63, 103, 246–8 (*see also Susan*)
  Persuasion, 253, 372–4
  Pride & Prejudice, 7, 57, 78, 122, 124–5, 128, 176–7, 181–2, 185–6, 223, 244–5, 310 (*see also First Impressions*)
  Scraps, 162, 167
  Sense & Sensibility, 7, 64, 78, 159, 176, 182, 185–7, 244, 366 (*see also Elinor and Marianne*)
  Sir Charles Grandison, 167
  Susan, 246, 366 (*see also Northanger Abbey*)

INDEX

The Watsons, 125, 268, 362, 366, 395n18
Austen, Leonora (1733-1783) Jane's aunt, 37–9, 44–5
Austen, Mary, née Gibson (wife of Jane's brother Frank), 367–8, 373
Austen, Mary, née Lloyd (1771-1843) 2nd wife of Jane's brother James, 59, 63, 252–3, 354–5, 361, 363–4, 370
Austen, Philadelphia. *see* Hancock, Philadelphia
Austen, Rebecca, née Hampson, earlier Mrs Walter (d. 1732) Jane's grandmother, 23, 37, 41
Austen, Stephen (d. 1750) bookseller, London, Jane's father's uncle, 37–9, 44
Austen, Susannah, née Kelk (2nd wife of Jane's grandfather, William Austen, m. 1736), 37
Austen, William (1701?-1737) surgeon, Jane's grandfather, 23, 28, 37
Austen family
 family life, 24, 33, 35–6, 61, 66, 133, 149, 158, 170, 185–6, 254, 290, 353–5, 360–1
 Jane's forebears & relatives, 24, 31, 37, 41, 44, 56, 67, 133, 136, 149, 176, 183, 361, 373
 Jane's nephews & nieces, 8, 160–1, 247, 354, 360, 363–5
 Jane's parents & siblings, 56, 60, 64, 119, 121, 163, 167–8, 175–6, 178–82, 246–7, 357, 373
Austen-Leigh, Rev (James) Edward (1798-1874) Jane's nephew, son of James Austen, 8, 176
 Memoir of Jane Austen (1869), 8, 24, 58–9, 61, 119, 160–1, 176, 254, 364, 405n74
 Recollections of the Early Days of the Vine Hunt, 8, 60, 119
Austen-Leigh, William (Jane's grand-nephew), 164
Australia. *see* New South Wales; Norfolk Island; Van Diemen's Land (Tasmania)

B
Baillie, Dr Matthew (specialist), 81, 361
Balmain, William (surgeon), 62, 105, 219, 257, 264–5, 268–9, 278, 283, 313–17, 321, 323–8, 330
Banks, Sir Joseph, 81, 197, 214, 221, 281, 295, 319, 321–2, 325, 335, 349, 404n46
Barrington, George, 154, 271–2
Bass, George (surgeon), 234, 271, 318
Bass Strait, 335, 341
Bath (Somerset), 23, 25, 109, 195, 222, 240, 248, 277
 Jane's visits & references to, 36, 58, 63, 103, 246, 353–4, 358–61, 363, 365, 368–73
Baudin, Nicholas, 335
Baughan, John (emancipist), 264, 267
Beaumarchais, Pierre-Augustin Caron de (1732-99), 87

Beddoes, Thomas, 81
Belfast, 14, 273, 306, 344
Bengal, Nawab of. *see* Siraj-ud-daula ('Sir Roger Dowlat')
Bennelong (or Bennillon), 221, 233–4
Beresford, John, 301, 304
Bertie, Lady Jane. *see* Mathew, Lady Jane, née Bertie (mother of Anne Austen)
Bessborough, Lady Catherine, Countess of, née Cavendish (mother of Countess Fitzwilliam, wife of 4th Earl), 285
Bessborough, William, 2nd Earl of (father of Countess Fitzwilliam, wife of 4th Earl), 285
Bigg sisters (Catherine & Alethea, of Manydown), 364–5, 371
Bigg-Wither, Harris (younger brother of Catherine & Alethea Bigg), 364–5
Blackall, Rev Samuel, 241
Blackheath, 95, 97, 100, 277
Blake, William, 79
Bligh, William (Governor of NSW), 213, 322, 347, 349, 351
Bond, Nicholas (magistrate), 146–7, 149–50, 158, 179
Boston, John, 256–7, 263, 268
Botany Bay (colony). *see* New South Wales
Botany Bay (NSW), 266, 270
Bow Street, Covent Garden
 magistrates, 99–102, 113, 116, 118, 144, 146–7, 149–50, 167, 178–9, 278
 Runners, 99–100, 102, 109, 111, 113–18, 153, 179, 345
Bridges, Edward (Elizabeth's brother), 370
Bridges, Elizabeth. *see* Knight, Elizabeth, née Bridges (1772/3-1808) wife of Jane's brother, Edward Knight, originally Austen
Bridges, Lady Fanny (Jane's brother Edward's mother-in-law), 370
Britannia (Third Fleet transport), 217, 220, 225–6, 228, 257–8, 278, 318
British Army, 247, 252, 267, 272, 347. *see also* New South Wales Corps ('Rum Corps')
Brooks, Richard (Captain) (c1765-1833), 326
'Brown, Mary,' 174
Brush Farm (NSW), 327, 333
Brydges, Sir Egerton (Anne Lefroy's brother), 367
Brydges, Mrs Jemima (mother of Anne & Deborah-Jemima), 134, 238
Buckey, Robert (convict), 334–5, 337, 339, 344, 350
Buckland, Samuel (William Lewer's clerk), 111–13
Burke, Edmund, 52–5, 249, 251, 287–9, 293, 295–6, 299, 301–3, 305, 409n46, 409n48, 409n50

417

Burney, Fanny (Madame d'Arblay) (1752-1840), 252, 296
Butler, Samuel, 91
Byron, George Gordon, Lord, 8, 97

C
Cadell & Davies (publishers), 254
Camden, Calvert and King (slave trading firm), 95, 98, 192–5, 202, 205, 210, 217
Camden, John Jeffreys Pratt, 1st Marquess (1759-1840) Secretary of State for War and the Colonies 1804-1805, 305, 322, 349, 357
Camp di Alange, Marchioness del (fl. 1792), 321
Campbell, Robert, 267, 269, 319
Campbell Clarke & Co (Calcutta), 266–7
Cape of Good Hope
  British Navy, 202
  cattle, 261
  Considen at, 343
  East India Company monopoly of trade, 190
  New South Wales trade with, 192, 205, 208–10, 220, 225, 227
  voyages to India, 42
  voyages to New South Wales, 197–9, 213, 217, 271, 328
Carlisle, Frederick Howard, 5th Earl of (1748-1825), 173, 285, 304
Castle Hill (NSW) revolt (1803-04), 331–2, 334
Catholic Defenders, 14, 256, 273
Catholics
  convicts, 221, 256
  England, 290, 305
  France, 32, 68, 248–9, 291
  Ireland, 13–14, 17, 273, 300–3, 306–7, 332, 357
  New South Wales, 332
Cawley, (Mrs) headmistress, 24–5
Champion, Alexander, 45
Chandos, 1st Duke of (great uncle of Jane's mother), 23–4
Chandos, Cassandra, Duchess of, née Willoughby (great aunt of Jane's mother), 24
Chard, George (music teacher), 59
Charlemont, Lord, 15, 17
Charles I, King of England, 11, 68–9, 71–6, 390
Charles X, King of France (earlier, Charles-Philippe, Comte d'Artois), 251
Charlotte, Queen (1744-1818) wife of George III, 229–30, 296
Charlotte (First Fleet ship), 104–5, 193, 195, 204
Chatham, William Pitt, 1st Earl of (1708-1778) 'Pitt the Elder.' Prime Minister 1766-68, 287–9
Chawton (Hampshire), 24, 58, 164
Chimney-Sweeper's Act, 130

China
  Macartney's embassy (1792), 49–50
  shipping, 105, 201, 205–6, 210, 212, 232, 242, 326, 341
  trade with Britain, 79, 98, 193, 208, 212
  trade with India, 45, 48–50
  trade with New South Wales, 190
Church of England. *see* Anglican Church
Church of Ireland, 13
Chute, William, 60
Clare, Anne Holles, Countess of, née Stanhope, 69, 75
Clare, John Holles, 1st Earl of (1564-1637), 69
  daughter (*see* Wentworth, Arabella, née Holles (1609-31) 2nd wife of 1st Earl of Strafford)
Clark, Ralph (Lieutenant), 210, 212–14, 221–2, 401n13, 401n23
Clark, Richard (Alderman), 107–8, 201
Clavering, Sir John, 47
Clerkenwell
  New Prison, 153
Clifford, Margaret. *see* Wentworth, Margaret, née Clifford, 1st wife of 1st Earl of Strafford (d. 1622)
Clive, Robert, 39–40, 44, 46
Coal River (NSW). *see* Hunter River
Cobbett, William, 62, 126
coffee-houses
  D'Arcy & Wickham at Kings Head, 86
  Fitzwilliam at the Mount, 20, 103, 130–2
  gambling, 92–3, 95, 106
  Jerusalem newsroom, 98
  medical men, 81, 93
  Oxford & Cambridge, Newman St, 108–9, 113, 115
  Paul Wentworth, 87
  politics, 55, 91
  social life, 90–3
  in York, 19
Coffin family, 217
Collins, David (Judge Advocate), 206, 220–1, 226, 233, 335–6, 345, 402n49, 403n78, 413n51
Colnett, James (Captain), 216, 218, 326–7
Considen, Dennis (d. 1815) surgeon, 105, 213–14, 219, 323, 327
constables (NSW), 268, 324, 327, 334
Constitution (Britain), 288–9, 292–3, 297, 304
convicts
  1st Fleet, 189
  2nd Fleet, 155, 192–3, 195, 199–203, 205–6, 210, 242
  3rd Fleet, 210, 217–18
  England, 104–5
  Grose's policy, 220, 226–8

INDEX

Irish (see Irish people)
New South Wales, 204, 222, 250, 255–6, 258–64, 266–72, 276–8, 281, 306, 311–13, 317, 325–7, 333, 344, 346
Norfolk Island, 207–12, 214, 216, 218–19, 221–4, 229–34, 263, 274, 334, 336–8, 343–5
Phillip's policy, 191–2, 205, 220
Port Phillip, 336
Portugal & Brazil, 190–1
Van Diemen's Land, 336, 342–3, 348–50
Cook, James (Captain), 190, 197, 208, 212
Cookney, Charles
as D'Arcy's London agent, 224, 232, 256–7, 262–3, 269, 309, 312, 335
D'Arcy's requests to return to England, 257, 281–2, 315–16, 323, 329, 343, 345, 347
Fitzwilliam's communications with, 154, 223–4
as guardian of D'Arcy's sons, 326, 343
as Hill's clerk, 154, 156, 224–5
Jane's meeting with, 155, 224
letters of introduction from, 272
Cookney, Thomasine (wife of Charles), 225, 343, 347
Cookney family, 225, 326
Cooper, Rev Edward (Jane's cousin), 27–9, 31, 63
Cooper, Jane (b. 1774) Jane's cousin, 24–5, 35, 63
Cornwallis, Charles, 1st Marquess (1738-1805), 110, 210, 291, 305–6, 330, 356, 367
Cowpastures (NSW), 261, 322
Cowper, William, 53, 208, 237, 248
Cox, William, 333
Craven, Charles (Governor of South Carolina), 63
Craven, William, Lord, 27, 63, 244
Crombie, Rev Dr Alexander (1762-1840), 347
Crosby, Richard & Co, 366
Crossley, George (1749-1823) convict, 327–8
Crowley, Ambrose (manufacturer), 95, 214–15
Crowley, Catherine (1773-1800) emancipist, 202–3, 206, 210–12, 214–16, 219, 221, 223, 232, 235, 255, 282–3, 311, 333
Crowley, Martha (Aug-Dec 1791) daughter of D'Arcy Wentworth & Catherine Crowley, 214, 232, 235
Crowley, William Charles. see Wentworth, William Charles (1790-1872)
Crown Inn, Portsmouth, 155–7
Cullum, Francis, 24
Cumberland, Anne, Duchess of (1743-1808), 32, 148, 150
Cumberland, Francis Clifford, 4th Earl of (1559-1641), 67
daughter (see Wentworth, Margaret, née Clifford, 1st wife of 1st Earl of Strafford (d. 1622))

Cumberland, Prince Henry, Duke of (1745-90), 32, 148, 299
Cumberledge, Elizabeth (Mrs) formerly Mrs Stephen Austen, & Mrs John Hinton, 38–9, 44
Cumberledge, Stephen Austen (bookseller), 44
Cunningham, Philip, 331–2
Curran, Sarah (1782-1808) Mrs Robert Henry Sturgeon, 251–2
Curtis, William (Alderman) ('Billy Biscuit'), 98–9, 101, 105, 107, 184, 193
son, 99
Curtis, William (apothecary & publisher), 125, 132–3
Botanical Magazine, 125

D
Dalrymple, Alexander, 208
d'Arblay, Madame. see Burney, Fanny (Madame d'Arblay) (1752-1840)
Darwin, Charles, 369
Darwin, Erasmus, 81
Davidson, Walter, 322
Davies, James (a.k.a. Davis, and Christopher Theakston), 345–6, 349–50
Dawes (Lieutenant), 204
Dawes Point (NSW), 262
Dawson, James (barrister), 106, 272
Dawson, Lieutenant Colonel Thomas, 15
Day, Jack, 144–6
Declaration of Independence (Ireland 1782), 15
Defoe, Daniel, 101, 359
Digweed, Harry, 60
Digweed, James, 60, 354
Dillon, Elizabeth. see Roscommon, Elizabeth, Countess of (sister of 1st Earl of Strafford)
Dillon, James. see Roscommon, James Dillon, 3rd Earl of
Dillon, Wentworth. see Roscommon, Wentworth Dillon, 4th Earl of
Dixon, Martha. see Wentworth, Martha (mother of D'Arcy)
Dog & Duck, St George's Fields (London), 94–5, 102–3
Doidge, Denis, 219
'Dowlat, Sir Roger.' see Siraj-ud-daula ('Sir Roger Dowlat')
Drake, Sir Francis, 77
Dring, William (emancipist), 210, 229–30
Dryden, John, 76, 298
Dublin, 12, 70, 89, 240, 243, 251, 301–3, 306, 330–1, 344, 382n2 (Ch 1)
duels, 194–5, 264, 304, 319–20, 322
Dundas, Lady Charlotte, née Wentworth-Fitzwilliam, 88–9, 310

Dundas, Rt Hon Henry (Secretary of State), 231, 283, 403n95, 406n29
Dundas, Sir Lawrence, 88
Dunn, John (stable-keeper), 116–17
Dutch East India Company, 198
Dutch East Indies, 198, 208–9, 213, 228, 320

E

East India Bill, 88
East India Company
  D'Arcy's dealings with, 15, 20, 84–5, 89, 104, 110, 130–1
  Hancock family and, 28, 38–9, 42
  history, 20, 39–41, 44–9, 51–3, 88, 98–9, 108
  monopoly of trade, 190, 193, 208, 212, 220, 227, 258, 281, 298, 312, 319–20
  surgeons, 15, 28, 85, 89, 104, 110, 130–1
Elder, James, 348–9
Elizabeth Farm, Parramatta (NSW), 259–60
Elizabeth I, Queen of England, 20, 76, 173, 300
Ellerington, William (chief mate of the *Neptune*), 202, 242, 248
elopement. *see* marriage
emancipists (former convicts), 229–31, 259–60, 264, 268–70, 272, 274, 278, 281, 311, 325, 334, 336, 338, 344–5
Emmet, Robert (d. 1803), 251–2, 331
Emmet, Thomas (brother of Robert), 251
Enderby, Samuel & family, 217, 281, 312, 318–19
England
  administration of Ireland (*see* Ireland)
  D'Arcy's attempts to return to from Norfolk Island, 244, 256, 309, 313, 323, 343, 346, 375
  D'Arcy's attempts to return to from Sydney, 233–4, 243, 256–7, 281–3, 311, 325, 328–9, 351–2, 361–4, 368, 372–3
  D'Arcy's sons at school in, 319, 326, 339, 342–3, 347, 351, 364
Erskine, Sir Thomas (Lord Chancellor), 55, 139–40, 151, 202, 296, 371
Evans, Thomas (Attorney), 202
exclusives (New South Wales), 275

F

Faithfull, William, 256–7
Faringdon, Huw Cook (Abbot of Reading), 26
Farquhar, Sir Robert (son of Sir Walter), 320
Farquhar, Sir Walter (father of Sir Robert), 252, 320, 322
Feuillide, Eliza de. *see* Austen, Elizabeth ('Eliza,' 'Betsy')
Feuillide, Hastings de (1786-1801) Eliza's son, 31, 33, 64, 154, 248, 356, 361
Feuillide, Jean-François Capot, Comte de (1751–94), 32, 248, 367

Fielding, Henry
  The Life & Death of Tom Thumb the Great, 34
  as magistrate, 99–100
  quoted, 91–2, 94, 96
Fielding, John, 100
First Fleet (Botany Bay), 98, 104–5, 190–5, 201, 203, 213, 347, 372
Fitzherbert, Mrs Maria, 301
Fitzroy, Charles (alias). *see* Wentworth, D'Arcy (1762-1827)
Fitzwilliam, Lady Anne, née Watson-Wentworth, Countess (wife of 3rd Earl), 285, 292
Fitzwilliam, Charles William Wentworth-Fitzwilliam, 5th Earl (1786-1857) earlier Viscount Milton, 87, 307–8, 310
Fitzwilliam, Lady Charlotte, Countess (formerly Lady Charlotte Ponsonby) (1747?-1822) wife of 4th Earl, 17, 87, 89, 285, 310, 316
Fitzwilliam, Hon George. *see* Wentworth-Fitzwilliam, Hon. George (1757-1786) only brother of 4th Earl Fitzwilliam
Fitzwilliam, Hon Louisa, Countess, 2nd wife of 4th Earl, née Molesworth, widow of William Brabazon, 1st Lord Ponsonby (1749/50-1824), 310
Fitzwilliam, Sir William (1526-99), 300
Fitzwilliam, William Wentworth-Fitzwilliam, 4th Earl (1748-1833)
  American interests, 77, 288, 290
  D'Arcy's relationship with, in England, 14, 16–20, 83, 85–7, 102–4, 106, 120, 130–2, 138–9, 141–2, 151–4
  D'Arcy's relationship with, in New South Wales, 205, 223, 228, 232, 235, 262–4, 293, 312, 315–16, 326, 347
  D'Arcy's requests to return to England, 224, 234, 257, 281–2, 309, 328–9, 351, 364, 372, 375
  family history, 16–18, 87–9, 252, 285–6
  Indian affairs, 52, 54, 83, 85, 104
  Irish interests (Lord Lieutenant 1794-95), 17–18, 264, 300–7
  Jane Austen's connections, 78, 122, 138–9, 141–3, 173, 184, 310
  New South Wales interests, 154, 234–5
  Whig politics, in Parliament, 14, 19–20, 88–9, 91, 249, 286, 288, 290, 292–310, 371
  Whig politics, in Yorkshire, 88–9, 124, 138–9, 148, 150, 293, 295, 297–9, 307–8
'Fitzwilliam, Henry Frederick Howard,' 173
Flinders, Matthew, 318
floggings, 212, 219, 222, 230, 255, 272, 274, 330–2, 337, 339
Forde, Louisa, 50
Foveaux, Joseph (Major), 221, 268, 274, 279, 313, 319, 321, 334, 336–40, 344, 349, 351

INDEX

Fowle, Charles, 63
Fowle, Fulwar-Craven, 27, 59, 63
Fowle, Jane, née Craven (Mrs), 63
Fowle, Rev Thomas (father of Tom), 63
Fowle, Rev Tom (d. 1797), 27, 59, 63, 244, 254
Fowle family, 27, 59, 63, 363
Fox, Charles James (1749-1806), 46, 52–3, 55–6, 88, 91, 249, 285, 293, 299, 303–4, 307
France. *see also* Napoleonic Wars
  British intelligence in, 86–7, 251
  Eliza & Phila in, 31–2, 34, 51, 55, 367
  Henry Austen in, 367
  India, 49, 52
  interests in New South Wales, 189, 207, 338, 340–1
  Irish relations, 251, 301, 330
  James Austen in, 34
  Jane's references to, 169
  North American relations, 86–7, 291
  shipping, 331, 335, 340–1, 371
  Thomas Paine in, 295–6
  wartime, 130, 233, 247, 263, 323, 343–4
  Wentworth family in, 76, 130, 172, 285
Francis, Sir Philip, 47–8, 53
Franklin, Benjamin, 86–7, 287, 295
French Revolution, 55, 172, 202, 213, 248–51, 273, 276, 293, 295, 299–300

G
Galvin, Thomas ('Paddy') convict, 274
Gambier, Admiral James, 247
Gambier, Mrs Jane (wife of James, sister of Louisa, cousin of Anne Austen), 247
Gambier, Mrs Louisa (wife of Samuel, cousin of Anne Austen), 247
Gambier, Samuel (Secretary of the Navy Board), 247
gambling, 76, 92–6, 104, 106, 128–9, 150, 153, 184, 275–6, 346, 359
Garrick, David, 21
  Bon Ton, 34–5, 133, 163
Garrow, William (barrister), 151–2
George III, King of England
  birthday celebrations, 229–30
  China, 49–50
  family, 148, 356
  Hanover, 276
  Ireland, 15, 17, 273, 301–2, 304–6, 344
  madness, health & regency, 80, 247, 297
  New South Wales colony, 189, 217, 264, 266–7, 280–1, 313–14, 324
  Parliament & government, 53, 109, 123, 225, 247, 286–91, 293–4, 296, 307
  sheep, 321–2
George IV, King of England
  birthday celebrations, 229
  as King, 101
  as Prince of Wales, 18, 54, 60, 124, 301
  as Prince Regent, 101, 138–9, 142, 148, 163, 250, 296–8, 310
  Whig connections, 298–9, 301
Germain, Lord George, 289
Gerrold (or Gerrard), Joseph, 250, 262
Gilbert, Thomas (Captain), 194–5
Ginders, Mrs Mary, 350
Godmersham (Kent), 24, 266, 354, 357, 363, 368–79
Gordon, Lord George (1751-93), 290–1
Gordon riots (1780), 166, 290, 294
Grand, George & Catherine, 48
Grattan, Henry, 302, 306
Gray, Thomas (jeweller), 185
Grenville, George (1712-70) Prime Minister 1763-65, 287
Grenville, William Wyndham Grenville, 1st Baron (1759-1834) Prime Minister 1806-1807, 195, 210, 215, 217, 250, 307, 402n35
Gretna Green (Scotland), 140, 143, 163, 170–2, 245
Grimes, Charles (surveyor), 231
Grose, Francis (Major), 219–20, 225–9, 231, 233–4, 259, 261, 268
Grosvenor Square (London)
  coffee house (The Mount), 20, 87, 103, 130–2
  Fitzwilliam's house, 20, 77, 86–7, 89, 102, 138–9, 155–6, 234, 290, 326
  riots (1792), 248
  stables, 116–17
  Sydney's house, 191
  Waterhouse family, 323
Grundy, Mrs Ann, 111–12, 116, 118
Guardian (Second Fleet transport), 197–9, 217

H
Haider Ali, Sultan of Mysore, 51
Hamilton, Catherine, Lady (d. 1782) 1st wife of Sir William, 285
Hamilton, Guy (Captain), 266–7
Hamilton, Sir William (1730-1803), 285
Hammersmith (London), 108
Hampson, Sir George, Bart. (d. 1733?) Jane's great grandfather, 28, 41
Hancock, Colbron (Tyso's brother), 41, 45
Hancock, Eliza. *see* Austen, Elizabeth
Hancock, Olivia. *see* Lightfoot, Olivia
Hancock, Philadelphia, née Austen (1730-92) Jane's aunt, 31–3, 37–46, 51, 56, 64, 140, 149, 154, 177, 248, 252, 361
Hancock, Dr Tyso Saul (1713-75) Jane's uncle, 28, 33, 38–46, 50, 56

Harewood, Henry Lascelles, 2nd Earl of (1767-1841) son of 1st Earl, 308
Harris, John (1754-1838) surgeon, 105, 137, 151, 157, 194–5, 199, 204, 311, 323–5
Hastings, George (son of Warren & Mary), 40–1
Hastings, Mary, née Elliott, earlier Mrs Buchanan, 39–40
Hastings, Warren, 40–1, 44–5, 47–8, 51–6, 85, 110, 120, 140, 213, 233
Hawkesbury River (NSW), 216, 231, 270, 277–80, 327, 331, 334
Heaney, Seamus, 330
Henry V, King of England (earlier, Prince of Wales), 97, 299
Henry VIII, King of England, 16, 26, 60, 80, 137, 249
Heywood, John Pemberton, 148–54, 184–5, 301
highway robbery
    1787 incidents, 97–103, 107–9, 111–13, 115–18, 120
    1788: Hounslow Heath, 56
    1789: D'Arcy's trial, 144–52
    1790: Davies, 345
    1790: Molloy, 277, 301
    D'Arcy's reputation, 128, 148, 180, 223, 242
    debt collection, 56
Hill, Thomas (Fitzwilliam's London agent), 120, 143, 152–5, 194, 224–5, 397n44
Hill, William (Captain), 193, 197, 199–201, 400n22, 400n34, 400n41
Hinton, John (bookseller), 38–9, 44
Hobart, Robert, Lord (later 4th Earl of Buckinghamshire) (1760-1816) styled Lord Hobart 1793-1804 (Secretary of State for War and the Colonies), 321, 327, 335–6, 339–40, 343, 372
Hogan, Michael (Captain), 256
Holles, Arabella. *see* Wentworth, Arabella, née Holles (1609-31) 2nd wife of 1st Earl of Strafford
Holt, Joseph, 270, 333–4, 344, 350, 407n55, 413n5
Home Office
    Fitzwilliam's relations with, 104, 143–4, 223–4, 263–4, 315
    Governor Hunter's relations with, 256, 264–5, 267, 269, 271, 273, 280
    Governor King's relations with, 223–4, 326
    Governor Phillip's relations with, 190–1, 213, 219, 221, 223
    Grose's relations with, 231
    Wickham's association with, 250–1
horse racing, 18–19, 27, 94, 120, 271, 297, 308, 351
hospitals

London, 20–1, 79–80, 83–4, 86, 93–4, 112, 130, 137, 144–6, 219
New South Wales, 200, 204–5, 262, 264, 274, 276–8, 283, 329, 345, 347, 361
Hounslow Heath, 56, 109, 111, 144–6, 162, 184
Howe, George (Government Printer), 274
Hunter, John (Captain) (1737-1821)
    1737-87: early life, 213
    1788-94: New South Wales under Phillip & Rum Corps, 190, 192, 208–9, 212–13, 223
    1794-1800: Governor of New South Wales, 223–35, 255–7, 259–76, 279–84, 309, 312–15, 408n104
    1800–21: returned to England, 319, 323, 343, 372
    meetings with Jane, 362, 364, 372–3, 375
Hunter, John (surgeon), 80–1, 93, 120
Hunter, William, 80
Hunter River (Coal River) (NSW), 271, 332, 348
Hurst, John & Mrs, 111–12, 116–18, 184
Hyatt, William (brandy merchant), 215

I
Iceland, 342
Imeerawanyee, 221, 403n104
India
    Austen family in, 138, 140
    British administration, 47, 50–1, 55, 108, 305
    D'Arcy's interest in, 15, 20–1, 28, 83–5, 89, 103–5, 130–1
    Hancock family in, 38–9, 42–6
    shipping, 98, 208–9, 276, 318, 320–1, 324, 326
    trade, 79, 95–6, 210, 225, 227, 257–8, 266–8, 315, 317, 325
    Warren Hastings in, 40–1, 48, 51–2, 55
India Bill 1783, 52–3, 293
Innet (or Inetts), Ann (convict), 218, 328
Ireland. *see also* *the names of Counties & other places*
    British troops in, 14, 272, 357
    Fitzwilliam's interest, 17–18, 264, 300–7
    pirates, 70
    Strafford's interest, 69–72
    unrest, 273, 330–2
    uprising (1798), 305–6, 330–1, 333, 356
    Wentworth family in (*see* Wentworth family)
    Wickham as Chief Secretary, 251
Irish Parliament, 15, 302–3
Irish people
    Barrington as, 271
    convicts, 217, 255–6, 271–4, 277, 301, 330–2, 337–8, 340–2
    D'Arcy as, 11–17, 27, 89, 102, 151, 213, 256, 273, 332–3, 345
    exiles, 251, 255, 273, 333, 342–3

INDEX

in Grenada, 247
Harris as, 137, 324
Hogan as, 256
Holt as, 333–4
Molloy as, 95, 301
Navy, 344
on Norfolk Island, 333, 337–8, 340–2, 344
Redfern as, 344
surgeons, 12–13, 213, 219, 275, 301
Tom Lefroy as, 240–1
Wentworth family (*see* Wentworth family)
Whigs, 301–2, 306
Irwin, James, 97–8, 102

J

Jamison, Thomas (surgeon), 214, 219, 225, 276, 316, 329, 407n85
Johnson, Rev Richard, 200–1, 218, 222
Johnson, Samuel, 21
Johnston, Major George, 220, 283, 319, 323, 325, 331, 412n61
Jones, James (slave trader), 98–9, 101
Jörgensen, Jörgen, 342

K

Kable, Henry, 269
Kempshott (Hampshire), 60, 124, 250
Kent, Mrs Eliza (wife of William), 275
Kent, William (Captain) nephew of Governor Hunter, 275, 283
Kenyon, Lord (Lord Chief Justice), 151, 271
King, Anna Josepha (Mrs) wife of Philip Gidley, 217–18, 223, 232, 319, 329–30, 351
King, John, Under-Secretary, Home Office, 224, 261
King, Norfolk (son of Philip Gidley King & Ann Innet), 218, 351
King, Philip Gidley (1758-1808)
  1788-90: Norfolk Island, 207, 214
  1790-91: England, 209–10, 217
  1791-96: Norfolk Island, 218–19, 221, 223–6, 228–31, 233–5, 271
  1796-99: England, 235, 271, 280–1
  1800-07: Governor of New South Wales, 311–32, 334–8, 340, 343, 346, 349, 351, 364, 399n1
  1807–08: return to England, 347, 351
King, Phillip Parker (son of Philip Gidley), 218, 351
King, Sydney (son of Philip Gidley King & Ann Innet), 218, 351
Kipling, Rudyard, 332
Knatchbull, Sir Edward (husband of Fanny Knight; father of Mary-Dorothea), 172
Knatchbull, Fanny (Frances Catherine), née Knight (1793-1882) wife of Sir Edward, 172, 246, 370
Knatchbull, Mary-Dorothea. *see* Knight, Mary-Dorothea, née Knatchbull (b. 1806/7) wife of Edward, Jane's nephew
Knight, Edward (1767-1852) Jane's brother, originally Austen, 23–4, 27–9, 31, 35, 60, 138, 172, 175, 180, 246, 354, 357, 363, 368–70
Knight, Edward (1794-1879) Jane's nephew, 172
Knight, Elizabeth, née Bridges (1772/3-1808) wife of Jane's brother, Edward Knight, originally Austen, 239, 246, 370
Knight, Fanny (Jane's niece). *see* Knatchbull, Fanny (Frances Catherine)
Knight, Mary-Dorothea, née Knatchbull (b. 1806/7) wife of Edward, Jane's nephew, 172
Knight, Thomas (Jane's father's cousin), 24
Knight family, 24, 35, 125, 246, 354, 357, 363
Knowlys, Newman, 114–17

L

La Perouse (French explorer), 207
La Tournelle, Mme (school principal), 27, 30–1
Lady Penrhyn (ship), 98, 104–5, 193
Lamb, Sir Matthew, 1st Baronet (1705-1768), 285
Lamplugh, Rev, 123
Lanchester, John, 9
Langlois, Benjamin (Henry Maxwell's uncle), 134
Lascelles, Henry. *see* Harewood, Henry Lascelles, 2nd Earl of
Laud, William, Archbishop of Canterbury, 69, 71, 94
Lee & Hurst (booksellers), 262
Leeds, Samuel (surgeon), 261
Lefroy, Anna (Jane-Anna-Elizabeth), née Austen (b.1793), 8
Lefroy, Anne, née Brydges (1749-1804) wife of Rev George, 134–8, 186, 237–42, 361, 367–9, 399n34
Lefroy, Rev George (m. Anne Brydges, 1751) Ashe Rectory, 134, 240
Lefroy, Tom (great-nephew of Rev George), 8, 59, 240–1, 251
Lefroy, William Thomas (1787-91), 136, 187–8, 399n34
Leigh, Eleanor, wife of Thomas, 2nd Baron Leigh of Stoneleigh, née Watson, 67, 76, 373
Leigh family, 41, 76–8, 171, 179, 359, 373
Leigh-Perrot, James (Jane's mother's brother), 358, 370
Leigh-Perrot, Mrs Jane, née Cholmondeley (d. 1805) wife of Jane's uncle James, 222, 358, 369–70
Leigh-Perrot, Richard (Jane's mother's brother), 63
wife, 63

Leigh (Worcestershire), 179
Lewer, William, 111–15, 117
Lezo, Don Blas de, 78
Lightfoot, Olivia, née Hancock (Tyso's sister), 41, 45
Liverpool, Charles Jenkinson, 1st Earl of (1729-1808), 281
Lloyd, Elizabeth (daughter of Nowes & Martha), 63
Lloyd, Martha, née Craven (Mrs), 63, 252, 369
Lloyd, Martha (daughter of Nowes & Martha), 63, 246, 369–70
Lloyd, Mary. *see* Austen, Mary, née Lloyd
Lloyd, Rev Nowes, 63, 252
The Loiterer (Oxford student magazine), 63, 65–6, 92–3, 138, 163, 179, 182
London, 7, 26. *see also the names of places & institutions in London*
   Austen family in, 37–8, 356, 369
   D'Arcy in (1785-88), 15, 19–22, 28, 77, 79–81, 83–7, 89–96, 100–18, 120–2, 130–3
   D'Arcy in (1789), 136–8, 143–56, 158, 178–9, 186, 195, 282
   D'Arcy's agent in (*see* Cookney, Charles)
   D'Arcy's attempts to return to (*see* England)
   Eliza in, 32–3, 55–6, 248–9, 252–3, 369
   Fitzwilliam's house (*see* Grosvenor Square)
   Hancock family in, 41, 43–4, 64
   Harris in, 195
   Hunter in, 323
   Jane's visits & interests, 56, 63–4, 134–9, 143–54, 161–2, 164, 167, 173, 176–7, 195, 308, 361
   Lefroy family, 134–8, 241
   New South Wales administration, 219–21, 224, 227, 231–5, 261, 263, 268–9, 271, 336, 364
   port of, 95–6
   shipping, 201
   Strafford in, 71
   Wentworth family in, 77, 86
   Wickham in, 124, 251
London Corresponding Society, 250, 296
Lord, Simeon, 268–9, 315, 333, 335
Lough Neagh (Ireland), 12
Louis, Sir Thomas, 1st Baronet (1758-1807) Rear-Admiral, 371
Louis XVI, King of France, 32, 86, 248, 251
Lyons, Sarah (convict). *see* Tunks, Mrs Sarah, née Lyons

M

Macarthur, Mrs Anna Maria, wife of Hannibal; née King, daughter of Philip Gidley & Anna Josepha, 223, 351
Macarthur, Edward (son of Captain John & Elizabeth), 194, 196, 203, 320
Macarthur, Elizabeth (daughter of Captain John), 320
Macarthur, Elizabeth (Mrs) wife of Captain John, 194–6, 203–4, 258–60, 319, 331
Macarthur, Hannibal (nephew of Captain John), 351
Macarthur, James (son of Captain John & Elizabeth), 260
Macarthur, John (Captain), 194–6, 203, 217, 220, 226–7, 259–61, 264–5, 267–8, 319–22
Macarthur, John (son of Captain John), 320
Macarthur family, 196–7, 217, 259, 331
Macartney, George, Lord, 49–50
Macaulay, Thomas Babington, 54
Macquarie, Lachlan (Governor of NSW), 349, 399n1
Magarot, Maurice, 250
Magellan, Ferdinand, 78
Mainwaring, Sir Philip (Lord Strafford's secretary), 298
Manning, Mrs Elizabeth, 101
Manning, William, 95, 99–101, 277
Mansfield, Lord (Lord Chief Justice), 51, 140, 290
Manydown (Hampshire), 60, 355, 364–6, 371
Marquis Cornwallis (ship), 255–6, 273, 275–6
marriage. *see also* Gretna Green (Scotland)
   Austen family, 168, 171, 173–4, 176–7, 180–1, 243, 245, 252–3
   English law, 170–4, 183
   Norfolk Island, 218, 222
Marsden, Rev Samuel, 274, 282, 331
Marshalsea (prison), 69
Martinez, Esteban Jose, 218
Mary Queen of Scots, 143, 239
Maskelyne, Neville, 81
Mathew, General Edward (d. 1805) father of Anne Austen, 246–7
Mathew, Lady Jane, née Bertie (mother of Anne Austen), 246
Maum (Captain) *Marquis Cornwallis*, 275–6
Maxwell, Deborah-Jemima, née Brydges (d. 1789) sister of Anne Lefroy, 134
Maxwell, Henry (husband of Deborah-Jemima), 134
Maynard, Samuel (Bow Street Patrol), 113–18
Melbourne, William Lamb, 2nd Viscount (1779-1848), 285
Melling, Catherine (convict), 311
Melville, Thomas (Captain), 217
Middleton, Sir Charles (Comptroller of the Navy), 107, 294
Midgley, Rev Richard, 326
Mileham, James (surgeon), 276, 327, 337
Milton, John, 76, 277

INDEX

Milton House (Northamptonshire), 148, 285, 310
Minerva (ship), 260, 268, 273–5
Ministry of All the Talents, 307, 371
Mitchell, James, 335, 337, 339
Moira, Francis Rawdon-Hastings, 2nd Earl of (1754-1826) Governor-General, Bengal, 108, 303–4
Molloy, John Francis (d. 1802), 95, 99–100, 102, 277–80, 301, 345–6
Molly Maguires, 14
Monro, Alexander (secundus) (1733-1817), 323
Monson, Sir George, 47
Montagu, Lady Mary Wortley, 137
Moore, John, Archbishop of Canterbury (1730-1805), 102
Moore, John, M.D. (1729-1802) father of Sir John Moore, 290
Moore, Sir John (1761-1809), 228
'Mortimer, Edmund Arthur William,' 173
Muir, Thomas, 250, 262–3
Murray, John (publisher), 8

N

Napoleonic Wars, 130, 228, 251, 275–6, 308, 321, 323, 342, 356–8, 366–8, 371
Nelson, Horatio, 1st Viscount (1758-1805), 202, 228, 323, 357, 371
Nepean, Evan, under-secretary, Home Office (brother of Nicholas), 104, 143, 152–4, 194–5, 218, 223–5, 250, 271, 277, 301–2, 320
Nepean, Nicholas (Captain) brother of Evan, 194–6, 204, 225–8
Neptune (Second Fleet ship), 153–8, 172, 181, 186, 192–202, 205–6, 210, 216, 226, 242, 248
New Hampshire, 20, 77, 86, 286
New South Wales (Botany Bay). *see also* Norfolk Island
 colonial administration (Phillip 1788-94), 189–92, 197, 200, 203, 205, 208–10, 212–17, 220, 222, 225, 227–9, 367, 372
 colonial administration (Rum Corps 1792-95), 226–8, 233
 colonial administration (Hunter 1795-1800), 233–5, 258, 260–1, 266–7, 269, 272, 274–5, 280–2, 284, 300, 361, 372
 colonial administration (King 1800-1807), 312–23, 325, 327–8, 334, 349, 351–2
 convicts (*see* convicts)
 D'Arcy in (*see* Wentworth, D'Arcy)
 exiles in, 255, 273, 333, 342–3
 Jane's knowledge of and references to, 163, 242–3
 social life, 271, 275, 330–1, 368
New South Wales Corps ('Rum Corps'), 203–5, 222, 225–8, 233, 255–61, 264–6, 268–70, 275, 278–9, 313–15, 317, 319–25
Norfolk Island, 203, 205, 210, 213, 219–20, 226, 229–31, 234, 339–40, 343, 345
Second Fleet, 155, 194, 213, 219
Third Fleet, 217
Van Diemen's Land, 336, 350
New Zealand, 192, 212, 225–6, 342
Newgate prison (London)
 D'Arcy in, 101, 111, 120, 149, 153, 155, 163, 165–6
 executions at, 112, 115
 Gordon riots (1780), 290
 Harvey in, 118
 New South Wales convicts in, 104, 155, 216
Nokes, David, 7, 24, 27, 183, 254, 358, 405n76, 414n24
Nootka Sound, 105, 217–18, 263, 318
Nore mutiny (1797), 344
Norfolk, Charles Howard, 11th Duke of (1746-1815), 124, 173, 298–9, 304–5
Norfolk, Edward Howard, 9th Duke of (1686-1777), 208
Norfolk, Mary Howard, Duchess of, née Blount (before 1712-1773) wife of Edward, 9th Duke, 208
Norfolk Island
 1788-90: British colony, 207–10, 221
 1790-96: D'Arcy on, 206, 210–14, 216, 218–19, 222–6, 228–32, 256, 262–4, 268, 309, 312–13, 323, 346
 1797-1802: British colony, 271, 315, 319, 321
 1802: D'Arcy posted to, 325
 1804-1806: D'Arcy on, 332–47, 375
 convicts on (*see* convicts)
 flax, 208, 212, 216, 225, 401n22
 relations with Sydney, 216, 219, 222, 224, 229, 232, 334–5, 375, 389
 Rum Corps on (*see* New South Wales Corps)
 rum trade, 226, 228, 230, 268, 335, 340
 surgeons (*see* surgeons)
 Sydney and, 216, 219, 222, 224, 229, 232, 334–5, 339, 375
Norfolk Island pine trees, 212, 216, 277, 334, 339, 347
North, Lord (Prime Minister), 15, 46, 53, 86–7, 288, 291, 293

O

Oakes, Francis, 268
O'Beirne, Rev Thomas Lewis (1749-1823), 277–8, 300–1, 407n95
Old Bailey (London)
 Company of Surgeons, 80, 107–8, 112
 courts, 108, 111–12, 114, 118, 121, 136, 150–4, 185, 195

425

opium, 48–9
Otaheite. *see* Tahiti
Oudh, Nawab of, 44–5
Oxford
  Jane & Cassandra at school, 24
  Jane's visits, 64
Oxford University
  Austen family, 23–4, 35, 64–6, 138, 179, 253
  Jane's references to, 64, 133, 246
  Tom Fowle, 59, 63
  Wickham, 123

P
Paine, Daniel, 257–8, 270, 405n13, 407n55
Paine, Thomas ('Tom') (b.1737), 263, 295–6
Palmer, John (Commissary), 265
Palmer, Thomas Fyshe (d. 1802), 250, 257, 262–3
Parramatta (NSW)
  constables, 268, 272
  D'Arcy in (1799-1802), 273, 275–7, 282–3, 329, 339
  D'Arcy in (1807-1808), 347–9
  hospital, 276
  Hunter, 260, 270, 275
  Macarthur family, 259–60, 322
  New South Wales Corps, 226, 324
Parramatta River (NSW), 276, 282, 331
Paterson, Elizabeth (Mrs) wife of William, 217, 320–1
Paterson, William (Colonel), 217, 220, 233, 258, 264, 278–9, 313–14, 319–20, 322, 336
Patton, Dr Alexander, 12–15, 17, 21–2, 106, 118
Pemulwuy (Pemelway), 260
Perryn, Sir Richard (judge) Baron of the Exchequer, 112, 116, 151, 154
Peterloo Massacre, 309
Phillip, Arthur (Captain) (1738-1814)
  D'Arcy's dealings with, 158, 194, 205–6, 210, 213, 223–4, 256
  early life, 190, 192
  Governor of New South Wales (1786-92), 104, 190–5, 200, 205–10, 213, 217–21, 312, 335, 401n14
  retirement, 226–7, 229, 233–4, 259, 367, 372
Pierrepont, Mary. *see* Montagu, Lady Mary Wortley
Pierrepont, William (brother of Lady Mary Wortley Montagu), 137
Piper, Captain John (1773-1851), 230, 320, 339–42, 345, 348–51
  family, 348
Piper, Mrs Mary Ann, née Shears, 350
pipes (anonymous letters or verses), 267–8, 325
Pitt, William, the Elder. *see* Chatham, William Pitt, 1st Earl of (1708-1778) 'Pitt the Elder.'

Prime Minister 1766-68
Pitt, William, the Younger (1759-1806) Prime Minister 1783-1801, 1803-06, 53, 86, 88–9, 99, 191, 218, 248, 251, 293–4, 296–7, 299–302, 304, 306–7, 371
Ponsonby, George (cousin of 4th Earl Fitzwilliam), 301
Ponsonby, William Brabazon, 1st Lord, 310
Ponsonby, William (cousin of 4th Earl Fitzwilliam), 301
Ponsonby family, 285
Pope, Alexander, 76
Portadown, County Armagh, 11–13, 17, 106
Portland, William Henry Cavendish-Bentinck, 3rd Duke of (1738-1809)
  1783: Prime Minister, 293
  1793: Secretary of State, 299–304
  1794-1805: Home Secretary, 231, 263–7, 269, 271–3, 280–1, 283–4, 313–14, 317, 320–1, 372, 406n29
  1807-1809: Prime Minister, 307
Portland Place (NSW), 270
Portpatrick (Scotland), 16, 170, 263
Portsmouth
  1st Fleet, 104–5, 192
  2nd Fleet, 150, 154–8, 178, 181, 186, 188, 190, 195, 200, 216
  Frank Austen, 35, 363
  Hunter, 372
  shipping, 42, 318, 356
Pott, Percival (surgeon), 20–1, 79–80, 84, 89, 107, 130
Price, John Washington (surgeon), 260, 274–7, 407n76, 407n87
Prince Regent. *see* George IV
Protestants
  England, 290 (*see also* Anglican Church)
  Ireland, 13–14, 17, 53, 273, 300–6, 324, 333, 357
  New South Wales, 332

Q
Quakers, 13, 84, 125, 214
Qianlong, Emperor of China, 49–50

R
Radcliffe, Ann: *The Mysteries of Udolpho*, 236, 239
Raleigh, Sir Walter, 77
Raven, William (Captain), 220, 225, 257
Reading, Jane & Cassandra in, 25–31, 35, 63, 121
Redfern, William (1774-1833) surgeon, 344–5, 347–8, 351
Reibey, Thomas, 279
Reliance (ship), 233, 235–6, 255, 271, 275, 315, 318
Remnant, Stephen, 97–8, 102

INDEX

Rhodes, Robert (Captain), 342
Riou, Edward (Captain), 197
Rockingham, Anne ('Nan'), Baroness, née Wentworth (b. 1627) daughter of 1st Earl of Strafford, 67–70, 72, 74–6
Rockingham, Charles Watson-Wentworth, 2nd Marquess of (1730-82) Prime Minister 1765-66 and 1782, 14–15, 17, 77, 86–9, 124, 172, 286–8, 290–3
Rockingham, Edward Watson, 2nd Baron (1630-89), 75–6
Rockingham, Mary Watson-Wentworth, Marchioness of, née Bright (wife of 2nd Marquess), 289
Rockingham, Thomas Watson-Wentworth, 1st Marquess of (1693-1750), 18
Rodes, Elizabeth. *see* Wentworth, Elizabeth, née Rodes (3rd wife of 1st Earl of Strafford)
Roe, Sir Thomas, 70–1
Roscommon, Elizabeth, Countess of (sister of 1st Earl of Strafford), 76
Roscommon, James Dillon, 3rd Earl of, 11, 76
Roscommon, Wentworth Dillon, 4th Earl of (d. 1684) poet, 76
Ross, Robert (Lt-Colonel), 210, 213, 228, 403n85
Rotherham (Yorkshire), 140, 163, 295
Russell, Sir Henry (lawyer), 107–8, 148–50

S

St Bartholomew's hospital, Smithfield, 20–1, 79–80, 84, 86, 112, 130, 137, 219
St George's Fields (London), 205, 290. *see also* Dog & Duck
St Thomas' Hospital (London), 94
Scarborough (ship), 105, 155, 193, 196, 200, 203, 206, 212–13
Scotland. *see also* Portpatrick
  Edinburgh University, 323–4, 343
  Jane & D'Arcy in, 143, 163–4, 171, 176, 178, 310, 361
  marriage laws, 170, 174, 177, 181 (*see also* Gretna Green)
  wars with England, 71
Scots people, 13, 95, 148, 213, 219, 266, 306, 358
Scott, Claude, 98–9, 102
Scottish Martyrs, 250, 257, 262–3
Sea Fencibles, 367–8
Second Fleet (New South Wales), 150, 154–5, 158, 188, 192–201, 210, 215–16, 219, 221, 226, 242, 324, 347
'Sentiment, Sophia.' *see* Austen, Jane (1775-1817): writings
Sergeant, Mary (convict), 326
Shakespeare, William, 298
  Henry IV Part I, 98–9, 111–12, 173–4

King Henry the Eighth, 156, 398n84
Measure for Measure, 156, 398n83
The Winter's Tale, 150
Shapcote, John, 193, 195–6
Shaw, George Bernard, 89
Shears, Mary Ann. *see* Piper, Mrs Mary Ann, née Shears
Shelburne, William Petty, 2nd Earl of Shelburne (1737-1805) Prime Minister 1782-83, 293–4
Sheridan, Richard Brinsley, 53, 55
Sherwin, Ann (convict), 338
Shippen, Joseph (1679 -1741) father of William, 84
Shippen, William ('Billey'), 83–5
Shooters Hill (London), 84, 97–9, 184
Sidmouth, Henry Addington, 1st Viscount (1757-1844) Prime Minister 1801-1804, 307, 367
Sinclair, Robert (brother of William), 19, 86, 89, 150–1, 306
Sinclair, Rev William (brother of Robert), 306
Siraj-ud-daula ('Sir Roger Dowlat'), Nawab of Bengal, 39–40
Sirius (First Fleet ship), 192, 197, 204–5, 207–14, 217, 233
Skirving, William, 250, 262
Smith, Abel, MP, 393n17
Smith, Adam, 225, 259
Smith, Joseph (convict), 223
'Smith, Jack,' 173–4
'Smith, Jane,' 173–4
Smithfield, 86, 118, 136–8. *see also* St Bartholomew's hospital, Smithfield
Smollett, Tobias, 21, 35–6, 77, 82, 90, 92, 107, 110, 219, 359
Smyth, Arthur Bowes, 105
'Sophia Sentiment.' *see* Austen, Jane (1775-1817): writings
Southey, Robert, 243
Spanish Armada, 173, 300
Speedy (ship), 280–1, 312
Stamp Act, 77, 286–8, 296
Stanhope, Philip Dormer, 50
Steventon (Hampshire)
  Austen family, 149, 170, 177–9, 353–5, 358, 361, 364–71, 373
  D'Arcy in, 155, 157–8, 186–7
  Eliza in, 55
  Jane's early life, 23–4, 31, 35, 44, 57–63, 65–6
  Jane's life after elopement, 126, 133, 155, 157–8
  Jane's life during D'Arcy's absence in New South Wales, 172–4, 177–9, 241, 353–5, 358, 361, 363, 365, 370–1, 373
  rectory school, 24, 27, 44, 57–60, 63, 67, 355
Stockdale, John (bookseller & publisher), 140, 151, 223

427

Strafford, Thomas Wentworth, 1st Earl of (1593-1641) a.k.a. Blacke Tom Tyrant of Ireland, 11, 16, 18, 30, 67–76, 292, 298, 300, 373
Strafford, William ('Will') Wentworth, 2nd Earl of (1626-95), 68, 70, 72, 74–5, 137
Strafford family, 28, 30
Sturgeon, Lady Harriot, née Wentworth (1736/7-89) wife of William, 172
Sturgeon, Robert Henry (Captain) cousin of Fitzwilliam, 252
Sturgeon, William, 172
Suffolk, Henry Howard, Earl of, 86–7
surgeons
  Army, 98, 195
  Company of Surgeons (*see* Old Bailey)
  Company of Surgeons' Court of Examiners, 15, 20, 105, 107, 219, 344, 346
  D'Arcy's apprenticeship in Ireland, 12–13, 102, 219, 277
  D'Arcy's training in London, 15, 20–2, 79–80, 83–5, 92–3, 105, 107, 112, 125, 130, 144–5, 219
  D'Arcy's work in Sydney & Parramatta, 257, 261–2, 276–7, 283, 311, 315, 325, 329, 337, 347, 349, 361
  D'Arcy's work on Norfolk Island, 205–6, 219, 223–4, 229, 235, 242–3, 262–3, 309, 325, 334–5, 337–8
  Hancock as, 28, 38–40, 42–3
  India, 15, 28, 48, 52, 85, 89, 104–5, 110, 130–1
  Irish, 12–13, 89, 95, 137, 213, 219, 275, 277–8, 301
  Navy, 105, 107–8, 110, 131, 137, 193, 195, 214, 234, 260, 274, 318, 324, 344
  New South Wales, 104–5, 154, 157–8, 177, 204, 209, 213, 234, 260–2, 274–5, 278, 315–16, 320, 324, 337
  Norfolk Island, 207, 213–14, 219, 263, 344–7
  slave ships, 193, 294
  training in London (walking the wards), 79–85, 89–90, 92, 95, 106, 278
Surprize (Second Fleet ship), 155, 157, 193, 195, 198–200, 204–6, 210–12, 221, 250, 256
Swift, Jonathan, 299
Switzerland, 123, 129–30, 250–1, 366
Sydney, Lord, 191–2, 209
Sydney, New South Wales
  1788-89: British settlement, 190–2
  1790: D'Arcy's arrival, 200–1, 203–5, 210
  1796-99: D'Arcy in, 235, 255–7, 276, 283
  1801-04: D'Arcy in, 311–17, 323, 326, 329, 331–2, 345, 361
  1806-: D'Arcy in, 347–52
  hospitals, 262
  shipping, 227–8, 232–3, 255, 266–8, 271, 313, 318, 324, 326, 335–6, 342–4, 346, 349
  social life, 260, 268, 275, 279
Sykes, Francis, 40

T
Tahiti (Otaheite), 213, 335, 342, 348–9
Tandragee (Ireland), 12–13, 106, 214
Tasmania. *see* Van Diemen's Land
Taylor, Samuel
  stenography, 83
'Taylor, Miss,' 179
Tedbury (Tjedboro), 260
Tench, Watkin (Captain), 192, 204, 209, 276, 407n86
Third Fleet (New South Wales), 210, 214, 217–19
Tippoo, Sultan of Mysore, 51–2
Tone, Wolfe, 251, 306
Toongabbie (NSW), 272, 331, 334
Tordesillas, Treaty of (1494), 217
Townson, John (Captain), 271
Traill, Donald (Captain of the *Neptune*), 193, 195–6, 201–2, 205–6, 242, 248
  wife, 196, 201
Trampe, Frederick Christopher, Count of (1779-1832), 342
tsunami (Norfolk Island), 345
Tuki (Maori), 225–6
Tunks, Mrs Sarah, née Lyons, 221–2
Tunks, William, 222
Twain, Mark, 55
Twisleton, Charlotte, née Wattell (wife of Thomas), 171
Twisleton, Hon Mary Cassandra (b. after 1773) Jane's cousin, 172, 359
Twisleton, Rev Thomas (after 1767-1815) Jane's cousin, 171

U
United Irishmen, 250–1, 273, 300, 305–6, 331–3, 344

V
Van Diemen's Land (Tasmania), 189, 217, 266, 318, 335–6, 338–9, 342–3, 346, 348–51, 375
Vancouver, George (Captain), 217, 225, 402n41, 403n77
Vansittart, Henry, 41–2
Venus (brig), 318
Vernon, Admiral, 77–8
Villiers, John, 86, 107, 110, 272, 343

W
Waaksamheyd (ship), 209, 213, 265
Walpole, Horace, 54, 91, 93, 103
Walter, James, 31, 34, 64

INDEX

Walter, Philadelphia (Phylly) (b.1761?) youngest child of William H. & Susanna, 34, 44, 55, 64
Walter, Susanna(h), née Weaver (wife of William H.), 43–4, 179
Walter, Rev Weaver (son of William H. & Susanna), 179
Walter, William Hampson (b.1721?) son of Jane's aunt Rebecca, 37, 43, 179
Washington, George, 291, 295
Waterhouse, Elizabeth (sister of Henry), 318
Waterhouse, Henry (Captain), 233, 236, 267, 315–16, 318, 343
Waterhouse, William (father of Henry), 233
Watling, Thomas, 191, 400n11
Watson family, 75, 78, 292
Watson-Wentworth, Lady Anne. *see* Fitzwilliam, Lady Anne, née Watson-Wentworth, Countess (wife of 3rd Earl)
Watson-Wentworth, Thomas (1665-1723) father of 1st Marquess of Rockingham, 75
Wellesley, Richard Colley Wellesley, Marquis of (1760-1842) Governor-General of India, 321
Wentworth, Anne ('Nan') (b.1627) daughter of 1st Earl of Strafford. *see* Rockingham, Anne ('Nan'), Baroness
Wentworth, Arabella, née Holles (1609-31) 2nd wife of 1st Earl of Strafford, 68–9
Wentworth, Arabella (b.1629) daughter of 1st Earl of Strafford, 68, 72, 74–5
Wentworth, 'Aunt.' *see* Wentworth, Elizabeth
Wentworth, D'Arcy (father of D'Arcy), 11–12, 15–16, 106
Wentworth, D'Arcy (1762-1827)
 (1762-85) birth & early life in Ireland, 11–15
 (1785-86) in England, 16–22, 77, 79–87, 89–90, 92–6, 309
 (1787-89) missing years, 120–5, 127–33, 135–8
 (1789-90) passage to New South Wales (Second Fleet), 143–4, 153–8, 160, 172, 177–8, 180–2, 186, 188, 193–6, 198–9, 202–3, 224, 309
 (1790) arrival in Sydney, 203–6
 (1790-95) Norfolk Island, 206, 210–14, 216, 218–19, 222–6, 228
 (1795-1804) Sydney & Parramatta, 234–6, 255–7, 261–5, 268–9, 271–7, 281–4, 311–17, 321, 323, 325–9, 331–2
 (1804-1806) Norfolk Island, 333–4, 336–47
 (1806-1807) Sydney, 347–52
 accused of highway robbery, **99–118,** 120, 128, 131, 144–55, 165, 176, 179–81, 195, 206, 301
 alias Charles Fitzroy, 110, 115, 117, 131–2
 alias John Smith, 145, 174
 alias Wilson, 143
 attempts to return to England (*see* England)

 correspondence with Jane Austen, 135, 199, 244, 283–4, 361–4, 367–8, 372–3, 375
 East India Company ambitions, 52, 84–5, 104, 106, 110
 Jane Austen (family), 67, 76–8
 Jane Austen (first meetings in 1786-89), 27–30, 67, 133, 136–42
 Jane Austen (Jane's writings), 66, 122–30, 159–63, 166–7, 175–88
 Jane Austen (links between lives), 9, 23
 Jane Austen (romance, elopement & marriage), 7, 123, 132, 143–58, 170–1, 195, 229
 Jane Austen (separated in Sydney), 205, 235–6, 242–5, 254, 310, 319, 352
 Jane Austen (separated on Norfolk Island), 218, 240, 242–5, 343
 Medical Notebook, 81, 120
Wentworth, D'Arcy (originally Dorset) (b. 1793) son of D'Arcy Wentworth & Catherine Crowley
 1793-96: birth & childhood on Norfolk Island, 214, 223, 232
 1796-1802: Sydney & Parramatta, 235, 255, 282–3, 311, 362
 1802-1810: at school in England, 342–3, 347, 351, 364
Wentworth, Dorothy (sister of D'Arcy), 11, 15
Wentworth, Elizabeth, née Lord (wife of General Thomas) 'Aunt Wentworth,' 78
Wentworth, Elizabeth, née Rodes (3rd wife of 1st Earl of Strafford), 70, 72, 74
Wentworth, Elizabeth (sister of 1st Earl of Strafford). *see* Roscommon, Elizabeth, Countess of
Wentworth, Frances (wife of Sir John), 289
Wentworth, Lady Henrietta Alicia ('Lady Harriot') (1736/7-89) sister of 2nd Marquess of Rockingham. *see* Sturgeon, Lady Harriot
Wentworth, Sir John (d. 1793) D'Arcy's American cousin, 20, 77, 86–7, 286
Wentworth, John (originally Matthew) (b. 1795) son of D'Arcy Wentworth & Catherine Crowley, 214, 232, 235, 255, 282–3, 311, 329, 333, 342–3, 347, 351, 362
Wentworth, Margaret, née Clifford, 1st wife of 1st Earl of Strafford (d. 1622), 67–8
Wentworth, Margaret (daughter of 1st Earl of Strafford), 70
Wentworth, Martha (mother of D'Arcy), 11–12
Wentworth, Michael (of South Elmsall, West Yorkshire & Ireland), 11
Wentworth, Paul (D'Arcy's American cousin), 20, 86–7
Wentworth, Peregrine (D'Arcy's cousin), 18–19, 88, 120

Wentworth, Robert (fl. 1730) D'Arcy's grandfather, 11–12
Wentworth, Thomas (1593-1641). *see* Strafford, Thomas Wentworth, 1st Earl of
Wentworth, General Thomas (d. 1747), 77–8
Wentworth, Sir William, Bart (1562-1614) father of 1st Earl of Strafford, 67–8
Wentworth, William ('Will') (1626-95) son of 1st Earl of Strafford. *see* Strafford
Wentworth, William (D'Arcy's eldest brother), 11, 15, 106, 136, 143, 243, 272
Wentworth, William (D'Arcy's nephew), 383 n20
Wentworth, William Charles (1790-1872) son of D'Arcy & Catherine Crowley
  1790-96: birth & early life on Norfolk Island, 206, 211–12, 214, 232
  1796-1802: childhood in Sydney & Parramatta, 235, 255, 276, 282–3, 311, 362
  1802-1810: at school in England, 326, 329, 339, 342–3, 347, 351, 364
  adult life, 309
Wentworth, William Charles IV ('Bill') (1907-2003) author's uncle, 7–9
Wentworth family
  in America, 15, 20, 76–7, 289
  in Australia, 7, 196–7, 232, 235, 256, 275, 282–3, 326
  in England, 17, 67–72, 74–8, 138, 183, 292, 301
  in Ireland, 7, 11–13, 17, 21, 76, 106, 136, 151, 172, 205, 243, 252, 292, 301
  Jane Austen's connections, 67, 78
  in Yorkshire, 16, 19, 76, 89, 142, 150–1, 293, 295, 298–9, 307–9
Wentworth-Fitzwilliam, Charles William. *see* Fitzwilliam, Charles William Wentworth-Fitzwilliam, 5th Earl
Wentworth-Fitzwilliam, Lady Charlotte. *see* Dundas, Lady Charlotte
Wentworth-Fitzwilliam, Hon. George (1757-1786) only brother of 4th Earl Fitzwilliam, 19, 28, 88–9, 91, 122
Wentworth House (Yorkshire). *see* Wentworth Woodhouse (house, Yorkshire)
Wentworth Woodhouse (house, Parramatta), 271, 347
Wentworth Woodhouse (house, Yorkshire)
  D'Arcy's & Jane's visits, 16–18, 120, 138–43, 173, 176, 310
  history, 11, 17, 67, 89, 123, 292, 295, 298–9
  Prince Regent at, 138–43, 297–9
Wesley, John, 13
whaling & sealing, 190, 217, 225, 281, 319, 337, 339, 342, 345, 349
Wharncliffe, Lord, 396n79

Whig party
  French Revolution, 249
  governments, 53, 289, 307, 371
  impeachment of Hastings, 55
  Ireland, 301–2, 306
  London coffee-houses & clubs, 91
  New South Wales interests, 242
  in Opposition, 53
  regency, 297
  Wentworth family, 14, 19, 88–9, 140, 150, 173, 234, 286, 292–3, 298-302, 304, 309
White, Gilbert, 126
White, John (Principal Surgeon), 104, 158, 204, 207–9, 213, 401n7, 278401n2
Wickham, Anne (sister of William), 121, 126
Wickham, Eléonore Medeline, née Bertrand (William's wife), 129–30
Wickham, Elizabeth, née Lamplugh (William's mother), 123
Wickham, Harriet (sister of William), 121, 126
Wickham, Henry (father of William), 123–4
Wickham, Henry Lewis (1789-1864) son of William, 130
Wickham, William (1761-1840), 86, 121–4, 126, 128–30, 249–52
Wickham family, 123–4, 126
Wilberforce, William, 201, 294–5, 307
Wilkes, John, 290–1
Wilkinson, Elizabeth (sister of Mary), 113–16
Wilkinson, John (coffee house proprietor), 108–9, 115
William III, King of England, 46, 297
Williamson, James (1758-1826) Commissary, 268, 275–6
Willoughby, Cassandra. *see* Chandos, Cassandra, Duchess of, née Willoughby (great aunt of Jane's mother)
Wilson (alias). *see* Austen, Jane (1775-1817); Wentworth, D'Arcy (1762-1827)
Winchester (Hampshire), 58–9, 62, 123
'window tax,' 297–8
Woodhouse family, 78, 292
Woolf, Virginia, 162, 182–3
Wordsworth, William, 79–80
Worgan (surgeon), 204
Wright, Sir Sampson, 99–100, 116, 145–6, 277
Wyatt, Jeffry (architect), 205
Wyvill, Rev Christopher, 293

Y
Young Slaughter's coffee-house (London), 81